The
COLLECTED
PLAYS *of*
Neil Simon
VOLUME III

The
COLLECTED
PLAYS *of*
Neil Simon

VOLUME III

With an Introduction
by Neil Simon

Random House
New York

Library of Congress Cataloging-in-Publication Data
(Revised for volume 3)
    Simon, Neil.
    [Selections. 1971]
    The collected plays of Neil Simon.

    Vol. 1 has title: The comedy of Neil Simon.
    Contents: [1] Come blow your horn. Barefoot in the park. The odd couple. The star-spangled girl. Promises, promises. Plaza suite. Last of the red hot lovers—[etc.]—v. 3. Introduction. Sweet Charity. They're playing our song. I ought to be in pictures. Fools. The odd couple, female version. Brighton Beach memoirs. Biloxi blues. Broadway bound.
    I. Title.   II. Title: Comedy of Neil Simon.

Library of Congress Cataloging-in-Publication Data
PS3537.I663A6   1979   812'.5'4   79-5081
ISBN 0-394-47364-7 (v. 1)
ISBN 0-394-50770-3 (v. 2)
ISBN 0-679-40889-4 (v. 3)

Manufactured in the United States of America
98765432
First Edition

TO GENE SAKS, MIKE NICHOLS,
BOB FOSSE, ROBERT MOORE,
HERBERT ROSS, AND STANLEY PRAGER,
ALL WONDERFUL DIRECTORS AND
GOOD FRIENDS

Contents

Introduction

The Art of Hindsight

On the night before the first day of rehearsal of *The Odd Couple*, director Mike Nichols and I sat down to dinner at a midtown restaurant to discuss last-minute preparations and to toast ourselves good luck. One always needs luck, of course, but not leaving any stones unturned will usually get you a better result than clinking two glasses of Beaujolais together. We had, as far as we could see, turned over every stone in sight, including a few pebbles just to make sure: We cast Walter Matthau and Art Carney in the two leading roles, had a wonderfully realistic set designed by the gifted Oliver Smith, handpicked the poker players from hundreds of eager and talented actors, and I personally went to England to find authentic "birds," as they were called in the early sixties, to play Gwendolyn and Cecily, the "coo-coo Pigeon Sisters," as Oscar Madison referred to them. Most importantly, Mike and I had worked and reworked the script for almost eight months. Our daily sessions always ended with my going home to rewrite a scene, which Mike would read the next day and generously laugh uproariously over, proclaiming it was brilliant, only to call me at two o'clock in the morning to suggest that I could improve it even more. Each day the script got better and better, Mike kept on laughing uproariously, and my phone kept ringing at two in the morning until finally the miracle came: The phone stopped ringing. It could only mean two things. Either the script was finished or Mike was dead. I called him at two-thirty to have either one of my suspicions corroborated and was much relieved to hear that he was alive and well but annoyed that I was thoughtless enough to call him at such an ungodly hour.

At that eventful dinner on D day minus one, after glasses were clunked, I looked at Mike and said, "Are you happy with the script now?" Mike looked at me and smiled confidently and said, "Completely," and then added suspiciously, "Why? Aren't you?"

"Oh, yes," I answered. "I'm happy with everything. The script, the cast, the set, the director, everything." . . . We had both just come off a number of successes, principally *Barefoot in the Park*, for which Mike won the Tony Award, his first of many to come. He had also directed a huge hit with Murray Schisgal's *Luv*, and I had two other nominally successful shows, *Come Blow Your Horn* and the musical *Little Me*. Four hits and no failures gave us the overwhelming confidence of the young and naive. "Then why are you looking so worried?" Mike asked reasonably. "Because," I answered, like a Talmudic scholar who weighs all the possibilities, "tomorrow morning at ten o'clock, the actors will read the play aloud for the first time and by twelve-thirty they will be through. And at a quarter to one, you and I will go to lunch, look at each other and say, 'we're in trouble,' and if we are, why don't we know it now?" Mike shrugged and said, "That's why this business is so much fun . . ."

At a quarter to one the next day, Mike and I went to lunch after the reading and he looked at me across the table and said, "We're in trouble." I said, "I know. And I don't find it much fun."

The Odd Couple was a three-act play, a species pretty much extinct by now. At the reading, the first act went enormously well. Big laughs from the actors, smiles of confidence from me and Mike. There are always about a dozen onlookers at these readings—producers; set, lighting, and costume designers; casting agents; stage managers; and a few well-wishing relatives. The reading of the second act went, if possible, even better than the first act and it felt more like a great opening night than the first reading of a play.

The producer, Arnold Saint-Subber, was feeling so optimistic at the break, he got up and said, "You don't need me around here. I'm going out to sell tickets," and left in a state of euphoria, feeling that even if the third act was less than wonderful, the play was a surefire hit no matter. . . . Or perhaps he was wise enough to foresee the disaster that lay ahead and wanted to avoid the carnage of confidence that was to follow. The third act was god-awful. This hilarious comedy had suddenly turned into a Moscow Art Company production of *Mourning Becomes Electra*. It gave new meaning to the word "grim." Actors began to cough, our well-wishers began to look at their watches, Mike began to think of food, and I began to think of airlines that flew to snowbound countries. Mike Nichols is not one to panic and he merely beamed at the actors and said, "You were all *won*derful," and I followed him out the stage door, expecting he was going to say to me, "Oh, I forgot to tell you. I'm doing a picture for Warner's on Monday. I won't be able to do the play. Do you mind?"

As I said, Mike is not one to panic. At lunch he seemed very cheerful and smacked down his linguini with white clam sauce with characteristic gusto. I looked at him pleadingly, hoping he would come up with the magic solution to our troubles, waiting for those sparks of genius that fly like Roman candles out of his brilliant mind. I could wait no longer and spewed out my plea. "What do you think we should do, Mike?" . . . And without a moment's hesitation, he smiled calmly and said, "Not to worry. I'll go back to the theater and direct the first two acts and you go home and write us a wonderful new third act." He then got up, leaving me with a smile, a look of encouragement, and the check.

Why hadn't we known the third act wouldn't work? We had loved it for weeks. Did the Typists tamper with it or did the Gods? It couldn't have been our fault because we were smart, talented, and successful. I could suddenly hear my father's *warning*. "What kind of a business is that for you? Writing? That's for writers, not for someone who wants to make a living." Why hadn't someone spoken up before? An unhappy actor or a nervous producer? There wasn't a clue from anyone . . . and for a very simple reason. No one knew. If all the best writers, directors, actors, and producers knew beforehand what worked and what didn't, there would never be an unsuccessful show. Yet the statistics tell us that eight or nine out of every ten shows that open on Broadway fail. How could they all not know? All that money and time invested in a business that had a success average of .107. If you were batting that on your Little League baseball team, they would promptly suggest you go home and take violin lessons. Except that kid, Isaac Stern, who really could hit. Shows you what they know.

Undaunted, I went home and wrote a new third act in

three and a half days. Adrenalin and potential abject failure can produce miracles of endurance and inspiration. I was congratulated by Mike and the cast for my achievement, my quick and fertile wit, my unending facility in finding new and clever plot twists, and the sparkling new ending for the play that would dazzle audiences and force critics back to their thesauruses to look up new superlatives. Then we sat down and read the new third act. It was like reading aloud the list of road fatalities on the Thanksgiving weekend. It made the old third act seem like Shaw. I was suddenly wondering if I could get my old job back thinking of whipped cream stunts on "Beat The Clock."

I was so desperate for help that I was willing to have Mike and the cast ad-lib any third act they wanted, while I hopped a freighter to some banana republic where I would earn my living writing letters home for illiterate Portuguese sailors.

Once again, Mr. Nichols and common sense prevailed. He suggested I stop thinking "wonderful" and just make it "good" . . . and from good we could proceed to make it wonderful. He was a born therapist, father, and saint. But even his simple suggestion seemed too tall an order for me to handle, and I asked if I could just make it "fair" before we went on to "good," not to mention such dizzying heights as "wonderful." . . . Mike said, "Fine. I'll settle for fair. But I need it by Thursday"—an awful thing to say to someone on a Tuesday. Thursday afternoon it was in his hands. It was better than fair. It was "not bad." "Not bad" was not good but "not bad" was better than not good at all. The reason Mike wanted it by Thursday was that we were opening in Wilmington, Delaware, on Saturday night. The cast had a day and a half to learn a completely new third act, written by someone that, by now, not even the stage doorman had any confidence in.

The tryout in Wilmington was just short of fair. The valiant actors expended so much energy trying to make the third act passable that they succeeded in making the first two acts merely bearable. So spake the reviews. We limped out of Wilmington, rehearsed the rewrites on the train, and proceeded to Boston, where the big-gun critics awaited us with howitzers at their aisle seats facing the stage. It was, however, not the roar of cannons we heard, but the roar of laughter from a packed opening night audience at the Colonial Theater. The third act sputtered here and there, misfired, exploded a few blanks, but hit enough bull's-eyes for us to get through by the skin of our teeth, a play I wish I had written instead. Elliot Norton, a venerated and extremely able critic, praised the play highly, but the headline of his review was "Oh, For a Third Act!" If he liked it so much, why not a headline like "Great First Two Acts" or "Mostly Brilliant"? I felt as if I just had a new baby and the doctor said "It's a fine, healthy child but I don't think it's going to be good at Ping-Pong." Come on, Elliot, give me a break. The truth was, he did. His review sold tickets and gave us enough time to work on the third act, where we had now passed "good" and were on our way to "wonderful." Exhausted, I returned to my hotel room, sat down at the typewriter, and burned the midnight oil; anything to keep from writing. This was twenty-seven years ago and *The Odd Couple* is still my greatest source of income royalty, greater than any of the other twenty-some-odd plays I've written since.

What did I learn from this experience? Everything and nothing. To go back for a moment to *Barefoot in the Park*, the first day's reading of that was horrendous from the first page to the last. I was certain the actors—Robert Redford, Elizabeth Ashley, and the others—were going to trip over each other trying to get to the phone to call their agents to get them a job doing radio in the Philippines, anything but this claptrap. The indomitable Mike Nichols remained calm and sanguine. "It'll be fine," he said. "How do you know it will?" I asked. "Because I want it to be," he replied. Life was so easy for Mike. The rehearsals proceeded with an air of doom. I had worked for years in television shows, watching the rehearsals of "The Sergeant Bilko Show" and "Your Show of Shows," and they were always filled with gales of laughter from cast and writers. The *Barefoot* rehearsals resembled *Medea* being performed by the Marat/Sade Players. I would sometimes wait outside the rehearsal hall, waiting for the sound of laughter, and when I heard it, I would rush in optimistically only to find the cast was on a break and

Mike was talking about anything at all and making it hilarious. "I don't get it," I said. "You're funnier than me. Why don't *you* write the play?" "Because," he answered, "you write it funnier than me." How could you help loving the man?

At the dress rehearsal on the stage of the Bucks County Playhouse in New Hope, Pennsylvania, where *Barefoot* was having its first public performance under the title of *Nobody Loves Me*—so in case the play really was bad, I would still be able to use the title *Barefoot in the Park* for a future one—I watched the proceedings glumly. Four weeks had gone by and I had yet to hear a single laugh, except from Mike, who loved everything the actors were doing. I saw Mike Ellis, the jovial manager of the Playhouse, sitting in a corner of the darkened theater, watching the rehearsal in ominous silence. I sidled over to him and asked, "Is this the *worst* play you've ever seen, Mike?" He thought for a second and said, "Well, maybe not the *worst.*" I was almost heartened by his corroboration that I was not mad and that my play was, indeed, terminally unfunny. The ushers, college freshmen all, were grouped together in the last row, watching the play with as much joy as if they had just found out they had all flunked every course they were taking. They just looked at each other and rolled their eyes skyward, a gesture I will not forget till my dying day, which I thought was going to be that night. At eight o'clock the curtain went up. The audience laughed from eight-oh-one until ten-fifteen, when the curtain came down and took its own bow, even before the performers. The play moved to Broadway, where it played almost four years. It is still done today in theaters all over the world, in igloos, caves, and mine shafts. Why didn't I know all that before?

One of the few times I was positive I had a smash hit on my hands was when I wrote *God's Favorite*, a contemporary telling of the Book of Job. I laughed writing it, I laughed at the rehearsals, and I laughed on opening night in New Haven. I was the only one. We ran eight weeks on Broadway. Why didn't I know before?

Wait. It goes on. . . . I had written an act and a half of a play called *The Sunshine Boys,* and then stopped, having lost faith in it, and sentenced it for life to the dark dungeon of my desk's bottom drawer. You need the excitement and enthusiasm you have on the first day you begin to write a play on each and every day you go back to the typewriter. You can have a bad day once in a while, but a bad day can lead to a bad week and one bad week can lead to abandonment. You start to search in your mind for the elements that made the other plays work, to follow the design you had laid out so clearly in other works. But every play has its own design and should not follow the blueprints of other houses. After all, you want to build castles, not Levittown. Six months after *The Sunshine Boys* had been laid aside and forgotten, I had dinner with Mike Nichols again, who was so successful by this time, he was using his Tony Awards as salt and pepper shakers. "What are you working on *now?*" he said, looking up from his home-grown escargot. "Nothing," I replied. "I've gone flat. I started this dumb thing about two old vaudevillians who haven't worked together in eleven years and have grown to hate each other, but then are asked to do their old act on the Ed Sullivan show, and start to fight again when they begin rehearsing their old routines, but I don't know, it all sounds so blah to me. It's dull, right?" . . . Without missing a bite, he said, "I love it. Finish it." . . . I was at the typewriter that night. The pages flew by effortlessly, sailed into rehearsal and straight into a successful run at the Schubert Theater, not to mention an Academy Award for George Burns in the film version. Sometimes all you need is one line of encouragement.

Brighton Beach Memoirs took me nine years from start to finish, but only eight months of the nine years were devoted to writing. I had written thirty-five pages and had just stopped. I didn't know where to go with it, or if I had written comedy or drama or something innovative or even soap opera. I gave it to my two daughters, Ellen and Nancy, to read. They loved it, anxiously awaiting to see how it all came out. But the wheels of inspiration had ground to a halt. The years went by and other plays came and went and still the girls persisted: "When are you going to finish the play about Eugene and Stanley? That's our favorite." . . . Nine years later I picked it up, read the thirty-five pages, knew exactly where I should go, and finished it in three months. Sometimes all you need is nine years of encouragement.

I certainly had no intention of writing a trilogy. If *Brighton Beach* was a failure, who would want to see a sequel? But *The New York Times,* though pointing out its flaws, was encouraging enough to say that "one hoped there would be a Chapter Two to *Brighton Beach.*" Out of a middling review, came *Biloxi Blues* and *Broadway Bound.* The birth and life of so many of these plays seem so fragile, as if their very existence depended on a single line of approval from someone I respected or cared for. Only once in my life have I written a play from start to finish without showing a page of it to anyone until it was completed. We'll come to that in a moment.

That play was not *Jake's Women,* although that was the work I was most proud of, at least in the writing stage. It was surely my most serious attempt at playwrighting on a grand scale. It was the story of a complex writer (is there another kind?) who feels that the people who most affected his life were all women. I did five rewrites before I sent it to anyone. I showed it first to Manny Azenberg, who has produced the last seventeen plays I've written. He showed it to his assistants, his wife, his closest confidants. No one said it was awful, no one said it was wonderful, but *everyone* said it *had* to be done. They all told me it was so personal, so self-revealing, that the reader felt he or she was almost intruding on my life, but that's exactly what I had intended. The overall feeling I got back from those who read it was that it was so compelling, it mesmerized you, but did not necessarily entertain you. A mixed blessing if I ever heard one. Gene Saks, the other most gifted director in my life, who had guided all three of the *Brighton Beach* plays so well that they earned him two Tony Awards, was also caught up with *Jake's Women,* but was well aware of its dangers. We decided to go into production and started casting sessions. Many of the scenes in the play sounded wonderful, and yet we had great difficulty in finding the right actors. Although casting is always a chore, and it usually takes anywhere from three to six months to cast a play well, we invariably came up with the people we wanted, without making concessions. But *Jake* gave us more trouble than we ever had before. We could not find anyone for the leading and most important role of Jake and I was not sure we had made the right decisions with the other roles. My radar kept giving off danger signals and I decided to call off the play. Manny Azenberg still had faith in it and sent it to Mike Nichols, who read it and thought it was the best play I had written. Once again my confidence came back and we proceeded to recast. This time we started to form a more interesting cast, but still I felt uneasy. This was not the usual fears of "Is it funny or is it not funny," but rather, "Will anyone understand it, and if they do, will they care at all about Jake and his self-absorbed life?" Mike and I decided to have a reading of the play and although we had not done any definite casting, Mike asked some of his friends to help us out and we had a blue-ribbon cast of actors who eagerly agreed to do the reading. It was held at the Michael Bennett Studios on lower Broadway on a hot, sultry day in late June. As we all sat around at the reading, we realized we couldn't hear a word above the din of the shaky wall air conditioners. We decided to turn them off, choosing words over comfort. It proved to be a mistake. The actors plunged into the reading with great energy and zest and after fifteen minutes, energy and zest turned into monosyllabic droning. As the temperature in the room rose, the sound of perspiration hitting the pages in the actors' hands in a slow, steady pattern turned the reading into a new form of Chinese torture. One could attribute the listlessness of the acting to the airlessness of the room, but I knew it was the aimlessness of the script. It roamed and strayed and meandered all over the pages, cresting like a wave coming in and then crashing on the craggy rocks.

We stopped after the first act for a break. The break lasted almost a year. At the reading I asked Mike not to go on with the second act, I had heard enough. After thanking the actors and making a very quick apology, I left the building, New York, and *Jake's Women,* not caring if I saw any of them again. After two years of trying, the play was saying to me, "Let me go, Neil. Stop holding me hostage. Put me in the bottom drawer and let me die in peace." I acceded to its wish, had a brief but tasteful funeral service, buried it forever, and went on with my life. I started a new comedy, a farce called *Rumors.* Things went well through the writing of the first half of the play; then one day I heard a knocking at the door. I opened it and saw no one there. Again the knocking came, but this time I could *tell* it wasn't the door at all, but rather was coming from the bottom drawer. I opened it slowly and *Jake's Women* peered up at me pleadingly and said, "I want to live. Give me another chance. I'll be good this time, I promise." . . . Who could refuse such poignant remorsefulness, such a sincere request for a second chance? Actually it had had nine or ten chances already but in a sense, an eleventh chance is really a second chance, if you're obstinate enough. One more time through the typewriter went *Jake,* all dressed up with new scenes, new coats of dialogue, and a double-gloss polishing of all the old rough edges . . . and there were enough of them to shave all the beards grown in the Old West.

Happy with my new, Frankensteinian gift of life, I faxed Manny Azenberg the happy message, "Jake Lives." . . . With that out of the way, I went on to finish *Rumors,* put it through its test in San Diego, and sent it on to New York, where it won the overwhelming approval of half the critics, if you subscribe to the "half full, half empty" theory of life. The other half of the critics who didn't care for it didn't stop it from running for almost fifteen months in New York. I was free at last to attend to what now seemed like my only reason for living—proving to the world that *Jake's Women* was a good play. I was so single-minded in purpose that, had I lived eighty or ninety years ago, I would have beaten Amundsen and Scott to the South Pole—without a dog team.

This time I made a wise decision. Not as wise as "Just forget about the damn thing," but wise enough. I decided to do something I had never done before. I wanted to have a reading of the play in front of a live audience. (Live as opposed to what?) With the help of a talented new director, Ron Link (*Stand-Up Tragedy*), we rented the Tiffany Theater in Los Angeles and invited an audience of about a hundred or so people to a staged reading of the play. I felt at ease because I had nothing to lose. If they didn't like it, it wasn't Broadway, I would not have to read scornful reviews and would save myself and our investors almost a million dollars. If it worked, "Look at me, Ma! Top o' the world!!" We gathered a pretty formidable cast of actors, read it through twice, and then waited for the audience to pour in at seven o'clock. Let me tell you something, folks, a hundred people coming for free to a tiny theater in Los Angeles with no critics, no reputation, and no money at stake, is just as scary as an opening night in New York. That's just the nature of the beast. We always want to do good.

And indeed, the night was fun. It went better than my wildest expectations. The audience laughed in all the right places, and there were plenty of them, thank goodness, and apparently they were moved and touched in the scenes where those responses were warranted. Manny was buoyed, Ron Link was buoyed, and I was buoyed. Three happy buoys were we. Manny proclaimed, "We're doing this play." I seconded the proclamation, a cast of first-rate actors were signed on aboard, and the good ship *Jake's Women* set sail for San Diego and New York, not bothering to check weather reports or to heed the dangers of sailing around Cape Horn in the dead of winter.

We rehearsed at the Henry Fonda theater on Hollywood Boulevard, a good omen if ever there was one. It would have been the John Wilkes Booth theater if the Gods wanted to warn me. The first day's reading of the play went splendidly. At the first act break, I thought Manny Azenberg was going to say, "You don't need me around here. I'm going out to sell tickets," but no such forewarning of tragedy occurred. Rehearsals went reasonably well, and there was nothing that couldn't be repaired with a wrench and a little oil, and four weeks later we were setting up shop at the Old Globe Theater in San Diego.

What happened next, only the survivors can tell you, and of those, there are a precious few. The six weeks we played there were the greatest seesaw ride of my life. One night up to the heavens; the next night, the Hindenburg crashed. The next night up, the next night down. Those of us who had to watch the play every night started to take Dramamine. Tuesday night the audience walked out, sought me out at the rear of the theater, and said,

"Brilliant. Your best play." Wednesday night the audience made a beeline for their cars, as if a monsoon were
about to hit. New pages went in daily, and after daily,
they went in hourly. The championship prizefight went
on. He's up, he's down, he's up, he's down. It looked like
I was headed for a no decision. The San Diego critics
came and liked it, with reservations. The Los Angeles
critics came and hated it, with no reservations. Good
friends came and told me they loved it. Better friends
came and told me to close it. The Old Globe directors,
Jack O'Brien and Tom Hall, were extremely affirmative.
Business was booming and positive phone calls were
coming in by the score. I wore out two typewriters and
wrote a new beginning to the play and a new ending.
Both worked. Cuts did wonders, and a complete new
slant on two of the women characters brought joyful
results. On a scale of ten, we had gone from a three to a
six and were pushing toward seven each night. One night
there was an after-the-performance discussion between
the cast and the audience. One man said it was the best
play he had seen at the Old Globe in the twelve years he
was a subscriber. Another woman said, "I don't get it. It
just seems self-indulgent to me." I popped down another
Dramamine, went back to the typewriter, and got the
play to 7.5. . . . But it's tough to get by in New York on
less than a 9.0. . . . I was spent, squandered, and bewildered. Should we leave the play or bring it on in? The
general consensus was, Let's bring it in. Finally, one
night I went up to the small balcony in that lovely theater
to watch the show from above, objectively. I sat quietly
and watched the play from beginning to end. Then I got
up, drove back to my hotel and, very calmly and full of
confidence in what I was doing, decided to close the
show. I called up Manny Azenberg in New York and told
him of my decision. It wasn't a long conversation. There
was anger and resentment from some of the actors, but
not all. The pros in the company knew it was coming
before I did. . . . I gave it every opportunity, for almost
two and a half years, and every time I threw it into the
water, it kept sinking to the bottom. . . . But questions still
remained. What about that wonderful reaction at the
Tiffany Theater? Was that cast better? Was that script
better? Why didn't I know?

As I write these pages, I am weeks away from going into rehearsals with a new play, *Lost In Yonkers*. This is the play that I wrote from beginning to end without showing a page of it to anyone until it was finished. I don't know if I did that from a desire not to stop the flow or because I had such confidence in what I was doing. But we've already seen what my confidence or lack of it can lead to. Betrayals, betrayals, time and time again. I like *Lost in Yonkers*. A lot. All those who have read it and signed on to be a part of the production are enamored of this play.

By the time this volume is published, the results should all be in. Will I be saying to myself, "I knew I was right about this one," or will it be, "Why didn't I know?"

A thought just came to me, another approach to fixing *Jake's Women*. Excuse me while I go inside and take another crack at it.

Neil Simon
Los Angeles
September 18, 1990

Sweet Charity

Book by Neil Simon
Music by Cy Coleman
Lyrics by Dorothy Fields

SWEET CHARITY *was first presented on January 29, 1966, by Fryer, Carr, and Harris at the Palace Theatre in New York City with the following cast:*

(In order of appearance)

CHARITY	Gwen Verdon
DARK GLASSES	Michael Davis
BYSTANDER	John Stratton
MARRIED COUPLE	Bud Vest, Elaine Cancilla
WOMAN WITH HAT	Ruth Buzzi
ICE CREAM VENDOR	Gene Foote
FOOTBALL PLAYER	John Sharpe
BALLPLAYERS	Harold Pierson, Eddie Gasper
CAREER GIRL	Barbara Sharma
SPANISH YOUNG MAN	Darrell Notara
FIRST COP	John Wheeler
SECOND COP	David Gold
HELENE	Thelma Oliver
NICKIE	Helen Gallagher
CARMEN	Carmen Morales
HERMAN	John Wheeler
DOORMAN	I. W. Klein
URSALA	Sharon Ritchie
VITTORIO VIDAL	James Luisi
WAITER	John Stratton
MANFRED	Bud Vest
RECEPTIONIST	Ruth Buzzi
OLD MAID	Elaine Cancilla
OSCAR	John McMartin
DADDY JOHANN SEBASTIAN BRUBECK	Arnold Soboloff
BROTHER HAROLD	Harold Pierson
BROTHER EDDIE	Eddie Gasper
POLICEMAN	Harold Pierson
ROSIE	Barbara Sharma
BARNEY	David Gold
MIKE	Michael Davis
GOOD FAIRY	Ruth Buzzi

THE SINGERS AND DANCERS OF TIMES SQUARE: I. W. Klein, Mary Louise, Alice Evans, Betsy Dickerson, Kathryn

Doby, Suzanne Charny, Elaine Cancilla, Carmen Morales, Christine Stewart, Charlene Ryan, David Gold, Gene Foote, Harold Pierson, Bud Vest, Darrell Notara, John Sharpe, Eddie Gasper, Michael Davis, Patrick Heim.

Conceived, staged, and choreographed by Bob Fosse
Scenery and lighting by Robert Randolph
Musical direction and dance music arranged by Fred Werner
Costumes designed by Irene Sharaff
Orchestrations by Ralph Burns
Production manager: Robert Linden
Associate producer: John Bowab
Based on an original screenplay by Federico Fellini, Tullio Pinelli, and Ennio Flaiano

SYNOPSIS OF SCENES

ACT ONE

ACT TWO

Act One

Collected Plays

of Neil Simon,

Volume III

"You Should See Yourself"	Charity
"The Rescue"	The Passersby
"Big Spender"	Nickie, Helene, and the Fan-Dango Girls
"Charity's Soliloquy"	Charity
"Rich Man's Frug"	The Patrons
"If My Friends Could See Me Now"	Charity
"Too Many Tomorrows"	Vittorio Vidal
"There's Gotta Be Something Better than This"	Charity, Nickie, and Helene

Act Two

"I'm the Bravest Individual"	Charity and Oscar
"Rhythm of Life"	Daddy Brubeck, Brother Harold, Brother Eddie, and Worshippers
"Baby, Dream Your Dream"	Nickie and Helene
"Sweet Charity"	Oscar
"Where Am I Going?"	Charity
"I'm a Brass Band"	Charity and her Brass Band
"I Love to Cry at Weddings"	Herman, Nickie and Helene, Girls and Patrons

Act One

SCENE I

The stage is in darkness. There is music, "Charity's Theme." A light picks up a girl, CHARITY. *She carries a shoulder bag. High on her left arm is a small heart-shaped tattoo. Across the heart, a man's name is tattooed. She begins to walk aimlessly about the stage. This soon develops into a dance. As she is dancing, a sign descends. (Periodically throughout the play, signs will appear. Some will fly, some will be pushed out from the portals, and some will be carried across the stage, perhaps done in fluorescent paint, to be seen in the dark.)*

A light hits this first sing. It reads: "THE ADVEN-TURES OF CHARITY." A second sign appears. It reads: "THE STORY OF A . . ." A third sign says: "GIRL WHO WANTED TO BE . . ."

There is a momentary pause. Then a fourth sign appears. It reads: "LOVED."

This fourth sign is decorated like a valentine. All four signs disappear. The dance ends.

The lights come up to reveal a park containing several groupings of trees and perhaps a bench or two. The audience should know that the orchestra pit is the lake.

CHARITY *begins to look around for someone. A young man wearing dark glasses enters. He too seems to be looking for someone. He has a great deal of black wavy hair which he combs constantly. Suddenly they both turn and see each other. He is about to speak when* CHARITY *holds up her hand.*

CHARITY   Charlie, don't—don't say a word. Because I know exactly what you're gonna say. I've been think-ing about it all day. You're gonna start off with (*She primps her hair, then sniffs*) . . . "Mmm, that heavenly odor. Is that perfume or is that you?" And then you're gonna look in my eyes and say (*She looks in his eyes,*

tigerlike), "You drive me crazy, did you know that?
Did you know you drive me crazy?" And then—you're
gonna take my hand and hold it in yours (*She takes his
hand in hers*) . . . and then—and this is the best part—
then you're gonna say, "Honey, you are the sweetest,
the softest, the prettiest girl in this whole cockeyed
crazy wide wonderful world." (*She sighs*) Oh, brother,
you sure know how to talk to a girl. (*She sings*)
　　Man! Man, oh, man!
　　Tst—tst—tst—
　　You should see yourself . . . You're a sight.
　　You're a hundred watt e-lec-a-tric light.
　　You're a block-buster, Buster; you got class.
　　And when *you* make a pass, man, it's a pass!
　　Man! Jack, you're mad! Mmmmmmmmmmmmm!
　　How those corny jokes turn me on!
　　And I laugh till I'm ga-ga-ga-ga-gone!
　　When you switch to a se-duc-a-tive mood
　　I'm not stuck on you, lover, I am glued!
　　In that college-type rah-rah-dee-dah tweed
　　Do I wilt? Boy, are you built!
　　You're so strong, you got muscles you don't need!
　　Yes . . . Yes, indeed!
　　Wild! Dad, you're wild! Grrrrrrrrrrrr!
　　You should see yourself in my eyes!
　　You're a blue ribbon Pul-it-itzer prize!
　　　(*Speaks*)
You know what I did today? I looked at furniture.
Bedroom sets, kitchen sets, bedroom sets, living room
sets, bedroom sets. (*They walk toward the orchestra pit*)
And I've got the money for the down payment right
here. My dowry. (*She sings*)
　　Dreams . . . I had not!
　　Dreams . . . now I got!
　　You're Old Glory, man; yes, you are!
　　In my flag, you're the fi-fifty-first star!
　　You should see yourself . . . and inspect yourself,
　　Get a mirror, man, and reflect yourself.
　　You should see yourself as I see you now!
　　　(*They stop at the "lake"*)
Charlie, doesn't the lake look beautiful? (*She takes off a
shoe and "dips" her toes into the "water"*) Oooh, it feels

nice . . . Hey, Charlie, let's throw something in the lake for luck. (DARK GLASSES *quickly looks around, then in one catlike movement, he grabs* CHARITY's *shoulder bag and shoves her into the "lake." A sign appears. It reads: "SPLASH!" It disappears.* DARK GLASSES *runs off.* CHARITY's *voice comes from the pit*) Help! Help!

> (*A sign appears. It reads: "THE RESCUE." It disappears. Music begins.*
>
> FIRST PASSERBY *enters. He hears the calls. He slowly walks to the edge of the stage and looks down. He shakes his head and says, "Tsk. Tsk." He exits.*
>
> *A* MARRIED COUPLE *strolls by. The cries for help continue*)

MARRIED WOMAN (*Pointing*) Look, Walter, there's a girl in there drowning.

MARRIED MAN (*Looks and turns away*) Don't look, dear.

MARRIED WOMAN But Walter—

MARRIED MAN Don't look, I tell you. Don't get involved. It's none of our business.
> (*They look away. The* FOOTBALL PLAYER *enters and sees* CHARITY *in the water*)

FOOTBALL PLAYER (*Calling to someone*) Hey, there's a girl in there. I think she's drowning.
> (*A* WOMAN WITH A HAT *rushes in and stands next to the* FOOTBALL PLAYER. *She peers into the pit*)

WOMAN WITH HAT Yes, it certainly looks like she's drowning.
> (*An* ICE CREAM VENDOR *rushes in*)

ICE CREAM VENDOR What's going on?

WOMAN WITH HAT (*Points*) That attractive young girl is drowning.

TALL MAN (*Entering*) What did she say?
> (*A crowd slowly begins to gather. They all ad-lib*

about CHARITY'*s drowning. Some are on bikes, some with baseball bats, one with a kite, another with a balloon*)

FOOTBALL PLAYER See! She's gone down two, three times already.

ICE CREAM VENDOR Ice cream! Get your ice cream!

TALL MAN Over here!

FOOTBALL PLAYER Jeez, I don't think she can even swim.

SECOND WOMAN Sure doesn't look like it.

WOMAN WITH HAT (*Cupping her hands, yells down to* CHAR-ITY) You should've taken swimming lessons. Now it's too late.

BASEBALL PLAYER (*To another*) Hey, I'll get my kid brother. He's never seen a drowning.

ICE CREAM VENDOR Soda! Ice cold soda!

GIRL Here.
        (*A* MAN WITH A DOG *enters*)

MAN WITH DOG What's going on? What's happened?

MARRIED MAN There's a girl in the lake. Looks like she's drowning.

MAN WITH DOG Drowning? There's a girl drowning and you all just stand around? My God, why doesn't some-body do something?

WOMAN WITH HAT Why don't you?

MAN WITH DOG (*Indignant*) I can't. I'm walking my dog.

SPANISH YOUNG MAN She's floating over here. I get her. Here, Señorita, here.
        (*He gets down on his knees*)

MARRIED MAN   What's happening now?

SECOND WOMAN   The Spanish man is going to help her.

WOMAN WITH HAT (*Disgusted*)   I certainly wouldn't let one of *them* help *me*.

SPANISH YOUNG MAN (*Leans way over*)   My ankles. Somebody hold my ankles.

ICE CREAM VENDOR   Peanuts! Hot roasted peanuts!

SPANISH YOUNG MAN   Over here, Señorita.
        (*Two* HUSKY YOUNG MEN *grab his ankles*)

SECOND WOMAN   I wish they'd hurry. I have a three o'clock dentist appointment.

FOOTBALL PLAYER   He's got her! He's got her!
        (CHARITY *hands reach for the* SPANISH YOUNG MAN'*s*)

AD LIBS   "Look, he's got her," etc.

BASEBALL PLAYER   Atta boy, baby.
        (*He slaps the* SPANISH YOUNG MAN *very hard on the back, causing him to drop* CHARITY. *There is another splash*)

FOOTBALL PLAYER   Aw, butterfingers!

BASEBALL PLAYER   Oh, oh. She's gone under.

ICE CREAM VENDOR   Last call for ice cream!

FOOTBALL PLAYER   There she is. He's got her again.
        (*And with a big heave, the* SPANISH YOUNG MAN *hauls* CHARITY *out of the water. All ad-lib their encouragement. She is soaking wet and in a state of semiconsciousness. They place her on the floor and the crowd gathers around her*)

ALL We did it.
(*There is a moment of contemplative silence*)

SECOND WOMAN She looks dead. Does she look dead to you?

MARRIED MAN I don't know. I never saw her before.

FOOTBALL PLAYER What'll we do?

MARRIED MAN Artificial respiration.

AD LIBS "Very good." "Good idea," etc.
(*A* DIRTY OLD MAN, *who looks like a dirty old man, steps forward. He has a lecherous smile*)

DIRTY OLD MAN No, no. Mouth to mouth—mouth to mouth resuscitation.
(*He starts to move toward* CHARITY *and a* THIRD WOMAN *shoves him back*)

MARRIED WOMAN Get away from her, you dirty old man.

DIRTY OLD MAN I just wanted to give her mouth to mouth—

MARRIED WOMAN I know what you wanted to give her. Get outa here!

BASEBALL PLAYER Upside down. We gotta get the water out.

FOOTBALL PLAYER Yeah, c'mon. Upside down.
(*Three or four men pick* CHARITY *up and hold her by the legs, upside down. Ad libs. They shake her.* CHARITY *begins to come out of it*)

WOMAN WITH HAT Look, she's beginning to open her eyes. (*Ad libs*) Quiet, everybody; quiet.
(CHARITY, *still upside down, opens her eyes. She looks around*)

CHARITY   . . . Oh, my God, I'm in Australia!

MARRIED WOMAN   She's all right.
   (Ad libs)

CHARITY   Put me down! Put me down! Will you put me
   down! (*They turn* CHARITY *over and put her down as she
   starts swinging at all the men*) What do you think you're
   doing, you—you bunch of degenerates.

WOMAN WITH HAT   I beg your pardon.

CHARITY   Is this how you get your kicks, lady?

FOOTBALL PLAYER   Take it easy. You was drowning.

BASEBALL PLAYER   Wow, what a stupid broad.

FOOTBALL PLAYER   Maybe she was trying to knock herself off.

BASEBALL PLAYER   Sure. Over some guy.

CHARITY (*Indignant*)   Ha. That's a laugh. I've got everything to live for. I'm a normal, desirable, and much
   sought after young woman who can have any man she
   wants at the snap of her fingers. (*She snaps her fingers
   twice, but there's no sound*) They're a little wet.
      (*They all laugh*)

FOOTBALL PLAYER   I think *you're* a little wet, lady.

CHARITY   How would you like a soggy fist right in your
   big mouth?
      (*She swings at him. There is about to be a fight when*
      TWO POLICEMEN *enter the crowd*)

FIRST COP   All right; all right, break it up. Let's break it
   up, heh? What's going on here?

SECOND COP   Let's break it up.
      (*All the people in the crowd now offer up their version*

of how the rescue took place. It is a garble. CHARITY *is now stretched out on the ground*)

BASEBALL PLAYER   Ah, this stupid broad was drowning, and I . . .
(CHARITY *swings at him again*)

FIRST COP   Hey, take it easy, lady.

CHARITY (*To* COP)   Where were you when I needed you?

FIRST COP   Let's move along, heh? The excitement's all over.

TALL MAN   Don't you push me. I'm a taxpayer.
(*The* SECOND COP *begins to shoo away the people, who leave reluctantly.* CHARITY *discovers she only has one shoe on and begins to look for the other one*)

FIRST COP (*To* CHARITY)   All right, lady?

CHARITY (*Looking for her shoe*)   I'm fine. Fine. I feel fine. I'm very fine. Put it down in your little book. "Crazy drowned lady feels fine."

SECOND COP   You wanna tell us what happened?

CHARITY   I lost my shoe, that's what happened.

SECOND COP (*To the* FIRST COP)   Hey, Monte, look for her shoe.

CHARITY   Yeah, look for it, Monte.

FIRST COP   What did it look like?

CHARITY (*Indicating the other shoe*)   Like this one! (*Mimicking*) What'd it look like?
(*The* FIRST COP *looks for the shoe*)

SECOND COP (*Writing in his book*)   What's your name, Miss?

CHARITY (*Looking for her shoe*)   Charity. Charity Hope Valentine.

FIRST COP (*Looks up and snickers*)   Charity Hope Valentine?

CHARITY   I wouldn't snicker at other people's names, Monte!

SECOND COP   Address?

CHARITY   615 West Ninety-fourth Street.

SECOND COP   Occupation?

CHARITY   . . . I'm a Social Consultant.

SECOND COP   Where?

CHARITY   The Fan-Dango Ballroom.

SECOND COP (*Looks at her, then writes in his book*)   Dance hall hostess.

FIRST COP   You mean you work in one of them tango palaces?

CHARITY   It's temporary.

SECOND COP   Length of employment?

CHARITY   Eight years. Oh, there's my shoe. In the water. Monte, would you be a sweet cop and—

FIRST COP (*Reluctantly*)   Yeah, yeah.
    (*He leans down into the "lake"*)

CHARITY   He's a sweet cop.
    (MONTE *has the shoe out. He hands it to her*)

SECOND COP   All right, I'd like to know what you were doing in the water.

CHARITY Actually, very little. You see, my fiancé, Charlie—that's his name on my tattoo—well, he's not really my fiancé. We're engaged to be wed the minute his own marriage breaks up, which, if you ask me, looks like it's on the rocks right now. Anyway . . . Thank you, Monte. (*Her shoe is on and she stands*) Anyway . . . Ich, they squish. Anyway—where was I?

SECOND COP (*Looks at his book*) Anyway—
    (*A sign appears. It reads: "FAN-DANGO BALL-ROOM . . . THAT NIGHT"*)

CHARITY . . . Anyway, we had an appointment to meet in the park because naturally we can't meet at his place—his wife is very peculiar. Well, I took my shoe off and . . . put my foot in the water . . .

End of scene

SCENE 2

The Hostess Room of the Fan-Dango Ballroom. It is a combination locker room, dressing room, and lounge. CHARITY *is now in front of her locker changing. Eight or nine dance hostesses are also changing and listening to* CHARITY's *sad story.*

CHARITY (*Continuing*) . . . my feet are always hot, you know . . . and I slipped.

GIRLS   Yeah. Sure.

CHARITY   He grabbed for me but all he got was my handbag and I fell in . . .

GIRLS   Oh, sure.

CHARITY   He started to come in after me but he didn't because of his bad back, which he received in the army—although he's very athletic, has a wonderful build, plays handball and the horses. Anyway, he ran off to get help—
  (*She is now out of her dress and into a robe. She takes a bath towel out of the locker. On the inside door of the locker there is a large, life-size picture of* DARK GLASSES)

HELENE   Honey, didn't you leave a tiny little detail out of that story?

CHARITY   Like what?

HELENE   Like there ain't one word of truth in it.
  (NICKIE *enters*)

NICKIE Hello, men.

CARMEN Hey, Nickie, did you hear about Charity and her new boyfriend?

NICKIE Oh! They're gonna be married! (*Embraces* CHARITY) Honey, all the luck in the world!

CARMEN He stole her money and pushed her in the lake.

NICKIE He wasn't for you!
(HERMAN, *the manager, sticks his head in*)

HERMAN Awright, ladies, Prince Philip just walked in, so stick your gum behind your ears and drag it out on the floor.
(*He exits*)

CHARITY (*Still trying*) I bet Charlie is out there right this minute. With a perfectly logical explanation. You'll see.

NICKIE Aw, baby, look—you know that I, Nickie Pignatelli, does not like to say harsh or cruel things. Despite the fact that I may have spent a few quiet years in an upstate government hotel, I am still warm, kindhearted, and basically sincere. (*To the others*) True?

HELENE True.

CARMEN True.

NICKIE True. So as a friend, someone who cares and loves you, I feel I owe ya this—you're a stupid broad! Your big problem is you run your heart like a hotel— you got guys checkin' in and out all the time.

CHARITY But this time it's different. I did slip. He wouldn't push me. He loves me. Every time I say to him, "I love you," he always says, "Ditto." "Ditto"; that's just the way he says it. Does that sound like a man who would push a girl in the lake for two hundred bucks?

NICKIE   Right.

HELENE   Ditto.

CARMEN   Forget him, honey. We got a living to make
  (*They start to exit*) . . . if you call this a living.

CHARITY (*Sits at the dressing table and sings*)
  You should see yourself, like tonight
  You're a hundred watt e-lec-a-tric light
  You're a block-buster. Buster, you got class
  And when you make a pass . . . man,
  It's a . . .
    (*She goes off. The Hostess Room disappears*)

End of scene

20

The Fan-Dango Ballroom. NICKIE, HELENE, SISSIE, *and the girls are on stage.*

FIRST GIRL Hey, mister, can I talk to you for a minute? What's the harm in a little talk?

SECOND GIRL Hey, good-looking, I like your hair.

THIRD GIRL Hey, mister, gotta cigarette for me?

FOURTH GIRL Hey, mister, you speak French? Come here, I wanna talk to you.

FIFTH GIRL Hey, fella, ya wanna dance? A little dance won't hurt ya.

SIXTH GIRL What's the harm in talking? It can't hurt ya, can it?

SEVENTH GIRL He's so tall . . . Must be six foot four . . .

EIGHTH GIRL Let's have some fun.

HELENE Psst . . .
        (NICKIE *whistles*)

ALL (*They sing*)
        The minute you walked in the joint
        I could see you were a man of distinction,
        A real big spender,
        Good-looking, so refined.
        Say, wouldn't you like to know what's going on in
            my mind?

So let me get right to the point.
I don't pop my cork for ev'ry guy I see.
Hey! Big spender,
Spend a little time with me . . . me . . .
Do you wanna have . . . fun?
How about a few . . . laughs?
I can show you a good time.
Do you wanna have fun . . . fun . . .
   (*They split up*)
Fun . . . fun . . . fun . . . fun . . .
   (*Singing together*)
How about a few . . . laughs . . . laughs . . .
Fun . . . laughs . . . fun . . . laughs . . . fun . . . laughs
   . . . fun . . . laughs . . .
I can . . . show you a . . . good time . . .

Fun . . . laughs . . . good time . . .
Hey! Big spender,
Spend a little time with me.

FIRST GIRL   What do you say to a . . .

SECOND GIRL   How's about a . . .

ALL   Laugh.

THIRD GIRL   I could give you some . . .

FOURTH GIRL   Are you ready for some . . .

ALL   Fun.

FIFTH GIRL   How would you like a . . .

SIXTH GIRL   Let me show you a . . .

ALL   Good time. (*They sing*)
   Hey! Big spender!
   Hey! Big spender!
   The minute you walked in the joint
   I could see you were a man of distinction,
   A real big spender,

Good-looking, so refined.
Say, wouldn't you like to know what's going on in
  my mind?
So let me get right to the point.
I don't pop my cork for ev'ry guy I see.
Hey! Big spender!
Hey! Big spender!
Hey! Big spender,
Spend a little time with me.
Fun, laughs, good time . . .
Fun, laughs, good time . . .
Fun, laughs, good time . . .

NICKIE How 'bout it, palsy?

ALL Yeah.
  (*A few of the girls walk off to the booths with men.*
  CHARITY *enters. She is looking for* DARK GLASSES)

CHARITY Anyone ask for me?

NICKIE (*To* CHARITY) Baby, Jack the Pusher ain't coming tonight.

CHARITY (*Still looking*) He'll come. Like he's come
every night for the last two months, with a gardenia in
his lapel and a cigarette dangling from his lips . . .

HELENE And a pound and a half of Vaseline in his hair.

NICKIE I bet that's why he never wore a hat. It kept
sliding off his head.

CHARITY He *will* be here tonight. I know it. He will. He
will. He will.

NICKIE He won't.

CHARITY I know he won't. (*In tears*) Oh, Nickie, I'm the
biggest pushover that ever lived.

HERMAN (*From the ticket booth*) Hey, c'mon!
  (*A customer enters and selects a girl*)

CARMEN   If he stole your purse, why don't you call the cops? They could still pick him up.

HELENE   Sugar, you know how many guys there are running around this city with pocketbooks?

CHARITY   Nickie!

NICKIE   Aw, baby!
  (*She embraces her*)

CHARITY   Nickie, why did he do it; why? I bought him everything he ever wanted. I even got him a midnight-blue mohair seventy-nine-dollar Italian suit that he could have bought for forty-five at Howard's. But that louse wouldn't wear a Howard's suit—

NICKIE   Go ahead, honey; get it out of your system.

CHARITY   The things I used to do for him. Getting up in the middle of the night to get him a provolone sandwich and a bottle of Yoo-Hoo chocolate milk.

NICKIE   Men—they got no feelings.

CHARITY (*To the picture of* DARK GLASSES)   Well, I've had it up to here, mister. You can slip and slide your greasy head on some other girl's shoulder.

NICKIE   You tell him, baby.

CHARITY   I hope your tight Italian pants choke you to death.

HELENE   *Ole!*

HELENE   The kid's gonna be all right.

NICKIE   Yeah.

CHARITY   It won't happen to me again. How did it all start anyway? (*She sings*)

Can I remember
How this song and dance began?
Yes, I can . . . Damned right I can.
It began, well, anyway, ya see,
There was this man . . .
Who stopped and asked me if I knew
Which way was Lexington Avenue.
He said: "I'm going to Bloomingdale's."
I said: "I'm going to Bloomingdale's!"
So . . . we hoofed it over to Bloomingdale's!
    (*Speaking*)
He wanted to buy some jockey shorts! (*Singing*)
Then he said: "Miss, would you like a cup
O' tea or maybe some Seven-Up?"
    (*She nods and smiles; a pause*)
I left the tip! Picked up the tab
For the jockey shorts
And a taxicab!
    (*Speaking*)

He dropped me off and I burned! Let that be a lesson to you. Lower the boom, girl! Lower the boom! (*Singing*)
But what can you do when he knocks on your door
'Cause they locked him out of his furnished room!
    (*Speaking*)
So he moves in! (CHARITY *moves into the Ballroom section. The music changes to a Bossa Nova. She smiles at a customer, takes his tickets, and dances with him. Her soliloquy continues*) He moves in with the jockey shorts in a paper bag! Nothing else! (*Singing*)
He needs toothpaste
And a toothbrush and pajama tops.
He needs razor blades, a razor, and a comb! Several!
He needs sistering and brothering
And fathering and mothering.
He needs a hat
To hang up in my flat
And call it home!

In no time at all
I find we're very much in love
And I'm blushing like a sentimental slob!

And he's kissing me
And hugging me
And all the time he's bugging me
To go out and try to find myself
A better-paying job!

Comes July, it's ninety-eight degrees,
He wants a coat!
Wants a fur-lined coat. Fur collar! Cuffs! The works
    (plus tax)!
While I really didn't begrudge it,
When I figured out my budget,
For that coat I had to dance
With something like eleven hundred jerks!
    (*Speaking*)
All right, Marvin—let's not get overheated.

MARVIN   Aw—I'm nuts about you, Charity. What do you say we spend the weekend together in Atlantic City? I'm crazy for you.

CHARITY   Sure. The next thing you know I believe him—and then I'm paying for the train tickets, the hotel bill, the salt-water taffy, three Turkish baths, and a massage.
    (*Singing*)
Pocket money! Poker money! Smoking money!
Skating money! Bowling money! Movie money!
Haircut money! Shoe shine money!
Money for a bill from Louie's Bar.
Money for a bill from Charlie's Bar.
Money for a bill from Maxie's Bar.
But, will he ask for subway money?
No! He don't want subway money!
    (*Speaking*)
'Cause it turns out the bum wants to go to Florida.
C'mon down!

MARVIN   What's your answer, Charity?

CHARITY   Here's my answer, Marvin. (*Singing*)
Now hear this!
And get this!

Oh, Susannah! Amen!
This big, fat heart
Ain't gonna be torn apart
Ever, ever, ever again! *Ole!*
(*Pushes* MARVIN *into a booth*)
My problem is I'm too giving. I'm always giving and
I never get. (*A* PANHANDLER *starts across*) Well, I'm
through giving. I already gave and *I'm not giving any
more.*
(*A* LADY *with a collection box crosses*)

LADY (*Pleadingly*) Could you please give to the Unwed
Mothers of New York?

CHARITY With humane pleasure.
(*She gives the* LADY *a dollar. The* LADY *starts off*)

LADY (*Tearfully*) Thank you and bless you.

CHARITY Er, are you an unwed mother?

LADY No, but my mother is!
(*She walks off*)

CHARITY (*Out front*) Sometimes we don't know when
we're well off.
(*Three people cross quickly*)

MAN (*With box*) Could you please give to wipe out
whooping cough?

CHARITY (*Gives*) Whooping cough? By all means.

ANOTHER LADY (*With box*) Stamp out sex in our schools.

CHARITY (*Giving*) I certainly want to do that.

ANOTHER MAN (*With box*) Help put a gypsy in Congress.

CHARITY (*Giving*) It's the least I can do.

End of scene

The street outside the Pompeii Club. A DOORMAN *stands outside by the Pompeii's canopy.*

CHARITY (*Out front*)   See what I mean? Now I'm starving to death and I gave away my last nickel. (*To the* DOORMAN, *cupping her hands as if begging*) Give to a hungry dance hall hostess.

DOORMAN   No soliciting, please.

CHARITY (*Making a fist*)   Now just a minute, Napoleon . . .
> (*Suddenly the door of the club bursts open and a beautiful, well-groomed girl,* URSALA, *storms out. She is fuming*)

URSALA (*Throws her sable around her, angrily*)   Get me a taxi right away. I'm going home.
> (*The door bursts open again and* VITTORIO VIDAL, *a mature, popular leading man in movies on both continents, rushes after her*)

VIDAL   Ursala! Ursala, wait a minute. (*He crashes into* CHARITY) Excuse me, Signorina. I'm very sorry. Forgive me.

CHARITY (*Suddenly her mouth drops as she realizes who he is*)   Vittorio Vidal! (*Rushes to the* DOORMAN, *pushing him*) That's Vittorio Vidal, the movie star!

VIDAL (*To* URSALA)   Ursala, you've got to let me explain.

CHARITY (*Punches the* DOORMAN)   Oh! It's really him. Look! Look!

VIDAL   I just said "Hello" to the girl. That's all.

URSALA (*Pulls away*)   Don't touch me. We're through, Vittorio. I hate you, do you hear? I hate the sight of you.

CHARITY (*To the* DOORMAN)   Gee, she really knows him.

VIDAL   Ursala, you can't walk out on me like this.

URSALA   No? Just watch me. *Just watch me!*

CHARITY (*To the* DOORMAN)   Watch! You're not watching!

VIDAL   You're coming back inside. (*Aside, angrily*) How will it look for a big star like me to be alone in a nightclub without a girl.

URSALA   That's *your* problem. (*To the* DOORMAN) Where's my taxi?

CHARITY (*Calls out*)   Taxi! Taxi!

DOORMAN (*To* CHARITY)   Will you get out of here!

VIDAL   You're coming inside!

URSALA   I'm not!

VIDAL   You are!

URSALA   I'm not!

VIDAL   Oh, yes, you are.
    (*He pulls her*)

URSALA   Oh, no, I'm not. You two-bit, "B" picture, fading Romeo. I wouldn't be caught dead seen with you. You wanna go back in there, get yourself another girl!

VIDAL   But Ursala. (*All the action freezes. A sign appears. It reads: "A STROKE OF LUCK"*) Ursala! (*He knocks into* CHARITY *again*) Signorina, I'm very sorry. Forgive me.

CHARITY   My pleasure.
  (*He turns and points to* CHARITY)

VIDAL   You. Are you busy tonight?

CHARITY (*Nudges the* DOORMAN)   He wants to know if you're busy tonight.

VIDAL (*Points*)   No. *You.* (CHARITY *looks around, then indicates herself*) Yes, you. Are you busy tonight?

CHARITY (*Gulps, then innocently*)   What time?

VIDAL   Now! Right now!

CHARITY   Right now is very good for me.

URSALA   You wouldn't dare. A girl off the streets?

VIDAL   Wouldn't I? (*To* CHARITY) Come.
  (*As he goes into the club*)

URSALA   Vittorio, you wouldn't! You wouldn't!

CHARITY (*Not viciously*)   He did. (*She takes* VIDAL'S *arm and starts to enter the club. Just as she is about to pass the bewildered* DOORMAN, *she stops and looks up at him and says proudly*) I'm with him.
  (*The rest of the stage unfreezes. The sign disappears and the street moves off*)

End of scene

SCENE 5

The interior of the Pompeii Club, with tables and a dance floor. There are about five couples on the floor doing the "Rich Man's Frug." They continue with bits and pieces of the dance interspersed throughout the dialogue of this scene.

As VIDAL *and* CHARITY *enter, the* DANCERS *all stop dead in their tracks from the shock of seeing this great celebrity with this strange little girl.* VIDAL *looks indifferent but* CHARITY *struts as proud as a peacock.*

The astounded WAITER *shows them to their table as the others form a group and start buzzing like hens.*

FIRST DANCER   Who's that with Vittorio?

SECOND DANCER   What happened to Ursala?

THIRD DANCER   That's not the girl he came in with.

FOURTH DANCER   I've never seen her before.

FIFTH DANCER   Who could she be?

SIXTH DANCER   She doesn't look familiar.

SEVENTH DANCER   Who is it?

EIGHTH DANCER   Who is it?

NINTH DANCER   Who is it?

TENTH DANCER   Who is it?

ELEVENTH DANCER   Who is it?

TWELFTH DANCER   Who is it?

ALL   Who is it?
(CHARITY, *passing by, chatting animatedly with* VIDAL, *looks up at them*)

CHARITY   It's me! (*She and* VIDAL *sit as the* WAITER *hands* CHARITY *a huge menu*) Oh, isn't this gay!

WAITER   Monsieur Vidal?

VIDAL   A double Scotch.

WAITER (*To* CHARITY)   And for Madam?

CHARITY (*She picks up the huge menu and sits*)   I'll just browse for a while.
(*She buries her head behind it*)

VIDAL (*Angrily, thinking of* URSALA)   I just wish I knew what she wanted. You know she gets insane if I just look at another woman? Wouldn't you call that psychotic?

CHARITY (*Reading from the menu*)   "Boy-yew de bwef oh natch-yew-rolle."

VIDAL   You tell me. What do *you* think it is?

CHARITY   Pot roast.

VIDAL   And yet in some ways she's so vital. So exciting and full of life . . .

CHARITY   Do you think we could have some rolls while we're waiting?

VIDAL (*Grabs her wrists*)   Talk to me.

CHARITY (*Quickly*)   Yes, Vittorio?

VIDAL   You look like a normal, sensible girl.

CHARITY (*A spark of hope*)   I try to dress simply.

VIDAL   Wouldn't you say she was vital and brimming with life?

CHARITY   That was my immediate reaction.

VIDAL   And yet she can be childish, neurotic, impossible.

CHARITY   That was my second impression.

VIDAL   Why are women like that? I've never met a man I couldn't depend on. Have you?

CHARITY   I depend on them all the time.

VIDAL   Is she worth all this? Is she?

CHARITY   Well, as you say, she *is* vital and brimming with life . . .

VIDAL   That's true. She *is* vital and brimming with life.

CHARITY   But of course, *you* know her better than I do.

VIDAL   No, no, you're right. She *is* vital and brimming with life.

CHARITY (*To herself*)   I think I just screwed myself up. (*The* WAITER *comes over with a telephone and plugs it in by their table*)

WAITER   Telephone, Monsieur Vidal.

VIDAL   Aha, it's her. Begging for forgiveness. She'll cry and plead for me to come to her apartment. What should I do? Should I be magnanimous or should I be aloof?

CHARITY   Aloof. The aloofer the better.

VIDAL   You're right. (*Into the telephone*) I'm not here. (*To* CHARITY *as he hangs up the phone*) Now I'm hungry. (*To the* WAITER) Bring us two Chateaubriand.

CHARITY (*To the* WAITER)   May I use the phone? I'd like to check with my telephone serv-eece!
(*She dials*)

WAITER   Very good, sir. Two Chateaubriand.

CHARITY   And trim the fat. (*Into the phone*) Hello, Nickie, Miss Valentine speaking. (*She is putting on airs*) Miss Valentine. Any messages for me? Charity, jerk! Who called? Jerry, the Greek? (*To* VIDAL) Must have been an overseas call. (*Back into the phone*) Oh, well, I don't know what time I'll be home. That's entirely up to Vittorio. Vittorio Vidal. Yes, the international film star. We're sitting together at a table at the Pompeii Club waiting for our rolls. Oh, all right. (*She hands* VIDAL *the phone*) Would you please say hello?

VIDAL (*Into the phone*)   Hello.

CHARITY (*Into the phone*)   There's your hello. Now good-bye.
(*She hangs up. The music starts*)

VIDAL   I seem to have done nothing but talk about my own problems. It must be very boring.

CHARITY   Well, I wouldn't want you to be bored. Talk about something else.

VIDAL   I don't want to talk.
(*He looks into her eyes*)

CHARITY (*Falling under his spell*)   What *do* you want to do?

VIDAL (*Soulfully*)   I want to dance.
(*She joins him on the floor. They start to dance and she steps on his foot*)

CHARITY   Oh, I'm sorry. I'm a little woozy—I haven't eaten since breakfast. Would you be kind enough to hold out your arms?

VIDAL   Why?

CHARITY   I'm going to faint.
   (*And she faints in his arms. He picks her up*)

FIRST DANCER   She's passed out!

SECOND DANCER   Somebody get some ammonia.

THIRD DANCER   Rub her wrists.

FOURTH DANCER   Loosen her collar.

FIFTH DANCER   Give her air. Give her air.
   (*There is general agreement*)

SIXTH DANCER   Put her down.

OTHER DANCERS   Yeah, lay her down.

VIDAL (*Looks around*)   Where?

CHARITY (*Opens her eyes eagerly*)   Your apartment!
   (*He carries her from the nightclub into his apartment*)

End of scene

VITTORIO VIDAL's *apartment. A light has remained on* CHARITY *and* VIDAL *as he carries her in. The room then lights up.* VIDAL's *apartment is large and in good taste. We are in a combination bedroom, sitting room, and dressing room.*

His bed is an oversized chaise covered with a fur throw and a great many pillows (that possibly spell out VIDAL *on the bed). There is a huge wardrobe closet with sliding doors and a smaller supplementary closet. In one corner of the room is a teacart which has been converted into an elaborate, well-stocked bar. There is a hi-fi. The overall effect is extravagance and sensualism.*

The music of the new scene has drifted away when the new set has come into place. VIDAL's MAN *is chilling some champagne when* VIDAL *carries* CHARITY *in.*

VIDAL   My apartment.

CHARITY   Hmm, cozy!

VIDAL   Good evening, Manfred.

MANFRED   Good evening, sir. (*Extends a hand toward* CHARITY *in* VIDAL's *arms*) I've laid out a small supper.

VIDAL   Thank you, Manfred. Were there any calls for me?

MANFRED   No, sir. No calls.

CHARITY   And let's keep it that way.

VIDAL   Good night, Manfred.

MANFRED   Good night, sir. Good night, ma'am.

CHARITY   Good night, Manny. (MANFRED *exits*) He's sweet. You're lucky to have someone worried about you all the time.

VIDAL   I'm worried about you right this minute. Do you want to lie down now?

CHARITY (*Coyly*)   It's your bed; whatever you say.

VIDAL (*Puts her down on the bed*)   I say you should have something to eat. (*Crosses to the table with the food*) What would you like? Chicken? Ham? Turkey? Genoa salami?

CHARITY   Isn't that funny? The minute Manny went to bed, I wasn't hungry any more.

VIDAL (*Taking off his jacket and crossing to the closet*)   You're a funny girl.

CHARITY   Yeah? Is that good or bad?

VIDAL   It's good, very good.

CHARITY (*Gets up, smiling*)   No kidding? Hey, keep talking.

VIDAL (*Puts on his robe*)   You know, I just realized. I don't know a thing about you.

CHARITY   Oh, I could tell you everything about me. Who I am and what I do, but it would be a waste of time 'cause I'm gonna lie.

VIDAL (*Crossing to the champagne bottle*)   Why would you lie?

CHARITY   Because I want to impress you and if I told you what I really did you wouldn't be very impressed.

VIDAL   Let me be the judge of that. What do you do?

CHARITY   I'm a dance hall hostess.

VIDAL   Oh.

CHARITY   You see. You shoulda let me lie. I was gonna be an assistant dental technician.

VIDAL (*Opening the champagne*)   That doesn't sound very impressive.

CHARITY   It is to a dance hall hostess.

VIDAL   *You're* the one who doesn't seem very impressed. (*Pours champagne*) Why did you ever take a job like that?

CHARITY   I don't know. Fickle finger of fate, I guess.

VIDAL   What?

CHARITY   Fickle finger of fate. Don't you know what that means?

VIDAL   Yes, I think so.

CHARITY   I don't. Not really. But so many things seem to happen to me and I don't know why or how. People always ask me, "Why did you take up with that guy?" or, "How did you wind up in that joint?" I got so embarrassed always saying, "I don't know." But it was the truth. I don't. (*She spits out an olive pit*) Scusi. But I guess you're supposed to know *why* you do things or *how* you wind up in places. (*She shrugs*) Anyway, now when anyone asks me why or how I just say, "Fickle finger of fate," and I don't get embarrassed any more.

VIDAL   I think you just like saying it.

CHARITY (*Delighted*)   I think you're right. Fickle finger of fate . . . Fickle finger of fate. (*She laughs*) Feels good. It cools the mouth. You wanna try it?

VIDAL   All right. Fickle finger of fate.

CHARITY   You like it?

VIDAL   Very nice.

CHARITY   I got lots of phrases I like to say, even when they don't exactly fit. Like if some wiseacre at the Fan-Dango says to me something fresh or something dirty and I just can't think quick enough to answer, I like to say, "Up yours."

VIDAL   (*A little surprised*)   You do?

CHARITY   Oh, yeah. That's a good one. Fits almost any question. Of course I wouldn't say it to a nice refined gentleman like you. I mean it wouldn't be right. You say to me, "Why did you ever take a job like a dance hall hostess?" And then I say, "Up yours." It just isn't nice. But I can say "Fickle finger of fate," can't I?

VIDAL   (*Laughs*)   You certainly can. (*Hands her a glass*) Here. Let's drink to it.

CHARITY   Okay.

VIDAL   (*Holds up his glass*)   To the fickle finger—

CHARITY   —of fate.
          (*They click glasses*)

VIDAL   Bottoms up!

CHARITY   Up yours! (*Puts her hand quickly over her mouth*) It just slipped out.

VIDAL   (*Laughs*)   You're wonderful. You're really wonderful.

CHARITY   Me? Me wonderful? Wow! Hey, that's really something coming from Vittorio Vidal.

VIDAL (*Pours more for himself*) What makes you think Vittorio Vidal is so special?

CHARITY Are you kidding? Have you ever seen you in the movies?

VIDAL (*Sits, holding his glass and the bottle*) Not recently. If nothing else, I have good taste.

CHARITY Well, you don't know what you're missing. You should've seen the picture you made with Monica Monicelli.
    (*She pronounces it "Munn-icker Munn-ickerlee"*)

VIDAL (*Corrects her pronunciation*) Monica Monicelli.

CHARITY Yeah. There was this scene. I couldn't see it too good 'cause it was very foggy. Anyway, you had just finished making wild love to her—which is why I think it was foggy—and she started to cry, like this (*She cries*) . . . "Mario. Mario." And then do you remember what you did?

VIDAL Fortunately, no.

CHARITY I will as long as I live. You bent down and kissed every one of her fingers. From pinkie to thumb. And then you said—and I remember every word exactly—you said, "Without love, life has no purpose!" Wow! Did that ever hit home. (*Pounds her chest*) You got me right where I live. I went through the whole picture and six Milky Ways just to hear that line again. "Without love, life has no purpose."

VIDAL Is that what you believe?

CHARITY Oh sure. Don't you? Doesn't everybody?

VIDAL Why? Why do you believe in love?

CHARITY (*Shrugs*) I don't know. You got to have some religion.

VIDAL   And so your religion is love?

CHARITY   Well, I'll tell you one thing, I sure go to the church a lot.

VIDAL (*Smiles, shaking his head*)   Signorina Valentine, I see you sitting there with my own eyes—but I find it hard to believe you really exist.

CHARITY   I don't believe I'm here either. Say, do you think I could have a personally autographed picture? Just so I could prove it to myself tomorrow.

VIDAL (*Gets up and goes to the dresser*)   It's the least I can do. (*Opens a drawer, taking out pictures*) With mustache or without?

CHARITY   Without.

VIDAL (*Starts to write*)   "For?"

CHARITY   Charity . . .

VIDAL   "For Charity . . ."
(*He looks at her to continue*)

CHARITY (*Dictating*)   "who was with me in my apartment tonight" (*He smiles and writes*) . . . "alone!" (*He writes*) "I swear it." (*Dictating*) . . . "Vittorio Vi—"

VIDAL   I know the rest. (*Hands her the picture*) *Eccola.*

CHARITY   Thanks. (*Takes the picture and looks at it proudly*) You move right into my locker tomorrow night. Gee, what a night for me. Champagne, dancing, personally autographed picture—but it may not be enough.

VIDAL   For what?

CHARITY   To prove to my girlfriends I was really here. Say, do you think I could have some small article of personal apparel? You know, like a tie, a handkerchief, an old camel's hair coat, anything.

VIDAL   I'll get something for you now. (*Starts for the door, then stops*) You won't leave?

CHARITY   Hurricane Hazel could strike, I'm not moving. (*He smiles and nods at her and exits.* CHARITY, *very contented with herself, looks around the room. The music starts*) The girls at the Ballroom would never believe me in a million years. (*She sings and dances*)
>   If they could see me now,
>   That little gang of mine—
>   I'm eating fancy chow
>   And drinking fancy wine—
>   I'd like those stumblebums
>   To see for a fact
>   The kind of top-drawer first-rate
>   Chums I attract!
>   All I can say is *wow*-
>   Eee, looka where I am!
>   Tonight I landed *pow!*
>   Right in a pot of jam!
>   What a setup! Holy cow,
>   They'd never believe it
>   If my friends could see me now!
>   They'd never believe it—
>   They'd never believe—
>   (VIDAL *comes in.* CHARITY *bumps into him and stops her dance*)

VIDAL (*He has a pop-up top hat which he snaps and "pops up"*)   I used this in my first picture, *Million Dollar Lips.*

CHARITY   What a beautiful black thing.

VIDAL   It's a hat. (*Opens it*) *Eccola.* (*Smiles*) Wait. There's some more.
>   (*He exits*)

CHARITY (*Singing*)
>   If they could see me now,
>   My little dusty group,

Traipsing 'round this
Million-dollar chicken coop!
I'd hear those thrift-shop cats say:
"Brother! Get her!"
Draped on a bedspread made from
Three kinds of fur!
All I can say is: "Wow!"
Wait till the riff and raff
See just exactly how
He signed this autograph!
What a buildup! Holy cow,
They'd never believe it
If my friends could see me now!
(*At the end of the second chorus and her dance,* CHAR-
ITY *is bouncing on the bed. She is caught, embarrassed,
by* VIDAL*'s return. He has a walking stick.* CHARITY
jumps off the bed)
Sealy Posturpedic.
(*Patting the mattress*)

VIDAL   I used this in *The Dancing Spy.* It's yours.

CHARITY   I couldn't.

VIDAL   You must.

CHARITY   I can't.

VIDAL   I insist.

CHARITY   I'll take it.
(*She takes the stick*)

VIDAL   Wait. There's more.
(*He goes back into the other room*)

CHARITY   *Ciao*, Vittorio, baby. (CHARITY, *with walking
stick and top hat, sings*)
If they could see me now,
Alone with Mr. V!
Who's waiting on me like he was a maitre d'!
I hear my buddies saying:

"Crazy! What gives?
Tonight she's living like the other half lives!"
To think the highest-brow,
Which I must say is he,
Should pick the lowest-brow,
Which there's no doubt is me,
What a step up! Holy cow!
They'd never believe it
If my friends could see me now!
   (*She dances. Near the end of her dance, she sings
   again*)
They'd never believe it
They'd never believe it
If my friends could see me now.
   (*She dances*)
Hi, girls—it's me—Charity!
   (*At the end of her song,* VIDAL *comes out again.* CHAR-
   ITY *has finished the last chorus on one knee with arms
   outstretched à la Al Jolson.* VIDAL *catches her like this*)

VIDAL Miss Charity Valentine. Come here. Please. (*He
takes her to the side*) In all my possessions, I find I have
nothing that truly expresses my warm feeling for you.
So I ask you, please to accept this.
   (*He gives her a light, simple, affectionate kiss on her
   forehead. She is overwhelmed*)

CHARITY I accept. And may I say I never received a gift
that came in such a gorgeous package.

VIDAL And now . . .

CHARITY Yes? And now?

VIDAL And now—shall we have dinner?

CHARITY Mr. Vidal, you've been so nice to me. Is there
any way—that I can return the favor?

VIDAL I don't understand.

CHARITY I mean—is there *anything* I can do? I mean,
anything you want me to do? Am I making myself
clear?

VIDAL   Perfectly. Now shall we have dinner?

CHARITY   I'm not making myself clear. Mr. Vidal, you've been so nice to me, is there *anything* . . .?

VIDAL (*Takes her hand*)   I *know* what you mean.

CHARITY   Oh. Okay. Let's have dinner. Of course, later on if you should change your mind about "you know," well, what the hell—you know what I mean? (*He smiles and nods*) You see, I know the heartbreak you're going through. I too have been to the well and have come up with an empty bucket.

VIDAL   You mean Ursala?

CHARITY   You're nuts about her, right?

VIDAL   Ha! I haven't given her a thought all night.

CHARITY   Yeah, she's got you gaga. I can tell by the way you say her name. You got little violins in your voice. (*She demonstrates with little violins in her voice*) Ursala! Ursala!

VIDAL   Nonsense!
        (MANFRED *rushes in*)

MANFRED   Sir, Miss March is at the door.

VIDAL (*With violins in his voice*)   Ursala?

CHARITY   See what I mean?

VIDAL (*To* MANFRED)   Get rid of her. Tell her I'm not in.

MANFRED   I did, sir, but she insists on seeing you anyway.

VIDAL (*To* CHARITY)   Why? Why does she torture me like this?

CHARITY (*Shrugs*)   Fickle finger of fate, I guess.

URSALA (*Offstage*) Vittorio, let me in. I must talk to you.

VIDAL Talk? You mean scream, don't you? (*To* CHARITY) What should I do? Help me.

CHARITY Be firm. Be strong. Be a man!

VIDAL (*Firmly*) Yes!

URSALA (*Pleading*) Please, Vittorio, I beg of you. Please.

VIDAL No.

URSALA Please.

VIDAL No.

URSALA Please.

CHARITY I can't stand it. Let her in.

VIDAL Yes, let her in.
    (MANFRED *starts for the door*)

CHARITY (*To* MANFRED) Wait a minute. (*To* VIDAL) I'd better get in the closet.

VIDAL Why?

CHARITY If she can't see me, I wasn't here.

URSALA Please.

VIDAL Thank you very much. You're wonderful. (*He opens the door of the closet.* CHARITY *jumps into the closet and shuts the door*) All right, Manfred.
    (*The closet door opens again and* CHARITY *sticks her head out*)

CHARITY Hey! This is just like that French picture you made, *Six in a Bed*.
    (*She shuts the door herself*)

MANFRED   Can I open it, sir?
(VIDAL *nods but—the closet door opens again*)

CHARITY   Oh! Hold it! (*She gets out, rushes to the food table and quickly makes herself a fat sandwich. Then she rushes back toward the closet*) . . . If you get a chance, I'd love a cold beer.
(*She gets back into the closet and* VIDAL *shuts the door and nods to* MANFRED, *who crosses and opens the other door.*
The audience can now see CHARITY *in the closet. We are in a split set. The closet is very small. Three or four coats are hanging up, along with several garment bags, the kind with a zipper up the side, and other assorted items.* MANFRED *opens the door and* URSALA *rushes in*)

URSALA   What's going on? I heard voices. Who are you talking to?

VIDAL   Is that why you came back? To accuse me again? (MANFRED *tiptoes out*) All right, it's that girl I picked up in front of the club. She's been with me all night and she's in that closet right now. (*He points to the closet*) Go on. Look for yourself.
(CHARITY *tries to hide behind a sports jacket*)

URSALA   All right, I will. (*She walks to the closet and opens it as* CHARITY *tries to hide further behind the jacket. But* URSALA *does not look in*) What's wrong with me? Thinking you could stoop so low as to hide a girl in a closet. (*She closes the door*) Oh, Vittorio, forgive me, forgive me. (CHARITY *takes the sleeve of the sports jacket and wipes her brow*) I don't know what comes over me. The thought of you with another girl drives me insane. (CHARITY *puts her ear right next to the door so she can hear better*) I try to fight it, Vittorio, but I can't. Why do I torture myself? *Why? Why? Why?* (*On the final "Why," she pounds on the closet door with her fist.* CHARITY, *with her head on the other side of the door, holds her head as though she's just been kicked by a horse*) Oh, Vittorio, if I knew you really cared, I'd forgive you anything.

VIDAL   Care? *Cara mia,* do you think a man as passionate as me could suddenly stop caring?
(VIDAL *has edged to the closet with a bottle of beer. He surreptitiously opens the door and passes it to* CHARITY, *who drinks a long draught*)

URSALA (*Smiles*)   Oh, Vittorio, and to think I was even jealous of that little nothing you picked up tonight.
(CHARITY *reacts and mouths,* "*Nothing?*" *Then she pantomimes* "*Up yours*" *to* URSALA)

VIDAL   Why do we say the things we do? Why do we torture each other like this?

URSALA   Because I'm an immature, foolish child, that's why.
(CHARITY *nods*)

VIDAL   It's my vanity. My stupid, egotistical vanity.
(CHARITY *shakes her head,* "*No*")

URSALA   No darling, it's my fault. It's all mine.
(CHARITY *nods*)

VIDAL   I don't know anymore. I just don't know *whose* fault it is.
(CHARITY *points to* URSALA *and mouths silently,* "*Hers!*")

URSALA   I never want to be away from you. Ever again.

VIDAL   It's no good without you, Ursala. No good at all.

URSALA   Without you, Vittorio, there is no love.

VIDAL (*Postures*)   And without love, life has no purpose!
(*He says it much the way* CHARITY *did before.* CHARITY, *in the closet, nods as if to say* "*Oh, well,*" *then lights a cigarette. The orchestra starts to play.* CHARITY *looks through the keyhole again*) Ursala, Ursala. My darling.

URSALA Oh, Vittorio, Vittorio.
>   (*They kiss.* CHARITY *watches the kiss, which is a long
>   one, and yawns.* VIDAL *sings to* URSALA)

VIDAL

Please don't go my love.
I'm frightened of
Too many tomorrows
Around this haunted place.
If I set you free,
What's left for me?
Too many tomorrows
I simply cannot face.
Those passionate words we find
To grieve each other
Do not mean
We'd leave each other.

So come fill my arms
And we'll forget
The meaningless sorrows
Each time we say we're through.
Darling, can't you see,
There can't ever be
Too many tomorrows
If you stay with me.

>   (*During the song, smoke starts to fill up the closet.*
>   CHARITY, *afraid that it will seep out through the
>   keyhole, puts her hand over the keyhole, but that will
>   not do. Neither will waving the smoke away. She tries
>   to hold in the next puff, letting a little dribble out of
>   the side of her mouth.*
>   *She looks for a place to hide the smoke. She sees a
>   garment bag. She unzips it and exhales into the gar-
>   ment bag. She zips it up. Another puff. Another zip
>   when she exhales. She zips it up*)

VIDAL (*Sings*)

So come fill my arms
And we'll forget
The meaningless sorrows
Each time we say we're through.

Darling, can't you see,
There can never be
Too many tomorrows
If you stay with me.
> (*He lies on the bed with* URSALA—*on half of the bed. A curtain drops, covering their side of the bed. From behind the curtain*)

VIDAL'S VOICE Ursala . . . my angel . . . my darling . . . my sweet . . .

URSALA'S VOICE Oh, Vittorio! You're *not* a fading Romeo, Vittorio. You're not . . .

> (CHARITY *cannot contain herself and looks through the keyhole again—with growing appreciation*)

CHARITY (*She whistles appreciatively*) Gee, talk about your foreign movies!
> (*She sings the line:* "If my friends could see me now." *The lights fade on the other half of the bed and the curtain falls around it.*
> *The lights have faded to blackout. A sign appears. It reads:* "A NEW DAY." *It disappears.*
> *The lights come up slowly to reveal the split set again. It is dawn.* URSALA *is asleep on the bed under the fur, smiling.* CHARITY *is asleep standing up in the closet, looking haggard.* VIDAL *tiptoes to the closet, opens it and* CHARITY *falls out. He catches her*)

CHARITY Wha—?

VIDAL Shh. (*He whispers*) Are you all right?

CHARITY (*Painfully smiles. She holds her back and whispers*) It's like those little roomettes that go to Florida.
> (*She gets out of the closet with his help*)

VIDAL (*Whispers*) Thank you very much for everything—and if there's anything I can do . . .

CHARITY (*Takes out his autographed picture*) You already did it.

(She starts to tiptoe out past URSALA. URSALA *extends an arm through the curtain and calls out sexily)*

URSALA Vittorio!
*(*VIDAL *crosses back and kisses* URSALA's *extended hand.* CHARITY *watches enthralled.* VIDAL *propels her to the door)*

CHARITY *(Whispers)* I've enjoyed your pictures, but in person!

VIDAL You mean, you watched? *Everything?*
*(*CHARITY *gives him a wink and an "O.K., Charlie" sign)*

CHARITY *Ciao!*
(She exits)

VITTORIO *Ciao!*

End of scene

During the scene change CHARITY *dances around the stage.*
She sings:

CHARITY
They'll never believe me
If they could see me now,
That little dusty group . . .
(*The lights come up on the hostess room of the Fan-*
Dango Ballroom.
BETSY, HELENE, *and* NICKIE *are getting dressed.*
CHARITY *walks in very excited, still clutching the cane*
and top hat)

CHARITY   . . . and then I left his apartment at five o'clock
in the morning and went home. And you know how
I got back to Ninety-fourth Street? I flew! My feet
never once touched the ground.

HELENE (*Putting on eye makeup*)   . . . Yeah, well, you
keep smoking them funny little cigarettes, you bound
to do a little flying.

CHARITY   You don't believe me? You don't believe I
spent the night with Vittorio Vidal!

NICKIE   You swear?

CHARITY   I swear.

NICKIE   On your mother's life?

CHARITY   On my mother's life.

NICKIE (*To* SISSIE)   Call up and find out how her mother is.

CHARITY (*Shows her the mementos*)   Here. He gave me these. His hat and his cane. They're mementos of our evening together.

BETSY   Is that all he gave you?
(CHARITY *nods*)

NICKIE   Honey, if I was you I'd pass the hat and beat myself to death with the cane 'cause you are dumb.

CHARITY   But you don't know what happened.

NICKIE   Forget it. What you do in bed is your business.

CHARITY   I wasn't in bed; I was in the closet.

NICKIE   To each his own.

BETSY   You coulda had a mink coat.
(*She exits*)

CHARITY   Why would he give me a mink coat?

HELENE   Well, if you're gonna mess with the details you ain't gonna get no results.

NICKIE   A hat and a cane. If it was me, I woulda walked outta there with my own beauty parlor.

HELENE   Now you'll never get out of here.

NICKIE   Baby, you're stuck. Stuck just like the rest of us.

HELENE   Yeah, and it ain't no use flappin' your wings, 'cause we are caught in the flypaper of life.
(*They all sit gloomily in silence for a moment. After the pause*)

NICKIE   . . . Not me.
(*They look at her*)

HELENE   What'd you say?

NICKIE (*Determined*)   I said not me. I'm not gonna spend the next forty years in the Fan-Dango Ballroom. I'm not gonna become the world's first little old taxi dancer. I'm gettin' out.

HELENE   Out. What a beautiful word—

NICKIE (*Singing*)

> There's gotta be something better than this.
> There's gotta be something better to do.
> And when I find me something better to do,
> I'm gonna get up; I'm gonna get out; I'm gonna get
>   up, get out and do it!
>
> There's gotta be some respectable trade.
> There's gotta be something easy to learn.
> And if I find me something a half-wit can learn,
> I'm gonna get up; I'm gonna get out; I'm gonna get
>   up, get out and learn it!
>
> All these jokers, how I hate them,
> With the groping, grabbing, clutching, clinching,
> Strangling, handling, fumbling, pinching . . .
>   (*Speaking*)
> Phooey. (*Singing*)
> There's gotta be some life cleaner than this.
> There's gotta be some good reason to live.
> And when I find me some kind of life I can live,
> I'm gonna get up; I'm gonna get out; I'm gonna get
>   up, get out and live it!

RECEPTIONIST   I got it! I got it! I'm gonna be a reception-ist in one of those glass office buildings like Lever Brothers. No, Seagrams. Nine to five! I'm gonna have my own typewriter—Underwood! Water coolers—office parties—coffee breaks!

CHARITY AND HELENE   Ooh!

RECEPTIONIST (*Sings*)

> When I sit at my desk on the forty-first floor,
> In my copy of a copy of a copy of Dior,

I'll receive big tycoons and I'll point to a chair.
I'll say "Honey, while you're waiting, how would
    you like to put it down over there."
    (*The girls hug each other*)

There's gotta be something better than this.
There's gotta be something better to do.
And when I find me something better to do,
I'm gonna get up; I'm gonna get out; I'm gonna get
    up, get out and do it!

Typewriter! Cover off!
    (*Pantomime*)

And if I find me something a half-wit can learn
I'm gonna get up; I'm gonna get out; I'm gonna get
    up, get out and learn it!

HELENE Me too—me too! I'm gonna get outta here and
go right to the top! I am gonna be a hat check girl. At
Sardi's East. I'll wear one of those cute lil' black numbers—cut up to there and down to there. All those hats
comin' in—derbies—homburgs—and that cute little
checked one with the skinny brim—and the feather.
(*She sings*)
    Check your hat, sir? Check your coat, sir? Check
        your vest, sir? Check your pants?
    Check your socks, sir? Check your shoes, sir? I can
        hold them while you dance!
    Check your eyes, sir? Check your ears, sir? Check
        and see if you are free.
    How about it; after hours I'll check you and you
        check me!
    (*She hugs the other girls and dances*)

CHARITY Me too!

HELENE AND NICKIE What?

CHARITY I'm getting out too!

NICKIE But, baby—what can you do?

CHARITY I dunno. Just get me out of here and I'll figure
it out later. (*She sings*)

There's gotta be some life cleaner than this.
There's gotta be some good reason to live.
And when I find me some kind of life I can live,
I'm gonna get up; I'm gonna get out; I'm gonna get
    up, get out and live it!
(*She dances*)

And when I find me some kind of life I can live,
I'm gonna get up; I'm gonna get out; I'm gonna get
    up, get out and live—
And live it!
(*After the song,* HERMAN *the manager enters*)

HERMAN Ladies, they have just announced the winners
of the 1966 Irish Sweepstakes. And since none of you
ladies are among the winners, get your ass out there.

CHARITY (*Angrily, to* HERMAN) In the *first* place, watch
your language! And in the *second* place, we're not so
sure we're comin' out.

HERMAN I can always find someone else.

HELENE *That's* the third place. I'm comin', Herman.
(HELENE *follows* HERMAN *out.* NICKIE *starts out too*)

CHARITY Wait a minute. What happened to all those
wonderful plans we just had?

NICKIE (*Forlornly*) Yeah, whatever happened to them?
(*They both exit, leaving* CHARITY)

CHARITY (*Shouting after them*) Well, I'm not giving up
without a fight. (*She picks up the hat and cane and looks
at it. A sign appears: "A BIG DECISION"*) . . . I've got
to get out of this dump. Go to new places . . . meet new
people. All I need is a different background . . . a little
culture . . . a little refinement . . . and I know just the
place to get it . . .
(*There is a blackout on* CHARITY *as a new sign immediately lights up:* "THE 92ND STREET 'Y' ")

End of scene

SCENE 8

The Ninety-second Street "Y." The lights come up on one corner of the stage. There is a booth with a GIRL *sitting behind it. Over the booth there is an "Information" sign. The* OLD MAID *approaches the booth.*

GIRL (*To the* OLD MAID) Yes? Can I help you?

OLD MAID (*Whispers*) I'm looking for sex in the later stages of marriage.

GIRL I beg your pardon?

OLD MAID (*Whispers*) The lecture. "On Sex in the Later Stages of Marriage."

GIRL Oh. Lecture Hall Two.

OLD MAID Thank you. (*Starts to go and then stops*) Is it all right if you're not married?

GIRL It's even better.
     (*The* SECOND WOMAN *approaches*)

SECOND WOMAN Excuse me. Could you tell me where Norman Mailer is reading his poetry tonight?

GIRL At home. Nobody showed up.

SECOND WOMAN Oh, dear.
     (*She exits.* CHARITY *enters and goes to the booth*)

CHARITY Hello. I'm interested in joining a cultural group.

GIRL   Certainly. Are you a member of the "Y"?
(*A shy, attractive man in his mid-thirties,* OSCAR, *approaches the booth*)

OSCAR   Excuse me, what room is the Free Thought in Action Society?

GIRL   One moment. This young lady was here first.

OSCAR   I'm sorry, but the class starts at eight and it's eight-fifteen now—

GIRL (*Coldly*)   When I'm through.

OSCAR (*Meekly*)   When you're through. Yes.
(*He looks at* CHARITY *and smiles with embarrassment. She smiles back. After all, he does have a nice face*)

GIRL (*To* CHARITY)   Now at nine o'clock we have Dr. Sidney Greenwald. Would you be interested in the Psychologists' Workshop?

CHARITY   No. I'm really not very good with my hands.

OSCAR   I, er, really hate to interrupt, but I'm going to be very late and—

CHARITY   He's going to be very late.

GIRL (*Annoyed*)   Oh, all right. Room 603.

OSCAR   603. Thank you very much. Thank you. (*To* CHARITY) And thank you—603 . . .
(CHARITY *smiles at him as he goes off. She continues to look after him*)

CHARITY (*To* GIRL)   What kind of group is that, Free Thought in Action?

GIRL   It's a self-analytical discussion group. People are prodded into saying anything that comes into their minds—under the careful supervision of a medical student. It can be very dangerous.

CHARITY (*Still looking after* OSCAR) Hmm, I think I'll take a crack at that. Room 603? (CHARITY *follows* OSCAR *off. The lights come up on a small self-service elevator. It is big enough to accommodate only three or four people at the most. It is constructed so as to give the illusion of being enclosed, but of course the interior of the elevator is in full view of the audience at all times. The elevator door opens and three people push out as* OSCAR *waits and then gets in.* CHARITY *comes running up, calling*) Going up! Going up! (OSCAR *holds the door back to keep it from closing on* CHARITY *and she gets in.* OSCAR *takes off his hat*) Thank you.

OSCAR (*About to press the button*) I'm going to six.

CHARITY (*Smiles*) Likewise.
(OSCAR *smiles back and presses the button. The elevator door closes and they ride up silently.* OSCAR, *with his hat in his hand, stares quietly ahead.* CHARITY *does too, but then slyly glances his way, then looks back out at nothing. Suddenly, they both jerk forward and we get the impression that the elevator has come to a sudden stop—but the door does not open. They are obviously between floors. It is plain to see from the blanched expression on* OSCAR's *face that he is not comfortable in this situation*)

OSCAR (*Nervously*) What was that?

CHARITY We stopped. Press the button. It'll start right in again.
(OSCAR *quickly presses the button but nothing happens. He presses it again and again. The elevator doesn't move*)

OSCAR Something's wrong. We're stuck.

CHARITY (*Cheerfully*) These old elevators. You never can trust them.

OSCAR (*Nervously wipes his forehead*) Oh, boy.

CHARITY I had a friend who was stuck in one for eight hours. With two German shepherds and a delivery boy.

OSCAR (*Is getting extremely tense. He loosens his tie*) It's kind of stuffy in here, isn't it? Isn't it stuffy?

CHARITY You think so?

OSCAR (*Unbuttons his top shirt button*) . . . You want to try pressing the buttons?

CHARITY No, that's all right. I'm sure you pressed them very well.

OSCAR (*Nods*) I did. I pressed them very well. I gave them a very good press. Soooo, I guess we're stuck.

CHARITY I guess so . . . (*She looks at the Inspector's Card on the wall and reads*) "Maximum weight in pounds, one thousand three hundred."

OSCAR (*Looks at her*) What do you weigh?

CHARITY A hundred and twenty-eight.

OSCAR We're all right.

CHARITY Sure.

OSCAR Yeah, we're fine. Fine. We're just stuck in the old elevator . . .
      (*He forces a little laugh*)

CHARITY Are you all right?

OSCAR (*Quickly*) Me? Me? Yes. Yes. Fine. Yes, I'm fine. Fine. Just have to get used to it, that's all. It's my first time *trapped* in an elevator. Trapped, trapped, trapped.

CHARITY   Hey! You don't have claustrophobia, do you?

OSCAR   (*Scoffing*)   Oh, no. No. No, nothing like that. Claustrophobia? No, I just don't like to be in small, tight places that I can't get out of.

CHARITY   Oh, I understand. I used to have that with zippers. I was once trapped in a dress for twenty minutes. I screamed all over Orbach's.

OSCAR   That's claustrophobia. You've got to watch out for that. No, I can handle this because I know we'll get out of here in a couple of minutes.

CHARITY   Sure we will.

OSCAR   (*Hopefully*)   You really think so?

CHARITY   I do. I really do.

OSCAR   But if you thought we were really trapped in here, what would you say?

CHARITY   But we're not trapped.

OSCAR   But if you thought we were, what would you say?

CHARITY   I'd say we were really trapped.

OSCAR   Oh, my God, I knew it; I knew it!

CHARITY   But we're not. You really shouldn't get so excited.

OSCAR   Isn't this awful? I never act this way. I'm really a very calm person. Highly organized. I can promise you that if it really comes down to it, you can depend on me. You understand that?

CHARITY   I do.

OSCAR I just hope it doesn't come down to it. Maybe I should yell for help?

CHARITY Why not?

OSCAR *I'm* all right, you understand. But I know that you suffer from claustrophobia and I realize you're very uncomfortable and I wouldn't want you to be stuck in here any longer than I have to be. Help! Help! Hel—
(CHARITY *touches him. He jumps violently*)

CHARITY My name is Charity Valentine. Hey, you're shaking.

OSCAR All over.

CHARITY Let me rub your wrists.
(*She rubs them*)

OSCAR You know what I feel like doing now? What my impulse is? To take off my clothes.

CHARITY Oh, well, I don't think that would do much good.

OSCAR (*Snappy*) You'd think they'd have a telephone in here, wouldn't you? Never again. I'll never go in an elevator without a telephone. I'll always check for a telephone.

CHARITY We really should change the subject. You wanna play actors and actresses?

OSCAR (*Yells down*) Hey, come on. We don't think it's funny anymore.

CHARITY Try not to think of it. Play the game. Awright, what actress was in *Sabrina Fair?* You get three guesses. Ready? Julie Andrews—

OSCAR I don't want to play. I really don't feel like playing. It's a stupid game for two people trapped in an elevator to play. No offense.

CHARITY   I'm just trying to pass the time.

OSCAR   If I could just get out for a few minutes. Just a few minutes outside and I'd be all right. Then I'd come back inside.

CHARITY   The best thing to do is to keep talking. Then you won't think about it. What's your name? (OSCAR *looks blank*) Your name? What's your name? You know, like Frank, Harry, Sidney, Bruce. That's a name.

OSCAR   Oh, Oscar. My name is Oscar. Whoo, it's stuffy. Stuffy, stuffy, stuffy.

CHARITY   Now, let's keep our clothes on, Oscar. What's your second name?

OSCAR   My what?

CHARITY   Your second name. Don't you have a second name?

OSCAR   No, I don't think so.

CHARITY   Sure you do. Like Oscar Minetti or Oscar Greenspan.

OSCAR   Greenspan—no, Lindquist. Oscar Lindquist. Look how quickly I'm breathing. You notice how quickly I'm breathing? What is that? What is that quick breathing?

CHARITY   That's quick breathing. Don't think about it. Where do you live?

OSCAR   Who?

CHARITY   You! You! Where do you live?

OSCAR   In an elevator.

CHARITY   No, you don't, Oscar. You live in a house.

OSCAR   Oh. Yes. 411 East Seventy-fourth Street. I gotta stop this breathing. I'm gonna use up all the air.

CHARITY   We got plenty, Oscar. Now keep talking. How old are you? Where do you work?

OSCAR   Heh? Yeah. Yeah. I work at thirty-eight years old—and I was a tax accountant for Gallagher and Perlmutter on my last birthday. Oh, boy, that's very quick breathing.

CHARITY   Keep talking. Oscar, what else?

OSCAR   It's not fair. You should breathe some of the air.

CHARITY   Are you married, Oscar? Do you have a wife?

OSCAR   What?

CHARITY   Married? Married? (*Losing control*) For God's sakes, are you *married?*

OSCAR   No. No, I'm not married.

CHARITY   (*Big smile*)   Oh, Oscar. You're gonna be all right.

OSCAR   Don't leave me.

CHARITY   Oh—I won't leave you. I'm gonna stay right here in the elevator with you. And you're gonna be all right, Oscar, because I'm gonna help you . . .

OSCAR   How? What should I do?

CHARITY   Just do what I do. (*She sings*)
   When I'm so jittery my knees buckle,
   Ice water tickles my spine,
   I'm trapped like a butterfly in a net,
   Then I say to myself:
   "I'm the bravest individual I have ever met!"
   I chew my fingernails to the knuckle,

Those teeth that chatter are mine.
So I stop and light up a cigarette,
And I say to myself:
"I'm the bravest individual I have ever met!"
This game makes very good sense;
I get results.

OSCAR
Isn't that great?

CHARITY
Get back my confidence and an even pulse—
Seventy-eight—
So when I panic and feel each day
I've come to the end of the line,
Then I say that fear hasn't licked me yet!
I keep telling myself:
"I'm the bravest individual I have ever met!"

OSCAR (*Excited*) Good. Listen, I have an idea. What do you think of this? Climbing out the top of the elevator, shimmying up the cable and forcing the door open on the floor above.

CHARITY I think it could work, Oscar, but gee, it sounds a little dangerous.

OSCAR Then don't try it. Stay here with me. (*He sings*)
Funny, but suddenly I can't swallow—
I think I'm going to die;
Sometimes, if you pardon the word, I sweat!

CHARITY
Then you say to yourself:

BOTH
"I'm the bravest individual I have ever met!"

OSCAR
"I'm the bravest individual I have ever met!"
Your game makes very good sense;
I get results!

CHARITY
　　Isn't that fine!

OSCAR
　　Got back my confidence and an even pulse!
　　　(*He touches his wrist*)
　　A hundred and nine!

CHARITY
　　So when you panic and think each day
　　You'll fail at whatever you try—

OSCAR
　　I just say that fear hasn't licked me yet!

CHARITY
　　And keep telling yourself:

OSCAR
　　"I'm the strongest, soundest, stoical,
　　Daringest, manliest, most heroical—"

OSCAR and CHARITY
　　"I'm the bravest individual I have ever met!"
　　　(*At the end of the song,* OSCAR's *spirits have been
　　　raised enormously by* CHARITY's *encouragement*)

OSCAR (*Beaming*)　I'm all right. I'm gonna be all right.

CHARITY　Of course you are.

OSCAR　I think I've got it licked. I've got it under control.

CHARITY　Atta boy, Oscar.

OSCAR　No matter what happens now, I'm going to be all
right. (*And on that line, the stage is thrust into total
darkness*) What was that?

CHARITY (*In the black*)　The lights went out.
　　　(*Suddenly two matches are struck by* CHARITY *and*

OSCAR. *As the two matches flicker pathetically in the dark, we hear both of them, in near panic, calling loudly, "Help!"*
A sign appears: "TO BE CONTINUED")

6 6

Curtain

Collected Plays

of Neil Simon,

Volume III

Act Two

SCENE I

As the curtain rises, the scene is still the "Y." The stage is in darkness except for the two lonely matches that continue to flicker.

A sign appears: "MEANWHILE BACK IN THE ELE-VATOR . . ."

We hear the tired, frightened, and weakened voice of CHARITY *singing a rather spiritless rendition of "Bravest Individual." During this* OSCAR *is calling weakly, "Help! Help!" At the end of the chorus, the lights suddenly go back on.*

CHARITY (*Excited*)   Oh! The lights are on. Press the button, Oscar, press the button!
> (OSCAR *presses the button. The car jerks and slowly begins to descend*)

OSCAR (*Beside himself with joy*)   It's moving! It's moving!

CHARITY   I told you, Oscar. I told you we'd be all right.
> (*He is straightening his tie as the elevator car disappears from view. They are down. The doors open and they emerge*) I knew it was just a matter of time.

OSCAR   Your big problem, actually, is panic. That's the cause of your greater number of accidents.

MAN (*Waiting at the elevator door, very nasty*)   Oh, so you finally came out, heh? I've been ringing for twenty minutes. Don't you have any consideration for other people?
> (*He gets into the elevator and presses the button. The door closes*)

OSCAR   Well, I'll see you—around.

CHARITY   Yeah. Around.

OSCAR   . . . Around where?

CHARITY   I don't know. Where are you going?

OSCAR   Well, I was going to Group Analysis, but I guess I missed it tonight.

CHARITY (*Worried*)   Will you be all right?

OSCAR   Oh, yes. It was my last session this week anyway. I'm finished.

CHARITY   Oh, good. What was your problem?

OSCAR   Well, one of my problems was—that I was painfully shy.

CHARITY   And now you're cured?

OSCAR   No. I just never had the nerve to bring it up in class. So I quit.

CHARITY   Oh. Well, shyness *ain't* one of my problems. If you noticed.

OSCAR   Oh, listen, I am not a nut or anything. I mean, after what happened in there; I can assure you, I'm not what I seem to be at all.

CHARITY   You seem to be very nice.

OSCAR   Oh, well, then I am what I seem to be because that's what I am—very nice. Well, if you're not doing anything now, would you like to come to church with me?

CHARITY (*Suspicious*)   What denomination did you have in mind?

OSCAR   It's the Rhythm of Life Church. Under the Manhattan Bridge. It was a jazz group in San Francisco and

turned into a religion. I hear it's an emotional experience.

CHARITY (*Smiles*)   I'm always looking for an emotional
experience.

OSCAR   Come on. (*About to ring the elevator bell*) We'll
walk down.
(*They start to run off as the elevator appears, then
stops with the* MAN *in it*)

MAN   Help! Help!
(CHARITY *and* OSCAR *laugh and point up*)

BOTH   Aha!
(*There is a blackout. In the black we hear a voice. It
is deep and powerful, reverberating and echoing like
Moses speaking from the mountain*)

VOICE   This is the Rhythm of Life Church. Tonight's
sermon is "Retribution and Absolution." And a one
and a two and a three . . .

End of scene

The Rhythm of Life Church. This is a garage converted for the evening into a pathetic, makeshift church. If possible, we should see the backs of a few automobiles protruding from the wings.

DADDY

Daddy started out in San Francisco
Tootin' on his trumpet loud and mean.

ASSISTANTS

Suddenly a voice said:
"Go forth, Daddy;
Spread the picture on a wider screen."

DADDY	BONGOISTS
And the voice said: "Daddy	Daddy . . .
There's a million pigeons	Go . . .
Waitin' to be hooked on	Go . . . go . . .
new religions.	go . . .
Hit the road, Daddy;	Tell . . . them . . .
Leave your common-law wife;	Ev . . . ry . . .
Spread the religion	Thing . . . you . . .
Of the rhythm of life."	Know . . .

GROUP A

And the rhythm of life
Is a powerful beat,
Puts a tingle in your fingers
And a tingle in your feet,
Rhythm in your bedroom,
Rhythm in the street.
Yes, the rhythm of life
Is a powerful beat!

GROUP A

Oh, the rhythm of life
Is a powerful beat,

Puts a tingle in your fingers
And a tingle in your feet,

Rhythm in your bedroom,

Rhythm in the street.
Yes, the rhythm of life

Is a powerful beat!

GROUP B

To feel the
rhythm of
life,

To feel the
powerful
beat,

To feel the
tingle
In your fingers,
To feel the
tingle
In your feet.

GROUP A

Oh: the rhythm
of life
Is a powerful
beat,
Puts a tingle
In your fingers
And a tingle
In your feet,
Rhythm in your
bedroom,
Rhythm in the
street.
Yes, the rhythm
of life
Is a powerful
beat!

GROUP B

To feel the

Rhythm of life,

To feel the
Powerful beat,

To feel the
tingle
In your
fingers,
To feel the
tingle
In your feet.

GROUP C

Daddy . . .

Go . . .

Go . . . go . .
Go . . .

Tell . . .
them . . .
Ev . . . ry . . .

Thing . . .
you . . .
Know . . .

DADDY

Daddy spread the gospel in Milwaukee,
Took his walkie-talkie to Rocky Ridge.

DADDY and BONGOISTS

Blew his way to Canton, then to Scranton,
Till he landed under the Manhattan Bridge.

GROUP D

Daddy was a new sensation,
Got himself a congregation,
Built up quite an operation
Down below.

With the pie-eyed piper blowing
While the muscatel was flowing,
All the cats were go-go-going
Down below.

GROUP D

Daddy was a new sensa-
tion,

Got himself a congrega-
tion,

Built up quite an opera-
tion
Down below.

GROUP E

Daddy was a
new
sensation,
Got himself
a congre-
gation,
Built up quite
an operation
Down below.

GROUP D

With the pie-eyed piper blowing
While the muscatel was flowing,
All the cats were go-go-going
Down below.

GROUP D

Daddy was a new sensa-
tion,

Got himself a congrega-
tion,

Built up quite a reputa-
tion

Down below.

With the pie-eyed piper blowing
While the muscatel was flowing,
All the cats were go-go-going
Down below.

GROUP E

With the pie-
eyed piper
blowing
While the
muscatel was
flowing,
All the cats
were go-
go-going
Down below.

ALL

Flip your wings and fly to Daddy!
Flip your wings and fly to Daddy!
Flip your wings and fly to Daddy!
Fly . . . fly . . . fly to Daddy!

Take a dive and swim to Daddy!
Take a dive and swim to Daddy!
Take a dive and swim to Daddy!
Swim . . . swim . . . swim to Daddy!

Hit the floor and crawl to Daddy!
Hit the floor and crawl to Daddy!
Hit the floor and crawl to Daddy!
Crawl . . . crawl . . . crawl to Daddy!

Do-do-do-do-do-we-do-we-do-we
Do-do-do-do-do-we-do-we-do-we
Do-do-do-do-do-we-do-we-do-we
Do-do-do-do-do-we-do-we-do-we

Do-do-do-do-do-we-do-we-do-we
Do-do-do-do-do-we-do-we-do-we
Do-do-do-do-do-we-do-we-do-we
Do-do-do-do-do-we-do-we-do-we

GROUP A

And the rhythm of life
Is a powerful beat,
Puts a tingle in your fingers
And a tingle in your feet,
Rhythm in your bedroom,
Rhythm in the street.
Yes, the rhythm of life
Is a powerful beat!

GROUP A	GROUP B
And the rhythm of life	To feel the
Is a powerful beat,	Rhythm of life,
Puts a tingle in your fingers	To feel the
And a tingle in your feet,	Powerful beat,
Rhythm in your bedroom,	To feel the
	tingle
Rhythm in the street.	In your fingers,

Yes, the rhythm of life   To feel the
tingle

Is a powerful beat!   In your feet.

GROUP A	GROUP B	GROUP C
And the rhythm of life	To feel the	Daddy . . .
Is a powerful beat,	Rhythm of life,	Go . . .
Puts a tingle	To feel the	Go . . .
In your fingers	Powerful beat.	Go . . .
And a tingle In your feet.		Go . . .
Rhythm in your bedroom,	To feel the tingle	Tell . . . them . . .
Rhythm in the street.	In your fingers	Ev . . . ry . . .
Yes, the rhythm of life	To feel the tingle	Thing . . . you . . .
Is a powerful beat!	In your feet.	Know . . .

ALL

To feel the rhythm of life,
To feel the powerful beat,
To feel the tingle in your fingers,
To feel the tingle in your feet.

Flip your wings and fly to Daddy.
Take a dive and swim to Daddy.
Hit the floor and crawl to Daddy.

Daddy, we've got the rhythm of life,
Of life, of life, of life . . .
Yeah . . . yeah . . . yeah . . . man!
(*All gather around* DADDY BRUBECK *and his two* ASSISTANTS, *who are standing on oil drums*)

DADDY BRUBECK   This is where it's happening, Baby. The Rhythm of Life—Number Seven in the Ten Top Religions.

EDDIE   We're gonna climb to Number One, Daddy.

BRUBECK   Time is running out on the big number called *Life*. And we are all coming to the last eight bars. And the leader man will soon take us by the hand where we will enter the flip side of life called *Eternity*.

HAROLD   Eternity.

EDDIE   The big coffee break in the sky.

BRUBECK   But before we play that final date and pile into that big black bus—we got to make our peace.

HAROLD   Make it, Daddy; make it.

BRUBECK   I shall not put my mother and father down.

GROUP   No, Daddy.

BRUBECK   I shall honor my debts, my grievances, and my alimony.

GROUP   Oh, yeah.

BRUBECK   I shall not falsify my name at the Unemployment Bureau.

GROUP   Oh, yeah!

BRUBECK   I shall respect my obligations and report each month to the Police.

GROUP   Oh, yeah.

CHARITY   (*To* OSCAR) They're a very devout group, aren't they?

OSCAR   Yes.
          (*The* GROUP *sings and hums rhythmically*)

BRUBECK   I shall not indulge in the evil marijuana weed commonly known as pot. It is sinful; it is harmful—and it is very expensive . . . (*Sirens and police whistles sound*)

And I suggest you dump the goods before the cops arrive.

> (*The congregation stamps out their cigarettes and there is a mad dash by all to escape*)

End of scene

OSCAR *and* CHARITY *are on a New York street, going crosstown. They are both breathless.*

OSCAR Gee. I'm sorry about that.

CHARITY Where do you find places like that?

OSCAR I'm on a mailing list. It's the Church of the Month Club. (*Looks at her warmly*) Look, will I—may I see you tomorrow night?

CHARITY Well, it depends what you have in mind. I mean if it's going to be a human sacrifice or something, I really don't—

OSCAR A movie. A plain, ordinary movie with a happy ending.

CHARITY (*Smiles*) I'm nuts about happy endings.
    (*They head toward the subway, joining a crowd of other passengers moving toward the trains*)

OSCAR I'll pick you up after work. At your office?

CHARITY (*Nervously*) What makes you think I work in an office?

OSCAR It's a hobby of mine. I could look at a person's face and in a second tell what they do. As a matter of fact, I know exactly what *kind* of an office you work in. If I'm wrong, you don't have to keep the date. You work in a bank, right?

CHARITY (*Smiles*)   You guessed it. First National City, Williamsburg Branch.

OSCAR   I knew it. I'm a great judge of character. How's six o'clock at the bank?

CHARITY   Oh, listen, I wouldn't want you to come all the way out to Williamsburg. Besides, tomorrow we have to take inventory. You know, count all the blotters and the pennies. All that jazz . . . Suppose I meet you in front of the "Y"?

OSCAR   Where?

CHARITY   In front of the "Y."

OSCAR   *Where?*

SUBWAY PASSENGERS   In front of the "Y"!
(*She steps out of the subway entrance*)

OSCAR (*He moves closer*)   I—I just want to say, I had a very nice time tonight, Charity—I mean, being with you.

CHARITY   So did I, Oscar . . .
(*They look at each other. There is a pause. A sign appears: "THE FIRST KISS"*)

OSCAR (*He moves closer*)   A very nice time.

CHARITY   That's what I had. A very nice time.

OSCAR   Well, good night.

CHARITY   Good night, Oscar.
(OSCAR *takes* CHARITY's *hand, then brings it up to his lips and kisses it*)

OSCAR   You're a lovely girl, Charity—*Sweet* Charity . . .
(*He turns and runs off.* CHARITY *looks after him, then at her hand*)

CHARITY (*Obviously touched*)   Gee, for a weirdo—he's very nice. (*She turns and walks into the next set as it moves in*) Sweet Charity? Sweet Charity. Sweet Charity, that's what he calls me.

End of scene

CHARITY'S *apartment.* SISSIE, NICKIE, *and* HELENE *are lounging around filing their nails, doing their eyes, and playing solitaire.* CHARITY'S *dialogue starts as she moves into the set.*

CHARITY   Can you imagine, I've gone out with the man now six times in the last two weeks and the most he ever tried was that hand-smooching business. Hey! that isn't a pass, is it?
(*She starts to change clothes*)

NICKIE   Noo . . . Is it, Helene?

HELENE   What?

NICKIE   If a man kisses your hand. Would you classify that as a pass?

HELENE   Well, that depends.

NICKIE   On what?

HELENE   On where your hand is when he kisses it.

NICKIE   Hey! where was your hand?

CHARITY   On the end of my arm. He has always behaved like a perfect gentleman.

HELENE   What's a perfect gentleman?

CHARITY   It's not my fault you've never met one.

NICKIE   Hey! If he kisses your hand all the time, maybe he's after something.

CHARITY   Like what?

NICKIE   Your wristwatch.

CHARITY   The only thing he's after is "Inner Contentment." And he wants me to help him find it.

NICKIE   Honey, you sure picked up a couple of hundred-dollar words since you been going around with this goofball.

CHARITY   Oscar is *not* a goofball! He is a highly complicated and very intelligent person.

NICKIE   All right, so besides slobbering over your knuckles, what else can he do?

CHARITY   He's in the tax accountancy profession. And he's also a graduate of C.C.N.Y.U. University . . .

NICKIE   Ooh! Sounds like a goofball to me.

HELENE   What does the goofball think of your vocation?

CHARITY   My what?

HELENE   Your chosen field of endeavor, child. Have you told him you're in the Rent-A-Body business?

CHARITY   Oh, he thinks *nothing* of it.

HELENE and NICKIE   She ain't told him.

CHARITY   In the first place, he's too highly educated to be bothered with things like that. And in the second place, he knows because I already told him.

NICKIE (*Shocked*)   That you're a dance hall hostess?

CHARITY   Yes, yes!

NICKIE   You told him?

CHARITY   (*Very defensive*)   Yes! Yes! I told him! I told him!

NICKIE   When?

CHARITY   *Next Sunday.* I'll tell him next Sunday—in Coney Island.
  (CHARITY *storms out. The girls look after her*)

HELENE   She won't listen. That girl just will not listen.

NICKIE   What do you think they talk about? When they're alone?

HELENE   Talk? Honey, that girl's built for everything but conversation.

NICKIE   Yeah. *He* probably does all the talking. Handing her those smooth lines like, "Baby, last night I dreamt you and I were in a cozy little cottage covered with clinging vines—"

HELENE   And there we were—clinging more than the vines.

NICKIE   And then he converts the convertible sofa and really goes to work.

BOTH   Quote—

HELENE
  Baby, dream your dream;
  Close your eyes and try it.

NICKIE
  Dream of furniture;
  Dream that I can buy it.

HELENE

    That fancy bed you prayed for,
    Not only bought but paid for.

NICKIE

    Dream we sign the lease,
    Leave a small deposit.

HELENE

    Three and one-half rooms
    With a walk-in closet.

BOTH

    We'll ask the local Jet Set
    To dine on our dinette set.
    Right across the street

NICKIE

    There's a friendly bank; you
    Make a friendly loan

HELENE

    And the bank says, "Thank you."

BOTH

    Every Saturday
    We'll spend all our money.

HELENE

    Join the P.T.A.

NICKIE

    They will love you, honey.

BOTH

    Life will be frozen peaches and cream;
    Baby, dream your dream.

NICKIE   Can't you see that little love nest in three years?

HELENE   Yeah. She's feeding the chicks and he's ready to
fly the coop!

BOTH
>Three fat, hungry kids,
>All in pink condition.

HELENE
>So! Who's in the red?

NICKIE
>That nice obstetrician.

BOTH
>Big Daddy's fav'rite pastime—
>He's had it for the last time.
>Soon Daddy don't come home;
>He says he's going bowling,
>But a bowling ball

NICKIE
>Is not what Daddy's rolling.

BOTH
>Every night they fight;
>Once they both exploded,
>Then they both got tight.

HELENE
>Tight? Hell, they got loaded!

BOTH
>Well, who knows what will sour the cream
>When you dream—your—
>   (*Both laugh*)
>But come to think of it,
>How happy I would be
>If someday I could find
>The kind of guy who'd say to me
>"Baby, dream your dream;
>Close your eyes and try it."

HELENE
>"Dream of three fat kids."

NICKIE

    Brother, would I buy it!

BOTH

    Life could be frozen peaches and cream
    If only I could dream,
    Dream, dream, dream, a dream!

End of scene

A sign appears: "CONEY ISLAND." A number of people with balloons, kewpie dolls, and ice cream cones pass by. One couple suddenly stops and looks up.

YOUNG MAN   Hey, look at that!
      (*Ad libs. A few other couples stop and look up. A* POLICEMAN *starts to push them back*)

POLICEMAN   All right, move back; move back. Let the emergency car through, heh?

GIRL   What's wrong, officer?

POLICEMAN   Can't you see? (*He points up*) There's a fellow and a girl stuck up there on the Parachute Jump!
      (*Ad libs. The lights black out on the group at the same time they come up on* CHARITY *and* OSCAR, *who are the couple stuck up on the Parachute Jump. They dangle from the sky strapped in a tiny two-seat contraption with a metal bar to hold onto. Perhaps the parachute above them can be seen.* OSCAR, *as usual, is in a panic*)

CHARITY   Don't panic, Oscar. It's not gonna do you any good to panic. You won't panic, will you?

OSCAR   No, I think there's a very good possibility I won't panic.

CHARITY   You see, it's not like the elevator, Oscar. You've got plenty of air to breathe. Look at all the air you've got.
      (*She looks around*)

OSCAR   You're right—we've got enough air to last us for hours.

CHARITY   You're all right?

OSCAR   I'm fine—fine.

CHARITY   Good.

OSCAR   Charity. You're shaking.

CHARITY   All over.

OSCAR   Are you worried about me?

CHARITY   No. About me. I can't stand—

OSCAR   Heights?

CHARITY   Oh! Don't even say it!

OSCAR   It's all right, Charity. I'm right here with you.

CHARITY   You won't leave me, will you? I stayed with you in the elevator. Fair is fair.

OSCAR   I won't leave. I'll stay as long as you need me.

CHARITY   Gee, I've never been this scared before. I'm usually very calm in these situations.

OSCAR   And I'm usually very scared.

CHARITY   Now *I'm* the one who's scared.

OSCAR   And I'm unusually calm.

CHARITY   Maybe that's why I'm scared.

OSCAR   Because I'm calm?

CHARITY   (*Nods*) When you know you have someone you can depend on, someone you know who can take care of you, you can afford to be scared. Oh, I've never had a someone like that before.

OSCAR I've never had anyone who depended on me before.

CHARITY Oh, boy! I'm depending on you now, Oscar.

OSCAR (*Manly*) Then sit back, relax, and be scared. 'Cause I'm very dependable. (*Yells down*) Don't worry about the girl. *I'm* up here.

CHARITY Oh, Oscar, you're such a comfort.

OSCAR I do what I can.

CHARITY Hold on to me.

OSCAR For as long as you like.

CHARITY I'd like it for as long as we're up here.

OSCAR Then I hope we never come down.

CHARITY I really don't know what happened to me.

OSCAR That's funny because I know exactly what's happened to me. (*He sings*)
    Here was a man
    With no dream and no plan;
    Then one crazy night I found
        Sweet Charity!

    You make life fun for me;
    Oh, what it's done for me,
    Having you around,
        Sweet Charity!

    Warm words I've never said
    Lately pop off the top of my head—
        Incredible!

    If, by and by,
    You and I should be *we*

I could touch the sky—quite easily.
    So, if you are free,
    Sweet Charity,
Please belong to me.
    Sweet, Sweet Charity,
Please belong to me!

CHARITY Oscar—maybe the reason I'm really scared is because I've got to tell you something about me that you may not like.

OSCAR There couldn't be anything about you I didn't like.
    (*He touches her hair*)

CHARITY You see, I'm not exactly with the Williamsburg Branch of the First National City Bank—

OSCAR You know, ever since I met you I knew there was something diffcrent about you. You have a quality in you, Charity, that I've never found in a girl before.

CHARITY In fact, I am definitely *not* with the Williamsburg Branch of the First National City Bank.

OSCAR Do you know what that quality is, Charity? It's purity. It's innocence. In you I have found pure innocence.

CHARITY As a matter of fact, I never, *never* been with the First National Williams of the Burg Bank.

OSCAR It's the truth, Charity. You're the last of a dying species. A virgin! Yes, a virgin in the most poetical sense of the word.
    (*They kiss*)

CHARITY . . . although we *do* have thirty-seven branches throughout the city.
    (*They kiss again*)

OSCAR and CHARITY
    Here was a man
    With no dream and no plan;

Then one crazy night I found
            Sweet Charity!

You make life fun for me;
Oh, what it's done for me,
Having you around,
            Sweet Charity!

Warm words I've never said
Lately pop off the top of my head—
            Incredible!

If, by and by,
You and I should be *we*,
I could touch the sky—quite easily!
            So, if you are free,
            Sweet Charity,
Please belong to me.
            Sweet, Sweet Charity,
Please belong to me!

BYSTANDERS
            Keep cool, you two up there.
            Know what I'd do up there,
            If I had you up there?
            They're quite a sight up there;
            They'll spend the night up there.
            They'll be all right up there.
            You wanna bet?
            He'll hold on to her!
            He'll hold on to her!

                        Blackout

The Fan-Dango Ballroom. HELENE *and the other hostesses are scattered about the lounge section. They are reading magazines, and they are all bored. There's not one customer in the place.*

HELENE   Oh, boy! Ya can't make a dime in this joint.

HERMAN   Psst. Psst. A live one.
> (*Suddenly a lone young man enters. They all spring up and start to sing*)

GIRLS   (*Sing*)
> Do you wanna have Fun, fun, fun?
> How's about a few Laughs, laughs . . .
> (*The boy selects a girl and retires into a booth*)

HELENE   Some business, heh? One fifteen-year-old dropout!
> (NICKIE *enters with* ROSIE, *a new girl. This is her first night as a hostess. She's attractive and very nervous*)

NICKIE   Girls! Girls! Good news. Besides stinkin' business, we now have a new, young, good-lookin' chick which we need like Idaho needs potatoes.

ROSIE (*Cheerfully to all*)   Hello. I'm Rosie.

HELENE   Not for long you ain't.
> (*The others all say "Hi."*)

ROSIE (*Looks around*)   So this is the Ballroom.

NICKIE   The Ballroom? That's right. This is where you'll meet Prince Charming who'll carry you off on his white horse to Scarsdale. You should live so long.

ROSIE   It's awfully dark in here, isn't it?

HELENE   That's called "merchandising." When the goods are a little shopworn, don't put 'em in the window.

NICKIE   *You* got no problems, honey. You're *worth* six-fifty a half hour.

ROSIE   Is that what the men pay to dance with us?

HELENE   Uh-huh. Which you split with the owner, a nice, kindly Argentinian gentleman named Adolf Hitler.

NICKIE   Every penny of which you will earn. You dance a little, talk a little, roll your eyes a little, swivel your hips a little—and like this, you kill a lifetime.

ROSIE   Oh, I only expect to stay a few weeks.

NICKIE   (*Sarcastic*)   Oh, sure.

ROSIE   My boyfriend's in California. When I save up enough money here, we're gonna get married.

HELENE   You'll make a sweet *old* couple.
            (CHARITY *enters, excitedly*)

CHARITY   Gather around, ladies—gather around and take a good look. It has happened to me. What every girl in this Ballroom dreams about, and it's happened to me.

HELENE   You've been drafted.

CHARITY   I'm in love. That's what's happened to me. I'm in love, I'm in love. I'm in love.

NICKIE That's the eleven o'clock news. We listen to it every night.

CHARITY Well, that was the last broadcast. This time it's different. This one is really serious.

CARMEN Has he—talked about marriage?

CHARITY Er—a—well, not in so many words.

ELAINE How many?

CHARITY None.

NICKIE And now we turn to the local weather and sports.

HELENE Look, kid, ya got any questions about this place—(*Pats* CHARITY) you just ask the housemother. She was with the original owners in 1794.

ROSIE There's just one thing. I'm not a very good dancer.

NICKIE Who dances? We defend ourselves to music.

CARMEN All you gotta know is when they touch you, make like you're excited.

NICKIE Of course a cute-lookin' thing like you can always go into the "extracurricular" business.

CHARITY What are you telling her a thing like *that* for? (*To* ROSIE) Hey, kid. You want some good advice, get out of this crummy joint—before you wind up like the rest of us.

HELENE Don't look at me; I was *always* like this.
(*A man enters the Ballroom alone.* HERMAN *signals from his booth*)

HERMAN Hey! C'mon.

FRENCHY   A live one!
(*They all get up*)

ROSIE   What do I do?

NICKIE   Sugar, from here on it's every man for himself.
(*All the girls move down to the rail.* ROSIE *and* CHAR-
ITY *are standing side by side*)

HELENE (*To the man*)   Hey, can I talk to you for a minute?

SUZANNE   Got a cigarette? Come here. I wanna tell you
something.

FRENCHY   Ooh, so tall. Americans always so tall.

NICKIE   Chicago, right? I can always tell a hometown
boy.

CARMEN (*Snapping her fingers*)   You look like a good
dancer.
(*The man walks silently up and down the lineup of
girls. He goes back and seems to be making up his
mind between* CHARITY *and* ROSIE. *The man finally
chooses* ROSIE, *gets his ticket, and goes off to a booth
with her*)

NICKIE   Sure learns fast, for a kid.

CHARITY   She doesn't look like such a kid to me.

HELENE   Ooh, touchy-touchy!

CARMEN   Sore just 'cause you came in second?

CHARITY   I'm sore 'cause I came in at all. Boy, am I sick
of this musical snake pit.

NICKIE (*Bryn Mawr-ish*)   Well. You can always go back
to Mummy and Daddy's place in Southampton.

CHARITY   I'll be getting out a lot sooner than any of you think.
    (*Two men walk in*)

HERMAN   Hey!

ELAINE   Psst. Psst. *Olé*, girls. Two more bulls in the ring.
    (*The other girls move down to the rail again.* NICKIE *goes to* CHARITY *and puts her arm around her shoulder*)

NICKIE (*To* CHARITY)   Look busy, Baby. Der Führer is watching.
    (*She means* HERMAN)

CHARITY   Let him watch. Let him fire me. You think I care?

NICKIE   Yeah, I think you care.

CHARITY   Well, I don't. I don't care. (*Angrily*) I cared for eight years but I do not care anymore. And I'll tell you why I don't care anymore. Because I don't like it here. I like you and I like Helene and I like the girls and I even like Herman. But *I don't like it here*. This-is-not-a-nice-place! And I do not intend to spend another day of my life in a place that is not a nice place!

NICKIE   What are you trying to say?

CHARITY   I am trying to say that I have made up what's left of my mind. I've made my decision. I know exactly what I have to do.

HELENE   What exactly do you have to do?

CHARITY   I have to get out. Understand? *Out!* Now! Tonight. This minute.

NICKIE   You mean you're goin'—

CHARITY   I mean, "You're damned right I'm goin'." (*She goes.* NICKIE *shrugs and moves down to the rail as the lights* dim and a single light hits CHARITY. *She moves downstage and the Ballroom moves off behind her*) The only trouble is, I don't know where. (*She sings*)

Where am I going?
And what will I find?
What's in this grab bag
That I call my mind?
What am I doing alone on the shelf?
Ain't it a shame, but
No one's to blame but myself!
Which way is clear?
When you've lost your way
Year after year . . .
Do I keep falling in love
For just the kick of it,
Staggering through the thin and thick of it,
Hating each old and tired trick of it?
Know what I am? I'm good and sick of it!
Where am I going?
Why do I care?
Run to the Bronx
Or Washington Square.
No matter where I run,
I meet myself there.
Looking inside me
What do I see?
Anger and hope and doubt.
What am I all about
And
Where am I going?
You tell me!

End of scene

SCENE 7

CHARITY *is in Times Square. At the end of the first chorus of her song, a phone booth moves on. She puts in a coin and dials quickly.*

CHARITY (*Into the phone, frantically*)   Hello? Western Union? I want to send a collect telegram. To Mr. Oscar Lindquist. 411 East Seventy-fourth Street. New York City. The message is: "Dear Oscar, I must talk to you right away but since I know you don't have a telephone, I am sending you this collect wire . . . I've got to know where I stand. What are your intentions? Are you just playing around with me? Because if you are, what the hell was with all that handkissing?" Handkissing! Yeah! I think it's one word . . . "Please, please meet me at one A.M. in Barney's Chile Hacienda so we can discuss a matter of utmost urgency . . ." Sign it: "Charity." No, make that *"Sweet* Charity." (*She hangs up and speaks to herself*) He's got to come. *He's got to!* He won't!
  (*She finishes the song*)
  Looking inside me,
  What do I see?
  Anger and hope and doubt.
  What am I all about
    And
  Where am I going?
  You tell me!

End of scene

A sign appears: "THE PROPOSAL." It disappears.
When the lights come up, we are in Barney's Chile Hacienda,
a small Mexican restaurant on Eighth Avenue. There are two
booths against the wall. OSCAR *sits alone in a booth, nervously*
glancing at his watch. CHARITY *enters. She looks at* OSCAR.
He sees her and gets up.

OSCAR Charity, I—
(*But* CHARITY *walks right past him and sits in the*
booth behind him so that they are directly back to
back)

CHARITY (*Doesn't look at him*) Sit down, Oscar.

OSCAR (*Surprised*) Aren't you going to sit with me?

CHARITY (*Tense*) I have some very important things to
say to you, Oscar, and if I have to look in your eyes I
don't think I'll be able to say them.
(OSCAR *wants to protest, but he sits down back to back*
with her. BARNEY *returns with a cup of coffee and*
looks quizzically at the way they are sitting)

BARNEY You alone, Miss?

OSCAR (*Without turning*) She's with me.
(BARNEY *looks at them both, puzzled at first; then he*
shrugs and exits)

CHARITY Oscar, I had to see you to tell you—I can't see
you anymore.

OSCAR (*Starts to turn*) What?

CHARITY   Don't look at me. Don't look at me. (*He turns back to back again*) Aren't you going to ask me why? Aren't you going to ask me why I can't see you anymore?

OSCAR   Why can't you see me anymore?

CHARITY   Never mind. I'll tell you. Because we're not getting anywhere, that's why. And we're not *going* to get anywhere either, because you don't even know where I've been. Oscar, I don't, never have, and probably never will *work in a bank.*

OSCAR   Oh?

CHARITY   I don't even have a bank *account.* I keep my money in an empty can of Chase and Sanborn coffee.

OSCAR   Charity—

CHARITY   And do you have any idea of how I earn that money? Do you? Heh?

OSCAR   You're a dance hall hostess.

CHARITY   I'm a dance hall hostess. I work in a dance hall. I dance with strange men and talk to them and drink with them and (*She suddenly realizes what he said*) That's right! How did you know?

OSCAR   I've known it for a week now. I was riding a bus one night, saw you, jumped off, and before I could catch you I saw you go into this dance hall. I went in and stood in the corner. You were sitting in a booth with some man. You were laughing and giggling. I didn't stay very long—an hour or so. That night when I went home, I tried very very hard to hate you, Charity—but I couldn't do it. I just couldn't hate you.

CHARITY   Maybe you'll have better luck tonight. Do you know what *other* business some of the girls are in?

OSCAR   I'm not interested.

CHARITY   Don't you want to ask me if I am too?

OSCAR   It's not important.

CHARITY (*Indignant*)   Not important? Well, it is to *me*. I'm in love with you, Oscar, and I'm not going to waste being in love with some jerk who isn't interested enough to find out if I really am what I'm hinting I *might* be. Don't look at me.

OSCAR   Charity, I don't care what you are or what you did. All I know is I want to marry you.

CHARITY   Let's settle one thing at a time, heh? I am *not* in any other business. All I sell is my *time*. But just to keep the record straight, I am not a poetical virgin! (*She suddenly bursts into tears*)

OSCAR   Charity, Charity, please don't cry. I believe you.

CHARITY (*Crying*)   I know you believe me. I'm crying about that other part.

OSCAR   What other part?

CHARITY   That *marrying* part! I didn't hear it the first time.

OSCAR   Marry me!

CHARITY (*Still crying*)   Oh, Oscar, you're not making fun of me, are you? Because asking a girl to marry her is one of her most sensitive areas. And you shouldn't say it unless you really mean it. Because you can seriously hurt people kidding around like that. And I'll tell you the truth, Oscar. I don't really think I can stand another injury of that nature.

OSCAR   Charity, for the first time I'm happy "inside." *Really* happy—and it's all because of you.

CHARITY (*Turns*)   Oh, Oscar—

OSCAR   Don't look at me! I can get pretty emotional too, you know! Give me your hand. (*She puts her hand down. He gropes backwards, feels it and clasps it into his*) You know what we're gonna do, Charity? We're gonna get out of this city.

CHARITY   Oh, I'd like that.

OSCAR   Get a little place in the country.

CHARITY   I'd like that.

OSCAR   We don't need much money. I could get a little gas station. I've always loved cars . . .

CHARITY   You'd like that.

OSCAR   Maybe get a Mobilgas franchise—with the big red and white sign.

CHARITY   I'd like that . . .

OSCAR   What really counts is that we'll be together.

CHARITY   That's what really counts.

OSCAR   Forget your past. Forget what you did before.

CHARITY   I forgot it. It's forgotten.

OSCAR   Some men could never do that, Charity. But not me.

CHARITY   Not you.

OSCAR   I promise I'll never mention it again as long as I live.

CHARITY   I'd like that.

OSCAR   Because I need you, Charity—I need you and I love you. (*The lights begin to fade on everything but*

CHARITY) There's this little place on Route 66 in Pass-
aic . . .

> (*He fades out.* CHARITY *walks out of the scene and
> comes downstage. The music helps build the moment*)

CHARITY   He loves me! (*She moves to one side*) Someone
loves me! (*She runs to the other side. She's shouting it to
the whole world now*) Someone loves me! (*All her joy
and emotion seem to pour out of her. She sings*)
Somebody loves me!
My heart is beating so fast;
All kinds of music is pouring out of me.
Somebody loves me at last!

I'm a brass band
I'm a harpsichord
I'm a clarinet
I'm the Philadelphia Orchestra
I'm the Modern Jazz Quartet
I'm the band from
Macy's big parade
A big Count Basie blast
I'm the bells of St. Peter's in Rome
I'm tissue paper on a comb.
And all kinds of music keeps pouring out of me
    'cause
Somebody loves me at last!
   (*She dances, then sings again*)
Somebody loves me at last!
   (*She dances again*)
Somebody loves me—at last!

End of scene

SCENE 9

The Fan-Dango Ballroom. Everyone is scurrying around.

ALICE   Shhhh, she's coming. She's coming!
(*Everyone ad-libs*)

HERMAN   Shhh. Okay, everybody, hide and be quiet. I want this to be a God-damned surprise party. (*Tells everyone where to go*) And keep your heads down!

MAN   Hey, Herman, what about you?

HERMAN   Oh, yeah; I forgot.
(*He ducks behind a banquette.* CHARITY *walks in carrying her suitcase. She looks around*)

CHARITY   Hey. Hello? Hello, I'm going. Anyone here to say goodbye to me? No? (*There is no answer. She shrugs*) Okay. Well, goodbye!
(*She turns to go when suddenly twenty-five people spring out of nowhere and shout, "Surprise!"* CHAR-ITY *screams in fright. All the hostesses are there and about ten men including* HERMAN, *a* COP, *a couple of* WAITERS, *a few* DELIVERY MEN, *a* DOORMAN, *and a couple of regular customers*)

HERMAN   You didn't think we'd let you go without givin' ya a little party, did ya?

CHARITY   A party? For me? Oh, you shouldn't have. You shouldn't have.

NICKIE (*To* HELENE)   I told you we shouldn't have.
(*There is a fanfare as two men pick* CHARITY *up.*

Someone else brings out a high stool and they set CHARITY *down on it in the center of the room. She yells out, "Hey, what're you doing? Put me down." They place a box down for* HERMAN, *who stands on it*)

HERMAN   And now, through the courtesy of the hostesses of the Fan-Dango Ballroom, Local 107, the waiters, the janitor, Joe the bouncer, Harry the Cop, and our three regular customers since 1954—we present (*Another fanfare*) . . . a seventeen-dollar cake.
   (*A huge cake is wheeled out on a cart, as everyone oohs and ahs. They place it in front of* CHARITY)

CHARITY (*Excited*)   Beautiful! (*She bends over and reads the inscription*) "Happy Birthday Angelo?"

NICKIE (*Whacks* HERMAN *across the shoulders*)   You couldn't get a new cake, you cheapskate?
   (*There are ad libs*)

HERMAN   All right, all right. I didn't know she was leavin' till this morning.
   (*They all shout "Cheapskate!" at* HERMAN)

CHARITY   Never mind. It's the sentiment that counts. Herman, Angelo and I thank you very much.

HERMAN (*Smiles at her*)   For a broad, you gotta lotta class.

CARMEN (*To* NICKIE)   The present. Give her the present.
   (*There are more ad libs*)

NICKIE   Awright. Awright. (HERMAN *gets off the box and* NICKIE *gets up on it*) Charity Hope Valentine, we who have lived with you, undressed with you, suffered the indignities of this crummy joint with you (*The girls all yell "Yeah!"*) . . . who have come to know you, and to love you—on this, your nuptial eve (*More ad libs*) . . . Ah shaddup. We just want to wish you—Oh, my God, I'm gonna cry.
   (*She cries*)

HELENE   Will ya quit slobberin' all over the cake.

NICKIE (*Crying*)   I can't help it. I'm gonna miss her.

HELENE   We all are. (HELENE *pulls her off the box*) Get down and I'll give the speech. (HELENE *gets on the box. There are ad libs*) Charity, honey (*She starts crying*) . . . Oh God, we're gonna miss you, kid.
(CARMEN *pulls her down and gets up*)

CARMEN   So we bought you this little present. Which I picked out.
(*She hands* CHARITY *a box*)

CHARITY   For me? A wedding gift?
(*They all yell, "Open it." *CHARITY *opens the box and, to her surprise, takes out a little baby's size-one snow-suit.* CHARITY *looks puzzled*)

NICKIE (*Angrily, to* CARMEN)   What the hell kind of wedding gift is that?

CARMEN (*Shrugs*)   I thought she was pregnant. Isn't that why she's getting married?
(*They all hoot her down*)

CHARITY   Oh, no! It's the best wedding present I ever got.
(*They all applaud and she cries*)

HERMAN (*Shouts for quiet*)   It ain't often that one of our girls leaves to marry a nice, respectable guy. In fact, this is the first time it ever happened. And so, as a parting gesture, our three regular customers since 1954 would like a farewell dance with our own bride-to-be, Miss Charity Valentine. (*The three regular customers all take turns dancing with* CHARITY. *In the midst of this,* OSCAR *walks in and watches.* HERMAN *sees him and walks over*) I'm sorry, Mac, this is a private party.

OSCAR   I know. I'm her—I'm here to take her away.

HERMAN   Yeah? Hey, Charity. Did you call for a cab?

CHARITY (*Sees him and rushes to him*) Oscar! It's him, everybody. This is the fellow. He's the one. It's him. (*She puts her arm in his*) He's it—him.

OSCAR (*Embarrassed*) Hello.
    (*The girls all circle him and ogle him*)

NICKIE (*While still shaking* OSCAR's *hand*) He's taking our baby away . . .
    (*She cries*)

CHARITY Oscar, I want you to meet our boss Herman, affectionately known as Der Führer!

OSCAR Pleasure.

HERMAN Likewise. How about a beer? Hey, somebody get a beer for Mr.—er—Mr.—?

CHARITY Lindquist.

HERMAN That's right, Lindquist. Sit down.
    (*He seats them. After seating them he begins a speech*)

ALL (*With general ad libs*) Yeah. Hear, hear. Give a speech. (*They sing*)
    It's tough for a loudmouth mug like me,
    Who all the time bellows like a bull,
    To make with the words
    About the "Missus-to-be!"
    When what *you* think is an empty heart—is full!
    Tomorrow when you say: "I do." . . . I'll die!
    I'm almost too ashamed to tell you why!

    I love to cry at weddings!
    How I love to cry at weddings!
    I walk into a chapel
    And get happily hysterical.
    The ushers and attendants,
    The family dependents,
    I see them and I start to sniff.
    Have you an extra handkerchief?
    And all through the service,

While the bride and groom look nervous,
Tears of joy are streaming down my face.

MIKE

Down his face.

HERMAN

I love to cry at weddings—
Anybody's wedding.

ALL

Any time! Any where! Any place!

ROSIE

I always weep at weddings!
I'm a soggy creep at weddings!
Ah! What's as sweet and sloppy as:
"Oh, Promise Me" . . . and all that jazz?

TWO GIRLS

The man you rest your head with,
The man you share your bed with
Is married to you—so you know
He won't jump up and dress and blow!

NICKIE

I could marry Herman—

HELENE

And be permanently sorry!

NICKIE

We would make a really lousy pair;
But, gee, I want a wedding,
Any kind of wedding—any time, any place, any
    where!

ALL

And all through the service,
While the bride and groom look nervous,
Tears of joy are streaming down my face.
I love to cry at weddings—
Anybody's wedding.
Any time! Any where! Any place!

I love to cry at weddings!
How I love to cry at weddings!
I walk into a chapel
And get happily hysterical.
The ushers and attendants,
The family dependents,
I see them and I start to sniff.
Please let me use your handkerchief!
And all through the service,
While the bride and groom are nervous,
I drink champagne and sing "Sweet Adeline."
I love to cry at weddings!
Everybody's wedding!
Just as long as it's not mine!
> (CHARITY *goes around saying her goodbyes.* HELENE
> *and* NICKIE *stand away.* CHARITY *comes up behind
> them and slips* VIDAL's *picture into* HELENE's *hand
> and the top hat into* NICKIE's)

ALL (*Sing softly*)
I love to cry at weddings—
Anybody's wedding.
Any time! Any where! Any place!
> (CHARITY *and* OSCAR *are gone*)
I love to cry at weddings!
How I love to cry at weddings!
I walk into a chapel
And get happily hysterical.
The ushers and attendants,
The family dependents,
I see them and I start to sniff.
Have you an extra handkerchief?
And all through the service,
While the bride and groom look nervous,
Tears of joy are streaming down my face.
I love to cry at weddings—
Anybody's wedding.
Any time! Any where! Any place!

End of scene

A sign appears. It reads: "PLANS." It disappears. Two lights pick up OSCAR *and* CHARITY, *hand in hand in the park. The rest of the stage is dark.* CHARITY *is glowing and speaks rapidly, filled with emotion. There is music playing underneath.*

CHARITY   Oh, Oscar. I didn't like the first half of my life much but the second half sure is getting good. (*Snaps her fingers, remembering something*) Oh, I knew I had something to show you (*Fishes through her purse and takes out a card*) —a joint bank account. I deposited the entire can of Chase and Sanborn. So that's my entire dowry. The point I'm trying to get across, Oscar Lindquist, is that I'm very happy.

OSCAR   (*Uncomfortably*)   Charity, there is something I have to tell you.

CHARITY   Oh, I've been doing all the talking. Okay, it's your turn, Oscar.

OSCAR   Charity, I'm very fond of you; you know that. And I find you unique—

CHARITY   That's me!

OSCAR   —and different and sweet and wonderful and tender—and I just can't marry you. Did you hear me, Charity?

CHARITY   (*Quickly*)   Yeah, I heard you. I heard you.

OSCAR   I can't, Charity—I can't go through with it.

CHARITY All right, Oscar, I know this isn't a joke because you certainly wouldn't joke about a thing like
that at a time like this. It couldn't be a joke because it
would be a very rotten joke. But I can't figure what else
it could be. Oscar, is it a joke?

OSCAR This is not easy for me, Charity. Not easy at all.

CHARITY I know it's not easy, Oscar—but is it a joke?

OSCAR (*Irritated*) It is *not* a joke. It is *no* joke!

CHARITY (*Mumbles*) It's no joke.

OSCAR I thought this time it would be different. But it's
not. It's the same. It's always the same.

CHARITY What's the same?

OSCAR The other men. I always get this far and then I
start thinking about the other men . . .

CHARITY What other men?

OSCAR (*Gently*) You know what other men!

CHARITY (*Pauses*) But Oscar, you said . . .

OSCAR Oh, I know I kept saying it didn't matter, because
I thought if I said it enough I could convince myself
it was true.

CHARITY That certainly makes sense to me, Oscar.

OSCAR It's not your fault, Charity. You're a wonderful
girl.

CHARITY (*Hopefully*) I am?

OSCAR But it's *my* problem, Charity. I have this neurosis—a mental block.

CHARITY   There's a lot of that going around.

OSCAR (*With self-anger*)   But I have this childish, incomprehensible, idiotic, fixation about purity. In this day and age? It's laughable, isn't it? (*She laughs*) It's not funny. But every time I think of you—with all those other men—

CHARITY   Oscar, you're making a mountain out of a couple of guys.

OSCAR   How many?

CHARITY   What?

OSCAR (*Shouts*)   How many? I want to know *exactly* how many.

CHARITY   Gee, when you yell like that, I can't think. (*She starts to count on her fingers*) Frank, Harry, Sidney . . . How far back do you want me to go?

OSCAR (*Covers his eyes in agony*)   Oh, my God, don't tell me. I don't want to hear.

CHARITY   Oscar, I know I'm not very bright. I could go to night school. We could be so happy in that gas station; I know it. On the days you felt "sick," you could stay in bed and I'd work the pumps. I've got so much to give. Let me give it to you.
(*She falls to her knees, pleading*)

OSCAR   Charity, get up. You're too good to be on your knees to me.

CHARITY (*With a weak smile*)   Give the little girl a break, heh?

OSCAR   Together, I'd destroy you. Sooner or later it would start again, and I'd hound you day and night. "What were their names?" "How long did you know them before?" "How did you feel when they—"

CHARITY   You could ask me *anything.* I won't hide a thing. I'll tell you everything you want to know.

OSCAR   You'd like that, wouldn't you? I'd get all the pretty details, wouldn't I? Give you quite a thrill, heh?

CHARITY   You won't get one word out of me, not a word. Don't you see, Oscar, I'm very flexible. I can go either way.

OSCAR   There's only one way to go with me. To destruction. Marry me and I'll destroy you, Charity.

CHARITY   That's okay. I'm not doing much now, anyway.

OSCAR   But the one shred of decency left in me won't let me destroy you. I must save you from me. I'm doing this for your own good, Charity. Run. Run. *I'm saving you, Charity—saving you!* (*He has forced her down to the apron. He pushes her into the orchestra pit. A sign appears: "DITTO."* OSCAR *leans over and looks down*) Woops. (*He starts running in all different directions, then goes back to the pit. He starts to run again, then goes back to the pit*) Charity, I feel sick about this. You may not believe that, but I feel just terrible. (*He backs away from the pit*) A wonderful girl—so understanding. They don't make them like that anymore.
      (*He goes off. The stage is empty for a moment. One of* CHARITY's *hands emerges from the pit. Then the other. Finally she lifts herself on the edge of the stage, her legs dangling into the pit. She is wringing wet*)

CHARITY   Did you ever have one of those days? (*She wrings some water out of her hair and her clothing. She sighs again*) At least I didn't get tattooed again. (*She picks herself up and starts to pull herself together, then she notices she still has her purse. She opens it up, looks inside and smiles*) . . . And I still have my dowry. (*Optimistically*) . . . Maybe things are beginning to pick up for me. (*Suddenly we see a shimmering light and hear an eerie musical effect—and lo and behold, before our very eyes at*

stage left appears, believe it or not—the GOOD FAIRY—
wearing a flowing gold cape and silver slippers and carry-
ing a wand. CHARITY *can scarcely believe her eyes. She rubs*
them and looks again. The GOOD FAIRY *is still there*) Hey!
Hey, you're really not—?

GOOD FAIRY (*She waves the wand at* CHARITY)   Tonight!
Tonight! It will *all* happen tonight!

CHARITY (*Believing, like a little girl*)   What? What'll happen tonight?

GOOD FAIRY   Dreams will come true tonight! Tonight!
Tonight!
> (*She waves the wand at* CHARITY *again and throws*
> *a handful of stardust at her. The* GOOD FAIRY *then*
> *turns and goes. On her back is a large sign that reads,*
> *"Watch 'The Good Fairy' tonight—8 o'clock—CBS."*
> *She flutters off the stage.* CHARITY *turns, smiles and*
> *shrugs as the music of "Charity's Theme" starts. The*
> *general lighting fades, leaving one light on* CHARITY.
> *She picks up her suitcase and begins to dance as she did*
> *in the beginning of the first act.*
> *As she dances, a sign appears in the same style as the*
> *first signs that appeared in the show. It reads:*
> "AND SO SHE LIVED
> ... HOPEFULLY
> ... EVER AFTER."
> *She strikes a pose in silhouette as in the opening scene*)

Curtain

They're
Playing
Our
Song

Book by Neil Simon
Music by Marvin Hamlisch
Lyrics by Carole Bayer Sager

THEY'RE PLAYING OUR SONG *was first presented in New York on February 11, 1979, by Emanuel Azenberg at the Imperial Theatre, with the following cast:*

VERNON GERSCH	Robert Klein
SONIA WALSK	Lucie Arnaz
VOICES OF VERNON GERSCH (BOYS)	Wayne Mattson, Andy Roth, Greg Zadikov
VOICES OF SONIA WALSK (GIRLS)	Helen Castillo, Celia Celnik Matthau, Debbie Shapiro

Directed by Robert Moore
Musical Numbers Staged by Patricia Birch
Scenery and Projections by Douglas W. Schmidt
Costumes by Ann Roth
Lighting by Tharon Musser
Music Direction by Larry Blank
Orchestrations by Ralph Burns, Richard Hazard, Gene Page

Synopsis of Scenes

Act One

Act Two

MUSICAL NUMBERS

ACT ONE

Overture

"Fallin' "	Vernon
"Workin' It Out"	Vernon, Sonia, Voices
"If He/She Really Knew Me"	Sonia, Vernon
"They're Playing Our Song"	Vernon, Sonia
"If She/He Really Knew Me" (Reprise)	Vernon, Sonia
"Right"	Sonia, Vernon, Voices
"Just for Tonight"	Sonia

ACT TWO

"When You're in My Arms"	Vernon, Sonia, Voices
"I Still Believe in Love"	Sonia
"Fill in the Words"	Vernon, Voices

Act One

SCENE I

A grand piano is onstage. A single spotlight is directed at it. At the piano is VERNON GERSCH, *about thirty-four. He wears slacks, sports shirt, cardigan sweater, loafers.*

He is playing a melody. A soft, sweet melody. He hums along with it, composing. He writes the music down on a sheet in front of him.

The doorbell rings. He is lost in his music. It rings again. With the pencil in his mouth and the sheet of music paper in his hand, he crosses to the door and opens it.

SONIA WALSK *comes in. Late twenties, attractive, although her clothes belie that fact. She dresses like a cross between Annie Hall and a gypsy tea reader. She carries a large shoulder bag and a leather portfolio.*

SONIA   Hi. Sonia Walsk. I tried to time it right, but I'm about ten minutes early.

VERNON (*Pencil in mouth*)   I'll be right with you. Sit down.

SONIA   I am really *soo* delighted—
(*He goes back to the piano and sits. He plays a few more bars and jots down his work. She sits and takes in the apartment, almost afraid to glance at him for fear of disturbing him. He finishes the musical phrase, then quickly gets up and crosses to her*)

VERNON   Hello. Vernon Gersch.

SONIA (*Jumps up*)   Hi. Sonia Walsk. I tried to time it right, but I'm about ten minutes early. I am really *soo* delighted—

VERNON   Actually you're twenty minutes late, but no problem. Can I take your jacket?

SONIA   I'm not wearing one. It's all part of the dress.

VERNON   Ahh. Very fashionable.

SONIA   No. Just thrifty. (*Gasps*) Oh, God. I can hardly catch my breath.

VERNON   You didn't *walk* up, did you?

SONIA   No. I'm just nervous. Didn't you notice when I shook your hand? It was a little clammy . . . mine, not yours . . .

VERNON   Did I do something to make you nervous?

SONIA   Yeah. You won two Grammies and an Academy Award.

VERNON   Oh? I'm sorry.

SONIA   It's not your fault. (*She picks up the Oscar*) They're lighter than I thought.

VERNON   They're chocolate on the inside. Would you like a drink? Some coffee? Coke?

SONIA   I used to go to a shrink in this building.

VERNON   No kidding? Me too. That's how I found this apartment.

SONIA   Dr. Tannenbaum?

VERNON   Dr. Markle.

SONIA   I went to Tannenbaum.

VERNON   He died last summer. Tannenbaum.

SONIA I didn't know . . . If you went to the funeral, he'd probably charge you for the hour. (*Looks out the window*) Nice view of the park.

VERNON I never look. I'm afraid of heights.

SONIA Then wasn't the fourteenth floor a mistake?

VERNON Except I always wanted to live in this building. Famous for musicians. Jerome Kern was one of the first tenants. Isaac Stern lived here. Leonard Bernstein. Where do *you* live?

SONIA West Eighteenth Street. Famous for poverty. Mostly artists. They keep painting pictures in the halls, I can never find my door. I wish I could afford something like this . . . Do you enjoy having money? Am I being too nosy?

VERNON No, no. You've been here almost three minutes . . . Sure I do. Well, not the money, but the things that come with it.

SONIA Well, I have all the things that *don't* come with it, and it stinks. Like having to buy my clothes second-hand. This is from *The Cherry Orchard*.

VERNON I don't know that store.

SONIA It's not a store. It's a play by Chekhov. My girl-friend wore it in the Brooklyn Academy production. It's practically new. She only wore it for thirty-eight performances and six previews.

VERNON You're lucky they didn't go out on tour.

SONIA I got my eye on a terrific dress that's in *Dracula*. It's all white with little black bats, perfect for New Year's Eve. (*Looks at the sheet music on piano*) How'd you like my lyrics?

VERNON Your lyrics?

SONIA You had them all weekend. Didn't you read them?

VERNON Oh. Yes. For a minute I forgot why you were here. I was very involved with the *Dracula* dress ... Listen, I have to be very honest with you. You don't look at all like what I expected.

SONIA What do I look like?

VERNON You're very pretty. I didn't expect someone very pretty.

SONIA Oh? You mean you found my lyrics unattractive?

VERNON I found them unhappy. A little sad. I expected someone very pale with a giant teardrop hanging from each eye.

SONIA When I write, it brings out my serious side. You'll notice I never wear anything from *Hello, Dolly!*

VERNON I never thought pretty girls had major problems.

SONIA They do when they turn thirty. That's for starters. Then I gave up smoking. *And* I just broke up with the fellow I was living with. I called my mother for the first time in a year and a half, and before I could say hello, she says, "Are you still fat?" ... And I'm in hock to my publisher for eight hundred dollars because I went to Tiffany's and bought myself a ring to celebrate my not committing suicide at turning thirty. So I guess I write sad songs.

VERNON Well, they're damn good. I really like your lyrics.

SONIA Well, we're batting a thousand because I really like your music.

VERNON Naturally, not *all* your lyrics.

SONIA   I wouldn't expect you to. I know how high your standards are . . . How many did you like?

VERNON   One.

SONIA   That many?

VERNON   *Part* of just one.

SONIA   I can live with that . . . Let me guess—"Fallin' "?

VERNON   Yes. Well, obviously you know that's the best.

SONIA   It's not the best, but it suits your style the best.

VERNON   Oh? You find my style somewhat limited?

SONIA   Not at all . . . I think you have great range. Great . . . unexplored range . . . Did that come out wrong?

VERNON   Only if you happen to hear it.

SONIA   What I mean is . . . Well, what I like about your music is that it's so fundamentally basic, so intrinsically melodic, so universally embraced . . . Oh, God, I just don't want to use the word "commercial."

VERNON   But I take it you do want to write popular songs. I mean, we're not here to write the score for *The Gulag Archipelago.*

SONIA   Oh, God. Yes. I've only had one hit in my whole life. That's why I want to write with you.

VERNON   Good. I've been working on a tune this morning. You might find it intrinsically melodic.
        (*Crosses to piano*)

SONIA   I heard something weird about you.

VERNON   What?

SONIA Well, there was a rumor that you were engaged to three different girls last year. Is there any truth to it?

VERNON Yes.

SONIA (*Shrugs*) Some people think everything is weird. If you're planning anything new, I've got this ring up for sale.

VERNON Thank you. I buy them by the gross. Listen, some of these lyrics are very clever. Very Dorothy Parker. Personally, I don't go for things like "Let's play two sets in Massachusetts," but I admire the skill.

SONIA I wrote that when I was eleven. If you have a tune you wrote when you were eleven, maybe we could do something with it.

VERNON Would you settle for a melody to "Fallin' "? I just finished it.

SONIA My God, you mean we wrote our first song together? I wish I knew, I would have dressed for the occasion.

VERNON No, no. *The Cherry Orchard* is fine. Before I start, are you sure you don't want something to eat?

SONIA I wouldn't want to be indebted to you in case I don't like the music.

VERNON Listen, we'd better settle that right now. You have to be completely honest with me. I'm a mature person. I have an ego, but I can take criticism. If you don't like it, you *must* tell me . . . It won't happen with *this* song because this one is fabulous . . . But please feel free to speak up. (*He sets up the music. She walks over to the window and looks out*) Don't you want to sit here? You can hear it better.

SONIA I don't listen with my ears.

VERNON   You don't? You found some other interesting part of the body in which sound enters?

SONIA (*Taps her chest*)   I listen in here . . . with the soul.

VERNON   I see . . . Well, I don't have a big voice, so could you turn your soul this way, please. (*He starts to play the intro*) This is very rough, you understand.

SONIA   I didn't expect to get it on the charts by tonight. (*He nods, takes a deep breath, and sings "Fallin' "*)

VERNON
    I'm afraid to fly
    And I don't know why.
    I'm jealous of the people who
    Are not afraid to die.
    It's just that I recall
    Back when I was small
    Someone promised that they'd catch me
    And then they let me fall.

    And now I'm fallin'
    Fallin' fast again.
    Why do I always take a fall
    When I fall in love?

    You'd think by now I'd learn
    Play with fire, you get burned.
    But fire can be oh so warm
    And that's why I return.
    Turn and walk away
    That's what I should do.
    My head says go and find the door
    My heart says I found you.

    And now I'm fallin'
    Fallin' fast again.
    Why do I always take a fall
    When I fall in love?

    It always turns out the same—
    Loving someone, losin' myself.
    Only got me to blame.

Help me, I'm fallin'
Fallin'
Catch me if you can.

Maybe this time I'll have it all
Maybe I'll make it after all
Maybe this time I won't fall
When I fall in love.
> (*He finishes the song gently, letting the last note linger, then drops off into silence. She still has her back turned to him, staring out the window . . . He waits patiently. Finally she turns and looks at him*)

SONIA It's good. I like it.

VERNON "It's good, you like it"? Try to control your enthusiasm. I wouldn't want you to froth at the mouth . . . I think it's *fantastic!*

SONIA You told me to be honest. Some of it is lovely. Some *not* so lovely.

VERNON Which part didn't you like?

SONIA The lyrics.

VERNON The *lyrics??* *You* wrote the lyrics. Didn't you ever hear them before?

SONIA Not with the music. The music is too good for the lyrics. It's beautiful. It made me cry. I would like to write you a different lyric.

VERNON I don't *want* a different lyric. I *love* this lyric. I heard the music in my head the minute I read them. I would like to keep this lyric.

SONIA Oh, God, Vernon, you are so gifted. I feel so inadequate. I can't write. I'm a fake, a fraud. I just put down anything. The first thought that pops into my mind. It's high school garbage. I don't know what the hell I'm doing in this business. I should be running a day-care center somewhere.

VERNON   You're not having a breakdown, are you? Tannenbaum is dead. Maybe you could see Markle?

SONIA   You mean you *really* like it? I have to know, Vernon. *The truth!*

VERNON   Yes. I like it. I think it's a first-rate song.

SONIA   Because I have such respect for your talent. That's why I was so nervous coming up here today. I put this dress on backward. I don't know if you noticed.

VERNON   Look, will you please stop telling me I make you nervous. Because it makes me nervous. I'm just plain Vernon Gersch. Not Mozart. Not Beethoven.

SONIA   Oh, but you are. How sweet that you don't realize how good you are. Your music is as important to *your* time as their music was to theirs. My God, you can't sit in a dentist's chair without hearing one of your songs. I think you're truly gifted. I think you are our only, our *only* contemporary living American composer.

VERNON   Well, thank you. That's very kind.

SONIA   Maybe Stephen Sondheim.

VERNON   Steve is good. I love Steve's work.

SONIA   And if you say to me you don't want me to touch those lyrics, then I will not touch those lyrics.

VERNON   Please . . . don't touch those lyrics.

SONIA   Well, then would you think about the first eight bars of the music? Somehow it doesn't work for me. (*She looks at her watch*) Oh, God. I have to run . . . I don't know how to fix it. That's your department. Listen, I'm not going to tell Mozart or Beethoven how to write . . . I'm having all my hair cut off in an hour.

You think I'm wrong? I trust your opinion. If you think I shouldn't have it cut off, I will not have it cut off.

VERNON   At this moment my feeling is, cut off anything you want.

SONIA   I respect your advice. I really enjoyed this session. It was very productive. When do you want to work again? I'm completely free and clear.

VERNON   Well, we should get started soon. I promised Barbra we'd have five songs by the eighteenth.

SONIA   No problem. I write quickly. Monday morning, ten A.M. sharp?

VERNON   (*Writes in his datebook*)   Sharp it is. Meet me at my studio. One eleven East Tenth Street. It's more relaxing there. See you Monday.

SONIA   Oh, Monday's bad. Make it Tuesday.

VERNON   All right. Tuesday at ten.

SONIA   Make it ten-thirty.

VERNON   Swell.

SONIA   Eleven is better.

VERNON   I already changed it.

SONIA   I'm going to the Hamptons for the weekend. Wow, this is really a great opportunity for me, Vernon. I thank God and our agents for putting us together. I'll make you proud of me, I swear. You inspire me like no one I've ever worked with. (*She shakes his hand vigorously*) If you get those first eight bars fixed, you can call me at Gurney's Inn, East Hampton. I think you can up the tempo a little, too. It's a little draggy. But you'll work it out. Have a nice weekend.

(And she is out the door. He stands there, numbed by his experience)

VERNON   A little *draggy* . . . She's out of her mind.
    (At the piano, he plays. Lights fade. She is out in the hall. She stops, sings)

SONIA
    God, he's such a genius
    When he played I almost cried.
    Imagine telling him
    How his music should begin.
    I'm gonna write this weekend
    And forget about Gurney's Inn.
    Next time he'll like me
    Next time my dress will be on straight
    I'll set my watch an hour fast
    And I won't be late!

SCENE 2

VERNON's *studio. Midmorning five days later. It is a gray, rainy day. An occasional clap of thunder.*

VERNON *appears, new sweater and shirt. He crosses impatiently to the window, looks out, then looks at his watch. He crosses back to a tape machine and presses the record button. He picks up the hand mike.*

VERNON   (*Into the mike*) Journal. Wednesday, May 17, eleven-twenty A.M. A date remarkable only in the fact that Sonia Walsk is now one day and twenty minutes late. The one day I could write off to eccentricity. It's the twenty minutes that *bugs* me . . . I have further concern for the future of our collaboration because of certain personality conflicts. She's a flake. And I'm a flake. Two flakes are the beginning of a snowstorm . . . Also of major consideration is that I can't stand working with people who just gave up smoking. (*The doorbell rings*) Doorbell at eleven twenty-two. I am showing signs of hives. (*Doorbell again, impatiently*) She rings impatiently. No doubt to put *me* on the defensive.
        (*She pounds on the door with her fist*)

SONIA   Open the door, for God's sake!

VERNON (*Into the mike*)   Suddenly Godzilla's outside. To be continued.
        (*He presses the off button, puts down the mike. He crosses to the door and opens it.* SONIA *rushes in, wearing another one of her "dresses"*)

SONIA   Where's your bathroom?

VERNON   Listen, I think you and I have to get a couple of things straight around—

SONIA (*Standing on a throw rug*)   If this is an expensive carpet, you'll tell me where your bathroom is.

VERNON   In there, first door on your left. (*She rushes off. He goes back to the tape machine, presses the "on" button and picks up the mike*) Eleven twenty-four. No attempt at explanation. She went directly to the toilet. She is wearing another one of those dresses that seem to cry out "Enter Olga Petrovka from stage right" . . . There is no doubt in my mind that collaboration is an ugly business. No wonder the word fell into disrepute during the Second World War.
    (SONIA *comes back in*)

SONIA   Whew! I just made it.

VERNON (*Into mike*)   Thank God! (*He clicks it off*) Listen, I think you and I have to—

SONIA   Who's N.K.G.?

VERNON   N.K.G.?

SONIA   Those are the initials on the hand towels.

VERNON   Natalie Klein. One of the girls I was engaged to. She kept all the gold and silver gifts, I got everything terry cloth . . . Does it bother you that it's twenty after eleven?

SONIA   Yes, I know. I'm late. I'm sorry. It's raining, I couldn't get a cab.

VERNON   It wasn't raining yesterday when you were supposed to be here.

SONIA   I had a rough weekend. I broke up with Leon. He's the fellow I was living with.

VERNON   You told me that on Thursday.

SONIA   I went back with him on Friday. I thought I'd give it one more chance. I don't give up easily on relationships.

VERNON   That's encouraging to know in case we get as far as this afternoon.

SONIA   I said I was sorry. It will never happen again. I will even try to go to the bathroom before I get here. Beyond that, I don't know what else to say.

VERNON   Is that the dress from *Dracula*?

SONIA   No. It's from *Of Human Bondage*.

VERNON   The movie?

SONIA   The play. They revived it in Dallas.

VERNON   And you didn't cut your hair?

SONIA   No. Leon talked me out of it. He likes it long.

VERNON   (*Puzzled*)   You still like to look good for the man you just broke up with?

SONIA   I can't stand his possessiveness, but I respect his taste.

VERNON   Well, I can only hope you and I begin as well as you and Leon ended. (*He crosses to piano*) Now, then . . . There was another song you left that first day. "Workin' It Out." I think I have an idea for something.

SONIA   "Workin' It Out"? Oh! Well, I'm glad you liked the lyric.

VERNON   I don't. I just like the title.

SONIA   (*Shrugs*)   I'll take what I can get.

VERNON I'm not quite sure where the song goes yet. (*He starts to vamp*) I hear some funky disco beat. Get 'em all nuts at Studio 54 . . . Real low-down, you know, like—
  (*He sings*)
  Ooh, workin' it out . . . la la la la la la la la
  Workin' it out . . . la la la la la la la la
  Workin' it out . . . la la la la la la la

SONIA (*Yells*) Hey! Whoa! Wait a minute! Hold it! Hold it! Save your la la la la's— (*He stops playing*) You can't come that fast at me. I'm a lyricist, not an IBM computer. I don't work that way.

VERNON No? How do you work?

SONIA I have to think about it. I deal in words. Thoughts. Ideas. Images. I have to sit down all by myself in a nice comfortable chair with a pad and a pencil and then I—
  (*She catches herself and stops*)

VERNON And then you what?

SONIA Well, I have this peculiar way of working. I talk it out with the girls.

VERNON What girls?

SONIA The other Sonias. The voices. The ones in my head. (*Shrugs*) The girls.

VERNON (*Nervously*) You mean there's an entire *group* of you?

SONIA Yes. In a way.

VERNON All dressed like that?

SONIA I guess. They're the other sides of my personality. We *all* have them. None of us is just one person. We have—ego. We have passion. We have skepticism.

VERNON   Are those their names?

SONIA   No. They're all Sonia. Just like you have other Vernons . . . Do you ever talk to yourself?

VERNON   A lot. When I'm waiting for you.

SONIA   Well, the one who's listening is another Vernon. When you write music and you can't hit that top note, who sings it in your head? When you're writing melody, who sings the harmony?

VERNON (*Thinks*)   The *boys?*

SONIA   Exactly.

VERNON   Why didn't you say so? I thought you were talking about somebody else. Now, can we get back to the song? (*He vamps*) See if you and the girls can come up with something . . .
      (*He sings "Workin' It Out"*)
   Ooh, workin' it out
   La la la la la la la la la
   Workin' it out
      (*Speaks*)
You'll put in some lyrics here.

SONIA
   The last thing I need to hear today
   Is a melody.

VERNON
   La la la la la la

SONIA
   I'm findin' out
   Nobody gives you their songs
   For free.

VERNON
   La la la la la la

SONIA

    He wants one thing
    He wants another
    I just wanna run and take cover.

    I need a little more time
    Just for me.

VERNON

    Can't you see I'm workin' it out

SONIA

    Workin' it out
    That's what I'm tryin' to do.
    Workin' it out

VERNON

    Dance for me, baby

SONIA

    For Leon, for me and you.
    Workin' it out

GIRLS

    It should be easy to do

SONIA

    But you never had to work it out

GIRLS

    You never had to work it out
    You never had to work it out

VERNON (*Speaks*) Work it out!

SONIA

    Work it out for two.

VERNON (*Speaks*) Listen, I think it could be like a Bee Gees record here. You know, about broken hearts or something like—

SONIA

    Look at the way he works.
    What would he know of a broken
    Heart?

<table>
<tr><td>VERNON</td><td>GIRLS</td><td></td></tr>
<tr><td> Do it for me, mama!</td><td>Ah . . .</td><td></td></tr>
</table>

SONIA and GIRLS

    To him "broken heart" is a phrase
    I should write for his goddamn
    Middle part.

VERNON (*Speaks*)   You'll fill it in here.

SONIA   GIRLS

    He's askin' me for
    words that are clever.   Ooh . . .
    Leon and me
    We had five years together.
    I need a little more time

GIRLS

    Time!

SONIA

    Just for me

GIRLS

    Can't he see

SONIA

    I'm workin' it out

VERNON

    Workin' it out

SONIA

    You gotta give me a chance.
    Just 'cause I hear your music

VERNON

    Baby

SONIA

    Don't mean I gotta dance.

SONIA	GIRLS
Workin' it out—	
It should be easy to do	It should be easy
But you never had to work it out	

VERNON (*Speaks*) Work it out!

SONIA

    Work it out for two.

VERNON (*Speaks*) Here's where my boys come in—

VERNON and BOYS

    La la la la la la la la la la la la
    La la la la la la la la la la la la
    La la la la la la

GIRLS

    Gotta give him something.

VERNON

    Hey, baby

SONIA

    He took my lyric
    Kept my title
    Threw out every word.

VERNON and BOYS

    Baby, ah . . .

SONIA

    He made some crazy disco thing.
    It's not at all the song I heard
    But—

GIRLS

    Maybe his way's better.

SONIA
>Who knows?
>I'm too unclear

SONIA and GIRLS
>Right now my mind's in such a mess,
>I hardly know I'm here.

VERNON and BOYS
>Hey, baby, la la la la la la
>La la la la la la
>La la la la la la

GIRLS
>Gotta find a lyric

SONIA
>Gotta give him something.

VERNON and BOYS
>La la la la la la
>La la la la la la

GIRLS
>Tell him you don't like it.

VERNON and BOYS
>Hey, baby

SONIA
>If someone else had
>written this
>I'd know just what to
>say.
>I'd say it's not my kind
>of song,
>
>Can't we write
>something
>Else today, but

BOYS

>Baby, ah . . .

GIRLS
>He might get insulted.

BOYS
　La la la la

SONIA
　His ego isn't small.

BOYS
　Baby

GIRLS
　If you don't write him something quick

SONIA and GIRLS
　We might not work at all

VERNON and BOYS
　Don't you know that I'm
　Workin' it out
　Workin' it out
　La la la la la la la la la la la la

SONIA and GIRLS
　I've got to work it out

VERNON and BOYS
　Workin' it out
　Workin' it out
　La la la la la la

SONIA and GIRLS
　Help me work it out

BOYS
　Bye, bye, baby

VERNON (*Speaks*)　The music is great. Now it's on you.

SONIA
　I'll try even harder
　That's all I can do.
　But you never had to work it out

VERNON (*Speaks*)　Let's go to work!

SONIA

Work it out for two.

BOYS and GIRLS

Workin' it out, workin' it out
La la la la la la la

VERNON   Anyway, that's the general idea . . . What do you think? About the song? . . . Hello? . . . Anything coming from the soul?

SONIA   Listen, Vernon. I think we have to sit down and have a serious talk.

VERNON   As opposed to all our gay, witty conversations of the past?

SONIA   How do you expect me to work with you if I don't even know who you are? Every time I walk in the door, you rush off to the piano. Why don't we just sit, talk, get to know each other?

VERNON   Because when I'm sitting here and talking, you're out somewhere breaking up with Leon.

SONIA   Leon is gone. Out of my life. Now I'm sitting and talking. Tell me about yourself. About your family, about school, about music, about what it really feels like to be Vernon Gersch.

VERNON   Look, you don't just *divulge* your entire personality. It's like toothpaste. It comes out a little bit at a time.

SONIA   So how come I'm having trouble getting your cap off?

VERNON   Look, if we don't work I'll have enough time to write my autobiography, and then you'll know everything about me.

SONIA   (*Not giving up*)   How old were you when you started playing the piano?

VERNON (*Disgruntled*) Four and a half.

SONIA And you didn't keep falling off the stool?

VERNON No. They tied me to a coatrack.

SONIA Did you ever have a desire to write really serious music? Like an opera?

VERNON Yes! I wish I were doing it *right now!*

SONIA Look, I think the problem is we're trying to get to know each other in a working atmosphere. I think the two of us have to get out and loosen up a bit.

VERNON Are you suggesting a gym?

SONIA I'm suggesting we meet somewhere in a more relaxed setting . . . I think it might be helpful if we had dinner together.

VERNON Heavy! Very heavy suggestion! I have never dated anyone I ever worked with . . . man *or* woman.

SONIA Who said anything about a date? I just said dinner. Dinner isn't necessarily a date.

VERNON Oh! You mean a *business* dinner.

SONIA No! That's our problem *now!* I don't want to discuss business. I want to have a nice sociable dinner.

VERNON *That's a date!*

SONIA A date is when two people get together socially in hopes of getting together again even more socially . . . I want to get together socially in hopes of getting together again so we can *work!*

VERNON You know, talking to you is like sending out your laundry. You never know what the hell is coming back! All right! I'll do it. I don't even want to know what it is . . . a dinner, a date. Surprise me!

SONIA Good. Thank you . . . I think having a nice casual dinner can be enormously helpful, and I appreciate your making this effort.

VERNON It's my pleasure . . . How about tomorrow night?

SONIA I'm busy tomorrow.

VERNON My shirts just came back without buttons.

SONIA Leon and I see our therapist tomorrow night.

VERNON I thought you broke up with him.

SONIA We'd like to split without any bitter feelings and we need help. So we're seeing a doctor.

VERNON (*Shrugs*) Well . . . it makes just as much sense as the date *we're* having. How about the night after?

SONIA Can't. It's Leon's birthday. I'm giving him a small party.

VERNON Look, you want to wait a few years until the breakup is firm and then try again?

SONIA It's over *now*. I am feeling guilty about it. *I'm* the one who walked out. I don't intend to see him after the party . . . I can have dinner with you tonight.

VERNON Fine. Should I make a reservation for three?

SONIA Believe it or not, I really can handle my life very well. I just have trouble with the people who can't handle theirs . . .

VERNON Well, up to now, I've been doing a bang-up job with mine, thank you. I'll make a reservation.
        (*He crosses to phone*)

SONIA You think I'm bizarre, don't you?

VERNON (*Picks up phone, dials. To* SONIA) Well, in this business I think we're all a little rococo. (*Into phone*) Hello. Is Fernando there? . . . Vernon Gersch . . . Yes, I'll hold.
(*She sings "If He Really Knew Me"*)

SONIA
    If he really knew me
    If he really truly knew me
    Maybe he would see the other side of me
    I seldom see.
    If there were no music
    If his melodies stopped playing
    Would he be the kind of man
    I'd want to see tonight?

    Does the man make the music
    Or does the music make this man
    And is he everything I thought he'd be?

    If he really knew me
    If he'd take the time to understand
    Maybe he could find me
    The part I left behind me
    Maybe he'd remind me of who I am.

VERNON (*Into phone*) Thanks, Fernando. (*He hangs up. To* SONIA) Eight-thirty. Ever been to Le Club? Or is that too dressy?

SONIA No. Terrific. I can finally get to wear my outfit from *Pippin.* Bye.
(*And she is gone.* VERNON *moves to his tape recorder and clicks it on*)

VERNON Eleven thirty-six . . . She's gone. Pulse rate normal again . . . Evaluation of Sonia Walsk. On positive side, she is extremely bright, speaks with candor and honesty, has enormous energy and enthusiasm . . . On the negative side, she is extremely bright, speaks with candor and honesty, enormous energy and enthusiasm . . . In short, this girl's a lot to deal with.
(*He sings "If She Really Knew Me"*)

If there were no music
If my melodies stopped playin'
Would I be the kind of man
She'd want to see tonight?

What the hell—it's just a dinner.
If this doesn't work—that's it!
And can I really be so hungry for a hit?

If she really knew me
If she'd take the time to understand
Maybe she would find me
The part I left behind me
Maybe she'd remind me
Of who I am.

THEY'RE

PLAYING

OUR SONG

Le Club.
Soft, sexy disco music in the background. On the walls, we
see the flickering shadows of dancers moving to the music.
   VERNON *is sitting alone at a table, a bottle of wine in front*
of him and two glasses. He looks at his watch and drums his
fingers on the table impatiently.

VERNON   This is not happening to me . . .

SONIA (*Rushes in, in* Pippin *outfit*)   I know. I'm late. I
   couldn't help it. I'm sorry. What is it, a quarter to nine?

VERNON   Ten to ten.

SONIA   Were you bored?

VERNON   No, they were playing a lot of Elton John
   . . . In fact *all* of Elton John.

SONIA (*Sits down*)   I don't blame you for being angry. I
   had a terrible scene with Leon. He doesn't want to
   break up. He wants me to come back. I couldn't get
   him out of my apartment. He was hysterical when I
   left. If I ever needed proof I'm doing the right thing,
   tonight was it . . . Oh, God, I'm famished.

VERNON   Shall we order dinner?

SONIA   The thing is, I don't think I can stay. I'm really
   scared about leaving him alone. When he gets like this,
   he's capable of doing anything.
      (VERNON *grabs wine bottle, wants to hit her*)

VERNON Well, I'm glad you dropped by . . . Maybe we can get to know each other one course at a time. A shrimp cocktail one night, a mixed green salad another . . .

SONIA Do you think I'm overreacting?

VERNON I don't know. Was Leon in the tub holding himself underwater?

SONIA Maybe I should just let him thrash it out up there. The thing is, he just refuses to accept our separation. Has anything like this ever happened to you?

VERNON I once changed my insurance man and he stopped sending me calendars. Nothing worse than that.

SONIA What about those three girls you were engaged to?

VERNON I wasn't really. The first girl was an actress who just liked to get her name in the papers. When you dialed her number, it also rang at the *New York Post* . . . Then there was Tina. We dated three times. Unfortunately her father was a caterer and very quick with announcements.

SONIA And then came Natalie Klein.

VERNON Well, Natalie was different.

SONIA How?

VERNON I'd rather not discuss it.

SONIA *I* told you about Leon. Why won't you tell me about Natalie?

VERNON Because I choose not to. Next subject, please.

SONIA Well, off to another great start, aren't we?

VERNON *I* started. You came in in the middle.

SONIA Is that why you're so belligerent?

VERNON Look, lady. I didn't suggest this. I told you it was dangerous. I thought it was better if we stayed in the apartment and wrote our five songs and nobody would get hurt.

SONIA *Lady??* That's a snide thing to say.

VERNON (*Turns away*) Oh, Jesus.

SONIA That's a really chauvinistic remark. Why did you call me "lady"?

VERNON Because I had two genders to pick from and I took a chance on the feminine. If I made a mistake, I'm sorry, Chuck.

SONIA That's as denigrating as if I called you "boy." How about writing a few songs, *boy*?

VERNON (*Looks around, embarrassed*) Will you lower your voice? Everyone is looking. I came here for dinner, I turned out to be the floor show.

SONIA Is that why you don't want to talk about Natalie? Is that where all your hostility toward women comes from?

VERNON (*Calmly*) Check! May I have the check, please? . . . Somebody?

SONIA Are you *leaving?* The minute we're beginning to get somewhere?

VERNON We haven't gotten past the first five minutes of *any* of our three meetings. It doesn't bode well for our future. (*Calls out*) Waiter! Can I find a waiter here who's on my side?

SONIA Don't go, please. At least we're bringing things up to the surface. I think there's something here worth fighting for.

VERNON (*Rises*) The Thirteen Colonies were worth fighting for . . . *Israel* is worth fighting for. Nowhere in our brief history can I find a reason for bearing arms. (*Yells off*) Do you want my lousy money or not?

SONIA (*Gets up*) Dance with me.

VERNON What?

SONIA I want to dance. Forget what I said. Forget everything. Let's just have a good time . . . Come on, Vernon, let's get it on.

VERNON I can't change moods that quickly.

SONIA Yes, you can. Don't hold on to your anger. (*She dances invitingly*) Let it all come out with the music . . . Come on . . . Dance with me.

VERNON To the Bee Gees? Why should I push *their* record? (*But he sees it's no use and she does seem so inviting. He gets up and they dance to slow, sensual rock . . . He is extremely awkward. As they dance*) I'm a lousy dancer.

SONIA Some things don't have to be said. (*He starts to walk away . . . She grabs him and pulls him back*) I find it attractive.
(*They resume dancing*)

VERNON That I can't dance?

SONIA Now I know you can't do everything. I'm not so in awe of you . . . And I find that attractive.

VERNON I also can't ski and I can't swim. You must be *nuts* about me now.

SONIA Not yet . . . but give a girl a chance.
(*He looks at her with renewed interest . . . They dance closer . . . She smiles*)

VERNON What are you smiling about?

SONIA You're fingering my back like you're playing the piano.

VERNON Oh. Sorry. I was working.

SONIA You mean you were composing on my spinal column?

VERNON I just wrote eight bars on your lower lumbar region.

SONIA Well, don't write any concertos. We're in a public place.

VERNON (*Smiles*) You know, for a dumb idea . . . maybe this wasn't such a dumb idea.
(*They look at each other. Their eyes connect. And for the first time, something even deeper connects between them . . . Suddenly she breaks away and goes back to their table.*)

SONIA I'm sorry . . .
(*She sits*)

VERNON What's wrong? What did I say now?

SONIA It wasn't you. It was Leon.

VERNON (*Looks*) Is he here?

SONIA I tell *you* not to hold on to your anger, but *I'm* the one who can't let go of the past . . . It's crazy, I know. Here I am enjoying myself for the first time in months and suddenly (*He sits*) I'm feeling guilty because Leon is so despondent. I've always been like that. If I got an A in history and my best friend got a C, I

would go home in tears. (*The music changes*) I feel personally responsible for the happiness of people I care about. I went to an analyst I hated for two years because I didn't want to hurt his feelings . . . I remember one time—
  (VERNON *holds up his hand for her to be quiet*)

VERNON Shh. Listen.

SONIA What is it?

VERNON Don't you hear what they're playing? Don't you recognize it? That was my first really big hit . . . three years ago this month.

SONIA *What?*
  (*He sings "They're Playing My Song"*)

VERNON
    Ho, ho, they're playin' my song
    Oh, yeah, they're playin' my song
    And when they're playin' my song
    Everybody's gotta shh shh shh.

    Don't say a word now.
    Listen to that sweet melody.
    I'm happy to say
    In my own humble way
    Every perfect note of that was written by me.

    Ah, ha, they're playin' my song
    That table's humming along.
    That couple half out the door
    Is coming back to hear
    More of my music.
    At first I thought this place was a dive.
    I chose it in haste
    But they showed they got taste
    As long as they're playin' my song.

    Who would have known nine months ago
    That I would give birth at my piano?
    In all honesty I've got to admit
    I knew this song would be an international hit.

Ah, ha, they're playin' my tune
Too bad it's ending so soon.
But when we all gotta go
It's good to know that
They'll be playin'
Oh, God, I'm prayin'
They'll be playin'
They'll be playin' my song.
    (*He finishes and sits down. He looks at her*)
I'm sorry. You were saying . . . ?

SONIA (*Slightly aghast*)   Do you *always* do that?

VERNON   Certainly. Don't you?

SONIA   Well, I get a thrill if I'm in a restaurant or an airplane and I hear one of my songs, but I don't get up in the aisle and stop lunch.

VERNON   It's been my dream since I was a kid. To walk into a club with Ingrid Bergman on my arm, the band spots me and plays all of my hits, and Ingrid looks at me adoringly and says, "I'm so lucky" . . . What was *your* dream?

SONIA   To go up and win a Grammy and not feel guilty about my friends who didn't.

VERNON   Well, maybe that's the difference between us. I don't get insane if people like or don't like me . . . as long as they like my music.

SONIA   You're lucky.

VERNON   Except for Natalie Klein. She was crazy about me. Hated my music. It drove me nuts. She would tear my clothes off in Grand Central Station. But in bed, I'd put on one of my tapes and she'd switch it to Alice Cooper.

SONIA   I can see why you called it off.

VERNON   When I told her it was over, she got hysterical. She said she would *force* herself to like my music. The ultimate put-down, right? Then one day last summer we were driving out to Bridgehampton and I happened to say—

SONIA   (*Holds up one hand*)   One second.

VERNON   What is it?

SONIA   What is it? It's my big one. Last summer, it's all they played. Talk about taking off—
      (SONIA *sings "They're Playing My Song"*)

SONIA
    Ho, ho, they're playin' my song.
    Oh, yeah, they're playin' my song.
    And when they're playin' my song
    Everybody's gotta shh shh shh.
    The magic of words
    Is weavin' its spell round this room.

    Nobody's dancin'
    They're all too entranced in
    Just listenin' to the perfect way
    My words fit that tune.
    Right now they're listenin' to me.
    My lyric reads like a poem.
    It surely stands on its own.

    It makes me proud to hear that music.
    It's a total expression of me.
    To be more specific
    This place is terrific
    As long as they're playin' my song.

    Who would have known two years ago
    When Leon asked, "Can't lovin' be fun?"
    Who would have known "Can't Lovin' Be Fun"
    Would be sung by everybody under the sun?

    You know this made the top ten.
    All good things come to an end.
    I wish they'd play it again and again.

Let 'em keep on playin'
Oh, God, I'm prayin'
They'll be playin' my song.
Ho, ho, they're playin' my song.

VERNON
Oh, yeah, they're playin' your song.

SONIA
I wish they'd play it again and again.
Let 'em keep on playin'
Oh, God, I'm prayin'
They'll be playin' my song.
  (*Speaks*)
You're right. That feels wonderful. I have to do that more often . . . Oh, God, you were talking about Natalie Klein. I *am* sorry. Go on.

VERNON   That's okay. I enjoy not talking about her. Would you believe I'm beginning to enjoy talking to you?

SONIA   Aha! A smile! A small victory for Sonia Walsk.

VERNON   No, no. I had my teeth cleaned today. I didn't want to waste it.

SONIA   Gee, it suddenly got—friendly in here.

VERNON   I must be maturing. If I met you in college, you would have scared the hell out of me.

SONIA   I know. It's a problem. I have a tendency to come on full-steam-ahead.

VERNON   That's why I always rush behind the piano . . . to get out of the way . . . Did you wear that perfume the first day we met?

SONIA   Yes.

VERNON   Funny. I didn't smell it till tonight.

SONIA   It's on a time-release. It goes to work when things begin to click.

VERNON   Oh? . . . Are we clicking?

SONIA   Well, you're not running and you're not hollering . . . So to me, that's clicking.

VERNON   You know, you have an incredible energy that's hard to resist. I have the feeling if there were a blackout in the city, you would be the only thing still lit up.

SONIA   You should see my electricity bills . . . You know, it's nice to see you finally coming out from behind the Steinway.

VERNON   It's a Yamaha. I got a break in the price.
(*They look at each other a moment. A romantic ballad is playing underneath*)

SONIA   My God! I've just spent five minutes without worrying about Leon . . . You know, when I first walked in your door—

VERNON   Wait a minute! . . . Listen to what they're playing.

SONIA (*She listens*)   Is that one of *your* songs?

VERNON   No.

SONIA   It's not one of mine . . . Nice romantic ballad . . . What is it?

VERNON   I don't know what it is, but I know what it's going to be.

SONIA and VERNON
   Oh, they're playin' our song
   Yeah, they're playin' our song.

VERNON
   I really like you tonight.

SONIA
   Ev'rybody, please—

BOTH
   Shh . . .

SONIA
   This man is a master.
   His music . . .

VERNON
   Her words are . . .

BOTH
   Divine.
   We started out shaky
   But we've broken the ice.
   On a bottle of wine,
   Well, you seem twice as nice.

SONIA *I'm* ready to work. Your place, ten o'clock tomorrow morning?

VERNON What's wrong with *your* place tonight? I suddenly have an overwhelming passionate desire to compose.

SONIA (*Looks at him*) Sure. Why not? (*He quickly gets up, helps her up. She stops*) We can't. Leon is still there.

VERNON (*Angrily*) Why don't you and I break up so we can spend more time together? . . . We'll go to my place!

SONIA No. Be at my place in an hour. (*She takes out an eyebrow pencil and writes it on the tablecloth*) Here's my address. If I don't get Leon moved out tonight, I never will.

VERNON And what if you never will?

SONIA Then I'll be the dumbest girl in New York. (*She runs off, stops, turns*) Better make it an hour and a half. (*She goes off. He takes off the tablecloth and folds it up and puts it in his pants pocket, most of it hanging out*)

VERNON Well, listen, if she thinks I'm going to spend the rest of my life waiting to hear how the continuing saga of Sonia and Leon is going to be resolved, she picked herself the wrong boy. I'm not something you rent at Avis, you know, where you can just pick me up and leave me when you want . . . This whole experience has left me so depressed, I don't know if I can work any—
    (*Music starts to play*—VERNON *sings*)
  Ho, ho, they're playin' my song.
  Oh, yeah, they're playin' my song.
  And when they're playin' my song
  Ev'rybody's gotta shh shh shh—
    (VERNON *exits*)

SCENE 4

Her apartment.
An hour and a half later.
It is a small, sloppy, and shoddy apartment. She is wearing
a robe, sitting on the sofa, wiping her teary eyes.
The doorbell rings.

SONIA (*Glumly*) It's open.
(VERNON *walks in very cautiously, looks around for*
LEON)

VERNON Hi! Any casualties?

SONIA It's okay. He's gone.

VERNON So is last winter, but it's coming back.

SONIA I don't ever want to go through a scene like that
again. He walked out of here so determined he was
going to make it on his own. He had the sweetest look
on his face. Like a twelve-year-old boy going off to
camp for the first time.

VERNON It's a picture I'll remember forever.

SONIA I'm sorry. I left you standing there. Please come
in. Close the door, sit down.

VERNON Is this where you live?

SONIA Certainly. What did you think it was?

VERNON Very charming.

SONIA It's a dump.

VERNON I find dumps charming.

SONIA Somehow I could never find a reason for fixing it up. Bespeaks of the relationship, don't you think?

VERNON Not necessarily. You could eat off my mother's floor and my father didn't speak to her for thirty years.

SONIA Would you like a drink? A glass of wine?

VERNON I'd better not. We forgot to have dinner during dinner.

SONIA You must be starved.

VERNON I'm okay. (*Takes a handful of tidbits from cocktail dish*) Oh, I love these. Those little pebble candies. (*He puts a few in his mouth*)

SONIA No. They're just pebbles. I collect them. (*He spits them out in his hand*)

VERNON You ought to put a sign up. A person could get gallstones.

SONIA You must think I'm an awful slob.

VERNON No, no. Call it "artistic license."

SONIA It's strange. But the only place I have orderliness in my life is with my lyrics. I have six months of unwashed laundry in the bathroom, but I'll spend four weeks looking for the right word in a song.

VERNON Why don't you write in the bathroom? Get them both done together.

SONIA I'm glad you're here, Vernon. I really needed someone to talk to.

VERNON Well, my intentions were other than verbal, but—I'm all ears . . . Well, maybe not *all*.

SONIA (*Turns away, more tears*) Damn! I'm sorry.

VERNON No, *I* am. I didn't mean to be glib. I'm beginning to see the side of you that isn't *Hello, Dolly!*

SONIA I am soo *dumb!* I've been trying to break up with the man for six months, and now that he's gone it's so painful. How did you say goodbye to Natalie Klein?

VERNON I'm not good at confrontations. I left a message on her service. (*This manages a smile from her*) Look, maybe this is the wrong time for me to—

SONIA No, please don't go. I have such mixed emotions about what I've done. And I feel this enormous need to just talk it out.

VERNON Wouldn't your analyst be better than a composer?

SONIA He's in Mexico getting divorced . . . All I need is a friend sitting in a chair . . . I was wondering if—well, no. That's silly.

VERNON What?

SONIA . . . Would you mind sitting in for him?

VERNON For your *analyst?*

SONIA You wouldn't have to do anything.

VERNON I can barely get *myself* through the day.

SONIA You wouldn't have to say anything. I just want you to listen. That's all *he* does. I listen to myself talk and then figure out things for myself. That's why he's such a good doctor.

VERNON   No wonder mine stinks. He's always giving me advice.

SONIA   If you're tired, you can even doze off.

VERNON   Really? Do you have any movie magazines?

SONIA   Gee, I really appreciate this. (*She moves a chair to the sofa*) You sit here, I'll be on the sofa.
(*She lies down on the sofa*)

VERNON   What are you doing? You're not going to lie down? I mean, that's really *official!*

SONIA   I don't have to, if it makes you uncomfortable.

VERNON   Well, I wouldn't want a malpractice suit . . . Go ahead, lie down.
(*She does*)

SONIA (*Takes a deep breath*)   Well, let's see . . . Where shall I begin?

VERNON   I feel I should have a pipe in my mouth.

SONIA   You have to be quiet. Otherwise I can't think.

VERNON   Sorry.

SONIA   Well, Leon and I had been living together close to five years now . . . I've known him almost *ten* years. We met back in—

VERNON (*Looks at watch, whispers*)   Excuse me. What time did we start?

SONIA   That's not important. Just listen.

VERNON   Sorry.

SONIA   We met back at college. At Middlebury. He was in the band. I was editor of the school paper.

VERNON   Yes, I know.

SONIA (*Turns around*)   How do you know that?

VERNON   Well, I assume you would have told me all that in previous sessions.

SONIA   No, no. Don't actually be my doctor. It's not going to get *that* confidential. Let me talk and you just listen, okay?

VERNON   Sure. That's easy . . . Hell of a way to make a living.

SONIA (*Lies back down again*)   Anyway, everything was fine for a while . . . And then, I don't know, the last year or so I've felt this need to be more . . . (*He keeps saying "Mm hm"* . . .) independent, to be out on my own . . . We were still writing together, but it just wasn't as good as it was in the beginning . . . So I began working with some other composers, had a few hits, I recorded some, played a few clubs . . . Please don't keep saying "Mm hm." It's very distracting. Okay?

VERNON   Mm hm . . . Sorry!

SONIA   I was nervous going out in front of a lot of people, but the exhilarating thing was this feeling of being in control of my own life. Once you step out there, you're all alone . . . and if you can cut that, you can cut anything . . . Well, it was just a few weeks ago I decided I was going to sever the umbilical cord forever . . . and that's about when I met you.

VERNON   Is "me" Vernon or the doctor?

SONIA   *Vernon!* You're always *Vernon.* The doctor is in Mexico.

VERNON   Gotcha. Just wanted to get it straight. Go on. This is fascinating.

SONIA   As I said, that's when I met you . . . and . . . I don't know, there was something different about you . . . a little intimidating . . . I'm always concerned with what you're thinking about . . . and I like that . . . (*Music sneaks in*) . . . Because it means I have to come up with the goods. I like challenges.
   (*She continues her speech and* VERNON *sings softly "If She Really Knew Me"*)

VERNON	SONIA
If she really knew me	. . . I had a contemporary
If she really truly knew	American literature
me	teacher in Middlebury. He
Maybe she would see the	had two eyes that could
Other side of me.	burn a hole right through
I hide of me.	me. He knew I had some
If there were no music	talent, but he wasn't going
If my melodies stopped	to let me get away with
playin'	anything. I really didn't
Would I be the kind of	like him, but I tried harder
man	for that man's approval
She'd want to see tonight?	than anyone I ever met
	before . . . He gave me an
	A-plus for the course, and
	on graduation day he said
	to me, "You got through
	by the skin of your teeth,
	Walsk. You'd better shape
	up" . . . That's what you
	make me do. Shape up
	. . . Oh, Jesus, I'm suddenly
	feeling very self-conscious.

SONIA   I'm sorry. This was a stupid thing to do. Can we stop now?

VERNON   Now? You still have forty-five minutes on your session.

SONIA   I keep saying I want to get to know you, and I'm
the one who's always doing the talking . . . How about
you lying down for a while?

VERNON   Oh, I gave that up. I'm into self-analysis now.

SONIA   You mean you analyze *yourself?*

VERNON   Mondays and Fridays, five to six.

SONIA   Are you serious?

VERNON   It saves a lot of time. I trust myself. I have a lot
of confidence in me. I can open up and not be ashamed
to hear what I have to say.

SONIA   I don't believe you.

VERNON   I swear. I'm really making some major break-
throughs. The only trouble is I have to stop soon. I go
on vacation in August.

SONIA   Come on, Vernon. What are you avoiding?

VERNON   I'm not avoiding anything.

SONIA   What is it you're so afraid to find out about yourself?

VERNON   I'm not afraid . . . I don't know. I've always had
this theory that all great talent is an outgrowth of some
deep-seated neurosis. And that if I were completely
secure and happy, I wouldn't be able to write music
anymore . . . For example, there's a place in Russia
where these smiling, happy yogurt-eating farmers live
to be a hundred and forty years old . . . But there's not
one of them who has a song in the top forty . . . and
that's since before Christ.

SONIA	VERNON
If he really knew me	I'm much more an instinc-
If he'd take the time	tual person than analytical.
To understand	If I started to analyze
Maybe he could show me	where it came from or how
Maybe he could find me	it got there, the well would
Maybe he'd remind me of	probably dry up and little
Who I am.	droplets of music would
	drip drip drip until my
	brain would crack and turn
	to parchment . . . There are
	some things in life that just
	shouldn't be analyzed. Like
	making love. I don't want
	to know *why* it feels nice to
	stroke a girl's hair or touch
	her skin. I just want to
	stroke and touch. Let her
	worry about why I'm
	doing it. I got enough trou-
	bles just getting her to let
	me do it . . .

VERNON (*He sits up*)   Anyway, I think you and I have a major decision to make.

SONIA   I love major decisions.

VERNON   Tomorrow is Thursday. We can either try to work this weekend . . .

SONIA   Or?

VERNON   Or—a friend of mine has this beach house in Quogue.

SONIA   I choose or!

VERNON   Realizing, of course, that I have only the basest interests at heart.

SONIA   If you don't, we might as well work.

VERNON   We'll leave tonight. Avoid the maniacs. I'll pick you up in an hour. If you're five minutes late, walk toward the ocean and turn left.

SONIA   Vernon, are you as excited as I am?

VERNON   Naturally. But I'm the fella. I'm acting cool.
  (*He starts to go*)

SONIA   Hey! (*He stops*) I kiss on first dates. (*He crosses back and kisses her gently*) Are you always so gentle?

VERNON   It's my classical training. I start with pianissimo and build to full orchestra . . . I'll be back with thirty-eight guys in tuxedos.
  (*He goes off*)

SONIA   (*To herself*) All right, don't get yourself all worked up, Sonia. You've been through all this before. (*She turns to go, then stops*) But God, it sure is starting off *right!!*
  (*She sings "Right," backed up by her* VOICES)
  Right
  Ev'ry-thing about this feels right.
  Ev'ry-thing is perfectly fine
  At this minute and this time.
  I'm finding that light
  Shining on me lookin' so bright
  Feelin' alive again
  Makin' me sure that he's more than
        All right for me.
  I can hear those voices inside of me
  Tellin' me my heart wouldn't lie to me.
  If I were to say in a word
  What I'm feelin' tonight I'd
  Say—

GIRLS
  Wrong, wrong, wrong
  Oh, baby, it's wrong now.
  Wrong, wrong, wrong
  Gonna do it again now.

Don't make the same mistake twice.
Ooo—

SONIA
Don't need nobody's advice

GIRLS
But if you're gonna do it, baby,
You better do it right.

SONIA
I'm gonna do it right

GIRLS
Get it on

SONIA
Got so much to pack now

GIRLS
Get him hot

SONIA
I better wear black now

GIRLS
Go for it and let him see what
Heaven can be

SONIA
He's gonna find a lot of woman
In me

GIRLS
And me
Make this right, right, right

SONIA
Lookin' for fun now

GIRLS
Check him out

SONIA

    This may be the one now

GIRLS

    Get him, honey, while you can
    Ooo—

SONIA

    This could be my magic man

GIRLS

    'Cuz if you're goin' for it, baby

SONIA

    I'm gonna get it right

GIRLS

    You better get it right

SONIA

    I'm gonna get it right

GIRLS

    You better get it right
    You better get it right
    You better get it right.

On the street.
A car drives up. VERNON *is in a green Austin, 1970 model.*
The top is down. He honks the horn, leaps out of the car, looks
at his watch . . . then stops himself.

VERNON   Okay, Vernon, buddy . . . Let's get a hold of
ourselves. Let's examine what's going on here . . . We
have either met ourselves one terrific woman . . . *or*
. . . we are about to step blindly into the old poopy-doo
once again! Caution! I suggest caution! Make no com-
mitments . . . Make no promises . . . Make *whoopee* and
then make a getaway! (*He starts to walk away.*) And
yet—
        (SONIA *appears in "normal" clothes. She carries a bag*
        and a tennis racket)

SONIA   You're ten minutes late. I've been waiting in the
lobby.

VERNON   I'm sorry. The car came unassembled. (*He*
reaches over and takes her bag) A tennis racket? Who's
going to have time for tennis?

SONIA   Shhh. It's for the neighbors.
        (*She gets into the car*)

VERNON   Those look like normal clothes. Where'd you
get normal clothes?

SONIA   I have a friend who does Geritol commercials.

VERNON (*Gets in the car*)   Any misgivings or second
thoughts before I blow two hundred bucks on gas?

SONIA   I am a fully committed woman.

VERNON   Good.

SONIA   I've never been to Quogue. What's it like?

VERNON   It's a fishing village founded by the Pilgrims in 1628. "Quogue" is an old Indian name.

SONIA   What does it mean?

VERNON   "Mess around on weekends."
          (*He starts the car. They drive off, singing "Right"*)

SONIA and VERNON
    Right, right
    Ev'rything about this feels right.
    Ev'rything is perfectly fine
    At this minute and this time.
    We're finding that light

VERNON
    Yeah! I can't remember feelin'
    This fine.

SONIA
    Did you say that to Natalie Klein?

VERNON (*Speaks*)   Sonia!

SONIA
    Hold me and tell me again.

SONIA and VERNON
    Tell me
    Just how sweet this weekend will be
    Just you and me
    Just you and me.
    Don't say a word
    Ev'rything's feelin' so right.
    Who'd ever thought we'd be here? Ooh!
    I can't wait 'till we get to Quogue.

We still aren't there
But we're sure doin' better than
We've done before
That's right.

SONIA
Do do do do do do
Do do
Do do do do do do.

SCENE 6

On the road. They drive along, quietly.

SONIA You've been quiet a long time. What are you thinking about?

VERNON Oh . . . nothing. It's okay. I'll handle it.

SONIA Does it concern me?

VERNON Well, yes. In a way.

SONIA Well, if it concerns me, it's important. What is it?

VERNON We're lost.

SONIA I thought we were. I just thought you were going a new way.

VERNON I am. No one ever went this way before. I haven't seen a sign in English for hours. I think we're in Bangladesh.

SONIA (*Looks around*) You better pull off the road.
        (*He pulls off the road. They come to a stop*)

VERNON I should have driven a piano. I'm safe behind a piano.

SONIA We'd better look for a gas station. I have to make a phone call, anyway.

VERNON Who are you calling?

SONIA   I forgot to tell Leon I was going out of town. He promised he'd take care of my plants whenever I was gone.

VERNON   I thought you sent Leon off to camp with the twelve-year-olds.

SONIA   He's the only one who has a key. I don't want my plants to die.

VERNON   So call the forest rangers! I don't understand you, Sonia. How can you call your ex-lover while you're spending the weekend with another guy?

SONIA   He's not my ex-*lover*. He is a warm, intimate, personal friend that I'm not emotionally attached to any more . . . Just as I hope you're not a "guy I'm spending the weekend with." I don't spend weekends with *guys!*

VERNON   Jesus, you really love to put a name tag on everything, don't you? You didn't happen to write "Look for the Union Label," did you?

SONIA   What is there about our relationship that you hate to see take a turn for the better?

VERNON   Talking! We're always talking about our relationship. Why don't we just have a relationship?

SONIA   Okay! Fine! Now that I know the rules, you won't hear a peep out of me until Monday morning! Quogue, please!
   (*She sits angrily. He tries to start the engine. It chokes but doesn't catch. He tries it again. No go. One more time and it dies*)

VERNON   Now see what you did. You got the car upset. (*He gets out, slams the door, goes to the hood, and lifts it up. He reaches inside and burns his finger. He winces and blows on it. He looks inside*) We burned our luggage! (*He looks around for help. To* SONIA) Do you know anything about engines? (*She looks away, doesn't answer*) May Day! May Day! We have to break radio silence here, we're in trouble. As I see it, we have two alternatives . . . A, we walk until we find a phone or a gas station, or B, we push the car until we get help.

SONIA   Good thinking. I'll take A, you try B!
(*She takes her things out of the car and starts walking away. And she is gone . . . He kicks the tire out of anger and starts to push . . . accompanied by the male* VOICES, *singing "Right"*)

VERNON
    Wrong!
    Ev'ry-thing about this feels wrong.
    God, I would give half my royalties
    Just for a phone booth—
    Maybe not half!

BOYS
    You're headed for trouble

VERNON
    I'd give a lot now

BOYS
    Let your fingers do the walkin'

VERNON
    Oh, so right

BOYS
    You better start dialin'

VERNON
    That's right now

BOYS
    You're headed for trouble. (BOYS *hand him a phone and exit*)

VERNON
    Thank you, boys.

VERNON (*Into phone*) Hello? . . . Automobile Club? . . . I have a dead English sports car that's lying in state here . . . Well, either a tow truck or a quick burial, that's up to you . . . Yes, I am a member of the club. I even go to the meetings . . . Where? Well, it's either Long Island or the planet Pluto. I haven't seen any earth people all night . . . Well, I don't know much about engines, but I think it's the distributor. The *distributor*, the crook who sold me the car . . . I don't *know* the exact location. The last sign I saw said "Fresh Clams, Four Dollars a Bucket." Does that help?

BOYS
    You're headed for trouble . . .

VERNON "Pepe's Foot-Long Hot Dogs," is that familiar?

BOYS
    Trouble . . .

VERNON "Cocker Spaniel Puppies for Sale," you know that place?

BOYS
    Trouble . . .

Beach house in Quogue. We hear the surf pounding against the shore.

SONIA   Hello? . . . Sonia Walsk . . . Any calls? . . . I'm in Quogue. The number is 516 653-0121 . . . but don't give it out to anyone . . . except, you know . . .

VERNON (*Enters with bags*)   Vernon Gersch . . . noted composer . . . died at seven-twenty A.M. this morning. Vice President and Mrs. Mondale will attend services. (*He drops bags, falls onto bed*)

SONIA   Listen, no more arguments. Let's just forget what happened. Come on. It's going to be a gorgeous day. Would you like to go for a dip?

VERNON (*Sits up*)   A *dip?* Yes. Possibly you could rent a crane and have me lowered into the water a few times . . . like a tea bag.

SONIA   Vernon . . . we can still salvage the rest of this weekend. If you drop the sarcasm, I'll drop the petulance. Except for the stinking miserable trip out here, I'm having a wonderful time. Come on, lazy. I'll race you to the beach.

VERNON   Please, I don't wanna play Sandra Dee. (*Holds his back*) Ooh, the pain. The Austin is not an economical car. It only gets two miles to the push. (*He sits up, looks around*) Where are we?

SONIA (*Starts to fix her hair*)   In Quogue. In your friend's house.

VERNON (*Gets up, looks around*) This isn't his house.

SONIA Of course it is. Two fifty-seven Sea View Road.

VERNON Two *sixty*-seven! *Sixty*-seven! How did you get in here?

SONIA The key didn't work, so I just *forced* it open.

VERNON (*Rushes to window, looks out*) *That's* the house! Next door . . . (*He grabs bags, groceries*) Jesus, breaking and entering, two to five years. Just when my career got going . . . Come on, will you?

SONIA Vernon! Let's stay here. I like this house much better than that one.

VERNON So does my friend, but he doesn't own this one . . . Hurry up, will you? And wipe off your fingerprints.

SONIA If we hear anyone, we'll run out the back way. Oh, Vernon, I can't think of anything more romantic than making love in a house you just broke into.

VERNON Really? How about making love in a house you can't get *out* of? Like a prison. Let's go, let's go.

SONIA It's the first time for us, Vernon. I want it to be special.

VERNON I do too. But I also want it to be legal . . . Will you get your things, and this time you push the car.

SONIA My God, Vernon, you are so—so—so *straight!*

VERNON *Me? Straight??* The man hasn't been *born* yet who's as neurotic as I am!! You've given me nothing but trouble since the moment I met you. And if I know you another fifty years, there isn't a day that'll go by where you won't drive me insane . . . And *still* I'm crazy nuts for you. So don't tell me about *straight*!!

SONIA   Then bend a little for me, Vernon. Please. Can't you bend?

VERNON   I've been bending since the Triboro Bridge.
(*She lies back on the bed. She raises her arms toward him. He doesn't make a move toward her . . . She sits back up*)

SONIA   Come on . . . All right . . . The last thing I want to do is tie you down to anything . . . especially a bed. I'll get my things.

VERNON   Wait a minute! (*She stops*) Stay there! Sex wins again. I'll put the bags in the next house. If I have to run, I'll have enough trouble with my zipper.
(*He turns and goes with the bags. She runs and calls after him*)

SONIA   Vernon! Bring back the pistachio nuts for afterward!
(*She sings "Just for Tonight"*)
Just for today
Let me love you.
Just for tonight
I'll close my eyes
And when I open them
My world will be all right.
It couldn't hurt anyone
It wouldn't hurt anyone

Just for today
I want to hold you.
Just for tonight
You'll be my dream.
And when the mornin' comes to wake me
That's all right.
It couldn't hurt anyone
It wouldn't hurt anyone

Takin' just one more chance
Tryin' for some fun.

Up to now
My life's been too much said
Too little done.

Just for today
I'll be my feelings
And I know they'll lead me home
And if we both come back a little wiser
It couldn't hurt anyone
It wouldn't hurt anyone
It shouldn't hurt anyone

Just for tonight
Just for tonight.
(VERNON *comes back in, breathless*)

VERNON   We better do this quickly. A couple of seagulls just spotted me. (*He removes his jacket and shoes and lies next to her on the bed. Telephone rings*) Oh, Jesus!

SONIA   I'll get it.

VERNON   What do you mean, you'll get it? It's for *them*, not us!

SONIA   It could be for me.

VERNON   What?

SONIA   I didn't know it was the wrong house. I called my service and left this number.

VERNON   You left this number??? Why?

SONIA   I don't know why. Force of habit, I guess . . . If it's Leon, I'll call him back.
(*She picks up phone receiver*)

VERNON   Sonia! I want you to put that phone down! I want you to hang up! And I don't want you calling him back . . . not today . . . not ever.

SONIA   Look, I'm sorry about today. It was stupid. But Leon is still my friend. I can't promise never to speak to him again. That's not fair of you, Vernon.

VERNON   I didn't say it was fair. I said it's what I wanted . . . Eventually we all have to cut ourselves loose from the coatrack.

SONIA   Look, I know I've got big trouble in that area. But if I do it when you want me to and not when I'm *able* to, it'll come back to haunt the both of us. It's happened to me before. When my father died, I was away in college and I never had a chance to say goodbye. I don't want any more unresolved relationships. Let me say goodbye in my own time . . . in my own way.

VERNON   It's your life . . . You do it any way you want, Sonia. (*He picks up his own bag*) I'll be next door . . . It suddenly doesn't feel like the right time to be in the wrong house.
    (*He turns and goes. She sits on the bed . . . then puts the phone to her ear*)

SONIA   Hello? . . . Leon? . . . Listen, I'm sorry but—this is a bad time to talk . . . *No!* Don't call back later . . . Later is a bad time too . . . It's *always* going to be a bad time, Leon . . . I *do* want to be your friend . . . I just don't know how to do it without hurting someone else . . . You take care of yourself, you hear me? I'm really counting on you to be good to yourself . . . Well, if you won't say it, I'll say it for both of us . . . Goodbye, Leon.
    (*She hangs up and sings "Just for Tonight"*)
    I'll be my feelings
    And I know they'll lead me home.

Okay, Vernon Gersch, if it's a relationship you want, get ready for the big time.

    It couldn't hurt anyone
    It wouldn't hurt anyone
    It shouldn't hurt anyone.
    (*Phone rings, continues ringing. She picks up her bag and runs off*)

Curtain

Act Two

SCENE I

VERNON's *living room. Four o'clock in the morning. The room is in semidarkness.*

VERNON, *in pajamas and open robe, is pacing wearily. He calls out to the city.*

VERNON   *Sleep!* I can't sleep! (*He crosses to piano, where his portable tape recorder is. He turns it on and speaks into it*) Journal . . . Monday, four o'clock in the morning . . . Well, it's happened . . . Just as I feared . . . LOVE FINDS VERNON GERSCH! CUPID STRIKES DOWN JUILLIARD GRADUATE . . . How do you like *them* apples, old faithful Panasonic tape recorder? . . . I have all the symptoms of a pubescent adolescent . . . I have gone from Mozart and Beethoven to ga-ga and goo-goo . . . That's what you get for not looking where you step . . . My greatest fear is that I will now have to adopt Leon . . . I've got to get some sleep . . . (*The doorbell rings*) Doorbell at four-oh-two . . . We know who that is, don't we?

　　　(*He crosses, turns on lights, opens door.* SONIA *steps in*)

SONIA (*Breathless and rapidly*)   Don't get nervous, Vernon. I know it's four o'clock in the morning, but I had to see you. I hope I didn't wake you. Oh, God, I can't catch my breath. I'm hyperventilating. (*She does*) I'm a wreck. I'm a nervous wreck. I haven't slept all night. I don't know how you do it. (*Takes scarf off her head*) Do you like my hair? I just had it cut.

VERNON   Just *now?* You found an all-night Vidal Sassoon?

SONIA   No. Earlier tonight. Then I went home and took a hot bath, me and the girls did some work and then I went to bed. Then at one o'clock in the morning my doorbell rings. I go to the door, open it up and you'll never guess in a million years who was standing there.

VERNON (*Thinks*) . . . I give up.

SONIA   Leon!

VERNON   Leon!! Of course! It never entered my mind. (*He rushes to the window, yells out, and waves*) Hey, Leon! Welcome home! We really missed you, buddy.

SONIA   He doesn't have a dime to his name. He doesn't have a place to stay. He looked like he'd been in a terrible fight, and Leon can't fight. He's got these teeny little fists . . . I couldn't kick him out on the street. I'm sorry, Vernon, I just couldn't.

VERNON   *I* could. Call *me* next time, I'd *love* to do it! Jesus, I haven't got the energy to participate in this yo-yo triangle any more, Sonia. Another few weeks of this, I'll be broke and Leon and I will end up sharing *your* apartment.

SONIA   That's more or less along the lines I wanted to discuss. I will not discard Leon like yesterday's garbage. On the other hand, I can't stay there with him. Not after what happened to us this weekend . . . Therefore, I was going to suggest—

VERNON   Don't tell me! (*He runs across the room*) Don't tell me!
        (*He runs out the door. He comes back in carrying two of* SONIA's *suitcases*)

SONIA   You don't have to say yes. It's just a suggestion.

VERNON   Pearl Harbor was a suggestion. (*He puts down suitcases*) A girl with packed suitcases is a very intimidating thing, Sonia.

SONIA I thought you might be pleased. I thought you might like the idea of my moving in with you. If nothing else, Vernon, I'd never be late again.

VERNON I adjusted to it . . . I set all my clocks back.

SONIA Listen, Vernon, I'm not asking you to take me in out of pity or charity. I'm not asking you to take care of me. I will pay for my room and board.

VERNON With what?

SONIA I was going to borrow money from you. You can take it out of my future royalties. And I will not leave my unwashed laundry in the bathroom.

VERNON By all rights, *Leon* should do our laundry. He's the only one not paying rent.

SONIA Does that mean yes, Vernon, because I feel an emotional sonic boom building up inside me and I don't want to crack your windows . . . and I'll be damned if I'm going to cry in an apartment I have not been invited to live in.

VERNON What do you want me to do, draw up a lease?

SONIA Can't you say it, damn it? I'll write it out for you. Just repeat after me: "Please, Sonia, won't you please—"

VERNON YES, I WANT YOU TO LIVE WITH ME. ALL RIGHT??

SONIA That's sweet of you to ask.

VERNON You don't wear jockey shorts, do you? I hate getting underwear confused.
    (*They kiss*)

SONIA Do you know what I'm going to do now?

VERNON What?

SONIA I'm going out in the hall and get the rest of my
things.

VERNON Sonia . . . (*She stops*) . . . I was going to ask you
to move in tonight. It was going to be a surprise. I was
going to go over myself while you were out, pack up
your things and have your apartment recycled . . . I
want to make you happy. I want to make you rich
. . . I want you to wear dresses that have never appeared
on any stage . . .
(SONIA *exits.* VERNON *plays piano and sings "When
You're in My Arms."*
During the second chorus of the song, VERNON *sings
while her* VOICES *help her move in and his help put
her things away. They move in posters, potted plants,
a bicycle, framed photos, a blender, and a grandfather
clock . . .*
*His apartment begins to take on a change of appear-
ance . . .*
*In the third chorus of the song, she changes into her
nightgown,* VERNON *into his pajamas. The male
and female* VOICES *continue backing them up in the
song . . .*
VERNON, *now in his pajamas, goes back to the piano,
still noodling with the song.* SONIA *crosses to him,
ready for bed.*
*The stage is now half the living room, half his bed-
room. The passage of time is about three weeks*)

VERNON
  When you're in my arms
  And I feel you close to me
  Life's what it's supposed to be.
  I'm in love
  And you are my song.

SONIA
  You're my melody
  You're every dream I locked away.

VERNON and **SONIA**

My whole world came alive
The day you walked into my life.
You are my song.
Sing it.
Let ev'rybody know I found you.
Let ev'rybody know I found that thing that people
     love to sing about.
Tell them
Tell them if they didn't hear by now
Tell 'em how I found that feeling that I waited for.
I've got the world and more
When you're in my arms.

VERNON

I wish I had the words to say

SONIA

I'll give 'em to you ev'ryday

VERNON and **SONIA**

Tonight you're in my arms
It feels good in your arms
Tonight you're in my arms.

GIRLS

When you're in love
The time keeps tickin'
But you got no time to see it go.

VERNON

I only got eyes for my sweet,
     sweet baby
So love's the only time I know.

VOICES (BOYS and **GIRLS)**

When you're in love
Your smile gets wider
You wear a kind of magic glow.
The clock on the wall,
Well, it don't matter at all
'Cause love's the only time
You know.

1 8 5

THEY'RE

PLAYING

OUR SONG

Somethin' so right 'bout lovin' together
Two hearts are better than one.
Good, good lovin' and sweet, sweet music
Sure makes wakin' up fun.
Sure feels good to be lovin' each other
Wonder why we waited so long.
Sonia and Vernon
The fire is burnin'
We got ourselves our own sweet song.

SONIA and VERNON
    When you're in my arms
    I see a world I've never
    seen.

VOICES
In your arms
Never seen.

VERNON
    I never knew that trees were green
    'Til you were in my arms.

ALL VOICES
    You are my song

SONIA
    Thank you
    For helpin' give my life some order.

VERNON
    But where'd you put my tape recorder?
    I want to write how good I feel tonight.

SCENE 2

VERNON *is at the piano.* SONIA *is getting ready for bed.*

VERNON   I'm still not sure about the middle eight bars . . . Listen to this again. Tell me what you think.
(*He continues playing. She slams the keyboard cover down*)

SONIA   No!!

VERNON (*Just getting his fingers out in time*)   Are you *crazy*?? My fingers don't work unless they're attached.
(*He rubs them protectively*)

SONIA (*She turns down bed covers*)   It's one o'clock in the morning. I've had enough music today. I don't want to hear any more music, Vernon. Let's go to bed.

VERNON   That's what you said *last* night. Then you got into bed and turned on *music.*

SONIA   When *other* people write it, it's music. When *we* write it, it's working. I'm through working today.

VERNON   How come when we're in bed and they're playing one of your old songs, you *love* it?

SONIA   Because that's already *written.* Then it's music. When it's still unwritten, it's not music. It's *working*!

VERNON (*He looks at her, then looks away, trying to figure out her logic*)   I *detest* it when a ridiculously illogical statement like that makes complete sense to me!

SONIA   Vernon . . . we've been working every day and every night since I moved in here three weeks ago. I saw you more socially when I didn't live with you. I want to go out to dinner. I want to go to a movie. I want to see people on the street and what girls are wearing these days. I want to see what the rest of the world is doing.

VERNON (*Looks out window at street*)   You can see from here. They're not doing much.

SONIA   You know what just occurred to me? The piano is your Leon. Don't talk to *me* about letting go.

VERNON   Never—*never*—refer to my piano as Leon! And the reason I've been working so much is because I never had so much fun working before . . . I *like* it when I look over and see you curled up in a chair with a scribbled pad on your lap and a pencil in your mouth—all chewed to pieces like a beaver got to it . . . I like it when you come over and touch the back of my neck when something I've written particularly pleases you . . . I can't find a good enough reason to go out when it's so terrific at home.

SONIA (*Touched*)   Well . . . you do the same thing to me.

VERNON   I don't chew my piano.
      (*They are both on the bed*)

SONIA   No . . . but you get the most incredible look in your face when you're searching for those first four bars in a song. I just watch you and wonder, "What's going on in his mind now? What does he hear inside his head that the rest of us can't hear?" And then your eyes roll upward and your tongue comes out to the corner of your mouth . . .

VERNON   I know that look. Usually I'm thinking about lunch.

SONIA   What are you thinking about right this minute?

VERNON (*He looks at her, smiles*) How to get Natalie
  Klein's initials off the towels.

BOTH (*Sing*) When you're in my arms

VERNON I wish I had the words somehow

SONIA Shh, not now

BOTH Tonight you're in my arms
  And you'll be wakin' up in my arms.

ALL VOICES When you're in my arms . . .

  (*He turns out bed lamp. Lights fade*)

THEY'RE

PLAYING

OUR SONG

SCENE 3

The bedroom.
The middle of the night.
The telephone rings . . . A pause. It rings again.
The light goes on over the bed. SONIA *looks at the clock.*

SONIA   It's a quarter to three. (*It rings again*) Aren't you going to answer it?

VERNON   There's no one I want to talk to who calls at this hour. (*It rings again. He picks it up*) Hello? . . . Who's this? . . . I'm sorry, I can't understand you . . . Who did you want? . . . Who? . . . Is this Leon? . . . Figures.

SONIA   Oh, God!

VERNON (*Into phone*)   No, not Mervyn. *Vernon!* . . . You know, you got a goddamn nerve!

SONIA   I'm sorry, Vernon.

VERNON (*Into phone*)   None of your business what we're doing. (*To* SONIA) He wants to know what we're doing.

SONIA   Don't tell him.

VERNON (*Into phone*)   Listen, *pal,* you know it's a quarter after three?

SONIA   It isn't. It's only a quarter of.

VERNON (*Into phone*)   Is that English? I don't know what the hell you're saying. (*To* SONIA) The man is either stoned or he's Greek. I can't understand him.

SONIA (*Crossing over*) Let me speak to him.

VERNON (*Handing her the phone*) He sounds like he's smoking one of your old dresses.

SONIA (*Into phone*) Leon? . . . It's me . . . Are you all right?

VERNON Why do you give him an unlisted number? My *mother* doesn't have this.

SONIA (*Into phone*) Leon, what's going on? . . . Are you alone? . . . You don't sound right to me . . .

VERNON Don't be nice to him! What are you being nice to him for?

SONIA (*Into phone*) What are you on, Leon? . . . You haven't done anything stupid, have you?

VERNON Hang up! It's my phone, I pay the bills. Hang up!

SONIA (*To* VERNON) Will you please stop! He's in trouble. (*Into phone*) Leon! I want you to lie down on the sofa and just close your eyes. I'm going to be there in ten minutes . . . Just hold on and wait for me, Leon. I'm on my way now. (*She hangs up*) I've got to get dressed. Could you please call downstairs and ask them to get me a cab?

VERNON Are you serious?

SONIA (*Getting dressed*) I've never heard him like this. He sounds manic. It's the last time, Vernon. I'll never go again, I swear. But I've got to go tonight.
(*She continues dressing*)

VERNON They have numbers you can call when you're in trouble. You dial "JUNKIE" or something.

SONIA Don't you understand? He doesn't want outside help. He wants *me*.

VERNON Funny, so do I. Maybe I should go in the other room and call this number.

SONIA I know what he's trying to do. I know how irrational he is. But somehow I just can't ignore it, knowing it's possible he just swallowed a bottle of pills.

VERNON He wouldn't be calling you if he was trying to kill himself. His plan is to do this at three o'clock every morning and kill *me*!
    (SONIA *puts on colorful knitted leg warmers, takes* VERNON'*s necktie from the bedstand and ties it around her waist, gathers up her nightgown to above her knees and tucks it under the tie. She then puts on shoes and a knee-length cape*)

SONIA I'm sorry, Vernon, I just have to go. (*She is dressed, crosses to him*) I just want you to know, aside from everything else, I love you for being so patient with me . . . No matter what I put down on paper, I still haven't expressed the way I feel about you . . . And let's not go out tomorrow night. I like things just the way they are. I'll be back in a half hour. Could you let me have five dollars for the cab?

VERNON (*Takes money off bureau*) You're going out like that? You look like you're going to the forest to visit your grandmother. (*He gives it to her. She kisses him quickly. And she is gone. Calls after her*) You'd better be back. We have a ten o'clock recording date in the morning. The demo, remember? I could understand all this if I were living with a doctor . . .

SCENE 4

Recording studio. Music is heard.
We hear a telephone ring through the receiver, then a voice
comes on . . .

WOMAN   Four-seven-one-six—Miss Walsk.

VERNON'S VOICE (*Impatient*)   Hello, four-seven-one-six.
Is she there?

WOMAN   There's no answer. Can I take a message,
please.

VERNON'S VOICE   It's Vernon Gersch again. Tell her I've
called seventeen times. Tell her I've— No, never mind.
Tell her to forget it. (*He hangs up angrily*) Cut the tape,
Phil. Cut the tape. (*The track music cuts off.* VERNON
enters) I called everywhere. I can't find her. How much
longer can I hold the studio?

PHIL (*Offstage*)   Maybe another twenty minutes.

VERNON   Unless she's in a terrible accident, I'm gonna
kill her! If she doesn't show in five minutes, I'll cut the
tape myself.
        (*He sits at piano as* SONIA *rushes in*)

SONIA (*Breathless*)   Don't say it! Whatever you're thinking, I agree with you. Only please don't say it.

VERNON   Sort of limits our conversation, doesn't it?
Okay. How'd the Yankees do last night?

SONIA   Oh, God, maybe you'd better say it. Get it all out,
because I deserve it.

VERNON (*Furious*) I have been sitting here since—How do you have the nerve not to even—Do you realize what it feels like to—If you were a guy right now—I've said enough!

SONIA It's all right. You're probably exhausted. Did you get any sleep at all?

VERNON I was going to take a Valium but I couldn't get my teeth unclenched. (*Into mike*) Phil, are you ready to go?

PHIL (*Offstage*) I've been ready all morning.

VERNON Couldn't you call me? Or would dialing endanger Leon's life?

SONIA I *tried* to call you. But when I picked up the phone, he went berserk. He ripped the wire out of the wall.

VERNON I did too, but I have a plug-in phone.

SONIA He's leaving for California tonight. I don't think he'll ever bother us again.

VERNON *Certainly* he will. Only now he'll bother us three hours earlier . . . He will keep bothering us just as long as you keep taking his phone calls.

SONIA I will never take his phone call again, Vernon. That's a promise.

VERNON (*Looks at her . . . Pushes a sheet of music in front of her and takes out a pen*) Put it in writing!

SONIA I said *I promised*!

VERNON That's not good enough. I need proof I can read before I go to bed. I can't sleep with one eye on the phone and the other eye on you.

PHIL (*Offstage*)   What do you say, Vernon? Time is running out.

VERNON (*Into mike*)   For everybody. (*To* SONIA) Write it, Sonia. Please. I think it's important.

SONIA   You're serious.

VERNON   Deadly!

SONIA (*Glares at him, grabs the pen*)   You want script or calligraphy?

VERNON   You can write it in Latin for all I care. I'll get the druggist to translate.

SONIA (*Writes*)   "I, Sonia Walsk, being of sound mind and body—"

VERNON   You don't have to leave him to me in your will. Just say you won't take his calls.

SONIA (*Writes quickly*)   "—will never take Leon Persky's calls again, so help me God!" Okay? Have you got a penknife? We can each drop a little blood on it, make it binding.

VERNON (*Takes paper*)   That won't be necessary.

SONIA   Would you like to have it notarized? How about a witness to cosign?

PHIL (*Offstage*)   I can witness that.

VERNON (*Into mike*)   Will you stay out of this, Phil! (*To* SONIA) Thank you. I appreciate this. It means a lot to me. (*Then he tears it up and throws it in the wastebasket*) Now maybe we can get on with our work. (*Into mike*) You can roll anytime, Phil. We're ready now.
   (*He sits at the piano*)

PHIL (*Offstage*)   Rolling tape . . . take one . . . "I Still Believe in Love." Gersch and Walsk.

(PHIL *plays the tape intro to the song,* VERNON *nods to* SONIA . . . *She begins to sing. But she is still so angry, she bites the words off sharply and bitterly. He stops playing*)

VERNON (*Into mike*)   Cut it, Phil! Hold it! Wait a second! (*Turns to* SONIA) That's a little hostile, isn't it? This is a ballad, not the official Nazi party song.

SONIA   It's a mood piece. This is the mood I'm in.

VERNON   Yeah? Well, gloom isn't selling so well these days. Can we try it a little more cheerful? Say, in the key of happiness. (*Into mike*) Okay, Phil.

PHIL (*Offstage*)   Take two . . . "I Still Believe in Love" . . . Gersch and Walsk.
　　　(SONIA *glares at him*)

SONIA   That was a lousy thing to make me do. Don't you ever do something like that to me again. I don't deserve that from anyone.

PHIL (*Offstage*)   I don't have that in my lyric. Is that a new lyric, Vernon?

VERNON (*Into mike*)   No. That's from life, Phil. Lyrics are with the music. (*To* SONIA) So far today it has cost me two hundred and forty dollars and all we've recorded is eight seconds of *vengeance*. Are we still on Leon? I'll write him into the song if that's the only way to get it on tape.

SONIA   No. We're well past Leon. We're into *us* now. Sonia and Vernon! You wanted five songs, we've written five songs. Every day and every night for a month. I think we've got a hell of a collaboration going, but our relationship could use a little working on.

VERNON   We're already living with each other, it's too late to start dating.

SONIA (*Suddenly nervous*) What's wrong, Vernon? Something is wrong when the dating was more fun than the living.

VERNON (*Turns away, soberly*) I don't know . . . I can't seem to get it straight in my mind. Am I living with the girl I work with, or working with the girl I live with?

SONIA I didn't know there was a difference.

VERNON Try "enormous" . . . I don't know which Sonia it is I'm so angry with right now. Which one do I complain to when the other one is driving me berserk?

SONIA Funny, but I've never thought of *you* as two people. And if I did, I would feel the same about both of them.

VERNON Well, you're much more liberal-minded than me. I'm just one of those old-fashioned monogamists . . . Are you hungry? I'm starved. (*Into mike*) Phil, is there any coffee and Danish left in there?

PHIL (*Offstage*) There's one Danish, but I've been using it as an ashtray.

SONIA Oh, God. I have that nervous feeling in my stomach you get when someone you care for is about to tell you something you don't care for.

VERNON Not at ninety dollars an hour. Let's make the tape.

SONIA (*Snaps at him*) *I'll pay for the goddamn tape.* Talk to me, Vernon. I'm here. Live! I don't want to be something you can erase when you get home.

VERNON (*Thinks*) I don't know . . . I've said it all . . . I think between you and me and me and you, we have one relationship too many.

SONIA   Jesus, Vernon, do you expect me to split myself down the middle and offer you the part of your choice? I am a fairly attractive, intelligent, twentieth-century woman, not, I pray to God, a broiled lobster. I am an entity. I come all assembled and complete. I work, walk, talk, make love, and drive some people berserk. I am Sonia Walsk. Leave out the battery and you can play with me all you want, but the eyes won't light up.

VERNON   Wait a minute. When I'm not at the piano, I'm just of average intelligence. Speak slowly, like I'm from Norway. I didn't get all of that. I didn't get *any* of that.

SONIA   I'm just asking you to be patient with me. If not, let's say goodbye now. I can't go through another one of those lingering five-year breakups.

VERNON   What you ask for, Sonia, isn't unreasonable.

SONIA   Well, that's encouraging.

VERNON   I just don't know if it's possible.

SONIA   All right . . . You want to try one me at a time? Okay! I can find someone else to work with. I've done it before. I'll get rid of my pads and pencils tonight. I can use the drawer space, anyway.

VERNON   It's not going to work, Sonia.

SONIA (*Near tears*)   Why not? You care for me, Vernon, I know that. What in God's name is it you're afraid of?

VERNON   Everything! I feel so damned threatened by you. I don't have your patience, your understanding, your incredible gift for still caring and worrying about a man that you no longer care or worry about. You're an emotional Florence Nightingale, and I don't know if I can measure up to your standards.

SONIA   Are we talking about the same person? You're the one I look up to with respect and admiration.

VERNON You want the God's honest truth, Sonia? You scare the hell out of me. I feel so competitive with you. When you tell me the last eight bars are no good, I want to quit the business and go back to Juilliard for another four years . . . Because I am so confused by you, I keep forgetting who *I* am . . .

SONIA (*Softly*) Ask me. I'll tell you.

VERNON I'd rather find out for myself.

SONIA (*Nods*) I understand . . .

VERNON I'm sorry, Sonia.

SONIA What the hell. I'm sure we'll both get a couple of good songs out of this . . . I'll get my things out tonight.

VERNON Oh, a package came for you this morning. From the Hanna Theater in Cleveland.

SONIA That'll be my gown from the *Rocky Horror Show.*

VERNON I will miss the Broadway melody in your closet. You still feel like cutting the demo? I've got the track laid down. Phil's all ready to go.

SONIA Sure. Why not? Might as well have a souvenir to take home.

VERNON I'll listen to it in the booth.
     (*He starts out*)

SONIA (*Nervously*) You're not leaving without saying goodbye, are you?

VERNON No . . . I will definitely say goodbye. That's a promise.
     (*He goes. She sits on the stool and signals to* PHIL *she is ready*)

PHIL (*Offstage*) Take three . . . "I Still Believe in Love" . . . Gersch and Walsk.

(We hear the musical intro and she sings "I Still Believe in Love")

SONIA

After all the tears I cried
You'd think I would give up on love
Get off this line.
But maybe I might
Get it right this time.

I was there as passion turned to pain
Sunshine turned to rainy days.
Yet here I am
Ready to begin once again.

All my life I've been a dreamer
Dreamin' dreams that always broke in two.
But I still believe in love
And I love believin'
Maybe you can make my dreams come true.

Here content with who I am
I'm reachin' out my hand to him
Once again.
At least I know I made myself a friend.

All my life I've been a dreamer
Dreamin' dreams that never quite came true
But I still believe in love
And I love believin'
I'll keep on dreamin'
Because I still believe in love
I still believe in love and me and you.
I still believe in love . . .

VERNON (*Offstage, over mike from the booth*) That was nice, Sonia . . . Thanks a lot . . . I'll, er . . . see you around.

SONIA Yeah? When?

VERNON (*Offstage*) I don't know . . . I think I'm going to get out of New York for a while.

SONIA Oh . . . Well, try not to get lost.

VERNON (*Offstage*)   Goodbye, Sonia.

SONIA   Gee . . . you kept your promise. Goodbye, Vernon . . . Phil? Would you play that back for me? I feel
like hearing a familiar voice.
(PHIL *plays back the beginning of the song*)

SONIA'S VOICE
   After all the tears I cried
   You'd think I would give up on love
   Get off this line
   But maybe I might get it right this time . . .
   (*We go to dark, the song continues . . . We hear the*
   VOICE *of Johnny Mathis . . .*)

VOICE
   All my life I've been a dreamer
   Dreamin' dreams that never quite came true
   But I still . . .
   (*We hear the* VOICE *of a disc jockey*)

VOICE   That was Johnny Mathis and "I Still Believe in
Love." Twelve weeks on the charts, and this week
number two.

VOICE (*In the scene change*)   Dr. Edwards . . . Dr. Lionel
Edwards, please check with the admitting office. Dr.
Edwards, please . . .

A hospital room. Late afternoon a few months later.
VERNON *is lying in bed in a hospital gown. His leg is in a cast. He is on the phone.*

VERNON (*Into phone*) Two-thirty in the afternoon . . . Crossing Sunset Boulevard. It said "walk," so I walked. Then it must have said "hit" because I got hit . . . a '72 Pinto with no insurance. Ten thousand Rolls-Royces in Beverly Hills and I get hit by an unemployed Mexican gardener with a sweet face . . . Well, I was going to fly back to New York Monday, but I'm not going unless I can take my leg . . . Listen, Lou, I'll talk to you later. They're taking me upstairs now for tap-dancing lessons . . . 'Bye. (*He hangs up. He picks up his tape recorder, presses on button and talks into mike*) Journal. January 16. Cedars Sinai Hospital. Los Angeles. They brought me fish for lunch today. I think they caught it in the intensive care ward. I am tied down to this bed in a marvel of medical science that was once used to get people to talk during the Spanish Inquisition. It makes going to the bathroom in the middle of the night the greatest adventure of my life. I thought of calling Sonia today. Oh, well. It was just a thought. (*There is a knock on the door*) Come in.
(*He turns off recorder.* SONIA *comes in carrying a gift-wrapped box*)

SONIA Hi! Volunteer song lady. Need any books, magazines, lyrical ideas?

VERNON Next to a waiter from the Stage Delicatessen, there is *no one* I'd rather see.

SONIA I'm still showing up late. I just heard about it this morning. I read it in the daily *Variety*.

VERNON Oh, good. Two breaks in one week. I heard you were in California. Doing your own album, someone said.

SONIA Yes. With Eclectic Records. Mark Rossetti's producing it.

VERNON The best in the business. You look terrific. How does it feel, wearing firsthand clothes?

SONIA They itch. I heard you were in Europe.

VERNON Yes. Paris, for two months. Scoring the Louis Malle picture.

SONIA How'd you like it?

VERNON I had a little trouble with the language. Every time I ordered breakfast, they'd bring me a bicycle.

SONIA This is really amazing, because I was on my way here this morning anyway. I was going up to the fifth floor to visit—a friend.

VERNON Don't tell me! Leon! (*She nods*) *Fan*-tastic! I knew we'd end up living together. Just out of curiosity, Leon doesn't drive a '72 Pinto, does he?

SONIA No. He's in for some tests. They're not crazy about his white-cell count.

VERNON I kept hearing the phone ring outside at two o'clock in the morning. Now I know who it was. I hope it's nothing serious.

SONIA I hope so too.

VERNON You're never going to let go of that responsibility, are you?

SONIA   I haven't seen him in three months. I think I'm making headway.

VERNON   Maybe I'll hobble up there one afternoon. I've always wanted to see what the Masked Stranger looked like . . . Where are you living?

SONIA   Mark has a house in Beverly Hills. I'm staying in the guest cottage.

VERNON   I have a place out at the beach.

SONIA   I thought you couldn't swim.

VERNON   Well, it's not *in* the water. It's back a little . . . I met a terrific girl jogging on the beach. We have a good relationship. She runs home every night.

SONIA   Saves the hassle of packing and unpacking.

VERNON   I sure miss the crispness of our conversations.

SONIA   I'll leave you one. You can put it in the freezer . . . Oh, I almost forgot. This is for you.
(*She puts the box on the table*)

VERNON   Oh, that's very sweet. Put it on the bed. I'll break it open with my leg.

SONIA   (*Starts to untie ribbon*)   Just to keep your mind occupied. (*She lifts off the cover and takes out a toy, a miniature piano, one that really plays. She hands it to him*) It's a Steinway grand. Someone left it out in the rain.

VERNON   I love it. (*He hits a few keys*) Perfect for writing "The Minute Waltz" . . . It's very thoughtful of you.

SONIA   True. I've thought of you a lot.
(*They look at each other . . . then she turns away*)

VERNON   I'm really glad you dropped by, Sonia.

SONIA It was nice of you to break a leg so I'd have a reason.

VERNON Right. Now I know how to get in touch with you.

SONIA Well, I've got to run.

VERNON I wish I could.

SONIA (*Extends hand*) Goodbye, Vernon.

VERNON (*Shakes it warmly*) Goodbye, Sonia.

SONIA Take care of yourself.

VERNON If not me, who then?

SONIA I don't know. Why don't you give it some thought?
　　　　(*She looks at him as though she were about to say more . . . then changes her mind and goes. He looks down at the small piano and tinkers with it. He begins to play . . . VERNON sings "Fill in the Words." And there singing along with him appear his three VOICES, all in hospital gowns*)

VERNON
　　　　You play a "C"
　　　　You get a "C."
　　　　That's simple
　　　　That's easy.
　　　　But there was you
　　　　There was me.
　　　　Not so simple
　　　　Not easy.

　　　　I'm never quite able to say what I feel.
　　　　I know that sounds absurd.
　　　　The only way you can hear me is to listen to my song
　　　　　　without words.
　　　　(*He plays*)

That's what I'm feelin' right now
And I'm writing this love song for you to
Fill in the words.
You were ev'rything good
I know you loved me.
I just couldn't make us work out
And all I could do was leave it to you
To fill in the words.

VERNON and BOYS
   Fill in the words

VERNON	BOYS
If I had the words	Ah—
I'd have a song	

   And maybe it would tell
      me where I belong.
   With you I had the words
      for free.
   It's just in lovin' you
   I was losin' me.
   I'm hopin' you'll un-
      derstand
   That until I can find
   those words for myself
   Will you fill in the words?

VERNON and BOYS
   Fill in the words

VERNON	BOYS
If I had the words	If I had the words
I'd have a song	I'd have a song
And maybe it would tell me	
Where I belong.	Maybe—tell me
	Where I belong.
With you and me I wasn't sure.	
Was I less?	Ah—

Were you more?
I'm hopin' you give me
    some time
And if that kid on the
    coatrack
Wants to come back,
Wants one more try,
Where will you be?

Will you still fill in the
    words?
Will you   Ah—
Fill in the words?

                          Ah—Ah.

207

THEY'RE

PLAYING

OUR SONG

Her New York apartment. A few months later. About ten in the evening.
It is winter. The apartment is dark. The phone rings.
She opens the door and enters. She crosses to the phone.

SONIA Hello? . . . Oh, hi . . . No, I was just out walking in the snow . . . How are you, Leon? . . . Well, you *sound* better . . . When did you check out? . . . You what? . . . You're worried about *me*? . . . That's a switch . . . Well, don't. I'm terrific . . . You got a job? Where? . . . Oh, that's wonderful . . . Leon, you don't have to pay me back anything . . . That's what old friends are for . . . Okay. Ten dollars a week for forty years . . . You know, we may not have had the healthiest relationship in the world, but at least it's reliable . . . I wish you the best of everything, Leon . . . I know you do . . . (*The doorbell rings*) Goodbye.
    (*She hangs up, crosses to the door, turns on the lights, and opens the door.* VERNON *stands there with a winter coat, collar up, gloves, and a cap with snow on it, leaning on a cane*)

VERNON Do you know I've waited my whole life to do this?

SONIA To do what?

VERNON Appear at the door with my coat collar up, snow in my hair, carrying a cane and walking with a limp. Tyrone Power in *A Yank in the R.A.F.*

SONIA And who am I?

VERNON   Betty Grable.

SONIA   Go out and pick another picture. I want to be Gene Tierney. (*He turns and starts to go*) No. I'm kidding . . . Oh, God, Vernon, I'm glad to see you.

VERNON   The doctors said I'm allowed to hug now.
    (*They embrace warmly*)

SONIA   What are you doing in New York? Isn't your picture opening in L.A. this week?

VERNON   Tomorrow night. I can catch the noon plane . . . It was important I see you quickly. In another couple of days, I won't be limping any more . . . I would love a drink.

SONIA   So would I. Anything special?

VERNON   Oh. Claret. Madeira. Anything that looks good with a coat collar up.
    (*She pours a drink and hands it to him*)

SONIA   Our timing's getting better. If you rang the doorbell two minutes sooner, you would have caught Leon again.

VERNON   Too bad. I would have said hello . . . We finally became buddies.

SONIA   You met him?

VERNON   Last week in the hospital. We took X-rays together. We were hoping you were there. We wanted a family portrait.

SONIA   You know, for someone you never met, we sure spent a lot of time together . . . What'd you think of him?

VERNON   Well, he was a lot better-looking than I'd hoped he'd be . . . He was actually quite witty and charming, which I found irritating as hell . . .

SONIA   What did you talk about?

VERNON   Well, I was very frank. I said, "Leon, old buddy, for a long time you've been a genuine pain in the ass to me" . . . And he looked at me and said, "Well, I guess there's got to be a Leon in everyone's life" . . . He said he was living with a girl now, and that if I wanted, I could call *him* at three o'clock in the morning.

SONIA   That's my Leon.

VERNON   He also told me what it was like growing up in Ithaca. Said it wasn't really worth the trouble. He told me how he met you at school. What you were like. He even remembered what you wore that first day he saw you running across the campus.

SONIA   I can't remember. What was it?

VERNON   A naval officer's uniform.

SONIA   Of course. *Mister Roberts.* I was late for dress rehearsal.

VERNON   So that's how it started . . . When he checked out, he came down and we shook hands and said good-bye . . . And the last thing he said to me was . . . "Take care of our girl."

SONIA   (*A little embarrassed*)   Leave it to Leon.

VERNON   Moving on to more mundane things, I hear your album's going to be very big. What's it feel like to finally have money?

SONIA   Old habits are hard to break. I flew home on economy.

VERNON   Well, now you can live it up. Get yourself a whole new wardrobe. Like all the costumes from *Annie.*

SONIA   Can I ask you a question, Vernon?

VERNON   Sure.

SONIA   What's wrong with us?

VERNON   Nothing. We're perfect. Well, *you're* perfect. I'm going to be perfect in eight months. I've been seeing a new therapist. A big, buxom, mother-earth analyst. When you break down and cry, she holds you in her arms and gives you cookies.

SONIA   I think that's terrific. What made you go back?

VERNON   Leon, probably. When I saw him walking out of my room looking happier than I was, I said to myself, "Vernon, I think it's time to pull into your friendly therapist for a thirty-four-year-old tune-up."

SONIA   You seem different, Vernon. I feel as though we're meeting for the first time. Does it seem like the first time to you?

VERNON   I don't know. Go out and come in twenty minutes late.

SONIA   I've gone through some changes myself. I've moved out of Mark's house . . . with no guilt, no sense of responsibility . . . I'm all alone for the first time in my life, handling it great and really proud of myself. In fact, tomorrow night I'm taking me out to dinner.

VERNON   I wish I was staying on. I was going to take myself out too. The four of us could have double-dated. (*They look at each other . . . an awkward pause*) I'd better go. Promise you'll go to the window and watch me limp away in the snow.

SONIA   With one hand holding back the curtains. A perfect Gene Tierney ending.

VERNON (*Reaches in his pocket*)   I thought it would be nice if we heard my love theme as I walked off. (*Hands her a cassette)* Would you put this cassette on as I get to the door?

SONIA You actually had it recorded?

VERNON Just eighteen pieces. No brass . . . I wrote it in the hospital . . . It's about you and me and Leon . . . I call it "You and Me and Leon"!

SONIA *(Looks at cassette)* I like it better than the one you erased. "Rhapsody in Blue Cross."

VERNON Everything good takes time . . . Goodbye, Sonia.

SONIA Goodbye, Vernon.
(He turns and limps to the door, opens it)

VERNON When you see me on the corner of Eighth Avenue, turn up the last eight bars. I want a big finish.

SONIA Good luck with the opening. I'll call you from London, see how it went.

VERNON You're going to London?

SONIA Tomorrow. There's a boy there they say is the new Elton John. He wants me to write with him.

VERNON Oh . . . well, you should love that. You'll get to wear things from *Private Lives* . . . Chin up and all that. *(He turns and goes. She puts on the cassette. We hear full orchestra play his "theme" . . . She crosses to the window. A perfect Gene Tierney ending . . . Her doorbell rings. She rushes to door and opens it. VERNON stands there)* I can't get home. I lost my cane!

SONIA What?

VERNON There was snow on the ground. I stepped off the curb, leaned on my cane, and it went right down a sewer!
(He leans against the door)

SONIA Are you all right?

VERNON I couldn't walk. I had to crawl back here on my hands and knees. People passed by and dropped me a dollar thirty in change . . .
(*She crosses to him*)

SONIA We'll get you to the sofa.
(*He puts his arm around her. They get to sofa*)

VERNON Can you imagine, on my hands and knees? A big dog came over and sniffed me, wondering what breed I was.

SONIA Let me get the boy next door. He's an intern. He'll take a look at your leg.
(*She rushes out the door*)

VERNON *Noo!!!*
(*But she is gone. He sits there, a pained expression on his face . . . A moment passes, and she walks back in deliberately . . . holding his cane. She looks at him*)

SONIA Look how much your cane loves you. It followed you all the way back to my door.

VERNON (*Shrugs*) So I tried sympathy. I didn't know any other way to stop you.

SONIA From what?

VERNON From going to London. Why would you want to write with the new Elton John when you can write with the new Vernon Gersch?

SONIA What happened to the *old* Vernon Gersch?

VERNON He didn't work out. He was driving me crazy. He wasn't sleeping at nights. He was coming late for appointments. He was writing and not enjoying it for the first time in his life . . . Oh, damn it, Sonia, come back! I've grown accustomed to your soul.

SONIA What makes you think we won't have the same problems as last time?

VERNON Because I've changed. I'm different. We'll have all *new* problems this time.

SONIA What happens if Mark Rossetti calls me in the middle of the night?

VERNON We'll change our schedule. We'll sleep during the day.

SONIA What happened to how difficult it is to work with someone you're living with?

VERNON We'll deal with it. Reasonably. Rationally. Intelligently . . . And I'll try to do the same.

SONIA It's going to be hard, Vernon.

VERNON Maybe impossible.

SONIA Things don't change overnight. It needs time.

VERNON Then why are we wasting any?

SONIA It needs commitment.

VERNON I'm ready to be committed right now.

SONIA No ego problems. No jealousies. No competitiveness. We each reserve the right to criticize the other's work without being accused of chauvinism or male domination.

VERNON I won't even notice you're a woman until lights out. Then it's every man for himself.

SONIA Well . . . London is cold now, anyway . . . Sure, let's give it a try. Hi. Sonia Walsk.

VERNON Yes. We met. I analyzed you once.

SONIA I thought you died.

VERNON No, that was Tannenbaum.

SONIA Oh, yes . . . So what'll it be? Your place tomorrow
at ten?

VERNON I think I'd better spend the night here. There's
ice out there and I don't have chains on my cane.

SONIA I'm glad you said that, Vernon. Because if you
started for that door, I would have broken your other
leg.

VERNON I am absolutely nuts for you, Sonia.

SONIA Not Sonia. Ingrid.

VERNON Ingrid?

SONIA (*The way he had said it*) I'm so lucky.
(*She throws her arms around him. Music swells*)

Curtain

I Ought to Be in Pictures

I OUGHT TO BE IN PICTURES *was first presented on January 17, 1980,*
at the Mark Taper Forum, Los Angeles, with the following cast:

LIBBY TUCKER	Dinah Manoff
STEFFY BLONDELL	Joyce Van Patten
HERB TUCKER	Tony Curtis

Directed by Herbert Ross
Scenery by David Jenkins
Lighting by Tharon Musser
Customes by Nancy Potts

I OUGHT TO BE IN PICTURES *was first presented in New York City*
on April 3, 1980, at the Eugene O'Neill Theatre, with the following
cast:

LIBBY TUCKER	Dinah Manoff
STEFFY BLONDELL	Joyce Van Patten
HERB TUCKER	Ron Leibman

Directed by Herbert Ross
Scenery by David Jenkins
Lighting by Tharon Musser
Costumes by Nancy Potts

Synopsis of Scenes

Act One

Act Two

Act One

SCENE I

The scene is a small bungalow in West Hollywood. It is a rather colorless affair with cheap, rundown furniture. There is a small kitchen off the living room, a small bedroom, and one tiny bathroom. A door leads to a small backyard, with three trees.

As the curtain rises, it is about nine o'clock in the morning, a bright, sunny California morning. The radio is playing. A young girl, short, about twenty, wearing sawed-off jeans, sweat socks, hiking boots, a backpack, an army jacket, and a beret, and carrying an old valise, stands outside the door. Her name is LIBBY TUCKER. *She has an energy and a vitality that will soon make themselves apparent.*

STEFFY BLONDELL, *a still-attractive woman close to forty, is in the bathroom combing her hair.*

LIBBY *rings the front doorbell.* STEFFY *turns off the radio, goes to the door and opens it.*

STEFFY   Yes?

LIBBY   Hi!

STEFFY   Hi! Can I help you?

LIBBY (*Looks into the room*)   I don't know. I'm not sure this is the place.

STEFFY   Who are you looking for?

LIBBY   Does Herbert Tucker live here?

STEFFY   Yes, he does.

LIBBY   Which Herbert Tucker is he?

STEFFY   I didn't know there were a lot of them. Which one are you looking for?
         (*She picks up a newspaper from the front steps*)

LIBBY   Is this the Herbert Tucker in show business?

STEFFY   Yes . . .

LIBBY   He's a writer?

STEFFY   Yes. What did you want?
         (*She comes back inside*)

LIBBY   I wanted to talk to him. Is he in?

STEFFY   He's sleeping. Listen, I'm kind of busy. Could you tell me what this is about?

LIBBY   It's personal . . . Are you his wife?

STEFFY   No, I'm not . . . Are you a friend of his?

LIBBY   No. I'm his daughter.
         (*There is a pause.* STEFFY *looks taken aback*)

STEFFY   His *daughter?*

LIBBY   Libby. Libby Tucker. From New York City.

STEFFY   I see.

LIBBY   I think I stunned you.

STEFFY   No, not at all.

LIBBY   A little, right?

STEFFY   Yes, a little . . . Please come in. Sit down. (LIBBY *comes in, puts her bag down*) He didn't mention you were coming.

LIBBY   That's because he didn't know. Is this like his office or something?

STEFFY   Well, both. He works here and he lives here.

LIBBY   I see.

STEFFY   It's not what you expected?

LIBBY   I don't know. You get this picture in your mind about Hollywood. I live this good in Brooklyn.

STEFFY   He usually has a woman come in and clean it a couple of times a week.

LIBBY   Couldn't make it this week, huh?

STEFFY   I don't know. I'm not here that often.

LIBBY   Oh. You don't live here?

STEFFY   No. (*Extending her hand*) My name is Steffy Blondell.

LIBBY   Glad to meet you, Steffy Blondell.
(*They shake hands*)

STEFFY   Are you just out for a visit?

LIBBY (*Looking around*)   No. I'm sort of out on business.

STEFFY   I see. Can I get you anything?

LIBBY   A glass of water would be swell. I think I swallowed the state of Arizona.

STEFFY (*Going to the sink*)   Wouldn't you like to take that thing off?

LIBBY   What thing?

STEFFY   That pack on your back.

LIBBY   Oh, Jeez, I forgot it was still there. (*She takes it off*) After you carry it for three weeks, you think it's a growth.

STEFFY   He should be up in a few minutes. I hate to wake him. He hasn't been sleeping too well lately.
(*She hands her the glass*)

LIBBY   Yeah? Is he all right?

STEFFY   Oh, sure. Just a little run-down.

LIBBY   All his various multiple projects, I suppose.
(*She drinks*)

STEFFY   Well, he keeps busy.

LIBBY (*Winces*)   Jesus, is this water? You could eat it with a spoon.

STEFFY   It probably tastes funny after the water in New York. He really should get a filter.

LIBBY   And a fishing pole.

STEFFY   That's something *he* would say. You sound a lot like him.

LIBBY   You mean the *Noo Yawk* accent?

STEFFY   No. Just the way you say things. I think you have his sense of humor.

LIBBY   Well, that's about all he left.
(*She looks around*)

STEFFY   You're not in school then, I take it.

LIBBY   You mean college? No.

STEFFY   Because your father mentioned a few weeks ago he thought you might be in college by now.

LIBBY   He's not exactly up on my current activities, is he? No, I just missing getting into Harvard by about three million kids . . . I'm an actress.

STEFFY   Really?

LIBBY   Yeah.

STEFFY   You mean professional?

LIBBY   Yeah. Sorta professional. I mean. I'm not a star. If I was a star you would have known who I was when I said "Libby Tucker."

STEFFY   What do you do, stage work mostly?

LIBBY   No, mostly I audition.

STEFFY   But you have studied.

LIBBY   You mean in acting school? No. I never had the time or the money. I had a part-time job in the notions department in Abraham and Straus. I was *almost* accepted for a scholarship at the Actors Studio.

STEFFY   What happened?

LIBBY   Nothing. They just didn't accept me.

STEFFY   I see. So you just decided to come. I mean, you didn't write or anything?

LIBBY   Yeah. When I was nine . . . He answered when I was twelve. (*Looking around*) Just one bedroom?

STEFFY   Yes. I was just about to go out shopping. Your father's not very good about keeping his refrigerator filled.

LIBBY   You don't have to go on my account. I mean, that water was a meal in itself.

STEFFY   If I don't do it, he never will. It's just down the block.

LIBBY   You know him long?

STEFFY   About two years. We date on and off.

LIBBY   Two years and you just see him "on and off"?

STEFFY   Well, I work and I raise two children. It's difficult.

LIBBY   Yeah, I know. My mother has the same problem. (STEFFY *lets that pass*) So what's he like?

STEFFY   You mean you have no idea?

LIBBY   No.

STEFFY   I'm sorry.

LIBBY   It's no big deal. I'm okay. I came very close to growing up neurotic but I got over it.

STEFFY   I'm glad . . . Your mother raised you?

LIBBY   (*Raises her hand waist-high*)   Up to here. The rest I did myself. Mom was working all the time and she had my brother Robby to take care of. Actually, my mother and my father was my grandmother. Grandma gave me a sense of direction. She gave me confidence in myself. I'm sure you noticed my confidence. It's the one thing about me you can't miss.

STEFFY   I noticed it the minute you said "Hi" . . . How'd you get out here?

LIBBY   I took the bus to Denver, then I hitchhiked. If you're not gorgeous, you hike more than you hitch. Listen, it wasn't bad. I got to see America, they got to see me. We both made a big impression.

STEFFY   Maybe I should wake him up, huh? Tell him you're here.

LIBBY   No, that's okay. I sort of have it all planned in my mind what I wanna say. I can handle it.

STEFFY   I was worrying how *he's* going to handle it.

LIBBY   Oh, you mean the shock? He doesn't have a bad heart, does he?

STEFFY   No.

LIBBY   Maybe I should slide a note under his door first.

STEFFY   Listen, he'll be fine. Maybe I just worry about him too much.

LIBBY   I don't even know what he looks like. I've never even seen a picture of him. I don't even know what to call him.

STEFFY   You don't know what to call him?

LIBBY   Well, he isn't exactly "Poppa" and I don't think "Mr. Tucker" is gonna win him over.

STEFFY   Look, if it's a problem, just tell him. He'll understand. He's really a nice man, you know.

LIBBY   Really? Like, what's nice about him?

STEFFY   Well, why don't you wait. Make up your own mind.

LIBBY   That's what Grandma told me to do last week at the cemetery.

STEFFY   Someone died?

LIBBY   Yeah. Grandma. About six years ago. But I go out there every few weeks to talk to her.

STEFFY   I'm not sure I understand.

LIBBY   I know. It sounds weird. When I told my mother Grandma still talks to me, she wanted me to take laxatives . . . It's hard to explain to most people. But I sort of always depended on Grandma. And when I need her the most, somehow she gets through to me. (STEFFY *stares at her*) You're looking at me funny. I swear I'm not one of those people who sees miracles. This isn't *The Song of Bernadette* or anything.

STEFFY   No, I think I know what you're saying.

LIBBY   She tells me if I'm eating too much or not getting enough sleep. Last week she didn't have much to say because she just had a fight with Grandpa. He's in the grave next to her.

STEFFY   Does he talk to you too?

LIBBY   He doesn't talk to Grandma, why should he talk to me?

STEFFY   I'll tell you the truth, it's something I've always wanted to do myself. Just go to the cemetery and talk to my mother, tell her what's going on with my life. But I always felt foolish.
(*She goes to the telephone and dials*)

LIBBY   Oh, don't I know. I had a girlfriend sleep over one night and three o'clock in the morning I had this conversation with Grandma. My friend didn't even stay for breakfast.

STEFFY (*Into the phone*)   Three-seven-seven. Did the studio call for me?

LIBBY   Are you in the business too?

STEFFY   Mm-hm. Makeup lady. I work over at Columbia.

LIBBY   Columbia Pictures? The movie studio? I'm having heart palpitations.

STEFFY (*Into the phone*) If the studio calls, tell them I'll be in at ten-thirty. Thank you.
(STEFFY *hangs up*)

LIBBY   Who do you make up? Any actual stars?

STEFFY   Sure.

LIBBY   Sure, she says. Like I have this conversation every day. Name me one star. A big one. Who was the biggest?

STEFFY   I don't know . . . Jane Fonda?

LIBBY   JANE FONDA? *You've touched Jane Fonda's face?* I mean, Jane Fonda is the one actress in the world I most identify with. I patterned my whole life after hers. I feel I have so many of her qualities. They just haven't surfaced yet.

STEFFY   Well, one day if you're not busy you can come out to the studio, I'll show you around.
(STEFFY *picks up her purse and goes to the front porch*)

LIBBY   (*Following after* STEFFY)   What do you mean, if I'm not busy? How many phone calls have I got since I'm here?

STEFFY   It's no problem. I'll set it up.

LIBBY   God's truth: I liked your face the minute I saw it through the door. Maybe I should forget my old man and move in with you.

STEFFY   Is that what you're planning to do? Move in with him?

LIBBY   I don't know. Let's see if I get a handshake first.
(STEFFY *stands on the doorstep pondering* LIBBY's *last remark as* LIBBY *goes into the house and closes the front door.* STEFFY *leaves.* LIBBY *looks around the room, then sits down. The telephone rings. She looks at the bedroom door, then rushes to answer it to avoid waking her father. Into the phone*) Hello? . . . Who? Oh, er . . . No. He's sleeping . . . No, this is er—sort of his daughter . . .

Yeah. Sure I know how to take a message. (*Picks up a pencil*) Wait a minute. I need a piece of paper. (*She starts to look through the mess on the desk. She finally finds paper in the top drawer. Into the phone*) Okay. Go ahead . . . "Stan Marx called. You got a turndown at NBC. Do you want to try CBS again?" Is that it? . . . Yeah, I got it . . . You're welcome. Goodbye. (LIBBY *hangs up. The bedroom door opens. A sleepy-eyed* HERB TUCKER *comes out in his pajama bottoms and an old T-shirt. He heads right for the coffee. She turns and notices him*) Oh! Hi!

HERB (*Doesn't look at her*)   I didn't hear you get up.

LIBBY   That's because I didn't sleep here.

HERB (*Looks at her*)   I thought you were Steffy. (*He calls out*) Steffy!

LIBBY   She went shopping.

HERB   Steffy did?

LIBBY   Yeah.

HERB   Who are you?

LIBBY   Libby.

HERB   You're the cleaning girl today, Libby?

LIBBY   No. Just Libby.

HERB   Steffy's niece.

LIBBY   No.

HERB   Come on, kid. It's too early. Don't play games with me. Libby who?

LIBBY   Libby Tucker.

HERB (*No reaction*)   Libby *Tucker*?

LIBBY   Libby Gladyce Tucker . . . Blanche's girl?

HERB   What are you saying to me?

LIBBY   I'm saying, I'm your daughter. I didn't mean to
sneak up on you like this. It must be an awful shock,
heh?

HERB   Yeah. A little. A little . . . Could you wait one
second? Let me get a little coffee down.
   (*He pours coffee and sips some*)

LIBBY   I suppose I should have called first, but it seemed
harder to say over the phone than in person . . . Are you
okay?

HERB   I'm fine. I'm fine. I just want to get a little more
coffee down.
   (*He drinks some more*)

LIBBY   I got out here yesterday, so I thought I'd just
come by and look you up.

HERB   You looked me up, heh?

LIBBY   I found your address in the telephone book.

HERB   Looked it up in the telephone book, heh?

LIBBY   Uh-huh . . . This is coming at you a little fast, isn't
it?

HERB   Yeah, a little. This is really terrific . . . Where's
what's-her-name?

LIBBY   Steffy?

HERB   Steffy. Where did she go?

LIBBY   Shopping. She'll be right back. She went to get
breakfast.

HERB   Oh, that's too bad. I wanted her to meet you.

LIBBY   We met.

HERB   Where do you know Steffy from?

LIBBY   From the door. She opened it and I came in.

HERB   Oh, I see. Just now.

LIBBY   When I came to look you up.

HERB   Okay, I got it. I got it. I'm up now . . . Jesus, what a surprise. Don't you feel like that?

LIBBY   No. I knew I was coming.

HERB   When did you decide all this?

LIBBY   About two years ago. That's how long it took me to save the money to come out here.

HERB   This is really incredible. I was just talking about you the other day to . . . what's-her-name?

LIBBY   Steffy?

HERB   To Steffy. I suddenly can't remember anybody's name. I'm sorry. I'm a little fuzzy. I took a sleeping pill about an hour ago.

LIBBY   An hour ago?

HERB   I like to wait until the last minute, in case I fall asleep on my own. Would you wait for one second? (*He goes to the sink and dashes water on his face*) Listen, could you pull down that window shade? It really bothers me.

LIBBY   You don't like the sun?

HERB   Not every day for sixteen years.

LIBBY   I love this kind of weather. Although I hear it rains a lot out here.
(*She pulls down the shade*)

HERB   Thirty inches of rain in two hours. The rest of the year is all sun.

LIBBY   I thought I'd find you all sunburned.

HERB   I hate it. It tries to get at me through the cracks in the door. I gotta hide.

LIBBY   Listen, after all those winters in New York, this is terrific.

HERB   Oh, well, this is temporary. I'm moving. I got a nice place picked out up in the Hollywood Hills. I'm supposed to move in a few weeks. I just gotta wait for a couple of things to come through.

LIBBY   What kind of things?

HERB   Oh, things. In the business, I got a very big deal on the fire right now. You wouldn't understand.

LIBBY   (*Picks up the message*)   Oh. There was a message for you. Stan Marx called. He said you got a turndown from NBC. Did you want to try CBS again?

HERB   Oh. (*He looks at the message*) Yeah, well, this wasn't important . . . This wasn't the deal I was talking about . . . You have a very nice handwriting. You make *w*'s like I do.

LIBBY   (*Proud*)   Yeah? I guess I inherited that, huh?

HERB   Jesus, I can't get over how grown up you've got. Turn around. Let me look at you.

LIBBY   This is it. I don't get any bigger.

HERB   You don't have to. You're perfect.

LIBBY   I'm a shrimp.

HERB   You're petite. I wouldn't want you any bigger. And you've got plenty of time to grow yet . . . How old are you now?

LIBBY   I was nineteen on my last birthday.

HERB   *Nineteen?* Already? Can you believe that?

LIBBY   Yeah. *I* can.

HERB   It was in December, wasn't it? December thirteenth, fourteenth . . .

LIBBY   July fifth.

HERB   July fifth. Of course. I remember that day. I was at the ball game. I just got home. Yankees–Red Sox. Yankees won it five-three in the bottom of the tenth. Hank Bauer hit a homer with Berra on second with one out.

LIBBY   Boy, you sure remember birthdays good.

HERB   And now you're this regular beautiful young lady.

LIBBY   Well, not so beautiful.

HERB   Of course you are. Who said you weren't beautiful?

LIBBY   Well, nobody ever said I *was.*

HERB   What do you mean? *I* just said it.

LIBBY   Well, that doesn't count. You're my father.

HERB   Yeah, but that was a long time ago.

LIBBY   Well, thank you. I'm glad you think I'm beautiful.

HERB   Very pretty. Healthy-looking, you know what I mean?

LIBBY   Yeah—fat!

HERB   You're not fat. You're . . . solid.

LIBBY   Same thing. Solid is hard fat.

HERB   Well, listen, you think what you want to think. I think you're beautiful. Jesus, look how I'm sitting here—in dirty pajamas. I mean, this is an important moment. I should put on a blazer or something.
(*He puts on an old jacket*)

LIBBY   Listen, I'm a little embarrassed . . .

HERB   Embarrassed? By what?

LIBBY   Well, I don't know what to call you.

HERB   You don't know what to call your father? Your own father? . . . You call me Herb, that's what you call your father.

LIBBY   Herb?

HERB   I mean, if you want to call me Pop or Dad, that's fine. I just didn't know how you felt about it. It's been a long time . . . But Herb is perfectly fine.

LIBBY   Okay, Herb. So isn't it time we shook hands or something? I mean, we're on a first-name basis. What do you think?

HERB   What do you mean, shake hands? Let me give you a kiss, for chrissakes. (*She steps forward eagerly. He takes her shoulders and kisses her on the side of her head. She is clearly disappointed. She moves away*) So how's your mother?

LIBBY   She's fine.

HERB   She never got married or anything?

LIBBY   No. She went with Mr. Slotkin, the butcher from Food Fair, for a couple of years. He was nice—he would bring over lamb chops, veal cutlets, things like that.

HERB   So what happened? Nothing serious?

LIBBY   No. When he started bringing over chicken wings, we knew the romance was over.

HERB   And how's Carl?

LIBBY   Who?

HERB   Carl. Your brother.

LIBBY   You mean Robby?

HERB   What do you mean, Robby? His name is Carl.

LIBBY   Not that I ever heard.

HERB   Of course. He was named after Carl Hubbell, the greatest screwball pitcher in the history of the National League.

LIBBY   Well, he shoulda spoken up. He thinks his name is Robert.

HERB   She changed his name? A beautiful name like Carl?

LIBBY   Well, you haven't seen him. He doesn't look like a Carl. He's kind of roly-poly like a Robert.

HERB   You know why, don't you? Because she hated baseball. Used to curse me every time I went out to a game. What—is that such a terrible thing, to want to go out to a baseball game? It's the most beautiful sport ever created by man.

LIBBY   You like the name Libby?

HERB   Sure I like Libby. I've always loved the name Libby.

LIBBY   What player was I named after?

HERB   You were named after my mother. You never saw her. She died before you were born . . . So what does Robby do? He goes to school?

LIBBY   Yeah.

HERB   Is he a jock? Is he a good ballplayer?

LIBBY   No. He plays piano.

HERB   The piano? He doesn't like to play ball?

LIBBY   He doesn't want to hurt his fingers.

HERB   He could play *soft*ball.

LIBBY   Once in a while he plays Ping-Pong.

HERB   Yeah? Is he any good?

LIBBY   He beat Grandma once.

HERB   Not exactly the *Wide World of Sports*. (*She's been munching on crackers*) Hey! What are you eating crackers for? I got fresh fruit here. I grow my own oranges. I have my own tree in the back. (*He takes an orange out of a basket, flips it to her*) Comin' at ya! (*She catches it*) Hey! Nice catch. Maybe *you're* the ballplayer in the family . . . Go on, taste that. (*She bites into it*) Juicy, isn't it?

LIBBY   You need a bathing suit to eat it.

HERB   Would you come here? I want you to see this. (*They go outside*) You see that? That's my orange tree. I grew that. I planted it. I fed it. I grew it. That's *my* tree.

LIBBY   I thought only God could make a tree.

HERB   That's back East. Out here, anyone can do it . . . And that's my lemon tree. I never thought I could do things like that. I grew up on the streets of New York. I used to play stickball and now I grow lemons and oranges.

LIBBY   What's the one next to it?

HERB   That one's a pain in the ass. It grows pits with no fruit. I didn't grow that one. It came with the house. Trees are like people. If they know you don't care about them, they're not going to give you anything back.

LIBBY   Yeah . . . I know a lot of people like that.
        (*He looks at her, getting the point of her irony*)

HERB (*Brightly*)   So what are you doing? Just visiting here? A holiday or something? Please sit. Where are you staying?

LIBBY   Last night I stayed at a motel. The Casa Valentino. You gotta use toilet paper for towels.

HERB   Well, that's crazy. I got room in here. Why don't you stay with me while you're out here?

LIBBY   I couldn't.

HERB   And I don't want to hear any back talk.

LIBBY   It's impossible. No.

HERB   It's settled. All right?

LIBBY   Sure. Thanks.

HERB   How long are you going to be out here?

LIBBY   The rest of my life.

HERB (*Looks at her. Smiles*)   What do you mean?

LIBBY   Well, it depends on how my career goes.

HERB What career is that?

LIBBY I want to be in pictures.

HERB You want to be in *what*?

LIBBY Pictures. Movies. I'm not ruling out television, but movies are my real goal.

HERB I see . . . Movies, heh. Well, you sure picked a tough business.

LIBBY So did you and you seem to be doing okay. (*She looks around, realizing what she has said*)

HERB What would you do?

LIBBY Act!

HERB Act? You want to be an *actress*? In the *movies*? That takes a little something called talent, you know.

LIBBY I've got talent. I've got plenty of talent. Some people think I'm kind of a female Dustin Hoffman.

HERB What people?

LIBBY Robby and Grandma.

HERB Where have you ever acted?

LIBBY Places.

HERB What places?

LIBBY Erasmus High School. We did *The Prime of Miss Jean Brodie.*

HERB Really? What part did you play?

LIBBY I didn't have a part. I was the understudy.

HERB   For Jean Brodie?

LIBBY   No. One of the girls in her class. Sandy.

HERB   Sandy? I see . . . Did you ever get on?

LIBBY   No. We only did two performances. And I had to work the lights.

HERB   Oh. You were the lighting girl.

LIBBY   *Assistant* lighting girl.

HERB   I see. So you were the assistant lighting girl who was the understudy to Sandy, for two performances of *The Prime of Miss Jean Brodie* at Erasmus Hall High School.

LIBBY   The summer session.

HERB   The summer session. Well, it's not exactly what I would call a *wealth* of experience.

LIBBY   No, it isn't. It's what you might call a "humble beginning." All I know is I believe in myself.

HERB   That's terrific. That's very important. Unfortunately, in this business everybody *else* believes in themselves . . . What are you going to do when they ask you for a résumé?

LIBBY   A what?

HERB   A résumé. A list of your credits. What you've done. I don't think it's enough to give them a picture of you working the lights at Erasmus High School.

LIBBY   I can read for them, can't I? I have this book of one-act plays that I read in my room every day. And I'm good too. I mean *really* good. Sometimes I even make myself cry. I *have* talent, I just need the outlet.

HERB   And you picked the *movies* as your outlet?

LIBBY   Yes. Because one thing I have is determination and confidence. Like, I have this tiny little flame burning deep inside of me, and I just need somebody to turn the gas jet up a little.

HERB   And who did you figure would do that?

LIBBY   I don't know. Someone out here. Someone in the business. Someone like a director—or a writer. Someone who's willing to give a young unknown kid from Brooklyn a chance.

HERB   (*Nods*) Does he have to be from this particular neighborhood?

LIBBY   I didn't say it was you.

HERB   I was just asking.

LIBBY   But if for any reason, you should want to make a phone call on my behalf, not out of any sense of loyalty or obligation or guilt, but just because you recognize some potential in me, I would appreciate it.

HERB   Who taught you to talk like that?

LIBBY   Like what?

HERB   Like coming around corners, going up over the roof, down into the basement, and coming up through the sewer. You got something to say to me, say it straight out.

LIBBY   Okay. Ordinarily I wouldn't be caught dead asking you for a favor, but it so happens that you owe me.

HERB   I what?

LIBBY   You owe me. You owe me for a lot. And Grandma said to me, "Go out to California and make sure that he pays you."

HERB   Oh, really. Is that what your grandmother told you?

LIBBY   Three weeks ago at Mount Hebron Cemetery.

HERB   What were you doing there?

LIBBY   That's where she lives. I mean, she's dead, but that's where she's buried. Next to Grandpa.

HERB   She died? I didn't know that. I'm sorry. When did this happen?

LIBBY   Six years ago, June fourteenth.

HERB   So when did you talk to her?

LIBBY   Last week.

HERB   Last *week*?

LIBBY   Last month. Last night. This morning. It's a little complicated.

HERB   I imagine it would be.

LIBBY   Forget Grandma. I'll explain it to you some other time. This is just me, Libby, the daughter you haven't seen in sixteen years asking you for a simple favor. Are you interested in helping me launch my career or not? Is that *straight* enough for you?

HERB   Hey, slow down! Slow down, will you? I've got a lot to digest here. I just found out my son Carl is called Robby, my ex-wife dated a man who brought her chicken wings, and my daughter talks to her dead grandmother. Let me catch up with all the news.

LIBBY   Look, if you don't want me to stay here, just say so. I didn't come here looking for any handouts.

HERB   Jesus! You are really something. Talking to you is like a two-hour workout in the gym. Why don't you just cool off, take that chip off your shoulder, and sit down? (*She glares at him*) Will you please sit down! *Please* sit down! (*She sits*) Now, can we start this entire morning right from the beginning again? Like you just walked in the door? Can we say hello to each other like average American people? . . . Hello.

LIBBY (*Still uptight*) Hello.

HERB Thank you. Can I get you something to drink?

LIBBY No, thanks. I just *ate* a glass of water.

HERB Look, about this movie business. Can we discuss it a little later? I really don't like being pressured into things. You understand?

LIBBY Well, I'm sorry if I made any *demands* on you. I won't do it again. It only comes *up* once every sixteen years.

HERB (*Glares at her*) You don't *look* like your mother but you sure *talk* like her.

LIBBY That's a crappy thing to say. Leave her out of this. My mother wasn't the one who walked out.

HERB You're right. I'm sorry. I apologize.

LIBBY Listen, I really think I better get out of here. This isn't turning out how I planned it at all. You're not what I expected, you know what I mean?

HERB No. I don't. I'm sorry if I'm a major disappointment to you. Maybe you had some image in your mind about what a father should look like and talk like, but I'm just plain old Herb Tucker, not somebody on *The Waltons*.

LIBBY I didn't mean that. I just thought you'd be a little friendlier. A little more "supportive."

HERB Why don't you give someone a chance? Why don't we get to know each other instead of just barging in here and telling me I've got to get you into the movies.

LIBBY You don't have to get me into anything. I couldn't even get a lousy kiss from you, so I sure as hell don't expect a phone call to your studio friends, because from the looks of this place, you don't got their number . . . And I don't have to get to know you because I know *everything* about you. Momma's been telling it to me since I was three years old. But I'm not interested. That's between you and her. I did fine without you. And I can manage on my own now too. You don't want to help me, swell. I happen to know people over at Columbia Pictures.

HERB Like who?

LIBBY Like Steffy Blondell . . . And you can keep your homemade oranges. I like mine from Florida.

HERB You're a fresh kid, you know that?

LIBBY And what are you? You make fun of your own daughter because she talks to her dead grandmother. I may be ditsy but I'm not the one with the tree that grows pits.

HERB Look, I don't care how you talk in your own house, but you change that tone of voice to me. I will not be talked to that way.

LIBBY I'll talk to you any way I please.

HERB Not to your father, you won't.

LIBBY My father? You're the last one in the world who's my father. My *grandmother's* my father. Boy oh boy, sixteen years of dreams down the toilet.
(STEFFY *enters and stands there, listening*)

HERB Who asked you to come? What is this, your mother's revenge? Do I get Robby and his piano tomorrow?

LIBBY Grandma was right again. I should have listened to her. "Once a shitheel, always a shitheel," she told me.

HERB That's how your grandmother talks to you?

LIBBY The language is mine, the wisdom is hers . . . I must have been nuts. Three thousand miles and all I get is a glass of mud.

STEFFY I hate to interrupt but you can hear this in the supermarket.

LIBBY (*To her father*) Well, let me tell you something, Mr. Herbert Tucker. The one who hasn't made it in show business is you, not me. I'm on the way up on the local and you're on the way-down express. It's possible, just possible, that one day I may be standing up there getting my Emmy Award or my Grammy or my Oscar or whatever the hell they get out here. And I'm going to smile and say to the entire world, "I want to thank everyone who helped me win this award. My grandmother, my mother, my brother Robby, my friends, my fans, and everyone else except my shitheel father. I think that about covers it!" . . . I apologize for my language, Steffy. It was very nice meeting you. I'm sorry I can't say that for everyone else in this house.
    (*She starts for the door.* HERB *catches her*)

HERB (*Angrily*) Wait a minute, you! You just listen to me a minute. I never figured I had anything coming to me. I gave you up, that was *my* loss. I left that house because if I had stayed it would have turned into a war zone and there would have been *no* survivors. You want to talk about guilts, regrets—I got enough to fill up my garage. But that's my business and I'll handle it my own way. I never expected anything from you *or* your brother. Outside this house, you can call me any goddamn thing you want to call me. But under this

roof is my domain, and if you talk to me, you show me some respect.
(*He walks away from her. She picks up her bag, walks out the door and then yells in*)

LIBBY (*Shouts*) I am now outside—and you are still a shitheel! Goodbye, Mr. Herbert Tucker!!
(*She starts to walk away*)

STEFFY Libby, wait! Wait, please!
(*She goes out after her*)

HERB Where does she get a *mouth* like that? (*He heads for his bedroom*) Crazy! That whole family was crazy from the minute I met them.
(*He goes in and slams the door*)

STEFFY (*Catches* LIBBY) Libby, don't go. Not like this. Please. Come on back in.

LIBBY (*On the verge of tears*) He didn't even listen. He just thinks I came out here to get something from him. Well, he doesn't have anything I want.

STEFFY You can't expect everything to happen in ten minutes. Give the man some time.

LIBBY And then he makes some crack about my mother. I don't have to listen to cracks about my mother . . . And he doesn't know everything about show business. Tells me I have to have a résumé. Well, my "résumé" is a lot better than the "telephone messages" he gets. I'm glad you think he's worth it, but maybe that's because you don't happen to be the daughter he walked out on.
(*She runs off.* STEFFY *watches her, then turns and goes back into the house. She starts for the kitchen, when* HERB *comes out of his bedroom. He has put on slacks and a shirt. They look at each other, silently.* STEFFY *starts to unpack the grocery bag*)

HERB Hell of a way to wake up.

STEFFY   I wanted to tell you she was here. But she wanted to surprise you. She had it all planned out what she was going to say.

HERB   You mean she's been *working* on that speech?

STEFFY   What happened, Herb?

HERB   (*After a pause*)   She tells me I'm not what she expected ... A strange kid walks in here in a mountain-climbing outfit, talks like Marlon Brando, tells me she was sent out here by her dead grandmother in Brooklyn, and *I'm* not what *she* expected!

STEFFY   Don't you realize how nervous she was? After all these years, seeing her father for the first time. She probably didn't know what to say.

HERB   Is that so? Well, she came up with "shitheel" three times without any trouble.

STEFFY   What did you expect from her? Don't you think the girl probably has a lot of hostility stored up in her?

HERB   Well, if she felt that way, why didn't she just write me a couple of threatening letters and let it go at that?

STEFFY   Sweet-looking girl. Don't you think she's sweet-looking?

HERB   I told her that. I swear to God. She says to me, "You can't even give me a kiss." I kissed her. I felt funny about putting my arms around her. I didn't know how she would feel about it.

STEFFY   You don't have to explain it to me.

HERB   After sixteen years she just walks in here. I don't even know how she found me. It took them twenty years to find Eichmann.

STEFFY   What are you going to do?

HERB   What do you *expect* me to do? I told her she could sleep here. She's the one who walked out. Why didn't she write to me first? Or call me. Tell me she's coming out.

STEFFY   Maybe she's afraid you would have said no.

HERB   That's right. I probably would have. After all these years, maybe it's better to leave things the way they were.

STEFFY   She wants to know who you are. She wants to know why you let her grow up without you. Are those unfair questions to ask, Herb?

HERB   She's interested in me for one thing, that's all. She wants me to get her into the movies. The *movies*, can you believe that? At first I thought she meant free passes.

STEFFY   Maybe saying "Get me into the movies" is just another way of saying "Let me back into your life."

HERB   What are you talking about?

STEFFY   I don't know. I'm no psychiatrist. Maybe she just wants you to do something for her to prove that you never really stopped caring.

HERB   Like getting her into the movies?

STEFFY   Yes. It's easier to ask for the impossible. When you ask for the possible, there's always the chance you'll get rejected.

HERB   When did you get so smart? You been going to UCLA on your lunch breaks?

STEFFY   I've been putting makeup on insecure people for years. After a while, you get pretty good at seeing what's underneath.

HERB   I can't handle her right now.

STEFFY   Why not?

HERB   It's a bad time for me. I'm trying to get this script finished. The thoughts don't come, the ideas aren't there. It takes me four weeks to get three words down on paper. I don't have time to start raising a daughter.

STEFFY   She looks raised enough to me. I think she just wants to find out who her father is.

HERB   She *knows* who it is. It's her grandmother.

STEFFY   Let her stay for a couple of days. It's none of my business, Herb, but you owe her that much. She's probably still on the corner waiting for the bus.

HERB   You were right before. It's none of your business.

STEFFY   (*She's stopped cold*)   Sorry.

HERB   Steffy, why do you bother with me? I'm hardly ever nice to you. I make love to you all night and don't say two civil words to you in the morning. You're still an attractive woman. (*Peeks at a clock*) It's only nine-twenty. If you get an early start, I bet you could find someone out there who would really appreciate you.

STEFFY   I thought I'd give you ten more minutes.

HERB   If you can say that after two years, you're a very patient lady.

STEFFY   Yeah. Either that or stupid.

HERB   I see other women, you know.

STEFFY   I know. But you didn't have to tell it to me.

HERB   Well, I *am* faithful in a way. I don't tell them about *you*.

STEFFY   I don't see other men, if you're interested.

HERB   I appreciate that.

STEFFY   It's not that I don't look. I'm just not crazy about what's out there.

HERB   I know. I'm really special, right?

STEFFY   I never really ask myself what the attraction is. The truth might scare the hell out of me.

HERB   Well, I know why *you* turn me on.

STEFFY   I do too: because I'm not looking for a husband.

HERB   Noooo . . . Well, that's part of it. You turn me on because you never make any demands. You never push me. Sometimes I wonder what you would say if I really asked you to marry me.

STEFFY   I don't know. Ask me.

HERB (*Laughs*)   Foxy. I love foxy ladies. (*He kisses her cheek*) You should be a writer.

STEFFY (*Pointedly*)   So should you. (*He turns away*) I mean it. You make me so damn furious sometimes. You've got more talent than ninety percent of the hacks in this town and you're too lazy or too scared to put it down on paper. Why won't you?

HERB   Because the other ten percent have all the jobs.

STEFFY   You know what you need? You need to have someone shove a ten-foot Roman candle up your rear end and set it off.

HERB   So how come every time I ask you to do kinky stuff in bed, you always get sore at me?

STEFFY   I'm going to work.
       (*She picks up her purse*)

HERB   Come on, give me a little smile?

STEFFY   It's impossible to have a serious discussion with you.

HERB   I'm being very serious. I would love to kiss you all over, including your pocketbook.

STEFFY   I think I'm going to take that picture in Hawaii. Three months out of the country may do us a lot of good.

HERB   Are you kidding? You couldn't go three months without me. It's not possible.

STEFFY   Damn it, Herb. I don't like you today.

HERB   Go on, you're crazy about me.

STEFFY   I know that, but I still don't like you today. (*Starts for the door*) Don't call me until you get five pages written. I don't care if it's lousy, I don't care if you copy it out of George Bernard Shaw, as long as it's five pages. And don't bother phoning because I won't take your calls.

HERB   Steffy! I'll call her. I'll call her today.

STEFFY   Because you want to or because it's another reason to get out of working?

HERB   Probably a little of both.

STEFFY   Do you know where she is?

HERB   Yes, I know where she is.

STEFFY   Well, don't wait. You don't want a kid like that wandering around the streets. You know what can happen in this town.

HERB   (*Moving toward her, smiling*)   Last night was terrific, wasn't it? I gave you five stars in my diary.

STEFFY   I still don't like you today . . . but it's very possible I can change my mind by tonight.
(*She goes out the door. He runs after her, calls out from the doorway*)

HERB   Hey, Steffy! You sure make one hell of a Roman candle!

Blackout

SCENE 2

It is later the same evening. The house is dark. HERB *is opening the door.* LIBBY *is behind him. She carries her pack; he carries her suitcase.*

HERB Fifteen years ago you couldn't get pastrami like that out here. Or real corned beef. They had to fly it in from New York. Thousands of hungry Jews would be waiting at the airport. (*He goes into the house. She waits outside. He looks for the wall switch*) We just got Thomas' English Muffins out here two years ago. This is still the wilderness. (*He turns on the light. Looks around*) Where is she? (*He goes to the door and looks outside*) What are you standing out there for?

LIBBY Are you sure about this?

HERB Fifteen bucks for dinner and a dollar and a half for parking, you think I'm fooling around?

LIBBY You never actually invited me formally.

HERB *Formally?* You want me to wake up a printer in the middle of the night and have something engraved?

LIBBY All you said to me was "Get your things and let's go." I've heard the *police* say that.

HERB Jesus! You're as difficult coming *into* a house as you are leaving it. All right. I am inviting you. You are invited into my humble abode wherein I shall make you welcome with lodgings and repast and pray that your slightest wish and desire will be met most hastily and graciously.

LIBBY   I like that. That's classy.

HERB   I mean it, Libby. I'm honestly glad you're here.

LIBBY   Thanks. (*They walk in*) I can only stay a couple of days.

HERB   What did I do now?

LIBBY   I just didn't want you getting the idea you were stuck with me for eternity.

HERB   In *California*? Don't worry. They don't give this whole place six weeks.

LIBBY (*Looks out the window*)   How come you never see any people on the streets out here? Where is everybody?

HERB   In their cars.

LIBBY   So how do you meet anyone? What do you have to do, crash?

HERB   You meet them at red lights, filling stations. At the Motor Bureau you meet terrific people.

LIBBY   It's so quiet. Don't you miss the noise?

HERB   The refrigerator rattles in the middle of the night. It's not much but it's all I got. (*Pointing to the bed in the alcove*) Libby, this is where you'll sleep.

LIBBY   Gee! My very own alcove. I love it . . . Do you own this house?

HERB   Me? Are you kidding? Six termites own it. They lease it to four mice and I sublet it from them.
(*She helps him make the bed*)

LIBBY   Because this place could be fixed up to look real cute. I have to be honest with you. This morning I hated it.

HERB   It came across.

LIBBY   But it's got potential. It just needs a few touches here and there. And it would hardly cost anything. I can paint. I can wallpaper. I can lay bricks. I can plaster.

HERB   Where did you learn to do that?

LIBBY   Back home in Brooklyn. They were going to condemn our whole block, but the tenants got together and fixed it up. We painted it, cleaned it up—you couldn't recognize it. All the rats came out of the sewer, thought they were in a rich neighborhood, and moved out to look for us.

HERB   I hope you didn't leave a forwarding address.

LIBBY   You should have seen our apartment. My bedroom looked like a night in Morocco. I painted my ceiling midnight-blue with little stars twinkling over my bed and a crescent moon hanging over my chest of drawers. Robby likes London, so I painted dark clouds on his ceiling and fog all over his walls. Would you like something like that?

HERB   No, thanks. I'm very happy with the weather in here.

LIBBY   Your car could use a tune-up, you know. I haven't heard coughing like that since the last flu epidemic. You got any tools? I can do it tonight.

HERB   You can tune up a car?

LIBBY   I can *make* one if I had the parts.

HERB   Terrific. Take the parts from *my* car and make me a Mercedes.

LIBBY   You think I couldn't do it?

HERB   I'm sure you can, but I couldn't afford the insurance.

LIBBY (*Getting tea bags*)   I'm making some tea. It'll be
ready in a minute.

HERB   Not for me, thanks. I think I'm going to turn in.

LIBBY   You're going to sleep? We haven't even talked to
each other yet.

HERB   We talked at dinner, didn't we?

LIBBY   "You want another cream soda?" is not exactly a
talk. We haven't seen each other since I'm three years
old. We have a lot of gaps to fill in.

HERB   Tonight? You want to fill in the entire sixteen
years *tonight*?

LIBBY   Well, we could spread it out. A couple of hours
every night for a week, like they did with *Roots*.

HERB   Okay. Swell. We'll start tomorrow night.

LIBBY (*Turns away*)   Yeah. Sure. I mean, if you don't
want to talk about things, I understand. If I were you,
I probably wouldn't want to talk about them either.

HERB   Listen, I'll make a deal with you.

LIBBY   Yeah?

HERB   If you stop trying to make me feel guilty, I'll stop
pretending I have nothing to feel guilty about.

LIBBY   I wasn't trying—

HERB   The hell you weren't.

LIBBY   Just a little.

HERB   Well, cut it out.

LIBBY   You mean I can *never* mention the fact that you walked out?
(*She serves the tea*)

HERB   Isn't there another way you can phrase that?

LIBBY   What? You "departed unobtrusively"?

HERB   You know, if I could write the way you talk, I'd have a house in Beverly Hills. See you in the morning. (*Going toward the bedroom*)

LIBBY   I don't think so. I want to leave the house about seven.

HERB   Where are you going?

LIBBY   I thought I'd get an early start on my career. Look for an agent.

HERB   You think there are agents wandering around the streets at seven o'clock in the morning? . . . You're really serious about this, aren't you? Why, Libby? Why show business?

LIBBY   Why not?

HERB   Because you can waste your life.

LIBBY   It's my life.

HERB   You like disappointment? You like rejection?

LIBBY   I wanted to be tall. I'm not. I wanted to be skinny. I'm not. I wanted to be gorgeous. I'm not. When you start off your life like that, what can they do to disappoint you?

HERB (*Looks at her; smiles*)   Come here. (*She goes toward him; stops a few feet away*) All the way. (*She moves close to him*) I'm sorry about this morning. I'm sorry if we got off on the wrong foot. And I'm sorry if I didn't give you a proper kiss—which I would like to do right now, if it's okay with you.

LIBBY Sure.
(He reaches out, takes her in his arms, embraces her, and kisses her cheek. She looks disturbed)

HERB What's wrong?

LIBBY Nothing. It's just a very heavy moment and I'm trying to deal with it.

HERB Listen, I understand how you feel. You've probably got a lot of mixed emotions. It's only natural you're going to have a lot of hostility towards me . . . Do you? Have a lot of hostility towards me?

LIBBY Not a lot. Some.

HERB Is that why you came? To let it out?

LIBBY No . . . to get rid of it.

HERB Thank you. I appreciate that . . . Listen, I'm going to get up at six-thirty and make you breakfast. You like waffles?

LIBBY You can make waffles? What kind of waffles?

HERB I don't know. I just pop 'em in the toaster. Good night, Lib.
(He goes into his room and closes the door)

LIBBY Don't you want to see a picture of Robby?

HERB *(Offstage)* Who?

LIBBY Robby! *Carl!* Your son. Don't you want to see what he looks like?

HERB Er, yeah, sure. I didn't know you had one.
(He comes back in)

LIBBY   Well, sit down. Put your feet up. Put your slip-pers on. (*He sits in a chair next to a lamp*) Do you have a pipe? I always pictured you smoking a pipe. With leather arm-patches and a couple of Great Danes. And a big library with old English books.

HERB   Who did you think I was? David Niven?

LIBBY   Yeah . . . sort of. (*He puts his glasses on*) Anyway, here's Robby . . . or Carl . . . or whatever his name is. (*She hands him the picture. He looks at it*)

HERB   Oh, he looks like a nice boy. Sweet face.

LIBBY   I think he looks a little like you.

HERB   Really? You think so? (*Looking again*) Yeah, there's a slight resemblance. He'll probably be a knock-out with the girls.

LIBBY   And that's Momma . . . You still recognize her?

HERB   How could I forget her? Hasn't changed much at all . . . What has she got, blond hair now?

LIBBY   She's been through every color. Changes it every two weeks. The kids in my school thought I had four-teen different mothers.

HERB   Well, we all want to stay young, I guess.

LIBBY   And that's Grandma. I had to sit in her lap, other-wise she wouldn't smile.

HERB   She got very thin, didn't she?

LIBBY   That was when she was sick. This was about three weeks before she died. She'll give me hell tonight. She'll say I should have shown you the picture of her in Miami Beach with the suntan.

HERB   Are you going to talk to her tonight?

LIBBY   Yeah. Probably. I mean, a lot of major events have happened today. If I didn't talk to her tonight, she'd pull my pillows off the bed.

HERB   She doesn't wander around the house, does she? I'm a very light sleeper.

LIBBY   No. She just wanders around in my head.
(*She goes into the bathroom*)

HERB   Well, I'm going to keep my door locked, just in case. Good night, Lib.

LIBBY   Good night, Herb.
(*He looks at her, then goes into his bedroom and closes the door. His door opens and he comes out*)

HERB   I don't like "Herb." Can we try "Pop"?
(*She comes out of the bathroom in an oversized football jersey*)

LIBBY   Sure. Whatever you say.

HERB   What's that?
(*He points at her jersey*)

LIBBY   My nightgown.
(*She goes back in*)

HERB   I got a boy who plays the piano and a girl who sleeps in a football uniform. Serves me right.
(*He goes back into the bedroom and closes the door.* LIBBY *takes out a paperback play from her suitcase, opens it to a page she has marked, stands in the center of the room, and begins to read aloud from the play*)

LIBBY   (*Reads sincerely but not well, using typewriter paper as a fan*) "I expect I shall be the Belle of Amherst when I reach my seventeenth year. I don't doubt that I shall have perfect crowds of admirers at that age. Then, at dances, how I shall delight to make them await

my bidding, and with what delight shall I witness their suspense while I make my *final decision*!"
(HERB's *door opens. He looks at her*)

HERB   Was that Grandma you were talking to?

LIBBY   No. I was just practicing acting. I won't do it if it keeps you awake.

HERB   No, that's okay. I don't mind ... How long a play is it?

LIBBY   I don't do the whole play. I just do the parts that I like. I can whisper.

HERB   No! Don't whisper. Don't get into bad habits. If you're going to act, learn to project.

LIBBY   Okay.

HERB   Good night, Lib.

LIBBY   Good night, Pop.
(*He looks at her again, and goes to his door. She turns the page and begins to read another section of the play, about twice as loud*) "THE ORCHARD IS FULL OF BLUEJAYS. TO SEE THEM FOLLOW THE HOSE FOR A DROP OF WATER IS A TOUCHING SIGHT. THEY WON'T TAKE IT IF I HAND IT TO THEM. THEY RUN AND SHRIEK AS IF THEY WERE BEING ASSASSINATED. BUT OH, TO *STEAL* IT! THAT IS BLISS!" (*She looks at him*) Too much projection?

HERB   I don't think I'm ever going to sleep unless I get something off my mind.

LIBBY   You mean, right now?

HERB   Yes. Right now.

LIBBY   Sure. What is it?
(*He gets a beer from the refrigerator*)

HERB   I thought you might want to know why it was I left your mother.

LIBBY   No. Not really. I mean, it's none of my business . . . Yeah, I *would* really like to know.
(*She sits. Looks at him*)

HERB   The truth is, I didn't like her very much . . . Oh, she was a good woman. Worked hard, never complained when we didn't have any money . . . The trouble was, she wasn't any fun. She had no humor at all. I could never make her laugh. That's what hurt me more than anything. We'd go to a party, I'd have a couple of drinks, in an hour, I swear, I'd have them all rolling on the floor. And I'd look over at her and she'd just be staring at me. A blank look on her face. Not angry, not upset, just not understanding. As if she walked into a foreign movie that didn't have any subtitles. She just didn't know how to enjoy herself. Oh, I know where it all came from. You're poor, you grow up in the Depression, life means struggle, hard work, responsibilities. I came from the same background, but we always laughed in my house. Didn't have meat too often, but we had fun. Her father never went to a movie, never went to a play. He only danced *once* in his entire life, at his wedding—and he did *that* because it was custom, tradition, not joy, not happiness. I give him a book to read and if he found in the middle he was enjoying it, he would put it down. Education, yes. Entertainment, no . . . Anyway, we were married about four years, and one day I was just sitting there eating her mushroom and barley soup, which happened to be delicious, and I decided I didn't want any more. Not the soup—my life. So I went inside, packed my bags, and said, "Blanche, I think I got to get out of here. And I don't think I'm ever coming back" . . . And I swear to you, Libby, if she had laughed I would have stayed. If she saw the craziness of what I was doing, the absurdity of it, I would have unpacked my bags and finished my soup. But she looked at me, cold as ice, and said, "If that's how you feel, who wants you?" So I put on my hat, left her whatever cash I had in my pocket, walked down the stairs, and I never came back . . . And that's it. As simple as that.

LIBBY   I see. Well, how did you feel about leaving me and Robby?

HERB   I loved you. I knew I'd miss you, but I knew if I stayed you'd grow up in a house where people didn't like each other. A week later I went out to California. I was going to write to you but you were three years old. What was I going to do, draw you pictures in crayon explaining why Daddy was gone?

LIBBY   You should have written me a letter. I could have saved it. It would have been something to hold on to. I never even had a picture of you. Momma tore them all up.

HERB   She was right. I was gone, I wasn't coming back, what did you want a picture for?

LIBBY   Didn't you want one of us?

HERB   I asked your mother, she wouldn't send me one. I called a few times, she wouldn't let me speak to you. She said if I wrote, she would tear up the letters. I couldn't argue with her. She was angry, she was vindictive . . . and she was right. After a while, I pretended I didn't have kids so it wouldn't hurt so much. Then I got so good at pretending, I finally believed it. Six, seven years went by. I was working a few shows, I came to New York a couple of times, thought about calling you up . . . Then I thought it wasn't fair. She put all the time in, you were her kids. I had no right to come busting in with an armful of presents to get a kiss and a hug and then make the next plane back to California.

LIBBY   What kind of presents? You should never throw away presents.

HERB   Libby, I'm being very honest with you. I never regretted leaving her. I'm just no good at marriage

. . . I know because I was married twice after that. One was a show girl, the other was a posturepedic mattress model on TV. Her name was Patty.

LIBBY Was *she* any fun?

HERB Oh, yeah. Terrific fun. Patty laughed at everything I said. Patty laughed at everything *anyone* said. Patty laughed in the bathtub, in the supermarket. She would laugh if the house was being carried away in a mudslide. Patty got a divorce, half my money, and drove away with another guy, laughing at everything *he* said.

LIBBY Tell me about the other one.

HERB Veronica. She was the show girl. Gorgeous body. The first year we were married, she spent seventy-one thousand dollars on clothes and jewelry. Considering I only made *fifty-eight* thousand dollars that year, I knew we had domestic problems. Six months later she was gone with the other half of my money, and when Patty heard about it, she laughed at *that* too . . . So there you are. *The Life Story of Herb Tucker,* condensed and edited for television.

LIBBY You didn't have to tell me all that, but I'm glad you did. They say confession is good for the soul.

HERB What do you mean, *confession*? I just left, I didn't murder the entire family.

LIBBY You know what I mean.

HERB Yeah. I know what you mean. I just hope you'll give me the chance to do a little better for you during the next sixteen years. Will you, Lib? Will you give me that chance?

LIBBY You don't have to do anything. I just like listening to you talk. I like the sound of your voice.

HERB Well, tomorrow morning, we'll have a long talk about this acting thing and all. Okay?

LIBBY Whatever you say.

HERB Well, I'm up. I'm never going to sleep tonight. Why don't you read me something? From one of your plays.

LIBBY You mean *audition*? For my own father? I would have heart failure.

HERB It's not an audition. I don't have any jobs to give you. I would just like to hear you read something.

LIBBY (*She gets the book*) Oh. Well, that's different. As long as I'm not on the spot here . . . This is from *The Belle of Amherst*. It's letters from the life of Emily Dickinson. Julie Harris did it on the stage. Anyway, this is one of my favorite parts. I've read it a thousand times. Are you ready?

HERB I am ready.

LIBBY (*Reads*) "I dream about Father every night, always a different dream, and forget what I'm doing daytimes—wondering where he is . . . His heart was pure and terrible, and I think no other like it exists. (*They look at each other*) I'm glad there is immortality, but would have tested it myself, before entrusting him . . . Home is so far from home—since my father died."

Curtain

Act Two

SCENE I

It is two weeks later, about 7 P.M.

The bungalow has virtually been transformed. It is clean, bright, and cheerful. A few inexpensive prints have been tacked on the walls. Some are modern art—a Picasso, a Braque, etc.

All the junk and refuse and old papers and magazines have disappeared from the place. The furniture has been rearranged and, in some instances, repaired. The kitchen also has been repainted, in a different and vibrant color. A seascape has been painted on the bathroom door.

HERB's *desk has been cleared of all debris, and all that remains is his typewriter, a fresh stack of typing paper, and a coffee mug filled with pens and pencils.*

LIBBY *is in a bathrobe, sitting at the typewriter at his desk. Her hair is up in curlers. She is slowly and very carefully pecking away at the keys.*

HERB *enters through the front door. The sun is just fading away. He is wearing a jacket with a folded-up racing form in his side pocket.*

LIBBY (*Without looking up from the typewriter*) Hi. How'd your meeting go today?

HERB Swell. Terrific coffee and Danish.
(*He looks through the mail*)

LIBBY Be careful in the bathroom. The walls aren't dry yet.

HERB You didn't paint my toothbrush, did you? I was very happy with the old color.

LIBBY No. But I changed your shower curtains. The old one looked like the one Janet Leigh was stabbed in in *Psycho.* I'm going to cut it up and make shower caps.

HERB Just what I need. Eighty-six new shower caps. (*He puts the mail down and turns toward the kitchen*) Where's the kitchen? I don't recognize this place since you turned it into the Museum of Modern Art.

LIBBY You can't tell me it's not cheerier in here now. It was so depressing. *Now* it looks like a happy house.

HERB (*Getting a beer from the refrigerator*) I know. I could hear it laughing from outside. (*He goes to the window and looks out*) Hey, look how gorgeous my trees look. I think this is going to be my best year for fruit.

LIBBY I'm using them for dinner. "Chicken à la Orange," "Salade à la Lemon"—you got anything out there I could use for dessert?

HERB How about "Pudding à la Pits"?

LIBBY How's the car driving now?

HERB Perfect. I may enter the Indy 500 this year.

LIBBY I was going to rotate the tires but I didn't have a chance yet.

HERB How'd I get so lucky? Suddenly I have a decorator, a mechanic, a typist, a cook. They don't have that much staff on *Upstairs, Downstairs*. What are you writing?

LIBBY Letters to Mom and Robby. I told them I saw Marlon Brando in the supermarket yesterday. My mother'll die.

HERB You saw Marlon Brando in the supermarket?

LIBBY Well, someone who looked like him. You want me to send regards to Robby?

HERB Sure.

LIBBY What should I say?

HERB   Say "Regards to Robby."

LIBBY   What about Mom?

HERB   What about her?

LIBBY   It would be kind of insulting to say something to Robby and not to her.

HERB   Yeah . . . Well, say I hope she's well.

LIBBY   Is that as far as you want to go?

HERB   What else? "Sorry about that misunderstanding sixteen years ago"? You want to write your own letters please?

LIBBY   I was just asking.

HERB   Maybe you could say I think she did a very nice job bringing up her daughter.

LIBBY   That's nice. She'll like that. Would you initial it so she doesn't think I'm making it up?

HERB   Would you just type your own letters? Leave me alone. What time is Steffy coming?

LIBBY   About seven, seven-thirty. (*She finishes typing her letter*) So tell me what happened at the meeting. Did they like your presentation?

HERB   Yeah. Loved it. Very impressed. They feel it needs a little work, but then what doesn't?

LIBBY   But do you have a deal? A contract? Are they going to pay you?

HERB   They don't work that way. They have to okay the treatment first. They go step by step. They're very cautious out here. I'm not worried. It was a good meeting.

LIBBY   Something went wrong. They didn't like it. You're covering up something. I can tell from your voice.

HERB   You've only heard my voice for two weeks, how can you tell anything?

LIBBY   Why can't you be honest with me? I'm honest with you. I tell you everything.

HERB   What have I been dishonest about?

LIBBY   They turned down your idea and you're afraid to tell me.

HERB   They didn't turn down my idea.

LIBBY   Swear to God?

HERB   I swear to God. They didn't turn it down . . . because I didn't go to the meeting.

LIBBY   You didn't go to the meeting?

HERB   Isn't that what I just said? I called them up and canceled. I had more important things to do.

LIBBY   What did you do?

HERB   I went to the races at Hollywood Park.

LIBBY   You went to the races at Hollywood Park?

HERB   What is this, the Berlitz School of English? You don't have to repeat everything I say. I went to the races. I picked three winners. Three hundred and forty-six bucks. That's three hundred and forty-six more than I would have made if I went to that meeting today because I had nothing to give them. I came up empty, do you understand?

LIBBY   You didn't even go to the meeting?

HERB I was not going to sit there with three teenage network executives and present them with forty-six pages of blank paper. I crapped out, okay?

LIBBY What do you mean, forty-six empty pages? I saw you working every day for two weeks. I heard the typewriter at night. I was worried your fingers would be bleeding today.

HERB It was no good, Libby. I didn't write forty-six pages. I wrote one page forty-six times.

LIBBY But you said it was a good idea. Why didn't you go to the meeting? You're a terrific talker. You could have told them the idea.

HERB Maybe seven, eight years ago. Not today. I dry up, I get nervous, I don't know what the hell I'm saying in there. You walk into a room and five smart-ass kids in Pierre Cardin suits and eighty-dollar haircuts sit there with their hands behind their heads and dare you to entertain them. I was making two grand a week, when they were pageboys at NBC. Screw 'em all when I can make a terrific living at Hollywood Park. I'm going to wash up.

LIBBY You know what really gets me mad? Would you like to know?

HERB No.

LIBBY What really gets me mad is when somebody stops believing in themselves. You won't even give yourself a break. Grandma always says to me, "You can't like other people until you like yourself."

HERB Really? For a woman who passed away, she certainly has a lot to say. Listen, I'm getting very antsy. I'd like to go out tonight. Would you mind if we forget about dinner at home? Let's go out and celebrate. You, me, and Steffy.

LIBBY Celebrate what?

HERB   I had a very big day today. Maybe not in my line of work, but a very big day.

LIBBY   It's up to you and Steffy. I wasn't going to be here anyway. I'm busy tonight.

HERB   Again? That's three nights this week. You're hardly ever home anymore.

LIBBY   Thanks. I'm glad you noticed.

HERB   Listen, it's okay with me. I want you to have a good time . . . Where are you going?

LIBBY   It's business.

HERB   What kind of business? *Show* business?

LIBBY   I can't discuss it with you.

HERB   You discuss *my* show business, why can't we discuss *your* show business? Where do you go every night?

LIBBY   Making contacts. Is it okay if I use the car?

HERB   Why not? You built it. Listen, Libby, L.A. is a very strange place at night. If you don't know your way around, you can get in a lot of trouble. Why can't you tell me where you're going?

LIBBY   Because it's important that I do this on my own. I really appreciate your letting me stay here. If I ever thought you owed me anything, you more than paid me back. But I had a long talk with Grandma over the weekend and we decided if I'm going to make it in this business I have to do it on my own.

HERB   Grandma's still here? I thought she left. You told me she missed New York.

LIBBY   She does. But she went out to this Hillside Cemetery the other day near the airport and she met some women she used to know from Prospect Park. They moved out here when their children did and then they died. So Grandma brings them up on the news in the old neighborhood. I've got to go. If you get stuck, maybe Grandma'll help you with the dinner.

(LIBBY *leaves through the front door*)

HERB (*Looks up to "Grandma"*)   I'll cook. You clean up.

Blackout

SCENE 2

It is about midnight. There is the sound of a car passing the house. HERB *comes out, wearing his robe and slippers. He seems distressed. He goes to the door and looks out.*

STEFFY *is wearing a short Japanese robe that she probably leaves there for such occasions. She stands in the doorway near the garden looking at* HERB, *sensing his distress.*

STEFFY   It's okay. I know how you feel.

HERB   You do?

STEFFY   It was a lousy day for me too. The big star came an hour and a half late and we all had to work overtime. I'm sorry if I spoiled the dinner.

HERB   You didn't spoil anything.

STEFFY   I did. I came late, the chicken was a little dry. I'm sorry.

HERB   It was timed for eight o'clock. I mean, the kid makes a chicken, baked potatoes, sour cream, chives, two vegetables, and a chocolate mousse, the least you could have done was call.

STEFFY   There were twenty grips trying to get at the phone. I thought I'd make better time on the freeway.

HERB   (*Picks up a handmade card*)   She even made this beautiful little menu—"Potatoes Germaine, Peas à la Libby . . ." All the artwork she did herself. She drew the chef's hat. She watercolored the little bunnies around the edges—

STEFFY   It's gorgeous. I don't know what else to say.

HERB   Would you leave her a note? Would you tell her the dinner was fantastic?

STEFFY   I'll tell her tonight. When is she coming home? (*She sits*)

HERB   I don't know. She's been out there three, four nights this week and I don't know where she is or what she's doing. What is it now, twelve-thirty? Don't you think that's kind of late?

STEFFY (*Smiles*)   No. I think it's kind of wonderful. Welcome to the World of Worried Parents. How does it feel, Herb?

HERB   I don't like it.

STEFFY   Being a parent or being worried?

HERB   Do I get a choice?

STEFFY   Nope. It's a package deal: To love someone is to be scared every minute of your life.

HERB   In two years with you, that was the first time I've been preoccupied in bed. It's very hard to keep stimulated while you're listening for a car to drive up.

STEFFY   For your information, it was one of the nicest times we've had together.

HERB   Well, you're weird. I like my sex without any distractions . . . I would call someplace, but I don't know where to call.

STEFFY   Interesting how worked up you're getting over a perfect stranger.

HERB   What do you mean stranger? She's my daughter, isn't she?

STEFFY She's been your daughter for sixteen years but you'd need a telescope to notice it.

HERB I didn't know what she was like. She wasn't real to me. I thought she hated me. Never thought she'd want to see me. I've lived all these years and I don't know a goddamned thing about life.

STEFFY How come you only have two trees?

HERB What?

STEFFY You've got a lemon tree and an orange tree. You've got room for a few more. You got one that's dying that you don't pay any attention to . . . I was wondering why you just have two trees?

HERB I don't know what the hell you're—Oh Jesus! Don't give me that. I give up my two kids so I grow two trees. So if I left sixteen kids I'd have Yosemite National Park back there, right? I don't think we should see each other anymore, Steffy. I'm not sure it's healthy to be having sex with your analyst.

STEFFY Don't look at me. I just raised the questions, not the trees.

HERB So what's your point? Libby is my Orange and Carl is my Lemon? And their mother is the dried-up one with the pits, is that it?

STEFFY I didn't mean it to be literal. I don't even know why I thought of it. I just thought of it.

HERB And who are you? I don't see *you* growing around here.

STEFFY (*With some resignation*) Yeah. I don't see me growing around here either.

HERB (*Annoyed*) Who do you want to be? A rose? A tulip? A rhododendron? I'll get a pot and plant you tomorrow.

STEFFY   I want to be Steffy. And I want to be somebody who sees you more than whenever it just suits your fancy. I want to move on with our relationship, Herb.

HERB (*Looks out the window*)   If she was lost, she would call me, wouldn't she?

STEFFY   What is it you're more worried about? Libby or answering my question?

HERB   What's wrong with our relationship? We've had a two-year run so far. To me, that's a big hit.

STEFFY   I lied to you a few weeks ago. I told you I don't see other men. I did. I had dinner twice with Monte Walsh—he's the cameraman on the picture. It was dinner, nothing else, but I found, much to my surprise, I enjoyed being with him. I enjoyed talking to him. I enjoyed enjoying myself.

HERB   I'm glad. What did you have for dinner?

STEFFY   Communication.

HERB   Oh, then you must have gone to Angelo's. They make it great.

STEFFY   There's your typewriter. There's the paper. All you've got to do is get those snappy answers down on the page and maybe someday *you'll* be able to afford to take *me* to Angelo's. I'm getting dressed.
(*She goes into the bedroom*)

HERB   Jesus Christ! Two weeks ago it was peaceful around here. Now suddenly they're moving in, moving out. I'm running the goddamn Beverly Hilton.

STEFFY (*Comes out, putting on her blouse*)   One daughter and one girlfriend is hardly a convention. I was hoping you could handle it.

HERB   Why now? Why now after two years do you come in here and throw pressure in my face? I thought you were happy. I thought we had the perfect arrangement. I thought you *liked* being the liberated woman.

STEFFY I'm going to be forty years old in June. As a choice, liberation is terrific. As a future prospect it's a little frightening.

HERB I won't get married again.

STEFFY I don't need you to *save* me. I need you to *want* me.

HERB I'll give up seeing other women. For good. I only did it once in a while anyway. Is that what you want?

STEFFY I didn't ask you to turn this into Lent! I just want something more permanent, Herb. Not marriage, just a commitment. I've got a house twice as big as this, I've got a room for you to work in. Move in with me. No financial obligations—I make more than you do anyway. I just miss you in the mornings. I get angry because I see a perfectly good talent gathering dust on your typewriter because you're the kind of man who needs a gentle, prodding push from behind. I care and I worry about you. I don't have to be your wife, but I think I'd make a terrific pusher.

HERB Why don't you like it the way it is anymore?

STEFFY Nothing stays the way it is. It all changes. It moves on and there's not a damn thing you or I can do about it.

HERB (*He's quiet. Looks away*) I miss 1948. I played stickball on the streets from seven in the morning till six at night. A summer lasted forever. And the pennant was going to fly over Yankee Stadium for the next two hundred years.

STEFFY I miss 1956. I wore a size-seven dress and never needed makeup. That's still not going to stop Monte Walsh from calling me tomorrow night. What do I do, Herb?

HERB   Change your number.

STEFFY   Sorry. You can't have it all your way. Not forever. When you're eighty-three and I'm seventy-seven, neither one of us is going to look forward to my coming over every Tuesday night. I put my kids on the school bus in the morning and they come home in the afternoon grown up. Don't ask me to settle for whatever it is *you're* willing to settle for. I want more for myself. I want it for *both* of us. But I'm just not going to wait around for *you* to make the decision for what *I* get.

HERB   Jesus, if it's anything I hate, it's someone who asks me to be fair. Maybe there's another way. Maybe there's some other arrangement we could make.

STEFFY   You know what I'm going to get you for Christmas, Herb? An "Exit" sign. I never saw a man who looked so hard for ways out.
    (*She goes into the bedroom and returns with her skirt and shoes*)

HERB   I got a kid missing on the streets. Can we talk about this tomorrow?

STEFFY   She's not missing. She's just *out* . . . All right, we'll talk about it tomorrow.
    (*She puts her skirt on*)

HERB   I *know* this place is a dump. I *know* I should get out of here. But it's just not that easy. I feel "comfortable" here.

STEFFY   Your lucky house?

HERB   Maybe it's what I think I deserve—"The House That Guilt Built."

STEFFY   Listen, we could take the trees with us. I know a guy who does great transplants. I have apples and pears. With your oranges and lemons, we'd make great fruit salad.

(HERB *looks at her warmly. She puts her arms around him and embraces him*)

HERB   Monte Walsh, heh?

STEFFY   Sorry . . . How does it make you feel?

HERB   Angry. Competitive. Scared. I've seen him around. Wears a cowboy hat, always looks like he's in Marlboro Country. What kind of cologne does he wear? Sagebrush?

STEFFY   He makes me smile but he's never made me laugh.

HERB   Yeah? Well, the bastard's making me nervous.

STEFFY   I know the feeling. That's what Libby's doing to me.

HERB   Libby?

STEFFY   (*Gets her shoes and starts putting them on*)   It's tough for a woman you've known for two years to compete with a daughter you haven't seen in sixteen.

HERB   Are you crazy? What's Libby got to do with you and me?

STEFFY   Don't ask me. I didn't make up nature.

HERB   I don't understand you. I don't understand women. To tell you the truth, I don't trust *anyone* who can't go to deep center field and catch a fly ball.

STEFFY   You know me. I say what's on my mind. She's got something I wish I had.

HERB   What?

STEFFY   *You* worrying about where I am at twelve-thirty.

HERB I *know* where you are. You're in the living room putting your clothes on instead of in the bedroom taking them off. Don't give me deadlines, Steffy. Don't tell me I have to make a decision this week. You want to have dinner with Monte Walsh, have dinner with him. You want to hunt buffalo with him, have a good time. See him as much as you want. I've got a script I not only have to finish, I have to *start*. I've got a daughter who wants to be a movie star by Sunday morning and I've got a dead grandmother in Brooklyn watching every move I make—that's all I can handle right now. You want a happy ending, you'll have to come up with it yourself.

STEFFY I'm not dumb enough to look for happy endings. I'd gladly settle for a promising middle.

HERB I'm sorry, Stef. I used up all my promises for this week.

STEFFY (*Nods, knowing there's no use pushing*) Sure. Forget it. I just thought I'd mention it in passing.
  (*She goes into the bedroom and gets her purse*)

HERB (*He looks out the window*) It looks cold out. I wonder if she's dressed warmly enough.

STEFFY She walked over the Rocky Mountains in shorts, she'll get through Wilshire Boulevard in a Mustang.

HERB How much do I owe her?

STEFFY For what?

HERB For waiting sixteen years before I started worrying if she's dressed warmly enough?

STEFFY I don't know. The minute you think you owe somebody something, you start paying them back for the wrong reasons. Forget the sixteen years, you can't make them up. In a way you're lucky. If you never left, she'd be nineteen years old anyway and still resent you for being a parent. I don't miss a breakfast with my kids and I'm going to end up in the same place you are.

HERB   You know what? You're one of the smartest ladies I know.

STEFFY   Then how come I'm going home alone at twelve-thirty at night?

HERB   You're just dumb when it comes to picking men. (*They stand there and look at each other, both feeling a little helpless. The lights fade and go to black*)

It is a little after 3 A.M. One lamp is on. The headlights of a car hit the house as it drives up. The car lights go off; we hear a door slam. LIBBY *enters the house and closes the door very gently. She starts to tiptoe quietly towards her room.* HERB *is sitting on the couch watching her.*

HERB   What's the point in tiptoeing? You could hear the car pull up in Denver.

LIBBY (*Softly*)   I didn't want to wake you.

HERB   You have to fall asleep before someone can wake you.

LIBBY (*Softly*)   Why didn't you take your pill?

HERB   I *took* a pill. The pill is more worried about you than *I* am.

LIBBY (*Softly*)   I'm sorry. I thought you'd be busy doing other things.

HERB   I *did* other things. What are you whispering for?

LIBBY   I don't want to wake Steffy.

HERB   She's not that light a sleeper. She went home two hours ago.
       (*He puts on the lights*)

LIBBY   How come? Doesn't she usually stay over?

HERB (*Edgy*)   Well, she's not usually staying over tonight.

LIBBY   What's wrong? Anything happen with you two?

HERB   Never mind Steffy. How about explaining where you've been till three o'clock in the morning?

LIBBY   I was out.

HERB   What do you mean, "out"? Three nights this week you come home two, two-thirty, three o'clock, I want to know where you've been.

LIBBY   I'm okay. I'm fine. What are you getting so huffy about?

HERB   *Huffy?* You walk out of here, don't tell me where you're going, you don't call, you don't know anybody in this city, you walk in three o'clock in the morning, and you don't think I have a right to be *huffy*?

LIBBY   (*Shrugs*)   You want to be huffy, be huffy.

HERB   Don't test me! Don't play games with me! If you think I'm going to keep paying through the nose for the sixteen years I owe you, you've got another guess coming. It's a bad debt. Forget it. You're never going to collect.

LIBBY   All I asked you for is one lousy introduction to some of your big-shot friends. Which I never got because you don't have.

HERB   You've been on my back asking for payoffs ever since you walked in here with that Orphan Annie look on your face. "You owe me and I'm here to collect"— that's what you said to me. (*Looks up*) Am I right, Grandma? Am I making that up? You're my witness. Is she listening now or do I have to dial an unlisted number?

LIBBY   Boy oh boy, *something* happened tonight.

HERB   I'm waiting for an answer.

LIBBY   I was out meeting people.

HERB   *What* people?

LIBBY   Important people . . . in the business.
(*She munches casually on a chicken leg throughout*)

HERB   *Show* business?

LIBBY   That's right.

HERB   I see. And what important people in show business did you meet tonight?

LIBBY   Producers, directors, actors . . .

HERB   Really? Anyone I might know?

LIBBY   I don't know if you *know* them, you may have *heard* of them.

HERB   Like who?

LIBBY   Like Jack Nicholson.

HERB   Jack Nicholson? . . . Yes, I've heard of him. You met him tonight?

LIBBY   That's right.

HERB   I see. Who else did you meet?

LIBBY   In movies or in television?

HERB   Either one.

LIBBY   James Caan.

HERB   Oh? You met "Jimmy"? How is he?

LIBBY   He looked terrific to me.

HERB   I'm sure he did. Anyone else I might have heard of?

LIBBY   Let me see . . . Candice Bergen, Suzanne Pleshette, someone who's a vice president at Columbia Pictures, that director who directed *Jaws* . . . A lot of others, I can't remember their names.

HERB   Well, you must have been so busy. Did you talk to these people?

LIBBY   Sure. I mean, we didn't have major conversations but I talked to them.

HERB   (*Looks at her*)   You mean the way you talk to Grandma?

LIBBY   No. Grandma's dead. These people were all dressed up. I know the difference.

HERB   I'm just asking. And where did you meet "Jack" and "Jimmy" and "Candy"?

LIBBY   At a party in Beverly Hills—11704 Benedict Canyon.

HERB   Who invited you?

LIBBY   Gordon Zaharias.

HERB   *Gordon Zaharias?* Who the hell is Gordon Zaharias?

LIBBY   He's the one who got me the job.

HERB   *What* job?

LIBBY   Parking cars at the party in Beverly Hills. I made thirty-two dollars plus tips—not including meeting Jack Nicholson.

HERB   That's where you met all these people? Parking their cars?

LIBBY   Well, for a while I was just the relay man. Like, George Segal would come out and say, " '78 blue Mercedes." Then I would run like crazy down the hill and yell to this other guy, " '78 blue Mercedes," and he would get to drive it up. But then I gave him ten dollars plus half my tips so I could get to drive the car up and meet George Segal. He was very nice. He smiled and said, "Thanks," just like in *A Touch of Class.* I made a lot of great contacts.

HERB   George Segal saying "Thanks" is what you consider making a good contact?

LIBBY   Well, it doesn't hurt. The important thing was leaving the cards on the windshield.

HERB   What cards?

LIBBY   Well, we had to leave this little card that says, "Sunset Valet Parking—No Party Is Too Big or Too Small." Only, on the back of each card I wrote, "Libby Tucker, New York–trained actress—No Part Is Too Big or Too Small." With my phone number. I must have left thirty of them. Even if only two people call, it was worth the money I spent.

HERB   (*Looks at her, then looks away, trying to figure her out*)   Libby, can I ask you a serious personal question? Do you honestly believe that anybody in this business—a director, a producer, a cameraman, *anybody*—is going to call someone for an audition because they left their name on the *back* of a valet parking ticket?

LIBBY   Not a *big* chance. But a better chance than if I left nothing at all.

HERB   YOU HAVE *NO* CHANCE! NONE! There are five thousand qualified agents in this town who can't get their clients a meeting with these people but *you* think they're going to call *you* because *you* left *your* name on the back of a stub they're going to throw out the window the minute they pull out of the driveway?

LIBBY   That's a very pessimistic attitude to take.

HERB (*Trying to control himself*)   Okay! For the sake of
argument, let us say someone looks at the card. Someone is looking for a valet service for his son's bar mitz-
vah. Someone just met a girl at the party and wants to
write down her number. Someone has a piece of spare-
rib in his teeth and is trying to pick it out with the card.
Only a small percentage of *that* group will look at the
back of the card. But let's say one does. He sees, "Libby
Tucker, New York–trained actress—No Part Is Too
Big or Too Small." Do you imagine he's going to slam
his foot on the brake, pull off the road, and say to his
wife, "That's exactly what I'm looking for. An actress
trained in New York who doesn't care if her part is too
big or too small. Right under my nose in my very own
car. What a break for me. I'll contact her first thing in
the morning and hope and pray that someone else with
spareribs in their teeth didn't get to her before me!"

LIBBY (*Shakes her head*)   With an attitude like that, I can
see why you don't get too much done.

HERB   Forget I mentioned it. I'm sorry I brought it up.
I'll stay out of this room tomorrow morning in case
you're swamped with phone calls.
    (*He starts for his bedroom*)

LIBBY   If I stayed in Brooklyn, I never would have come
out here. If I never came out here, I never would have
met Steffy. If I didn't meet Steffy, she never would
have told me about the Los Angeles Academy of Dramatic Arts. If I didn't go over to the Los Angeles
Academy of Dramatic Arts, I never would have met
Gordon Zaharias of Peoria, Illinois. If I didn't meet
Gordon Zaharias, I never would have gotten a job
driving George Segal's car. If I didn't drive all those big
shots' cars, the name and number of Libby Tucker
would never be stuck in their windshields. Where is
your number stuck? If you don't pick yourself up and
do something in this world, they bury you in Mount
Hebron Cemetery and on your tombstone it says,

"Born 1906—Died 1973 . . . and in between HE DIDN'T DO NOTHIN' "!

HERB (*Losing his temper*) Leaving cards in windshields is *not* how you become an actress.

LIBBY And going to Hollywood Park Racetrack is not how you get a script written.

HERB Don't you tell me what to do! I haven't asked you for your advice or your help.

LIBBY And I stopped asking for yours. I'm an independently self-employed woman!

HERB You're a dreamer, that's what you are. You paint Morocco on your ceiling and pretend you don't live in Brooklyn. You pretend your father is the King of Hollywood and you're going to march out here and become the Princess. Well, life isn't pretending. It's goddamned hard work.
(*He goes into his bedroom*)

LIBBY (*Calls out*) Sorry! (*He reenters*) I'm sorry. I didn't mean to get you upset. I thought you'd be pleased with how well things are going for me.

HERB I don't know. Maybe you're right. Maybe sheer determination is all you need. Are you going to be parking any more cars this week?

LIBBY Saturday night in Beverly Hills. There's a big party.

HERB Well, if it's not too much trouble, mention me on one of your cards. See you in the morning.
(*He goes into his bedroom. She watches after him, then goes to his door*)

LIBBY I was wondering if I could discuss something else with you.

HERB (*Offstage*) I just took my pill.

LIBBY It's kind of an emergency. It's something that came up tonight and I'm not sure I know how to handle it.

HERB (*Offstage*) My eyes are starting to close.

LIBBY Yeah. Okay. Never mind. I'll try to work it out for myself. Good night.

HERB (*Comes out*) Would you *stop doing that!* Okay, what's it about?

LIBBY Sex!

HERB Sex?

LIBBY Don't get nervous. If you get nervous, I'll get nervous.

HERB What do you mean, sex?

LIBBY (*Shrugs*) Sex! Things that have to do with things sexual.

HERB Are you in any kind of trouble?

LIBBY Yeah. I think so.

HERB What kind of trouble?

LIBBY I don't know how to do anything sexual.

HERB *That's* the trouble you're in?

LIBBY Most of the people left the party. And Gordon and I were sitting at the bottom of the hill in Suzanne Pleshette's car. And he wanted to fool around. He's not gorgeous but he's kinda cute. And I felt very grateful to him, and I didn't want to hurt his feelings. And I wanted to fool around too. Only I didn't know what was right. I didn't want to be one of those girls they call "easy," but I didn't want to be impossible either. So I just kissed him and got out of the car and decided not to deal with it. But this Saturday night I think I'm going to have to deal with it.

HERB   And you want to discuss this with me?

LIBBY   It doesn't have to be this minute. But Sunday morning'll be too late.

HERB   You never talked about these things with your mother?

LIBBY   She doesn't trust men too much. You can guess why.

HERB   What about your grandmother?

LIBBY   Well, sex isn't her best subject. I brought it up a couple of times but she pretended she was dead.

HERB   Are you telling me that you don't know the first thing about sex?

LIBBY   No. I know how it works. I don't have any mechanical problems. I've seen five X-rated movies. I could pass a test on it. I just don't know what to expect—emotionally.

HERB   I see. Would you feel more comfortable talking to Steffy about it?

LIBBY   Probably. But it's more important I talk to you.

HERB   Why?

LIBBY   Because you're my father. And what you think means a lot to me.

HERB   That's a very nice thing to say. I appreciate that.

LIBBY   If it's a major trauma for you, I understand. I mean, I could always take a couple of glasses of wine and just plunge in.

HERB   You're not plunging into anything. I'd just like to know, is Gordon, what's-his-name, important enough to be the first time in your life?

LIBBY   It's got to be the first time sometime. If it's not him, I could always use the information.

HERB   You know what you are, Libby? Unique. Uni-quest kid I ever met . . . I don't know where to start this thing.

LIBBY   Should I ask you some questions?

HERB   Good idea. Ask me some questions.

LIBBY   Like what?

HERB   How do I know? I have to hear the questions.

LIBBY   Well . . . Emotionally, is it different for the man than it is for the girl?

HERB   Is it different for the man than it is for the girl? . . . Yes!

LIBBY   It *is*?

HERB   Am I wrong?

LIBBY   This isn't a test. I just want to know the answer. How old were you the first time?

HERB   Fifteen.

LIBBY   FIFTEEN?

HERB   I grew up in a tough neighborhood. A fifteen-year-old virgin was considered gay.

LIBBY   Who was the girl?

HERB   I didn't notice. It was very dark and I just wanted to get it over with.

LIBBY   What was it like with Mom? . . . That's a very personal question, isn't it?

HERB   So far it tops the list . . . Well, she was different from anyone I had ever met before. She was respectable. I liked that. Her family had *Time* magazine on the table—to me, that was cultured.

LIBBY   Did you do it with her before or after you were married?

HERB   I didn't think you could top the other question. What did she say?

LIBBY   She said after.

HERB   She did? . . . Yeah. We did it after.

LIBBY   No, you didn't. I knew she lied. She just couldn't talk to me about those things. That's why I'm talking to you. I wanted to know how she felt. If she was scared or excited. Was it fun? Was it painful? I didn't think it was an unreasonable question. I mean, if she could teach me how to walk, why couldn't she teach me how to love?

HERB   I don't know.

LIBBY   So what was she like? Making love.

HERB   Libby, there's just so much I can handle.

LIBBY   Because she was so angry when you left. So bitter. I don't think she ever slept with another man after you were gone.

HERB   You never can tell. She's not unattractive.

LIBBY   It's like when you left, you took her with you. That's why I was so angry with you. It was bad enough you were gone, but you could have left my mother there for me.

HERB She *was* there for you. Look, if she didn't see other men, that was *her* choice. Maybe *you* were the other men in her life.

LIBBY Yeah. No wonder I grew up to be a fruitcake.

HERB Don't talk like that.

LIBBY She used to hug me so hard sometimes. Like she was trying to squeeze all the love out of me that she wasn't getting anywhere else. So instead of growing up to be me, I grew up to be a substitute—

HERB You're no substitute. You're first-string all the way. I never saw a girl your age who was so sure of herself. Jesus, if I had *half* your confidence, maybe you'd have been parking *my* car at that party tonight.

LIBBY Confidence? . . . I'm scared from the minute I wake up every morning.

HERB Of what?

LIBBY Of everything. I get up an hour before you just to check if you're still there . . . I know Grandma's dead. I know she probably can't hear me. But I speak to her every day anyway because I'm not so sure anyone else is listening. If I have to go for an interview, my heart pounds so much you can see it coming through my blouse. That thing about writing my name on the valet stubs? It wasn't my idea. It was Gordon's. He did it first, so I just copied him . . . If you want the God's honest truth, I don't even want to be an actress. I don't know the first thing about acting. I don't know *what* I want to be . . . (*Beginning to break down*) I just wanted to come out here and see you. I just wanted to know what you were like. I wanted to know why I was so frightened every time a boy wanted to reach out and touch me . . . I just wanted somebody in the family to hold me because it was *me*, Libby, and not somebody who wasn't there . . .

(*She is sobbing. He quickly reaches out and grabs her in his arms*)

HERB   I'm here, baby, I'm here. It's all right. Don't cry. I'm holding you, baby, I'm holding you.
(*He cradles her in his arms as she sobs silently*)

LIBBY   Don't let go yet . . . please.

HERB   You can stay in my arms as long as you like. You can move in tonight—put all your clothes in my pockets.

LIBBY   I love Mom so much. I didn't mean to say anything against her.

HERB   I know that.

LIBBY   It's just that she won't let me inside. When she holds me, all I can feel is her arms . . . but I never feel what's inside.

HERB   I understand.

LIBBY   (*Crying openly now; turns away*) Boy oh boy . . . Really opened up the old waterworks. I never expected to do that. I hope you have flood insurance.

HERB   Libby. It can also be wonderful.

LIBBY   What can?

HERB   Giving yourself to someone . . . loving them, giving them pleasure, making them happy . . . making yourself happy. It's that way with me and Steffy. Every time. Haven't missed yet.

LIBBY   Really?

HERB   I wouldn't lie to you.

LIBBY   Then why do you only ask her to come over once a week?

HERB   You're not the only one with shaky confidence.
(*They embrace as the lights fade to black*)

SCENE 4

It is Sunday morning, a few days later, about 11 A.M.

HERB (*Coming out of the bedroom and calling toward the bathroom*) Libby? You up? C'mon, we're going to Nate and Al's for breakfast. I want a mushroom and onion omelette, bagels, cream cheese, and a pot of hot coffee. We're going to the Dodger game. I got tickets yesterday. Dodgers. Phillies. (*He looks out into the garden*) What a gorgeous day. Nice and cloudy. You know what I was thinking? Maybe you could make a sunroof for the car? I mean, it's ready to fall in anyway, it shouldn't be too big a job. What do you think? (LIBBY *emerges, wearing her original outfit*) Is that what you're going to wear? We're not going to *hike* to Dodger Stadium . . . You don't look too happy. You don't want to go to the game? It's okay. You don't have to go. I just thought you might enjoy it.

LIBBY (*Tentatively*) I would. I would really love to go with you.

HERB So why the long face?

LIBBY It's not a long face . . . It's a goodbye face. I'm going home.
(*She begins to tie on her hiking boots*)

HERB What do you mean?

LIBBY I mean, I'm going back home. To New York.

HERB When?

LIBBY   Today. Now. I was waiting for you to get up. I called Steffy to say goodbye. She said she would try to get over before I left.

HERB   You mean for good?

LIBBY   I hope not. I hope you'll invite me to come out again sometime . . . I hope you'll come out to visit me in New York. I hope I'll have my own place by then. Maybe you can sleep in *my* alcove.

HERB   When did you decide all this?

LIBBY   Last night. I couldn't sleep. I was lying in bed and suddenly I heard a voice say to me, "Libby, it's time to go home. You got what you came for." And I suddenly realized it wasn't Grandma's voice. It was mine. So I got up this morning and packed my bags.

HERB   What do you mean you got what you came out for? What did you get? A job parking cars? Is that what this whole trip was for?

LIBBY   No. It was to get something from you. I thought it was a career or maybe just to tell you that I thought you were a shitheel. But the other night when you held me in your arms and said I could stay there as long as I wanted, I could feel your heart beating, I could feel what was *inside*—and I knew then, when you were holding me, that that's what it was I came out for.

HERB   Then why do you have to go back? Why now? It took us sixteen years to get to this place. It doesn't seem right to go back the way we were.

LIBBY   We're not going back the way we were. I'm just going back to New York. We have a relationship now. I know who you are; you know who I am. That's a whole new place for us.

HERB   What's in New York for you? What are you going to do there?

LIBBY Start to think about what I want to do with my life instead of wasting my time being angry with what I didn't get.

HERB But you just got here. A couple of lousy weeks, what's that? Stay a month, two more weeks. Go to the Dodger game with me, Libby. Don't go home today. Please . . . Jesus. I'm just going to miss you so damn much.

LIBBY We can call each other. We can write. I always imagined you wrote the most wonderful letters, being a professional and all. I'll save them up and make a book out of them. You know, like Groucho Marx's letters to his son.

HERB "The Postcards of Herbert Tucker."

LIBBY That's not a bad title.

HERB You'll need money for the plane.

LIBBY I saved it. I made a lot this week. I'm going to take the bus to Chicago and hitch the other half.

HERB You're not going to hitch. (*Reaching for his wallet*) Here's some money.

LIBBY No, Daddy. I don't want it. Please.

HERB It was worth it just to hear you call me Daddy. Christ, I think I would have been better off if you never came.

LIBBY Don't say that.

HERB Well, I'm mad, damn it. I'm pissed off at you. You could have given me some warning. If I knew you were only going to stay two weeks, I never would have—

LIBBY What?

HERB Never mind.

LIBBY   You never would have what? Gotten so attached?

HERB   I didn't say that.

LIBBY   But you were going to . . . Why couldn't you say it? What is it about attachments that scares you so much?

HERB   Unattachments.

LIBBY   Listen. You want to go to the game, I'll go to the game. I can leave tomorrow.

HERB   No. What's the point? I'll give the tickets to Steffy's kids.
        (*He sits and holds his stomach with a grimace*)

LIBBY   What's wrong? Are you all right?

HERB   I just have an empty feeling in my stomach— maybe I'm hungry.

LIBBY   You're not going to go back to not eating again, are you? Not taking care of yourself? I'm going to mail you sandwiches every day from New York.

HERB   Mail them early in the morning. I can't stand cold pastrami.

LIBBY   These have been the best two weeks of my life. I wouldn't have traded them for anything.
        (STEFFY *appears at the door*)

STEFFY   I ran out of gas two blocks away. I was afraid I'd miss you. Oh God, am I out of shape.

LIBBY   It looks plenty good to me. Doesn't it look good to you, Dad?
        (HERB *gets up and goes into the garden*)

STEFFY   How does he feel about your leaving?

LIBBY   Terrible. Isn't it wonderful?

STEFFY   You look different than that first day you got here. Taller. Did you get taller?

LIBBY   Yeah. Inside. I also got gorgeous but it didn't come out yet.

STEFFY   You could have fooled me. Oh. This is for you.
(*She hands her a manila envelope*)

LIBBY   What is it?

STEFFY   It's a present. Open it.
(LIBBY *opens it and takes out an eight-by-ten glossy photograph of Jane Fonda*)

LIBBY   "To Libby . . . From what I hear, a girl after my own heart. Best wishes, Jane Fonda." Well, that did it. You have just destroyed a tall, gorgeous girl from Brooklyn. In two weeks everything I ever wanted came true. This is some place to live.
(LIBBY *goes to her knapsack on the coffee table and puts the picture in it*)

STEFFY   I almost got Candice Bergen's for you too.

LIBBY   Oh that's okay. I know Candice. We already met.
(HERB *comes in from the garden with three oranges in his hand. He goes to the kitchen, and puts them into a bag*)

HERB   Here's some oranges. You ought to take some oranges to eat on the trip.

LIBBY   Jeez. I forgot to tell Mom I'm coming home. Dad? Can I call long distance? I'll pay you back.
(LIBBY *rushes to the phone and dials*)

STEFFY   Should I wait outside?

LIBBY   No. Stay. It's okay. (*Into the phone*) Hello, Mom? . . . Hi, Mom. It's me. Libby . . . No. Everything's terrific . . . How are you? . . . Your feet are bothering you? . . . Well, don't stand on them so much . . . (*Hand over the phone, to* STEFFY) She says, "So what should I stand on?" (*Back into the phone*) Mom? Listen. I just wanted to tell you I'm coming home . . . I'm leaving today . . . No, no, no—things are *wonderful.* I'll tell you all about it when I get there . . . Well, I've missed you too . . . I think about you all the time . . . There's so many things I want to talk to you about now . . . I've become very enlightened in California . . . *Enlightened* . . . Forget it, I'll explain it Wednesday . . . Listen, Mom, could you hold on for one second? Don't go away. (*She puts her hand over the phone. To* HERB) You don't have to say yes. I know it's an imposition, but it would mean an awful lot to me . . . Would you say hello to her?

HERB   Libby!

LIBBY   It doesn't have to be a conversation. Just a plain hello. She's feeling kind of low. I can hear it in her voice. It would be a nice gesture—with Mother's Day coming up in three weeks.

HERB   What's the matter with you, Libby? I haven't spoken to the woman in sixteen years. You don't just pick up a phone and say hello.

LIBBY   It's only the first few seconds that's hard.

HERB   Don't do this to me, Libby. Don't do this to your mother. It's embarrassing for both of us.

LIBBY   I'm not trying to make a *match.* I just thought it would be nice if everybody didn't spend the rest of their lives hung up on something that happened sixteen years ago.

HERB   Steffy, would *you* please explain it to her!

LIBBY   Let me ask Mom. If she says okay, will you say okay?

HERB   She's not going to say okay. Why would she say okay?

LIBBY   She might surprise you. You never know. Can I ask her?

HERB   Go ahead. Ask her. I know the woman.

LIBBY   (*Into the phone*)   Mom? There's somebody here who wants to say hello to you . . . Yeah. He's standing right here . . . How do you feel about it? . . . Uh-huh . . . Uh-huh . . . All right, wait a minute. (*Hand over the phone, she moves toward* HERB) She says if you would like to say hello, she won't stop you.

HERB   You see! What did I tell you?

LIBBY   That's a *yes*! She said yes.

HERB   *That's the worst "yes" I ever heard!*

LIBBY   She's waiting on the phone. If you don't say hello *now*, that would *really* be a lousy thing to do.

HERB   (*He glares at her*)   You're something! You're really something! Two more weeks of you and *I* would have hitchhiked back to New York. (*He goes toward her*) Gimme the phone!

LIBBY   (*Into the phone*)   MOM? . . . Here's—him.
        (*She hands him the phone. He takes it and looks around despairingly*)

STEFFY   I have to wash my hands.
         (*She goes into the bathroom*)

LIBBY   I have to make your bed.
        (*She goes into his room and closes the door.* HERB *is alone. He looks at the phone, takes a deep breath, and plunges in*)

HERB   Hello? . . . Blanche? . . . It's Herb . . . Yeah . . . Yeah, it's a surprise for me, too . . . How have you been? . . . Oh? . . . Yeah, well, I have trouble with my feet sometimes too . . . Libby showed me a picture of you. You looked very well . . . You were wearing a blue dress with an orange sweater . . . No. You didn't look heavy at all . . . You looked the same as ever to me . . . The thing I wanted to say was . . . Well, I think Libby's a terrific kid . . . A little outspoken, you know, but er . . . Well, you did a wonderful job with her, Blanche, and you should be very proud . . . Very, very proud . . . Yes. Well, it was nice talking to you too . . . Take care of yourself, Blanche . . . Who? . . . Sure. Sure, if he's there, put him on . . . (*He waits, takes another deep breath*) Hello? Hello, Robby, how are you? . . . Well, it's nice meeting you too . . . I hear you play the piano . . . You like it? . . . Yeah, I like it. It's a nice instrument . . . What's that? . . . Yeah. Yeah, I'm working on a script right now, as a matter of fact . . . Oh, you saw that one? That was about three years ago . . . I'm glad you liked it . . . I didn't know you saw it . . . No kidding? Really? Well, if you do, you just look me up . . . Your sister has the address . . . Okay. I have to go too . . . It was good speaking to you . . . Say goodbye to your mother . . . Goodbye, Robby. (*He cries a moment; then*) . . . You can come out now!

(*Both* STEFFY *and* LIBBY *come out at exactly the same time*)

LIBBY Thank you. that was very nice what you said about me. What'd you think of Robby?

HERB He didn't sound like a Carl. He has a very high voice, hasn't he?

LIBBY It gets that way when he gets nervous. Don't worry. He's not what you're thinking.

HERB Who said anything? He may come out here next summer. He may go to school out here. He said he'd like to come by and see me.

LIBBY You see! You see! Now aren't you glad you said "Hello"?

HERB   I suppose this means your mother comes out the summer after Robby.

LIBBY   No. You'd never get Mom out of her apartment. She'll live in Brooklyn until the day she dies, and then they'll bury her next to Grandma.

HERB   Then starts the three-way conversations. You'll have to put in another line.

STEFFY   I'm leaving now too. I can drop you off wherever you want.

LIBBY   No, thanks. I want to leave the way I came. On my own. A girl has to be independent these days. Have I got everything?

HERB   The fruit. Don't forget your fruit.

LIBBY   (*Looks at them*)   Thanks. You really grow great oranges and lemons.

HERB   I'm sure glad this was the right Herb Tucker you were looking for that morning.

LIBBY   Listen, if you ever do a picture in New York, we have a spare room for you. It used to be Grandma's. I did it over in French Riviera.

STEFFY   I *love* French Riviera. I have to wash my hands again.
       (*She goes into the bathroom*)

LIBBY   Sooo . . . Here it is again. Another one of those goodbye days.

HERB   (*Looks around*)   I feel like I should be giving you something more to take with you . . . I don't know what else to give you.

LIBBY   I can think of something.

HERB   You can? What?

LIBBY Your picture.

HERB My picture? (*He looks around*) Gee, I don't know if I have any good ones. (*Opens drawers*) I had some publicity shots but they're about six years old. I had a mustache. It doesn't even look like me.
(LIBBY *takes out a Kodak Instamatic*)

LIBBY I came all prepared. All you have to do is stand there.

HERB Oh, God. I hate taking pictures.

LIBBY You're not. *I'm* taking it. You're just posing. (*She focuses the camera. He poses uncomfortably*) Can't you do something? You look like you're being booked for prison.

HERB What do you want me to do? Dance on the ceiling?

LIBBY No. Just give me a smile. Come on. Force yourself. That's a smile? That's how they look at Mount Hebron Cemetery. A big smile for Libby, okay? (*He smiles. She snaps*) Stay there! One more for Robby. (*He smiles. She snaps*) And one for Mom.

HERB Oh, come on.

LIBBY For Mother's Day. Be a sport. (*He smiles. She snaps*) Thank you. The rest I'm going to use for America. Well, I think I'm going to go very quickly because in five more minutes I'm going to take root and grow into a New York apple tree . . . Goodbye, Daddy. I love you.
(LIBBY *runs out the door. The bathroom door opens and* STEFFY *comes out*)

STEFFY Well, I think I'll be going myself. Would it be all right if I borrow your car for a few minutes? I have to pick up a can of gasoline. I'll be right back.

HERB Sure.

STEFFY I was going to take in a picture with the kids, and a Chinese dinner. You interested?

HERB I don't know. I thought I might get a few pages done today.

STEFFY On a Sunday?

HERB The typewriter doesn't know. It could be Wednesday to him.

STEFFY Sure. Well, maybe some other time.

HERB Yeah.

STEFFY You got something you're working on?

HERB Yeah. I think so.

STEFFY I'm glad to hear it . . . Something new?

HERB No. It's an old idea. Actually, it came to me about sixteen years ago.

STEFFY I like it already. (*She turns and goes to the car.* HERB *goes to his desk and sits.* STEFFY *returns*) I forgot the keys . . . I see you've gone in for advertising.

HERB What?
(STEFFY *hands him a small red card*)

STEFFY That was on your steering wheel. (*She hands the card to* HERB. *He reads it, smiles, and hands it back to* STEFFY, *who reads it aloud*) "Herbert Tucker. New York–trained writer. No script too big or too small."

Curtain

Fools

FOOLS *was first presented on April 6, 1981, at the Eugene O'Neill Theatre, New York City, with the following cast:*

(In order of appearance)

LEON TOLCHINSKY	John Rubinstein
SNETSKY	Gerald Hiken
MAGISTRATE	Fred Stuthman
SLOVITCH	David Lipman
MISHKIN	Joseph Leon
YENCHNA	Florence Stanley
DR. ZUBRITSKY	Harold Gould
LENYA ZUBRITSKY	Mary Louise Wilson
SOPHIA ZUBRITSKY	Pamela Reed
GREGOR YOUSEKEVITCH	Richard B. Shull

Directed by Mike Nichols
Scenery by John Lee Beatty
Costumes by Patricia Zipprodt
Lighting by Tharon Musser

Act One

SCENE I

Kulyenchikov, about 1890, a remote Ukrainian village.
LEON TOLCHINSKY, about thirty, carrying a battered old suitcase and some books tied together, arrives over a small bridge in the town square. He looks around, seems pleased, then turns to the audience.

LEON (*Smiles*) Kulyenchikov, I like it! It's exactly as I pictured: a quiet, pleasant village, not too large . . . the perfect place for a new schoolteacher to begin his career . . . Well, to be honest, I did spend mornings for two years in a small children's school in Moscow teaching tiny tots rudimentary spelling and numbers, but this, *this* is my first bona fide, professional appointment as a full-time schoolmaster. Actually, I never even heard of Kulyenchikov until I saw the advertisement that a Dr. Zubritsky placed in the college journal. Although the position was in a remote village in the Ukraine, I jumped at the chance, but I don't mind telling you that my heart is pounding with excitement. I have this passion for teaching . . . Greek, Latin, astronomy, classic literature. I get goose bumps just thinking about it . . . (*He looks around*) I don't see anyone around . . . Maybe I arrived a little early—I'm one of those extremely eager and enthusiastic people who's up at the crack of dawn, ready to begin his work. This is a very, very auspicious day in my life. (*We hear a ram's horn offstage*) Oh! Excuse me.
(SNETSKY *the shepherd enters, carrying a ram's horn and a staff*)

SNETSKY Elenya! Lebidoff! Marushka! Olga! Where are you?

LEON   Good morning.

SNETSKY   Good morning. Did you happen to see two dozen sheep?

LEON   Two dozen sheep?

SNETSKY   Yes. There were fourteen of them.
   (*He continues looking*)

LEON   No. I'm sorry.

SNETSKY   Well, if you see them, would you give them a message?

LEON   A message for the sheep?

SNETSKY   Yes, tell them the shepherd is looking for them and they should tell you where they are and I'll come and get them. Thank you.
   (*He starts to walk off*)

LEON   Wait, wait. Excuse me—what is your name, please?

SNETSKY (*Stops*)   Snetsky.

LEON   And your first name?

SNETSKY (*Thinks*)   How soon do you need it?

LEON   Never mind. Forget your first name.

SNETSKY   I did.

LEON   I am Leon Steponovitch Tolchinsky and I am to be the new schoolteacher.

SNETSKY   Is that a fact? (*He shakes* LEON's *hand vigorously*) I'm very honored to meet you, Leon Steponovitch Tolchinsky. I am Something Something Snetsky . . . Will you be staying the night?

LEON You don't understand. Kulyenchikov will be my new home. I'm going to live here and teach here. I am, if I may say so, an excellent teacher.

SNETSKY Oh, they all were. They came by the thousands, but not one of them lasted through the first night. (*He blows the horn hard*) Oh, it's so hard to blow these, I don't know how the sheep do it.

LEON You've had thousands of teachers?

SNETSKY More. Hundreds! We're unteachable. We're all stupid in Kulyenchikov. There isn't a town or village more stupid in all of Mother Poland.

LEON Russia.

SNETSKY Whatever. All good people, mind you, but not a decent brain among them. (*He blows the horn with difficulty*) Oh, that feels so good. I just opened up my ears. I thought you were whispering. What were you saying?

LEON Are you telling me that every man, woman, and child—

SNETSKY All stupid. Including me. Talk to me another ten minutes and you'll begin to notice.

LEON (*Ignores it*) I was hired by Dr. Zubritsky to teach his young daughter.

SNETSKY (*Bursts out laughing*) Teach his daughter? Impossible. The girl is hopeless. Nineteen years old and she just recently learned to sit down . . . She's hopeless. She doesn't even know the difference between a cow and a duck. Not that it's an easy subject, mind you.

LEON (*To the audience*) Something is up here! (*He takes the ad out of his pocket*) I thought nothing of it then, but when I first read it I *did* notice that every word in the advertisement was misspelled . . . I'm sure Dr. Zubritsky will explain it all to me. (*He steps back and turns to* SNETSKY) You've been most helpful, Citizen Snetsky. I enjoyed our chat.

SNETSKY   As did I, Master Tolchinsky. (*He turns to the audience*) He's not the only one who can have private thoughts. I can have private thoughts as well. (*He tries to think*) The trouble is, I can never think of a thought to have in private. Oh, I must be on my way. Good day, schoolmaster.

LEON   I'm sure we'll meet again.

SNETSKY   Oh, of course. Just mention my name to anyone. Snetsky the sheep loser.
(*He leaves. A* MAGISTRATE, *ringing a bell, enters.* LEON *tries to stop him, but is ignored*)

MAGISTRATE   Nine o'clock and all's well . . . Nine o'clock in the village of Kulyenchikov and all's well . . . Nine o'clock and all's well.
(*He is gone*)

LEON (*To the audience*)   It may have been all well with him, but I was beginning to have my doubts.
(*He leaves. A butcher,* SLOVITCH, *comes out of his shop with a broom. He sweeps the dirt into a pile and then sweeps it* into *the shop. The postman,* MISHKIN, *appears*)

SLOVITCH   Good morning, postman.

MISHKIN   Good morning, butcher.

SLOVITCH   A beautiful, sunny day, isn't it?

MISHKIN   Is it? I haven't looked up yet. (*He looks up*) Oh, yes. Lovely. Very nice.

SLOVITCH   Do I have any mail?

MISHKIN   No. I'm sorry. I'm the postman. I have all the mail.

SLOVITCH   My sister in Odessa hasn't been feeling well. I was hoping I would hear from her.

MISHKIN   It's very hard to hear all the way from Odessa. Perhaps she wrote a letter. I'll look.
(*He starts to look through the mail. We hear* YENCHNA, *a vendor, calling "Fish!" offstage before she appears*)

YENCHNA (*Calling out, selling her wares*)   Fish! Fresh fish! Nice fresh flounder and halibut! A good piece of carp for lunch.

SLOVITCH   Good morning, Yenchna.

YENCHNA   How about a nice piece of haddock? Is that a beautiful fish?

SLOVITCH   What do you mean fish? Those are flowers.

YENCHNA   They didn't catch anything today. Why should I suffer because the fisherman had a bad day? Try the carp, it smells gorgeous.

MISHKIN   I don't have any letters from your sister, Slovitch. But I have a nice letter from the shoemaker's cousin. Would you like that?

SLOVITCH   Is she sick? I hate reading bad news.

MISHKIN   No, no. In perfect health. Take it. You'll enjoy it.

YENCHNA   Can you believe my daughter hasn't written to me in over a year?

MISHKIN   Doesn't your daughter live with you?

YENCHNA   It's a good thing. Otherwise I'd never hear from her.
       (LEON *enters*)

LEON (*To the townspeople*)   Good morning. My name is Leon Steponovitch Tolchinsky. I'm the new schoolmaster.

MISHKIN (*Bows*)   Mishkin the postman.

SLOVITCH (*Bows*)   Slovitch the butcher.

YENCHNA   Yenchna the vendor.

LEON   How do you do. I was just talking to a shepherd named Snetsky.

MISHKIN   Oh, yes. Something Something Snetsky. We know him well.

LEON   He was pleasant enough, although—and I hope I don't seem unkind—somewhat deficient in his mental alertness.

YENCHNA   That's Snetsky, all right. (*She taps her head*) He was kicked in the head by a horse.

LEON   Oh, well. What a pity. When was that?

YENCHNA   Tuesday, Wednesday, twice on Friday, and all day Saturday.

LEON (*Looks at* YENCHNA's *flowers*)   What lovely and fragrant wares you have to sell, madame. Perhaps I might buy some for my new employer. How much are they, please?

YENCHNA   The flounder is two kopecks and the halibut is three.

LEON   I beg your pardon?

YENCHNA (*Holds up a white flower*)   If it's too much, I have a nice whitefish for one and a half.
(*She wraps it in a newspaper and hands it to him. He pays*)

LEON (*To the audience*)   Perhaps the dialect is a little different in this part of the country. (*To the group*) I'm very eager to begin my new duties. Will one of you be so kind as to direct me to the home of Dr. Zubritsky?
(*They all point in different directions*)

ALL THREE   That way!

LEON   Thank you. Perhaps I'll go in the one direction you haven't pointed to . . . A pleasure meeting you all. (SNETSKY *appears*) Oh. Hello again. Have you found your sheep?

SNETSKY   Not yet. (LEON *leaves*) Who was that?

MISHKIN   The new schoolteacher.

SNETSKY   Another one? I just met one a few minutes ago, they must be having a convention here.

YENCHNA   Count Yousekevitch up on the hill isn't going to be very happy about this.

SLOVITCH   That's right. Count Yousekevitch doesn't like new schoolteachers.

SNETSKY   Why?

MISHKIN   He's afraid they'll break the curse.

SNETSKY   What curse?

SLOVITCH   The one that made us stupid since the day we were born.

SNETSKY   Oh, that one.

MISHKIN   Yes. I've been stupid for fifty-one years . . . What about you, Snetsky?

SNETSKY   I'll be dumb forty-three next July.

MISHKIN   And you, Slovitch?

SLOVITCH   Forty-one for me. What about you, Yenchna?

YENCHNA   I just turned the corner of twenty-six.

SLOVITCH   That corner must be about forty miles from here.

(They all exit)

The home of DR. ZUBRITSKY. *The* DOCTOR *is examining a patient,* MAGISTRATE KUPCHIK. *The* DOCTOR *is administering an eye-chart test.*

MAGISTRATE (*Covering one eye*) K . . . E . . . 5 . . . L . . . A . . . R . . V . . . Is that right?

DOCTOR   I don't know. It sounds good to me. (*Listening to the* MAGISTRATE's *heart*) Yes . . . Yes . . . Very interesting.

MAGISTRATE   Then I'm in good health?

DOCTOR   The best. The best of health. You'll live to be eighty.

MAGISTRATE   I'm seventy-nine now.

DOCTOR   Well, you've got a wonderful year ahead of you.

MAGISTRATE (*Gets dressed*)   Good. I must keep up my strength. I'm a magistrate. Law and order must be preserved.

DOCTOR   Did you want a prescription?

MAGISTRATE   For what?

DOCTOR   I don't know. Some people like prescriptions. Here, take this to the druggist. Pick out something you like and take it three times a day with a little water. Goodbye, sir.

MAGISTRATE   How much do I owe you, Doctor?

DOCTOR   Oh, forget it. Forget it. If I ever go to medical school you can send me a little something.

MAGISTRATE   Oh, thank you. Goodbye.
(LENYA *enters. She is exuberant and excited*)

LENYA   Nikolai! Nikolai! He's here. He's come! He arrived not two minutes ago. He's young. He looks strong, determined. Maybe he'll be the one, Nikolai. Maybe this one will finally be our salvation.

DOCTOR   Calm yourself, Lenya. Who's come? Who'll be our salvation?

LENYA   The new—er—The new—what do you call them? They come and they—er—The ones who—We had one once but no more.

DOCTOR   Oh, God. I know. I know who you mean.

LENYA   They have a place, and then you go to the place—

DOCTOR   And they point to you and they say—er—they ask you if you—er—

LENYA   And if you don't they say, "Why didn't you? Next time I'll *make* you."

DOCTOR   And he's outside?

LENYA   He's just down the street.

DOCTOR   Well, show him in, Lenya. Show him in. And pray God this is the one who will deliver us and all of Kulyenchikov from this dreadful—er—this—er—Oh, God, what is it we have again?

LENYA   I know. I know what you mean. It sounds like *nurse* . . .

DOCTOR   Nurse.

LENYA   Or *hearse* . . .

DOCTOR   Hearse.

LENYA   Something like that.

DOCTOR   Or something like that. (*There is a knock*) Or is it a knock?

LENYA   We have a knock?
(*She goes to the door*)

DOCTOR   Yes, yes. Open the knock. (*She* pushes *on the door*) The other way, the other way.
(*She opens it.* LEON *stands there*)

LENYA   Won't you come in, young man?

LEON   Dr. Zubritsky? Madame Zubritsky? I am delighted to be in Kulyenchikov. I am Leon Steponovitch Tolchinsky.

DOCTOR   So you are the new—the new—

LEON   Yes! I am he.

DOCTOR   It's he, Lenya, the new—the new—

LENYA   But you look so young to be a—to be a—

LEON   Not at all. I think in time you will find that I am, if I may say so, one of the best young—well, I don't want to seem immodest.

DOCTOR   No. Please. Be immodest. We *love* immodesty.

LENYA   The more immodest the better. The best young what? *What?*

LEON   The best young teacher in all of Russia!

DOCTOR (*Excited*) *A teacher!!!* He's a teacher!! The new teacher is here.

LENYA *Thank God the teacher is here!!*

LEON Thank you. Thank you. I'm most gratified at this most warm and overwhelming reception.

DOCTOR Make yourself at home, teacher. Take off your coat, teacher. Lenya, bring the teacher a cup of tea. Sit down, teacher.

LENYA Would you like some tea, teacher? Or maybe some paper and pens, teacher? Perhaps you would like to start teaching right away, teacher?

LEON Well, no one's more eager than I am. Madame Zubritsky, this is for you.
(*He hands her the flowers*)

LENYA Oh, whitefish. I saw them on sale today. Thank you.
(*She takes them.* LEON *looks at the audience, bewildered*)

DOCTOR How can we help you?

LEON Well, there are a few questions I wanted to ask you first.

DOCTOR Questions! That's what they ask. When they point to you and you don't know. He knows. He knows what questions are. I can tell this one's going to be a good teacher.

LENYA Would you be so kind, Master Tolchinsky, to— to ask us a question. Any question at all.

DOCTOR It means a lot to us. It's been so long since anyone has asked us a good "school" question . . . *Please!*
(*They all sit*)

LEON   Well, there are questions and there are questions. Do you want a question on mathematics or a question dealing with science or perhaps a philosophical question?

DOCTOR   The first one. The first one sounds good. The philosophical question. Ask us that one.

LEON   Very well, if you wish . . . What is the purpose of man's existence?

DOCTOR   What a question . . . Lenya, did you ever hear such a beautiful question?

LENYA   I'm speechless . . . To think someone would ask *us* a question like that.

LEON   Are you interested in the answer?

DOCTOR   Not today, thank you. To be asked one question like that in a lifetime is more than we ever expected. The answer should be given to someone much more worthy than we are.

LEON   But it's your birthright. Knowledge is *everyone's* birthright.

DOCTOR   Everyone not born in Kulyenchikov.

LEON   I don't understand.

LENYA   You would if you knew about the nurse.

LEON   What nurse?

DOCTOR   Not the nurse, the hearse.

LEON   The hearse?

LENYA   He means the purse.

LEON   What kind of purse?

DOCTOR The kind of purse that inflicts the wrath of God upon all those poor souls who were unfortunate enough to be born in this pitiful village.

LEON Do you mean, perhaps, a curse?

DOCTOR *Curse!!* That's what it is! I *knew* it sounded like that.

LENYA We were so close. *So* close!

LEON What is this curse you speak of, Dr. Zubritsky?

DOCTOR Lenya, bolt the door. Draw the curtains.

LENYA I can't draw curtains. I can draw a cat or a fish—

DOCTOR Never mind. Lower your voice.

LENYA (*Bends her knees, making herself shorter*) How low do you want my voice?

DOCTOR That's low enough. Bring the book, it's on the shelf. (*She goes over to the bookshelf, knees bent as she walks. To* LEON) Young man—have you ever heard of the Curse of Kulyenchikov?

LEON I can't say that I have.

DOCTOR You can't say that? It's not hard. Even Lenya can say that.

LENYA (*Standing by the bookshelf*) "The Curse of Kulyenchikov."

LEON What is this curse, Doctor?

DOCTOR Two hundred years ago, a curse was put on this village that struck down every man, woman, child, and domestic animal, including all their ancestors for generations to come, leaving each and every one of them— and this you'll find hard to believe—with no more intelligence than a bump on a log.

LEON   Doctor, I don't believe in curses. Curses are old wives' tales.

DOCTOR   You're thinking of Noychka. In Noychka all the old wives have tails. That was *their* curse. Ours is altogether different.

LEON   But where did the curse come from? And who would inflict such cruel punishment on such a peaceful and simple village?
(LENYA *has returned with the book*)

DOCTOR   Who indeed? It's all documented in *The Book of Curses*. (*He blows dust off the cover into* LEON's *face. To* LENYA) I thought you said you dusted this.

LENYA   I did. I put dust on it yesterday.

DOCTOR (*To* LEON)   Here. Read it for yourself. The page is marked.

LEON (*Opens the book. The page is sticky and gummy*)   It's all stuck together.

LENYA   We marked it with maple syrup. Read it to us.
(*They all sit on the* DOCTOR's *sofa*)

LEON (*Reading*)   "On the morning of April 11, in the year 1691, in the village of Kulyenchikov, two young people fell hopelessly in love."

LENYA   I knew it. Whenever young people fall in love, you know a curse is coming.

LEON   But surely you've heard all this before?

DOCTOR   Many times. But we never understood it. It's a very well thought-out curse.

LENYA   So what happens?

LEON   "The boy was a young, handsome, but illiterate farmer named Casimir Yousekevitch. The girl was the daughter of the most learned man in the town, Mikhail Zubritsky."

LENYA   Zubritsky! I've heard that name before.

DOCTOR   I've seen it! I've seen it! On a front door somewhere. In this neighborhood.

LEON   It's on your front door. *Your* name is Zubritsky.

DOCTOR (*With profound insight*)   Wait a minute! That means that the young man in the curse may possibly be related—to our front door.
(*He and* LENYA *walk over to the door, open it, and look out*)

LEON (*To the audience*)   Mind you, I'm dealing with the intelligentsia now! . . . I continue: "The young girl's name was Sophia Zubritsky." (*To the* DOCTOR) May I ask the name of your young daughter?

DOCTOR   Sophia.

LEON   Sophia? Sophia Zubritsky! The identical name of the girl in the curse over two hundred years ago.

DOCTOR   I can't believe it. Unless our daughter has been lying about her age.
(*He and* LENYA *have come back. Each stands behind a chair*)

LEON   "The match was doomed from the start. When Sophia's educated father learned that young Casimir was illiterate, he forbade Sophia ever to see Casimir again. Six months later Sophia married a young student, and that winter Casimir, distraught and despondent, took his life by plowing his own grave and planting himself in it. Upon hearing of his son's death, Casimir's father, Vladimir Yousekevitch—"

THE ZUBRITSKYS (*Shaking the chairs*)   Tremble, tremble, tremble, tremble.

LEON   "—Casimir's father, Vladimir Yousekevitch—"

THE ZUBRITSKYS   Tremble, tremble, tremble, tremble.

LEON   "—Casimir's father, Vladimir Yousekevitch—"

THE ZUBRITSKYS   Tremble, tremble, tremble, tremble.

LEON   "—who caused people to tremble at the mention of his name—"

LENYA   Next time don't mention his name.

LEON   "—Casimir's father, Vla—"

THE ZUBRITSKYS (*With a short chair shake*)   Trem—

LEON   "—and So-and-So, sometimes known as the Sorcerer because of his ability to summon the powers of the Devil himself, brought all his wrath and fury down upon Kulyenchikov . . ."

DOCTOR   Here it comes! Here it comes!

LEON   " 'A curse! A curse upon all who dwell in Kulyenchikov!' he cried out. 'May the daughter of Mikhail Zubritsky, murderer of my only son, be struck down by the ignorance that caused my son's death! May stupidity engulf her brain! May incompetence encumber her faculties! May common sense become uncommon and may reason become unreasonable!! May her children be cursed as well. And may all their children be cursed for eternity! May all who live in Kulyenchikov be born in ignorance and die in ignorance, unable to leave this cursed village until my final vengeance has been satisfied!' "

LENYA   That would explain why the train doesn't stop here.

LEON (*To the audience*)   My initial impulse was to panic, even my secondary impulse was to panic . . . To educate is one thing, to break curses is another.

DOCTOR   Excuse me, but are you all right, Master Tol-
    chinsky?

LEON   Yes. I'm fine. I—I was just thinking.

DOCTOR   Lenya . . . he was thinking.

LENYA   He was thinking.

DOCTOR (*To* LEON)   What's it like?

LEON   You mean you don't know what thinking is?

DOCTOR   I don't and she certainly doesn't.

LEON   *Thinking?* It's the thoughts that come to one's
    mind. It's the process which enables us to make deci-
    sions.

DOCTOR   Decisions? No. I don't think we're capable of
    that.

LEON   But surely you know what it is you want.

LENYA   Oh, dear God, yes. We desperately want some-
    one to help us. Not so much for us, we've already lived
    our lives. But for your child, our sweet daughter,
    Sophia.

LEON   Did you hear what you just said?

LENYA   No, I wasn't listening.

LEON   It was a decision. You decided to help your daugh-
    ter because you thought about it. You are capable of
    thought. You think.

LENYA   No, I don't think so. It just came out.

LEON   Yes. Out of your head where your brain is lodged.
    The center of thoughts. And if it's possible to have even
    one tiny infinitesimal insignificant thought, then it's

possible to expand those thoughts to ideas—and ideas into comprehension—comprehension into creativity—and finally, supreme *intelligence*!!

DOCTOR   Would I be able to open up jars? I have terrible trouble opening up jars.

LEON (*Aside*)   Be firm, Leon. Be staunch . . . (*To the* DOCTOR) Patience! We will break this curse, I promise you! By the simple, everyday, painstaking work of education. We must begin at once. I should like to start by seeing your daughter, Sophia.

DOCTOR   Sophia?

LEON   Yes, it occurs to me that since the curse started with the young Sophia two hundred years ago, perhaps the key to ending it lies with her direct descendant. Can I see Sophia?

LENYA   Not from here. She's up in her room. We would have to send for her.

DOCTOR   Do what the schoolmaster asks.

LENYA   She may be taking her singing lesson now.

LEON   She takes singing lessons? From whom?

LENYA   A canary. He does the best he can.

DOCTOR   No words, mind you. Just the tunes.

LEON   I understand. The girl, madame. Please.

DOCTOR (*To* LENYA)   Remember, sweetheart, upstairs and to the left. (*She goes. To* LEON) You'll find her a most delicate and sensitive girl. Not like the others in the village. She has so many interests, always occupied.

LEON   Occupied with what?

DOCTOR   Oh, she likes to do interesting things . . . like touching things—wood, paper, metal. She likes drinking water.
     (LENYA *returns*)

LENYA   Master Tolchinsky. May I present our daughter . . . (*She looks at piece of paper in her hand to remind her of* SOPHIA's *name*) Sophia Irena Elenya Zubritsky. (SOPHIA *enters*) Sophia, this is the new schoolmaster, Leon Tolchinsky.

LEON   Miss Zubritsky! (*He turns aside, dazed*) Is that my breath that has just been taken away? Is that vision before me human or have I too been cast under the spell? Never have I felt such a stirring beneath my breast . . . Watch yourself, Leon! She is your pupil, not the object of your dormant feelings of passion. (*He turns back to them*) Excuse me.

DOCTOR   Do you know what he was just doing, Sophia? He was *thinking*! Isn't that wonderful?

SOPHIA   Yes, Mama.

DOCTOR   Papa! She is Mama and I am Papa.

LEON   Won't you please sit down, Miss Zubritsky?
     (*She sits slowly, carefully, and when she is down, the* DOCTOR *embraces* LENYA *and says, "She did it! She did it!" then turns to* LEON)

DOCTOR   Wasn't that a beautiful sit?

LEON   Yes. Very nice. Lovely. (*To* SOPHIA) Miss Zubritsky—may I call you Sophia?

SOPHIA   Sophia?

DOCTOR   It's your name, sweetheart.

LENYA   Say "Yes," darling. Say, "Yes, you may call me Sophia."

LEON   Please, madame. We must allow the girl to speak for herself. (*To* SOPHIA) I should like very much to be your friend. Would it please you if I called you Sophia? (SOPHIA *looks puzzled*)

DOCTOR   It's been so long since she's taken a test.

LEON   I think she wants to say something.

SOPHIA   I—I would be very pleased to have you call me Sophia.

DOCTOR   There you are!

LENYA   I'm so proud. So proud!

LEON   Please. It's very distracting to the girl's concentration. (*To* SOPHIA) I've come a very long way to help you with your education. I have every reason to believe that under ordinary circumstances, you have the capability of being an extremely bright and intelligent young woman, that deep inside you somewhere is an intellect just crying to be heard, that you have enormous powers of reason. But someone has put a cloud over these powers and it is my intention to remove this cloud so that enlightenment can once more shine through those unbelievably crystal-clear blue eyes once again . . . But I need your help, Sophia. Will you give me that help?

SOPHIA   Yes. You may call me Sophia.

DOCTOR   She did it again. That's two in a row.

LEON (*Aside*)   Get a grip, Leon. Nothing in life comes easy . . . (*To* SOPHIA) I should like to ask you a few very simple questions. If we are to begin your education, it is important that I know at what point to begin. It won't be taxing, I promise you. I would never want to be the cause of a furrow or frown on that fair face . . . Now, then—what is your favorite color?

SOPHIA   My favorite color?

LEON Yes, is it red or blue or green or orange? Any color at all. Which one is your favorite?

DOCTOR I used to know that one.

LEON I'll ask you once again, Sophia. What-is-your-fa-vorite-color?

LENYA Why is he being so hard on her? This isn't a university.

SOPHIA My favorite color—

LEON Yes?

SOPHIA —is yellow.

LEON Yellow! Her favorite color is yellow! Why, Sophia? Why is yellow your favorite color?

SOPHIA Because it doesn't stick to your fingers as much.

LENYA (*Aside, to the* DOCTOR) I think she's wrong. I think it's blue that doesn't stick to your fingers as much.

LEON That's a very interesting answer, Sophia. There is a certain logic to her response. The fact that that logic escapes me completely doesn't alter the fact that she has something in mind. Sophia, I'm going to ask you something quite simple now. I'm going to ask you to make a wish. Do you know what a wish is?

SOPHIA Yes. A wish is something you hope for that doesn't come true.

LEON Well, perhaps we can change all that. If you could make a wish that did come true, anything at all, what would you wish for?

SOPHIA What would I wish for?

LEON Yes, Sophia, what would you wish for?

SOPHIA   I would wish that I could fly like a bird . . . to soar over buildings and trees . . . to float on the wind and be carried far away . . . over mountains and lakes . . . over forests and rivers . . . to meet people in other villages . . . to see what the world was like . . . to know all the things that I shall never know because I must always remain here in this place.

LEON   Sophia, that is the most beautiful wish I have ever heard. (*To the* ZUBRITSKYS) Don't you see what her wish means? To fly like a bird means to sever the bonds that chain her to ignorance. She wants to soar, to grow, she wants knowledge! And with every fiber of my being, from the very depths of my soul, I shall gather all my strength and patience and dedication, and I make this promise that I, Leon Steponovitch Tolchinsky, shall make Sophia Zubritsky's wish come true.

SOPHIA   If you could do that, schoolmaster, I would be in your debt—forever.

LEON   She touches me so. Your daughter has such a sweet soul and such a pure heart. We must begin as soon as possible. Not another moment must be lost. I shall return in the morning at eight o'clock sharp. (*To* SOPHIA) What subject shall we begin our studies with, Sophia?

SOPHIA   I should like to begin with—languages.

LEON   Languages! Of course! Even I should have thought of that. Languages it shall be, my dear, sweet Sophia . . . And what language shall we begin with first?

SOPHIA (*Thinks*)   Rabbit, I think.

LEON   *Rabbit?*

DOCTOR   A very hard language, rabbit. Hardly anyone speaks it anymore.

LENYA   As long as she gets a few phrases, it's enough to begin with.

SOPHIA   Am I through for today?

LEON   Yes.

SOPHIA   Then I shall go to my room.

LENYA   Watch how she gets up from the chair. Watch! You didn't see it. Sophia, do it again.

LEON   It's not necessary. She's already past getting up from chairs.

DOCTOR   They're so much smarter than in our day.

SOPHIA   Until tomorrow, schoolmaster.

LEON   In all my life, I have never looked forward to a morning as much as tomorrow's.

SOPHIA   I think you are the most beautiful schoolteacher I have ever seen, Master Tolchinsky. I pray that you don't despair of Kulyenchikov . . . and that you will stay with us forever.
   (*She leaves*)

LENYA   She found the door! She found the door!

DOCTOR   I've never seen Sophia so radiant . . . Lenya, are you thinking what *I'm* thinking?

LENYA   I'm not even thinking what *I'm* thinking. What are you talking about?

DOCTOR   I think our Sophia has taken a liking to the new schoolmaster.

LEON   If it is true, Dr. Zubritsky, then standing before you is the happiest man on the happiest planet in the universe. Tell me, is she spoken for?

DOCTOR   Spoken for?

LEON   Does she have any suitors? Any young men desperately in love with her?

DOCTOR   We—we don't talk of such things.

LEON   Why not?

DOCTOR   There is no one. No one at all. Not even *him.*

LEON   *Him?*

LENYA   He didn't mean him. He meant someone else who isn't him.

LEON   There is someone. Who is it? I must know. It's of the greatest concern to me.

DOCTOR   If I told you who him was, you must promise never to say it was I who told you it was him.

LEON   I promise.

DOCTOR   Have you ever heard of . . . Count Gregor of Kulyenchikov?

LEON   I can't say that I have.

DOCTOR   You can't say that? It's not that hard. Even Lenya can say that.

LENYA   Count Gregor of Kul—

LEON   (*Annoyed*)   Yes! Yes! I can say it. Who is he?

LENYA   He's—he's one of them. The ones who put the purse on us.

LEON   You mean—a Yousekevitch?

DOCTOR   The last of his line.

LEON Tell me about him and Sophia.

DOCTOR He proposes marriage twice a day.

LEON Twice a day?

LENYA Six-fifteen in the mornings, seven-twenty at nights.

LEON He cares for her that much?

DOCTOR He cares only about avenging his ancestors. If a Zubritsky marries a Yousekevitch, they will be satisfied and the nurse will be over.

LEON Does Sophia care for him?

DOCTOR She has said no for many years, but she can't resist much longer. The poor girl wants to sleep late just one morning.

LEON What kind of a man is this Count Yousekevitch?

LENYA You know . . . like the rest of us.

LEON You mean he is cursed as well?

DOCTOR He still lives in Kulyenchikov. He's not permitted to leave here either.

LEON I understand. If I have a rival, I am more determined than ever to break this curse. God bless you both for your faith in me. Tomorrow the education of Sophia Zubritsky begins. In all my excitement, I forgot to ask. What about lodgings?

DOCTOR Oh, don't worry about it. We'll be very comfortable right here.

LEON Of course. I'll see you in the morning.

LENYA Master Tolchinsky! Please! Ask us again! Ask us the question. It makes us feel . . . important.

LEON   Yes, certainly. What is the purpose of man's existence?

LENYA   I'm all choked up again. I'm sorry I asked.

DOCTOR   One moment! I—I think I know. I think I know the answer.

LEON   To the purpose of man's existence?

LENYA   What are you talking about?

DOCTOR   It's true. The first time I heard it I didn't understand. But now, suddenly something came to me. I know my limitations, but still, I think I really know the answer . . . Oh, my God, what if I'm right?

LEON (*Excitedly*)   Tell me, Dr. Zubritsky. Tell me what you think the answer is.

DOCTOR   I think—it's *twelve!*

LEON   *Twelve?*

DOCTOR   It's wrong; I can tell by your face. Fourteen?

LEON   I think you missed the point.

DOCTOR   It's less than a hundred, I know that. Even *I'm* not that stupid. Eighty-three . . . forty-six.

LEON (*Moving on*)   We'll discuss it when we get to philosophy. Don't think about it. Get some sleep. Good night. Until tomorrow. (*He walks out to the street and screams*) TWELVE?

LENYA   Why didn't you leave well enough alone? Why must you have answers? Aren't questions beautiful enough?

LEON (*In the street*)   *TWELVE!*

DOCTOR   But what if I am right? I could have sold the answer. We could have made a fortune.
(*They leave . . . the set goes off.* LEON *reappears*)

LEON (*To the audience*)   That's it. I'm leaving now, so I'll say goodbye. I *was* going to stay and try to break the curse, but when he said "Twelve," I knew it was time to go . . . What I must do now is try to forget Sophia. I must!

SOPHIA'S VOICE   Schoolmaster!

LEON   Sophia? Where are you?
(*She appears on the balcony*)

SOPHIA   Down here. I had to see you once more.

LEON   Without a wrap? In the cold night air, you'll come down with a chill.

SOPHIA   Oh, I never catch colds.

LEON   You don't?

SOPHIA   I've tried. I've just never learned how to do it.

LEON   Be grateful . . . Some things are not worth knowing.

SOPHIA   I know that something has happened a long time ago that prevents me from knowing what happened a long time ago. If only you knew me the way I might have been instead of the way I am.

LEON   But if you were not the way you are, then I would not have come here to help you to become the way you might have been. (*Aside, quickly*) Careful! You're beginning to think like her.

SOPHIA   Could you—could you ever care for someone who never became the way I might have been?

LEON Could I ever care for someone who never became—I see what you mean. I see what you're getting
at. Yes. Yes, I could. I would. I shall. I will. I have. I
do.

SOPHIA Is that rabbit you're speaking? It's hard to follow.

LEON If it sounds like gibberish it's because you do that
to me, Sophia. When thoughts come from the heart
they sometimes trip over the tongue.

SOPHIA Then I must watch where I walk when you
speak . . . I must go. Everything depends upon tomorrow.

LEON And if not tomorrow, then the tomorrow after
tomorrow. And all the tomorrows for the rest of my
life, if that's what it takes.

SOPHIA No. It all rests on tomorrow. If we fail, we shall
never see each other again.

LEON Never see each other? What do you mean?

SOPHIA I never know what I mean. I do have thoughts
but they seem to disappear when they reach my lips.

LEON If I ever reached your lips, I would never disappear.

SOPHIA Would you like to kiss me?

LEON With all my heart.

SOPHIA No. I meant with your lips.

LEON An even better suggestion.

SOPHIA Hurry. Hurry.
            (*He climbs up to the balcony*)

LEON   I'm climbing as fast as I can.
  (*She disappears*)

LEON (*Arrives on the balcony*)   Where are you?

SOPHIA (*Appears below*)   Up here.

LEON (*To the audience*)   If only she were ugly, I'd be
  halfway home by now. (*To* SOPHIA) Stay where you
  are. I'll come to you.

SOPHIA   All right.
  (*But he doesn't move*)

LEON (*To the audience*)   After a while you get the hang
  of it.

SOPHIA (*Reappears on the balcony*)   Here I am.

LEON   My kiss, sweet Sophia.
  (*They kiss*)

SOPHIA   As we kissed I felt a strange flutter in my heart.

LEON   So did I.

SOPHIA   You felt a flutter in my heart as well? How alike
  we are. And yet your hair is so much shorter . . . I must
  go. I'm about to fall asleep and I want to get to bed in
  time.
  (*She leaves*)

LEON (*To the audience*)   I know the dangers of loving
  such a simple soul. It would mean a lifetime of sweet,
  blissful passion—and very short conversations at breakfast. (*There is a clap of thunder*) I'd best find some comfortable lodgings.
  (*He descends. There is another clap of thunder*)

SNETSKY (*Running onstage*)   Was that you?

LEON   I beg your pardon?

SNETSKY   Were you responsible for making that dreadful noise?

LEON   Of course not. That was thunder and lightning. It's caused by extreme atmospheric pressures in the skies above us.

SNETSKY   Well, whoever did it is going to get Count Yousekevitch very angry at us.

LEON   Count Yousekevitch?

SNETSKY   He's the one who lives in the big house on top of the hill. Every time he hears someone make that noise, he throws water down on us.

LEON   No, no, Snetsky, that's rain. Rain!
   (YENCHNA *appears*)

YENCHNA   Umbrellas! Umbrellas for sale! Get your umbrellas before he throws the water.

LEON   Yenchna, no one throws water. It's rain from the skies caused by a buildup of condensed moisture.

YENCHNA   You can tell that to these fools, but I used to be a substitute teacher . . . Umbrellas!

LEON   Excuse me, but would either one of you know of a place to stay?
(SLOVITCH *appears with* MISHKIN)

SLOVITCH   What's going on? What's all the racket?

MISHKIN   I knew it. I knew he would throw water down on us today. Every time I wash my cow, you know he's going to throw water.

LEON   Mishkin, would you happen to know—
(*Prelude chimes, which precede the actual ringing of the steeple bell*)

SLOVITCH   Oh-oh. It's time for Count Yousekevitch to propose again.

MISHKIN   This could be the day. One yes from her and we could all be smart again.

LEON   You mean you want Sophia to marry him?

SNETSKY   Not unless she wanted to. But it would be nice to remember my first name.

LEON   But that's a terrible sacrifice to ask of Sophia. Surely you wouldn't ask that of her.

YENCHNA   What kind of sacrifice? To live in a big house up on the hill . . . To have little macaroons whenever you want . . . To have a maid brush your teeth in the morning . . .

LEON   But does she love him?

SNETSKY   I beg your pardon?

LEON   Does she love him?

SLOVITCH   We don't have any.

LEON   You don't have any what?

SLOVITCH   Love! It's part of the curse.

LEON   I don't understand.

MISHKIN   I hear him coming. You'd better leave, school-master. He doesn't like people around.
(SLOVITCH, MISHKIN, *and* SNETSKY *leave*)

LEON   Yenchna! Is it true there is no love in Kulyen-chikov?

YENCHNA   I wouldn't know. My late husband's been gone almost fourteen years.

LEON   I'm sorry.

YENCHNA   That's a long time to be late. I wish he was dead.
(*She leaves*)

LEON   I'm breaking out in a cold sweat. The possibility of losing Sophia terrifies me ... I'm going to eavesdrop.
(*He hides behind a tree*)

GREGOR (*Offstage*)   Sophia! (*Strumming a balalaika,* GRE-GOR YOUSEKEVITCH *appears*) Sweet Sophia! Time to wake up, my pretty one . . . time to get proposed to. She's asleep! Perhaps a pebble will awaken her.
(*He picks up a pebble and tosses it up to the balcony. We hear a crash of glass.* DR. ZUBRITSKY *appears in a nightshirt, holding a candle*)

DOCTOR   Who did that?

GREGOR   It is I, Count Yousekevitch.

DOCTOR   Good evening, sir.
(*He bows and knocks his head on the railing*)

GREGOR   I've come to propose.

DOCTOR   Well, you're a little late. I'm married almost twenty-six years.

LENYA (*Offstage*) Nikolai! Nikolai!

DOCTOR I'm out here, Lenya. What did you want?
(LENYA *appears*)

LENYA Some bandages. My feet are bleeding . . . Who
are you talking to?

GREGOR It is I, Madame Zubritsky. Count Yousekevitch. I've come to propose to Sophia.

LENYA She's busy throwing water on the drapes.
They're on fire.

DOCTOR The drapes are on fire?

LENYA I had to light something . . . I couldn't find my
candle.
(SOPHIA *comes out*)

SOPHIA Papa, what's going on?

DOCTOR Did we wake you, darling?

SOPHIA No. I was reading by the light of the drapes.

GREGOR I must be crazy marrying into this family.

DOCTOR Count Yousekevitch wants to propose to you,
darling. Go ahead, Count Yousekevitch.

GREGOR Can't we be alone?

DOCTOR No. No. I think Sophia should hear this, too.

GREGOR Very well. Will you marry me, Sophia?

LENYA Oh, my God, this is so romantic. I just wish my
feet weren't bleeding.

SOPHIA I'm sorry, Count Yousekevitch, but marriage is
a very great step to take and I don't wish to make it

while I do not have the intelligence to know what I am stepping into. Good night, sir. Good night, Mama, good night, Papa.

LENYA   Good night, son. When you're through reading, darling, put out the drapes.

GREGOR   I do not give up easily. I'll be back in the morning.

DOCTOR   Good night, your grace.

LENYA   Good night, Grace.
        (*They bow low*)

DOCTOR   Watch what you're doing, you're burning my mustache.

GREGOR   (*Aside*)   Having them for in-laws is a curse worse than the curse.

LEON   Pray God it never happens.

GREGOR   Who's that? Who's there? Come out, I say!

LEON   Forgive me, sir. I was just passing by. May I introduce myself. I am—

GREGOR   I know who you are. You're the new schoolmaster who has come here in a pathetic attempt to break the curse of Kulyenchikov.

LEON   As I have just witnessed your pathetic attempt to win Sophia.

GREGOR   Everyone's a critic. The curse can only be broken if you can educate her, which you can't . . . or if she marries me.

LEON   Which apparently she won't. Why don't you pursue some other girl?

GREGOR   Because Sophia is beautiful. Did you ever see the other girls in the village? They look like me!

LEON   For a man so powerful, you seem to have an inordinate lack of self-esteem. I am sorry for you. Good day, sir.

GREGOR   Not *good* day. *One* day.

LEON   I beg your pardon?

GREGOR   Were you not aware that if at the end of one brief day you have not succeeded to raise her intellect you must be gone from our village? To remain for even one second past the allotted time means you will fall victim to the curse yourself. (*To the audience*) I love that part.

LEON   I cannot believe such nonsense. Threaten me all you want, sir, but I will never leave. To be quite honest, I love Sophia Zubritsky.

GREGOR   Love??? There is no love in Kulyenchikov. It's all part of the curse.

LEON   You mean Sophia cannot love me?

GREGOR   You have one day to find that out, sir. One single day. Twenty-five measly hours.

LEON   Twenty-four.

GREGOR   What?

LEON   There are twenty-four hours in a day.

GREGOR   I believe you are thinking of February, sir. Good night.

LEON   But is it true? If I cannot teach Sophia to think in twenty-four hours, she will never be able to love me?
(SOPHIA *appears on the balcony*)

SOPHIA Leon!

LEON Sophia! Are you all right?

SOPHIA I must talk to you. Someplace where we'll not be seen.

LEON Wherever you say.

SOPHIA Can you meet me here?

LEON Yes. When?

SOPHIA Now!

LEON Now? Yes. Of course. That's where I am.

SOPHIA Come up here. Hurry, Leon, hurry. It's of the utmost importance. I overheard your conversation with the Count. (*He climbs up to the balcony*) Leon, I cannot be taught. You must leave Kulyenchikov at once.

LEON Never without you.

SOPHIA Then take me with you. Tonight.

LEON But the curse—

SOPHIA It cannot be broken. But we can live in the swamp and eat brown roots and I will become old and ugly and more stupid and more ignorant and never love you but at least we'll be together.

LEON Well, that wasn't exactly what I had in mind.

SOPHIA Then we are lost.

LEON No, no, Sophia. I will teach you. I will break this curse. Tomorrow, I promise you.

SOPHIA Oh, Leon, I wish I could love you.

LEON You will, Sophia. Tomorrow. I promise.

SOPHIA Until tomorrow.
      (*She goes inside. He climbs down*)

LEON   I wish she'd sleep in the kitchen.
(SOPHIA *reappears*)

SOPHIA   Leon! Come back! Hurry, hurry.
(*He climbs back up*)

LEON   What is it?

SOPHIA   I couldn't sleep. I'm so frightened.

LEON   Don't be frightened, Sophia.

SOPHIA   If I could know the feeling of loving you for just
one day, I would endure a hundred thousand years of
curses . . . Good night, Leon. God bless you and keep
you.
(*She leaves*)

LEON (*To the audience*)   She asks not to *be* loved but to
know what it means to give her love to another. I think
I have wandered into a very special place. I love Yenchna, I love Snetsky and Mishkin, and yes, even Count
Yousekevitch. *All* of them. God give me the strength
to break this curse—and to get up and down this balcony. (*He gets down*) By the way, I urge you to give
the matter some thought yourselves. I have no wish to
alarm you, but you are, after all, sitting within the
bounds of Kulyenchikov. Therefore, I wish us both the
best of luck.
(*He starts to leave*)

SOPHIA (*Reappears on the balcony*)   Leon! I forgot to tell
you something!

LEON (*Gasping*)   Tomorrow, Sophia! I can't *take* any
more news tonight!
(*He walks off, clutching his chest*)

Curtain

Act Two

SCENE I

The town square, early next morning. A rooster crows. SNETSKY *appears and yawns in unison with the crowing.* SLOVITCH *comes out of his shop.*

SNETSKY   Slovitch, any news?

SLOVITCH   About what?

SNETSKY   About what? About the curse, of course. Has it been lifted yet?

SLOVITCH   How would I know?

SNETSKY   Let's see if there's anything in the newspaper.

SLOVITCH   Good idea. It rained during the night.

SNETSKY   Where does it say that?

SLOVITCH   I can feel it. The paper's all damp.

SNETSKY   Maybe your dog did that.

SLOVITCH   No, no. He's housebroken. He only does it inside. (YENCHNA *appears, pulling a cow that is upside down*) What's wrong with your cow?

YENCHNA   He's tired. I've been milking him since four o'clock.

SLOVITCH   Upside down?

YENCHNA   You get a little more cream that way! (*She starts to leave*) Cream! Fresh cream right from the top.

Drink it right from the spigot, two kopecks a mouthful! Fresh cream . . . right from the udder.

(*She is gone. We move to the* DOCTOR's *house. He and* LENYA *appear, carrying lit candles*)

DOCTOR   Come. Let us pray, Lenya. Pray for deliverance. Dear Lord, who art in heaven. We art in Kulyenchikov, and we art in trouble.

(*They are on their knees in front of the sofa*)

LENYA   We art a simple people, dear Lord.

DOCTOR   But we're not so simple that we don't believe in you.

LENYA   Forgive us our sins, dear Lord.

DOCTOR   We know not what we do because we know not what we do.

BOTH   God bless us, God bless our daughter, God bless the schoolmaster, and God bless yourself, whoever you are. Amen.

(*There is a knock*)

DOCTOR   Was that the door?

LENYA   No, I think it was someone knocking.

DOCTOR   Well, open it, open it! It must be the schoolmaster. (*He calls out*) Sophia! It's time. Wake up! Give yourself a nudge. (*To* LENYA, *as* LENYA *pushes against the door*) The other way! The other way!

(LEON *enters, breathless*)

LEON   Do you know what time it is?

DOCTOR   Ten to six?

LENYA   Eight-fifteen?

DOCTOR   A quarter to nine?

LENYA   We don't have a clock.

DOCTOR   Pick any one you want. Ten-twenty, eleven-forty. Is there something in there you like?

LEON   You don't understand. The Count said I had only twenty-four hours to break the curse after I arrived in Kulyenchikov. I arrived yesterday morning at exactly nine o'clock. It's eight o'clock now. That means I have only one hour. It doesn't even *leave* me one hour. I've just used up an entire minute telling you how much time I haven't got left . . . Dear God, help me. Help me, dear Lord.

DOCTOR   What a shame. You just missed him. We finished services two minutes ago.

LEON   Get Sophia! We can't lose another moment. Hurry, I beg of you.
      (*We hear footsteps*)

DOCTOR   Listen! I hear footsteps coming down the stairs.
      (SOPHIA *rushes in*)

SOPHIA   Good morning, Mama. Good morning, Papa. Good morning, schoolmaster.

DOCTOR   She got all three right! This is going to be her day, I know it!

LEON   And looking more radiant than ever.

LENYA   Where shall we sit?

LEON   Doctor, with all due respect, I need Sophia's full concentration this morning. I must ask the parents to leave the room.

DOCTOR   By all means. We'll see that you're not disturbed. Goodbye, Sophia.
      (LENYA *and the* DOCTOR *walk over to the door*)

LENYA   Goodbye, my little angel.

DOCTOR   Do as the schoolmaster tells you.

LENYA   We'll be praying for you every minute.

DOCTOR   If you succeed, schoolmaster, give us the signal by rapping on the window three times, followed by two short ones—

LENYA   —followed by six long ones.

DOCTOR   If you fail, rap seven times quickly—

LENYA   —followed by three times slowly.

DOCTOR   If you want lunch—

LEON   *Will you please leave!*
       (*He gently pushes them out*)

BOTH   We're going! We're going!
       (*They are on the other side of the closed door*)

LENYA   Something's not right, I can feel it in my bones.

DOCTOR   He can hear you. Lower your voice.
       (LENYA *bends her knees, lowering herself*)

LENYA   I'm a mother. I know about these things. Why do you look taller to me lately?
       (*They exit*)

LEON   Sophia . . . Last night I decided that the task before us is one step beyond impossible. I knew I would fail and that I had to leave Kulyenchikov, like all those who have failed before me . . . but today, looking into your eyes, I know there is no life for me without you. Therefore, we must not think of failure, we cannot afford to despair. Only a miracle can save us, Sophia, but with a majestic, supreme effort, we must try to make that miracle happen.

SOPHIA   What is a miracle?

LEON   A miracle is a wish that God makes. You are a miracle, Sophia.

SOPHIA   You mean God wished for me?

LEON   In one of his most sublime moments . . . We must hurry, Sophia. (*He picks up a book*) This is a primary book of mathematics. It's used to teach very small children very simple problems in arithmetic.

SOPHIA   Do you think it's too advanced for me?

LEON   I don't think so, Sophia. We can't go back any further than this book. Now, let us begin . . . (*He opens the book to the first page. A large number one fills up the page*) One is the figure, the word, the symbol for a single item. One finger, one Sophia, one Leon, one book . . . Now then, I am holding up one finger, Sophia. Now I am holding up a second finger. One plus one is two. Would you repeat that for me, Sophia.

SOPHIA   Which part?

LEON   One—

SOPHIA   One.

LEON   Plus one—

SOPHIA   Plus one.

LEON   Is two!

SOPHIA   Is two!

LEON   Yes! Yes! Yes! Wonderful. We're making headway. Slow, invisible headway. . . . I'm very, very proud of you, Sophia. Are we ready to go on?

SOPHIA   Yes. History, please. I hope I can master it as well as I have mathematics.

LEON Well, I honestly don't think we've conquered mathematics yet. There are problems that could come up. Let's continue. One plus two is three.

SOPHIA Am I finished with one plus one?

LEON You are if you remember the answer.

SOPHIA I remembered it before. Is it necessary to remember it again?

LEON Of course it's necessary to remember it again. It's necessary to remember it for *always.*

SOPHIA You mean you will always be asking me what one plus one is?

LEON No! Once you tell me, we can move on to other things. Like one plus two and one plus three, and so on. But if you can't remember what one plus one is, then the answer to one plus two is meaningless.

SOPHIA Do you know how much one plus one is?

LEON Certainly.

SOPHIA Then why is it necessary for me to know? Certainly, if you have such esteem and affection for me, you will tell me the answer whenever I ask you.

LEON But I won't always be around to tell you. You have to know for yourself. In case other people ask you.

SOPHIA No one here ever asks questions like that. Even if I told them, they wouldn't know if it was the right answer.

LEON Because they are cursed with ignorance. And we are trying to lift that debilitating affliction.

SOPHIA You're getting angry with me. What's the point of being educated if you get angry? When you didn't ask me such questions, you always said the loveliest things to me. Is this what it's like to be intelligent?

LEON   No, Sophia. It is I who am not being intelligent. It's frustration and impatience that drives me to such crude behavior. Forgive me. We'll start from the beginning again. One plus one is two. Repeat.

SOPHIA   One plus one is two. Repeat.

LEON   *No!!* Don't repeat the word "repeat." Just repeat the part before I say "repeat" . . . Now watch me carefully: One plus one is two. *Repeat!!*

SOPHIA   What were you like as a little boy?

LEON *(Angrily)*   What was I like as a little boy?

SOPHIA   You're shouting again.

LEON *(Tries to placate her)*   I was inquisitive. Probing. Wondering why we were put on this earth and what the purpose of man's existence was.

SOPHIA   The purpose of man's existence . . . !

LEON *(Shouts)*   *I've had enough of that.* Sophia, you must stop asking me questions. Our time is nearly gone.

SOPHIA   Then how am I to learn?

LEON   Sophia, you must answer what I ask, not what you want me to answer.

SOPHIA   Then I will learn only what *you* want me to know. Why can't I learn what I want to know?

LEON   Because what you want to know is of no practical value. What I want to teach is acceptable knowledge.

SOPHIA   Is knowing what you were like as a little boy not acceptable knowledge?

LEON   Of course not. It's of no significance at all.

SOPHIA   But it's much more interesting than that which is significant.

LEON   But I'm not trying to interest you. I'm trying to educate you.

SOPHIA   I know. But while you fail to educate me, you never fail to interest me. I find that very significant.

LEON   There is nothing like the logic of an illogical mind! Let's try one more time.
(*The* DOCTOR *and* LENYA *appear outside.* LENYA *peers through the transom*)

DOCTOR   She must be speaking rabbit like a bunny by now.
(SLOVITCH *comes out of his shop*)

SLOVITCH   How much longer is this going to take? I haven't sold a sausage all morning.
(MISHKIN *appears*)

MISHKIN   Good morning, Dr. Zubritsky.

DOCTOR (*To* LENYA)   What's going on?
(LEON *is on the floor banging his head in dismay*)

LENYA   I think he's teaching her gymnastics.

MISHKIN   Dr. Zubritsky, I have an urgent letter for schoolmaster Tolchinsky.

DOCTOR   Quiet, please. This is a school zone.
(YENCHNA *and* SNETSKY *appear*)

MISHKIN   I have an important letter for him. It's marked urgent, so I only went to three wrong houses first.

DOCTOR   Can't you see he's busy? Bring it back later.

LENYA   I don't like the way it's going. I just don't like the way it's going.

DOCTOR   Let us pray. Let us all pray to the Lord that this young man will deliver us from bondage. Let us ask for his blessing. Very religious on this side, semireligious on the other . . . (LEON *comes out*) Quiet! Quiet, everyone! The schoolmaster wants to speak . . . Please, God, let this be the answer to our prayers.

SNETSKY   Ah-men!

LENYA and YENCHNA   Ah women!

DOCTOR (*To* LEON)   Is my daughter—you know—empty or full?

LEON   She is the same as always. I have only moments and I must ask this quickly, because I may not have the intelligence to ask this later. Because of my deep and unbounded devotion for your daughter, Sophia, I would like to ask for her hand in marriage. I ask this of you now while I still love her. In a few minutes I may not know the meaning of the word. When the clock in the church steeple strikes nine, I hope you will have an answer for me.
    (*He goes back inside*)

DOCTOR   He's a nice young man. I'll say that. Very ambitious. Lenya, what do you think?

LENYA   If the man can't break a simple curse, how's he going to put bread on the table?

MISHKIN   And what about Tremble?

DOCTOR   Who?

MISHKIN   Tremble Tremble. You know, up on the hill. The one who throws the water.

SNETSKY   Mishkin's right. It's his curse. He would never permit such a marriage.

MISHKIN   Wait! There is one chance. If a stranger marries a Kulyenchikovite before he becomes like us, then he is free to take her away from here.

DOCTOR   I didn't know that.

MISHKIN   It was added to the curse two years ago . . . to make it more exciting.

SLOVITCH   You would never see your daughter again, but you would know she was happy and getting smarter every day.

SNETSKY   Oh, give it, Doctor. Give her your permission.

YENCHNA   If you don't give it to her, give it to me.

DOCTOR   I don't know. It's a decision, and I can't make decisions. Let's leave it to God. Let God make the decision.
(*They get on their knees and pray*)

SOPHIA   What are you doing, Leon?
(LEON *sits, musing*)

LEON   Having my last thoughts. One final pleasurable moment of reason.

SOPHIA   Then I was right. A wish is something you hope for that doesn't come true.

LEON   I'm sorry. I cannot help you soar over mountains and lakes, Sophia. But I will not leave you. I will remain here for the rest of my days, not basking in the light of your beauty but cowering in the darkness of my own ignorance . . . for that is the measure of my esteem and affection for you.

SOPHIA   I would do anything to save you from this calamity . . . anything! (*Prelude chimes*) Oh, run, Leon. Run for your life. There are ignorant girls in other villages you could learn to love.

LEON Listen to me carefully and remember it forever. I love you with all my heart.
(*The bells begin*)

SNETSKY Listen! The church bell!

LEON I may never say these words again.
(*Bell*)

SLOVITCH The time is up!

LEON Savor it, Sophia. Keep the memory of what I say.
(*Bell*)

YENCHNA Her last chance to marry. I know the feeling.

LEON The way I gaze lovingly into your eyes as I do now.

LENYA Say it, husband. Give them permission to marry. Quickly.
(*Bell*)

LEON All the love I would have given you in a lifetime must be compressed into a final instant.
(*Bell*)

DOCTOR Yes. I'll give it. I'll go in there and give my permission right now.

LEON Goodbye, sweet Sophia. I did not love you long, but I loved you well.
(*Bell*)

DOCTOR I'll just wait to see what time it is first.

LEON Tell everyone in Kulyenchikov that I—
(*Bell.* LEON *freezes, a dumb look on his face*)

MAGISTRATE (*On the balcony*) Nine o'clock and all's well!
(*They all rush into the house*)

DOCTOR   Wonderful news, Master Tolchinsky!

SOPHIA   Mama! Papa! Everyone! The schoolmaster has something to say. Let us all listen . . . Leon, didn't you want to say something?

LEON   (*Bewildered, befuddled*)   Yes, but you said we should all listen.
  (*The* MAGISTRATE *has joined them*)

YENCHNA   Oh, oh!

SNETSKY   He's got a look on his face I've seen before.

SLOVITCH   It's the same one you've got on your face.

SOPHIA   (*To* LEON)   No, I meant that we will all listen while you tell us what you have to say.

LEON   Oh! I see . . . Thank you . . . Actually, I don't have much to say.

SNETSKY   There's no fool like a new fool.

DOCTOR   Young man, do you still want to marry my daughter?

LEON   Marry your daughter? Oh, no, sir, you do me too great an honor.

YENCHNA   I knew he'd never make it when he bought the whitefish from me.

MAGISTRATE   All right, move along. Break it up, you've all seen a ninny-poop before. Let's keep it moving. Come on.
  (YENCHNA, *the* MAGISTRATE, SNETSKY, *and* SLOVITCH *leave*)

MISHKIN   (*To* LEON)   If you ever want this urgent letter, let me know. Not that anything in your life is urgent anymore.
  (*He puts the letter back in his pouch and leaves*)

LENYA Sophia, darling, go in the garden and plant some vegetables. We'll have salad tonight for dinner.
(*She leaves*)

DOCTOR So, young man—what are your plans now that everything has fallen apart at the top?

LEON I'm not sure. This absence of thought will take some getting used to.

DOCTOR Well, you might try politics. You sound very well suited for it.

LEON Oh, this is an old suit. If I went into politics I would need all new clothes.

DOCTOR This is really just one doctor's opinion, but when you catch a curse you really catch a curse. (*To* SOPHIA) Don't stay up too long. I want you to go up on the roof later and take the canary for a walk.
(*He leaves*)

LEON I'm sorry, Sophia. Weren't we in the middle of a lesson when the clock began to chime? What were we saying?

SOPHIA You said that you loved me and that I should savor it and keep it as a memory because soon you would not love me ever again. Do you not love me now, Leon?

LEON Love you? I'm not quite sure I know what the word means. Perhaps if you kissed me. Would you like to?

SOPHIA With all my heart.

LEON No, I meant—

SOPHIA I know what you meant. (*They kiss, warmly*) Oh, Leon! The less you know, the better you kiss!

LEON   And the better I kiss, the more brilliant I become!
Oh, my dear sweet Sophia, look at me! Look at me and
tell me what you see!
(*He has jumped up on the* DOCTOR'*s sofa*)

SOPHIA   I see a very good kisser dirtying my father's sofa.

LEON   No, Sophia. You see a man of intellect inspired by
love. I am not cursed, Sophia. I still have my intelligence. I only pretended to be stupid.

SOPHIA   You pretended to be stupid?

LEON   Yes.

SOPHIA   That doesn't sound very intelligent to me.

LEON   It will soon, I promise.

SOPHIA   But the curse . . .

LEON   It had no effect on me. Oh, I was plenty worried,
I admit. Especially when the clock struck nine. But
when nothing happened, I suddenly realized—you
can't be cursed unless you *permit* yourself to be. Kulyenchikov's lack of intelligence is self-inflicted, caused
by fear and guilt and the relinquishing of your own
self-esteem to a tyrannical power. Do you understand
what I'm saying?

SOPHIA   Everything but the explanation.

LEON   If a parent tells you you are a naughty child from
the day you were born, you will grow up believing you
are a worthless human being. And from the day *you*
were born, you were told you were all stupid. Now do
you understand?

SOPHIA   Not as well as before.

LEON   I know that telling it doesn't change it. You must
be shown. When I was standing there, I suddenly be-

came inspired. I hit upon a plan that will break this curse and save you from Yousekevitch.

SOPHIA   What is it?

LEON   You must marry Yousekevitch.

SOPHIA   Are you still pretending to be stupid?

LEON   No, Sophia. I don't mean Count Gregor.

SOPHIA   Oh, thank goodness. You had me frightened half to death.

LEON   You will marry me, Sophia. I will be Yousekevitch. Do you understand?

SOPHIA   Don't ask me that question anymore.

LEON   Trust me, Sophia. The wedding will take place tomorrow. Tomorrow the curse will be over. Tomorrow you will be intelligent. Tomorrow you will love me, Sophia.

SOPHIA   Could I have a kiss just to tide me over?

LEON   Of course, my sweet. I must go set my plan in action.

SOPHIA   I'm so excited, Leon. Tonight I will clear all the nonsense out of my head to prepare for all the knowledge that will be coming in. I love rearranging things.
        (*She leaves*)

LEON (*To the audience*)   The plan begins. I must find Count Yousekevitch.
        (*He leaves.* YOUSEKEVITCH *appears, and addresses the audience*)

GREGOR   Was he just talking about me? You like him, don't you? Better than me, right? Admit it . . . I would give up all my wealth and powers if I could be the hero.

I wouldn't have to wear this dumb outfit . . . people would applaud when I come on. You're not even listening to me, are you? All you care about is getting those two kids together . . . I hope it's raining when you leave here.

(*He starts to leave.* LEON *rushes onstage*)

LEON   Oh, good day, Count Yousekevitch. You remember me? Something Something Tolchinsky.

GREGOR (*To the audience*)   Listen to this conversation. What is it, Something?

LEON   I couldn't help overhearing what you just said. I want you to know that even though I've lost most of my intelligence—

GREGOR   —all of it.

LEON   —all of it—I am not without some feelings. It pains me to know that being disliked makes you so unhappy.

GREGOR   Oh. That's easy for you to say. You don't like me either, do you?

LEON   Well, I don't dislike you.

GREGOR   But do you like me?

LEON   No. Not much.

GREGOR   You see!

LEON   Because you never do anything redeeming. Why not?

GREGOR   I don't know. I was brought up that way, I guess. My father taught me since I was a little boy, if you want to hold your power over these people, you must never be nice to them. Always make them fear and tremble.

LEON   Did you like your father?

GREGOR   Oh, he was all right, I guess.

LEON   You didn't like him, did you?

GREGOR   Don't tell anyone. When I was nine months old I tried to crawl away from home.

LEON   There you are! Then, the answer to being liked is to do something redeeming. Isn't there something good you could do for the village?

GREGOR   You mean like a barbecue?

LEON   Well, it's a start. But I was thinking of something on a much grander scale. Like lifting the curse.

GREGOR   How can I? It won't be lifted unless Sophia marries me.

LEON   Or another Yousekevitch.

GREGOR   There is none. I'm the last of the line.

LEON   Unless you had a son.

GREGOR   But I'm not even married. I may be a villain, but I don't fool around. Maybe that's why I'm so unhappy.

LEON   You don't have to be married. You can adopt a son.

GREGOR   Adopt a son? Who?

LEON   Me!

GREGOR   You?

LEON   I'm single, available, ready, and willing. I'm not very intelligent but I will be once the curse is lifted.

GREGOR   I've always wanted a son. Someone to take on
fishing trips.

LEON   I never really had a father.

GREGOR   My boy, Leon. I'd spoil you like anything.

LEON   That's okay, Dad.

GREGOR   And then people would like me, wouldn't they?

LEON   They do now. Look at their faces. They're smiling at you. Even up there.
(*He points to the audience.* GREGOR *looks out,
pleased*)

GREGOR (*To the audience*)   Yes! I see! Oh, God bless you.
You don't know what this means to me.

LEON   Then, let us go and sign the adoption papers and
notify Sophia's family. Are you ready, Dad?

GREGOR   Let me just watch them smiling at me again.
(*To the audience*) Thank you. Thank you all of you.
Maybe we can all have lunch together next week
. . . In the meantime, you're all invited to my son's
wedding! (*To* LEON, *as they exit*) The first thing I'm
going to do is have your shoes bronzed!
(*They are gone. Wedding decorations fly in as we hear
bright, cheerful music.* SNETSKY, SLOVITCH, MISHKIN,
and YENCHNA *are dancing, all dressed in their best.*
GREGOR *and* LENYA *approach from opposite sides of
the stage. The music has slowed down to a proces-
sional*)

MISHKIN   Doesn't Mrs. Zubritsky look beautiful?

YENCHNA   Isn't it bad luck for the mother of the bride to see the postman before the wedding?
(*He hides behind* YENCHNA)

SNETSKY   This is it, Slovitch—after two hundred years the curse will finally be gone.

SLOVITCH   I just had a terrible thought.

SNETSKY   What's that?

SLOVITCH   Suppose they lift the curse and I find out I was really dumb in the first place?

LENYA   They're coming! They're coming! Quiet, everyone! I have a sponge cake in the oven.
(LEON *appears*)

LEON (*To the audience*)   Remember, if I still appear stupid, I'm only pretending. It's all part of the plan.

LENYA (*To* GREGOR)   You must be very proud of him.

GREGOR   He's been my son for ten minutes and he's never given me a moment of trouble.
(*The* DOCTOR *and* SOPHIA, *in bridal gown, appear*)

YENCHNA   There but for me goes her.

MISHKIN   I hope she remembers to give me her change of address.
(*The* MAGISTRATE *appears*)

MAGISTRATE   We are gathered here today, dear friends, to witness the joining of two souls in holy matrimony. It is only the good will and generous benevolence of our dear friend the Count that makes this blessed union possible.

ALL   Thank you, Count.

MAGISTRATE   Will the groom step before me.

GREGOR   That's you, *mein kind.*
    (LEON *steps forward*)

MAGISTRATE   And will the bride step forward.
    (SOPHIA *steps out, but* LENYA *restrains her*)

LENYA   No, Sophia, the bride! The bride!

DOCTOR (*To* LENYA)   What's the matter with you?
    (*He places* SOPHIA *next to* LEON)

SOPHIA   Leon, your plan was brilliant.

LEON   Thank you, Sophia.

MAGISTRATE   And who giveth away this bride?

DOCTOR   I giveth away this bride.

MAGISTRATE   Why do you giveth away this bride?

DOCTOR   Because he asketh me for her. And I noddeth my head. And he taketh her.

MAGISTRATE   Do you, Leon, son of Count Gregor Mikhailovitch Breznofsky Fyodor Yousekevitch—

ALL (*Shaking*)   Tremble, tremble, tremble, tremble . . .

GREGOR   No, no. Not today! You don't have to do it today. It's a holiday.

ALL   Oh, thank you . . . Very kind . . . How nice of you . . .

MAGISTRATE   Do you, Leon, take Sophia, to have and to hold from this day on?

LEON   I have.

MAGISTRATE   No. I do.

LEON   You do?

MAGISTRATE   No, *you* do.

DOCTOR   He will. He does. Say it.

LEON   "He will, he does." I said it.

DOCTOR   Don't say what I say. Say what he says.

LEON   What did he say?

GREGOR   "I do." Just say "I do"!

LEON   My papa says I do!

GREGOR   I'm beginning to hate this curse, I swear to God.

MAGISTRATE   And do you, Sophia, take Leon, in sickness and in health, for better or for worse, for as long as you both shall live?

SOPHIA   I do.

LENYA   With a brain like that she could have gotten anyone.

MAGISTRATE   The ring, please.

GREGOR   I have it. The ring that Casimir Yousekevitch was going to place on the young Sophia two hundred years ago.
      (*He gives* LEON *a huge ring*)

LENYA   What an onion!

MAGISTRATE   Place the ring on her finger.
    (LEON *has great difficulty getting it on her finger*)

LENYA   He's not going to be very handy around the
house.

MAGISTRATE   Repeat after me, please: "With this ring, I
thee wed."

ALL   With this ring, I thee wed.

MAGISTRATE   Just the bride and the groom, thank you.

LEON and SOPHIA   With this ring, I thee wed.

MAGISTRATE   Before I pronounce this holy union, is
there any among you who has just cause or reason why
Leon and Sophia should not be joined in eternal wed-
lock? (*Pause*) Then with the power invested in me as
Chief Magistrate of the village of Kulyenchikov, I now
pronounce thee—

GREGOR (*Stepping forward*)   Welllll, maybe there's one
tiny little thing.

MAGISTRATE   You have an objection to this marriage?

GREGOR   You bet I have! This boy is not my son ... This
son is not my boy!

LEON   What are you saying, Father?

GREGOR   You think I'm crazy? Why should I give up a
cute little bundle of noodle brains like her?

LEON   But the adoption papers . . .

GREGOR   They're false. You trusted me so much you
didn't even read them. Here are the documents as
proof. I did not adopt him, I divorced him! According
to these documents, we are not father and son, we are
no longer husband and wife!

LENYA Dear God, my daughter almost married a divorced woman.
(*She faints in the* DOCTOR's *arms*)

SOPHIA Leon . . . Is this part of the plan?

LEON No, Sophia. I'm sorry.

GREGOR But fear not, dear friends. I may be a venomously treacherous snake, but I'm not a wet blanket. There will be a wedding.

DOCTOR My daughter will not marry an impostor.

GREGOR An impostor, no. But a Yousekevitch, yes! You have pledged your daughter's hand in marriage, good doctor, to a Yousekevitch. And a pledge once given must be honored.

MAGISTRATE That is the law. I helped write it myself.

DOCTOR It's true. I even voted for it.

GREGOR And I am the only true Yousekevitch here.

SOPHIA Leon, will you not object to this marriage?

LEON What can I do, Sophia? I am helpless.

MAGISTRATE Come on. Come on. I haven't all day.

GREGOR Say the words. Let's get it over with. There's been a hotel room booked for this honeymoon for two hundred years.

DOCTOR I'm sorry, daughter. With all my heart, truly sorry.
(*He places* SOPHIA *next to* GREGOR)

LENYA At least she'll get better dinners at his place.

MAGISTRATE Dearly beloved—

GREGOR   We did that part. We heard that. I do. Ask her, she's the one.

MAGISTRATE   And do you, Sophia, take Count Gregor, for as long as you both shall live.

LENYA   Say it, darling. You'll be rich and smart. It's better than happiness.

SOPHIA   Goodbye, Leon . . . goodbye forever. I do.

MAGISTRATE   Then with the power invested in me as chief magistrate of the village of Kulyenchikov—

LEON   You didn't say the other part.

MAGISTRATE   What other part?

LEON   The part if anybody objects, and I object.

GREGOR   What's that?

MAGISTRATE   On what grounds?

LEON   On the grounds that I didn't receive my urgent letter yet.

GREGOR   What kind of grounds is that?

MISHKIN   I have an urgent letter for schoolmaster Tolchinsky.

LEON   For me? Whatever could it be?

GREGOR   Finish the ceremony while he's reading the letter.

MAGISTRATE   I can't do that. It's against the law.

DOCTOR   It's true. I even voted for it.
           (LEON *has taken the letter from* MISHKIN. *He sits down to read it. All except* GREGOR *surround him and listen*)

LEON   It's bad news, I'm afraid. My uncle and sole remaining relative has just died in St. Petersburg leaving me nothing but all his debts.

SNETSKY   When you're going downhill, it gets faster at the bottom.

LEON   Before he died, he said he blamed all his misfortunes on the selfish and vindictive character of his distant relatives and that even changing his name to Tolchinsky never helped him escape destiny's finger.

DOCTOR   What was his name before Tolchinsky?

LEON   Yousekevitch.

YENCHNA   Oh-oh!

GREGOR   Those distant relatives will haunt you every time!

SOPHIA   Leon! Do you realize what this means?

LEON   No. What?

DOCTOR   He'll know in a few minutes. Schoolmaster, take your place next to my daughter. This time she's going to marry the right one!

LEON (*To the audience*)   It didn't say that at all. It's a bill from my former college saying I still owe them for last year's tuition.

SOPHIA   Hurry, Leon, hurry.

LEON (*To the audience*)   I have planted the bomb in their minds. I now pray God—for the explosion!
(*He rushes to* SOPHIA's *side*)

MAGISTRATE   Hurry up. Places, everyone. I don't want to spend the rest of my life marrying this girl . . . Are we ready, everyone!

ALL Ready!

MAGISTRATE Do you, Leon—

LEON I do.

MAGISTRATE And do you, Sophia—

SOPHIA I do.

MAGISTRATE If there is anyone here who objects—

ALL No one objects!

MAGISTRATE Going once . . . Going twice . . . Going three times . . . That's it! I now pronounce you *man and wife*!
      (*There is a loud thunderclap. The stage darkens, then gets lighter. All have fallen to the ground except* LEON, *who watches them*)

SNETSKY I have never heard a noise like that in all my life.

SLOVITCH It felt as though my head had cracked open.

SNETSKY Like what?

SLOVITCH Like my—head had cracked open. (*He and* SNETSKY *look at each other*) I'm afraid to ask it.

SNETSKY Go ahead. Ask it.

SLOVITCH But what if we're wrong?

SNETSKY And what if we're right? . . . Ask it! . . . *Ask it!*

SLOVITCH Cat!

SNETSKY Cat. C-a-t, cat!

SLOVITCH Dog!

SNETSKY   Dog. D-o-g, dog!

SLOVITCH   Oh, my God, it's a miracle!

SNETSKY   Miracle. M-i-r-a-c-l-e, miracle!

MISHKIN   Yenchna! . . . Yenchna—seven and five?

YENCHNA   Twelve.

MISHKIN   And twelve?

YENCHNA   Twenty-four.

MISHKIN   And forty-eight?

YENCHNA   Seventy-two! . . . Name five world capitals.

MISHKIN   Athens, Bucharest, Cairo, London, and—
      (*He is stuck*)

LEON   You can do it!

MISHKIN   Constantinople!
      (*They all cheer*)

MAGISTRATE   (*Rises*) The quality of mercy is not
   strained; it droppeth like the gentle rains from heaven.
      (SLOVITCH *and* SNETSKY *are up*)

SLOVITCH   That's beautiful. Did you make that up?

MAGISTRATE   I think so. Where else would it have come
   from?

LENYA   Nikolai! I—I feel funny. Weak in the knees. A
   dizziness in my head.
      (*The* DOCTOR *helps her up*)

DOCTOR   It's all right, my dear. Your blood is just pulsat-
   ing from the excitement. Sometimes that can cause the
   adrenal glands to oversecrete, resulting in a sudden
   rush to the head.

LENYA I—I never knew you were such a brilliant doctor.

DOCTOR I'm just an average doctor. I worry about you because—I love you, my dear.

LENYA And I love you, Nikolai. Even when I couldn't say it, in my heart I knew I loved you.

SOPHIA Leon . . . Are you now as you were before I became what I am?

LEON I am more than I have ever been or dreamed could be possible.

SOPHIA I love you, Leon.

LEON I adore you, Sophia.

GREGOR You mean it's over? The curse is over?

DOCTOR See for yourself, Count Gregor.

YENCHNA Land! I should have put my money in land. You can never go wrong with real estate.
    (SNETSKY *and* SLOVITCH *leave*)

MISHKIN It depends, of course, on the political situation. With a czarist government, land reform is a very delicate issue.
    (YENCHNA *and* MISHKIN *leave*)

GREGOR Such brilliant conversation. All my power over them is gone.

DOCTOR Power is a useless weapon over the enlightened, Count Gregor. We are all equal citizens here.

LENYA You mean men are all equal citizens. Women have been subjugated long before there were any curses.

DOCTOR   Lenya, you know I love you, but that's a very radical point of view.
(*The* DOCTOR *and* LENYA *leave*)

SOPHIA   It was your faith and courage that won over ignorance.

LEON   No, it was your pure heart and trusting soul that gave me that faith and courage. It was love that destroyed the curse, Sophia, not my puny efforts.

SOPHIA   I don't wish to argue the point, Leon. I just think you should allow me room to express my own views.

LEON   I welcome your views, Sophia, but I think you should have all the facts before you become so adamant.
(SOPHIA *leaves*)

GREGOR   Well, you got your wish, schoolmaster.

LEON   Yes . . . What about you, Count Yousekevitch? What are your plans now that you're intelligent?

GREGOR   Thanks to you, I'll probably have to work for a living now. Well, cousin, my congratulations. I wish you a long and happy marriage.

LEON   Thank you . . . and may I wish the same good fortune to you.

GREGOR   Please. I've been cursed once in my life, I know when I'm well off.
(*He leaves*)

LEON (*To the audience. During his speech, the cast members appear as he mentions them*)   When you think of it, it's not such a bizarre story, after all. Be honest. Haven't you all met someone in your life who came from a place like Kulyenchikov? An aunt, an uncle, a neighbor . . . your boss! Of course, once the curse was lifted, we became like any other small town or village in any other part of the world, susceptible to all the "ups and downs" of normal life—well, the magistrate, for example.

(*The* MAGISTRATE *appears*)

After two more years in office, greed got the better part of him and he was convicted for taking bribes for political favors. He served two years in jail and eventually sold his memoirs for a fortune.

(MISHKIN *appears*)

Mishkin gave up the postal service and became a writer. He wrote a six-hundred-page story about the Curse of Kulyenchikov and sent it off to a publisher. Unfortunately, it got lost in the mail.

(YENCHNA *appears*)

Yenchna, a shrewd businesswoman, put all her money in real estate and now owns seventeen houses in Kulyenchikov, including Count Gregor's. And as an investment for the future, she bought land in six other towns that had curses on them.

(SLOVITCH *appears*)

Slovitch, with all his life savings, bought four more butcher shops in a village that really needed only one and went bankrupt in a month, confirming his greatest fears that with or without a curse, he didn't have much brains.

(SNETSKY *appears, walking like a dandy*)

Snetsky, with his newly acquired intelligence, found his sheep, gathered his wool, and became a wealthy philanthropist.

(GREGOR *appears in a monk's robe*)

Count Yousekevitch became more and more lovable, studied theology, and is now the local monk. During the drought seasons he goes up on the hill and prays to God to throw water down on us.

(LENYA *appears, looking officious*)

My dear mother-in-law, Mrs. Zubritsky, suddenly found a voice of her own. She became the first woman mayor of Kulyenchikov and eventually consul governor of the Northern Ukraine Sector. Her husband sees her by appointment only.

(*The* DOCTOR *appears*)

Dr. Zubritsky became one of the finest doctors in all of

Russia. He became the personal physician to the royal family and was recently elected to the Academy of Sciences. However, he still has trouble opening jars.

(SOPHIA *appears, carrying a baby*)

As for Sophia, she was—and still is—a miracle. Not that we don't have our differences, not that all our days are blissfully happy, but she has a wisdom that can never be found in books. She has, in turn, become my teacher, and I have learned there is no spirit on earth, evil or otherwise, that can destroy a pure heart or devoted love.

As for myself, I remained a schoolmaster and dedicated my life to the education of the unenlightened . . . After all, there are so many Kulyenchikovs in this world.

Curtain

The Odd Couple (Female Version)

THE ODD COUPLE (FEMALE VERSION) *was first presented on October 4, 1984, at the Majestic Theatre in Dallas, Texas, with the following cast:*

SYLVIE	Jenny O'Hara
MICKEY	Mary Louise Wilson
RENEE	Kathleen Doyle
VERA	Marilyn Cooper
OLIVE MADISON	Rita Moreno
FLORENCE UNGER	Sally Struthers
MANOLO COSTAZUELA	Lewis J. Stadlen
JESUS COSTAZUELA	Tony Shalhoub

Directed by Gene Saks
Scenery by David Mitchell
Costumes by Ann Roth
Lighting by Tharon Musser

Synopsis of Scenes

Time: The present
Place: Olive Madison's Riverside Drive apartment

ACT ONE
A hot summer's night

ACT TWO

SCENE 1: Two weeks later, about 11 p.m.
SCENE 2: A few days later, about 8 p.m.
SCENE 3: The next evening, about 7:30 p.m.

Act One

A hot summer's night.

We are in the apartment of OLIVE MADISON, one of those six-room affairs on Riverside Drive, New York, in the eighties. The building is about forty years old and still has vestiges of its once-glorious past: high ceilings, walk-in closets, and thick walls.

We are in the combination living room–dining room. Two steps up is the front door and next to that, a hall closet. A window at stage left holds a broken air conditioner. Toward center rear, a doorway leads to the kitchen. At stage right, a hallway leads to the back bedrooms and the bathroom.

The apartment is quite unkempt. Books are a mess in the bookshelves. Magazines and old newspapers litter the floors and tables. Unopened mail and unopened laundry packages lie about.

A dining table at stage right is being used for the girls' weekly Trivial Pursuit game. Four women are at the table playing, two on each side. RENEE and SYLVIE, a compulsive smoker, are on one side; VERA and MICKEY, a uniformed policewoman, on the other. Food and drinks, none too appetizing, are on the table. MICKEY is standing.

MICKEY (*She shakes the dice in her hand*)   C'mon, baby, we need a piece of the pie. (*She throws the dice*) . . . Five! (*She counts off spaces on the board*) One—two—three— four—five! . . . Science and Nature. (*She sits.*)
   (RENEE *takes a card from the box and looks at it*)

RENEE   Oh, you're going to love this . . . "How many times a year does a penguin have sex?"
   (MICKEY *looks at her partner,* VERA, *puzzled*)

MICKEY   Do you know any penguins? . . . Intimately?

VERA   That shouldn't be Science and Nature. That should be gossip.

MICKEY   I'll say they do it six times.

VERA   Why only six times?

MICKEY   Did you ever see what they look like?

VERA   They live on icebergs. What else could they do all winter? (*To opponents*) I say twenty times.

RENEE   Wrong. They do it once.

SYLVIE   *Once?* Jesus, I married a penguin.

RENEE   Christ, it's hot in here. When is she going to fix her air conditioner?

SYLVIE (*Hands the dice to* RENEE)   Your roll.

RENEE   I'm going to pass out, I swear.

VERA   Someone told me you were seeing a doctor. Is it anything serious?

RENEE   No. We only had two dates. (*She rolls the dice*) Four. (*Counting off with the marker*) One—two—three—four . . . Oh, Christ. Sports!

SYLVIE   Go the other way. (*To* VERA) We take Science. (RENEE *moves the marker the opposite way*)

MICKEY   Two minutes to go and counting down.

SYLVIE (*To* MICKEY)   Do you mind if she asks the question first? (*To* VERA) Go on, Vera.

VERA (*Reads from a card*)   "What does C mean in Einstein's Theory of Relativity, E equals MC squared?" (SYLVIE *and* RENEE *look at her with their mouths open, dumbfounded*)

SYLVIE   We'll try sports.

VERA   You can't change after you've heard the question.

RENEE   She picked it on *my* turn. I pick sports.
(*She moves the marker back*)

MICKEY (*Looks at her watch*)   A minute thirty and count-ing down.

VERA (*Reads*)   "Who pitched back-to-back no-hitters for the Cincinnati Reds in 1938?"
(SYLVIE *and* RENEE *stare again with mouths open, dumbfounded*)

SYLVIE (*To* RENEE)   You want to take a crack at MC squared?

RENEE (*To* VERA)   Give us a hint.

VERA   What kind of hint?

RENEE   Is it baseball or football?

VERA   It's baseball. I'll give you another hint. He has a Dutch name . . .

SYLVIE   . . . Dutch Schultz.

MICKEY   Dutch Schultz was a gangster.

RENEE   Joe Rembrandt.

VERA   Is that your answer?

SYLVIE   Peter Windmill.

VERA   Is that your answer?

MICKEY   Sixty seconds and counting down.

SYLVIE   What is this, liftoff at Cape Canaveral?
(*Calls off toward the kitchen*) Olive, we need help.

OLIVE (*Offstage*) I'm coming. I'm coming.

VERA Do you give up?

RENEE Not yet ... Bobby Amsterdam ... Tony Tulips.

VERA Give up. You'll never get it. I have to leave by twelve.

SYLVIE Where the hell are you running?

VERA I told you that when I sat down. I have to leave by twelve. Mickey, didn't I say that when I sat down? I had to leave by twelve.

MICKEY I'm really starting to worry about Florence. She's never been this late before.

VERA I told Harry I'd be home by one the latest. We're making an eight o'clock plane to Florida.
(SYLVIE *glares at her*)

MICKEY Who goes to Florida in July?

VERA It's off-season. There are no crowds and you get the best rooms for one-tenth the price.

SYLVIE Some vacation. Six cheap people in an empty hotel.

MICKEY Maybe Florence is sick. I'm really getting nervous.

VERA Do you give up?

SYLVIE Mickey Dikes ... I hate this game.

MICKEY Did you know Florence once locked herself in the bathroom overnight in Bloomingdale's? She wrote out her entire will on a half a roll of toilet paper ... (*She looks at her watch*) Time is almost up.

SYLVIE (*Calls out*) Olive! We're running out of time.
(OLIVE *comes out of the kitchen with a tray of food and soft drinks*)

OLIVE Alright, what's the question?

MICKEY You only have four seconds.

VERA Who pitched back to back no-hitters—

OLIVE (*In one breath*) Johnny Van Der Meer on June 11th against the Boston Braves, three-nothing, and on June 15th against the Brooklyn Dodgers, six-nothing, his overall record for the year was fifteen wins and ten losses, I have one second left over, ask me another question.

RENEE She's incredible.

SYLVIE You really love sports, don't you?

OLIVE I love big men in tight pants . . . Who gets a no caffeine NutraSweet one calorie Pepsi?

MICKEY I do.

OLIVE (*She brings her the can*) One can of chemicals for Mickey the Cop.

MICKEY (*Holding the can*) It's warm.

RENEE Because her refrigerator's been broken for two weeks.

OLIVE So it drips a little, who wants food?

MICKEY What have you got?

OLIVE (*Looks at the sandwiches*) I got brown sandwiches and green sandwiches.

MICKEY What's the green?

OLIVE (*Looks*) It's either very new cheese or very old meat.

MICKEY I'll take the brown.

RENEE You're going to eat food from that refrigerator? I saw milk standing in there that wasn't even in the bottle.

OLIVE What are you, some kind of health nut? Eat, Mickey. Eat.

SYLVIE (*To* RENEE) We go again. Roll 'em.

RENEE (*To* OLIVE) I thought you had a new maid starting to work on Monday.

OLIVE No. I didn't pass the interview.

RENEE (*Shaking the dice . . . to the others*) The woman produces a prime time news show and she doesn't have a maid. (*She throws the dice*) Five. One—two—three—four—five . . . Science and Nature.

VERA Oh, this is good . . . "What closes when a frog swallows?"
    (RENEE *and* SYLVIE *look at* OLIVE)

SYLVIE HIS EYES!! . . . They close their eyes.

MICKEY That's right. How did you know that?

SYLVIE I went out with a guy who looked like a frog.

MICKEY (*To* RENEE) Your turn again. Roll 'em.

RENEE Hey, Olive, can we make a rule? Every six months you have to buy fresh potato chips.

OLIVE I do. Eat those until September.

RENEE At least at Florence's house you get decent food.

OLIVE My food isn't decent?

RENEE It's not even food.

OLIVE Alright, I'm through being the nice one. You owe
me six dollars apiece for the buffet. (*They all react deri-
sively*)

SYLVIE Buffet? Hot diet colas and two sandwiches left
over from when you went to high school?

RENEE (*Moves her marker*) One—two—three . . . Again
sports.

MICKEY (*Reads the card*) "What did Forrest Smithson
carry in his hand for inspiration while running the
hurdles at the 1908 Olympics?"
(RENEE *and* SYLVIE *turn and look at* OLIVE)

OLIVE . . . Extra jockey shorts.

VERA Is that your answer?

SYLVIE (*To* VERA) If you say that one more time, I'm
taking you hostage, I swear to God.

MICKEY Sixty seconds and counting down.

OLIVE He carried a Bible.

VERA That's right.

RENEE The woman's unbelievable.

MICKEY (*To* OLIVE) How could you know about the
1908 Olympics?

OLIVE From Phil. Phil knew more about sports than any
man I ever knew . . . I think we'd still be married today
if only I could have won the Kentucky Derby.
(*She looks off, thinking of Phil*)

RENEE   Don't get that mournful look in your eye again. The man lost your entire life savings at the track.

RENEE   Two. Science and Nature.

VERA   What's the strongest muscle in a man's body?

SYLVIE   Before or after?

MICKEY   You're not still sending Phil money, are you?

OLIVE   Nah.

MICKEY   Yes she does.

OLIVE   . . . a few hundred dollars. Just until he gets his life straightened out.

MICKEY   He's been trying to get straightened out for two years. How bent was he?

OLIVE   I can't help it. Every time I hear his voice on the phone, I end up sending him a check. He's so good at it. He puts a little whimper in because he knows it gets to me.

RENEE   I would never support an ex-husband. Not until women are getting equal pay with men.

SYLVIE and MICKEY   Right!

VERA   Well, you have to look at it both ways. What's sauce for the goose is sauce for the gander.

SYLVIE (*Looks at her*)   You're going to be some big hit in Florida.

VERA   You give up on the strongest muscle?

RENEE   The tongue.

VERA   That's right.

RENEE (*Throws the dice*)   Don't ask me how I know that. Three. One—two—three . . . Sports and Leisure.
   (*The phone rings*)

VERA (*Reads*)   "What's the southern dish made of pigs' small intestines called?"

OLIVE   Airplane food.

SYLVIE   Chitlins.

OLIVE (*She picks up the phone*)   Hello? Oh, my God. Phil! . . . I was just talking about you.

MICKEY   Somebody hide her checkbook.
   (RENEE *throws the dice again. She moves the marker during* OLIVE's *conversation*)

OLIVE (*Into phone*)   How have you been, Phil? . . . You sound good. Tired? . . . Yeah, you sound like you have a little cold . . . Haven't been sleeping, heh? (*Hand over phone, to the girls*) He's whimpering. This is going to cost me.

MICKEY   Don't give in. Remember the Alamo.

OLIVE (*Into phone*)   So what have you been doing, Phil? . . . Mostly thinking of me. Ah, that's sweet. (*Hand over phone, to the girls*) We're talking about four figures here. (*Back into phone*) You're in a bind? What kind of bind?

SYLVIE   You want us to cut the wire?

OLIVE (*Holds up her hand to quiet* SYLVIE. *Into phone*)   You owe two months' back rent? Oh gee, I'm sorry . . . How much does it come to?

RENEE (*To the girls*)   A million six.

OLIVE (*Into phone*)   Gee, I wish I could help you out, Phil, but I'm broke myself. I just paid the last two years' taxes.

MICKEY   That's it. Hang in, girl. Win this one for the Gipper.

OLIVE (*Into phone*)   I know . . . I know you hate to ask, Phil. And I hate to turn you down.

SYLVIE   Hang up. Hang up before his voice cracks.

OLIVE (*Into phone*)   What's wrong with your voice, Phil? . . . Oh, gee. Phil, don't do that . . . Please don't, Phil . . . Listen, I'll send you three hundred dollars, is that alright?

RENEE   Gloria Steinem hates you!

OLIVE   Stop coughing, Phil . . . Sympathy is not going to work with me . . . I'm sending you five hundred dollars and that's it.

SYLVIE (*To the girls*)   Even money she goes to six-fifty.

OLIVE (*Into phone*)   Phil, I've got to go . . . It was nice speaking to you . . . It's what? . . . Our anniversary? . . . When? . . . My God, next week, you're right . . . Oh . . . Well, the same to you, Phil . . . Sure. Six-fifty's fine . . . G'bye, Phil. (*She hangs up. She looks at the girls, embarrassed and ashamed*) He sounded like Orphan Annie in a snowstorm, what do you want from me?

RENEE (*Holding potato chips*)   You give your ex-husband six hundred and fifty dollars and your best friends get to eat the Dead Sea Scrolls?

OLIVE   I have a fatal flaw in my character. Him. Go ahead and shoot me.

MICKEY   If you mean it, I have my gun here.

VERA (*Reads*)   "What's the oldest known vegetable in the world?"
    (*Everybody stares at her, astonished*)

SYLVIE ... *You* are!!

RENEE (*To* OLIVE) There's other men around, you know.

OLIVE (*Pacing*) You think I don't know? There's two Spanish brothers in this building who are crazy about me. Sexiest guys you ever saw ... I must be crazy. Why am I sending a shiftless gambler like Phil seven hundred and fifty dollars?

MICKEY (*To* RENEE) Hand me my purse. I'll shoot her now.

VERA (*To* SYLVIE *and* RENEE) Is that your final answer?

SYLVIE Yes! You are the oldest vegetable known to man.

VERA Wrong. It's the pea.

SYLVIE Then you're runner-up.
        (VERA *tosses the dice and moves her marker*)

OLIVE The kids today are smarter than us. Why go through all the trouble of marriage when you can have a roommate? I'm going to start looking around on the bus tomorrow.

VERA Entertainment.

RENEE (*Reads*) "What group starred in the movie *Rock Around the Clock*?"

OLIVE Everybody, all together!

ALL FIVE WOMEN (*All raise their fists in air*) BILL HALEY AND THE COMETS!!!

OLIVE (*Snaps her fingers*) Yeah! God, give me one more night in the back of a T-Bird! Whoo-hoo!

SYLVIE Remember Danny Flannigan? Hot! Hot stuff!

MICKEY He wore size 28 jeans on a 32 body.

RENEE I remember the first time I danced close with him. He kept saying, "It's not what you think. I got two packs of cigarettes in my pocket" . . . I had to go to confession the next day.

OLIVE Always had a pound of grease in his hair. Remember the winter he went out and his head froze? He had to comb his hair with a hammer and chisel.

VERA You know who I thought the cutest one in the school was? . . . Mr. Schwartzman, the principal.
(*The girls look at each other*)

OLIVE Jesus, I hated being seventeen . . . until I got to be thirty-five. You know what I mean?
(*They all get lost in thought*)

MICKEY Yeah.

SYLVIE Yeah.

RENEE Yeah.

VERA Yeah.
(SYLVIE, RENEE, *and* MICKEY *nod . . . Then they all become quiet as they ponder this thought quietly. They are all momentarily lost in memories of their youth.*

The phone rings. It's as though they don't hear it.

It rings again.* OLIVE *crosses and picks it up*)

OLIVE (*Into phone*) The Chubby Checker Fan Club. Hello. (*She suddenly smiles, lowers her voice, turns away from the others*) Oh, hello, sweetheart. (*She becomes very seductive. The others listen*) I told you not to call me tonight . . . I can't talk to you now . . . You *know* I do, darling . . . Alright. Just a minute. (*She turns*) Mickey! It's your husband. (*She lays down the phone*)

MICKEY (*Gets up and crosses to the phone*)   I wish you *were* having an affair with him. Then he wouldn't bother *me* all the time. (*She picks up the phone*) Hello, Stanley. What's wrong? Did you make yourself dinner? . . . What'd you have? . . . Lamb chops? That's very good, Stan.

VERA   Your husband can make lamb chops?

MICKEY (*Hand over phone*)   He boils them in water. (*Back into phone*) Who? . . . No, she didn't show up tonight. What's wrong? . . . You're kidding! . . . How should I know? . . . Alright. I will . . . Yes. Goodbye. (*To the others*) What did I tell you?

RENEE   What's the matter?

MICKEY   Florence is missing.

RENEE   Oh, my God!

MICKEY   I *told* you something was up.

SYLVIE   What do you mean, missing?

MICKEY   She wasn't home all day today. She canceled her facial appointment and her pedicure. She never showed up for her yoga class or her spiritual adviser. No one knows where she is. Stan just spoke to her husband.

OLIVE   Wait a minute. No one is missing for one day.

RENEE   That's right. You've got to be missing for forty-eight hours before you're missing.

SYLVIE   She loves the Museum of Modern Art. Maybe she went there.

VERA   Maybe she got locked in the museum. I once talked to a security guard there for twenty minutes until I found out he was a statue.
    (SYLVIE *glares at her*)

RENEE Maybe she had an accident.

OLIVE They would have heard.

RENEE If she's lying in a gutter somewhere? Who would know who she is?

OLIVE She's got charge plates for forty-seven stores. If eight hours go by without her shopping, New York shuts down.

RENEE Maybe she was mugged.

OLIVE Do you know what she carries in her handbag? Tear gas, a siren, and a police radio. If you tap her on the shoulder, a squad car shows up.

MICKEY I don't know. I have a feeling in my bones she's someplace in trouble right now.

OLIVE What are we guessing for? I'll call Sidney.
(*She starts for phone*)

SYLVIE Wait a minute! Don't start anything yet. Just because *we* don't know where she is doesn't mean somebody *else* doesn't know . . . Is she seeing someone? On the side?

VERA You mean like a hypnotist?

SYLVIE (*Glaring at her*) Are you on Valium? . . . Did you ever think of taking speed so you can keep up with the rest of us?

OLIVE Florence doesn't play around. She didn't even take her clothes off when she had her children . . . Please.

SYLVIE You never can tell. It's a different world we live in today. What a man can do, a woman can do . . . I've never personally done it myself, but I've gotten the itch once in a while. Admit it. We all have.

VERA I haven't.

SYLVIE I'm talking about *normal* women.

OLIVE (*Dialing*) We're wasting time. I'm going to call Sidney and find out what's what. (*Into phone*) Hello? Sidney? . . . Olive. I just heard. Listen, Sidney, do you have any idea where she could be? . . . She what? . . . You're kidding? . . . Why? . . . No, I didn't know . . . Gee, that's too bad . . . Alright, listen, Sid. You just sit tight and the minute I hear anything I'll let you know . . . Right. Goodbye. (*She hangs up. They all look at her with great suspense. She crosses wordlessly to the end of the sofa, lost in thought. They just stare at her. Finally she turns to them*) They broke up.

VERA Who?

OLIVE *Who*??? . . . Florence and Sidney, that's who. They broke up. The marriage is over.

VERA Don't tell me.

RENEE I can't believe it.

SYLVIE After fourteen years.

VERA They were such a happy couple.

MICKEY Fourteen years doesn't mean you're a happy couple. It just means you're a *long* couple.

SYLVIE What happened?

OLIVE The man wants out, that's all.

MICKEY She'll go to pieces. I know Florence. She's going to try something crazy.

SYLVIE She used to say, "Our marriage will last a hundred years" . . . What happened?

OLIVE She missed by eighty-six years.

MICKEY   She'll kill herself. You hear what I'm saying. She's going to go out and try to kill herself.

SYLVIE   Will you shut up, Mickey? Stop being a police-woman for two minutes. (*To* OLIVE) Where'd she go, Olive?

OLIVE   She went out to kill herself.

MICKEY (*To* SYLVIE)   What'd I tell you?

RENEE (*To* OLIVE)   Are you serious?

OLIVE   That's what the man said. She went out to kill herself. She didn't want to do it at home because her mother was sleeping over.

VERA   Why did she want to kill herself?

OLIVE   Why? Because she's an hysteric.

SYLVIE (*To* OLIVE)   You mean she actually said, "I'm going out to kill myself"? What did she do, leave a note?

OLIVE   No. She sent a telegram.

MICKEY   A suicide telegram?

RENEE   If she wants to kill herself, why does she send a telegram?

OLIVE   Because the quicker it gets there, the quicker she has a chance to be saved.

VERA   Oh, I get it. She really doesn't want to kill herself. She just wants sympathy.

MICKEY   We get people like her all the time. They crave attention. We have a man who calls us every Saturday afternoon from the top of the George Washington Bridge. We don't even answer it.

RENEE   I don't know. There's always a first time. Maybe this is the one time she really means it.

OLIVE   Please. She's too nervous to kill herself. She wears her seat belt in a drive-in movie.

SYLVIE   Well, we can't sit here and do nothing.

VERA   Isn't there someplace we could look for her?

SYLVIE   Where? Where would you look for a suicidal person who wants to live?
        (*The doorbell rings*)

OLIVE (*Lowering her voice*)   Of course! If you're going to kill yourself, where's the safest place to do it? . . . With your friends.

VERA (*Starting for the door*)   I'll let her in.
        (*All talk quickly, nervously*)

RENEE   Wait a minute! She may be hysterical. Let's play it nice and easy. If we're calm, maybe *she'll* be calm.

MICKEY   That's right. That's how they talk to those people out on ledges. Gentle and soothing, like a priest.

VERA   What'll we say to her?

MICKEY   Nothing. We say nothing. As if we never heard a thing.

SYLVIE   Maybe we should notify the police.

MICKEY (*Angrily*)   What the hell do you think *I* am, for crise sakes?

OLIVE   Are you girls through with this discussion? Because she already could have died of old age out in the hall . . . Everybody, sit down. (*They all rush into their chairs.* VERA *crosses to the door.* OLIVE *sits with* RENEE *and* SYLVIE . . . *To* MICKEY)   Alright, ask us a question.

MICKEY   You have to roll the dice first. Get your category.

OLIVE   Who gives a crap what the category is? Just ask a question.

MICKEY   My mind is too logical. I can't ask a question till someone gives me a category.

RENEE   Sports and Leisure.
         (*The bell rings again*)

SYLVIE   Not Sports and Leisure—it's too tough.

OLIVE   I can't believe this.

VERA   Should I tell Florence to wait a minute?

OLIVE (*To* MICKEY)   Movies! Entertainment! *Open the door!*
         (MICKEY *picks up a card as* VERA *opens the door.* FLORENCE *stands there, dressed neatly. She carries a purse. She tries to act as if everything is fine but we can sense the tension and anxiety underneath*)

FLORENCE   Hello, Vera.

VERA   Oh, hello, Florence. We practically forgot all about you.
         (*She scurries back to her seat.* FLORENCE *steps into the apartment*)

OLIVE   One more piece of the pie is all we need.

FLORENCE   Hello, girls.
         (*The girls barely look up. They throw her a perfunctory "Hello, Florence," but their attention is on the game*)

SYLVIE (*To* MICKEY)   Could you repeat the question, please?

MICKEY   I didn't ask it yet . . . "Name three actors who played Charlie Chan on the screen."

FLORENCE (*Wanders around*)   I'm sorry I'm late.

OLIVE   Five, ten minutes. Big deal . . . There are some sandwiches there if you're hungry.

FLORENCE   Yes, I am. I didn't eat all day. (*She crosses to the sandwiches; looks in a sandwich*) No. Never mind.

OLIVE   What was the question?

RENEE   Three actors who played Charlie Chan.

FLORENCE   Is there anything to drink?

OLIVE   Sure. Coke, Pepsi, 7-Up, anything.

FLORENCE   I meant hard stuff. Do you have any hard stuff? . . . A Dubonnet?

OLIVE   Dubonnet? . . . No, I just killed my last case.

FLORENCE   It's not important. (*As she turns away from them, an audible sigh*) Nothing is very important.

OLIVE (*Back to the game*)   . . . Three actors who played who?

MICKEY   Charlie Chan! Charlie Chan! How many times do I have to say it? Charlie Chan!

SYLVIE   Alright, take it easy, everyone. Calm down.

FLORENCE (*She stands behind* VERA *and plays with* VERA'S *hair*)   . . . Anyone call about me?

OLIVE   Call? Not that I can remember. (*To the others*) Did anyone call for Florence? (*They quickly mumble they "can't remember"*) Why? Were you expecting a call?

FLORENCE   Me? Who would call for me?

OLIVE (*Turning back to the game*) Er, three actors who played Charlie Chan, is that it?

MICKEY That's it. That's the question. You got it!

OLIVE You mean in the same picture?

MICKEY (*Losing patience*) How can they play in the same picture? What do they want three Charlie Chans in the same goddamn picture for?

VERA They had two Tarzans in the same picture once.

MICKEY (*Attacking her*) Never! Never two Tarzans in one picture.

VERA One of them pretended to be Tarzan.

MICKEY (*Losing control*) Then it wasn't two Tarzans. It was *one* Tarzan and one pretending to be Tarzan.

RENEE Alright, take it easy. Take it easy.

OLIVE Calm down, everyone, alright?

MICKEY I'm sorry. I can't help it. Everyone makes me nervous.

SYLVIE That's because you make everybody *else* nervous.

MICKEY (*Sarcastically*) I'm sorry. Forgive me. I'll go kill myself!

OLIVE (*Warning her*) Mickey!
(*She motions her head to* FLORENCE.
They all sit in silence a moment as FLORENCE *crosses to the window*)

FLORENCE Gee, it's a pretty view from up here. What is it, twelve floors?

OLIVE (*Gets up very quickly*) No. It's only eleven. (*She closes the window quickly*) It says twelve but it's only eleven . . . Want to sit down and play, Flo? It's still early.
(*As* OLIVE *crosses back to table*)

FLORENCE No . . . I don't think I could concentrate tonight.

SYLVIE It's your favorite category. Movies.

FLORENCE I wouldn't know one movie from another tonight.

OLIVE You'd know this one . . . "Name three actors who played Tarzan in the movies."

MICKEY Charlie Chan! *CHARLIE CHAN!!*

FLORENCE Sidney Toler, Warner Oland, and Peter Ustinov . . . Excuse me.
(*She crosses*)

OLIVE Where are you going?

FLORENCE I have to go to the bathroom.

OLIVE Alone?

FLORENCE I always go alone . . . Why?

OLIVE No reason . . . You gonna be in there long?

FLORENCE . . . As long as it takes.
(*She goes into the bathroom*)

MICKEY Are you crazy? Letting her go in there alone?

OLIVE How is she going to kill herself in the john?

SYLVIE What do you mean, how? She could take pills. She could slash her wrists.

OLIVE It's the guest bathroom. There's nothing in there. What is she going to do, swallow a towel?

MICKEY She could jump.

VERA That's right. Isn't there a window in there?

OLIVE It's only six inches wide.

MICKEY She could stick her head out and slam the window on her neck.

OLIVE She could also flush herself into the East River. I'm telling you she's not going to try anything.

VERA Shh! Quiet! (*They all listen. We hear* FLORENCE *sobbing in the bathroom*) She's crying.

RENEE We should do something. She shouldn't be in there crying all alone.

OLIVE You want to go in there and cry *with* her? (*We hear the toilet flush*)

VERA She's coming out! (*They all make a mad dash for the table and sit. They're all in the wrong seats. They get up and quickly change seats. They resume positions of being relaxed and even bored.* FLORENCE *comes out and wipes her eyes and nose*)

OLIVE (*Reading from a card*) "What picture did Claude Rains and Bette Davis—"

FLORENCE *Mr. Skeffington.* I think I'm going to take a little walk. (*She gets her coat and bag*)

OLIVE Where are you going to walk this time of night?

FLORENCE I don't know. Along the river is nice.

OLIVE The *river*??

FLORENCE   You heard something, didn't you?

OLIVE   No.

FLORENCE   Yes. You're worried I'm going to try something because Sidney dumped me after fourteen years of marriage, the dirty bastard! (*She bursts into tears and rushes for the front door*) I've got to go!

OLIVE   Florence, no!!

RENEE   Don't do it, Florence, please!
(*They all plead with her*)

FLORENCE   Don't stop me. Don't try to stop me.
(FLORENCE *is trying to get out the door; they are pulling her back in*)

MICKEY   Florence, we're your friends. You can talk to us.

FLORENCE (*Tearfully*)   I can't live without him. There's no point in going on.
(MICKEY, *the cop, grabs* FLO *and pulls her arm back behind her. With her free arm,* FLORENCE *jabs* MICKEY *in the ribs with her elbow.* MICKEY *doubles over in pain. Leaving* MICKEY *behind, she breaks away from them and rushes across the room to the bathroom on the opposite side. They all rush after her in single file because there's only room behind the table and chairs to run that way. They all follow* FLORENCE *into the bathroom. The last one in closes the door. There is a loud commotion inside, unseen by the audience. Suddenly it stops. The first one out is* OLIVE, *who holds her hand in pain. She is followed out by* RENEE)

RENEE   You didn't have to hit her so hard.

OLIVE   She was biting my neck. What did you want me to do, lick her face?

MICKEY (*She comes out walking backwards, directing with her hands as if she was directing traffic*) Lay her down on the sofa.

 (SYLVIE *comes out carrying the unconscious* FLORENCE *on her shoulders, followed by* VERA)

SYLVIE   Rub her wrists.

RENEE   She's coming around.

FLORENCE   Leave me alone, will you? I'll work it out. Just please, everybody, leave me alone . . . Oh, God! Oh, my stomach.

MICKEY   What's the matter with your stomach?

VERA   She looks sick. Look at her face.

FLORENCE   I'm not sick. I'm alright. I didn't take anything, I swear.

OLIVE   What do you mean you didn't take anything? What did you take?

FLORENCE   Nothing!

OLIVE   Do you swear?

FLORENCE   I swear.

OLIVE   On your children's life?

FLORENCE   No. On my husband's.

MICKEY   You hear that? She took pills.

FLORENCE · Just a few, that's all.
 (*All react in alarm and concern for the pills*)

OLIVE   How many pills?

MICKEY   What kind of pills?

FLORENCE I don't know. Little green ones. I just grabbed anything out of Sidney's cabinet. I must have been crazy.

OLIVE I'm gonna call Sidney. He'll check the cabinet.

FLORENCE NO!! Don't call him! If he hears I took a whole bottle of pills—

MICKEY A WHOLE BOTTLE?? A WHOLE BOTTLE OF PILLS?? . . . Quick! Call for an ambulance!
        (RENEE *picks up the phone and dials*)

OLIVE You don't even know what kind.

MICKEY What's the difference? She took a whole bottle.

OLIVE Maybe they were vitamins. She could be the healthiest one in the room . . . Take it easy, will you.

FLORENCE Don't call Sidney. Promise me you won't call Sidney.

MICKEY Slap her face. Open the window. Give her some air.

SYLVIE Walk her around. Don't let her go to sleep.
        (SYLVIE *and* MICKEY *pull* FLORENCE *up, drape her arms over their shoulders, and begin to walk her around the room*)

MICKEY (*Waiting on the phone*) Rub her wrists. Keep her circulation going. Keep walking. Keep her blood moving.

RENEE The hospital is busy.
       (*She hangs up.*
       OLIVE *has been sitting on the sofa watching this madhouse contemptuously*)

SYLVIE (*To* OLIVE) Isn't there a doctor in the building?

OLIVE He's an optometrist. If she goes blind, I'll call him.
       (*They continue to walk her*)

FLORENCE   Please let me sit down. I can't walk this much without my Nikes.

MICKEY   You're not sitting down till we get those pills out.

FLORENCE   I got them out. They're out.
    (SYLVIE *and* MICKEY *stop and look at her*)

MICKEY   When did they come out?

FLORENCE   I had a pizza on Broadway. I threw up in the elevator. (SYLVIE *and* MICKEY *look at her, then walk away, leaving her alone*) I'm sorry. They'll think a dog did it . . . Can I have a drink, somebody?

VERA   I'll get it. Do you want a Fresca or a Sprite?

SYLVIE (*Yells*)   Will you just get her a drink?

VERA   Alright.
    (*She scurries into the kitchen.* FLORENCE *is sitting in a club chair*)

FLORENCE (*Crying*)   Fourteen years! Did you know we were married fourteen years, Renee?

RENEE   Yes, Florence. I knew.

FLORENCE   And now it's over. Just like that. Fourteen years out the window.

SYLVIE   Maybe it was just a fight. You've had fights before.

FLORENCE   No. It's over. He's getting a lawyer tomorrow . . . *My* cousin.

MICKEY   It's alright, darling. Let it out. Let it all out.

FLORENCE   Twelve hours I've been crying. I don't know where it's all coming from. I think it's all the same tears just going around in circles.

VERA   Is Dr. Pepper alright?

FLORENCE   Don't call him. I'm fine.

VERA   No, it's a drink.

FLORENCE   Oh. Thanks, Vera.
    (*She takes soda and slowly drinks entire can. She burps*)
Pardon me.

OLIVE   Florence, everyone's been worried sick about you. Where have you been for the whole day?

FLORENCE   I don't know. I just wandered around the city . . . I ended up in the Museum of Modern Art. I talked to this security guard for an hour, he just stood there listening to everything I said. So patient.
    (*They all look at* VERA. *She shrugs*)

MICKEY   Alright, let's not stand around looking at her. Let's break it up, heh?

OLIVE   Yeah. Come on. She's alright. Let's call it a night.
    (MICKEY, SYLVIE, RENEE, *and* VERA *cross back to the table to get their things*)

FLORENCE   I'm so ashamed. Please forgive me, girls.

VERA   It's okay. We understand.

MICKEY (*Lowering her voice*)   Do you know the number for the suicide hotline?

OLIVE (*Looks at her*)   I'll get it from Florence, she has an account there . . .
    (MICKEY *nods and goes. The other girls file out*)

GIRLS   Goodnight, Flo . . . Take care, honey . . . We'll call you tomorrow.
    (*They all leave. The door closes. Then it opens as* RENEE *sticks her head in*)

RENEE   If anything happens, Olive, just call me.
(OLIVE *nods;* RENEE *goes, and closes door. It reopens and* SYLVIE *sticks her head in*)

SYLVIE (*To* OLIVE)   I'm three blocks away. I could be here in five minutes.
(OLIVE *nods;* SYLVIE *leaves and closes the door. It opens again and* VERA *comes in*)

VERA   If you need me, I'll be at the Meridian Motel in Miami Beach.

OLIVE   You'll be the first one I call, Vera.
(VERA *nods and leaves*)

MICKEY (*To* OLIVE)   You sure?

OLIVE   I'm sure.

MICKEY (*Loud, to* FLORENCE)   Goodnight, Florence. Try to get a good night's sleep. I guarantee you things are going to look a lot brighter in the morning. (*To* OLIVE, *whispering*) Hide all your belts and plastic bags.
(OLIVE *closes the door, looks at* FLORENCE, *then slowly crosses into the room*)

OLIVE   Ohh, Florence, Florence, Florence, Florence.

FLORENCE   I know, I know, I know, I know . . . What am I going to do, Olive?

OLIVE   You're going to wash down those pills with some hot black coffee. I'll make it.

FLORENCE   The terrible thing is, I still love him. It's a lousy marriage, but I still love him. I didn't want this divorce.

OLIVE   You want a brownie? A chocolate brownie? It's about three weeks old but I could toast it.

FLORENCE   If Sidney and I break up, I'll be the first one in my family to be divorced.

OLIVE   You told me your mother and father were divorced.

FLORENCE   I mean since them . . . My sister is still married . . . Separated but married.

OLIVE   How about some espresso? With Stella D'Oro cookies?

FLORENCE   How *dare* he treat me like this? How *dare* he? (*In anger, she bangs her fist down on the arm of the chair and suddenly grabs her neck in great pain*) Oh! Oh, my neck! My neck!

OLIVE   What did you do?

FLORENCE (*Holding her neck*)   It's a nerve spasm. I get it in the neck. Oh, God. Oh, God, it hurts.

OLIVE   What can I do?

FLORENCE   A towel. Get me a hot towel. Very hot.

OLIVE   Right. What about some aspirins?

FLORENCE   Aspirin is good . . . And some brandy . . . I can't move my neck.

OLIVE   Hot towel, aspirin, and brandy. Anything else?

FLORENCE   Ben-Gay. To rub in after.

OLIVE   Right.
(*She starts inside*)

FLORENCE   And a scarf. A woolen scarf . . . Cashmere is better if you have one. (*She paces, rubbing her neck*) I knew something was coming, Olive. I knew we were in trouble. In the middle of the night I'd tiptoe into the bathroom and I would pray, "Please, God, please help me save my marriage. Please, God, tell me what to do. Tell me what I'm doing wrong. Please, God, help me"

. . . And then I'd hear Sidney in the bedroom saying, "Please, God, make her shut up. Tell her to be quiet, please, God" . . .

OLIVE (*Comes back in with tray of medicants*) . . . Here. Put the scarf on. Take your aspirins.

FLORENCE (*Sits at the table*) I'm not a complainer. I've never once tried to change Sidney . . . He wears a toupee two sizes too big, he looks like an English sheep-dog, I never said a word.

OLIVE Drink them down with brandy.

FLORENCE Now he's into cowboy boots. Five foot three and a half, he wears cowboy boots. They come up to his knees . . . He looks like he jumped off a hundred-foot horse. He's also into languages. He's studying Russian at the New School. Instead of yes, he says "Da." Everything is "Da."

OLIVE You're tensing up again, Florence. Stop tensing.

FLORENCE I'm married to a five-foot-three-inch man with an oversized toupee and boots up to his knees who walks around saying, "Da," and he walks out on *ME*???

OLIVE Will you relax!! RELAX, dammit! Your neck feels like Arnold Schwarzenegger.

FLORENCE Sometimes I think I'm crazy. Sometimes I think I should be put in an institution.

OLIVE Later, if the massage doesn't work.

FLORENCE That doesn't smell like Ben-Gay.

OLIVE (*She looks at the tube*) You're right. It's toothpaste.

FLORENCE I don't think this is helping me.
(*She wipes off the toothpaste with towel*)

OLIVE   Because you won't relax. Have you always been this tense?

FLORENCE   Since I was a baby. I could chew a thick sirloin steak just with my gums.

OLIVE   Bend over.
(FLORENCE *bends over.* OLIVE *begins to massage up and down her back*)

FLORENCE   I do terrible things, Olive. I cry. I panic. I get hysterical.

OLIVE (*Still massaging*)   If this hurts just tell me because I don't know what the hell I'm doing.

FLORENCE   I take advantage of you, Olive. I abuse our friendship. I know I drive you crazy.

OLIVE   No, you don't.

FLORENCE   Yes, I do.

OLIVE   You don't.

FLORENCE   I do. I see you grit your teeth together when I talk to you. You used to have much longer teeth.

OLIVE (*Stops massaging*)   Okay. How does your neck feel?

FLORENCE   Better.

OLIVE   Good.

FLORENCE   But it never lasts long.

OLIVE   Maybe this time.

FLORENCE   No. It just came back.
(OLIVE *rubs her neck again*)

OLIVE (*She shakes her head in despair*) Drink your brandy.

FLORENCE   I don't think I can. It doesn't go down.

OLIVE   I'll get you a plunger . . . Come on, drink the brandy. You'll feel better.

FLORENCE   Thank God the kids are away at summer camp. They'll be spared this until September.

OLIVE   Please drink your brandy.

FLORENCE   I don't want to get divorced, Olive. I don't want to suddenly change my whole life. Talk to me. Tell me what to do.

OLIVE   Alright, alright. First of all, you're going to calm down and relax. Then you and I are going to figure out a whole new life for you.

FLORENCE   Without Sidney? What kind of a life is there without Sidney?

OLIVE   I don't live with Sidney and I'm very happy. You can do it, Florence, believe me.

FLORENCE   Olive, you've been through it yourself. What did you do? How did you get through it?

OLIVE (*She drinks some brandy*) I drank for four days and five nights. I couldn't work. I ate a quart of Häagen-Dazs jamocha almond fudge every night. I gained fourteen pounds, seven on each hip. I looked like I was carrying my laundry in my pockets . . . But I got through it.

FLORENCE   And what about Sidney? He's human too. How's he going to get through this?

OLIVE   He's a man. Men have freedom. He can meet women anywhere. *We* have to donate a kidney and hope the man is grateful and single.

FLORENCE You think Sidney is thinking of other women? At a time like this?

OLIVE I guarantee you by tomorrow night he'll be at a singles bar sitting on a stool on top of two telephone books.

FLORENCE You think so?
(She's been playing with her ear. She suddenly starts to make strange noises as she tries to unplug her ear)

OLIVE What's the matter now?

FLORENCE *(Standing)* My ears are closing up. It's a sinus condition. I'm allergic.
(She makes the sinus sound again, then crosses to the open window. OLIVE *follows nervously behind)*

OLIVE What are you doing?

FLORENCE I'm not going to jump. I just want to breathe. *(She takes deep breaths)* I was even allergic to perfume. I had to wear Sidney's after-shave lotion. Old Spice Menthol . . . I always felt like I just sailed home from Singapore.
(She suddenly bellows like a moose)

OLIVE *(Looks dumbfounded)* What are you doing?

FLORENCE I'm trying to clear my ears. You create a pressure inside and then it opens up.
(She bellows again)

OLIVE Did it open up?

FLORENCE A little. *(Rubs her neck)* I think I strained my throat.

OLIVE Florence, leave yourself alone. Don't tinker.

FLORENCE I can't help myself. I drive everyone crazy. A marriage counselor once kicked me out of his office. He wrote on my chart, "Lunatic"! . . . I don't blame Sidney. It's impossible to be married to me.

OLIVE   It takes two to make a lousy marriage.

FLORENCE   What'll I do with the rest of my life, Olive? I have so much of it left. If only I was seventy, seventy-five, I could get through it.

OLIVE   I'll tell you what you're going to do. You're going to start your life over and stand on your own two feet. Be independent!

FLORENCE   You're right.

OLIVE   Of course I am.

FLORENCE   That's what I was before I was married. I was a great bookkeeper. I could have been Price Waterhouse today. You're right. Go back to work. Be independent. A self-sufficient woman.

OLIVE   You're damn right.

FLORENCE   Maybe I should ask for my old job back.

OLIVE   Why not? Who did you work for?

FLORENCE   Sidney. God, the mistakes I've made. Goddamn idiot!! I hate me.

OLIVE   You don't hate you. You love you. You think no one has problems like you.

FLORENCE   You're wrong. I happen to know I hate my guts.

OLIVE   Come on, Florence. I've never seen anyone so in love. If you had two more legs, you'd take yourself out dancing.

FLORENCE   I thought you were my friend.

OLIVE   I am. That's why I can talk to you like this. I love you almost as much as you do.

FLORENCE   Then help me.

OLIVE   How can I help you when I can't help myself? You think you're impossible to live with? I was sloppy since I was a kid. I got married in a white gown with Coca-Cola stains on it . . . My mind is into other things . . . I like to write, I like to paint, I like photography. I *don't* like to clean up. I leave a mess after I read a book.

FLORENCE   I don't do it for myself. I liked Sidney to come home to a clean house. I want my children growing up having respect for things. How else will they learn?

OLIVE   But what's the point of it all? When you're dead, they're going to throw dirt on you anyway.

FLORENCE   If only I could change . . . Maybe I should call Sidney.

OLIVE   What for?

FLORENCE   To talk it out again. Maybe we left something unsaid.

OLIVE   Where's your self-respect? You want to crawl back on your hands and knees?

FLORENCE   He wouldn't notice. He'd think I was scrubbing the floors.

OLIVE   Florence, listen to me . . . Tonight you're going to sleep here. Tomorrow you're going to go home, pack up your sinus medicines and your after-shave lotions, and move in here with me.

FLORENCE   Won't I be in the way?

OLIVE   Of course you will.

FLORENCE   I'm a pest.

OLIVE   I *know* you're a pest. I was the one who gave you the name.

FLORENCE   Then why do you want me to live with you?

OLIVE   Because—I can't stand living by myself either . . . Because I'm lonely, that's why.

FLORENCE   I never thought of you being lonely. You have so many friends.

OLIVE   Friends go home at eleven o'clock . . . Come on, Florence, I'm proposing to you. What do you want, a goddamn ring?

FLORENCE   If you really mean it, Olive, there's a lot I can do around here. I could turn this place into something out of *Architectural Digest.*

OLIVE   Florence, *Sports Illustrated* is fine with me.

FLORENCE   I want to do something, Olive. Let me do something.

OLIVE   Alright. Tomorrow you can build me a terrace. Anything you want.

FLORENCE   (*She begins to tidy up*)   You'll eat like you never ate before. You like hot Russian blinis? Or Shashlik Caucasian? I'll make it for dinner.
(*She picks up the dirty dishes*)

OLIVE   You don't have to cook. I like eating out.

FLORENCE   Breakfast and dinner at home, we'll save a fortune. We'll need it. Because I'm not taking one single penny from Sidney.

OLIVE   Wait a minute. Let's not be hasty.

FLORENCE   You told me to have self-respect, didn't you? How am I going to have self-respect if I take money from Sidney?

OLIVE   Money is the one aréa where self-respect doesn't work.

FLORENCE   I don't need anything from Sidney. I'll show him. I'll show him what I can do. (*The telephone rings. She looks at it*) That's him. That's Sidney. I can tell his ring.
(*It rings again.* OLIVE *crosses and picks it up*)

OLIVE   Hello? Oh, hello, Sidney.
(*She nods to* FLORENCE)

FLORENCE (*She waves her arms frantically*)   I'm not here. You didn't see me. You don't know where I am. I didn't call. You can't get in touch with me. I'm not here.

OLIVE (*Into phone*)   Yes. She's here.

FLORENCE   DON'T TELL HIM THAT! DIDN'T I TELL YOU NOT TO TELL HIM THAT?

OLIVE (*Into phone*)   Yes, she told me everything.

FLORENCE   How does he sound? Is he worried? What is he saying? Does he want to speak to me? Because I don't want to speak to him.

OLIVE (*Into phone*)   I agree with that, Sidney.

FLORENCE   You agree with *what*? Don't agree with him. Agree with *me*! *I'm* your friend. I can't believe you agreed with him.

OLIVE (*Into phone*)   Well, personally I think she's taking it very well, Sidney.

FLORENCE   I am *NOT* taking it well. I'm taking it like a crazy woman. You call this taking it well?

OLIVE (*Into phone. Warmly*) Oh, I know you have, Sidney. You've been wonderful that way, God bless you.

FLORENCE WHAT DO YOU MEAN, "GOD BLESS YOU"? DON'T "GOD BLESS HIM"!!

OLIVE (*To* FLORENCE) He sneezed, what do you want from me??

FLORENCE I'm sorry. Does he want to speak to me? Ask him if he wants to speak to me?

OLIVE (*Into phone*) Er, Sidney, would you like to talk to her?

FLORENCE (*Reaching out*) Give me the phone. I'll talk to him.

OLIVE (*Into phone*) Oh, you *don't* want to talk to her.

FLORENCE (*Shocked*) He doesn't want to talk to me?

OLIVE (*Into phone*) Yes. I see . . . I understand . . . I agree . . . You're absolutely right . . . Okay. You take care too . . . Goodbye.
   (*She hangs up*)

FLORENCE He didn't want to speak to me?

OLIVE (*Sympathetically*) No.

FLORENCE Then why did he call?

OLIVE He just wanted to make sure you were alright.

FLORENCE He did?

OLIVE He said he loves you very much and that you're a wonderful mother and a wife.

FLORENCE He said that? . . . What else did he say?

OLIVE It wasn't important.

FLORENCE   What else did he say?

OLIVE   It was nothing.

FLORENCE   What else did he say?

OLIVE   But as a woman, you're crazy as a bedbug.

FLORENCE (*She walks to the kitchen door, stops, and says deliberately*)   Oh, really? . . . Is that what the short, hairless cowboy said? . . . Well, tell him he'll never find another woman like me if he lives to be a thousand.
    (*She goes into the kitchen with the dishes*)

OLIVE   . . . Which bedroom do you want? One you can see New Jersey, the other you can see a guy who sleeps naked.

FLORENCE (*She comes out of the kitchen*)   You know, I'm glad. Because he finally made me realize. It's over! It didn't sink in until just this minute.
    (*She continues to tidy up*)

OLIVE   You want some sleeping pills? Take some sleeping pills.

FLORENCE   I can't swallow them.

OLIVE   You can *suck* on them all night.

FLORENCE   I don't think I believed him until just now. My marriage is really over.

OLIVE   Florence, let's go to bed. I have another career besides you.

FLORENCE   Somehow it doesn't seem so bad now. I mean I think I can live with this thing.

OLIVE   Good. Live with it tomorrow. Go to bed tonight.

FLORENCE   I will. I just want to start rearranging our life. Get things in order. Do you have a pad? I want to make out the menus for the week.

OLIVE   NO MENUS! Don't plan my food. I don't want to make any promises to a roast chicken. *Please go to bed*!!

FLORENCE   Can I please be alone for a few minutes? I have to collect my thoughts. (*She starts to pick up the debris from the game*) I think better when I'm cleaning.

OLIVE   I won't sleep if I hear you in here. You want to clean, go downstairs and clean the elevator.

FLORENCE   You'll appreciate it in the morning. Once I get this junk out of here, you'll see furniture you never knew you had. Go on. Go to bed. I'll see you for breakfast.
      (*She is on her hands and knees cleaning up under the table*)

OLIVE   You're not going to do anything big, are you? Like putting up wallpaper?

FLORENCE   Ten minutes. That's all I'll be. I promise. (*Kiss*) Olive!

OLIVE (*Who has started for the bedroom*)   What?
      (FLORENCE *climbs onto the dining table and begins dusting the light fixture*)

FLORENCE   I never realized you were so lonely. It must have been awful for you without anyone else here.

OLIVE (*She reenters, and looks at her with foreboding*)   Well . . . We'll see!!

Curtain

Act Two

SCENE I

Two weeks later. About 10:00 P.M.

The Trivial Pursuit game is in progress. OLIVE, VERA, *and* MICKEY *are on one side of the table,* RENEE *and* SYLVIE *on the other. An empty chair, presumably* FLORENCE's, *is on* SYLVIE's *team's side.*

The appearance of the room is decidedly different than in the first act. It is sterile, spotless, and shining. No laundry bags around, no newspapers on the floor or old magazines, no dirty dishes.

MICKEY *tosses the dice, then moves her marker six spaces.*

MICKEY   Entertainment!

OLIVE   My meat. Go ahead.

RENEE (*She looks back toward the kitchen*)   How long does it take Florence to make coffee?

OLIVE   Well, first she has to go to Colombia to pick the beans. Come on, come on. What's the question?

SYLVIE (*Reading from a card*)   ... "In the 1940's, who was known as the 'Queen of Republic Pictures'?"

OLIVE   Oh. Oh. Easy. I know that. Don't tell me. It's er ... what's her name? ... Oh, Christ, I know it. Big blonde. Lousy actress. I think her husband owned the studio.

VERA   Give us a hint.

OLIVE   NO!! No hints. I don't want hints ... Alright, give us a hint.

SYLVIE She had the same name as a cereal.

MICKEY A cereal?

VERA . . . A cold cereal or a hot cereal?
(MICKEY *and* OLIVE *glare at* VERA. FLORENCE *appears from the kitchen. She is wearing a frilly apron. She carries a tray with glasses, food, and linen napkins. After putting the tray down,* SHE *takes the napkins one at a time, flicks them out at full length, and starts to lay them out on each player's lap, one at a time from left to right around the table*)

MICKEY (*To* SYLVIE) What do you mean? Like Grape-Nuts?

VERA There's no actress named Grape-Nuts. I would remember.
(FLORENCE *continues spreading the napkins on them as they play*)

OLIVE No . . . It's the name of the company. Kellogg. Kitty Kellogg . . . Nabisco . . . Nora Nabisco.
(FLORENCE *pours a Pepsi into a glass with ice in it*)

FLORENCE An ice-cold Pepsi for Mickey.
(SHE *crosses to* MICKEY)

MICKEY Thank you.

FLORENCE (*Holds back the glass*) Where's your coaster?

MICKEY My what?

FLORENCE Your coaster. I just bought a beautiful new set of plastic coasters.

VERA (*Holds up a brown coaster*) Here. I thought they were big chocolate mints.

FLORENCE Always try to use your coasters, girls . . . Sherry on the rocks?

SYLVIE (*Raises her hand*) Sherry on the rocks. (*Holds up a coaster*) And I have my coaster.

FLORENCE (*Crosses back to the food tray*) I hate to be a pest but wet glasses eat right through the polish. Ruins the finish.

OLIVE (*Still on the game*) Farina? (*To* VERA *and* MICKEY) Is it Farina?

VERA Wasn't Farina in the *Our Gang* comedies?

MICKEY Right. The cute little black girl with a circle around her eye.

FLORENCE Aaaand we have a clean ashtray for Sylvie ...

SYLVIE Thanks.

OLIVE ... It's three names. Something something cereal.

FLORENCE Aaaand a sandwich for Vera.
(*She wipes the bottom of the dish with a napkin and places it in front of* VERA)

VERA That smells wonderful. What is it, Florence?

FLORENCE It's crab salad with curry sauce and a little dash of dill on Swedish rye.

VERA You went to all this trouble just for me?

FLORENCE It's no trouble. Honest. You know how I love to cook. (VERA *is about to bite in when* FLORENCE *pushes* VERA's *head forward*) I just vacuumed the rug, try to eat over the dish ... Olive, what did you want?

OLIVE Peking duck for seven! ... Can't you see I'm trying to concentrate?

FLORENCE Gin and tonic. I'll be right back. (*She starts for kitchen, stops at metal box on table*) Who turned off the Pure-A-Tron?

MICKEY   The what?

FLORENCE   The Pure-A-Tron. (*She turns it back on*) Don't play with this, girls. I'm trying to get some of the grime out of the air. (*She flicks the air with her napkin*)

OLIVE (*Losing patience*)   You're purposely doing this, aren't you? You're trying to distract me so your team can win.

FLORENCE   No, I'm not. I don't even know the question.

MICKEY   Who was the Queen of Republic Pictures?

FLORENCE   Vera Hruba Ralston.
    (*She goes into the kitchen.* OLIVE *yells*)

VERA   Ralston! *That's* the cereal.

OLIVE (*Stands and shouts*)   THAT'S NOT HER QUESTION!!! THAT WAS *MY* QUESTION!!! . . . I did all the hard work and she gets the fun of saying Vera Hruba Ralston!!! (*She throws her napkin down on the table*) Goddamn it! . . . Mickey? What would it cost me to hire a hit man?

SYLVIE (*Gets up*)   I can't take this anymore. In three hours we haven't got past four questions . . . I can't think. I get nervous she's going to sneak up behind us and shampoo our hair.

RENEE (*Holds her throat*)   I can't breathe. That lousy machine has sucked all the air out of here.

VERA (*Tastes her sandwich*)   This is delicious. The toast is crisp without being dry.

MICKEY   You know what I hear? I hear Sidney looks terrible. Sends out for Chinese food every night. Stanley saw him on the street with soy sauce on his mouth.

VERA (*Still eating*)   Everything on the sandwich is so fresh. Where does she get fresh crab?

OLIVE   We raise them in the bathtub.

SYLVIE   Is that hotel in Florida still open? I think I may go.

RENEE (*Indicating the Pure-A-Tron*)   I'm telling you that thing could kill us. They'll find us here in the morning with our tongues on the floor.

SYLVIE   Do something, Olive! She's turned a nice friendly game into the Christian Science Reading Room.

VERA   I was just in the bathroom. The towels are so clean and fluffy. And they smell so good. Does she do that too, Olive?

OLIVE   No, she sends them to India and they beat them on rocks.

MICKEY   The trouble is, Florence should have lived a hundred years ago. She would have been appreciated in that world.

OLIVE   I'm trying to arrange it.

RENEE (*Standing near the window, she touches the drapes*)   Jesus, that machine has cleaned the drapes. It's probably vacuuming our lungs right now.

SYLVIE (*Putting on her jacket*)   Listen. Forget it. I'm going home.

OLIVE   Sit down. She's coming out.

SYLVIE   When? She's probably putting up shelf paper.

OLIVE   Don't leave, Sylvie. The game isn't over.

SYLVIE   Listen, I don't even like this game that much. But it's the one night a week I can spend with the girls. I'll talk sex. I'll talk gossip. I will even talk *National*

Enquirer ... But I will *not* talk crispy toast and fluffy towels. (*She puts her shoulder bag on*) There are two kinds of people who drive you crazy in this world. Those who just gave up smoking and those who just got separated.

VERA (*to* SYLVIE) You really have to learn to have more compassion.

SYLVIE (*points to* VERA) And people who say that are the third kind.
    (*She heads for the door*)

OLIVE Don't go, Sylvie. Not yet.

SYLVIE It's your own fault. You're the one who stopped her from killing herself. (*She opens the door and goes*)

OLIVE She's right. The woman is right.

VERA I would have talked sex. No one brought it up.

RENEE I hope I have my wallet so they can identify my body.

OLIVE (*Yells into the kitchen*) Florence, goddammit, we're all waiting. Close up the kitchen and get out here.

RENEE (*She picks up the question cards*) What's that smell? (*She smells the cards*) Disinfectant! ... It's the cards. She washed the cards.
    (*She throws them down.*
    FLORENCE *comes in with a drink for* OLIVE)

FLORENCE Alright, what's the question?

RENEE (*Getting up*) Name a Philip Marlowe movie starring Robert Mitchum.

FLORENCE *Farewell, My Lovely.*

RENEE And goodnight to you, sweetheart.
    (*She puts on her jacket and goes*)

FLORENCE   Gee, I'm sorry. Is it my fault?

VERA   No. I guess no one feels much like playing to-night.

MICKEY   I gotta get up early for work anyway.
(*She puts on her jacket and shoulder bag*)

FLORENCE   Does your husband like you being a cop, Mickey?

MICKEY (*Getting up*)   Well, all he wants to do is kinky things.

FLORENCE   Like what?

MICKEY   Like handcuffing you to the bed.

VERA   Did you ever do it?

MICKEY   Once. But he fell asleep and I slipped a disk trying to get to the bathroom. (*Heading for the door*) If you ask me, you two are the lucky ones. I envy the both of you.

FLORENCE   Envy us? Why?

MICKEY   Because you're free. You can do what you want, go where you like. Live out your fantasies.

FLORENCE   Is that how you feel, Vera?

VERA   I'm not good at fantasies. Harry makes one up and gives it to me.

MICKEY (*Nearing the door*)   Believe me, this is the time to be single. I look around. Men are better looking today than they ever were before.

FLORENCE   Why do you think that is?

MICKEY   Because they're eleven years younger today.
(VERA *and* MICKEY *exit*)

FLORENCE (*She starts to clean up the table*) That's something, isn't it, Olive. They think we're lucky. They think we're enjoying this. They don't know, Olive. They don't know what it's like.

OLIVE (*Flat and cold*) I'd be immensely grateful to you, Florence, if you didn't clean up just now.

FLORENCE (*Still cleaning up*) It's only a few things . . . Can you imagine they actually *envy* us?

OLIVE Florence, leave everything alone. I'm not through dirtying up for the night.

FLORENCE It's just a few dishes. You want me to leave them here all night?

OLIVE I don't care if you have them cleaned by your dentist. But don't make *me* feel guilty about it.

FLORENCE I'm not asking you to do it.

OLIVE That's why you make me feel guilty. You're always in my bathroom hanging up my towels. Whenever someone smokes, you follow them around with an ashtray. Last night I found you washing the kitchen floor, shaking your head and moaning, "Footprints! Footprints!" . . .

FLORENCE I didn't say they were yours.

OLIVE Well, they *were* mine, dammit. I have feet and they make prints. What did you want me to do, climb across the cabinets?

FLORENCE No. I want you to walk on the floor.
(*She crosses to clean the telephone*)

OLIVE Can I? Oh, that's wonderful.
(FLORENCE *cleans the phone with a rag and then cleans the wire as well*)

FLORENCE I'm just trying to keep the place livable. I don't want to irritate you.

OLIVE Then don't wipe the telephone. Some of my favorite fingerprints are on that telephone.

FLORENCE (*She looks at* OLIVE, *puts down the cloth, and sits in a chair. Self-pity is coming on*) . . . I was wondering how long it would take.

OLIVE How long *what* would take?

FLORENCE Before I got on your nerves.

OLIVE I didn't say you got on my nerves.

FLORENCE Well, it's the same thing. You said I irritated you.

OLIVE *You* said you irritated me. *I* didn't say it.

FLORENCE Then what *did* you say?

OLIVE I don't know what I said. What's the difference what I said?

FLORENCE It doesn't make any difference. I was just repeating what I thought you said.

OLIVE (*Angrily*) Well, don't repeat what you *thought* I said. Repeat what I SAID!! . . . My God, that's irritating.

FLORENCE (*She picks up a cup and paces*) I'm sorry. Forgive me, Olive. I don't know what's wrong with me.

OLIVE And don't pout. If you want to fight, we'll fight. But don't pout. Fighting *I* win, pouting you win.

FLORENCE You're right. Everything you say about me is absolutely right.

OLIVE (*Getting angry*)   And don't give in so easily. I'm *not* always right. Sometimes *you're* right.

FLORENCE   You're right. I do that. I always figure I'm in the wrong.

OLIVE   Only this time you *are* wrong and I'm right.

FLORENCE   Oh, leave me alone.

OLIVE   And don't sulk. That's the same as pouting.

FLORENCE   I know. I know. (*She squeezes the cup with anger*) Damn me! Why can't I do one lousy thing right?
(*She suddenly cocks her arm back angrily, about to hurl the cup against the wall, then thinks better of it and stops herself*)

OLIVE (*Watching this*)   Why didn't you throw it?

FLORENCE   I almost did. I get so insane with myself sometimes.

OLIVE   Then why didn't you throw the cup?

FLORENCE   Because I'm trying to control myself.

OLIVE   Why?

FLORENCE   What do you mean, why?

OLIVE   Why do you have to control yourself? You're angry, you felt like throwing the cup, why don't you throw it?

FLORENCE   Because there's no point to it. I'd still be angry and I'd have a broken cup.

OLIVE   How do you *know* how you'd feel? Maybe you'd feel *wonderful*. Why do you have to control every single thought in your head? Why don't you let loose once in your life? Do something that you *feel* like doing and not what you're *supposed* to do . . . Stop keeping books. Relax! Get drunk! Get angry! . . . C'mon! BREAK THE GODDAMN CUP!!

(FLORENCE *suddenly gets a surge of anger, faces the wall, and with all her might, throws the cup against the wall. It smashes to bits.* SHE *suddenly grabs her arm in pain*)

FLORENCE   Ohh, my arm! I hurt my arm!
(*She is in agony*)

OLIVE (*Throwing up her hands*)   You're hopeless! You're a hopeless mental case!

FLORENCE   I'm not supposed to use this arm. I have bursitis.
(*She rubs it*)

OLIVE   You're not going to cry, are you? I think all those tears dripping on the arm is what gave you bursitis. (*She throws her a napkin*) You know what you are, Florence? You're a human accident.

FLORENCE (*Dabbing at her knee*)   Uh huh. Who just happens to cook and clean and take care of this house. I save us a lot of money, don't I?

OLIVE   Thank you, Paine Webber.

FLORENCE (*She limps over to the table and puts the broken pieces of the cup on tray*)   Okay, I may be compulsive but I'm not a grouch. We have our good times too, don't we?

OLIVE   Good times?? . . . Florence, getting a clear picture on Channel Two is not my idea of whoopee.

FLORENCE   What are you talking about?

OLIVE   I've spent enough nights watching you put paper strips between your toes. The night was made for better things.

FLORENCE Like what?

OLIVE Like the smell of a good cigar circling under my nose. Listen to me good. There are two sexes in this world. We're one of them. I didn't make this up, but nature demands that our sex sometimes has to get in touch with their sex.

FLORENCE You mean men?

OLIVE If you want to give it a name, alright. Men!

FLORENCE That's funny. I haven't thought about men in weeks.

OLIVE I fail to see the humor.

FLORENCE You think I don't find men attractive? I find plenty of men attractive.

OLIVE Like who? Name one.

FLORENCE I always thought Adlai Stevenson was attractive.

OLIVE Yes, but he doesn't date anymore . . . Florence, we can't stay home alone every night like this.

FLORENCE Listen, I intend to go out. I get lonely too. But I'm just separated a few weeks. Give me a little time.

OLIVE What am I asking? I would just like to have dinner one night with a couple of nice guys.

FLORENCE Who would I call? The only single man I know is my hairdresser and he's into other things.

OLIVE Leave that to me. There are two brothers who live in this building. They're Spanish. They used to live in Spain. They're a million laughs.

FLORENCE How do you know?

OLIVE   I was trapped in the elevator with them last week. They asked me to dinner. This'll be perfect.

FLORENCE   What do they look like?

OLIVE   Real gentlemen. They wore double-breasted suits.

FLORENCE   Double-breasted suits doesn't mean you're a gentleman.

OLIVE   These had cuffs on the pants.

FLORENCE   But are they young or old? Are they nice-looking?

OLIVE   I'm trying to tell you, these are two classy Spanish guys. No taps on their shoes.
(*She finds the number*)

FLORENCE   Which one do I get?

OLIVE   Take whoever you want. When they come in, point to the Spaniard of your choice.
(*She crosses to the phone and starts to dial*)

FLORENCE   I wouldn't know what to say to them.

OLIVE (*Stops dialing*)   Will you relax. They're easy to be with. I talked to them for a half hour and didn't even understand a word they said.

FLORENCE   They don't speak English?

OLIVE   They speak *perfect* English—every once in a while . . . Just promise me one thing.

FLORENCE   What?

OLIVE   Don't call one of them Sidney. Forget Sidney. It's Manolo and Hay-zoos?

FLORENCE   Manolo and Hay-zoos?

OLIVE   You don't pronounce the J.

FLORENCE *(Thinks)*   Where is there a J in Manolo and Hay-zoos?

OLIVE   Stop worrying, will you? We're going to have a night out on the town. They know the best Spanish restaurant in New York.

FLORENCE   I'm not going out to a restaurant and being seen by everyone in this city.

OLIVE   You think people are lining the streets waiting to see who we go out with?

FLORENCE   I'm talking about my friends. My family. What if my mother-in-law walks in and sees me drinking tequilas with Manolo and Hay-zoos?

OLIVE   Your mother-in-law lives in Florida!!!

FLORENCE   THIS COULD BE THE ONE NIGHT SHE COMES TO TOWN.

OLIVE   Florence . . . I need a date *real bad.* Time is going by. My hormones are going tick-tock, tick-tock . . . Give me your hand.

FLORENCE   What?

OLIVE   Give me your hand. *(She takes* FLORENCE's *hand and puts it on her chest)* Do you feel my breast?

FLORENCE   Yes.

OLIVE   Well, it's not good enough. I want to feel a bigger hand with knuckles . . . Please!

FLORENCE   Alright. Alright . . . But not outside. We'll eat here.

OLIVE   HERE??? . . . Florence, this is not a date about *food.* It's about nibbling fingertips. It's about fighting for a woman's honor and making sure we *lose*!

FLORENCE   I don't intend to lose anything. You want dinner, I'll make dinner. I'll make a roast chicken Valencia with Spanish rice, eggplant, squash, potato dumplings, and lemon soufflé.

OLIVE   Are you crazy? You'll blow them up. They'll need help to get out of the chairs. I want them romantic, not diabetic.

FLORENCE   My food is light. My food is fluffy. Don't tell me how to cook. You want them to nibble on your fingers, I'll spread pâté on them.
(*She crosses to the phone*)

OLIVE   Who are you calling?

FLORENCE   My kids. I want them to know what I'm doing. In case their friends tell them their mother is a tramp. (*She finishes dialing. As she waits for the phone to ring*) Manolo and who?

OLIVE   Hay-zoos.

FLORENCE   How do you spell it?

OLIVE   J-E-S-U-S!

FLORENCE   That's Jesus! His name is JESUS???

OLIVE   It's a different Jesus. Will you stop worrying, for God's sakes!

FLORENCE   You didn't tell me his name was Jesus . . . I'll make something simpler. Fish and loaves or something.

Curtain

A few days later. Early evening.

No one is onstage. The dining table looks like a page out of House and Garden. *It's set up for dinner for four, complete with linen tablecloth, candles, and wine glasses. There is a floral centerpiece, flowers about the room, crackers and dip on the coffee table.*

The front door opens and OLIVE *enters. She carries her purse, briefcase, a paper bag with wine. She looks around the room with a gleeful smile.*

OLIVE (*Aloud, to the kitchen*) Oh, God, it's gorgeous . . . It looks like a Noel Coward play.

> (*She kicks off her shoes, then takes off her jacket and throws it on a chair, but it misses and hits the floor. She starts to take off her skirt. She has already put her briefcase on the dining table*)

I feel alive again . . . I feel glamorous . . . I feel like somebody on "Dynasty" . . .

> (*She crosses into the bathroom carrying the dress in the plastic bag from the cleaners that she brought in with her.*
>
> FLORENCE *comes in from the kitchen. She is carrying a large green garbage bag. She looks around at the mess* OLIVE *has left. She goes around and picks up the items—the briefcase, the skirt, blouse, shoes—and, one by one, puts them in the garbage bag. Then she twirls it into a knot, crosses to the hall closet, opens the door, and throws the bag in along with five or six other filled garbage bags. Then she crosses back into the kitchen.*
>
> OLIVE *comes out of the bedroom, zipping up her dress, brushing back her hair. She crosses to the table against the wall and gets out bobby pins and her shoes from one of the drawers.*

FLORENCE *comes out holding a wooden ladle and glares at* OLIVE. FLORENCE *sits*)

OLIVE (*Doing up her hair*)   Oh, you look beautiful. I love the big earrings. Very Espanol . . . What's the matter, Florence? . . . Something's wrong. I can tell by your conversation . . . Alright. Come on. What is it?

FLORENCE   What is it? Let's start with what time do you think it is?

OLIVE   What time? I don't know. Seven-thirty? Eight?

FLORENCE   Try eight-twenty!

OLIVE   Alright, so it's eight-twenty. So?

FLORENCE   You said you'd be home by seven.

OLIVE   Is that what I said?

FLORENCE   That's what you said. "I will be home at seven" is what you said.

OLIVE   Okay. I said I'd be home by seven and it's eight-twenty. So what's the problem? . . .

FLORENCE   If you knew you were going to be late, why didn't you call me?

OLIVE   I couldn't call you. I was busy.

FLORENCE   Too busy to pick up a phone? Where were you?

OLIVE   I was running up and down Sixth Avenue looking for a pair of earrings.

FLORENCE   I have dozens of earrings. I could have loaned you a pair.

OLIVE   I told you. I can't wear pierced earrings. My earlobes closed up.

FLORENCE   I could have *bitten* them open. When Sidney was late, he always called me.

OLIVE   Late?? I'm not late!! I was the first one in the room . . . What difference does it make what time it is?

FLORENCE   I'll tell you what difference. You told me they were coming at seven-thirty. You were going to be here at seven to help me with the hors d'oeuvres. At seven-thirty they arrive and we have cocktails. At eight o'clock sharp we sit down and have dinner. It is now eight-twenty-one and I have a big beautiful bird that's ready to be served. If we don't eat in five minutes, it might as well fly the hell out of here.

OLIVE (*Looks up*)   Oh, God, help me!

FLORENCE   Never mind helping you. Tell him to save my twelve pound capon.

OLIVE   Twelve pounds?? You cooked twelve *pounds*??? They'll fall asleep without us.

FLORENCE   When I have company, I serve the best. And tonight I'm serving the best dried capon money can buy.

OLIVE   Can't you keep it moist for a while?
         (FLORENCE *exchanges the wine bottle*)

FLORENCE   MOIST??? Don't you understand, it DRIES UP!! . . . Food can't be cooked forever. It turns into fossils.

OLIVE   Well, then slice it up now and we'll serve cold capon.

FLORENCE (*Slightly crazed*)   Cold capon?? . . . COLD CAPON??? . . . For a sit-down dinner? . . . You think I'm some kind of BARBARIAN? . . .

OLIVE   It was just a suggestion.

FLORENCE   Really? How about franks and beans? What about four Big Macs and some milk shakes? You think I went to Elizabeth Arden's today for a leg wax so I could serve COLD CAPON??

OLIVE   You asked my advice, I'm giving it to you.

FLORENCE (*She waves the ladle in her face*)   Why don't we have a bag of Halloween candy and let them grab what they want?

OLIVE   Alright, Florence, get ahold of yourself.

FLORENCE   You think it's easy? Go on. Go out and shop and clean and make floral arrangements and stamp little Spanish designs on the butter patties. I'm slaving in a hot kitchen all day and you're in an air-conditioned office giving out baseball scores.

OLIVE   *Baseball scores*?? . . . I'm responsible for getting important news out to the public. Do you know there was a major revolution today in Baggi? A *major revolution!*

FLORENCE   Where the hell is Baggi?

OLIVE   It's a new African country.

FLORENCE   Since when?

OLIVE   Since Thursday.

FLORENCE   No kidding? Well, I have a capon that's older than Baggi.

OLIVE   Who tells you to cook? We could have been at the Casa mi Casa watching Flamenco dancers instead of your lousy twirling ladle.
       (*The doorbell rings. They both freeze*)

FLORENCE   Well, they're here. Our dinner guests. I'll get a chain saw and cut the wings off.
       (*She starts for the kitchen*)

OLIVE STAY WHERE YOU ARE!!

FLORENCE I'm not taking the blame for this dinner.

OLIVE Who's blaming you? Who even cares about the dinner? We're having a date tonight, not a bake-off.

FLORENCE I take pride in what I do. I'm known all over New York for my cooking. And you're going to explain to them exactly what happened.

OLIVE I'll write a full confession on their dinner napkins. Now take off that Peter Pan apron because I'm opening the door.

FLORENCE Why don't we send out to Arthur Treacher's for some fish sticks?

OLIVE Are you through?

FLORENCE I am through.
(FLORENCE *forces a smile as* OLIVE *opens the door. Two gentlemen in dark double-breasted suits, each with a mustache and each holding a box of candy and a bouquet of roses, stand there. They are extremely polite, good-natured, good laughers, and have engaging personalities. They speak with Castilian accents. They are, of course,* MANOLO *and* JESUS)

OLIVE Well, hello there. Or should I say, "Buenas dias"?

MANOLO You can, but ees wrong. Say "Buenas tardes."

JESUS Días ees morning.

MANOLO Tardes ees evening.

OLIVE Got it. I capeesh.

MANOLO No. You "comprendo."

JESUS Capeesh ees Italian.

MANOLO   Comprendo ees Spanish.

OLIVE   I understand.

MANOLO   I understand is English.
    (*The boys and* OLIVE *laugh*)

OLIVE   Well, come on in, "amigos."

MANOLO   Amigos! Very good! (*They come in*) Jesus? You
    have something to say?

JESUS   Sí. With our deep felicitations, Manolo and I have
    brought you fresh flowers and fresh candy.

MANOLO   And red roses for your red hair.

OLIVE   Oh, how sweet.

JESUS   And the candy. I hope you like them. They are
    no good.

OLIVE   They're no good?

JESUS   Sí.

OLIVE   The candy is no good?

MANOLO   Sí. Very chewy.

OLIVE   Do you mean *nougat*?

MANOLO   Ah, yes! *Nou-gat*! (*To* JESUS) Not no good.
    Nougat!

JESUS   I'm sorry . . . We are still new at English.

OLIVE   But very thoughtful. I'll put them in water.

MANOLO   Just the flowers. Candy in water is no good.

JESUS (*To* MANOLO)   I thought it was *nougat.*

MANOLO   No, this time I meant no good was no good.

OLIVE (*Holding two bunches of flowers and two boxes of candy*)   Well, they certainly are beautiful. I feel like Miss America.

JESUS   I feel the same. I miss Spain sometimes.

MANOLO (*To* JESUS)   No. She means the girl in the bathing suit. We'll talk later. (*To* OLIVE) Are you alone tonight?

OLIVE   No. Where is she? . . . Manolo! Jesus! I'd like you to meet my roommate and chef for the evening, Florence Unger.

FLORENCE   *Mrs.* (*She extends her hand*) How do you do?

MANOLO   My pleasure is most extreme. (*He bows and kisses her hand*) I am Manolo Costazuela. (*He bows and kisses her hand again*) And thees ees my very dear brother, Hayzoos Costazuela.

FLORENCE (*Extends her hand*)   How do you do?

JESUS   I am filled with much gratification to meet you. (*He kisses her hand and bows. Her foot automatically bends up behind her*)

OLIVE (*Extends her hand*)   And one for me.

JESUS   Always a pleasure.
(*He bows and kisses* OLIVE's *hand*)

MANOLO   And I double the pleasure. (*He bows and kisses her hand*) Thees ees a charming surprise for me, Mrs. Unger.

OLIVE   Why don't we all sit down, boys?

MANOLO   Gracias. You like me een thees chair?

OLIVE   I don't know. Park it anywhere.

JESUS   We did. The car is outside.

MANOLO   No. No. She means park yourself.
    (*The boys laugh*)

OLIVE   Hayzoos, why don't you sit on the sofa?

JESUS   Of course, eef eet's not too much trouble.

OLIVE   Well, do it the easiest way you can. (*The boys laugh*) And, Florence, why don't you sit on the sofa next to Hayzoos? . . . or the chair. (FLORENCE *sits in the single club chair.* JESUS *sits*) Manolo, aren't you going to sit?

MANOLO   After you, Olivia.

JESUS (*Gets up*)   Oh, excuse me.

OLIVE (*To* JESUS)   You don't like that chair?

JESUS   No, I love this chair. Perhaps you like this chair.

OLIVE   No, no. I *gave* you that chair. Please sit.

JESUS   Of course.
    (*He sits*)

MANOLO (*To* JESUS)   Not until Olivia sits.

JESUS (*He gets up*)   I'm so stupid. Forgive me.

MANOLO (*To* OLIVE)   Now you sit, Olivia.

OLIVE   Good. It's my turn.
    (*She sits*)

MANOLO   Now I sit. (*He sits. To* JESUS) Now you sit.
    (*He sits.* FLORENCE *gets up*)

FLORENCE   Would anyone like anything?
    (MANOLO *and* JESUS *get up*)

OLIVE   Why don't we just see if we can all sit at the same time?

MANOLO   Of course.
(*He sits*)

OLIVE (*Snaps her fingers*)   Florence, sit! (FLORENCE *sits as* MANOLO *and* JESUS *rise in deference*) Down, boys, down.
(*The boys sit*)

MANOLO   Thees happens all the time een Spain. That's why we have to take siestas . . . Olivia! I am so much impressed with your home.

OLIVE   Oh? You like it?

MANOLO   Like it? No. *Love* it! (*Kisses his fingers*) Beautiful, like an El Greco.

OLIVE   Who?

MANOLO   El Greco. The painter, no?

OLIVE (*Looks around, shrugs*)   I don't remember *who* painted it.
(MANOLO *and* JESUS *laugh uproariously*)

MANOLO   You lie to me, Olivia. You say to us eet ees too—er, sloppy—here to invite us. Ees not sloppy.

OLIVE   Yes, but since then I have a woman who cleans every day.

MANOLO   I have the same thing. It's Hayzoos.
(*He points to* JESUS. *They all enjoy this*)

JESUS   Ees true. I like my house very clean. Manolo and I are very different. I am neat, he is not. I am always on time, he is always late. Ees very difficult to live together, you understand?

OLIVE   I've heard of people like that, yes . . . You've heard of people like that, haven't you, Florence?

FLORENCE (*Pauses . . . then, to* MANOLO) You mean El Greco, the great Spanish painter, don't you?

MANOLO (*A little confused*) Sí . . . You wish to go back a little een the conversation?

FLORENCE No. I caught up.
    (*There is an awkward moment of silence*)

OLIVE Well, this is really nice . . . I was telling Flo the other day how we met.

MANOLO Ahh . . . Who ees Flo?

OLIVE She is.

FLORENCE I am.

OLIVE Flo is short for Florence.

JESUS Noo. She is not too short.

OLIVE No. Her name is.

JESUS Her name ees too short?

OLIVE No. It's like er . . . a nickname. Like my name is Olive. But sometimes they call me Ollie. It's shorter.

JESUS Ollie ees shorter than Olive?

OLIVE . . . It's a tricky language.

FLORENCE . . . Actually, El Greco was Greek.

MANOLO Sí.

JESUS Ah!

FLORENCE That's what the name El Greco means . . . "*The*—Greek"!

MANOLO (*Nods*) Yes, we know. We speak Spanish.

FLORENCE   I know. I was speaking about art. I read about him in a travel guide. He lived in a Spanish city called Toleedo.

JESUS (*Correcting*)   Tolaydo.

FLORENCE   I thought it was Toleedo.

JESUS   No. Ees pronounced Tolaydo.

OLIVE (*Sings*)   "She says Toleedo and you say Tolaydo, she says Tomeeto and you say Tomayto . . ."
(*She and the boys laugh*)

FLORENCE   . . . We have a Tolaydo in Ohio . . . Tolaydo, Ohio.

JESUS   No . . . I think that's Toleedo.

FLORENCE   Oh.

MANOLO   You see, Castilian Spanish, you pronounce different than English. Barselona ees Bar*th*elona. San *J*o-say is San Ho-say. *V*ery *v*ery good *v*itamins ees berry berry good bitamins . . . So—they haf berry berry good bitamins in San Ho-say but berry berry bad bodka martinis in Barthelona . . . I do good, Hay-zoos?

JESUS   Berry berry nith. (*They laugh . . . Then—there is an awkward silence*)

OLIVE   Say—hasn't this been one shitty summer? . . . Oh. I'm berry berry sorry.

MANOLO   Oh, eet ees the most hot I can remember. Last night Jesus and I sleep with nothing on.

OLIVE (*Sexily*)   Is that right?

MANOLO   The old couple next door see us naked. We leave the door open for the breeze. They see us, they theenk we are—what ees the word when you theenk two men love each other?

Cut

FLORENCE   Brothers?

MANOLO   No. Not brothers. You know. *Happy* people.

OLIVE   Gay?

MANOLO   Sí. Gay. Yes. They think we are gay.

JESUS   We are not gay, believe me. (*They laugh*) We are the opposite. What is the opposite of gay?

OLIVE   *Not* gay.

JESUS   Sí. Yes. We are *not* gay.

MANOLO   We are the most not gay that ees possible. (*They laugh at this*)

JESUS   Tell me, Florence—because you live with Olivia, do people think you are gay?

FLORENCE   Of course not. That's ridiculous . . . Why do you ask?

MANOLO   Because each Friday night you only have women to veesit you, people say funny things.

FLORENCE   We used to play cards, now we play Trivial Pursuit. What's wrong with that?

MANOLO   That ees a good point. Florence makes a good point.

FLORENCE   Why is it when *men* play poker, no one thinks that *they're* gay?

MANOLO   That ees another good point. Florence makes two good points.

JESUS   In America, people are very suspicious of people who are not married.

MANOLO   Yes. Ees true. Jesus makes a very good point.

OLIVE   So Florence is leading two points to one . . .
Listen, I'm sure the boys would like a cocktail first
. . . Wouldn't you, boys?
(She gets up)

MANOLO   That would be very nice.

OLIVE   Good. What would you like?

MANOLO   I don't wish to put you to trouble. You have
perhaps a double vodka.

JESUS   Manolo! You promise me. No more double vod-
kas.

MANOLO   You hear? My brother ees like my mother
sometimes. But he's right. I'm not good with liquor. I
get very aggressive. Sometimes I attack people.

OLIVE   Come on, let the kid have a drink . . . And for
Jesus?

JESUS   Jesus will have a very, very, very, dry martini.

OLIVE   I'll put a sponge in the glass. Coming right up.
(She starts for the kitchen)

FLORENCE *(Following her)*   Where are you going?

OLIVE   To get the refreshments. I'll give you plenty of
time to get acquainted.
(She exits into the kitchen. FLORENCE *seems lost. She
looks over at the* BOYS; *they smile at her. She crosses
back to her chair and sits, crossing her legs. There is
a long, awkward silence)*

FLORENCE   So . . . You're brothers, are you?

MANOLO   Oh, yes . . . Both of us.

FLORENCE   That's nice . . . Where are you from?

JESUS Barthelona.

FLORENCE Ah . . . And how long have you been in the United States of America?

JESUS Tres anyos. Three years.

FLORENCE Three years . . . You're on a holiday?

MANOLO No, no. We work here, yes, Jesus?

JESUS Yes. Iberia.

FLORENCE You work in Siberia?

JESUS No. *I*beria. The Spanish airlines.

FLORENCE Oh. I didn't understand . . . Are you pilots?

MANOLO No, no. Sales and administration.

FLORENCE I'm really going to have to learn Spanish. Today everyone in New York does. If you don't know what Caballero means, you're afraid to go to the bathroom.

MANOLO That's another very good point. Now you have three good points, Fly.

FLORENCE Fly?

MANOLO Isn't that your name for short?

FLORENCE Flo.

MANOLO Flo! I am so much sorry, Flo.

FLORENCE That's alright, *Manny*.

MANOLO Manny? . . . Oh, ees short for Manolo. Very good, yes, Jesus?

JESUS   Not Hayzoos . . . *Hayz*!
(*They all three laugh, then* FLORENCE *calls out*)

FLORENCE   *OLIVE*?? YOU NEED HELP?

OLIVE (*Peeking in through the door*)   I'm fine. I'm just having a little trouble with the ice cubes.
(*She disappears*)

JESUS   So, Flo . . . What occupation are you?

FLORENCE   I'm separated.

JESUS   From your job?

FLORENCE   No, from my husband.

JESUS   Forgive me, I didn't understand.

FLORENCE   I used to work but then I stopped to become a mother.

MANOLO   You have children?

FLORENCE (*Explaining to foreigners*)   Yes. Mothers-have-children.

MANOLO   How many?

FLORENCE   *All* mothers have children.

MANOLO   No. How many children have *you*?

FLORENCE   Oh . . . er, three . . . No! Two . . . I was counting my husband. (*She laughs embarrassedly. They do too*) But now that I'm separated, I'm going to look for a job again.

MANOLO   That ees where Spain ees very different than America. Spain is still very traditional, very old-fashioned. They feel eet ees the man who should steal the cake.

FLORENCE   Steal the cake?

MANOLO   The cake stealer?

FLORENCE   The breadwinner?

MANOLO   Sí. The breadwinner . . . But Jesus and I are very up-to-date. Very new-fashioned. Tell her, Jesus.

JESUS   Manolo and I are very up-to-date. Very new-fashioned. That ees why we divorced our wives. That ees why we come to this wonderful country to start our lives over. We still love Spain but it was time to say adiós.

FLORENCE   How sad . . . Are there any children still over there?

JESUS   Oh, yes. Millions of children. They have plenty of children.

FLORENCE   No, I meant *yours*.

JESUS   Ah. No. No children. We are honorable men. If we had children, we would have stayed there with our wives and family and been miserable forever.

FLORENCE   It's hard, isn't it? When you lose a spouse?

MANOLO   Ah, yes . . . What ees a spouse?

FLORENCE   (*Realizes they don't understand*)   A spouse! (*She thinks*) . . . My husband is a spouse.

MANOLO   Did you know he was a spouse before you marry him?

FLORENCE   No. The person you're married to *is* a spouse. Your *wife* was a spouse.

MANOLO   I don't think so. We did not keep secrets from each other.

FLORENCE   No, you see, when you get married the person you're married to becomes your spouse.

JESUS   Ya comprendo. Your spouse is your "mareedo." Your husband. Sí?

FLORENCE   Sí. Sí. Grathias. Mucho thank God.

JESUS   You are unhappy to be separated from your spouse?

FLORENCE   Well, after fourteen years, sure. It's so wrenching, isn't it?

JESUS   Wrenching? (*Looks puzzled*) Que es wrenching?

MANOLO (*Shrugs*)   Wrenching . . . No comprendo.

FLORENCE   (*Illustrates tearing apart with her hands*) Wrenching. Tearing apart.

JESUS   Your husband tore you apart?

FLORENCE   No. *Life* tore us apart. Problems tore us apart. I'm still not over it. It's been a very difficult time. You understand?

JESUS   Oh, yes. It's nougat.

MANOLO (*Correcting*)   No good.

JESUS   It's no good.

MANOLO (*To* FLORENCE)   You are unhappy now, Flo, but in time eet will be better. In Spain we have an expression. "The house is not built until smoke comes from the chimney" . . . You understand?

FLORENCE   No.

MANOLO   Maybe thees will explain . . . "The bull does not cry till his horns touch the sky" . . . Yes?
    (*Still puzzled, she shakes her head*)

JESUS   "The ship comes home when the sailor is lost"
. . . (*She shakes her head*) "The dog drinks water when
the—"

MANOLO   Never mind, Jesus.
   (FLORENCE *takes pictures from the table and shows
   them to the boys*)

FLORENCE   This is the worst part of breaking up.

MANOLO (*He gets up and looks at the pictures*)   Ah. You
were childhood sweethearts?

FLORENCE   No. That's my little boy and girl.

MANOLO   Ohh. Preciosos. Such pretty children. Look,
Jesus. Preciosos, no?

JESUS   Oh. Sí. Muy preciosos. (*Points*) The little girl
looks like you.

FLORENCE   That's the little boy.

MANOLO   Ahh . . . They live with their father?

FLORENCE   No. They're still in summer camp. He's a
wonderful father. He's very strict with them but he's
always fair. Sidney's a very exceptional man. One day
he—oh, what am I saying? You don't want to hear any
of this.

MANOLO   But of course we do. Eet ees good to get everything up. *We* got it up. You have to get it up too, Flo.

FLORENCE   I'm trying. (*Takes out another picture and
shows it to them*) That's him. Sidney.

MANOLO (*He looks at the picture, a little skeptical*)   Oh.
Very distinguished. Jesus, distinguished, no?

JESUS (*Looks. He is just as skeptical*)   Oh, yes . . . Very
distinguished . . . He ees a cowboy?

FLORENCE   No. He just likes to wear boots.

JESUS (*Looking at the picture*)   He has beautiful thick black hair. Is he Spanish?

FLORENCE   No, but I think the hair is. (*She picks out another picture*) Isn't this nice?
   (JESUS *looks at it. He is puzzled. He shows it to* MANOLO, *who is puzzled too. They turn it upside down, then right side up*)

JESUS   There ees no one een this picture.

FLORENCE   I know. That's a picture of our living room. We had a gorgeous apartment.

MANOLO   Oh, yes. Ees very beautiful.

JESUS (*Looks at picture*)   The lamps are very beautiful.

FLORENCE   We bought those lamps in Italy. Very rare lamps. I loved my apartment so much, I never wanted to go out. It was such a happy place, everybody laughing, everybody talking to each other. I thought it would go on forever . . . And suddenly it's all gone . . . Sidney, the laughter, the lamps—
   (*She can't finish. She breaks down, sobbing*)

JESUS   . . . Don't be sad, Flo . . . There's a place in Brooklyn you can get the same lamps.

FLORENCE   Please forgive me. I didn't mean to get so emotional. Would you like some guacamole dip?
   (*She hands them a dish as the tears flow again*)

MANOLO   Eet ees good to cry. It washes the pain away, ees true, Hayz?

JESUS   Sí. When Manolo say goodbye to his spouse, he cried for three days.

FLORENCE   Really?

MANOLO I loved her like no man could love a spouse. (*His voice starts to crack with emotion. He cries*) Every night I still theenk of her. Is this true, Zoos?

JESUS Hayz! . . . Ees true. Every night I hear him thinking of her.

MANOLO (*Wiping his eyes*) Sometimes I theenk I have made a mistake. Eef I loved Salina so much, why did I leave her? I was insane. And now ees too late. (*He is sobbing*)

FLORENCE Maybe it's *not* too late.

MANOLO Eet ees too late . . . (*Tearfully*) She got married last month.

JESUS For me ees the same. Only was much worse. My Consuela was—forgive me—unfaithful. (*Crying*) But today I would forgive her. Because I loved her so very much. I will never find another woman like Consuela.

FLORENCE Did you know who the other man was?

JESUS Sí. (*He points to* MANOLO) His ex-wife's new husband.

FLORENCE My God!!
(*All three are crying.* OLIVE *suddenly walks into the room with the drinks*)

OLIVE Is everybody happy? (*She stops dead at the sight of the maudlin scene. They all try to pull themselves together*) What the hell happened? What did you say to them?

FLORENCE Nothing.

OLIVE Well, if you really want to cry, go inside and look at your dead bird.

FLORENCE (*Jumps up*) Oh, my God! Why didn't you call me? I told you to call me.
(*She rushes into the kitchen*)

OLIVE   I should have warned you, boys. She's the high-est-rated soap opera in New York.

MANOLO   I think she is the most sensitive woman I have ever met.

JESUS   So fragile. So delicate. So Spanish. She is the kind of woman you find only in Barthelona.

OLIVE   Well, when she comes out of that kitchen, that's where she may head for.
(*The kitchen door opens and* FLORENCE *comes out. She wears pot-holder gloves*)

FLORENCE   I hope everybody likes dark meat.

OLIVE   Wait a minute. Maybe we can save it.

FLORENCE   Save what? The Black Bird? It looks like the Maltese Falcon.

MANOLO (*Sympathetically*)   Can *we* look at it, Flo?

JESUS   Please?
(FLORENCE *reluctantly goes into the kitchen, then comes out with the dark, smoldering bird. She shows them the remains*)

MANOLO (*He crosses, looks at it*)   Hmmm . . . Thees ees a berry berry burnt bird.

JESUS   Ees no problem. We can have chicken paella up-stairs in my house in ten minutes.

FLORENCE   With *this*?

JESUS   No. I have Stouffer's frozen paella. Ees better than real food.

MANOLO   Then we see you upstairs. Apartment 14B.

OLIVE   We won't even wait for the elevator.

MANOLO   Ees true. There's always dogs in there.
(*Hand kisses. They both rush to the door and are gone in a flash.* OLIVE *turns to* FLORENCE, *beaming*)

OLIVE   Are they cute?? . . . ARE THEY CUTE??? . . . Our time has come, Florence. This is going to be a great year for women . . . Come on, get the guacamole dip.
(*She grabs the wine bottle*)

FLORENCE   I'm not going.

OLIVE   What?

FLORENCE   I don't know how to talk to them. I don't understand them . . . "The ship comes home when the sailor is lost"? What does that mean?

OLIVE   I don't know. I'm not a Spanish philosopher. I'm a frustrated American woman . . . Now take the guacamole dip.

FLORENCE   I can't. I feel too guilty. Emotionally I'm still tied to Sidney.

OLIVE   Florence . . . defrosting paella with Jesus is not adultery. Now, take the guacamole dip.
(*She starts for the door*)

FLORENCE (*She gets the guacamole dip. She starts for the door*)   All right, all right, but it's not going to be any fun. I'm tense as a board. Even my dress feels hard.

OLIVE   Stop it, Florence. You'll get sick in the elevator again.
(FLORENCE *grabs her back on the first step*)

FLORENCE   OHH!! . . . OH, GOD!!! . . . OH, MY BACK!!! . . . OHH! It's broken. My back is broken. It feels broken.

OLIVE   Your back isn't broken . . . Let's get to the chair.
(FLORENCE *can't move from the pain*)

FLORENCE (*At the top of the stairs*)   NO!!! . . . I can't move! Don't move me!
    (*She leans against the wall*)

OLIVE   Damn it, you're going to ruin my whole evening . . . I can't leave you like this.

FLORENCE   I *want* you to go. You're just making me tenser. *Please*, just go.

OLIVE   I'll get you some aspirin.
    (*She goes into the kitchen.* FLORENCE *stands there, immobile*)

FLORENCE   . . . Please, God, don't let me fall. Don't let me die here, God, please, I still have two children to raise, please, God . . .

OLIVE (*From the kitchen*)   Please, God, make her shut up. Please, God make her be quiet.

Curtain

SCENE 3

The next evening, about 7:30 P.M.

The room is once again set up for the game, the chairs set around it. FLORENCE *is vacuuming the living room rug. The door opens and* OLIVE *comes in looking a little weary. She wears a raincoat over her slacks and shirt. She carries the evening newspaper.* FLORENCE *is oblivious to* OLIVE. OLIVE *takes off her raincoat, then crosses to the wall plug and unplugs the vacuum.* FLORENCE *notices it and turns and sees* OLIVE. OLIVE *sits in the wing chair and opens her newspaper.*

FLORENCE *takes the vacuum cleaner and crosses into the kitchen with it.*

OLIVE *steps on the cord, as* FLORENCE *yanks from the kitchen. On the third yank,* OLIVE *lifts her foot and we hear a loud crash from the kitchen.*

FLORENCE *comes out limping as* OLIVE *smiles and sits on the sofa.* FLORENCE *is carrying a tray with a steaming dish of spaghetti on it. She sits at the table and puts cheese on the spaghetti and begins to eat.*

OLIVE *gets up, takes a deodorizer can, and crosses. She sprays all around* FLORENCE *to erase the scent of the spaghetti and gives one final spray into the dish of spaghetti itself . . .* FLORENCE *puts down her fork and napkin, trying to contain her anger.* OLIVE *has resumed her seat on the sofa and continues reading.*

FLORENCE   Alright, how much longer is this going to go on? Are you going to spend the rest of your life not talking to me?

OLIVE   You had your chance to talk last night. I begged you to come upstairs with me. I was looking for romance and instead I got a petrified woman standing in my doorway. I never want to hear the sound of your voice again, do you understand?

FLORENCE   Si. Yo comprendo. Gracias.

OLIVE (*She takes a key out of her pocket and crosses to* FLOR-
ENCE)   There's a key to the back door. Stick to the
hallway and your room and you won't get hurt.

FLORENCE (*Indignant*)   Oh, really? Well, let me remind
you that I pay half the rent and I'll go into any room
I want.

OLIVE   Not in my apartment. I don't want to see you.
Cover the mirrors when you walk through the house
. . . (*Threatening*) And I'm sick and tired of smelling
your cooking. I've had it up to here with your polyun-
saturated oils. Now get that spaghetti off of my table.

FLORENCE (*Laughs*)   That's funny. That's really funny.

OLIVE   What the hell's so funny about it?

FLORENCE   It's not spaghetti. It's linguini.
(OLIVE *looks at her as if she's crazy. Then* OLIVE *picks
up the plate of pasta, crosses to the kitchen door, and
hurls it into the room against the far, unseen wall*)

OLIVE   Now it's garbage!!
(OLIVE *looks self-satisfied.* FLORENCE *looks into the
kitchen, aghast*)

FLORENCE   Are you CRAZY??? . . . I'm not cleaning that
up . . . It's *your* mess . . . Look at it hanging all over
the walls.

OLIVE (*Looks at it*)   I like it.

FLORENCE   You'd just let it hang there, wouldn't you?
Until it turns hard and brown and yich—I'm cleaning
it up!
(*She starts in*)

OLIVE (*Yells*)   You touch one strand of that linguini and
I'll break every sinus in your head.

FLORENCE Why? What is it I've done? What's driving you crazy? The cooking? The cleaning? The crying? What?

OLIVE I'll tell you exactly what it is. It's the cooking, the cleaning, and the crying. It's the moose calls that open your ears at two o'clock in the morning. I can't take it anymore, Florence. I'm cracking up. Everything you do irritates me. And when you're not here, the things I know you're going to do when you come in irritate me . . . You leave me little notes on my pillow. "We're all out of corn flakes. F.U." . . . It took me three hours to figure out that F.U. was Florence Unger . . . It's no one's fault, Florence. We're just a rotten pair.

FLORENCE I get the picture.

OLIVE That's just the frame. The picture I haven't even painted yet . . . Every night in my diary I write down the things you did that day that aggravate me . . . This is June and so far I filled up till January . . . And I haven't even put down the Gazpacho Brothers yet.

FLORENCE Oh! Is that what's bothering you? That I loused up your sex life last night?

OLIVE What sex life? I can't even have dirty dreams. You come in and clean them up.

FLORENCE (*She shakes her finger in* OLIVE's *face*) Don't blame me. I warned you not to make that date in the first place.

OLIVE Don't point that finger at me unless you intend to use it.

FLORENCE Alright, Olive, get off my back. Off! You hear me?
(*She turns away as if she's just won a major battle*)

OLIVE What's this? A display of temper? I haven't seen you really angry since the day I dropped my eyelashes in your pancake batter.

FLORENCE Olive, you're asking to hear something I don't want to say . . . But if I say it, I think you'd better hear it.

OLIVE (*Sarcastically*) I'm trembling all over. Look how I'm trembling all over.
(*She sits in a chair and crosses her legs calmly*)

FLORENCE Alright, I warned you . . . You're a wonderful girl, Olive. You've done everything for me. If it weren't for you, I don't know what would have happened to me. You took me in here, gave me a place to live and something to live for. I'll never forget you for that. You're *tops* with me, Olive.

OLIVE (*Motionless, thinking it over*) . . . If I've just been told off, I think I may have missed it.

FLORENCE It's coming now.

OLIVE Good.

FLORENCE You are also one of the biggest slobs in the world.

OLIVE I see.

FLORENCE And completely unreliable.

OLIVE Is that so?

FLORENCE Undependable.

OLIVE Is that it?

FLORENCE Unappreciative, irresponsible, and indescribably inefficient.

OLIVE What is that, a Cole Porter song?

FLORENCE That's it. I'm finished. *Now* you've been told off. How do you like that?
(*She walks away*)

OLIVE   Good. Because now I'm going to tell *you* off
... (FLORENCE *rushes back, sits in the chair, and crosses
her legs calmly*) For eight months I've lived all alone in
this apartment. I thought I was miserable. I thought I
was lonely. I took you in here because I thought we
could help each other ... And after three weeks of close
personal contact, I have hives, shingles, and the heartbreak of psoriasis ... I am growing old at twice the
speed of sound ... I have seven new liver spots on my
hand that look like the Big Dipper ... I can't take any
more, Florence ... Do me a favor and move into the
kitchen. Live with your pots, your pans, your ladle, and
your meat thermometer ... I'm going inside to lie
down now ... My teeth are coming loose and I'm afraid
if I drop them in here, you'll get out your vacuum
cleaner again.
     (*She goes off, a wreck*)

FLORENCE (*Waits, then*)   Walk on the papers, will you?
I just washed the floors in there. (OLIVE *comes back out,
seething, a maniacal look in her eyes, bent on murder. She
comes after* FLORENCE) Keep away from me. I'm warning you, don't you touch me.

OLIVE   In the kitchen! I want to get your head in the
oven and cook it like a capon.

FLORENCE   You're going to find yourself in one sweet
lawsuit, Olive.

OLIVE   It's no use running, Florence. There's only six
rooms and I know all the shortcuts.
     (OLIVE *chases* FLORENCE, *who runs into the bathroom
     and closes the door.* OLIVE *chases, but instead of going
     into the bathroom, she goes back into the bedroom. The
     stage is empty for a moment. Then* FLORENCE *screams
     as* OLIVE *has apparently entered the bathroom through
     the other door.* FLORENCE *runs out into the living
     room*)

FLORENCE   Is this how you settle your problems, Olive?
Like an animal? (*She grabs her pocketbook, takes out an*

object, and points it at her) Stand back! That's tear gas. You lay one finger on me and you'll be using eyedrops the rest of your life.

OLIVE   You want to see how I settle my problems? I'll show you how I settle them.
(*She runs into* FLORENCE's *bedroom.* FLORENCE *takes a siren out of her pocketbook*)

FLORENCE (*Calling out*)   Alright. I warned you. I'm turning on my siren. (*She presses the switch but it doesn't scream. She holds it to her ear and listens*) What's wrong with this? Have you been playing with my siren? (*She bangs it on the table three or four times in despair*) God-damn it! Twenty-two fifty for a piece of Japanese shit!
(OLIVE *comes out of* FLORENCE's *room with an empty suitcase. She throws it on the table*)

OLIVE   I'll show you how I settle them! (*She opens up the suitcase and stands back*) There! That's how I settle them.

FLORENCE (*Confused, looks at the suitcase*)   Where are you going?

OLIVE (*Apoplectic*)   Not me, you idiot! You!! You're the one who's going. I'll fix your siren so it can whistle for a cab.

FLORENCE   What are you talking about?

OLIVE   The marriage is over, Florence. We're getting an annulment. I don't want to live with you anymore. I want you to pack your things, tie them up with your Saran Wrap, and get out of here.

FLORENCE   You mean actually move out?

OLIVE (*Heading for the kitchen*)   Actually, physically, and immediately. (*She gets pots and pans in the kitchen. She comes out with the utensils, drops them in the bag, and slams the bag closed*) There! You're all packed.

FLORENCE   You know, I've got a good mind to really leave.

OLIVE (*Looks up to heaven*)   Why doesn't she hear me? I know I'm talking, I recognize my voice.

FLORENCE   In other words, you're throwing me out.

OLIVE   Not in other words. Those are the perfect ones. (*She hands the suitcase to* FLORENCE, *who doesn't take it*)

FLORENCE   Alright. I just wanted to get the record straight. Let it be on *your* conscience. (*She goes into her bedroom*)

OLIVE   Let *what* be on my conscience?

FLORENCE   That you're throwing me out. (*She comes out, putting on her jacket*) "Get out of the house" is what you said. (*She crosses to her purse and puts in her siren and tear gas*) But remember this: Whatever happens to me is *your* responsibility. Let it be on *your* head!

OLIVE   What did you put on my head? Don't put things on my head! Take it off! (*She swats at her hair as if trying to get insects out*)

FLORENCE   I left you plenty of food, you just have to heat it up. You can ask the neighbors how to light a match. (*She heads for the doorway*)

OLIVE (*She rushes to the door and blocks the way*)   You're not leaving till you take it back.

FLORENCE   Take what back?

OLIVE   "Let it be on your head" . . . What the hell is that, "The Curse of the Cat People"?

FLORENCE   I'd like to leave now. (*The doorbell rings*) . . . That's your bell . . . Aren't you going to answer it?

OLIVE   Florence, we've been good friends too long to end it this way. We're civilized people. Let's shake hands and part like gentlemen . . .

FLORENCE   There's nothing gentle about being kicked out.

OLIVE (*Nods*)   Okay . . . I tried.
   (*She opens the door.* MICKEY *and* VERA *peer in, then come in*)

MICKEY   What's going on? (*Looks at* FLORENCE) Florence, you look white as a ghost.

FLORENCE (*To the girls*)   Olive will explain everything to you. Have a nice game. If you're hungry, Olive'll get you a plate of linguini. Don't forget to duck . . . Goodbye, everyone.
   (*She goes, closing the door*)

MICKEY   Isn't Florence playing tonight?

OLIVE   She's too busy. She has to go out and spread guilt throughout the land . . . Alright, let's get started. Get the game out.
   (VERA *gets the Trivial Pursuit game and opens it on the table.*
   MICKEY *goes into the kitchen, then stops when she sees what's on the opposite wall*)

VERA (*Putting the game out*)   I know what you're going through. Harry and I had a big fight this morning too.

OLIVE   About what?

VERA   He's very jealous. He thinks I dress too sexy.

OLIVE (*Looks at her*)   Hold on to Harry. He's an unusual man.
   (*The front door opens and* RENEE *enters, looking harassed*)

RENEE Hi . . . Listen, can I please have a scotch. I've got really bad news. I broke up with the doctor.

OLIVE Did he leave you with a curse on your head?

RENEE He's not a witch doctor. He's a gynecologist.
(*The door opens and* SYLVIE *comes in*)

SYLVIE Everybody sit down. I've got major news to tell you.

OLIVE Jesus, this place is like group therapy.

VERA Is it good news or bad news?

SYLVIE It depends what your income is . . . I'm pregnant.

MICKEY Hey! Congratulations.

SYLVIE Isn't it great? The penguin came through.

RENEE Are you sure you're pregnant? I don't trust gynecologists.

SYLVIE Where's Florence? I want to tell her the big news.

OLIVE She left. She's angry because she didn't like what I said.

VERA What did you say?

OLIVE I said, "Get out of my house!"

RENEE You threw her out?

OLIVE I couldn't help it. I couldn't take it anymore . . . It was bad enough watching her straightening out the telephone cord, but when she put nuts in a bowl, she would arrange them—almond next to cashew,

cashew next to peanut, peanut next to pecan, pecan next to Brazil nut, Brazil nut next to almond—

SYLVIE Alright! Stop it, Olive. You're getting yourself sick.

OLIVE —walnuts around the edges—

SYLVIE That's enough!!!
(She puts an arm around OLIVE *and comforts her)*

MICKEY Okay, we all know she's impossible, but she's still our friend and she's still out on the street and I'm still worried about her.

OLIVE And I'm not? I'm not concerned? I'm not worried? Who do you think sent her out there in the first place?

MICKEY Sidney.

OLIVE What?

MICKEY Sidney sent her out in the first place. *You* sent her out in the second place. And whoever she lives with next will send her out in the third place. Don't you understand? It's Florence. She does it to herself.

OLIVE Why?

MICKEY I don't know. There are people like that. There's a tribe in Africa who hit themselves on the head with rocks all day.

OLIVE . . . I'll bet they don't arrange their nuts.

SYLVIE I wonder where she'll go this time?
(The doorbell rings)

OLIVE It's her. I knew it. She wants to come back. New York City didn't want her either.

VERA I'll get the door.

OLIVE   Start the game! I'm not giving her the satisfaction of knowing we were worried about her. Everybody sit down, like nothing happened.
   (*They all sit*)

SYLVIE (*Holding her stomach*)   I hope my baby's not listening to this. She'll think women are crazy.

OLIVE (*To* VERA)   Open it! Open it!
   (VERA *opens the door.* MANOLO *stands there*)

VERA   Oh, hello . . . It's not her, Olive.

MANOLO   Buenas tardes.

VERA   Olive, it's Mr. Tardes.

OLIVE (*She gets up*)   Oh, hello, Manolo . . . Girls, I'd like you to meet my neighbor, Manolo Venezuela.

MANOLO   *Costa*zuela. Manolo *Costa*zuela. (*To* OLIVE) Olibia, may I see you a moment, please.

OLIVE (*Crosses*)   Certainly, Manolo. (*He takes her aside*) What's the matter?

MANOLO   I theenk you already know. I have come to pick up Flo's clothes.

OLIVE (*Looking at him in disbelief*)   Flo's clothes??? . . . *My* Flo's clothes?

MANOLO   Yes. Florence Unger, that sweet tortured woman who ees een my apartment now wrenching her heart out to Jesus . . . You've been a very naughty spouse, Olibia . . . Friendship is more important than capons . . . She is in our apartment now getting it up.

OLIVE (*She turns to the girls*)   I'll translate all this later.
   (JESUS *comes in, pulling a reluctant* FLORENCE)

JESUS   Manolo, Florence doesn't want to stay. Please tell her to stay. (*He notices the girls*) Excuse my intrusiveness, por favor.

FLORENCE   Really, fellows, this is very embarrassing. I can go to a hotel. (*To the ladies*) Hello, girls.

GIRLS (*Quietly awed*)   Hi, Florence.

MANOLO (*To* FLORENCE)   Nonsense. I told you we have a spare room nobody ever uses. You cannot refuse our invitation.

JESUS   We were not raised to allow a woman to wander the streets alone.

FLORENCE   You sure I wouldn't be too much trouble?

MANOLO   It is *we* who are the trouble. Jesus snores and I talk in my sleep.

OLIVE (*To the girls*)   That should sound great with her moose calls.

MANOLO (*To* OLIVE)   I do not weesh to be rude, Olibia, but in Spain, to throw one's friend out of the house is like killing a bull with a pistol. (*To* FLORENCE) Please, Flo. Just for a few days.

JESUS   Just until you get settled.

FLORENCE   Well—maybe just for one night. I have to look for a job tomorrow.

MANOLO   Oh, that ees wanderful.
        (*He kisses her hand*)

JESUS (*To* FLORENCE)   Shall we help you up weeth your clothes?

FLORENCE (*She looks at her dress*)   *These* clothes?? . . . Oh, the ones inside. No, thanks. I'll get them.

MANOLO   Very well. Come up as soon as you are ready—Flosy!

OLIVE   *Flosy*???

JESUS   Don't be late. Cock-a-tails een fifteen minutes.

MANOLO   And keep studying the Spanish language book I gave you.

FLORENCE   Monto bastante bien.

MANOLO   Oh, good. I like to ride horses too. Buenas tardes.
   (*The* BOYS *leave with a flourish.* FLORENCE *turns and looks at the girls on her way toward the bedroom*)

RENEE   Hey, Florence. Are you really going to move in with two guys?

FLORENCE   One kicks you out, two take you in. Women are finally making progress.
   (*She goes into the bedroom proudly*)

SYLVIE (*Amazed at* FLORENCE)   I think I'm going to give birth right here on the floor.

OLIVE   Well, it's cleaner than a hospital.

VERA   I'm really impressed. I never saw such a change come over a woman so fast in my life.
   (FLORENCE *comes out with her dresses in a plastic bag*)

FLORENCE (*Beaming happily*)   I don't know, I suddenly feel so high. I feel like I'm floating—like when you take cough syrup . . . Olive, I want to thank you.

OLIVE   Thank me? For what?

FLORENCE   For the two greatest things you ever did for me. Taking me in and kicking me out. (*The phone rings.* MICKEY *gets up to answer it*) That must be the boys. Spanish blood is so hot.
   (MICKEY *picks up the phone*)

MICKEY (*Into phone*)   Hello? . . . Just a minute.

FLORENCE (*She takes items out of her purse*) Olive, here's my mace and my siren. I think I can handle men on my own now.

MICKEY It's your husband.

FLORENCE Oh! . . . Well, do me a favor, Mickey. Tell him I can't speak to him now. But tell him I'll be calling him in a few days because I think we have a lot to talk about. And tell him if I sound different to him it's because I'm not the same woman who left that house three weeks ago. Go ahead, Mickey, tell him.

MICKEY I will when I see him. This is Olive's husband.

FLORENCE (*Embarrassed*) Oh! (OLIVE *crosses to the phone*) Goodbye, girls. I'll send you down a box of nougat. (*She starts for the door.* OLIVE *stops her*)

OLIVE Florence, don't go yet. (*Into phone*) Hello, Phil . . . Look, I can't talk now. Can I call you back? . . . What check? . . . Phil, I am positively through sending you any more checks. There's a limit to—what? You sent *me* a check? . . . You mean you repaid *everything*? . . . Gee, I'm glad you had a big winner, Phil, but I never expected you to pay back all the—no, no . . . I know what you mean by self-respect. (*She and* FLORENCE *exchange glances*) . . . Does that mean you won't be calling me anymore, Phil? . . . Good. I hope you will . . . G'bye, Phil. (*She hangs up. She looks a little sad, but tries to force a smile*) Isn't that nice? I guess he doesn't need me anymore.

FLORENCE Liking you is better than needing you.

OLIVE (*Wipes her eyes*) Listen, you'd better go. You're starting to talk like a fortune cookie.

FLORENCE (*To the girls*) Are you starting the game now?

VERA Yeah. You want to play?

FLORENCE   I would but I'm berry, berry busy . . .
(*She exits.*
SYLVIE comes out of the bedroom holding a towel.
OLIVE takes it and folds it up neatly)

OLIVE   . . . Come on, let's start the game . . . (*She sits*) Renee and me against you three . . . Roll 'em, Renee . . .

RENEE (*Rolls them*)   Four . . . Entertainment.

VERA (*Picks up a card and reads*)   "According to the 1962 Four Seasons' smash hit, who doesn't cry?"
(OLIVE *begins to sing the song "Big Girls Don't Cry."* SYLVIE *joins in . . . then* VERA, *then the others. They are singing as—*)

Curtain Falls

The Brighton Beach Trilogy

Brighton Beach Memoirs

Biloxi Blues

Broadway Bound

Brighton Beach Memoirs

BRIGHTON BEACH MEMOIRS *was first presented on December 10, 1982, at the Ahmanson Theatre, Los Angeles, and on March 27, 1983, at the Alvin Theatre, New York City, with the following cast:*

EUGENE	Matthew Broderick
BLANCHE	Joyce Van Patten
KATE	Elizabeth Franz
LAURIE	Mandy Ingber
NORA	Jodi Thelen
STANLEY	Željko Ivanek
JACK	Peter Michael Goetz

Directed by Gene Saks
Setting by David Mitchell
Lighting by Tharon Musser
Costumes by Patricia Zipprodt

SYNOPSIS OF SCENES

ACT ONE

Brighton Beach, Brooklyn, New York
September 1937—6:30 P.M.

ACT TWO

Wednesday, a week later
About 6:30 in the evening

Act One

Brighton Beach, New York. September 1937. A wooden frame house, not too far from the beach. It is a lower-middle-income area inhabited mostly by Jews, Irish, and Germans.

The entrance to the house is to the right: a small porch and two steps up that lead to the front door. Inside we see the dining room and living-room area. Another door leads to the kitchen . . . A flight of stairs leads up to three small bedrooms. Unseen are two other bedrooms. A hallway leads to other rooms . . .

It's around six-thirty and the late-September sun is sinking fast. KATE JEROME, *about forty years old, is setting the table. Her sister,* BLANCHE MORTON, *thirty-eight, is working at a sewing machine.* LAURIE MORTON, *aged thirteen, is lying on the sofa reading a book.*

Outside on the grass stands EUGENE JEROME, *almost but not quite fifteen. He is wearing knickers, a shirt and tie, a faded and torn sweater, Keds sneakers, and a blue baseball cap. He has a beaten and worn baseball glove on his left hand, and in his right hand he holds a softball that is so old and battered that it is ready to fall apart.*

On an imaginary pitcher's mound, facing left, he looks back over his shoulder to an imaginary runner on second, then back over to the "batter." Then he winds up and pitches, hitting an offstage wall.

EUGENE   One out, a man on second, bottom of the seventh, two balls, no strikes . . . Ruffing checks the runner on second, gets the sign from Dickey, Ruffing stretches, Ruffing pitches—(*He throws the ball*) Caught the inside corner, steerike one! Atta baby! No hitter up there. (*He retrieves the ball*) One out, a man on second, bottom of the seventh, two balls, one strike . . . Ruffing checks the runner on second, gets the sign from Dickey, Ruffing stretches, Ruffing pitches—(*He throws the ball*) Low and outside, ball three. Come on, Red! Make him a hitter! No batter up there. In there all the time, Red.

BLANCHE (*Stops sewing*) Kate, please. My head is splitting.

KATE I told that boy a hundred and nine times. (*She yells out*) Eugene! Stop banging the wall!

EUGENE (*Calls out*) In a minute, Ma! This is for the World Series! (*Back to his game*) One out, a man on second, bottom of the seventh, three balls, one strike . . . Ruffing stretches, Ruffing pitches—(*He throws the ball*) Oh, no! High and outside, JoJo Moore walks! First and second and Mel Ott lopes up to the plate . . .

BLANCHE (*Stops again*) Can't he do that someplace else?

KATE I'll break his arm, that's where he'll do it. (*She calls out*) Eugene, I'm not going to tell you again. Do you hear me?

EUGENE It's the last batter, Mom. Mel Ott is up. It's a crucial moment in World Series history.

KATE Your Aunt Blanche has a splitting headache.

BLANCHE I don't want him to stop playing. It's just the banging.

LAURIE (*Looks up from her book*) He always does it when I'm studying. I have a big test in history tomorrow.

EUGENE One pitch, Mom? I think I can get him to pop up. I have my stuff today.

KATE Your father will give you plenty of stuff when he comes home! You hear?

EUGENE All right! All right!

KATE I want you inside *now!* Put out the water glasses.

BLANCHE I can do that.

KATE   Why? Is his arm broken? (*She yells out again*) And I don't want any back talk, you hear?
(*She goes back to the kitchen*)

EUGENE (*Slams the ball into his glove angrily. Then he cups his hand, making a megaphone out of it, and announces to the grandstands*) "Attention, ladeees and gentlemen! Today's game will be delayed because of my Aunt Blanche's headache . . ."

KATE   Blanche, that's enough sewing today. That's all I need is for you to go blind.

BLANCHE   I just have this one edge to finish . . . Laurie, darling, help your Aunt Kate with the dishes.

LAURIE   Two more pages, all right, Ma? I have to finish the Macedonian Wars.

KATE   Always studying, that one. She's gonna have some head on her shoulders. (*She calls out from the kitchen*) Eugene!!

EUGENE   I'm coming.

KATE   And wash your hands.

EUGENE   They're clean. I'm wearing a glove. (*He throws the ball into his glove again . . . then he looks out front and addresses the audience*) I hate my name! Eugene Morris Jerome . . . It is the second worst name ever given to a male child. The first worst is Haskell Fleischmann . . . How am I ever going to play for the Yankees with a name like Eugene Morris Jerome? You have to be a Joe . . . or a Tony . . . or Frankie . . . If only I was born Italian . . . All the best Yankees are Italian . . . My mother makes spaghetti with ketchup, what chance do I have?
(*He slams the ball into his glove again*)

LAURIE   I'm almost through, Ma.

BLANCHE   All right, darling. Don't get up too quickly.

KATE (*To* LAURIE)   You have better color today, sweetheart. Did you get a little sun this morning?

LAURIE   I walked down to the beach.

BLANCHE   Very slowly, I hope?

LAURIE   Yes, Ma.

BLANCHE   That's good.

EUGENE (*Turns to the audience again*)   She gets all this special treatment because the doctors say she has kind of a flutter in her heart . . . I got hit with a baseball right in the back of the skull, I saw two of everything for a week and I still had to carry a block of ice home every afternoon . . . Girls are treated like queens. Maybe that's what I should have been born—an Italian girl . . .

KATE (*Picks up a sweat sock from the floor*)   EUGENE!!

EUGENE   *What??*

KATE   How many times have I told you not to leave your things around the house?

EUGENE   A hundred and nine.

KATE   What?

EUGENE   You said yesterday, "I told you a hundred and nine times not to leave your things around the house."

BLANCHE   Don't be fresh to your mother, Gene!

EUGENE (*To the audience*)   Was I fresh? I swear to God, that's what she said to me yesterday . . . One day I'm going to put all this in a book or a play. I'm going to be a writer like Ring Lardner or somebody—that's if things don't work out first with the Yankees, or the

Cubs, or the Red Sox, or maybe possibly the Tigers
. . . If I get down to the St. Louis Browns, then I'll
definitely be a writer.

LAURIE Mom, can I have a glass of lemonade?

BLANCHE It'll spoil your dinner, darling.

KATE A small glass, it couldn't hurt her.

BLANCHE All right. In a minute, angel.

KATE I'll get it. I'm in the kitchen anyway.

EUGENE (*To the audience*) Can you believe that? She'd
better have a bad heart or I'm going to kill her one day
. . . (*He gets up to walk into the house, then stops on the
porch steps and turns to the audience again . . . confi-
dentially*) Listen, I hope you don't repeat this to anybody . . . What I'm telling you are my secret memoirs.
It's called, "The Unbelievable, Fantastic, and Completely Private Thoughts of I, Eugene Morris Jerome,
in this, the fifteenth year of his life, in the year nineteen
hundred and thirty-seven, in the community of Brighton Beach, Borough of Brooklyn, Kings County, City
of New York, Empire State of the American
Nation—"

KATE (*Comes out of the kitchen with a glass of lemonade and
one roller skate*) A roller skate? On my kitchen floor?
Do you want me dead, is that what you want?

EUGENE (*Rushes into the house*) I didn't leave it there.

KATE No? Then who? Laurie? Aunt Blanche? Did you
ever see them on skates? (*She holds out the skate*) Take
this upstairs . . . Come here!

EUGENE (*Approaches, holding the back of his head*) Don't
hit my skull, I have a concussion.

KATE (*Handing the glass to* LAURIE) What would you tell
your father if he came home and I was dead on the
kitchen floor?

EUGENE   I'd say, "Don't go in the kitchen, Pa!"

KATE (*Swings at him, he ducks and she misses*)   Get upstairs! And don't come down with dirty hands.

EUGENE (*Goes up the stairs. He turns to the audience*)   You
see why I want to write all this down? In case I grow
up all twisted and warped, the world will know why.

BLANCHE (*Still sewing*)   He's a boy. He's young. You
should be glad he's healthy and active. Before the
doctors found out what Laurie had, she was the same
way.

KATE   Never. Girls are different. When you and I were
girls, we kept the house spotless. It was Ben and Ezra
who drove Momma crazy. (*We see* EUGENE, *upstairs,
enter his room and take out a notebook and pencil and lie
down on his bed, making a new entry in his "memoirs"*)
. . . I've always been like that. I have to have things
clean. Just like Momma. The day they packed up and
left the house in Russia, she cleaned the place from top
to bottom. She said, "No matter what the Cossacks did
to us, when they broke into our house, they would have
respect for the Jews."

LAURIE   Who were the Cossacks?

KATE   The same filthy bunch as live across the street.

LAURIE   Across the street? You mean the Murphys?

KATE   *All* of them.

LAURIE   The Murphys are Russian?

BLANCHE   The mother is nice. She's been very sweet to
me.

KATE   Her windows are so filthy, I thought she had black
curtains hanging inside.

BLANCHE   I was in their house. It was very neat. *Nobody* could be as clean as you.

KATE   What business did you have in their house?

BLANCHE   She invited me for tea.

KATE   To meet that drunken son of hers?

BLANCHE   No. Just the two of us.

KATE   I'm living here seven years, she never invited *me* for tea. Because she knows your situation. I know their kind. Remember what Momma used to tell us. "Stay on your own side of the street. That's what they have gutters for."
    (*She goes back into the kitchen*)

EUGENE (*Writing, says aloud*)   "That's-what-they-have-gutters-for" . . . (*To the audience*) If my mother knew I was writing all this down, she would stuff me like one of her chickens . . . I'd better explain what she meant by Aunt Blanche's "situation." You see, her husband, Uncle Dave, died six years ago from (*He looks around*) this thing . . . They never say the word. They always whisper it. It was (*He whispers*)—cancer! I think they're afraid if they said it out loud, God would say, "I HEARD THAT! YOU SAID THE DREAD DIS-EASE! (*He points his finger down*) JUST FOR THAT, I SMITE YOU DOWN WITH IT!!" . . . There are some things that grownups just won't discuss. For ex-ample, my grandfather. He died from (*He whispers*)—diphtheria! Anyway, after Uncle Dave died, he left Aunt Blanche with no money. Not even insurance. And she couldn't support herself because she has (*He whispers*)—asthma . . . So my big-hearted mother in-sisted we take her and her kids in to live with us. So they broke up our room into two small rooms, and me and my brother Stan live on this side, and Laurie and her sister Nora live on the other side. My father thought it would just be temporary, but it's been three and a half years so far and I think because of Aunt

Blanche's situation, my father is developing (*He whispers*)—high blood pressure!
(*He resumes his writing*)

KATE (*Comes out of the kitchen with a pitcher and says to* LAURIE) Have some more lemonade, dear.

LAURIE (*Sits up*) Thank you, Aunt Kate.

BLANCHE Drink it slowly.

LAURIE I am.

KATE (*Looks at* BLANCHE) Blanche, that's enough already. Since seven o'clock this morning.

BLANCHE I was just stopping.

KATE You'll sew your fingers together.

BLANCHE It's getting dark anyway. (*She stops, sits back, and rubs her eyes*) I think I need new glasses.

LAURIE Our teacher said you should change them every two years.

KATE (*To* BLANCHE) Would it kill you to put a light on?

BLANCHE I don't have to run up electric bills. I owe you and Jack enough as it is.

KATE Have I asked you for anything? You see anybody starving around here? If I go hungry, you'll give me something from your plate.

BLANCHE Kate! I'm going to pay you and Jack back someday. I don't know when, but I keep my word.

KATE From your lips to the Irish Sweepstakes . . . Go in and taste the soup. See if it needs salt.
(BLANCHE *goes into the kitchen*)

LAURIE Should I put out the water glasses or is Eugene going to do it?
> (EUGENE, *having heard, slams his "memoirs" shut angrily*)

KATE (*Yells up*) EUGENE! It's the last time I'm going to tell you! (*To* LAURIE) Just do the napkins, darling.
> (*She goes into the kitchen.* LAURIE *gets up and starts to set out the napkins*)

EUGENE (*Sits up on his bed and addresses the audience*) Because of her "condition," I have to do twice as much work around here. Boy, if I could just make the Yankees, I'd be in St. Petersburg this winter . . . (*He starts out and down the stairs*) Her sister Nora isn't too bad. She's sixteen. I don't mind her much. (*He is downstairs by now*) At least she's not too bad to look at. (*He starts taking down some glasses from the open cupboard*) To be absolutely honest, this is the year I started noticing girls that weren't too bad to look at. Nora started developing about eight months ago . . . I have the exact date written in my diary.
> (*Suddenly we hear a voice. It is* NORA)

NORA Mom! Laurie! Aunt Kate! (*We see* NORA, *an absolutely lovely sixteen-and-a-half-year-old girl, with a developed chest, bound across the front steps and into the house. She is bubbling over with enthusiasm*) I've got incredible news, everybody!!

EUGENE Hi, Nora!

NORA Eugene! My sweet adorable handsome cousin! Wait'll I tell you what's happened to me. (*She throws her arms around him, hugs him close, and kisses his cheek. Then she rushes into the other room to* LAURIE) I'm fainting! I'm absolutely fainting!

EUGENE (*Still stunned from the hug, turns to the audience*) I felt her chest! When she grabbed me, I felt my first chest.

NORA   I can't believe this whole day!

LAURIE   What happened?

NORA   Where's Mom? Aunt Kate? I have to tell everyone. (*She rushes to the kitchen door*) Everybody inside for
the big news!
  (KATE *and* BLANCHE *come out of the kitchen.* KATE
  is mashing potatoes in a pot)

KATE   What's all the excitement?

BLANCHE   You're all red in the face.

NORA   Sit down, Mom, because I don't want you fainting on the floor.

KATE   Sit down, Blanche.

LAURIE   Mom, sit down.
  (BLANCHE *sits*)

NORA   You too, Aunt Kate. Okay. Is everybody ready?

LAURIE   Stop dragging it out. The suspense is *killing* me.

BLANCHE   Don't say things like that, Laurie.

KATE (*To the others*)   Can I hear what the girl has to say?
(*To* NORA) Go ahead, darling.

NORA (*A little breathless*)   Okay! Here goes! ... I'm going
to be in a Broadway show! (*They look at her in a stunned
silence*) It's a musical called *Abracadabra.* This man, Mr.
Beckman, he's a producer, came to our dancing class
this afternoon and he picked out three girls. We have
to be at the Hudson Theater on Monday morning at
ten o'clock to audition for the dance director. But on
the way out he took me aside and said the job was as
good as mine. I have to call him tomorrow. I may have
to go into town to talk to him about it. They start
rehearsing a week from Monday and then it goes to

Philadelphia, Wilmington, and Washington . . . and
then it comes to New York the second week in December. There are nine big musical numbers and there's
going to be a big tank on the stage that you can see
through and the big finale all takes place with the entire
cast all under water . . . I mean, can you believe it? I'm
going to be in a Broadway show, Momma!
(*They are all still stunned*)

BLANCHE (*To* KATE) What is she talking about?

KATE Do I know? Am I her mother?

LAURIE How can you be in a show? Don't you have to
sing and act?

NORA I can sing.

LAURIE No, you can't.

NORA A little.

LAURIE No, you can't.

NORA I can carry a *tune*.

LAURIE No, you can't.

NORA Well, I probably won't have to. They're just looking for dancers.

LAURIE On Broadway you have to sing and act.

NORA How do *you* know? You never saw a Broadway
show.

BLANCHE Did you tell him how old you were?

NORA He didn't ask me.

BLANCHE He didn't ask if you were sixteen?

NORA He just asked me to audition. My God, isn't anybody excited?

EUGENE I am. It's the most fantastic thing I ever heard.

NORA Thanks, Eugene. I'm glad somebody's excited.

EUGENE (*Turns to the audience*) My God! I'll be sleeping right next door to a *show girl!*

BLANCHE How can you go to Philadelphia? What about school?

NORA School? Momma, this is a Broadway show. This is what I want to do with my life. Algebra and English isn't going to help me on the stage.

LAURIE *Aren't?*

NORA Will you stay out of this!

BLANCHE You mean not finish school? Not get a diploma? Do you know how hard it is today for a girl to get a good job without a high school diploma?

NORA But I've *got* a job. And I'll be making more money than *ten* girls with diplomas.

LAURIE You don't have it yet. You still have to audition.

NORA It's as good as mine. Mr. Beckman told me.

BLANCHE And what if you, God forbid, broke a leg? Or got heavy . . . How long do you think they'll keep you? Dancing is just for a few years. A diploma is forever. I know. I never had one. I know how hard it is to find a decent job. Aunt Kate knows. Tell her, Kate.

KATE It's very hard.

NORA Then why did you send me to dancing school for three years? Why do I spend two hours a day on a subway, four days a week after school, with money that you make going half blind over a broken sewing machine? Why, Momma?

BLANCHE   Because it's my pleasure . . . Because I know how you love it . . . Because you asked me.

NORA   Then I'm asking you something else, Momma. Let me do something for *you* now. I could be making almost sixty dollars a week. Maybe even more . . . In two years when I get out of high school, I wouldn't make that much with a *college* diploma.

BLANCHE (*Takes a deep breath*)   I can't think now. It's almost dinnertime. Uncle Jack will be home soon. We'll discuss it later.
      (*She gets up*)

NORA   I have to know *now*, Momma. I have to call Mr. Beckman and let him know if I can go to the audition on Monday . . . At least let me audition. Let me find out first if they think I'm good enough. Please don't say no until Monday.
      (*They all look at* BLANCHE. *She looks down at her hands*)

EUGENE (*Turns toward the audience*)   It was a tense moment for everybody . . . I love tense moments! Especially when I'm not the one they're all tense about.
      (*He turns back and looks at* BLANCHE)

BLANCHE   Well, God knows we can use the money. We all owe Aunt Kate and Uncle Jack enough as it is . . . I think they have as much say in this as I do. How do you feel about it, Kate?

KATE (*Shrugs*)   Me? I never voted before in my life, why should I start with my own family? . . . I have to heat up the potatoes.
      (*She goes into the kitchen*)

BLANCHE   Then we'll leave it up to Uncle Jack. We'll let him make the decision.
      (*She starts for the kitchen*)

NORA   Why, Momma? I love him but he's not my father.

BLANCHE   Because I need help. Because I don't always know what the right thing to do is . . . Because I say so, that's why.
(*She goes into the kitchen, leaving* LAURIE *and* EUGENE *standing there staring at the forlorn* NORA)

EUGENE   Eugene M. Jerome of New York casts one vote for "yes." (NORA *looks up at him, breaks into tears, and runs out of the room and up the stairs.* LAURIE *follows her up. He turns toward the audience*) What I'm about to tell you next is so secret and private that I've left instructions for my memoirs not to be opened until thirty years after my death . . . I, Eugene M. Jerome, have committed a mortal sin by lusting after my cousin Nora. I can tell you all this now because I'll be dead when you're reading it . . . If I had my choice between a tryout with the Yankees and actually seeing her bare breasts for two and a half seconds, I would have some serious thinking to do . . .

KATE (*Comes out of the kitchen*)   I need bread.

EUGENE (*Turns quickly*)   What?

KATE   I don't have enough bread. Run across the street to Greenblatt's and get a fresh rye bread.

EUGENE   Again? I went to the store this morning.

KATE   So you'll go again this afternoon.

EUGENE   I'm always going to the store. When I grow up, that's all I'll be trained to do, go to the store.

KATE   You don't want to go? . . . Never mind, I'll go.

EUGENE   *Don't* do that! Don't make me feel guilty. I'll go.

KATE   And get a quarter pound of butter.

EUGENE   I bought a quarter pound of butter this morning. Why don't you buy a half pound at a time?

KATE   And suppose the house burned down this afternoon? Why do I need an extra quarter pound of butter?
(*She goes back into the kitchen*)

EUGENE   (*Turns toward the audience*)   If my mother
taught logic in high school, this would be some weird
country.
       (*He runs out of the house to Greenblatt's. Our atten-
       tion goes to the two girls upstairs in their room.* NORA
       is crying. LAURIE *sits on the twin bed opposite her,
       watching*)

LAURIE   So? What are you going to do?

NORA   I don't know. Leave me alone. Don't just sit there
watching me.

LAURIE   It's my room as much as yours. I don't have to
leave if I don't want to.

NORA   Do you have to stare at me? Can't I have any
privacy?

LAURIE   I'm staring into space. I can't help it if your
body interferes. (*There is a pause*) I bet you're worried?

NORA   How would you feel if your entire life depended
on what your Uncle Jack decided? . . . Oh, God, I wish
Daddy were alive.

LAURIE   He would have said "No." He was really *strict*.

NORA   Not with me. I mean, he was strict but he was fair.
If he said "No," he always gave you a good reason. He
always talked things out . . . I wish I could call him
somewhere now and ask him what to do. One three-
minute call to heaven is all I ask.

LAURIE   Ask Mom. She talks to him every night.

NORA   Who told you that?

LAURIE   She did. Every night before she goes to bed. She puts his picture on her pillow and talks to him. Then she pulls the blanket halfway up the picture and goes to sleep.

NORA   She does not.

LAURIE   She does too. Last year when I had the big fever, I slept in bed with the both of them. In the middle of the night, my face fell on his picture and cut my nose.

NORA   She never told me that . . . That's weird.

LAURIE   I can't remember him much anymore. I used to remember him real good but now he disappears a little bit every day.

NORA   Oh, God, he was so handsome. Always dressed so dapper, his shoes always shined. I always thought he should have been a movie star . . . like Gary Cooper . . . only very short. Mostly I remember his pockets.

LAURIE   His pockets?

NORA   When I was six or seven he always brought me home a little surprise. Like a Hershey or a top. He'd tell me to go get it in his coat pocket. So I'd run to the closet and put my hand in and it felt as big as a tent. I wanted to crawl in there and go to sleep. And there were all these terrific things in there, like Juicy Fruit gum or Spearmint Life Savers and bits of cellophane and crumbled pieces of tobacco and movie stubs and nickles and pennies and rubber bands and paper clips and his gray suede gloves that he wore in the wintertime.

LAURIE   With the stitched lines down the fingers. I remember.

NORA   Then I found his coat in Mom's closet and I put my hand in the pocket. And everything was gone. It was emptied and dry-cleaned and it felt cold . . . And that's when I knew he was really dead. (*She thinks for a moment*) Oh, God, I wish we had our own place to live. I hate being a boarder. Listen, let's make a pact . . . The first one who makes enough money promises not to spend any on herself, but saves it all to get a house for you and me and Mom. That means every penny we get from now on, we save for the house. We can't buy *anything*. No lipstick or magazines or nail polish or bubble gum. *Nothing* . . . Is it a pact?

LAURIE (*Thinks*) What about movies?

NORA Movies too.

LAURIE Starting when?

NORA Starting today. Starting right now.

LAURIE Can we start Sunday? I wanted to see *The Thin Man*.

NORA Who's in it?

LAURIE William Powell and Myrna Loy.

NORA Okay. Starting Sunday . . . I'll go with you Saturday.
> (*They shake hands, sealing their "pact," then both lie down in their respective beds and stare up at the ceiling, contemplating their "future home."*
> EUGENE *returns with a paper bag containing the milk and butter under his arm. He stops, pretends to be a quarterback awaiting the pass from center. The bread is his football*)

EUGENE Sid Luckman of Columbia waits for the snap from center, the snow is coming down in a near blizzard, he gets it, he fades back, he passes (*He acts all this out*)—AND LUCKMAN'S GOT IT! LUCKMAN CATCHES HIS OWN PASS! HE'S ON THE FIFTY, THE FORTY, THE THIRTY, THE

TWENTY . . . IT'S A TOUCHDOWN! Columbia wins! They defeat the mighty Crimson of Harvard, thirteen to twelve. Listen to that crowd!
(*He roars like a crowd . . .*)

KATE (*Comes out of the kitchen. She yells out*) EUGENE! STOP THAT YELLING! I HAVE A CAKE IN THE OVEN!
(*She goes back into the kitchen.* STANLEY JEROME *appears.* STAN *is eighteen and a half. He wears slacks, a shirt and tie, a zip-up jacket, and a cap*)

STAN (*In half whisper*) Hey! Eugie!

EUGENE Hi, Stan! (*To the audience*) My brother Stan. He's okay. You'll like him. (*To* STAN) What are you doing home so early?

STAN (*Looks around, lowers his voice*) Is Pop home yet?

EUGENE No . . . Did you ask about the tickets?

STAN What tickets?

EUGENE For the Yankee game. You said your boss knew this guy who could get passes. You didn't ask him?

STAN Me and my boss had other things to talk about. (*He sits on the steps, his head down, almost in tears*) I'm in trouble, Eug. I mean, really big trouble.

EUGENE (*To the audience*) This really shocked me. Because Stan is the kind of guy who could talk himself out of *any* kind of trouble. (*To* STAN) What kind of trouble?

STAN I got fired today!

EUGENE (*Shocked*) Fired? You mean for good?

STAN You don't get fired temporarily. It's permanent. It's a lifetime firing.

EUGENE   Why? What happened?

STAN   It was on account of Andrew. The colored guy who sweeps up. Well, he was cleaning the floor in the stockroom and he lays his broom against the table to put some junk in the trash can and the broom slips, knocks a can of linseed oil over the table and ruins three brand-new hats right out of the box. Nine-dollar Stetsons. It wasn't his fault. He didn't put the linseed oil there, right?

EUGENE   Right.

STAN   So Mr. Stroheim sees the oily hats and he gets crazy. He says to Andrew the hats are going to have to come out of his salary. Twenty-seven dollars. So Andrew starts to cry.

EUGENE   He cried?

STAN   Forty-two years old, he's bawling all over the stockroom. I mean, the man hasn't got too much furniture upstairs anyway, but he's real sweet. He brings me coffee, always laughing, telling me jokes. I never understand them but I laugh anyway, make him feel good, you know?

EUGENE   Yeah?

STAN   Anyway, I said to Mr. Stroheim I didn't think that was fair. It wasn't Andrew's fault.

EUGENE (*Astounded*)   You said that to him?

STAN   Sure, why not? So Mr. Stroheim says, "You wanna pay for the hats, big mouth?" So I said, "No. I don't want to pay for the hats." So he says, "Then mind your own business, big mouth."

EUGENE   Holy mackerel.

STAN   So Mr. Stroheim looks at me like machine-gun bullets are coming out of his eyes. And then he calmly sends Andrew over to the factory to pick up three new hats. Which is usually my job. So guess what Mr. Stroheim tells *me* to do?

EUGENE   What?

STAN   He tells me to sweep up. He says, for this week I'm the cleaning man.

EUGENE   I can't believe it.

STAN   Everybody is watching me now, waiting to see what I'm going to do. (EUGENE *nods in agreement*) Even

Andrew stopped crying and watched. I felt the dignity of everyone who worked in that store was in my hands. So I grit my teeth and I pick up the broom, and there's this big pile of dirt right in the middle of the floor . . .

EUGENE   Yeah?

STAN   . . . and I sweep it all over Mr. Stroheim's shoes. Andrew had just finished shining them this morning, if you want to talk about irony.

EUGENE   I'm dying. I'm actually dying.

STAN (*Enjoying himself*)   You could see everyone in the place is about to bust a gut. Mrs. Mulcahy, the bookkeeper, can hardly keep her false teeth in her mouth. Andrew's eyes are hanging five inches out of their sockets.

EUGENE   This is the greatest story in the history of the world.

STAN   So Mr. Stroheim grabs me and pulls me into his back office, closes the door, and pulls down the shades. He gives me this whole story how he was brought up in Germany to respect his superiors. That if he ever— (*With an accent*) "did soch a ting like you do, dey would beat me in der kopf until dey carried me avay dead."

EUGENE   That's perfect. You got him down perfect.

STAN   And I say, "Yeah. But we're not in Germany, old buddy."

EUGENE   You said that to him?

STAN   No. To myself. I didn't want to go too far.

EUGENE   I was wondering.

STAN   Anyway, he says he's always liked me and always thought I was a good boy and that he was going to give me one more chance. He wants a letter of apology. And that if the letter of apology isn't on his desk by nine o'clock tomorrow morning, I can consider myself fired.

EUGENE   I would have had a heart attack . . . What did you say?

STAN   I said I was not going to apologize if Andrew still had to pay for the hats . . . He said that was between him and Andrew, and that he expected the letter from me in the morning . . . I said good night, walked out of his office, got my hat, and went home . . . ten minutes early.

EUGENE   I'm sweating. I swear to God, I'm sweating all over.

STAN   I don't know why I did it. But I got so mad. It just wasn't fair. I mean, if you give in when you're eighteen and a half, you'll give in for the rest of your life, don't you think?

EUGENE   I suppose so . . . So what's the decision? Are you going to write the letter?

STAN   (*Thinks*) . . . No!

EUGENE   Positively?

STAN   Positively. Except I'll have to discuss it with Pop. I know we need the money. But he told me once, you always have to do what you think is right in this world and stand up for your principles.

EUGENE   And what if he says he thinks you're wrong? That you should write the letter.

STAN   He won't. He's gonna leave it up to me, I know it.

EUGENE   But what if he says, "Write the letter"?

STAN   Well, that's something we won't know until after dinner, will we?
    (*He walks into the house*)

EUGENE (*Looks after him, then turns to the audience*)   All in all, it was shaping up to be one heck of a dinner. I'll say this though—I always had this two-way thing about my brother. Either I worshiped the ground he walked on or I hated him so much I wanted to kill him . . . I guess you know how I feel about him today.
    (*He walks into the house as* KATE *comes out of the kitchen carrying a water pitcher for the table.* STAN *has stopped to look at the small pile of mail*)

KATE (*To* EUGENE)   All day it takes to bring home bread? Give Aunt Blanche the butter, she's waiting for it.

EUGENE   I was home a half hour ago. I was talking to Stan.
    (*He goes into the kitchen*)

STAN   Hey, I got a letter from Rosalyn Weiner. Remember her? She moved to Manhattan. They live up on Central Park West.

KATE   Why not? Her father's a gangster, her mother is worse. I don't get a kiss "Hello"?

STAN   Nope. I was going to save it up and give you a giant one for Christmas.

KATE   We don't have Christmas. I'll take it now, thank you. (*He puts his arms around her and kisses her warmly, then embraces her*) A hug too? When do I ever get a hug from you? You must have done something wrong.

STAN   You're too smart for me, Mom. I robbed a barber-shop today.

KATE   Is that why you look so tired? You don't get enough sleep. Running around all night with your two hundred girl friends.

STAN   A hundred and thirty. That's all I have, a hundred and thirty.

KATE   How do you get any work done?

STAN   I get it done.

KATE   And your boss doesn't say anything to you? About being tired?

STAN   About being tired? No. He doesn't.
       (*He starts toward the stairs*)

KATE   Did you ask him about Thursday?

STAN   What?

KATE   You were going to ask him about getting paid this Thursday so I can pay Greenblatt's on Friday. Saturday is a holiday.

STAN   Oh. No. I forgot . . . I'll ask him tomorrow.

KATE   If it's a problem, don't ask him. Greenblatt can wait. Your boss is more important.

STAN   That's not true, Mom. My boss isn't any more important than Mr. Greenblatt.
       (*He goes upstairs and on to his room, where he lies down, tries to read his letter, then puts it down and*

stares up at the ceiling wondering about his predicament.

EUGENE *bursts out of the kitchen and practically staggers out of the house. He sits on the steps, his head down, looking very disconsolate. He addresses the audience)*

EUGENE   Oh, God! As if things weren't bad enough . . . and now this! The ultimate tragedy . . . liver and cabbage for dinner! A Jewish medieval torture! . . . My friend Marty Gregorio, an A student in science, told me that cooked cabbage can be smelled farther than sound traveling for seven minutes. If these memoirs are never finished, you'll know it's because I gagged to death one night in the middle of supper. (*We suddenly hear a crash of broken dishes in the kitchen.* EUGENE *turns toward the sound, then to the audience)* You're all witnesses. I was sitting here, right? But I'll get blamed for that, anyway.

(*The kitchen door opens and* KATE *comes out helping* BLANCHE, *who is wheezing and gasping quite badly. She can't catch her breath)*

BLANCHE   I'm all right. Just let me sit a minute.

KATE   Didn't I tell you to get out of that hot kitchen? *I* can't breathe in there and *I* don't have asthma. (*She calls out)* NORA! LAURIE! Come help your mother!!
(NORA *and* LAURIE *jump up from their beds)*

BLANCHE   I'm sick about the plates. I'll replace them. Don't worry about the plates.

KATE   Plates I can always get. I only have one sister.
(*The girls have come down the stairs)*

NORA   What happened?

BLANCHE   I'm all right. Don't run, Laurie.

KATE   It's another asthma attack. It's the second one this week. Nora, maybe you'd better get the doctor.

BLANCHE   I don't need doctors . . .

KATE   This is no climate for you, near the beach. What you need is someplace dry.

LAURIE   Like Arizona, Momma.

NORA   Should I get the doctor?

BLANCHE   No. No doctors. It's better. It's going away.

LAURIE   I can still hear the whistle.

NORA   Will you shut up!

BLANCHE   (*To* NORA)   Help Aunt Kate in the kitchen, Nora. I broke her good plates.

KATE   Never mind—Eugene will do it. You go up and get your mother's medicine . . . Laurie, you sit there quiet and watch your mother. You look pale as a ghost. Eugene!

EUGENE and KATE   Come in here and help me!

JACK   (*Offstage*)   Hello, Mrs. Kresky, how are you?

EUGENE   (*Gets up, looks off down the street*)   In a minute, Ma. Pop's home!

LAURIE   (*Sits next to her mother. To the audience*)   I would now like to introduce my father, a real hard worker. He was born at the age of forty-two . . . Hi, Pop! How you doin', Pop?
        (JACOB "JACK" JEROME *appears, a man about forty, who could pass for older. He wears a wrinkled suit, brown felt hat, and black shoes. The* BROOKLYN EAGLE *sticks up out of his side coat pocket. He carries two large and very heavy cardboard boxes, tied around with hemp cord. He appears to be very tired*)

JACK   How am I doin'?

EUGENE   Let me carry these for you, Pop.
(*He reaches for one of the boxes*)

JACK   They're too heavy, you'll hurt yourself.

EUGENE   No. I can do it easy. (*He takes one of the boxes, tries to lift it. It weighs a ton*) Ugh! I just have to get a good grip.
(JACK *stops and sits. He wipes his forehead with a handkerchief and holds his chest*)

JACK   I want to sit a few minutes.

EUGENE   Are you okay, Pop?

JACK   I'm resting, that's all . . . Get me a glass of cold water.

EUGENE (*Struggles with the first box toward the house*)   I'll be out for the other box in a minute, Pop. (*To the audience*) I don't know how he does it. King Kong couldn't lift these . . . You know what's in here? Noise-makers and party favors. Pop sells them to nightclubs and hotels after he gets through every day with his regular work, which is cutting material for ladies' rain-coats.

JACK   Did you do your homework today?

EUGENE   Not all of it. Mom sent me to the store fifteen times. *Amos 'n' Andy* is on tonight.

JACK   Do your homework, then we'll discuss *Amos 'n' Andy*.
(EUGENE *continues into the house as* NORA *comes down the stairs with her mother's medicine*)

NORA   Here's your medicine, Mom. Laurie, go get some water.

BLANCHE   Laurie shouldn't be running.

EUGENE (*The hero*) I'll get it, Nora.

NORA You sure you don't mind?

EUGENE No. No trouble at all. (*To the audience*) Two and a half seconds, that's all I ask. (*He goes into the kitchen*)

NORA (*To* BLANCHE) When are you going to speak to Uncle Jack, Mom?

BLANCHE When I speak to him, that's when I'll speak to him.

NORA Tonight? I have to know tonight.

BLANCHE I'll see . . . If he's not too tired, I'll talk to him tonight.

KATE (*Comes out of the kitchen*) Jack's home. We'll eat in ten minutes. Nora, darling, go get Stanley . . . How's your mother, Laurie?

LAURIE Much better. The whistling's stopped.
(KATE *walks to the front door and goes out.* JACK *is sitting on the stoop, wiping his neck.* NORA *goes upstairs*)

KATE What's wrong? Eugene said you were holding your chest.

JACK I wasn't holding my chest.

KATE You have to carry that box every day? Back and forth to the city. You don't work hard enough, Jack?

JACK You want the box, it's yours. Keep it. I don't need it anymore.

KATE What do you mean?

JACK Del Mars Party Favors went out of business. They closed him out. The man is bankrupt.

KATE   Oh, my God!

JACK   He never even warned me it was coming.

KATE   You told me he lived up on Riverside Drive. With a view of the river. A three-hundred-dollar-a-month apartment he had. A man like that.

JACK   Who are the ones you think go bankrupt? You live in a cold-water flat on Delancey Street, bankruptcy is the one thing God spares you.

KATE   All right . . . You can always find good in something. You don't have to lug that box anymore. You don't have to get up at five-thirty in the morning. We can all eat dinner at a decent hour. You still have your job with Jacobson, we won't starve.

JACK   I can't make ends meet with what I make at Jacobson's. Not with seven people to feed.

KATE   (*Looks back toward the house*)   They'll hear you. We'll talk later.

JACK   I can't get by without that extra twenty-five dollars a week. I can't pay rent and insurance and food and clothing for seven people. Christmas and New Year's alone I made a hundred and fifty dollars.

KATE   (*Nervous about someone hearing*)   Stop it, Jack. You'll only get yourself sick.

JACK   He didn't even pay me for the week, the bastard. Five salesmen are laid off and he's going to a Broadway show tonight. I stuffed every hat and noisemaker I could carry in that box and walked out of there. At his funeral I'll put on a pointy hat and blow a horn, the bastard!

KATE   Don't talk like that. Something'll come up. You'll go to temple this weekend. You'll pray all day Saturday.

JACK (*Smiles ironically*) There's men in that temple who've been praying for forty years. You know how many prayers have to get answered before my turn comes up?

KATE (*Rubs his back where it pains him*) Your turn'll come up. God has time for everybody.
　　(EUGENE *has come out of the kitchen with two glasses of water. He walks over to* BLANCHE)

EUGENE Here's your water, Aunt Blanche.

BLANCHE Thank you, darling.

EUGENE Where's Nora?

LAURIE She went up to call Stanley for dinner.

EUGENE Hey, Laurie—you want to take a walk on the beach tonight?

LAURIE I have homework. What do you want to walk with me for?

EUGENE You, me, and Nora. I just felt like taking a walk.

LAURIE I think Nora has a date with Larry Clurman.

EUGENE *Larry Clurman??* She likes Larry Clurman?

LAURIE I don't know. Ask her yourself.

EUGENE Larry Clurman is my father's age.

LAURIE He's twenty.

EUGENE Same thing . . . You think he's good-looking?

LAURIE I don't think *anybody's* good-looking.

EUGENE Larry Clurman? He doesn't even have a chin. His tie comes all the way up to his teeth.

KATE (*Calls out*) Eugene! Where's your father's water?

EUGENE I'm coming! I'm coming. (*As he walks through the front door, he turns to the audience*) Now I've got Larry Clurman to contend with. (*He comes out*) Here's your water, Pop. I put ice in it.
(*He hands a glass of water to his father, who drinks it all*)

KATE Don't drink so fast.

EUGENE Do you have time to look at my sneakers, Pop?

KATE What does he want to look at your sneakers for?

EUGENE They have no soles. They're hanging on by a tiny piece of rubber. I have to clench my toes when I run out for a fly ball.

JACK I bought you new sneakers last month.

EUGENE Last year, Pa. Not last month. I can only wear them two hours a day because my toes can't grow in them.

KATE This is no time to talk to your father about sneakers. He's got enough on his mind. Turn the light down on the liver. (EUGENE *goes inside and into the kitchen. To* JACK) We'll talk about this tonight. You'll eat a nice dinner, relax, and when everybody's asleep, we'll figure things out calmly. I don't like it when you get upset.

BLANCHE I'm feeling better. Come, dear, help me with dinner.

JACK (*Looks at the house*) You think she'll ever get married?

KATE Blanche?

JACK She's not unattractive. I see men look at her on the beach. What does she want to waste her life in this house for?

KATE   She's raising two children.

JACK   Why doesn't she ever go out? If she wants to meet people, I know plenty of single men.

KATE   Blanche isn't the type to get married.

JACK   She was married once, wasn't she? Those are the type that get married.

KATE   Dave was different. She's not interested in other men.

JACK   What about that Murphy fellow across the street? He's plenty interested, believe me.

KATE   That drunk! The man can't find his way into the house at night. He slept in the doorway once. In the rain. He was there when I went out to get the milk.

JACK   He's got a good-paying job, lives alone with his mother. So he takes a drink on a Saturday night. Maybe what he needs is a good woman.

KATE   Not my sister. Let him meet someone lying in the next doorway. I don't want to discuss this anymore.
   (*She goes inside and into the kitchen.* JACK *sighs, gets up slowly and follows her in. Our attention goes to* STANLEY *on his bed still reading the letter from Rosalyn Weiner. He suddenly sits up.* NORA *knocks on the door*)

STANLEY   Come in.

NORA (*Entering*)   Are you busy? I wanted to talk to you.

STANLEY   That's funny, because I wanted to talk to *you*.

NORA   About what?

STANLEY   I need a favor. Real bad. You're the only one who can help me.

NORA   What is it?

STANLEY   Well, when Pop comes home tired, he doesn't usually pay too much attention to me and Eugene. He's different with you. He's always interested in what you have to say.

NORA   Really? I hope so.

STANLEY   Oh, sure. You never noticed that?

NORA   Not really. What's the favor?

STANLEY   This may sound dumb, but at dinner, do you think you could steer the conversation in a certain direction?

NORA   What direction?

STANLEY   Well, something like how much you "admire people who stand up for their principles."

NORA   *What* people?

STANLEY   *Any* people. "Principles" is the important word. If you could work it in three or four times, I'd be very grateful.

NORA   Three or four times??

STANLEY   It'll be easy. I'll mention someone like Abraham Lincoln and you look up and say, "Now there's a man who really stood up for his principles."

NORA   I have my *own* things to bring up at dinner. I don't want to get into a discussion about Abraham Lincoln.

STANLEY   Not his whole life. Just his principles.

NORA   Why would I do such a stupid thing?

STANLEY Because as of tomorrow I'm unemployed . . . unless someone besides me mentions "sticking up for your principles."

NORA What happened? Did you get fired?

STANLEY I will be unless I write Kaiser Wilhelm a letter of apology. It's really up to my old man. I've decided to do whatever he tells me . . .

NORA When are you going to ask him?

STANLEY Tonight. Right after dinner.

NORA *Tonight?* Does it have to be tonight?

STANLEY That's the deadline. I have to give my answer to Mr. Stroheim in the morning. Why?

NORA Couldn't you ask your father in the morning?

STANLEY He gets up at five-thirty. My mother has to line up his shoes at night because he can't make decisions at five-thirty. (*She is about to break into tears*) What's wrong, Nora?

NORA (*Angrily*) I don't know what *you* have to complain about. At least your father is alive and around the house to make decisions. You don't know when you're well off, Stanley. Sometimes you make me sick!
(*She runs out of the room, slamming the door behind her.* STANLEY *sits there looking bewildered.*
EUGENE *walks into the dining room facing the audience. He looks at them and speaks*)

EUGENE Chapter Seven—"The Infamous Dinner"! (*The others drift into the dining room, taking their seats.* BLANCHE *and* KATE *bring most of the dishes, passing them around. They are all seated as he continues his narrative*) It started out like a murder mystery in Blenheim Castle. No one said a word but everyone looked suspicious . . . It was so quiet, you could hear Laurie's soup going down her esophagus. (*They sit silent, eating*) Everyone had one eye on their plate and the other eye on Pop. Except me. I sat opposite Nora. (*He sits opposite* NORA) I kept dropping my napkin a lot so I could bend down to get a good look at those virginal creamy-white legs. She was really deep in thought because she left herself unguarded a few times and I got to see halfway up her thighs that led to the Golden Palace of the Himalayas.

KATE Eugene! Keep your napkin on your lap and stop daydreaming.

EUGENE (*To the audience*) Stanley knew what I was doing because he's the one who taught it to me. But he was busy with his own problems, like everyone else. You could hear the clock ticking in the kitchen. The tension in the air was so thick, you could cut it with a knife. Which is more than I could say for the liver.
(*He tries to cut his liver*)

JACK Ketchup . . . mustard . . . pickles . . .

EUGENE I'm through. I'll help with the dessert.

KATE Finish your liver.

EUGENE I finished. Do you see liver on my plate?

KATE You buried it under the mashed potatoes. I know your tricks. Look how Laurie ate hers.

EUGENE (*To the audience*) I had a major problem. One more bite and I would have thrown up on the table. That's a sight Nora would have remembered forever. A diversion was my only escape from humiliation. (*To* STANLEY) So how's things down at Stroheim's, Stanley? (STANLEY, *who is drinking water, slams down the glass, splashing it. He glares at* EUGENE, *who continues to address the audience*) I felt bad about that, but for the moment, attention had shifted away from my liver.

JACK (*To* STANLEY) How long have you been working there now?

STANLEY Where?

JACK At Stroheim's.

STANLEY At Stroheim's? Let me see . . . part-time a year and a half before I graduated high school. And a year since then.

JACK So what's that?

STANLEY Two and a half years, counting part-time.

JACK And he likes you?

STANLEY Who?

JACK (*Impatiently*) Mr. Stroheim.

STANLEY Yeah. Usually he likes me. Sometimes I'm not sure.

JACK You come in on time?

STANLEY Yeah.

JACK You do your work?

STANLEY Yeah.

JACK You get along with the other people?

STANLEY Yeah.

JACK So why shouldn't he like you? How much are you making now?

STANLEY Seventeen dollars a week.

JACK It's time you moved up. Tomorrow you go in and ask him for a raise.

STANLEY A RAISE???

JACK   If you don't speak up, people take advantage of you. Tomorrow morning you go into his office, you're polite, you're respectful, but you're firm. You tell him you think you're worth another five dollars a week.

STANLEY   *FIVE DOLLARS????*

JACK   He'll offer you a dollar and a quarter, you settle for two-fifty. I know how these things work. You're a high school graduate, he's lucky he's got you.

STANLEY   I don't think this is the time to ask him for a raise, Pop. I think his wife is very sick.

JACK   You're afraid to ask him? You want me to take you by the hand and walk into his office and say, "My little boy wants a raise"?

STANLEY   I'm not afraid.

KATE   Your father wouldn't ask you if he didn't think it was the right thing. Believe me, Stanley, now is the time to ask for it.

EUGENE   (*Choking*)   Ma, I think I have a bone in my throat.

KATE   There are no bones in liver.
(*He runs into the kitchen*)

LAURIE   So what's new at dancing school, Nora?

NORA   (*Glares at her*)   *Nothing* is new. Mind your own business.

LAURIE   I'm just trying to introduce the subject.

NORA   I don't need your help. Will you tell her to be quiet, Mother.

BLANCHE   Laurie, you may be excused if you're finished.

JACK   What happened at dancing school?

BLANCHE Nora received a very nice compliment from her teacher. She said Nora had professional potential.

LAURIE He didn't say "potential." "Potential" is the future. Mr. Beckman is interested in Nora's "immediate present."

JACK (*Still eating*) Isn't that something! Mr. Beckman is your teacher?

NORA No. He's one of the most widely known and respected producers on Broadway.

JACK Broadway? Imagine that. That's wonderful. And how are you doing in school otherwise?

NORA (*Looks at her mother*) I'm doing fine.

BLANCHE She's doing very well.

LAURIE I wish *I* was as smart as she is.

EUGENE Isn't that the same Mr. Beckman who's producing the great Broadway extravaganza *Abracadabra?* I hear if a girl gets hired for the chorus of a show like that, not only is her career practically guaranteed, but the experience she gains is equal to a four-year college education.

KATE Eugene, that's enough.

JACK Only a four-year college education is equal to a four-year college education.

STANLEY I don't think Abraham Lincoln went to college.
     (NORA *goes into the kitchen*)

JACK What about you, Laurie? You're feeling all right?

LAURIE Yes, Uncle Jack.

JACK   You getting plenty of fresh air?
(NORA *returns*)

LAURIE   As much as I can hold in my lungs. Nora, did you tell Uncle Jack about the big tank that's filled with water?

BLANCHE   Girls, why don't we just let Uncle Jack eat his dinner? If we have something to discuss, we can discuss it later.

JACK   Somebody has something to discuss? If there's a problem, this is the time to bring it up. This is the family hour.

EUGENE   What a great idea for a radio show. *The Family Hour.* Every Wednesday night you hear a different family eating dinner discussing their problems of the week. And you get to hear different recipes. (*As announcer*) "WEAF presents dinner at Brighton Beach starring the Jacob Jerome Family and featuring tonight's specialty, liver and cabbage, brought to you by Ex-Lax, the mild laxative."

KATE   The whole country's going to hear about a fifteen-year-old boy gagging on liver?

JACK   Nothing to discuss? Nobody has any problems? Otherwise I want to turn on the news.

STANLEY   Well, as a matter of fact . . .

JACK   What?

STANLEY   Nothing.

EUGENE   I'll help with the dishes.

KATE   You sit there and finish your liver.

EUGENE   I can't swallow it. It won't go down. Remember the lima-bean catastrophe last month? Does anybody want to see a repeat of that disgusting episode?

JACK   Why does he always talk like it's a Sherlock Holmes story?

STANLEY   He thinks he's a writer.

EUGENE   And what do you think *you* are?

KATE   Eat half of it.

EUGENE   Which half? They're both terrible.

KATE   A quarter of it. Two bites.

EUGENE   *One* bite.

KATE   *Two* bites.

EUGENE   I know you. If I eat one bite, you'll make me eat another bite . . . I'll take it to my room. I'll eat it tonight. I need time to chew it.

JACK   These are not times to waste food. If you didn't want it, Eugene, you shouldn't have taken it.

EUGENE   I didn't take it. They gave it to me. It comes attached to the plate.

NORA   If it's so important to everybody, I'll eat your liver, Eugene.
(*They all look at her*)

EUGENE   You *will*?

NORA   It seems to be the only thing this family is worried about. (*She takes his plate*) Give me your liver so we can get on with more important things in our lives.

JACK   Nora's right. Take the liver away. If nobody likes it, why do you make it?

KATE (*Angrily*)   Because we can't afford a roast beef for seven people.
(*She heads for the kitchen*)

EUGENE (*To the audience*) I suddenly felt vulgar and cheap.

JACK Stanley, turn on the news.

BLANCHE Laurie, get off your feet. You look tired to me.

STANLEY Can I talk to you a minute, Pop? It's something really important.

JACK More important than what's going on in Europe? (*He turns on the radio*)

STANLEY It's not more important. It's just coming up sooner.

JACK (*Fiddles with the dial*) Hitler's already moved into Austria. In a couple of months the whole world will be in it . . . What's the matter with this radio? (*It is barely audible*)

KATE (*Comes out of the kitchen*) Someone's been fooling around with it. Haven't they, Eugene?

EUGENE Why "Eugene"? Pop had the news on last night.

KATE You weren't listening to the ball game this afternoon?

JACK He's talking about Poland . . . Dammit! I don't want anyone touching this radio anymore, you understand?

EUGENE (*To the audience*) Guess who's gonna get blamed for the war in Europe?

KATE Eugene! Bring in the knives and forks. (*He does.* JACK *turns off the radio*)

STANLEY You really think there'll be war, Pop? I mean, America too?

JACK   We're already in it. Not us maybe. But friends, relatives. If you're Jewish, you've got a cousin suffering *somewhere* in the world.

KATE (*Wiping the table*)   Ida Kazinsky's family got out of Poland last month. The stories she tells about what's going on there, you don't even want to hear.

STANLEY   How many relatives do we have in Europe?

KATE   Enough. Uncles, cousins. I have a great-aunt. Your father has nephews.

JACK   I have a cousin, Sholem, in Poland. His whole family.

BLANCHE   Dave had relatives in Warsaw. That's where his mother was born.

STANLEY   What if they got to America? Where would they live?

JACK   Who?

STANLEY   Your nephews. Mom's cousins and uncles. Would we take them in?

JACK (*Looks at* KATE)   What God gives us to deal with, we deal with.

STANLEY   Where would we put them?

KATE   What are you worrying about things like that now for? Go upstairs and work on your speech.

STANLEY   What speech?

KATE   How you're going to ask Mr. Stroheim for a raise tomorrow.

STANLEY (*Looks apprehensively at* EUGENE)   Can I talk to you later, Pop? After you've rested and read your paper?

EUGENE (*Has taken part of his father's paper, opens it*) Lou Gehrig got two hits today. Larrupin Lou is hitting three-oh-two!

KATE (*Grabs the paper away*) Is that your paper? How many times have I told you you don't read it until your father is finished?

EUGENE I didn't break it. The print doesn't come off if I take a quick look at it.

JACK Don't be fresh to your mother. Upstairs.

STANLEY Pop?

JACK Everybody.

STANLEY I'll come down later, okay, Pop?

EUGENE C'mon, Stan. I have to talk to you anyway.
(*They start toward the stairs*)

STANLEY (*To* EUGENE) You're a pest! Did anyone ever tell you you're a pest?

EUGENE Yeah. I have a list upstairs. You wanna add your name to it?
(*He taps* STANLEY *on the forehead with his forefinger. It is annoying and* STAN *chases him up the stairs*)

KATE (*To* JACK) Maybe you should lie down. There's nothing in that paper that's going to cheer you up.

JACK (*Thoughtfully*) What *would* we do, Kate? Where would we put them if they got off the boat and knocked on our door? How would we feed them?

KATE The boat didn't get here yet. I can't deal with boats that haven't landed yet.
(*NORA bursts out of the kitchen, apparently having just argued with her mother. She is followed by* BLANCHE *and* LAURIE)

NORA (*Determined*) Uncle Jack! I know you're tired and you have a lot of things on your mind, but the rest of my life may depend on your decision and I have to know tonight because I have to call Mr. Beckman and let him know if I can go or not.

JACK Who's Mr. Beckman?

NORA The Broadway producer we talked about at dinner.

LAURIE *Abracadabra?* Remember?
(*We see* STANLEY *walk to the bathroom—*EUGENE *walks into the bedroom*)

BLANCHE Laurie! Upstairs! This minute . . . Nora, not now. This isn't the time.

NORA (*Angrily*) It's *never* the time. You won't make a decision and I don't have anyone else I can talk to. Well, I'll make my own decision if no one else is interested. I'm sixteen and a half years old and I'll do what I *want* to do.
(*The tears begin to flow as she runs out the front door to the yard*)

JACK What is this all about?

KATE Go on out, Jack. Talk to her.

BLANCHE I'll take care of it. Nora's right. It's my decision.

KATE What are you going to tell her? That she can leave school? That she can throw her future away? Is that what you want to do?

BLANCHE What if I'm wrong? What if she's got talent? What is it I'm *supposed* to say?

JACK She can't talk to me? It's all the same family, isn't it? I'm her uncle, for God's sake.

KATE　She doesn't need an uncle tonight. She needs a father . . . Go on. She'll tell you.
　　　(JACK *looks at them both, then walks out to the front yard.* NORA *is sitting on the bench, tearfully*)

BLANCHE　I never learned . . .

JACK (*To* NORA)　You mind if I sit with you?

BLANCHE　I wrapped my life up in Dave so much, I never learned to be their mother.

JACK　If you want to talk, we'll talk; if not, not.

KATE　We have enough mothers here. This is a family. The world doesn't survive without families . . . Laurie, do your homework. Blanche, make me some tea. You're the only one here who makes decent tea.
　　　(LAURIE *goes up to her room.* BLANCHE *and* KATE *have gone into the kitchen*)

JACK　Listen . . . I know what it's like, Nora. Not to be heard.

NORA　You do?

JACK　I grew up in a family of four children. My father, before he died, never could remember our names. My oldest brother was "the big one," I was "the little one." My brother Sol was "the rotten one," Eddie was "the skinny one."

NORA　Who am I?

JACK　The pretty one . . . What's the problem?
　　　(STANLEY *walks from the bathroom into the bedroom*)

NORA　I don't know. It doesn't seem very important now.

JACK　I've never seen you cry over something that wasn't important. I know I'm not your father. It's not my place to make decisions for you. But I can offer advice. Advice is free. If it doesn't fit, you can always return it.

NORA   Can we walk down the block?

JACK   Sure. We'll take a look at the ocean. My father always used to say, "Throw your problems out to sea and the answers will wash back up on the shore."

NORA   Did they?

JACK   Not in Brighton Beach. Orange peels and watermelon pits washed up. That's why it's good to take someone who knows how to give advice.
(*She gets up and they walk off toward the beach.* STANLEY *is lying on his bed, hands under his head, deep in thought.* EUGENE *sits on his bed, banging a baseball into his glove*)

STANLEY   Will you stop that? I'm trying to think.

EUGENE   I'm glad I don't have your problems.

STANLEY   How'd you like an official American League baseball in your mouth?

EUGENE   I've got to talk to you, Stanley. I mean a really serious, important talk.

STANLEY   Everybody in this house has to have a talk with somebody. Take a number off the wall and wait your turn.

EUGENE   I had a dream last night. It was about this girl. I can't tell you her name but she's gorgeous. We were really kissing hard and rubbing up against each other and I felt this tremendous buildup coming like at the end of *The Thirty-nine Steps.* And suddenly there was an explosion. Like a dam broke and everything rushed and flowed out to sea. It was the greatest feeling I ever had in my life . . . and when I woke up, I was—I was—

STANLEY All wet.

EUGENE (*Surprised*) Yeah! How'd you know?

STANLEY (*Unimpressed*) It was a wet dream. You had a wet dream. I have them all the time.

EUGENE You do? You mean there's nothing wrong with you if it happens?

STANLEY You never had one before?

EUGENE Yeah, but I slept through it.

STANLEY Didn't you ever try to do it by yourself?

EUGENE What do you mean?

STANLEY Didn't you ever diddle with yourself?

EUGENE No. Never.

STANLEY Baloney. I've heard you. You diddle three, four times a week.

EUGENE You're crazy! What do you mean, diddle?

STANLEY Whack off. Masturbate.

EUGENE Will you be quiet! Laurie might hear you.

STANLEY There's nothing wrong with it. Everybody does it. Especially at our age. It's natural.

EUGENE What do you mean, everybody? You know guys who do it?

STANLEY Every guy I know does it. Except Haskell Fleischmann, the fat kid. He does it to the other guys.

EUGENE I can't believe I'm having this conversation.

STANLEY You can't grow up without doing it. Your voice won't change.

EUGENE Where do you get this stuff from? Is it in a medical book or something?

STANLEY It's puberty.

EUGENE It's what?

STANLEY Puberty. You never heard that word before? You don't read books?

EUGENE Yeah. *The Citadel* by A. J. Cronin. He never mentioned puberty.

STANLEY Even Pop did it.

EUGENE Pop? *Our* pop? You know what, Stanley? I think you're full of shit.

STANLEY (*Sits up*) Hey! Don't you use that language. Who do you think you are? You're just a kid. Never let me hear you say that word again.

EUGENE I don't get you. You mean it's okay for you to say "puberty" but I can't say "shit"?

STANLEY "Puberty" is a scientific word. "Shit" is for those guys who hang around the beach.

EUGENE What do you expect me to say when you tell me that Pop whacks off?

STANLEY I don't mean he still does it, because he's married now. But when he was a kid. Fourteen or fifteen. The whole world whacks off.

EUGENE President Roosevelt too?

STANLEY Rich kids are the worst. They whack off from morning till night. In college, they sit around in their dorms drinking beer and whacking off.

EUGENE   Stanley, this is the most useful information you ever taught me . . . What about girls?

STANLEY   Five times as much as boys.

EUGENE   *Five* times as much? Is that an actual figure? Where do you know all this from?

STANLEY   You pick it up. You learn it. It's handed down from generation to generation. That's how our culture spreads.

EUGENE   Five times as much as boys? Some of them don't even say hello to you and they're home all night whacking off.

STANLEY   They're human just like we are. They have the same needs and desires.

EUGENE   Then why is it so hard to touch their boobs?

STANLEY   If you were a girl, would you like some guy jumping at you and grabbing your boobs?

EUGENE   If I had boobs, I would love to touch them, wouldn't you?

STANLEY   I've got my own problems to think about.

EUGENE   How do girls do it?

STANLEY   I can't explain it.

EUGENE   Please, Stanley. I'll be your slave for a month. Tell me how they do it.

STANLEY   I need a pencil and paper. I'll do it later.

EUGENE (*Quickly hands him his notebook and a pencil*)   Do you want crayons? Maybe you should do it in color?

STANLEY   Hey, Eugene. I have a major problem in my life. I haven't got time to draw girls masturbating for you.

EUGENE   I'll bet Nora doesn't do it.

STANLEY   Boy, could I win money from you. You think she's in the bathroom seven times a day just taking showers?

EUGENE   She does it in the bathroom?

STANLEY   I knew two girls who used to do it in English class. I saw a girl do it during a final exam and she got a ninety-eight on her paper . . . Is she the one you were thinking about last night?

EUGENE   No. It was somebody else. One of the beach girls.

STANLEY   It was Nora. I see what's going on. I knew why you dropped your napkin twelve times at dinner tonight.

EUGENE   She drives me crazy. I think I'm in love with her.

STANLEY   Yeah? Well, forget it. She's your cousin.

EUGENE   What's wrong with being in love with your cousin?

STANLEY   Because it's against the laws of nature. If she was your stepsister, it would be dirty, but it would be okay. But you can't love your own cousin. Let me give you a piece of advice: When you're going through puberty, don't start with anyone in your own house.

EUGENE   Who made up those rules? Franklin Roosevelt married his cousin.

STANLEY   Maybe she was his second or third cousin. But you can't marry your first cousin. You get babies with nine heads . . . I wish Pop would get back. I got to talk to him tonight.

EUGENE   I still would love to see her naked. Just once. There's nothing wrong with that, is there?

STANLEY   No. I do it all the time.

EUGENE   *You've seen Nora naked?*

STANLEY   Lots of times. I fixed the lock on the bathroom door, then opened it pretending I didn't know anyone was in there.

EUGENE   I can't believe it. What a pig! . . . What did she look like?

STANLEY   All I can tell you is I was pretty miserable she was my first cousin.
      (*He lies back on his bed.* EUGENE *turns and looks out at the audience*)

EUGENE   That was the night I discovered lust and guilt were very closely related. (*To* STANLEY) I have to wash up.

STANLEY (*Teasingly*)   Have a good time.

EUGENE   I don't do that.
      (BLANCHE *and* KATE *come out of the kitchen. They each have a cup of tea. They sit at the dining table*)

KATE   I'm sorry. I forgot it was this Tuesday. I'll change my doctor appointment.

BLANCHE   You don't have to change anything. The girls will be with me.

KATE   Have I ever missed a year going to the grave? Dave was my favorite in the whole family, you know that.

BLANCHE   You realize it'll be six years? Sometimes I forget his birthday, but the day he died I never forget.

KATE   There wasn't another one like him.

BLANCHE   Laurie asks me questions about him all the time. Was he funny? What was the funniest thing he ever said, she asked me. I couldn't remember. Isn't that awful, Kate?

KATE   Sometimes you talk like your life is over. You're still a young woman. You're still beautiful, if you'd ever stop squinting so much.

BLANCHE   I went with him for two years before we were married. What was I waiting for? That's two married years I didn't have with him.

KATE   Listen. Jack's company is having their annual affair in New York next Wednesday. At the Commodore Hotel. You should see how some of those women get dressed up. Jack wants you to come with us. He told me to ask you.

BLANCHE   Me? Who do I know in Jack's company?

KATE   You'll be with *us*. You'll meet people. Max Green'll be at our table. He's the one whose wife died last year from (*She whispers*)—tuberculosis . . . He's their number one salesman. He lives in a hotel on the Grand Concourse. He's a riot. You'll like him. Maybe you'll dance with him. What else are you going to do here every night?

BLANCHE   I don't have a dress to wear for a thing like that.

KATE   You'll make something. Jack'll get you some material. He knows everybody in the garment district.

BLANCHE   Thank you, Kate. I appreciate it. I can't go. Maybe next year.

KATE   Next year you won't have any eyes altogether. What are you afraid of, Blanche? Dave is dead. You're not. If God wanted the both of you, you'd be laying in the grave next to him.

BLANCHE   I've made plans for next Wednesday night.

KATE   More important than this? They have this affair once a year.

BLANCHE   I'm having dinner with someone.

KATE   You're having dinner? With a man? That's wonderful. Why didn't you tell me?

BLANCHE   With Mr. Murphy.
     (*This stops* KATE *right in her tracks*)

KATE   Who's Mr. Murphy? . . . Oh, my God! I don't understand you. You're going to dinner with that man? Do you know where he'll take you? To a saloon. To a Bar and Grill, that's where he'll take you.

BLANCHE   We're going to Chardov's, the Hungarian restaurant. You never even met the man, why do you dislike him so much?

KATE   I don't have to meet that kind. I just have to smell his breath when he opens the window. What do you think a man like that is looking for? I grew up with that kind on Avenue A. How many times have Stanley and Gene come home from school black and blue from the beatings they took from those Irish hooligans? What have you got to talk to with a man like that?

BLANCHE   Is that why you don't like him? Because he's Irish? When have the Jews and the Irish ever fought a war? You know who George Bernard Shaw is?

KATE   I don't care who he is.

BLANCHE   One of the greatest Irish writers in the world? What would you say if *he* took me to Chardov's next Wednesday?

KATE   Is Mr. Murphy a writer? Tell him to bring me some of his books, I'll be glad to read them.

BLANCHE Kate, when are you going to give up being an older sister?

KATE I've heard stories about him. With women. They like their women, you know. Well, if that's what you want, it's your business.

EUGENE (*To the audience*) I decided to go downstairs and quiet my passion with oatmeal cookies.

BLANCHE We took a walk along the beach last Thursday. He hardly said a word. He's very shy. Very quiet. He told me where his parents came from in Ireland. Their life wasn't any easier than Momma and Poppa's in Russia.

KATE *Nobody* had it like they had it in Russia.

BLANCHE He holds down a decent job in a printers' office and he didn't smell of liquor and he behaved like a perfect gentleman.
(EUGENE *comes down the stairs. He had been listening*)

KATE (*Without turning*) No cookies for you. Not until you eat that liver.

EUGENE You're still saving it? You mean it's going to be in the icebox until I grow up?

KATE No cookies, you hear me?

EUGENE I just want a glass of water.

KATE You have water in your bathroom.

EUGENE There's toothpaste in the glass. It makes me nauseous.
(*He goes into the kitchen*)

KATE (*To* BLANCHE) Listen, there's no point discussing this. I'm going to bed. Do what you want.

BLANCHE Kate! . . . I don't want to do anything that's going to make you unhappy. Or Jack. I owe too much to you. I can't live off you the rest of my life. Every decent job I've tried to get, they turn me down because of my eyes. The thought of marrying Frank Murphy hasn't even occurred to me. Maybe not even to him. But I don't think one dinner at Chardov's is the end of the world.

KATE I just don't want to see you get hurt. I never mean you harm. I can take anything except when someone in the family is mad at me.

BLANCHE (*Embraces her*) I could never be mad at you, Kate. That I promise you to my dying day.

KATE Go on. Have dinner with Frank Murphy. If Poppa ever heard me say those words, he'd get up from the cemetery and stand in front of our house with a big stick.
(BLANCHE *kisses her again*)

BLANCHE I told him to pick me up here. Is that all right?

KATE *Here?* In *my* house?

BLANCHE For two minutes. I wanted you to meet him. At least see what he's like.

KATE Tell his mother to wash her windows, maybe I'd know what he's like.
(*We see* NORA *hurriedly cross the front yard and open the front door. She looks upset.* NORA *walks over to her mother, determined*)

NORA Can I see Mr. Beckman tomorrow? Yes or no?
(JACK *crosses the front yard*)

BLANCHE Did you talk to Uncle Jack?

NORA I talked to Uncle Jack. I want an answer from *you*, Mother. Yes or no?
(JACK *enters the house*)

BLANCHE   What did he say?

NORA   It doesn't matter what he said. It's your decision or mine. Who's going to make it, Mother?

JACK   I said if I were her father, I'd tell her to finish high school. If she's got talent, there'll be plenty of other shows. I never got past the eighth grade and that's why I spend half my life on the subway and the other half trying to make a few extra dollars to keep this family from being out on the street.

NORA (*To* BLANCHE)   I don't want this just for myself, Momma, but for you and for Laurie. In a few years we could have a house of our own, instead of all being cooped up here like animals. We could pay Uncle Jack for what he's given us all these years. I'm asking for a way out, Momma. Don't shut me in. Don't shut me in for the rest of my life.
   (*They all turn and look at* BLANCHE)

BLANCHE   You promised you'd do what Uncle Jack said.

NORA   He doesn't make decisions—he offers advice. I want a decision, Momma. From you . . . Please!

BLANCHE   You finish high school. You tell Mr. Beckman you're too young. You tell him your mother said "No" . . . That's my decision.

NORA (*Looks at her, frustrated*)   I see. (*To* JACK) Thank you very much, Uncle Jack, for your advice. (*To* BLANCHE) I'll let you know in the morning what *my* decision is.
   (*She rushes upstairs to her room.* BLANCHE *starts to go after her*)

KATE   Let her go, Blanche. Let her sleep on it. You'll only make it worse.

BLANCHE   It seems no matter *what* I do, I only make it worse.

(She turns, starts up the stairs. NORA *has slammed the door of her room.* STANLEY *hears it and opens his door and starts down)*

JACK *(To* KATE*)*   What could I tell her? What could I say?

KATE *(Shrugs)*   You inherit a family, you inherit their problems.

EUGENE *(Comes out of the kitchen)*   Well, good night.

KATE   Put the cookie on the table.

EUGENE   What cookie?

KATE   The oatmeal cookie in your pocket. Put it on the table.

EUGENE   You can smell an oatmeal cookie from ten feet away?

KATE   I heard the jar moving in the kitchen. Suddenly everybody's doing what they want in this house. Your father's upset, Aunt Blanche is upset, *put the cookie on that table!*
    *(*EUGENE *puts the cookie on the table and starts up the stairs to his room. He passes* STANLEY*)*

STANLEY *(To* EUGENE*)*   I heard a lot of yelling. What happened?

EUGENE   I don't know, but it's my fault.
    (He goes on up and into the bathroom. NORA *is on her bed, crying.* LAURIE *sits on her bed and watches her)*

LAURIE   What are you going to do? (NORA *shakes her head, indicating she doesn't know)* Do you want *me* to speak to Mom? I could tell her I was getting flutters in my heart again.

NORA *(Turns, angrily)*   Don't you ever say that! Don't you pretend to be sick to get favors from anyone.

LAURIE   I'm not pretending. They're just not *big* flutters.
(STANLEY *has been sitting at the top of the stairs
trying to work up courage to talk to his father.*
JACK *is sitting in the living room, disconsolate.* KATE
is puffing up pillows)

JACK   Stop puffing up pillows. The house could be burning down and you'd run back in to puff up the pillows.

KATE   Let's go to bed. You're tired.

JACK   When does it get easier, Kate? When does our life
get easier?

KATE   At night. When you get seven good hours of
sleep. That's the easiest it ever gets.
(NORA *has put on her robe, left her room, and opens
the bathroom door. We hear a scream from* EUGENE)

EUGENE   *CLOSE THE DOOR!!!*

NORA   Oh. I'm sorry. I didn't know anyone was in there.
(*She rushes out, back to her room.* STANLEY *moves
into the living room*)

STANLEY   Dad? Do you think I could talk to you now?
It'll just take five minutes.

KATE   He's tired, Stanley. He's practically asleep.

STANLEY   Two minutes. I'll tell it as fast as I can.

JACK   Go on, Kate. Go to bed. The boy wants to tell me
something.

KATE   Turn out the lights when you're through. (*She
kisses* JACK's *head*) Don't worry about things. We've
always made them work out.
(*She leaves the room just as* EUGENE *darts out of the
bathroom, rushes into his own room, and slams the
door*)

EUGENE She saw me on the crapper! Nora saw me on the crapper! (*He falls on his bed*) I might as well be dead.

STANLEY I have a problem, Pop.

JACK If you didn't, you wouldn't live in this house.

STANLEY It must be tough being a father. Everybody comes to you with their problems. You have to have all the answers. I don't know if *I* could handle it.

JACK Stop trying to win me over. Just tell me the problem.

STANLEY I got fired today!

JACK *What???*

STANLEY Don't get excited! Don't get crazy! Let me explain what happened.

JACK What did you do? You came in late? You were fresh to somebody? Were you fresh to somebody?

STANLEY I'm not fired yet. I can still get my job back. I just need you to help me make a decision.

JACK Take the job back. I don't care what it is. This is *not* the time for anybody to be out of work in this family.

STANLEY When I was twelve years old you gave me a talk about principles. Remember?

JACK All night you waited to tell me this news?

STANLEY This is about principles, Pop.

JACK How long were you going to go without telling me?

STANLEY Will you at least hear my principles?

JACK   All right, I'll hear your principles. Then you'll hear mine.

STANLEY   Just sit back and let me tell you what happened. Okay? Well, it was on account of Andrew, the colored guy who sweeps up.
    (JACK *sits back and listens.* STANLEY *sits with his back to the audience, talking, but we can't hear him. Our attention is drawn to* EUGENE *up in his room*)

EUGENE (*To the audience*)   . . . So Stanley began his sad story. Pop never said a word. He just sat there and listened. Stanley was terrific. It was like that movie, *Abe Lincoln in Illinois*. Stanley was not only defending his principles, he was defending democracy and the United States of America. Pop must have been bleary-eyed because not only did he have to deal with Stanley's principles, Nora's career, the loss of his noisemaker business, how to get Aunt Blanche married off, and Laurie's fluttering heart, but at any minute there could be a knock on the door with thirty-seven relatives from Poland showing up looking for a place to live . . . Finally, Stanley finished his story.

STANLEY   So—either I bring in a letter of apology in the morning or I don't bother coming in . . . I know it's late. I know you're tired. But I didn't want to do anything without asking you first.

JACK (*After a few moments of silence*)   Ohh, Stanley, Stanley, Stanley!

STANLEY   I'm sorry, Pop.

JACK   You shouldn't have swept the dirt on his shoes.

STANLEY   I know.

JACK   Especially in front of other people.

STANLEY   I know.

JACK   He's your boss. He pays your salary. His money helps put food on our dining table.

STANLEY   I know, Pop.

JACK   And we don't have money to waste. Believe me when I tell you that.

STANLEY   I believe you, Pop.

JACK   You were sick three days last year and he only docked you a day and a half's pay, remember that?

STANLEY   I know. I can see what you're getting at. I'll write the letter. I'll do it tonight.

JACK   On the other hand, you did a courageous thing. You defended a fellow worker. Nobody else stood up for him, did they?

STANLEY   I was the only one.

JACK   That's something to be proud of. It was what you believed in. That's standing up for your principles.

STANLEY   That's why I didn't want to write the letter. I knew you'd understand.

JACK   The question is, Can this family afford principles right now?

STANLEY   It would make it hard, I know.

JACK   Not just on you and me. But on your mother. On Aunt Blanche, Nora, Laurie.

STANLEY   Eugene.

JACK   Eugene. Eugene would have to get a part-time job. Time he should be using studying books to get himself somewhere.

STANLEY He wants to be a writer. He wants to go to college.

JACK I wish I could have sent *you*. I've always been sick about that, Stanley.

STANLEY I like working, Pop. I really do . . . Listen, I made up my mind. I'm going to write the letter.

JACK I'm not saying you should . . .

STANLEY I know. It's *my* decision. I really want to write the letter.

JACK And how will your principles feel in the morning?

STANLEY My principles feel better already. You told me you were proud of what I did. That's all I really cared about.

JACK You know something, Stanley—I don't think there's much in college they could teach you that you don't already know.

STANLEY Guess who I learned it from? . . . Thanks for talking to me, Pop. See you in the morning. You coming to bed?

JACK I think I'll sit here for a while. It's the only time of day I have a few minutes to myself.
        (STANLEY *nods, then bounds up the stairs to his room.*
        JACK *sits back in his chair and closes his eyes.*
        STANLEY *enters his room.* EUGENE *is writing in his book of memoirs*)

EUGENE How'd it go? Do you have to write the letter?

STANLEY Yeah.
        (*He gets out a pad and his fountain pen*)

EUGENE I *knew* that's what he'd make you do.

STANLEY   He didn't *make* me do it . . . Be quiet, will ya! I have to concentrate.

EUGENE   What are you going to say?

STANLEY   I don't know . . . You want to help me? You're good at those things.

EUGENE   People used to get paid for that in the old days. Professional letter writers.

STANLEY (*Indignant*)   I'm not going to pay you money.

EUGENE   I don't want money.

STANLEY   Then what *do* you want?

EUGENE   Tell me what Nora looked like naked.

STANLEY   How horny can you get?

EUGENE   I don't know. What's the highest score?

STANLEY   All right. When we finished the letter.

EUGENE   I don't trust you. I want to get paid first.

STANLEY   You know, you're a real shit!

EUGENE   Don't talk like that in front of me, I'm just a kid.

STANLEY   What do you want to know?

EUGENE   Everything. From the time you opened the door.

STANLEY   It happened so fast.

EUGENE   That's okay. Tell it slow.

STANLEY   Jesus! All right . . . I heard the shower running. I waited for it to stop. I gave a few seconds for the water to run off her body, then I knew she'd be stepping out of the shower. Suddenly I just opened the door. She was standing there on the bath mat, a towel on her head and nothing else in the whole wide world.

EUGENE   Slower. Don't go so fast.

STANLEY   Her breasts were gorgeous. Like two peaches hanging on the vine waiting to be plucked . . . Maybe nectarines. Like two nectarines, all soft and pink and shining in the morning sun . . .

Curtain

Act Two

Wednesday, a week later. About six-thirty in the evening.
KATE *comes down the stairs carrying a tray of food. She looks a little haggard.*
LAURIE *is lying on the sofa in the living room with a book.*
EUGENE *is in the backyard, sitting on the beach chair, writing in his book of memoirs.*

KATE   Laurie! You should see your mother. She looks gorgeous.

LAURIE   I'm waiting for her grand entrance . . . How's Uncle Jack?

KATE   He's resting. He ate a nice dinner. You can go up and see him later. (*She yells*) Eugene! Your father's resting. I don't want to hear any ball playing against the wall.

EUGENE   I'm not playing. I'm writing.

KATE   Well, do it quietly.
(*She goes into the kitchen*)

EUGENE (*To the audience*)   She wants me to write quietly. If that was the only sentence I published in my memoirs, it would be a best-seller . . . Everybody's been in a rotten mood around here lately . . . Three days ago Pop had a (*He whispers*)—heart attack. It wasn't a major (*He whispers*)—heart attack. It was sort of a warning. He passed out in the subway and a policeman had to bring him home. He was trying to make extra money driving a cab at nights and he just plain wore out . . . The doctor says he has to stay home for two or three weeks, but Pop won't listen to him. Mr. Jacobson has a brother-in-law who needs a job. He's filling in for Pop temporarily, but Pop's afraid that three weeks in bed could turn into permanently.

(STANLEY *appears, coming home from work. He looks distraught. He half whispers to* EUGENE)

STANLEY   I have to talk to you.

EUGENE   What's up?

STANLEY   Not here. In our room. Don't tell anybody.

EUGENE   What's the big secret?

STANLEY   Will you shut up! Wait'll I get upstairs, then follow me.

(*He goes into the house*)

EUGENE   If it's about Nora, I'm not interested. (*To the audience*) I forgot to tell you, I hate my cousin Nora. She's been real snotty to everybody lately. She doesn't say hello in the morning and eats her dinner up in her room. And she's been seeing this guy Larry No Chin Clurman every night. And she's not as pretty as I thought she was . . .

KATE (*Walking out of the kitchen*)   Eugene! Did you bring your father his paper?

EUGENE   I'm coming. My knee hurts. I fell down the stairs at school.

KATE   Well, bring it up. Your father's waiting for it.

(*She goes back into the kitchen*)

EUGENE (*To the audience*)   If I told her I just lost both my hands in an accident she'd say, "Go upstairs and wash your face with your feet" . . . I guess she's sore because she and Pop can't go to the affair at the Commodore Hotel. They had Glen Gray and his orchestra . . . I feel sorry for her 'cause she doesn't get to go out much. (*He gets up, starts toward the house*) And she's nervous about Frank Murphy coming over to pick up Aunt Blanche.

She's angry at the whole world. (*He enters the house*) That's why she's making lima beans for dinner.

KATE (*Walks into the living room with a dish of nuts*) Would you like a cashew, Laurie?

LAURIE Oh, thanks. (*She takes one*) And a Brazil nut too? (*She takes one*) And one almond? (*She takes one*)

KATE You must be starved. We're having dinner late tonight. We'll wait till your mother goes out.

EUGENE (*Limps into the living room*) Can I have some nuts, Mom?

KATE Just one. It's for the company. (*He takes one, starts upstairs*) We're eating in the kitchen tonight. You and Stanley help with the dishes.
(*He goes upstairs*)

KATE (*To* LAURIE) You look all flushed. You don't have a fever, do you? (*She feels* LAURIE's *head*) Let me see your tongue. (LAURIE *shows her her tongue*) It's all spotted.

LAURIE That's the cashew nut.

KATE Don't you get sick on me too. If you're tired, I want you in bed.

LAURIE I have a little stomach cramp. Maybe I'm getting my "ladies."

KATE Your what?

LAURIE My "ladies." That thing that Nora gets when she can't go in the water.

KATE I don't think so. Not at your age. But if your stomach hurts real bad, you come and tell me. I made

a nice tuna-fish salad tonight. Call me when your mother comes down.
(*She starts toward the kitchen*)

LAURIE   Aunt Kate! . . . Does Momma like Mr. Murphy?

KATE   I don't know, darling. I don't think she knows him very well yet.

LAURIE   Do you like him?

KATE   I never spoke to the man.

LAURIE   You called him a Cossack. Are those the kind who don't like Jewish people?

KATE   I'm sure Mr. Murphy likes your mother, otherwise he wouldn't be taking her out to dinner.

LAURIE   If Mom married him, would we have to live in that dark house across the street? With that creepy woman in the window?

KATE   We're not up to that yet. Let's just get through Chardov's Restaurant first.
(*She goes into the kitchen.* EUGENE *rushes into his room.* STANLEY *is lying on his bed, hands under his head, staring at the ceiling*)

EUGENE   Pop's feeling better. He threw the newspaper at me because I didn't bring him the evening edition.

STANLEY (*Sits up*)   Lock the door.

EUGENE (*Locking the door*)   You look terrible. You were crying. Your eyes are all red.

STANLEY   I'm in trouble, Eug. I mean, real, *real* trouble.
(*He takes a single cigarette out of his shirt pocket, puts it in his mouth, and lights it with a match*)

EUGENE   When did you take up smoking?

STANLEY I smoke in the stockroom all the time. Don't let me see you do it. It's a bad habit.

EUGENE So how come *you* do it?

STANLEY I like it.

EUGENE What brand do you smoke?

STANLEY Lucky Strikes.

EUGENE I knew you would. That's the best brand.

STANLEY Swear to God, what I tell you, you'll never tell a living soul.

EUGENE (*Raises his hand*) I take an oath on the life of the entire New York Yankees . . . What happened?

STANLEY (*He paces before he can speak*) . . . I lost my salary.

EUGENE *What?*

STANLEY The entire seventeen dollars. It's gone. I lost it.

EUGENE Where? In the subway?

STANLEY In a poker game. I lost it gambling.

EUGENE IN A POKER GAME?

STANLEY *Will you shut up??* You want to kill Pop right in his bedroom?

EUGENE You never told me you gambled.

STANLEY We would just do it at lunch hour. For pennies. I always won. A dime. A quarter. It wasn't just luck. I was really good.

EUGENE   Seventeen dollars!!

STANLEY   When Pop got sick, I thought I could make
some extra money. To help out. So I played in this
game over in the stockroom at Florsheim Shoes . . .
Boy, did I learn about poker. They cleaned me out in
twenty minutes . . .

EUGENE   What are you going to tell them?

STANLEY   I don't know. If Pop wasn't sick, I would tell
him the truth. Last week he tells me how proud he is
of me. He's driving a cab at nights and I'm playing
poker at Florsheim's.
        (*He puts his head down and starts to cry*)

EUGENE   Yeah, but suppose you won? Suppose you won
fifty dollars? You just had bad luck, that's all.

STANLEY   I had no chance against those guys. They were
gamblers. They all wore black pointy shoes with clocks
on their socks . . . If Pop dies, I'll hang myself, I swear.

EUGENE   Don't talk like that. Pop isn't going to die. He
ate three lamb chops tonight . . . Why don't you just
say you lost the money? You had a hole in your pocket.
You can tear a hole in your pocket.

STANLEY   I already used that one.

EUGENE   When?

STANLEY   In November when I lost five dollars. He said
to me, "From now on, check your pockets every morning."

EUGENE   What happened to the five dollars? Did you
gamble that too?

STANLEY   No. I gave it to a girl . . . You know. A pro.

EUGENE   A pro what? . . . A PROSTITUTE??? You
went to one of those places? Holy shit!

STANLEY   I'm not going to warn you about that word again.

EUGENE   Is that what it costs? Five dollars?

STANLEY   Two-fifty. I went with this guy I know. He still owes me.

EUGENE   And you never told me? What was she like? Was she pretty? How old was she?

STANLEY   Don't start in with me, Eugene.

EUGENE   Did she get completely naked or what?

STANLEY   (*Furious*)   Every time I get in trouble, I have to tell you what a naked girl looks like? . . . Do me a favor, Eugene. Go in the bathroom, whack off, and grow up by yourself.

EUGENE   Don't get sore. If you were me, you'd ask the same questions.

STANLEY   Well, I never had an older brother to teach me those things. I had to do it all on my own. You don't know how lucky you are to be the younger one. You don't have the responsibilities I do. You're still in school looking up girls' dresses on the staircase.

EUGENE   I work plenty hard in school.

STANLEY   Yeah? Well, let me see your report card. Today's the first of the month, I know you got it. I want to see your report card.

EUGENE   I don't have to show you my report card. You're not my father.

STANLEY   Yes, I am. As long as Pop is sick, I am. I'm the only one in the family who's working, ain't I?

EUGENE   Really? Well, where's your salary this week, Pop?

STANLEY (*Grabs* EUGENE *in anger*)   I hate you sometimes. You're nothing but a lousy shit. I help you all the time and you never help me without wanting something for it. I hate your disgusting guts.

EUGENE (*Screaming*)   Not as much as I hate yours. You snore at night. You pick your toenails. You smell up the bathroom. When I go in there I have to puke.

STANLEY (*Screaming back*)   Give me your report card. Give it to me, goddammit, or I'll beat your face in.

EUGENE (*Starts to cry*)   You want it? Here! (*He grabs it out of a book*) Here's my lousy report card . . . you fuck!!
  (*He falls on the bed crying, his face to the wall.* STAN-LEY *sits on his own bed and reads the report card. There is a long silence*)

STANLEY (*Softly*)   Four A's and a B . . . That's good. That's real good, Eugene . . . You're smart . . . I want you to go to college . . . I want you to be somebody important someday . . . Because I'm not . . . I'm no damn good. (*He is crying*) I'm sorry I said those things to you.

EUGENE (*Still faces the wall. It's too hard to look at* STAN)   Me too . . . I'm sorry too.
  (JACK *appears at the top of the stairs. He is in his pajamas, robe, and slippers. He seems very shaky. He holds on to the banister and slowly comes down the stairs.*
  He looks around, then sees LAURIE *and walks into the living room. His breath does not come easy*)

LAURIE (*Sees him*)   Hi, Uncle Jack. Are you feeling better?

JACK   A little, darling. Your mother's not down yet?

LAURIE   No.

JACK   I wanted to see her before she goes out.
       (KATE *comes out of the kitchen with a bowl of fruit.
       She sees* JACK)

KATE   Oh, my God! Are you crazy? Are you out of your
       mind? You're walking down the stairs?

JACK   I'm all right. I was tired lying in that bed. I wanted
       to see Blanche.
       (*He sits down slowly*)

KATE   How are you going to get upstairs? You think I'm
       going to carry you? The doctor said you're not even
       supposed to go to the bathroom, didn't he?

JACK   You trust doctors? My grandmother never saw
       one in her life, she lived to be eighty-seven.

KATE   She didn't have high blood pressure. She never
       fainted on the subway.

JACK   She used to faint three, four times a week. It's in
       our family. We're fainters. Laurie, darling, go get your
       Uncle Jack a glass of ice water, please.

LAURIE   Now?

JACK   Yes. Now, sweetheart. (LAURIE *gets up and goes
       into kitchen*) That child is pampered too much. You
       should let her do more work around the house. You
       don't get healthy lying on couches all day.

KATE   No. You get healthy driving cabs at night after
       you work nine hours cutting raincoats. You want to
       kill yourself, Jack? You want to leave me to take care
       of this family alone? Is that what you want?

JACK   You figure I'll get better faster if you make me feel
       guilty? . . . I was born with enough guilt, Katey. If I
       need more, I'll ask you.

KATE   I'm sorry. You know me. I'm not happy unless I can worry. *My* family were worriers. Worriers generally marry fainters.

JACK   (*Takes her hand, holds it*)   I'm not going to leave you. I promise. If I didn't leave you for another woman, I'm certainly not going to drop dead just to leave you.

KATE   (*Lets go of his hand*)   What other woman? That bookkeeper, Helene?

JACK   Again with Helene? You're never going to forget that I danced with her two years in a row at the Commodore Hotel?

KATE   Don't tell me she isn't attracted to you. I noticed that right off.

JACK   What does a woman like that want with a cutter? She likes the men up front. The salesmen. She's a widow. She's looking to get married.

KATE   You're an attractive man, Jack. Women like you.

JACK   Me? Attractive? You really must think I'm dying, don't you?

KATE   You don't know women like I do. Just promise me one thing. If anything ever happened with you and that Helene, let me go to my grave without hearing it.

JACK   I see. Now that you're worried about Helene, you've decided you're going to die first.
(LAURIE *comes back in with a glass of ice water*)

LAURIE   I had to chop the ice. I'm all out of breath.

JACK   It's good for you, darling. It's exercise.
(*He takes the ice water.*
NORA *comes out of her room and goes bounding down the stairs*)

NORA (*Coldly*) I'm going out. I won't be having dinner. I'll be home late. I have my key. Good night.

KATE Nora! Don't you want to see how your mother looks?

NORA I'm sure she looks beautiful. She doesn't need me to tell her.

KATE What about Mr. Murphy? I know your mother wants him to meet you and Laurie. He'll be here any minute.

NORA I have somebody waiting for me. I can meet Mr. Murphy some other time.

JACK I think it would be nice if you waited, Nora. I think your mother would be very hurt if you didn't wait to say goodbye.

NORA I'm sure that's very good advice, Uncle Jack. I know *just* how my mother feels. I'm not so sure she knows how *I* feel.
(*She turns and goes out the front door.* JACK *and* KATE *look at each other*)

KATE Jack! What'll I do?

JACK Leave it alone. It's between Nora and Blanche. It's something *they* have to work out.

KATE Who is she going out with? Where does she go every night?

LAURIE With Larry Clurman. He borrows his father's car and takes her to the cemetery.

KATE What cemetery?

LAURIE Where Daddy is buried. She goes to see Daddy.
(BLANCHE *has come out of her room and appears at*

the head of the stairs. She is all dressed up and looks quite lovely. She comes down the stairs)

KATE   What'll I tell her? I don't want to spoil this evening for her.
(BLANCHE *appears in the room*)

BLANCHE   Jack? What are you doing down here?

JACK   We have company coming. Where else should I be?

BLANCHE   I looked in your room. I got scared to death.

JACK   Well, you don't look it. You look beautiful.

KATE   Ohh, Blanche. Oh, my God, Blanche, it's stunning. Like a movie star. Who's the movie star I like so much, Laurie?

LAURIE   Irene Dunne.

KATE   Like Irene Dunne.

LAURIE   I think she looks like Rosalind Russell. Maybe Carole Lombard.

JACK   I think she looks like Blanche. Blanche is prettier than all of them.

BLANCHE   I had such trouble with the makeup. I couldn't see my eyes to put on the mascara. So I had to put my glasses on. Then I couldn't get the mascara on under the glasses.
(STANLEY *gets up from his bed, goes out to the bathroom, and closes the door*)

KATE   Where are your glasses? Have you got your glasses?

BLANCHE   In my purse. I thought I'd put them on in the restaurant, when I'm looking at the menu.

KATE   Make sure you do. I don't want you coming home telling me you don't know what he looks like.

BLANCHE   I'm so glad to see you up, Jack. Then you're feeling better?

JACK   It was nothing. I needed a rest, that's all. Besides, I wanted to meet this Murphy fella. A stranger comes in, he likes to meet another man. Makes him feel comfortable.

BLANCHE   Thank you, Jack. That's very thoughtful of you.

KATE   (*Takes something out of her pocket*)   Here. Wear this. Don't say no to me. Just put them on, Blanche. Please.

BLANCHE   Kate! Your pearls. Your good pearls.

KATE   What are they going to do? Sit in my drawer all year? Pearls are like people. They like to go out and be seen once in a while.

BLANCHE   You were going to wear them to the affair tonight. I'm so wrapped up in myself, I forgot you're missing the affair this year.

KATE   I can afford to miss it. I don't see Jack there the whole night anyway.

JACK   Let's see how they look.

BLANCHE   I'm so nervous I'll lose them.
(*She puts them on. They all look*)

KATE   All right. Tell me I don't have a beautiful sister.

JACK   Now I feel good. Now I feel I got my money's worth.

LAURIE   Definitely Carole Lombard.

BLANCHE   Laurie, go up and get Nora. I want to show them to Nora.

LAURIE   . . . She's not here. She left.

BLANCHE (*Looks at* KATE *and* JACK)   What do you mean, she left? Without saying goodbye?

KATE   She had to meet somebody. She wanted to wait for you.

BLANCHE   She could have come into my room. She knew I wanted to see her.

JACK   She'll see you when you get home. You'll look just as good at twelve o'clock.

BLANCHE   What did she say? Did she say anything?

KATE   You're going out. You're going to have a good time tonight. We'll talk about it later.

BLANCHE   She's making me pay for it, isn't she? She knows she can get to me so easily . . . That's what I get for making decisions.

JACK   I feel like ice cream for dessert. Laurie, you feel like ice cream for dessert?

LAURIE   Butter pecan?

JACK   Butter pecan for you, maple walnut for me. Go up and tell Eugene I want him to go to the store.

LAURIE   I'll go with him.

KATE   Don't run, darling.

JACK   Let her run. If she gets tired, she'll tell you. Let's stop worrying about each other so much.
        (LAURIE *knocks on* EUGENE's *door*)

LAURIE   Eugene! Your father wants us to go to the store.

EUGENE   Tell him I'm sick. My stomach hurts.

LAURIE   You don't want any ice cream?

EUGENE (*Thinks*)   Ice cream? Wait a minute. (*He sits up, looks out at the audience*) It's amazing how quickly you recover from misery when someone offers you ice cream.

JACK   She's only sixteen, Blanche. At that age they're still wrapped up in themselves.

EUGENE   How am I going to become a writer if I don't know how to suffer? Actually, I'd give up writing if I could see a naked girl while I was eating ice cream.
(*He comes out of his room and goes down the stairs with* LAURIE. STANLEY *comes out of the bathroom and goes back into his own room*)

BLANCHE   What time is it?

KATE   Six-thirty. He'll be here any minute. Get your mind off Nora, Blanche. Don't wear my pearls out tonight for nothing.

JACK   Eugene! Go to Hanson's. Get a half pint of butter pecan, a half pint of maple walnut, a half pint of chocolate for yourself. Kate, what do you want?

KATE   I'm in no mood for ice cream.

JACK   Get her vanilla. She'll eat it. And whatever Stanley likes.

EUGENE   I need money.

JACK   I just paid the doctor fifteen dollars. Go up to Stanley. He got paid today. Ask him for his salary.

EUGENE (*In shock*)   What???

KATE   Here. Here's a dollar. (*She takes it out of her pocket*) Hurry back so Laurie can meet Mr. Murphy. But don't run.
   (*They take the money and leave by the front door*)

BLANCHE   You know what I worry about at night? That she'll run off. That I'll wake up in the morning and she'll be gone. To Philadelphia. Or Boston. Or God knows where.

KATE   Look how the woman's going out on a date. Is that what you're going to talk about? He'll start drinking in five minutes.

BLANCHE   You think so? What'll I do if he gets drunk?

KATE   You'll come right home. Do you have money? Do you have carfare?

BLANCHE   No. I didn't take anything.

KATE   Wait here. I'll get five dollars from Stanley. Now I have something *else* to worry about.
   (*She starts up the stairs*)

JACK   I could use a cup of hot tea.
   (*He gets up*)

BLANCHE   Sit there. I'll make it.

JACK   We'll both make it. Keep me company. We can hear the bell from the kitchen.
   (*They go off to the kitchen.* KATE *is at* STANLEY'S *door. She knocks on it*)

KATE   Stanley? Are you in there? (*She opens the door.* STANLEY *is lying on his bed*) Open the window. You never get any air in this room . . . (*She extends her hand*) I need five dollars for Aunt Blanche. (*He stares at the floor*) . . . Stanley? Did you get paid today?

STANLEY   Yes. I got paid today.

KATE Take out your money for the week, let me have the envelope.

STANLEY (*Still stares down*) I don't have it.

KATE You don't have the envelope?

STANLEY I don't have the money.

KATE What do you mean, you don't have the money?

STANLEY I mean I don't have the money. It's gone.

KATE (*Nervously, sits on the bed*) It's gone? . . . Gone where?

STANLEY It's just gone. I don't have it. I can't get it back. I'm sorry. There's nothing I can do about it anymore. Just don't ask me any more questions.

KATE What do you mean, don't ask any more questions? I want to know what happened to seventeen dollars, Stanley!

STANLEY You'll tell Pop. If I tell you, you're going to tell Pop.

KATE Why shouldn't I tell your father? Why, Stanley? I want to know what happened to that money.

STANLEY I gambled it! I lost it playing poker! All right? You happy? You satisfied now?
        (*He starts to weep*)

KATE (*Her breath goes out of her body. She sits there numb, then finally takes a breath*) I'm not going to deal with this right now. I have to get Aunt Blanche out of the house first. I have your father's health to worry about. You're going to sit in this room and you're going to think up a story. You were robbed. Somebody stole the money. I don't care who, I don't care where. That's what you're going to tell your father, because if you tell

him the truth, you'll kill that man as sure as I'm sitting here . . . Tonight, after he goes to sleep, you'll meet me in the kitchen and we'll deal with this alone.
(*She gets up, moves to the door*)

STANLEY (*Barely audible*) . . . I'm sorry.
(*She goes, closes the door.* STANLEY *sits there as if the life has gone out of him.*
KATE *walks down the stairs and into the living room. She goes over to the window, looks out, and breaks into sobs.*
BLANCHE *comes out of the kitchen. She looks around the living room*)

BLANCHE I left my purse in here. Without my glasses, I'm afraid to pour the tea. (*She notices* KATE *wiping her eyes with her handkerchief*) Kate? . . . What is it? What's wrong?

KATE Nothing. I'm just all nerves today.

BLANCHE You're worried about Jack. He shouldn't have come down the stairs.

KATE He knows he's not supposed to get out of bed. What did we need a doctor for? He doesn't listen to them.

BLANCHE I shouldn't have asked Mr. Murphy to come over. That's the only reason he came down.

KATE It's not just Mr. Murphy. It's Stanley, it's Eugene, it's everybody.

BLANCHE I'm sorry about Nora. Jack told me what she said when she left.

KATE Why don't you get your purse, Blanche. He'll be here any minute.

BLANCHE Did Nora say anything to hurt you, Kate? I know she's been very difficult these last few days.

KATE (*Suddenly turns, angrily*) Why is it always *Nora?* Why is it only *your* problems? Do you think you're the only one in this world who has troubles? We *all* have troubles. We *all* get our equal share. (*It hits* BLANCHE *like a slap in the face*)

BLANCHE I'm sorry. Forgive me, Kate. I'm sorry.

KATE Maybe you're stronger than I am, I don't know. You survived Dave's death. I don't know if I could handle it if anything happens to Jack.

BLANCHE He'll be all right, Kate. Nothing's going to happen to him. He's still a young man. He's strong.

KATE When Dave died, I cried for his loss. I was so angry. Angry at God for taking such a young man ... I never realized until now what *you* must have gone through. How did you get through it, Blanche?

BLANCHE I had you. I had Jack ... But mostly, you live for your children. Your children keep you going.

KATE (*Almost smiles*) My children.

BLANCHE I wake up every morning for Nora and for Laurie.

KATE Nora hurts you so much and you can still say that?

BLANCHE Why? Don't you think we hurt *our* parents? You don't remember how Momma cried when Celia left home? Sure it hurts, but if you love someone, you forgive them.

KATE Some things you forgive. Some things you never forgive.
(LAURIE *comes back into the house. She has a letter in her hand*)

LAURIE Is the ice cream here yet?

BLANCHE   No, darling. Didn't you go with Eugene?

LAURIE   No. I was across the street in the creepy house. It's just as creepy inside.

BLANCHE   In Mr. Murphy's house? You were just in there? Why?

LAURIE   She called me from the window. The old lady. I think it's his mother. She told me she had a letter for you. I had to go inside to get it.
   (*She hands the letter to* BLANCHE)

KATE   What did she say to you?

LAURIE   She offered me a cookie but it was all green. I said I wasn't hungry.
   (EUGENE *appears outside the house. He carries a brown paper bag with four small cartons of ice cream.* BLANCHE *opens the letter*)

EUGENE   (*To the audience*)   "Dear Mrs. Morton, I send regrets for my son Frank. I tried to reach you earlier, then realized you had no phone. Frank will be unable to keep his dinner engagement with you this evening. Frank is in hospital as a result of an automobile accident last night, and although his injuries are not serious, the consequences are. As a devoted mother I would end this letter here and forward my apologies. Despite all my son's faults, honesty and sincerity have never been his failings. He wanted me to tell you the truth. That while driving a friend's motorcar, he was intoxicated and was the cause of the aforementioned accident. The truth would come out soon enough, but Frank has too much respect and fondness for you to have you hear it from some other source. I hope you will not think I am just a doting mother when I tell you my boy has a great many attributes. A great many. As soon as Frank can get out of his difficulties here we have decided to move to upstate New York where there is a clinic that can help Frank and where we have relatives with whom we can stay. Frank sends, along with his regrets, his regard for a warm, intelligent, friendly, and most delightful neighbor across the way . . . Yours most respectfully, Mrs. Matthew Murphy."

KATE   What is it?
   (BLANCHE *hands the letter to* KATE)

BLANCHE   He's not coming. He's . . . in the hospital.
   (KATE *reads the letter*)

EUGENE (*To the audience*)   It was a sad letter, all right, but it sure was well written. Maybe I should have been born in Ireland.
   (*He walks into the house*)

KATE (*As she reads*)   I knew it. I said it right from the beginning, didn't I?

LAURIE   Why is he in the hospital?

BLANCHE   He was in a car accident . . . Oh, God. That poor woman.

LAURIE   Does that mean you're not going out to dinner?

KATE (*Nods her head as she finishes*)   It could have been you in that car with him. I warned you the first day about those people.

BLANCHE   Stop calling them "those people." They're not "those people." She's a mother, like you and me.

KATE   And what is he? Tell me what he is.

BLANCHE   He's somebody in trouble. He's somebody that needs help. For God's sakes, Kate, you don't even know the man.

KATE   I know the man. I know what they're *all* like.

BLANCHE   Who are you to talk? Are we any better? Are we something so special? We're *all* poor around here, the least we can be is charitable.

KATE   Why? What have *I* got I can afford to give away? Am I the one who got you all dressed up for nothing? Am I the one who got your hopes up? Am I the one they're going to lock up in a jail somewhere?

LAURIE   They're going to put him in jail?

KATE   Don't talk to me about charity. Anyone else, but not me.

BLANCHE   I never said you weren't charitable.

KATE   All I did was try to help you. All I *ever* did was try to help you.

BLANCHE   I know that. Nobody cares for their family more than you do. But at least you can be sympathetic to somebody else in trouble.

KATE   Who should I care about? Who's out there watching over *me?* I did enough in my life for people. You know what I'm talking about.

BLANCHE   No, I don't. Say what's on your mind, Kate. What people?

KATE   You! Celia! Poppa, when he was sick. Everybody! . . . Don't you ask *me* "What people"! How many beatings from Momma did I get for things that you did? How many dresses did I go without so you could look like someone when you went out? I was the workhorse and you were the pretty one. You have no right to talk to me like that. No right.

BLANCHE   This is all about Jack, isn't it? You're blaming me for what happened.

KATE   Why do you think that man is sick today? Why did a policeman have to carry him home at two o'clock in the morning? So your Nora could have dancing lessons? So that Laurie could see a doctor every three weeks? Go on! Worry about your friend across the

street, not the ones who have to be dragged home to keep a roof over your head.
(*She turns away.* JACK *walks in from the kitchen*)

JACK   What is this? What's going on here?

BLANCHE (*To* KATE)   Why didn't you ever tell me you felt that way?

KATE (*Turns her back to her*)   I never had the time. I was too busy taking care of everyone.

JACK   What is it, Blanche? What happened?
(*She hands* JACK *the letter. He starts to read it*)

BLANCHE   It took all these years? It took something like that letter for you to finally get your feelings out?

KATE   I didn't need a letter . . . I just needed you to ask me.
(BLANCHE *is terribly hurt and extremely vulnerable standing there*)

BLANCHE   Laurie! Please go upstairs. This conversation isn't for you.

EUGENE   The ice cream is ready.

BLANCHE   Eugene, put the ice cream in the icebox. I have to talk to your mother.
(EUGENE *goes into the kitchen*)

JACK (*Finishes the letter*)   I never spoke to the woman. They've lived in that house for three years, and I never exchanged a word with her.

KATE (*To* JACK)   What are you walking around for? If you're out of bed, at least sit in a chair.

BLANCHE   If I could take Nora and Laurie and pack them out of this house tonight, I would do it. But I can't. I have no place to take them.

JACK Blanche! What are you talking about? Don't say such things.

BLANCHE (*Looks straight at* KATE) If I can leave the girls with you for another few weeks, I would appreciate it. Until I can find a place of my own, and then I'll send for them.

JACK You're not sending for anybody and you're not leaving anywhere. I don't want to hear this kind of talk.

KATE Stay out of this, Jack. Let her do what she wants.

BLANCHE I know a woman in Manhattan Beach. I can stay with her for a few days. And then I'll find a job. I will do *anything* anybody asks me, but I will *never* be a burden to anyone again.
(*She starts for the stairs*)

JACK Blanche, stop this! Stop it right now. What the hell is going on here, for God's sakes? Two sisters having a fight they should have had twenty-five years ago. You want to get it out, Blanche, get it out! Tell her what it's like to live in a house that isn't yours. To have to depend on somebody else to put the food on your plate every night. I know what it's like because I lived that way until I was twenty-one years old . . . Tell her, Kate, what it is to be an older sister. To suddenly be the one who has to work and shoulder all the responsibilities and not be the one who gets the affection and the hugs when you were the only one there. You think I don't see it with Stanley and Eugene? With Nora and Laurie? You think I don't hear the fights that go on up in those rooms night after night? Go on, Kate! Scream at her! Yell at her. Call her names, Blanche. Tell her to go to hell for the first time in your life . . . And when you both got it out of your systems, give each other a hug and go have dinner. My lousy ice cream is melting, for God's sakes.
(*There is a long silence*)

BLANCHE   I love you both very much. No matter what Kate says to me, I will never stop loving her. But I have to get out. If I don't do it now, I will lose whatever self-respect I have left. For people like us, sometimes the only thing we really own is our dignity . . . and when I grow old, I would like to have as much as Mrs. Matthew Murphy across the street.
(*She turns and goes up the stairs, disappearing into her room*)

JACK   What did it, Kate? Something terrible must have happened to you tonight for you to behave like this. It wasn't Blanche. It was something else. What was it, Kate?

KATE (*Stares out the window*)   Tell the kids to come down in five minutes. We're eating in the kitchen tonight.
(*She walks into the kitchen.* JACK *stands there, staring after her.* EUGENE, *coming out of the kitchen, passes his father*)

JACK   Get Stanley and Laurie. Dinner is in five minutes.
(JACK *goes into the kitchen.* EUGENE *walks to the stairs and up toward his bedroom*)

EUGENE (*To the audience*)   It was the first day in my life I didn't get blamed for what just happened. I felt real sorry for everybody, but as long as I wasn't to blame, I didn't feel all *that* bad about things. That's when I realized I had a selfish streak in me. I sure hope I grow out of it. (*He enters his bedroom and says to* STANLEY) Aunt Blanche is leaving.

STANLEY (*Sits up*)   For where?

EUGENE (*Sits on his own bed*)   To stay with some woman in Manhattan Beach. She and Mom just had a big fight. She's going to send for Laurie and Nora when she gets a job.

STANLEY   What did they fight about?

EUGENE I couldn't hear it all. I think Mom sorta blames Aunt Blanche for Pop having to work so hard.

STANLEY (*Hits the pillow with his fist*) Oh, God! . . . Did Mom say anything about me? About how I lost my salary?

EUGENE You told her? Why did you tell her? I came up with twelve terrific lies for you.
 (STANLEY *opens his drawer, puts on a sweater*)

STANLEY How much money do you have?

EUGENE Me? I don't have any money.

STANLEY (*Puts another sweater over the first one*) The hell you don't. You've got money in your cigar box. How much do you have?

EUGENE I got a dollar twelve. It's my life's savings.

STANLEY Let me have it. I'll pay it back, don't worry.
 (*He puts a jacket over the sweaters, then gets a fedora from the closet and puts it on.* EUGENE *takes the cigar box from under the bed, opens it*)

EUGENE What are you putting on all those things for?

STANLEY In case I have to sleep out tonight. I'm leaving, Gene. I don't know where I'm going yet, but I'll write to you when I get there.

EUGENE You're leaving home?

STANLEY When I'm gone, you tell Aunt Blanche what happened to my salary. Then she'll know why Mom was so angry. Tell her please not to leave, because it was all my fault, not Mom's. Will you do that?
 (*He takes the coins out of the cigar box*)

EUGENE I have eight cents' worth of stamps, if you want that too.

STANLEY   Thanks. (*He picks up a small medal*) What's this?

EUGENE   The medal you won for the hundred-yard dash two years ago.

STANLEY   From the Police Athletic League. I didn't know you still had this.

EUGENE   You gave it to me. You can have it back if you want it.

STANLEY   It's not worth anything.

EUGENE   It is to me.

STANLEY   Sure. You can keep it.

EUGENE   Thanks . . . Where will you go?

STANLEY   I don't know. I've been thinking about joining the army. Pop says we'll be at war in a couple of years anyway. I could be a sergeant or something by the time it starts.

EUGENE   If it lasts long enough, I could join too. Maybe we can get in the same outfit. "The Fighting 69th." It's mostly Irish, but they had a few Jewish guys in the movie.

STANLEY   You don't go in the army unless they come and get you. You go to college. You hear me? Promise me you'll go to college.

EUGENE   I'll probably have to stay home and work if you leave. We'll need the money.

STANLEY   I'll send home my paycheck every month. A sergeant in the army makes real good dough . . . Well, I better get going.

EUGENE (*On the verge of tears*)   What do you have to leave for?

STANLEY   Don't start crying. They'll hear you.

EUGENE   They'll get over it. They won't stay mad at you forever. I was mad at you and *I* got over it.

STANLEY   Because of me, the whole family is breaking up. Do you want Nora to end up like one of those cheap boardwalk girls?

EUGENE   I don't care. I'm not in love with Nora anymore.

STANLEY   Well, you *should* care. She's your cousin. Don't turn out to be like me.

EUGENE   I don't see what's so bad about you.

STANLEY (*Looks at him*)   Take care of yourself, Eug. (*They embrace. He opens the door, looks around, then back to* EUGENE) If you ever write a story about me, call me Hank. I always liked the name Hank.
     (*He goes, closing the door behind him.*
     EUGENE *sits there in silence for a while, then turns to the audience*)

EUGENE   I guess there comes a time in everybody's life when you say, "This very moment is the end of my childhood." When Stanley closed the door, I knew that moment had come to me . . . I was scared. I was lonely. And I hated my mother and father for making him so unhappy. Even if they were right, I still hated them . . . I even hated Stanley a little because he left me there to grow up all by myself.

KATE (*Yelling*)   Eugene! Laurie! It's dinner. I'm not waiting all night.

EUGENE (*To the audience*)   And I hated her for leaving Stanley's name out when she called us for dinner. I don't think parents really know how cruel they can be sometimes . . . (*A beat*) At dinner I tried to tell them about Stanley, but I just couldn't get the words out . . . I left the table without even having my ice cream . . . If it was suffering I was after, I was beginning to learn about it.

> (KATE *and* JACK *come out of the kitchen, heading upstairs*)

JACK   It's ten o'clock, where is Stanley so late?

KATE   Never mind Stanley. You should have been in bed an hour ago.

JACK   Why won't you tell me what happened between you and that boy?

KATE   I'm tired, Jack. I've had enough to deal with for one day.

JACK   I want him to go to temple with me on Saturday. They stop going for three or four weeks, they forget their religion altogether.

> (*They go into the bedroom*)

EUGENE   The house became quieter than I ever heard it before. Aunt Blanche was in her room packing, Pop and Mom were in their bedroom, and I had to talk to somebody or else I'd go crazy. I didn't have much choice. (*He walks over to her room and knocks on the door*) Laurie? It's Eugene. Can I come in?

LAURIE   What do you want? I'm reading.

EUGENE (*Opens the door*)   I just want to talk to you.

LAURIE   I didn't say yes, did I?

EUGENE   Well, I'm already in, so it's too late . . . What are you reading?

LAURIE   *The Citadel* by A. J. Cronin.

EUGENE I read it. It's terrific . . . I hear your mother's leaving in the morning.

LAURIE We're going too as soon as she finds a job.

EUGENE I can't believe it. I'm going to be the only one left here.

LAURIE You mean you and Stanley.

EUGENE Stanley's gone. He's not coming back. I think he's going to join the army.

LAURIE You mean he ran away?

EUGENE No. Only kids run away. When you're Stanley's age, you just leave.

LAURIE He didn't say goodbye?

EUGENE My parents don't even know about it. I'm going to tell them now.

LAURIE I wonder if I'll have to go to a different school.

EUGENE You'll have to make all new friends.

LAURIE I don't care. I don't have any friends here anyway.

EUGENE Because you're always in the house. You never go out.

LAURIE I can't because of my condition.

EUGENE You don't look sick to me. Do you *feel* sick?

LAURIE No. But my mother tells me I am.

EUGENE I don't trust parents anymore.

LAURIE Why would she lie to me?

EUGENE   To keep you around. Once they find out Stanley's gone, they're going to handcuff me to my bed.

LAURIE   I wouldn't leave my mother anyway. Even when I'm older. Even if I get married. I'll never leave my mother.

EUGENE   Yeah? Mr. Murphy across the street never left his mother. And he ended up going to jail.

LAURIE   None of this would have happened if my father was alive.

EUGENE   How did you feel when he died?

LAURIE   I don't remember. I cried a lot because I saw my mother crying.

EUGENE   I would hate it if my father died. Especially with Stanley gone. We'd probably have to move out of this house.

LAURIE   Well . . . then you and your mother could come and live with us.

EUGENE   So if we all end up living together, what's the point in breaking up now?

LAURIE   I don't know. I have to finish reading.
         (*She goes back to her book.* EUGENE *gets up and looks at the audience*)

EUGENE   You don't get too far talking to Laurie. Sometimes I think the flutter in her heart is really in her brain. (*He leaves the room, closes the door, and heads down the stairs*) I went into their bedroom and broke the news about Stanley. The monumental news that their eldest son had run off, probably to get killed in France fighting for his country. My mother said, "Go to bed. He'll be home when it gets cold out." I couldn't believe it. Their own son. It was then that I suspected that Stanley and I were adopted . . . They finally went to bed and I waited out on the front steps until it got cold, but Stanley never showed up.

(*He goes out the front door.*
It is later that night, after midnight. We see NORA *enter the front yard.* BLANCHE *comes down the stairs in a nightgown and a robe. She waits at the foot of the stairs as* NORA *comes into the house and sees her*)

BLANCHE   I wanted to talk to you.

NORA   Now? It's late.

BLANCHE   I know it's late. We could have talked earlier if you didn't come home at twelve o'clock at night.
(BLANCHE *walks into the living room.* NORA *follows her in and stands in the doorway*)

NORA   How was your dinner?

BLANCHE   I didn't go. Mr. Murphy was in an accident.

NORA   I'm sorry. Is he all right?

BLANCHE   He's got his problems, like the rest of us . . . I was very hurt that you left tonight without saying goodbye.

NORA   I was late. Someone was waiting for me.

BLANCHE   So was I. You knew it was important to me.

NORA   I'm not feeling very well.

BLANCHE   You purposely left without seeing me. You've never done that before.

NORA   Can we talk about this in the morning?

BLANCHE   I won't be here in the morning.

NORA   Then tomorrow night.

BLANCHE I'm leaving, Nora. I'm moving out in the morning.

NORA What are you talking about?

BLANCHE Aunt Kate and I had a fight tonight. We said some terrible things to each other. Things that have been bottled up since we were children. I'm going to stay with my friend Louise in Manhattan Beach until I can find a job. Then I'll send for you and Laurie.

NORA I can't believe it. You mean it's all right for you to leave *us* but it wasn't all right for me to leave *you*?

BLANCHE I was never concerned about your leaving *me*. It was your future I was worrying about.

NORA It was *my* future. Why couldn't *I* have something to say about it?

BLANCHE Maybe I was wrong, I don't know. I never made the decisions for the family. Your father did. Aunt Kate was right about one thing: everyone always took care of me. My mother, my sisters, my father, even you and Laurie. I've been a very dependent person all my life.

NORA Maybe that's all I'm asking for. To be *in*dependent.

BLANCHE (*Sternly*) You *earn* your independence. You don't take it at the expense of others. Would that job even be offered to you if somebody in this family hadn't paid for those dancing lessons and kept a roof over your head and clothes on your back? If anyone's going to pay back Uncle Jack, it'll be me—doing God knows what, I don't know—but one thing I'm sure of. I'll *steal* before I let my daughter show that man one ounce of ingratitude or disrespect.

NORA So I have to give up the one chance I may never get again, is that it? I'm the one who has to pay for what you couldn't do with your own life.

BLANCHE (*Angrily*)   What right do you have to judge me like that?

NORA   *Judge* you? I can't even talk to you. I don't exist to you. I have tried so hard to get close to you but there was never any room. Whatever you had to give went to Daddy, and when he died, whatever was left you gave to—
(*She turns away*)

BLANCHE   What? Finish what you were going to say.

NORA   . . . I have been jealous my whole life of Laurie because she was lucky enough to be born sick. I could never turn a light on in my room at night or read in bed because Laurie always needed her precious sleep. I could never have a friend over on the weekends because Laurie was always resting. I used to pray I'd get some terrible disease or get hit by a car so I'd have a leg all twisted or crippled and then once, maybe just once, *I'd* get to crawl into bed next to you on a cold rainy night and talk to you and hold you until I fell asleep in your arms . . . just once . . .
(*She is in tears*)

BLANCHE   My God, Nora . . . is that what you think of me?

NORA   Is it any worse than what you think of me?

BLANCHE (*Hesitates, trying to recover*)   I'm not going to let you hurt me, Nora. I'm not going to let you tell me that I don't love you or that I haven't tried to give you as much as I gave Laurie . . . God knows I'm not perfect, because enough angry people in this house told me so tonight. But I am *not* going to be a doormat for all the frustrations and unhappiness that you or Aunt Kate or anyone else wants to lay at my feet . . . I did *not* create this universe. I do *not* decide who lives and dies, or who's rich or poor, or who feels loved and who feels deprived. If you feel cheated that Laurie gets more than you, then I feel cheated that I had a husband who

579

BRIGHTON

BEACH

MEMOIRS

died at thirty-six. And if you keep on feeling that way, you'll end up like me—with something much worse than loneliness or helplessness and that's self-pity. Believe me, there is no leg that's twisted or bent that is more crippling than a human being who thrives on his own misfortunes . . . I am sorry, Nora, that you feel unloved and I will do everything I can to change it except apologize for it. I am *tired* of apologizing. After a while it becomes your life's work and it doesn't bring any money into the house. If it's taken your pain and Aunt Kate's anger to get me to start living again, then God will give me the strength to make it up to you, but I will *not* go back to being that frightened, helpless woman that *I* created! I've already buried someone I love. Now it's time to bury someone I hate.

NORA   I didn't ask you to hate yourself. I just asked you to love me.

BLANCHE   I do, Nora. Oh, God, why can't I make that clear to you?

NORA   I feel so terrible.

BLANCHE   Why?

NORA   Because I think I hurt you and I still want that job with Mr. Beckman.

BLANCHE   I know you do.

NORA   But I can't have it, can I?

BLANCHE   How can I answer that without you thinking I'm still depriving you?

NORA   I don't know . . . Maybe you just did.

BLANCHE   I hope so, Nora. I pray to God it's so.
         (KATE *is coming down the stairs*)

KATE   I heard voices downstairs. I didn't know who it was.

BLANCHE   I'm sorry if we woke you . . . Go on up to bed, Nora. We'll talk again in the morning.

NORA   All right . . . Good night, Aunt Kate.
   (NORA *goes upstairs*)

KATE   Is she all right?

BLANCHE   Yes.

KATE   She's not angry anymore?

BLANCHE   No, Kate. No one's angry anymore. (NORA *goes into the bedroom*) I just explained everything to Nora. The girls will help you with all the housework while I'm gone. Laurie's strong enough to do her share. I've kept her being a baby long enough.

KATE   They've never been any trouble to me, those girls. Never.

BLANCHE   I'll try to take them on the weekends if I can . . . It's late. We could both use a good night's sleep.
   (*She starts out of the room*)

KATE   Blanche! Don't go! (BLANCHE *stops*) I feel badly enough for what I said. Don't make me feel any worse.

BLANCHE   Everything you said to me tonight was true, Kate. I wish to God you'd said it years ago.

KATE   What would I do without you? Who else do I have to talk to all day? What friends do I have in this neighborhood? Even the Murphys across the street are leaving.

BLANCHE   You and I never had any troubles before tonight, Kate. And as God is in heaven, there'll never be an angry word between us again . . . It's the girls I'm thinking of now. We have to be together. The three of us. It's what they want as much as I do.

KATE   All right. I'm not saying you shouldn't have it. But you're not going to find a job overnight. Apartments are expensive. While you're looking, why do you have to live with strangers in Manhattan Beach?

BLANCHE   Louise isn't a stranger. She's a good friend.

KATE   To me good friends are strangers. But sisters are sisters.

BLANCHE   I'm afraid of becoming comfortable here. If I don't get out now, when will I ever do it?

KATE   The door is open. Go whenever you want. When you got the job, when you find the apartment, I'll help you move. I can look with you. I know how to bargain with these landlords.

BLANCHE (*Smiles*)   You wouldn't mind doing that?

KATE   They see a woman all alone, they take advantage of you . . . I'll find out what they're asking for the Murphy place. It couldn't be expensive, she never cleaned it.

BLANCHE   How independent can I become if I live right across the street from you?

KATE   Far enough away for you to close your own door, and close enough for me not to feel so lonely.
        (BLANCHE *looks at her with great affection, walks over to* KATE *and embraces her. They hold on dearly*)

BLANCHE   If I lived on the moon, you would still be close to me, Kate.

KATE   I'll tell Jack. He wouldn't go to sleep until I promised to come up with some good news.

BLANCHE   I suddenly feel so hungry.

KATE   Of course. You haven't had dinner. Come on. I'll
fix you some scrambled eggs.
   (*She heads toward the kitchen*)

BLANCHE   I'll make them. I'm an independent woman
now.

KATE   With your eyes, you'll never get the eggs in the
pan.
   (*They walk into the kitchen.* EUGENE *appears in the
   front yard. He is carrying two bags of groceries. It is
   late afternoon. He stops to talk to the audience*)

EUGENE   So Aunt Blanche decided to stay while she was
looking for a job. Nora went back to school the next
morning, gave me a big smile, and her legs looked as
creamy-white as ever. Laurie was asked to take out the
garbage but she quickly got a "flutter" in her heart, so
I had to do it. Life was back to normal.
   (*He goes into the house.* KATE *comes out of the
   kitchen*)

KATE   Eugene! Go back to Greenblatt's. I need flour.

EUGENE   How much? A teaspoonful? (*She glares at him,
takes the bags, and goes back into the kitchen. He turns to
the audience*) Stanley didn't come home that night, and
even though Mom didn't say anything, I knew she was
plenty worried. She told Pop how Stanley lost the
money playing poker, and from the sounds coming out
of their room, I figured Stanley should forget about the
army and try for the Foreign Legion. (STANLEY *appears
down the street*) And then all of a sudden, the next night
about dinnertime, he came back. I was never so happy
to see anyone in my whole life.

STANLEY   Hi! (*He looks around*) Where's Mom and Pop?

EUGENE   Mom's in the kitchen cooking. Pop's upstairs
with his prayer book. They figured if God didn't bring

you home, maybe her potato pancakes would . . . What happened? Did you join up?

STANLEY I came pretty close. I passed the physical one two three.

EUGENE I knew you would.

STANLEY They were giving me cigarettes, doughnuts, the whole sales pitch. I mean, they really wanted me.

EUGENE I'll bet.

STANLEY But then, just as I was about to sign my name, I stopped cold. I put down the pen and said, "I'm sorry. Maybe some other time"—and walked out.

EUGENE How come?

STANLEY I couldn't do it to Pop. Right now he needs me more than the army does . . . I knew Mom didn't really mean it when she said she'd never forgive me for losing the money, but if I walked out on the family now, maybe she never would.

EUGENE Gee, I thought you'd be halfway to training camp by now . . . but I'm real glad you're home, Stan.
      (*They stand there looking at each other for a moment as* KATE *walks out of the kitchen to the yard*)

KATE Eugene. I need a pint of sweet cream. And some more sugar.

EUGENE Stanley's home.

STANLEY Hello, Mom.

KATE (*Looks at him, then to* EUGENE) Get a two-pound bag. I want to bake a chocolate cake.

EUGENE   A two-pound bag from Greenblatt's? I'll need identification.
(*He looks at* STANLEY, *then goes*)

KATE (*To* STANLEY)   Are you staying for dinner?

STANLEY   I'm staying as long as you'll let me stay.

KATE   Why wouldn't I let you stay?? This is your home. (KATE *walks into the house,* STANLEY *follows.* JACK *comes down the stairs and goes over to his favorite chair. He opens up his paper*) Your father's been very worried. I think you owe him some sort of explanation.

STANLEY   I was just about to do that. (KATE *looks at him, wants to reach out to touch him, but can't seem to do it. She goes back into the kitchen as* STANLEY *walks into the living room*) Hi, Pop. How you feeling? (JACK *doesn't turn. He keeps reading his newspaper*) I'm sorry about not coming home last night . . . I know it was wrong. I just didn't know how to tell you about the money. I know it doesn't help to say I'll never do it again, because I won't. I swear. Never . . . (*He takes money out of his pocket*) I've got three dollars. Last night I went over to Dominick's Bowling Alley and I set pins till midnight and I could make another six on the weekend, so that makes nine. I'll get the seventeen dollars back, Pop, I promise . . . I'm not afraid of hard work. That's the one thing you taught me. Hard work and principles. That's the code I'm going to live by for the rest of my life . . . So—if you have anything you want to say to me, I'd be very glad to listen.
(*He stands there and waits*)

JACK (*Still looking at the paper*)   Did you read the paper tonight, Stanley?

STANLEY   No, Pop.

JACK   There's going to be a war. A terrible war, Stanley.

STANLEY   I know, Pop.
(*He moves into the room, faces his father*)

JACK The biggest war the world has ever seen. And it frightens me. We're still not over the last one yet, and already they're starting another one.

STANLEY We don't talk about it much in the store because of Mr. Stroheim being German and all.

JACK My brother, Michael, was killed in the last war. I've told you that.

STANLEY You showed me his picture in uniform.

JACK He was nineteen years old. The day he left, he didn't look any older than Eugene. He was killed the second week he was overseas . . .

STANLEY I know.

JACK They didn't take me because I was sixteen years old, both parents were dead, and I lived with my Aunt Rose and Uncle Maury. They had two sons in the navy, both of them wounded, both of them decorated.

STANLEY Uncle Leon and Uncle Paul, right?

JACK (Nods) My brother would have been forty years old this month. He was a handsome boy. Good athlete, good dancer, good everything. I idolized him. Like Eugene idolizes you.

STANLEY No, he doesn't.

JACK He does, believe me. I hear him outside, talking to his friends. "My brother this, my brother that" . . . Brothers can talk to each other the way fathers and sons never do . . . I never knew a thing about girls until my brother taught me. Isn't it like that with you and Eugene?

STANLEY Yeah, I tell him a few things.

JACK   That's good. I'm glad you're so close . . . I missed all that when Michael went away. That's why I'm glad you didn't do anything foolish last night. I was afraid maybe you'd run away. I hear you talking with Eugene sometimes about the army. That day will come soon enough, I'm afraid.

STANLEY   I did think about it. It was on my mind.

JACK   Don't you know, Stanley, there's nothing you could ever do that was so terrible, I couldn't forgive you. I know why you gambled. I know how terrible you feel. It was foolish, you know that already. I've lost money gambling in my time, I know what it's like.

STANLEY   You did?

JACK   You're so surprised? You think your father's a perfect human being? Someday I'll tell you some other things I did that wasn't so perfect. Not even your mother knows. If you grow up thinking I was perfect, you'll hate yourself for every mistake you ever make. Don't be so hard on yourself. That's what you've got a mother and father to do.

STANLEY   You're not hard on me. You're always fair.

JACK   I try to be. You're a good son, Stanley. You don't even realize that. We have men in our cutting room who haven't spoken to their sons in five, six years. Boys who have no respect for anyone, including themselves; who haven't worked a day in their lives, or who've brought their parents a single day's pleasure. Thank God, I could never say that about you, Stanley.

STANLEY   I gambled away seventeen dollars and you're telling me how terrific I am.

JACK   Hey, wait a minute. Don't get the wrong idea. If you were home last night when your mother told me, I would have thrown you and your clothes out the window. Today I'm calmer. Today I read the newspaper. Today I'm afraid for all of us.

STANLEY   I understand.

JACK   After dinner tonight, you apologize to your mother and give her the three dollars.

STANLEY   I will.

JACK   And apologize to your Aunt Blanche because she was worried about you too.

STANLEY   I will.

JACK   And you can thank your brother as well. He came into my bedroom this afternoon and told me how badly you felt. He was almost in tears himself. The way he pleaded your case, I thought I had Clarence Darrow in the room.

STANLEY   Eugene's a terrific kid.

JACK   All right. Go wash up and get ready for dinner. And tonight, you and I are going to go out in the backyard and I'm going to teach you how to play poker.

STANLEY (*Smiles*)   Terrific!
    (*He turns to go when* KATE *comes out of the kitchen*)

KATE   Is Eugene back yet?

STANLEY   No, Mom.

KATE   You look tired. Did you get any sleep?

STANLEY   I got enough. I slept at a friend's house. Can I talk to you after dinner, Mom?

KATE   Where am I going? To a nightclub?

STANLEY   I'll wash up and be right down.
(*He turns and starts up the stairs*)

KATE   Stanley! You didn't join anything, did you?

STANLEY   No, Mom.

KATE   You've got time yet. The family's growing up fast
enough.

STANLEY   Yes, Mom.
(*He turns and rushes up the stairs.* KATE *turns and
looks at* JACK)

JACK   It's all right. Everything is all right.

KATE   Who said it wasn't? Didn't I say he'd be home?
(*She calls up*) Laurie! Call your sister. Time to set the
table.
(EUGENE *comes running into the house with a small
bag and some letters*)

EUGENE (*Out of breath*)   I just broke the world's record
to Greenblatt's. Next year I'm entering the Grocery
Store Olympics. Here's some mail for you, Pop.

KATE   Is that my sweet cream?

EUGENE   Never spilled a drop. The perfect run. (*She
takes the bag and goes into the kitchen*) Where's Stanley?

JACK (*Takes the mail*)   He's cleaning up. (*He looks at the
mail*) Oh, my God, I've got jury duty next week.
(*He sits and opens up a letter.* EUGENE *rushes up the
stairs and runs into his room.* STANLEY *is taking off
his two sweaters*)

EUGENE (*Closing the door*)   Are you back in the family?

STANLEY   Yeah. Everything's great.

EUGENE   Terrific . . . You want to take a walk on the boardwalk tonight? See what's doing?

STANLEY   I can't tonight. I'm busy.

EUGENE   Doing what?

STANLEY   I'm playing poker.

EUGENE   Poker? Are you serious?

STANLEY   Yeah. Right after dinner.

EUGENE   I don't believe you.

STANLEY   I swear to God! I got a poker game tonight.

EUGENE   You're crazy! You're genuinely crazy, Stanley . . . If you lose, I'm not sticking up for you this time.

STANLEY   If you don't tell anybody, I'll give you a present.

EUGENE   What kind of present?

STANLEY   Are you going to tell?

EUGENE   No. What's my present?
            (STANLEY *takes something wrapped in a piece of paper out of his jacket and hands it to* EUGENE)

STANLEY   Here. It's for you. Don't leave it lying around the room.
            (EUGENE *starts to open it. It's postcard size*)

EUGENE   What is it?

STANLEY   Open it slowly. (EUGENE *does*) Slower than that . . . Close your eyes. (EUGENE *does. It is unwrapped*) Now look!
            (EUGENE *looks. His eyes almost pop out*)

EUGENE   OH, MY GOD!! . . . SHE'S NAKED! YOU CAN SEE *EVERYTHING*!!

STANLEY   Lower your voice. You want to get caught with a thing like that?

EUGENE   Where did you get it? Who is she?

STANLEY   She's French. That's how *all* the women are in Paris.

EUGENE   I can't believe I'm looking at this? You mean some girl actually *posed* for this? She just lay there and let some guy take a picture?
   (BLANCHE *comes out of the kitchen*)

BLANCHE   Laurie! Nora! Time for dinner.
   (*The girls come out of their room*)

STANLEY   It belongs to the guy who owes me two and a half bucks. I can keep it until he pays me back.

EUGENE   Don't take the money. Let him keep it for a while.
   (*He lies back on the bed, staring at the picture.* NORA *and* LAURIE *go down the stairs as* KATE *comes out of the kitchen with plates and starts to set up the table*)

STANLEY   That's my appreciation for being a good buddy.

EUGENE   Anytime you need a favor, just let me know.

STANLEY   Put it in a safe spot . . . Come on. It's dinner.

EUGENE   In a minute. I'll be down in a minute.
   (*He lies there, eyes transfixed.* STANLEY *starts down the stairs.* NORA *and* LAURIE *set out napkins and utensils.* BLANCHE *starts to arrange the chairs.* JACK, *with a letter in his hand, gets up, looking excited, walks into the dining room*)

JACK   Kate? Where's Kate?

KATE   Don't run. You're always running.

JACK (*Holds up the letter*)   It's a letter from London. My cousin Sholem got out. They got out of Poland. They're free, Kate!

BLANCHE   Thank God!

JACK   His wife, his mother, all four children. They're sailing for New York tomorrow. They'll be here in a week.

KATE   In a week?

LAURIE   Do they speak English?

JACK   I don't think so. A few words, maybe. (*To* KATE) They had to sell everything. They took only what they could carry.

STANLEY   Where will they stay?

JACK   Well, I'll have to discuss it with the family. Some with Uncle Leon, Uncle Paul—

KATE   With us. We can put some beds in the dining room. It's easier to eat in the kitchen anyway.

BLANCHE   The little ones can stay with Laurie. Nora can sleep with me—can't you, dear?

NORA (*Pleased*)   Of course, Momma.

STANLEY   Don't worry about money, Pa. I'm going to hit Mr. Stroheim for that raise.

JACK   They got out. That's all that's important. They got out.
(JACK *sits down at the table to reread the letter.* NORA, STANLEY, *and* LAURIE *look over his shoulder.* BLANCHE *and* KATE *set the table*)

KATE (*Yells up*) Eugene! We're all waiting for you!

EUGENE (*Calls down*) Be right there! I just have to write down something. (*He looks at photo again, then picks up a fountain pen and his memoir book and reads as he begins to write*) "October the second, six twenty-five P.M. A momentous moment in the life of I, Eugene Morris Jerome. I have seen the Golden Palace of the Himalayas . . . Puberty is over. Onward and upwards!"

Curtain

Biloxi
Blues

BILOXI BLUES *was first presented on December 8, 1984, at the Ah-manson Theatre, Los Angeles, and on March 28, 1985, at the Neil Simon Theatre, New York City, with the following cast:*

ROY SELRIDGE	Brian Tarantina
JOSEPH WYKOWSKI	Matt Mulhern
DON CARNEY	Alan Ruck
EUGENE MORRIS JEROME	Matthew Broderick
ARNOLD EPSTEIN	Barry Miller
SGT. MERWIN J. TOOMEY	Bill Sadler
JAMES HENNESEY	Geoffrey Sharp
ROWENA	Randall Edwards
DAISY HANNIGAN	Penelope Ann Miller

Directed by Gene Saks
Setting by David Mitchell
Lighting by Tharon Musser
Costumes by Ann Roth

ACT ONE

ACT TWO

The action takes place in Biloxi and Gulfport, Mississippi, in 1943.

Act One

The coach of an old railroad train, pressed into service because of the war.

It is 1943.

(All set pieces are representational, stylized, and free-flowing. We have a lot of territory to cover here . . .)

Four soldiers, dressed in fatigues, from eighteen to twenty years old, are stretched out across the coach seats, facing each other, their legs reaching out onto the opposite seats. Three of the soldiers are sleeping. They are JOSEPH WYKOWSKI, ROY SELRIDGE, *and* DON CARNEY. *The fourth boy is* EUGENE MORRIS JEROME. *He is awake and sitting up, writing in a school notebook. It is quiet except for the rumbling of the train along the tracks. A fifth boy,* ARNOLD EPSTEIN, *sleeps in the baggage rack above the others.*

It is night and a single light illuminates the group. ROY, *in an effort to get more comfortable, turns, and his shoeless foot crawls practically into* WYKOWSKI'S *mouth.* WYKOWSKI, *annoyed, slaps* ROY'S *foot away.*

SELRIDGE (*Waking*) Hey! What the hell's with you?

WYKOWSKI Get your foot out of my mouth, horseface.

SELRIDGE Up your keester with a meathook, Kowski.

CARNEY Knock it off, pissheads.

WYKOWSKI Go take a flying dump, Carney.

CARNEY Yeah. In your mother's hairnet, homo!
(*They all return to sleeping*)

EUGENE (*Aloud to the audience*) . . . It was my fourth day in the army and so far I hated everyone . . . We were on a filthy train riding from Fort Dix, New Jersey, to Biloxi, Mississippi, and in three days nobody washed.

The aroma was murder. We were supposed to be fighting Germany and Japan but instead we were stinking up America.

> (*The train rumbles along* . . . ROY *peers out the window*)

SELRIDGE   Where the hell are we? (EUGENE *is still engrossed in his writing.* ROY *kicks him*) Hey! Shakespeare! Where the hell are we?

EUGENE   West Virginia.

SELRIDGE   No shit? . . . Where's that near?

EUGENE   You don't know where West Virginia is? Didn't you ever take geography?

SELRIDGE   I was sick that day.

EUGENE   You don't know what part of the country it's in?

SELRIDGE (*Rises and grabs his crotch*)   Yeah. *This* part. Up yours, Jerome.

EUGENE (*Reads what he has written*)   "Roy Selridge from Schenectady, New York, smelled like a tunafish sandwich left out in the rain. He thought he had a terrific sense of humor but it was hard to laugh at a guy who had cavities in nineteen out of thirty-two teeth."

> (*The train rumbles on*)

WYKOWSKI (*Opens his eyes*)   Jesus Christ! Who did that?

EUGENE   What?

WYKOWSKI   Someone let one go! . . . Holy Jeez. (*He fans his cap in front of his face*) I need a gas mask . . . (*He lights a match*) You writing all this stuff in your diary? "Major fart in West Virginia."

EUGENE   It's not a diary. It's my memoirs.

WYKOWSKI Well, you don't have to write it down because *that* one will stay in your book forever . . . Whoo! Jeez!
(*He goes back to sleep*)

EUGENE (*To the audience*) Joseph Wykowski from Bridgeport, Connecticut, had two interesting characteristics. He had the stomach of a goat and could eat anything. His favorite was Hershey bars with the wrappers still on it . . . The other peculiar trait was that he had a permanent erection. I'm talking about night and day, during marching or sleeping. There's no explaining this phenomenon unless he has a unique form of paralysis.
(*The train rumbles on in the night*)

CARNEY (*His eyes are closed and he suddenly starts to sing the opening lines of "Chattanooga Choo-Choo" with practically full voice*)

WYKOWSKI Wake him up! Wake him up, for crise sakes!
(ROY *kicks* CARNEY *in the chest with his foot.* CARNEY *jumps*)

CARNEY What the hell's wrong with you?

SELRIDGE It's two-thirty in the goddamn morning. You were singing again.

CARNEY I was not.

SELRIDGE What do you mean, "You was not"? You practically made a record.

CARNEY What was I singing?

SELRIDGE "Chattanooga Choo-Choo."

CARNEY I don't even know the words to "Chattanooga Choo-Choo."

WYKOWSKI Maybe not awake. But you know them when you're sleeping.

CARNEY (*To* EUGENE) Hey, Gene. Was I singing "Chattanooga Choo-Choo"?

EUGENE Yeah.

CARNEY . . . Was I good?

EUGENE Well, for a guy who was sleeping, it wasn't bad.

CARNEY Damn. I wish I heard it.

EUGENE (*To the audience*) Donald Carney from Montclair, New Jersey, was an okay guy until someone made the fatal mistake of telling him he sounded like Perry Como. His voice was flat but his sister wasn't. She had the biggest breasts I ever saw. She came to visit him at Fort Dix wearing a tight red sweater and that's when I first discovered Wykowski's condition.
(*The train rumbles on*)

WYKOWSKI (*Sits up*) Goddamn it. Someone let go again . . . Was it you, Carney?

CARNEY I was singing, wasn't I? I'm not going to do that while I'm singing.

WYKOWSKI Yeah? Well, maybe you sang to cover it up.

SELRIDGE Wait a minute. Wait a minute. (*He looks up*) It's coming from up there.
(*They all look up.* EPSTEIN *has been sleeping on the grilling of the baggage rack with his rear end to the audience.* WYKOWSKI *whacks his cap hard against* EPSTEIN'*s butt*)

WYKOWSKI Hey! Bombardier! Kill Germans, not G.I.s.
(EPSTEIN *turns around. He is slight of build*)

EPSTEIN I'm sorry. I'm not feeling very well.

SELRIDGE   Yeah? Well, now we're *all* not feeling very well.

EUGENE   Leave him alone. He didn't do it on purpose.

SELRIDGE (*To* EPSTEIN)   You hear, Epstein? He's your buddy. Aim the next one at him, okay?

EPSTEIN   Does anyone have an Alka-Seltzer tablet?

WYKOWSKI   Plugging it up ain't gonna help, Epstein.
   (*He and* ROY *laugh. They all go back to their sleeping positions*)

EUGENE (*Stops writing and looks at the audience*)   Arnold Epstein of Queens Boulevard, New York, was a sensitive, well-read, intelligent young man. His major flaw was that he was incapable of digesting food stronger than hard-boiled eggs . . . I didn't think he'd last long in the army because during wartime it's very hard to go home for dinner every night . . . (*The train rumbles on*) Hey, Arnold! What's the best book you ever read?

EPSTEIN   *War and Peace* . . . The fifth time.

EUGENE   If I wanted to become a writer, who do you recommend I read?

EPSTEIN   The entire third floor of the New York Public Library.

WYKOWSKI   Hey, Epstein? Can you read lips? Read this!
   (*He gives Epstein a Bronx cheer.* SELRIDGE *laughs*)

EUGENE (*To the audience*)   If the Germans only knew what was coming over, they would be looking forward to this invasion . . . I'm Eugene Morris Jerome of Brighton Beach, Brooklyn, New York, and you can tell I've never been away from home before. In my duffel bag are twelve pot roast sandwiches my mother gave me . . . There were three things I was determined to do in this war. Become a writer, not get killed, and lose my virginity . . . But first I had to get through basic training in the murky swamps of Mississippi . . .

(There is silence for a moment, then CARNEY, *eyes closed, begins to sing "Paper Doll." Lights dim as the train rumbles on. As* CARNEY's *singing slowly fades, we hear the sound of men marching and chanting out the cadence rhythms so familiar in the military. Lights come up in the barracks as the sound of marching men fades.*

EUGENE, WYKOWSKI, EPSTEIN, SELRIDGE, *and* CARNEY *amble into the barracks carrying their heavy barracks bags. They are hot, sweaty, and tired. They look around at their new "home" for the next few months)*

EUGENE   Boy, it's hot. This is hot! I am really hot! Oh, God, is it hot!
(He puts his duffel in a lower bunk)

WYKOWSKI   You can cool off on the top 'cause that's *my* bunk down there.
(He throws EUGENE's *duffel on top and throws his own on the lower.* EPSTEIN *throws his duffel on the top bunk next to* EUGENE. *He looks at the rolled-up mattress and picks off a bedbug. They have all put their duffels on bunks and sit or lie down)*

CARNEY   I'm so tired I'm just gonna sleep on the springs.

EUGENE   It never got this hot in Brooklyn. This is like Africa-hot. *Tarzan* couldn't take this kind of hot.

SELRIDGE   Where's the phone? Call the manager. There's no ice water.

SERGEANT TOOMEY *(Enters with a clipboard)*   Dee-tail, at-tenSHUN!!
(The boys slowly get to their feet)

SELRIDGE   Hi, Sarge.

TOOMEY   I think it's in your best interests, men, to move your asses when I yell ATTENSHUN!! MOVE IT!!! I want a single line right there! (*They all jump and line up in front of their bunks.* TOOMEY *paces up and down the line, looking them over*) Until the order "At Ease," is given, gentlemen, you are not "At Ease," is that understood? 'Tenshun! (*They snap to attention. He looks at them a moment*) At Ease! (*They stand "At Ease" . . .* TOOMEY *looks them over, then consults his clipboard*) Answer when your name is called. The answer to that question is "Ho." Not yes, not here, not right, not sir or any other unacceptable form of reply except the aforementioned "Ho," am I understood? Wykowski, Joseph T.

WYKOWSKI   Ho!

TOOMEY   Selridge, Roy W.

ROY   Ho!

TOOMEY   Carney, Donald J.

CARNEY   Ho!

TOOMEY   Jerome, Eugene M.

EUGENE   Ho!

TOOMEY   Epstein, Arnold B.

EPSTEIN   Ho Ho!
         (TOOMEY *looks at him*)

TOOMEY   Are there two Arnold Epsteins in this company?

EPSTEIN   No, Sergeant.

TOOMEY   Then just give me one goddamn Ho.

EPSTEIN   Yes, Sergeant.

TOOMEY   Epstein, Arnold B.

EPSTEIN   Ho!

TOOMEY   One more time.

EPSTEIN   Ho!

TOOMEY   Let me hear it again.

EPSTEIN   Ho!

TOOMEY   Am I understood?

EPSTEIN   Ho! (*as if to say "Of course"*)

EUGENE (*To the audience*)   Arnold Epstein was the worst soldier in World War Two and that included the deserters . . . He just refused to show respect to those he thought were his intellectual inferiors.

TOOMEY (*To the men*)   . . . My name is Toomey, Sergeant Merwin J. Toomey, and I am in charge of C Company during your ten weeks of basic training here in beautiful Biloxi, Mississippi, after which those of you who have survived the heat, humidity, roaches, spiders, snakes, dry rot, fungus, dysentery, syphilis, gonorrhea, and tick fever will be sent to some shit island in the Pacific or some turd pile in Northern Sicily. In either case, returning to your mommas and poppas with your balls intact is highly improbable. There's only one way to come out of a war healthy of body and sane of mind and that way is to be born the favorite daughter of the President of the United States . . . I speak from experience, having served fourteen months in the North African campaign where seventy-three percent of my comrades are buried under the sand of an A-rab desert. The colorful ribbons on my chest will testify to the fact that my government is grateful for my contribution, having donated a small portion of my brains to this conflict, the other portion being protected by a heavy steel plate in my head. This injury has caused me to become a smart, compassionate, understanding, and sympathetic teacher of raw young men—or the cruelest, craziest, most sadistic goddamn son of a bitch you ever saw . . . and that's something you won't know until ten weeks from now, do I make myself clear, Epstein?

EPSTEIN   I think so.

TOOMEY   DO I MAKE MYSELF CLEAR, EP-STEIN??

EPSTEIN   Ho!

TOOMEY   DO I MAKE MYSELF CLEAR, JEROME?

EUGENE   Ho yes!

TOOMEY   Ho *what?*

EUGENE   Ho nothing.

TOOMEY   Goddamn right, boy.

EUGENE (*To the audience*)   I hated the lousy movies. I thought I was going to get a nice officer like James Stewart.

TOOMEY (*Looks at* EUGENE)   Are you paying attention to me, Jerome?

EUGENE (*Nervously*)   Yes ho. I mean Ho, sir. Just plain Ho.

TOOMEY   Where are you from, Jerome?

EUGENE   1427 Pulaski Avenue.

TOOMEY   In my twelve years in the army, I never met one goddamn dogface who came from 1427 Pulaski Avenue. Why is that, Jerome?

EUGENE   Because it's my home. Only my family lives there. I'm sorry. I meant I live in Brighton Beach, Brooklyn, New York.

(TOOMEY *notices* EPSTEIN *shifting from foot to foot*)

TOOMEY   Hey, Fred Astaire! You trying to tell me something?

EPSTEIN   I have to go to the bathroom, Sergeant.

TOOMEY   Now how are you going to do that? We don't have bathrooms in the army.

EPSTEIN   They had them in Fort Dix.

TOOMEY   Not bathrooms, they didn't.

EPSTEIN   Yes, they did, Sergeant. I went in them a lot.

TOOMEY   Well, I'm telling you we don't have any bathrooms on this base. Do you doubt my veracity?

EPSTEIN   No, Sergeant.

TOOMEY   Then you've got a problem, haven't you, Epstein?

EPSTEIN   Ho ho.

TOOMEY   You bet your ass, ho ho . . . Do you know why you've got a problem, Epstein?

EPSTEIN   Because I have to go real bad.

TOOMEY   No, son. You've got a problem because you don't know army terminology. The place where a U.S. soldier goes to defecate, relieve himself, open his bowels, shit, fart, dump, crap, and unload is called the la-trine. La-trine! (EUGENE *smiles*) Want to tell us what's funny about that, Jerome?

EUGENE   Well . . . that you said all those words in one sentence.

TOOMEY   That's why these ribbons are pinned on my shirt. Because I'm an experienced army man. Do you understand that, Jerome?

EUGENE   Ha.

TOOMEY   What?

EUGENE   Ho.

TOOMEY   Where are you from, Wykowski?

WYKOWSKI   Bridgeport, Connecticut.

TOOMEY   Do you know where that is, Selridge?

SELRIDGE   It's er . . . in Connecticut. Bridgeport, I think.

TOOMEY   Is that right, Wykowski?

WYKOWSKI   Ho.

TOOMEY (*Looks directly at* ROY)   And what did you do in Bridgeport, soldier?

SELRIDGE   I was never there, Sergeant.

TOOMEY   I wasn't talking to you, Selridge.

SELRIDGE   Oh. You were looking at me.

TOOMEY   I may be looking at you but I am talking to the soldier from Bridgeport. (*He looks into* ROY'S *face*) Now, what did you do there, Wykowski?
    (*They all look confused*)

WYKOWSKI   I drove a truck. A moving van. I was a furniture mover.

TOOMEY   That's just what they need in the South Pacific, Wykowski. Someone who knows how to move furniture around in the jungle. (EPSTEIN *half raises his hand*) I believe Private Epstein has a question.

EPSTEIN   May I go to the latrine, Sergeant?

TOOMEY   No. I am addressing the new members of my company, Epstein. (*He looks directly into* WYKOWSKI's *face*) What's your name again, soldier?

WYKOWSKI   Wykowski.

TOOMEY   I am talking to the man next to you.

SELRIDGE   Selridge!

TOOMEY (*Points to* CARNEY)   *You,* boy! You are the one I am directing my question to.

CARNEY   Carney, sir. Donald J . . . Ho!

TOOMEY   I didn't ask if you were here. I can *see* that you're here. I asked where you're from, Carney, Donald J.

CARNEY (*Thinks*)   I don't remember . . . Er, Montclair, New Jersey.

TOOMEY   And what was your civilian occupation in Montclair, New Jersey, Private Carney, Donald J.?

CARNEY   I didn't have any.

TOOMEY   No occupation? You were unemployed then, is that right?

CARNEY   No, Sergeant. I worked in a shoe store. In the stock room.

TOOMEY (*Stares at him*)   Did I not hear you just say you didn't have an occupation?

CARNEY   Not in Montclair. I *lived* in Montclair. I worked in Teaneck. You just asked what my occupation was in Montclair.

TOOMEY   I see . . . Is it your intention, Private Carney, Donald J., to humiliate and ridicule me in front of my company?

CARNEY   No, Sergeant.

TOOMEY   And yet that is precisely what you did. As I stand here in front of my newly arrived company, you took this opportunity, assuming that because of my Southern heritage, I was an uneducated and illiterate cotton picker, you purposefully and deliberately humiliated me. Did you think for one second you would get away with that, Private Carney, Donald J.?

CARNEY   I wasn't trying to get away with—

TOOMEY   Well, I can assure you, YOU DID NOT AND WILL NOT! You just got your ass in a sling, boy! *Does everyone understand that?*

ALL TOGETHER   HO!!!

TOOMEY   What?

ALL TOGETHER (*Louder*)   HO!!!

TOOMEY   I am, strictly speaking, Carney, old army. And old army means discipline. Can you do push-ups, Private Carney?

CARNEY   Yes, Sergeant.

TOOMEY   What is the highest total of push-ups you ever achieved in one session, Private Carney?

CARNEY   I'm not too strong in the arms. About ten . . . maybe fifteen.

TOOMEY   Congratulations, Carney. You are about to break your old record. I want one hundred push-ups from you, Carney, and I want them *now*. AM I UNDERSTOOD?

CARNEY   One hundred? Oh, I couldn't possibly do one hu—

TOOMEY   HIT THE FLOOR, SOLDIER!!!

CARNEY   I could do, say, twenty a day for five days—

TOOMEY   Count off, goddammit, and move your ass!

CARNEY   (*Starts doing push-ups*)   One . . . two . . . three . . . four . . . five . . .

TOOMEY   (*Looks into* EPSTEIN's *eyes*)   Nobody eats, drinks, sleeps, or goes to the latrine until I hear one hundred.

CARNEY   Six . . . seven . . . Oh, God . . . nine . . . ten . . .

TOOMEY   Eight. You forgot eight, didn't you, boy?

CARNEY   I did it. I just didn't say it.

TOOMEY   Well, say them all, Donny boy. Let's start again from one. Let's hear it.

CARNEY   One . . . two . . . three . . .
          (CARNEY *continues this throughout the scene with great difficulty*)

TOOMEY   (*Shouting*)   *Private Jerome!* Do you think this is cruel, unfair, and unjust punishment being inflicted on Private Carney?

EUGENE   Oh, gee, I don't know. It's my first day—

TOOMEY   I want the God Almighty truth from you. Is this punishment unfair and unjust, Private Jerome?

EUGENE (*To the audience*)   If only I had a heart murmur, I wouldn't be in this trouble.

TOOMEY   Your answer, boy.

EUGENE   Well, I think it was a misunderstanding . . . I think er—(*He feels his head*) I think I have swamp fever, sir.

TOOMEY   Yes or no, Jerome. Am I being unfair to the young man who is breaking his ass on the floor?

EUGENE   In my opinion? . . . Yes, Sergeant.

TOOMEY   I see . . . Apparently, Jerome, you don't understand the benefits of discipline. It is discipline that will win this war for us. Therefore, until you learn it, soldier, I will just have to keep teaching it to you . . . *Selridge!* One hundred push-ups. *Hit* the floor!

SELRIDGE   Me??? . . . I didn't say nothin'.

TOOMEY   When we do battle, we are sometimes called upon to sacrifice ourselves for the sake of others.

SELRIDGE   Yeah, but we didn't do battle yet.

TOOMEY   ON YOUR FACE, SOLDIER!!

SELRIDGE (*On the floor*)   One . . . two . . . three . . . four . . . five . . .
     They continue)

TOOMEY (*To* EUGENE)   What I have done to Private Selridge may seem even more unfair and unjust than what I did to Private Carney. Is that your opinion, Private Jerome?

EUGENE (*Takes a deep breath*)   . . . No, Sergeant.

TOOMEY   Hold it, boys. (*To the others; they stop*) You all heard that. Private Jerome approves of my method of discipline. He thinks what I am doing is fair, moral, and just. Therefore, with his approval and endorsement, Private Wykowski will join us for one hundred push-ups. Hit the deck, Wykowski! I can see how grateful you are. You can thank your buddy, Private Jerome.

WYKOWSKI (*Glaring at* EUGENE) I will. Later.
(*He starts push-ups*)

TOOMEY Back to work, boys.

WYKOWSKI One . . . two . . . three . . . four . . .

EUGENE (*To* WYKOWSKI) I'm sorry.
(CARNEY *is struggling*)

CARNEY I—I don't think I can do any more, Sergeant.

TOOMEY I realize that, son, and I sympathize with you. If only there were some way I could help you.

EUGENE I could finish it for him, Sergeant.

TOOMEY That's damn decent of you, Jerome, but I think Private Carney doesn't expect other men to shoulder his responsibility.

CARNEY I would be willing to make an exception, Sergeant.

TOOMEY What I think you need, Carney, is inspiration. Therefore, I am asking volunteers to join Privates Carney, Selridge, and Wykowski on the barracks floor. All volunteers take one step forward and shout, "Ho!" Sound off!

EUGENE (*Takes one step forward*) Ho!
(EPSTEIN *remains silent and doesn't move*)

TOOMEY We have one volunteer . . . and one inconclusive. (*He turns to* EPSTEIN *and moves in face to face*) Does your silence mean you are not volunteering, Private Epstein?

EPSTEIN   I have a slight deformity of the spine which escaped the medical exam—

TOOMEY   ON YOUR FACE, EPSTEIN!!! (ARNOLD *drops to the floor*) Ready . . . Ho!

EPSTEIN   One . . . two . . . three . . . four . . .
   (*All four men are doing push-ups.* CARNEY *and* EP-STEIN *struggle the most.*
   TOOMEY *paces back and forth, nodding happily*)

TOOMEY   Now we're moving ahead in our quest for discipline . . . As the sweat pours off your brows and your puny muscles strain to lift your flabby, chubby, jellied bodies, think of Private Jerome of Brighton Beach, New York, who is *not* down there beside you. *Not* sharing your pain, *not* sharing your struggle . . . Fate always chooses someone to get a free ride. The kind of man who always gets away with all kinds of shit. In this company it seems to be Private Eugene M. Jerome. Eventually we get to hate those men. Hate them, loathe them, and despise them. How does Private Jerome learn to deal with this cold wall of anger and hostility? By learning to endure it alone. That, gentlemen, is the supreme lesson in discipline. You're slowing down, boys. The sooner you finish, the sooner you'll get to our fine Southern cooking . . . Up down . . . Up down . . . Carry on instructions, Jerome. Up down . . . up down . . .
   (TOOMEY *leaves*)

EUGENE (*To the audience*)   It was then I decided I had to get out of the army . . . I thought of shooting off a part of my body I might not need in later life but I couldn't find any . . . But the worst was still to come . . .
   (*Lights out on* EUGENE.
   Lights up on a section of the mess hall. WYKOWSKI, SELRIDGE, CARNEY, *and* EPSTEIN *are sitting at a wooden table, staring frozen-faced at the aluminum*

tray filled with "supper" in front of them. Nobody moves. The forks in their hands are raised motionless above the tray)

CARNEY   What do you think it is?

WYKOWSKI   My brother had this in the marines. It's S.O.S.

CARNEY   What's S.O.S.?

WYKOWSKI   Shit on a shingle.

CARNEY *(Inspecting it)*   Yeah, that's what it looks like all right.

SELRIDGE   What do you mean? They take a shingle and they put—shit on it?

WYKOWSKI   It's beef. Creamed chipped beef.

EPSTEIN   Why would you chip something after it's been creamed?

WYKOWSKI   It doesn't look so bad to me. Hell, I'm hungry. *(He takes a forkful and eats it. They all watch him)* . . . It's terrific . . . It needs ketchup, that's all.
     (He puts ketchup on it)

SELRIDGE   They oughta drop this stuff over Germany. The whole country would come out with their hands up.
     (EUGENE appears, carrying his tray. His mouth is agape, his face aghast as he looks at what's on his tray)

EUGENE   I saw this in the Bronx Zoo. The gorillas were throwing it at each other.

EPSTEIN   If you can't eat this, you can get something else. It's government regulations. Enlisted men must be served palatable food.

WYKOWSKI Why don't you ask them for some matzoh ball soup, Epstein. I hear the army makes great matzoh ball soup.
(*He and* SELRIDGE *laugh.* EUGENE *looks emphatically at* EPSTEIN)

EPSTEIN It's my right to speak up. (*He looks around*) I'm going to speak to the sergeant.

CARNEY Sit down, would you, please?

EUGENE Don't start in with him, Arnold. He's crazy. This was probably his recipe.

WYKOWSKI (*To* EUGENE *and* EPSTEIN) Listen, you two guys. Don't give the sergeant any more crap. 'Cause when he doesn't like you, he doesn't like the rest of us. Any guy who screws up in this platoon is in deep shit with me, understand?

EPSTEIN Who made you lieutenant colonel?

WYKOWSKI *I* did. I promoted myself. If I have to do any more push-ups on account of you, Epstein, you're going to be underneath me when I'm doing them.

SELRIDGE Well, now we know who the fruits are.
(*He laughs*)

EPSTEIN I'm not even supposed to be in the army with my stomach. No one's going to make me eat this if I don't want to.
(JAMES HENNESEY, *a soldier their own age, on KP, comes over to refill their sugar jars*)

HENNESEY You guys hear what happened over at Baker Company? Some kid went nuts. Said he was going home, didn't want no part of this army. An officer tried to stop him and the kid belted him one, broke the Captain's nose. They said this guy's sure to get five to ten years in Leavenworth. They don't crap around in the army, you find that out real fast.

CARNEY   I hope they ship us out to the Pacific. At least we'd get Chinese food.

HENNESEY   My name is Hennesey. I'm in your platoon. They gave me eight straight days of KP.

HENNESEY   I left over two spoonfuls of barley soup. Two lousy spoonfuls . . . Be careful, you guys.
    (*He turns and moves away quickly as* SGT. TOOMEY *approaches the table*)

TOOMEY   How my boys doing? (*All except* EPSTEIN *smile and greet him warmly*) How's the chow?

WYKOWSKI (*Sounding overly cheerful*)   First-rate, Sarge.

SELRIDGE   They don't give you enough.

EUGENE   Surprisingly interesting food, Sarge.

TOOMEY   Not hungry, Epstein?

EPSTEIN   I find enough nourishment in bread and water, Sergeant.

TOOMEY   Well, you're all going to need plenty of nourishment with ten back-breaking weeks ahead of us, starting tonight.

CARNEY   Tonight?

TOOMEY   Worked out a little surprise for you. Something to work off tonight's dinner. We're going on a midnight hike, men.

EUGENE   Midnight?

TOOMEY   Not too far, this being your first night in camp. Just a short fifteen-mile walk around the marshes and swamps. How does that sound to you, Jerome? You think that's a reasonable request of me to make?

EUGENE   We've sort of elected Wykowski our leader. I think he should answer that.
(WYKOWSKI *glares at* EUGENE)

TOOMEY   Is that right, Wykowski?

WYKOWSKI   I don't question orders, Sergeant. I just follow them.

TOOMEY   That's a good answer, Wykowski. It's a chicken-shit one, but a good answer . . . How about you, Epstein? You up to a fifteen-mile walk around the swamp?

EPSTEIN   . . . No, Sergeant.

TOOMEY   No??? Epstein's not up to it, men . . . Why is that, Epstein?

EPSTEIN   We've been on a train for five days and five nights. We haven't had one good night's sleep since we left Fort Dix.

TOOMEY   I see . . . Okay. Fair enough, Epstein . . . You're excused from the hike. I appreciate a man who speaks up.

EPSTEIN   Thank you, Sergeant.

TOOMEY   You get a good night's sleep just as soon as you've washed, scrubbed, and shined every john, urinal, and basin in the latrine. If it doesn't sparkle when we get back, then Wykowski and Selridge are going to do two hundred push-ups. That'll put you in good with the boys, Epstein . . . Anyone else care to stay home for the evening? . . . Okay then, let's get moving. Full field packs in front of barracks at twenty-four hundred hours, ready to march. LET'S GET CRACKING! (*They all jump up, except* EPSTEIN) HOLD ON ONE

GODDAMN MINUTE!!! (*They all stop*) Nobody—but NOBODY—leaves here with good U.S. Army chow untouched, uneaten, and unfinished. You can sit there poking at it with your fork till it sprouts weeds, but by God, you will sit there until that tray is empty . . . Line up in front of me, trays extended for inspection. (*They quickly line up in front of* TOOMEY *in single file.* WYKOWSKI *is first.* TOOMEY *looks into his tray*) Okay, Wykowski, move! (SELRIDGE *is next*) Right, Selridge, move. (*He follows* WYKOWSKI *out.* CARNEY *is next. His food is untouched*) Something wrong with your dinner, Carney?

CARNEY   Yes, Sarge. It's the first food I was ever afraid of.

TOOMEY   You'll like it about a month from now 'cause that's how long you'll be sitting there. Back to your seat! (CARNEY *glumly goes back and sits at the table.* EUGENE *steps in front of* TOOMEY, *tray extended*) Don't approve of our *cuisine,* Jerome?

EUGENE   It's not that, Sarge. It's a religious objection. This is the week that my people fast for two days.

TOOMEY   This is March, Jerome. Rosh-Ahonah and Yom Kippur are in September. I have an all-religion calendar in my barracks room. Don't you try that shit on me again!

EUGENE   It's a different holiday. It's called El Malagueña.

TOOMEY   El Malagueña??

EUGENE   It's for Spanish Jews.

TOOMEY   Carney!

CARNEY   Yes, Sarge?

TOOMEY   Put half your tray onto Jerome's.

CARNEY (*Smiles*) Yes, Sergeant.

TOOMEY (*To* EUGENE) Eat in good health, Jerome, and Happy El Malagueña to you. (CARNEY *eagerly scrapes half his tray into* EUGENE'*s.* EUGENE, *looking miserable, sits.* EPSTEIN *steps in front of* TOOMEY) Okay, Epstein, what's your story? And don't tell me today is La Coocharacha.

EPSTEIN I have a legitimate excuse, Sergeant. I have a digestive disorder, diagnosed as a nervous stomach.

TOOMEY Is that right? And how come you passed the army medical examination?

EPSTEIN It only gets nervous while I'm eating food. I wasn't eating food during the examination. I brought a chicken salad sandwich along to show them what happens when it enters the digestive tract . . .

TOOMEY Are you a psycho, Epstein? You sound like a psycho to me. That's a psycho story.

EPSTEIN (*Reaches into his breast pocket*) I have a letter from my internist who's on the staff of Mount Sinai Hospital on Fifth Avenue—
    (TOOMEY *grabs the letter from* EPSTEIN *and quickly reads it*)

TOOMEY Did you show this to the army medical examining officer?

EPSTEIN Yes, Sergeant.

TOOMEY What did he say?

EPSTEIN He said don't eat chicken salad sandwiches and then he accepted me.

TOOMEY Then this letter ain't worth the paper it's written on. (*He tears it up and shreds it over* EPSTEIN'*s food*) I expect to see everything on that tray gone, Epstein,

including that letter. The corporal at the door will be watching you. Good appetite, men. (*Turns briskly and starts out*) "El Malagueña" . . .
(EPSTEIN *sits, and the three men sit in stony silence*)

EUGENE   I've got an idea.

CARNEY   Yeah?

EUGENE   We dump it under the table. We'll be gone by the time they find it.

CARNEY   Great idea. But we have to time it right. When no one's looking.

EUGENE   I'll tell you when.

CARNEY   Remember. Timing's everything.

EUGENE (*Looks around*)   . . . Okay. *Now!*
(*In unison they lower their trays under the table. They are about to dump the food when the voice of the* CORPORAL *calls out*)

VOICE (*Sharp*)   GET THOSE TRAYS BACK ON THE TABLE.
(*They bring trays quickly back up*)

CARNEY   . . . Work on your timing.

EPSTEIN   Give it to me.

CARNEY   What?

EPSTEIN   I'm not going to eat mine. No point in all of us suffering. Scrape it onto my tray.

EUGENE   You mean it?

EPSTEIN   This is lunacy. I'm an intelligent human being. I refuse to capitulate to the lunatics. One day when this war is over, there will be investigations . . . (*To the boys*) Go on. Give it to me.
(*They scrape their food onto* EPSTEIN's *tray*)

CARNEY   I like you, Epstein, but you're weird as hell
. . . But I'll tell you one thing. I'm sitting next to you
every meal we get.
(*He leaves*)

EUGENE   I could have used you when my mother made
lima beans.
(*He leaves*)

EPSTEIN   . . . I won't eat slop . . . I won't eat slop . . . I
WON'T EAT SLOP! I WON'T EAT SLOP!

EUGENE (*Appears in field equipment*)   Arnold didn't eat
the slop. They gave him K.P. for five straight days
including cleaning the latrines. But that was better than
the midnight march through the murky swamps of
Mississippi. (*We hear the sound of eerie birds and strange
animals.* EUGENE *looks up*) The only time I heard
strange sounds like that was at Ebbets Field when the
Dodgers played . . . Toomey made Wykowski carry me
the whole fifteen miles just so Wykowski would hate
me more . . . But maybe Toomey was right. If nobody
obeys orders, I'll bet we wouldn't have more than
twelve or thirteen soldiers fighting the war . . . We'd
have headlines like "Corporal Stanley Leiberman in-
vades Sicily" . . . (*Lights off on* EUGENE. *Lights up on the
barracks.* EPSTEIN *enters from the latrine,* EUGENE *goes to
his locker*) Hey, Arnold, it was incredible. You missed
it. We were in the swamps up to our necks. There were
water snakes and big lizards that crawled up your pants
and swooping swamp birds that swooped down and
went right for your eyeballs . . . What's wrong, Arnold? . . . Arnold? . . .

EPSTEIN (*Sitting down*)   Leave me alone!

EUGENE   What is it? Are you sick?

EPSTEIN   Get away from me. You're like all the rest of
them. I hate every goddamn one of you.

EUGENE   Hey, Arnold, I'm your friend. I'm your buddy.
You can talk to me.

EPSTEIN (*Sits up and looks around*) . . . I'm getting out. I'm leaving in the morning. I'm going to Mexico or Central America till after the war . . . I will not be treated like dirt, like a maggot. I'm not going to help defend a country that won't even defend its own citizens . . . Bastards!

EUGENE Because you pulled latrine duty? We all have to pull latrine duty. You have to adjust . . . It's all a game, Arnold. Only it's their ball and their rules. And they know the game better than we do because they've been playing it since Valley Forge.

EPSTEIN . . . I was in the latrine alone. I spent four hours cleaning it, on my hands and knees. It looked better than my mother's bathroom at home. Then these two non-coms come in, one was the cook, that three-hundred-pound guy, and some other slob, with cigar butts in their mouths and reeking from beer . . . They come in to pee only instead of using the urinal, they use one of the johns, both peeing in the same one, making circles, figure-eights. Then they start to walk out and I say, "Hey, I just cleaned that. Please flush the johns." And the big one, the cook, says to me, "Up your ass, rookie," or some other really clever remark . . . And I block the doorway and I say, "There's a printed order on the wall signed by Captain Landon stating the regulations that all facilities must be flushed after using" . . . And I'm requesting that they follow regulations, since I was left in charge, and to please flush the facility . . . And the big one says to me, "Suppose you flush it, New York Jew Kike," and I said, "My ethnic heritage notwithstanding, please flush the facility" . . . They look at each other, this half a ton of brainless beef, and suddenly rush me, turn me upside down, grab my ankles and—and—and they lowered me by my feet with my head in the toilet, in their filth, their poison . . . all the way until I couldn't breathe . . . then they pulled off my belt and tied my feet onto the ceiling pipes with my head still in their foul waste and tied my hands behind my back with dirty rags, and they left me there, hanging like a pig that was going to be slaughtered

. . . I wasn't strong enough to fight back. I couldn't do it alone. No one came to help me . . . Then the pipe broke and I fell to the ground . . . It took me twenty minutes to get myself untied—twenty minutes!—but it will take me the rest of my life to wash off my humiliation. I was degraded. I lost my dignity. If I stay, Gene, if they put a gun in my hands, one night, I swear to God, I'll kill them both . . . I'm not a murderer. I don't want to disgrace my family . . . But I have to get out of here . . . Now do you understand?

EUGENE But you can't go AWOL. They'll catch you. They have agents all over the world . . . You'll get back at them one day. Don't you believe in justice?

EPSTEIN . . . You're so damn naïve, Eugene.
(WYKOWSKI *and* SELRIDGE *come out of the latrine in their underwear, carrying towels, toothbrushes, and toothpaste*)

WYKOWSKI (*Scratching*) I got a hundred and twelve goddamn mosquito bites.

SELRIDGE (*Shivering*) I pulled twelve leeches off me. I pulled one off near my crotch, it wasn't a leech. Maybe I pulled something else off.
(*He gets into bed, still shivering.* CARNEY *and* HENNESEY *come out in their underwear, towels*)

CARNEY I heard a top-secret rumor today. I'm not supposed to repeat it.

WYKOWSKI What is it?

CARNEY I can get in trouble if it gets out.

WYKOWSKI No one's gonna talk. What is it?

CARNEY I hear they're getting ready to invade Europe and Japan on the same day.

HENNESEY Where'd you hear that?

CARNEY   On the radio. It was one of them small stations.

EUGENE   Why on the same day?

CARNEY   Surprise attack. You hit them both at dawn. Then they don't have enough time to warn each other.

EUGENE   Hey, Carney. When it's dawn in Europe, it's a day later in Japan. They don't have dawn at the same time. Japan could read about it in their newspapers.

HENNESEY   Besides, we're not ready. We don't have enough trained men to invade both places on the same day.

EPSTEIN   You know what *Time* magazine estimates the casualty rate of a full-scale invasion would be? Sixty-eight percent. Sixty-eight percent of us would be killed or wounded.

WYKOWSKI   No shit? . . . So out of this group, how many is that?

EPSTEIN   Of the six of us here, about four point three of us would get it.

CARNEY   What part of your body is point three?

SELRIDGE   Hey, Wykowski. We know what part of *your* body is point three.
  (*He giggles*)

EUGENE   Listen, if you knew you were one of the guys who wasn't coming back, if you knew it right now, what would you do with the last few days of your life? It could be anything you want . . . I give everyone five seconds to think about it.

CARNEY   I thought about it. I'm not dying. You think I'm gonna kill myself to entertain *you?*

EUGENE   Why not? It's like a fantasy. I'm giving you the opportunity to do anything in the world you ever dreamed of . . . Come on.

SELRIDGE   I think it's a good idea. Let's play for money.

HENNESEY   For *money?*

SELRIDGE   Yeah. Five bucks a man. The guy with the best fantasy collects the pot.

HENNESEY   That's morbid.

WYKOWSKI   Okay, I'm in. We need a judge.

EUGENE   I'll be the judge.

WYKOWSKI   Why you?

EUGENE   Because I thought of the game. Ante up, everyone. Come on, Hennesey. (*They all put up money except* EPSTEIN) Come on, Arnold. I *know* you have some great fantasies.

EPSTEIN   I don't sell my fantasies.

WYKOWSKI   Burn his bunk!

EUGENE   Come on, Arnold . . . for me.

SELRIDGE   I love this. I'm gonna clean up.

EUGENE (*Jubilantly*)   Okay, Carney. You're first. You're dead. Killed in action . . . What would you do with your last days on earth?

CARNEY   How much time do I have to do it in?

EUGENE   A week.

SELRIDGE   I need ten days.

EUGENE   It's my game. You only get a week . . . What would you do with it, Donny?

CARNEY   (*Thinks*) Okay . . . I would sing at the Radio City Music Hall. Five shows a day, my own spot. In the audience are four thousand girls and one man. Every girl is gorgeous. Every girl is size 38-24-36 . . . And they all want me . . . real bad.

HENNESEY   Who's the man?

CARNEY   The president of Decca Records. He wants me too. I have a choice. After the last show, I could have all four thousand girls . . . or a contract with Decca Records.

HENNESEY   Which one do you take?

SELRIDGE   (*Urging him on*) The record contract. I would take the record contract.

CARNEY   Right. I take the record contract.

SELRIDGE   (*Laughs*) MORON!! He believed me. He could have humped four thousand girls and now he's got a record contract that ain't worth shit.

CARNEY   Wrong! Because now I'm a big star and stars get all the girls they want anyway.

SELRIDGE   Yeah? How? You're dead. Girls never go out with dead record stars.

CARNEY   Bullshit! I paid five bucks for my fantasy. I can do what I want . . . What's my score, Gene?

EUGENE   Well, you started off with an A-minus but you finished with a B.

CARNEY   B. Not bad—better than I ever did in school.

EUGENE   All right. Selridge is next.

SELRIDGE   Okay . . . Here we go . . . I make it with the seven richest women in the world. And I'm so hot, each dame gives me a million bucks. And at the end of a week, I got seven million bucks. Pretty good, heh?

EUGENE   If you're dead, what are you going to do with seven million dollars?

SELRIDGE   I told you. That's why I need ten days. I need a long weekend to spend the money. Give up, suckers, I got you all beat.

EPSTEIN   Moronic. It's beyond moronic. It's submoronic.

SELRIDGE   Break their hearts, Jerome, and tell 'em my score.

EUGENE   It lacks poetry. I give Selridge a B.

SELRIDGE (*Angrily*)   A *B?* You give me a B? That creep signs a record contract that ain't worth shit and he gets a B? (*He heads for the money*) I want my money back.

WYKOWSKI   Touch that money and you're dead.

SELRIDGE   I was kidding. You think I was serious? I was kidding. (*He lies on his bunk*) Who's next?

EUGENE   Hennesey.

HENNESEY   Me? I'm not ready yet.

EUGENE   It's your turn.

HENNESEY   I'm not good at things like this.

EUGENE   Come on. Just say it.

HENNESEY   I can't think of anything.

SELRIDGE   He can't think of anything. So he's out. Tough shit. Give him an F . . . Who's next?

HENNESEY   Okay. Okay . . . I'd spend it with my family.

WYKOWSKI   Is this guy serious?

CARNEY   Damn, I wish we were playing for big dough.

SELRIDGE   What an asshole.

HENNESEY   It's my last week. I can spend it any way I want. I'd like it to be with my family.

CARNEY (*Mimicking him*)   I'd like it to be with my family.

SELRIDGE   Go ahead, Jerome. What do you give him for *that* crap?

EUGENE   It's not interesting but at least it's honest . . . I give him a B-plus.

SELRIDGE   Okay. This game is fixed. I'm calling in the Military Police. I get a B for screwin' seven millionairesses and *he* gets a B-plus for goin' home to his mother? . . . I change my answer. I want to visit sick children in the hospital.

WYKOWSKI   Knock it off, Selridge. You had your turn.

EUGENE   It's yours now, Wykowski.

CARNEY   Don't let us down, Kowski. To some of us you're a hero.

WYKOWSKI   Okay . . . I always wanted to make it with a world-famous woman that nobody else could have. It didn't make no difference if she was beautiful or not, as long as I was the only one.

HENNESEY   Have you got someone in mind?

WYKOWSKI (*Smiling*) Yeah. I got someone in mind.

EUGENE I think we're heading for an A-plus.

CARNEY Who's the woman, Kowski?

WYKOWSKI (*Does a grind and a bump*) . . . The Queen of England!
　(*They all stare at him, dumbstruck*)

CARNEY The Queen of England????

SELRIDGE That is disgusting. That's like making it with your grandmother.

EUGENE Besides, you wouldn't be the only one. What about the *King* of England?

WYKOWSKI Kings and Queens just do it once a year. To make a Prince. But I'd have her every day and every night for a week.

SELRIDGE You couldn't get near her. They keep her under guard at Rockingham Palace.

WYKOWSKI Not for me. She would say—(*In a high-pitched voice*) "Let that sexy Wykowski in my chamber."

EPSTEIN Apes and gorillas. I'm living with apes and gorillas.

HENNESEY What's his score? Give him his score.

CARNEY (*In a high-pitched English voice*) Yes. Give the Earl of Meatloaf his score.

EUGENE This is a tough one. I find it completely unredeeming in every way. Morally, ethically, and sexually . . . but it's got style . . . *A*-minus!

SELRIDGE (*Furiously*) Okay. I want my five bucks back. I'm not getting beat out by a guy who humps the Mother of the British Empire.

HENNESEY Boy, I'm learning a lot about you guys to-night.

SELRIDGE And versa visa, jerk-off.

WYKOWSKI So I'm winning, right?

EUGENE It's not over yet. There's two more to go.

SELRIDGE Epstein's next. I want to hear what *his* last week on earth would be like. Probably wants to take an English exam at City College.

EUGENE It's your turn, Arnold.

EPSTEIN There's no point to this game.

EUGENE Yes, there is.

EPSTEIN What's the point?

EUGENE I like it . . . Come on. It's your last week on earth. You're going to get killed overseas. What's your secret desire?
     (*They all look at* EPSTEIN *. . . He thinks carefully*)

EPSTEIN . . . I don't want to say. If I say it, it might not come true.

CARNEY He doesn't have one. All he does is complain.

WYKOWSKI And pass gas. That's his secret desire. He wants to bend over and blow up the world.
     (SELRIDGE *loves that one*)

EUGENE Wait a minute. Give him a chance. He has one . . . What is it, Arnold? What's the last thing you want to do on this earth?
     (*All attention is on* EPSTEIN)

EPSTEIN . . . I would like to make Sergeant Merwin J. Toomey do two hundred push-ups in front of this platoon.
   (*There is stunned silence*)

WYKOWSKI That's good . . . I hate to admit it, but it's good.

SELRIDGE It's okay. Five hundred would have been better.

EUGENE I think it's terrific. I give Epstein an A-plus.

CARNEY A-plus? You're crazy. Now you can't beat him.

EUGENE I can still tie him.

WYKOWSKI If it's a tie, all bets are off. Nobody wins.

EUGENE Fair enough. Somebody else has to judge me. Pick a judge, Wykowski.

WYKOWSKI (*Smiles*) Sure, I pick Selridge.

SELRIDGE I love it. No matter what crap he says, he gets an A-plus. Your money is safe, boys.

HENNESEY Go on, Gene . . . Let's hear yours.

EUGENE Okay. (*He takes a deep breath. They listen intently*) . . . I'm going to get mine wiping out a whole battalion of Japanese marines. They'll put up a statue of me at Brighton Beach. (*He poses*) Maybe name a junior high school after me, or a swimming pool.

SELRIDGE All they'd give you is a locker room. The Eugene M. Jerome Locker Room.

HENNESEY Let him finish. Go on, Gene.

EUGENE Well . . . if it's my last week on earth . . . I would like to fall in love.

CARNEY   With who?

EUGENE   The perfect girl.

WYKOWSKI   There is no perfect girl.

EUGENE   If I fell in love with her, she'd be perfect.

WYKOWSKI   I told you. Jewish guys are all homos.

CARNEY   Incredible! . . . Okay, the game is over. Tell him
what he got, Roy, and we'll all take our money back.
(*They look at* SELRIDGE)

WYKOWSKI   Go on. Tell him his score.

SELRIDGE   I give him a C-minus.

WYKOWSKI   What??

SELRIDGE   I'm sorry. I'm not gonna let him beat me with
that pissy story. I came up with something "hot," I'm
not gonna give him an A-plus for "Love in Bloom."

WYKOWSKI   Jesus, you are a moron. Go look in the latrine and see where you dropped your brains.

SELRIDGE   I couldn't help it. I couldn't.

EUGENE   You win, Arnold. It's your money.
(EPSTEIN *starts for the money*)

WYKOWSKI   It never fails. It's always the Jews who end
up with the money. Ain't that right, Roy?

SELRIDGE   Don't ask me. I never met a Jew before the
army.

WYKOWSKI   They're easy to spot. (*To* EPSTEIN) There's
one . . . (*To* EUGENE) . . . And there's another one. (*To
all*) They're the ones who slide the bacon under their

toast so no one sees them eat it. Ain't that right, Jerome?

EPSTEIN (*Calmly*)   I'm tired of taking that Jew crap from you, Wykowski. I know you can probably beat the hell out of me, but I'm not going to take it from you any- more, understand?

WYKOWSKI   Sure you will. You'll take any shit from me . . . Come on. Come on. Let's see how tough you are. I'll knock the Alka-Seltzer right out of your asshole.

HENNESEY   Cut it out, Kowski. What difference does it make what religion he is?

WYKOWSKI   I didn't start it. Epstein's the one who thinks he's too good to take orders, isn't he? Well, I'm not doing a hundred push-ups for any goddamn goof-up anymore. If he doesn't shape up, I'll bust his face whether he's got a Jew nose or not.
   (*They both go for each other, but are restrained by the others*)

CARNEY (*Seeing* TOOMEY *coming*)   Ten-HUT!
   (*Suddenly* SERGEANT TOOMEY *appears in his pants and an undershirt. All snap to attention*)

TOOMEY   What the hell is going on here?

HENNESEY   Nothing, Sergeant.

TOOMEY   What do you mean nothing? I heard threats, challenges, and an invitation to bust the nose of mem- bers of minority races. Now are you still telling me that nothing was going on here?

HENNESEY   Yes, Sergeant.

TOOMEY   I think you'd better sleep on that answer, boy. And to make sure you get a good night's sleep, you get yourself good and tired with one hundred push-ups. On the floor, dogface, and let me hear you count. (HEN-

NESEY *gets on the ground and immediately starts to do push-ups*) If I hear any more racial slurs from this platoon, some dumb bastard is going to be shoveling cow shit with a teaspoon for a month. Especially if I hear it from a Polack! LIGHTS OUT!!

(The lights suddenly go out, leaving only a tiny spot on EUGENE)

EUGENE *(To the audience)* . . . I never liked Wykowski much and I didn't like him any better after tonight . . . But the one I hated most was myself because I didn't stand up for Epstein, a fellow Jew. Maybe I was afraid of Wykowski or maybe it was because Epstein sort of sometimes asked for it, but since the guys didn't pick on me that much, I figured I'd just stay sort of neutral . . . like Switzerland . . . Then I wrote in my memoirs what every guy's last desire would be if he was killed in the war. I never intended to show it to anyone, but still I felt a little ashamed of betraying their secret and private thoughts . . . Possibly the only one who felt worse than I did was Hennesey on the floor.

HENNESEY *(Doing push-ups)* . . . forty-one . . . forty-two . . . forty-three . . . forty-four . . . forty-five.

(It is weeks later, in a section of the latrine. SELRIDGE *and* CARNEY *are finishing shaving.* HENNESEY *is brushing his hair. They are in their underwear, some with their trousers on)*

SELRIDGE   Forty-eight-hour pass, hot damn! If I make it with one woman every four hours, that means I could have . . . er . . . I could have . . . *(He thinks)*—a lot of women!

HENNESEY   I'd be careful. You know what you could get.

SELRIDGE   Yeah. Relief.

WYKOWSKI *(Comes in looking very angry)*   Son of a bitch! goddamn son of a bitch!!

SELRIDGE   What's wrong?

WYKOWSKI (*Holds up the empty wallet*) Someone broke into my footlocker last night. They emptied my wallet. They took my pay and every cent I had in the world. Sixty-two bucks. Dirty bastard.

CARNEY How do you know it was stolen? Maybe you lost it.

WYKOWSKI I counted it before I hit the sack. I was saving it for the big weekend. Don't think I'm not wise to who did it. Maybe they both did it together.

HENNESEY How do you know it was them? Maybe it was one of us.

WYKOWSKI ... Was it? Was it?

SELRIDGE You think I'm crazy enough to tell you if I stole your money?

WYKOWSKI It was Epstein, I'm telling you. He's trying to get back at me for what I said that night.

HENNESEY Maybe he's sore at you but he's not the kind that steals money.

WYKOWSKI Who asked you, Hennesey? What are you, one of those Irish Jews? All I did was call him a couple of names. Where I come from we're all polacks, dagos, niggers, and sheenies. That stuff doesn't mean crap to me. You're a mick, what do I care?

HENNESEY Half mick, half nigger.
(WYKOWSKI *and* SELRIDGE *look at each other*)

WYKOWSKI Are you serious?

HENNESEY Yeah. My father's Irish, my mother's colored.

SELRIDGE You can't be colored. They wouldn't let you in with us.

HENNESEY   I never told anybody.

WYKOWSKI   Yeah, but I guessed it. It was something I couldn't put my finger on but I knew something was wrong with you.

HENNESEY   I'm black Irish, that's as colored as I am. But now we know how you think, don't we, Kowski?

WYKOWSKI   I'm laying for you, Hennesey. After I get the bastard who stole my money, I'll settle my score with you.

CARNEY   Does Toomey know?

WYKOWSKI   I think so. He must have heard me. Somebody steals sixty-two bucks, people hear about it.
        (TOOMEY *appears*)

TOOMEY (*Calmly*)   Gentlemen, I think we have a problem. All those wishing to help me solve it, get your asses in here before the firing squad leaves for the weekend. ON THE DOUBLE!!! Ten-hut!! (*The lights go up on the barracks area, off on the latrine. All six soldiers rush in and line up at attention in front of their bunks.* TOOMEY, *dressed for weekend leave, walks slowly in front of them, thinking very seriously*) . . . I've been in this man's army now for twelve years, four months, and twenty-three days and during my tenure as a noncommissioned officer, I have put up with everything from mutiny to sodomy. I consider mutiny and sodomy relatively minor offenses. Mutiny is an act of aggression due to a rising expression of unreleased repressed feelings. Sodomy is the result of doing something you don't want to do with someone you don't want to do it with because of no access to do what you want to do with someone you can't get to do it with.

EUGENE (*To the audience*)   It makes sense if you think it out slowly.

TOOMEY   Burglary, on the other hand, is a cheap shit crime. And I frown on that. In the past thirty-one days, you boys have made some fine progress. You're not fighting soldiers yet, but I'd match you up against some Nazi cocktail waitresses any time. That's why it was my recommendation that this platoon receive a forty-eight-hour pass . . . But until we clear up the mystery of Private Wykowski's missing sixty-two dollars, there will be no forty-eight-hour passes issued until you are old and gray soldiers of World War Two, marching as American Legionnaires in the Armistice Day Parade. I am asking the guilty party to place sixty-two dollars on this here footlocker within the next thirty seconds . . . I offer no leniency, no forgiveness, and no abstention from punishment. What I do offer is honor and integrity, and the respect of his fellow soldiers, knowing that it was *his* act of courage that enabled them to enjoy the brief freedom they so richly deserve. (*He looks at his watch*) I am counting down to thirty . . . It is of this time that heroes are made. One . . . two . . . three . . . four . . . five . . . (*They all look at each other silently*) six seven . . . eight . . .

(*Suddenly* EPSTEIN *takes out his wallet, removes some bills, counts off sixty-two dollars, and puts it on the footlocker in front of him. The others look silently ahead*)

EPSTEIN   There's sixty-two dollars, if anyone cares to count it.

TOOMEY   I don't think that will be necessary, Private Epstein . . . Wykowski, pick up your money. (WYKOWSKI *picks it up and starts to count*) I SAID DON'T COUNT IT, BOY!!!! (WYKOWSKI *stops, folds it and puts it in his pocket, and returns to attention*) Private Epstein, do you have anything to say?

EPSTEIN   No, Sergeant.

TOOMEY   May I ask why you decided to return the money?

EPSTEIN   I chose to.

TOOMEY   You chose to. Knowing full well that swift and just punishment may be inflicted upon you when and if this is reported to the commanding officer?

EPSTEIN   I know it only too well.

TOOMEY   You could have kept quiet about this incident. Chances are no one would have found out or been the wiser.

EPSTEIN   I didn't see any reason why five innocent men should suffer a loss of privilege because of one guilty one.

TOOMEY   Private Wykowski . . . Is it your wish that I report this incident and the guilty party to the commanding officer?

WYKOWSKI   I just want my money, Sergeant. I can deal with the bastard who took it on my own.
     (TOOMEY *stares at him, then reaches into his pocket and takes out some folded bills*)

TOOMEY   Last night at 0100 hours I wandered through this barracks and saw carelessness and complacency. Wykowski's wallet was lying in an open footlocker inviting weakness, avarice, and temptation. *I* took your sixty-two dollars, Wykowski, and returned the empty wallet in its place. I did it to teach you a lesson . . . Instead, *I* got . . . submarined. (*He goes nose to nose with* EPSTEIN) Private Epstein, are you such a goddamn ignorant fool to take the blame for something you were completely innocent of?

EPSTEIN   The army has its logic, I have my own.

TOOMEY   The army's "logic," as you call it, is to instill discipline, obedience, and unquestioned faith in superiors. What the hell is yours?

EPSTEIN   Since I'm not guilty of a crime, I reserve the privilege to keep my own motives a matter of confidentiality.

TOOMEY   That's where you're wrong, soldier. Confessing to a crime you didn't commit is no less an offense than *not* confessing to one you *did* commit. That is called obstruction of justice. You may not like our rules, boy, but by God, you're going to clean every toilet and pisspot until you learn them. Confined to barracks until further notice. The rest of you are on forty-eight hours' leave. Fall out! . . . Epstein, I would like a word with you in private. (*The others break up and move to their bunks to discuss the event.* EPSTEIN *follows* TOOMEY *to the latrine.* TOOMEY *turns, faces* EPSTEIN, *lowers his voice*) Listen to me, you flyspeck on a mound of horse shit. You're taking me on, ain't you? Well, you're making a big mistake because I have a nutcracker that crunches the testicles of men who take me on . . . How the hell do you think you can beat me?

EPSTEIN   I'm not trying to beat you, Sergeant. I'm trying to work with you.

TOOMEY (*Looks at him sideways*)   I think you're low on batteries, Epstein. I think some plumber turned off your fountain of knowledge. What the hell do you mean, *working* with me?

EPSTEIN   I don't think it's necessary to dehumanize a man to get him to perform. You can get better results raising our spirits than lowering our dignity.

TOOMEY   Why in the hell did you put back money you knew you didn't take?

EPSTEIN   Because I knew that *you* did. I saw you take it. I think inventing a crime that didn't exist to enforce your theories of discipline is Neanderthal in its conception.

TOOMEY (*Gets closer*)   I can arrange it, Epstein, that from now on you get nothing to eat in the mess hall except cotton balls. You ever eat cotton balls, Epstein? You can chew it till 1986, it don't swallow . . . Men do not face enemy machine guns because they have been treated with kindness. They face them because they have a bayonet up their ass. I don't *want* them human. I want them obedient.

EPSTEIN   Egyptian Kings made their slaves obedient. Eventually they lost their slaves *and* their kingdom.

TOOMEY   Yeah, well, I may lose mine but before you go, you're going to build me the biggest goddamn pyramid you ever saw . . . I'm trying to save these boys' lives, you crawling bookworm. Stand in my way and I'll pulverize you into chicken droppings.

EPSTEIN   It should be an interesting contest, Sergeant.

TOOMEY   After I crush your testicles, you can replace them with the cotton balls. (*He glares at* EPSTEIN, *then exits quickly*) . . . Neanderthal in its conception, Jesus Christ!

CARNEY (*Tying his tie*)   So who really stole the money?

SELRIDGE (*Brushing his shoes*)   Toomey stole Wykowski's sixty-two bucks but Epstein stole Toomey's *idea* of stealing Wykowski's sixty-two bucks.

HENNESEY   Why?

SELRIDGE   Did you ever see a big fat walrus screw another big fat walrus? There's no point to it but they do it anyway . . . You comin', Kows?

WYKOWSKI   In a minute.

CARNEY   I'll tell you something. The army is really dumb. If the navy is this dumb, we're gonna have to take a train to Europe.
      (CARNEY *and* HENNESEY *leave.* EPSTEIN *returns to the room*)

WYKOWSKI   I don't get you, Epstein. What'd you do a dumb-ass thing like that for?

EPSTEIN   You wouldn't understand.

WYKOWSKI   Why not? Am I too dumb? Dumb polack is that what I am? Now who's calling who names?

EPSTEIN   You are. If no one confessed, no one goes on leave. If any of the other guys really did it, I'd end up cleaning the toilet bowls anyway. He's trying to break my spirit.

WYKOWSKI   How'd you figure that out?

EPSTEIN   Talmudic reasoning.

WYKOWSKI   What?

EPSTEIN   Talmudic. You weigh both sides of an issue, then choose the one that's the most interesting. Unless, of course, the other guy picks that one first.

WYKOWSKI   Yeah? Well, whatever . . . Anyway, I owe you one. You stuck your neck out for us. (*He extends his hand*) I like to pay back my debts.

EPSTEIN   (*Looks at the extended hand*)   You really want to shake my hand, Wykowski?

WYKOWSKI   Listen, it's not going to come out again, so take your chance while you got it.

EPSTEIN   Let's not be hypocritical. I did what I did for me, not for you.

WYKOWSKI   (*Smiles*)   I'm not going to make any more Jew cracks at you, Epstein. 'Cause you're a shitheel no matter what you are.
     (*He goes. The others go off.* EUGENE *sits on his bed, smiles, and shakes his head at* EPSTEIN)

EUGENE   Why do you always have to do things the hard way?

EPSTEIN   It makes life more interesting.

EUGENE   It also makes a lot of problems.

EPSTEIN   Without problems, the day would be over at eleven o'clock in the morning.
(EPSTEIN *starts to change into fatigues*)

EUGENE   I admire what you did back there, Arnold. You remind me of my brother, sometimes. He was always standing up for his principles too.

EPSTEIN   Principles are okay. But sometimes they get in the way of reason.

EUGENE   Then how do you know which one is the right one?

EPSTEIN   You have to get involved. You don't get involved enough, Eugene.

EUGENE   What do you mean?

EPSTEIN   You're a witness. You're always standing around *watching* what's happening. Scribbling in your book what other people do. You have to get in the middle of it. You have to take sides. Make a contribution to the fight.

EUGENE   What fight?

EPSTEIN   *Any* fight. The one you believe in.

EUGENE   Yeah. I know what you mean. Sometimes I feel like I'm invisible. Like The Shadow. I can see everyone else but they can't see me. That's what I think writers are. Sort of invisible.

EPSTEIN   Not Tolstoy. Not Dostoyevsky. Not Herman Melville.

EUGENE   Yeah. I have to read those guys.

TOOMEY (*Offstage*)   EPSTEIN! I DON'T HEAR NO GODDAMN FLUSHING!!

EPSTEIN   I'd better go. I have to get involved with toilet bowls.

EUGENE   I'd love to talk to you more, Arnold.

EPSTEIN   I'm available.

EUGENE   Well, maybe when I get back Sunday night.

EPSTEIN   Sure. Anytime you want . . . Just make sure you don't come back pregnant.

EUGENE   Are you kidding? I'm wearing three pairs of socks.

EPSTEIN   Make sure you put them on the right place.
          (*He leaves*)

EUGENE (*To the audience*)   Soo—I was off to Biloxi to live out my fantasies. Love or sex, I'd settle for either one . . . I put powder and Aqua Velva in and under every conceivable part of my body.
          (CARNEY *comes back in*)

CARNEY   I've been waiting for you.

EUGENE   Okay. Let's go!

CARNEY   Wait—wait! I need a favor from you.

EUGENE   What is it?

CARNEY   Sit down. I need your opinion. And please, tell me the truth. (EUGENE *waits*, CARNEY *lowers his head and begins to sing "Embraceable You." The curtain starts to descend as* EUGENE *looks helplessly at the audience*)

Curtain

Act Two

A section of a small, tacky room in a cheap hotel. There are two worn armchairs at angle, to each other. Seated are EUGENE *and* CARNEY. SELRIDGE *paces impatiently. All three are smoking cigarettes, puffing away nervously.*

SELRIDGE (*Looking at his watch*)   Almost a half hour he's been in there. It doesn't take a half hour. She couldn't make any money that way.

CARNEY   Maybe he went twice. Or three times.

SELRIDGE   Wykowski could keep going for six months straight. That's not the point. They charge you every time, that's the point.

CARNEY   Maybe she gave him a free one because of his unusual condition.

EUGENE   You mean she charges you every time you have a—

SELRIDGE (*Pacing*)   That's right.

EUGENE   How does she know when you have one?

SELRIDGE (*Stops and looks at him*)   Because your eyes spin around and when they stop on two pineapples, you just had one. (*To* CARNEY) Is this guy for real?

CARNEY   And he's from New York City too. Can you believe it?

EUGENE (*Defensively*)   I make out on my own. I just never go to places like this . . . And you mean, if you have a—a thing more than once, she keeps count?

CARNEY Yeah. Actually, every time you do it, she makes an X on your head with her lipstick.
(*He blows smoke in* EUGENE'*s face*)

EUGENE Hey, don't blow smoke in my face. I'll stink up from tobacco.

CARNEY Stop worrying. Nothing can penetrate your Aqua Velva . . . If you don't like it, what are you smoking for?

EUGENE (*Looks at the cigarette in his hand*) I didn't know I was. Somebody must have handed it to me. (*He puts it out hard in the ashtray. He gets up and paces. To* SELRIDGE) You want to sit down?

SELRIDGE And break my concentration? (*He looks at his watch*) Hurry up, dammit, I'm going to pass my peak.

EUGENE What if she's ugly? I mean really ugly.

SELRIDGE . . . Close your eyes and think of some girl in high school.

EUGENE I don't want to close my eyes. That's the same as doing it to yourself.

SELRIDGE Not if you're feeling somebody underneath you . . . Or on top of you.

EUGENE (*Stops*) What do you mean, on *top* of you. Who would be on top of me?

SELRIDGE She would. She could be anywhere. Under a table. On a chair or an ironing board.

EUGENE *An ironing board???* What kind of girl is this? I thought we were going just to a regular place.

SELRIDGE I didn't mention anything that wasn't regular. I mean don't you know anything? Do you have any idea of how many possible positions there are?

EUGENE   Yeah. Sure. I'm not an ignoramus.

CARNEY (*To* EUGENE)   How many positions are there?

EUGENE (*Looks at* CARNEY, *then points to* SELRIDGE)   I'm having this conversation with him.

SELRIDGE   Okay. How many positions are there?

EUGENE (*Thinks*)   . . . American or Worldwide?

SELRIDGE (*Laughs*)   You don't know shit, Jerome.

EUGENE   Maybe not actual experience. But I have all the information I need.

SELRIDGE   Then how many positions are there, in this galaxy?

EUGENE   For how much?

SELRIDGE   Loser pays for the bang.

EUGENE   Don't call it a bang. I'm here for pleasure, not to get banged.

CARNEY (*Laughs*)   This guy's a riot.

SELRIDGE   For five bucks. How many positions are there?

EUGENE   I'm thinking. Give me a minute.

SELRIDGE   You want me to tell you?

EUGENE   No.

SELRIDGE   Well, I'll tell you. Seventeen.

EUGENE   How do you know?

SELRIDGE   Because I've tried them all.

EUGENE   You're wrong. There's at least *fifty-two* different positions.

SELRIDGE   *Fifty-two??* . . . You're crazy! . . . Where'd you get that from?

EUGENE   I saw a dirty deck of cards once.

SELRIDGE (*To* CARNEY)   This guy's worse than Epstein.

EUGENE   You owe me five bucks.

SELRIDGE   Listen, twerp. You're lucky if you do *one* position.

EUGENE   I'm not going to do *anything* if it's on an ironing board.

CARNEY   Why not? You'll get your shirt pressed for free.

SELRIDGE (*Looks at his watch*)   Thirty-four minutes. Damn Wykowski! We should have let the normal guys go first.

EUGENE (*To the audience*)   I didn't want my first time to be like this . . . I really tried to meet somebody nice but there are twenty-one thousand soldiers on leave in Biloxi and fourteen girls . . . Those are tough odds. Especially since the fourteen girls all go to Catholic school and are handcuffed to nuns.
    (WYKOWSKI *appears with a know-it-all look on his face. He straightens his tie as he chews gum*)

SELRIDGE   Well??? . . . Tell us!

WYKOWSKI   She wants to see me again after the war.
    (*He puts on his cap and disappears*)

SELRIDGE (*Looks around*)   Okay, whose turn is it?

EUGENE   You go ahead. I just had lunch. I don't want to get cramps.
    (CARNEY *nods assent*)

SELRIDGE (*Straightens himself up*) I'll try to leave a little something for you guys. (*He disappears*) Hey! How are you?

CARNEY (*Looks at* EUGENE) We don't have to do this, you know. There's a dance over at the U.S.O.

EUGENE This isn't your first time, is it? I mean, you've done it before, haven't you?

CARNEY Oh, yeah. Sure. Are you kidding? . . . Not a lot. About five or six times.

EUGENE So why are you doing it again?

CARNEY You're not through after five or six times. If you live long enough, you've got twelve thousand more left.

EUGENE I don't know why I'm so scared. I'm never going to see her again. I just don't want to seem foolish. I think I'm afraid she's going to laugh at me.

CARNEY Not if she gets paid. If she laughed at you, you would be entitled to a refund.
     (SELRIDGE *comes out, buttoning his shirt*)

EUGENE You're through already? That was fast.

SELRIDGE (*Unhappy*) I didn't make it to the bed. I knew I hit my peak too soon.
     (*And he is gone*)

CARNEY (*Looks at* EUGENE) Listen, I think I'm gonna go to the dance.

EUGENE How come?

CARNEY I said before I did it five or six times but it was all with the same girl. We're sort of engaged. She might not like it.

EUGENE   I bet she wouldn't. I didn't know you had a girl. That's terrific. What's her name?

CARNEY   Charlene.

EUGENE   Charlene! Wow! Sounds sexy. You think you'll get married?

CARNEY   Well, it's a fifty-fifty chance. She's got another boyfriend in Albany . . . So what are you going to do?

EUGENE   Well, the thing is, I don't have a girl. I've got to learn on my own. Epstein says I have to get more involved in life. I think I'm in the perfect place for an involvement.

CARNEY   Okay. Maybe I'll see you later. (*He puts on his cap*) Listen. Don't expect too much the first time. What I mean is, if it doesn't go all that terrific, don't give up on it for good.

EUGENE   I'm not a quitter. I'm dedicating my life to getting it right.

CARNEY   You putting this in your memoirs?

EUGENE   Sure. I put everything in my memoirs.

CARNEY   That's smart. Because people don't like books unless there's sex in them . . . Good luck, kid.
          (*He takes a photo of* EUGENE *with his hand on the door*)

EUGENE (*To the audience*)   . . . And thus, the young man they called Eugene bade farewell to his youth, turned, and entered the Temple of Fire.
          (*The scenery changes to* ROWENA's *room.* EUGENE *is hidden behind a screen.* ROWENA *is sitting at her vanity, smoking and trying to be patient*)

ROWENA (*Calls out*)   How you doing, honey?

EUGENE (*From behind the screen*)   Okay.

ROWENA   You having any trouble in there?

EUGENE   No. No trouble.

ROWENA   What the hell you doing for ten minutes? C'mon, kid. I haven't got all day. (EUGENE *appears. He is wearing his khaki shorts, shoes, and socks. A cigarette dangles from his lips.* ROWENA *looks at him*) Listen. You can keep your shorts on if you want but I have a rule against wearing army shoes in bed.

EUGENE (*Looks down*)   Oh. I'm sorry. I just forgot to take them off. (*He sits on the bed and very slowly starts to unlace them. To the audience*) I started to sweat like crazy. I prayed my Aqua Velva was working.
     (ROWENA *sprays around her with perfume from her atomizer*)

ROWENA   You don't mind a little perfume, do you, honey? The boy before you had on a gallon of Aqua Velva.

EUGENE (*Looks at the audience, then at her*)   No, I don't mind. You can spray some on me. (*She smiles and sprays him playfully*) Gee, it smells good.

ROWENA   If you'd like a bottle for your girlfriend, I sell them. Five dollars apiece.

EUGENE   You sell perfume too?

ROWENA   I sell hard-to-get items. Silk stockings. Black panties . . . You interested?

EUGENE (*Earnestly*)   Do you carry men's clothing?

ROWENA (*Laughs*)   That's cute. You're cute, honey . . . You want me to take your shoes off?

EUGENE   I can do it. Honest. I can do it.
(*He gets his first shoe off*)

ROWENA   Is this your first time?

EUGENE   My first time? (*He laughs*) Are you kidding?
That's funny . . . Noo . . . It's my second time . . . The
first time they were closed.

ROWENA   You don't smoke cigarettes either, do you?
(*She takes the cigarette out of* EUGENE's *mouth*)

EUGENE   How'd you know?

ROWENA   You looked like your face was on fire . . . If you
want to look older, why don't you try a mustache?

EUGENE   I did but it wouldn't grow in on the left side
. . . What's your name?

ROWENA   Rowena . . . What's yours?

EUGENE   My name? (*To the audience*) I suddenly pan-
icked. Supposing this girl kept a diary.

ROWENA   Well?

EUGENE (*Quickly*)   Jack . . . Er . . . Jack Mulgroovey.

ROWENA   Yeah? I knew a *Tom* Mulgreevy once.

EUGENE   No. Mine is Mulgroovey. Oo not ee.

ROWENA   Where you from, Jack?

EUGENE (*With a slight accent*)   Texarkana.

ROWENA   Is that right?

EUGENE   Yes, ma'am.

ROWENA   Is that Texas or Arkansas?

EUGENE Arkansas, I think.

ROWENA You *think*?

EUGENE I left there when I was two. Then we moved to Georgia.

ROWENA Really? You a cracker?

EUGENE What's a cracker?

ROWENA Someone from Georgia.

EUGENE Oh, yeah. I'm a cracker. The whole family's crackers . . . Were you born in Biloxi?

ROWENA No. Gulfport. I still live there with my husband.

EUGENE Your husband?? . . . You're married?? . . . My God! If he finds me here he'll kill me.

ROWENA No he won't.

EUGENE Does he know that you're a—you're a—

ROWENA Sure he does. That's how we met. He's in the navy. He was one of my best customers. He still is.

EUGENE You mean you *charge* your own husband??

ROWENA I mean he's my best lover . . . You gonna do it from there, cowboy? 'Cause I'll have to make some adjustments.

EUGENE I'm ready. (*To* ROWENA) Here I come.
     (*She holds the open blanket. He gets into the bed and clings to the side*)

ROWENA If you're gonna hang on the edge like that, we're gonna be on the floor in two minutes.

EUGENE   I didn't want to crowd you.

ROWENA   Crowding is what this is all about, Tex. (*She pulls him over. He kneels above her*) Okay, honey. Do your stuff.

EUGENE   What stuff is that?

ROWENA   Whatever you like to do.

EUGENE   Why don't you start and I'll catch up.

ROWENA   Didn't anyone ever tell you what to do?

EUGENE   My brother once showed me but you look a lot different than my brother.

ROWENA   You're sweet. I went to high school with a boy like you. I had the biggest damn crush on him.

EUGENE   (*He is still above her*)   Do you have a hanky?

ROWENA   Anything wrong?

EUGENE   My nose is running.
            (*She takes the hanky and wipes his nose*)

ROWENA   Better?

EUGENE   Thank you. Listen, please don't be offended but I really don't care if this is a wonderful experience or not. I just want to get it over with.

ROWENA   Whatever you say . . . Lights on or off?

EUGENE   Actually I'd like a blindfold. (*She reaches over and turns off the lamp*) . . . Oh, God . . . Oh, MY GOD!!! (*He slumps down*) . . . WOW! . . . I DID IT! . . . I DID IT!!

ROWENA   Anything else, honey?

EUGENE (*Calmer, more mature*)   Yes. I'd like two bottles of perfume and a pair of black panties.

Blackout
(*Lights up on a section of the barracks. It's late Sunday night.* SELRIDGE, CARNEY, *and* EPSTEIN *are lying on their bunks.* WYKOWSKI, *pacing, has* EUGENE'*s notebook of memoirs.* CARNEY *is on his stomach reading a letter and* EPSTEIN *is reading a worn paperback of Kafka*)

WYKOWSKI   . . . I can't believe what this creep's been writing about us . . . Listen to this . . . "No matter how lunatic I think Sergeant Toomey is, there is method in his madness. He is winning the game. Each day we drop a little of our own personalities and become more obedient, more robotlike, until what was once an intelligent, thinking human being is now nothing but a khaki idiot. Yesterday, in front of everybody, he made Epstein unscrew the top of his head and take his brains out."

EPSTEIN (*Without looking up from his book*)   I fooled him. I only took out my mucous membranes.

WYKOWSKI (*Continues reading*)   . . . "I am fighting hard to retain my identity, and the only time I am able to hold on to who I is in the still, still of the night."
(HENNESEY *comes in from outside*)

HENNESEY   Wow, what a weekend. How'd you guys do?

WYKOWSKI   Hey, Hennesey. You ought to listen to this. You're in this too.

HENNESEY   What is it?
(*He starts loosening his tie*)

WYKOWSKI   *The Secret and Private Memoirs of Eugene M. Jerome.*

HENNESEY   He let you read it?

WYKOWSKI   No, but we're going to ask him if it's all right when we get through.
(*He and* SELRIDGE *laugh*)

HENNESEY   You have no right to read that. That's like opening someone's mail.

WYKOWSKI   Bullshit. It's all about us. Private things about every one of us. That's public domain like in the newspapers.

EPSTEIN (*Without looking up from his book*)   A newspaper is published. Unpublished memoirs are the sole and private property of the writer.

WYKOWSKI   I thought all Jews were doctors. I didn't know they were lawyers too.

EPSTEIN   I'm not a Jew anymore, Wykowski.

WYKOWSKI   What do you mean?

EPSTEIN   I converted to Catholicism yesterday. In six weeks I hope to become a priest and my first act of service to the Holy Father is to have you excommunicated, so get off my ass.

SELRIDGE (*Laughs*)   That's good. That's funny. Goddamn Jews are really funny. Hey, Epstein, I'm beginning to like you, I swear to Christ.

WYKOWSKI (*Annoyed*)   You guys interested in hearing the rest of this or not?

HENNESEY   No, I'm not. (*He starts toward the latrine, stops*) I thought you were Gene's friend, Epstein.

EPSTEIN   He didn't lock his locker. Why then would he leave something so private in an open locker? There's no logic to it. I have no interest in illogical things.

HENNESEY (*To* EPSTEIN) You tell Gene I had nothing to do with this. You hear me?
  (*And he is off to the latrine*)

SELRIDGE Go on. After ". . . still, still of the night."

WYKOWSKI (*Reading*) . . . "At night I listen to the others breathing in their sleep and it's then that their fears and self-doubts become even more apparent than during their waking hours . . . One night a sudden scream from Selridge that sounded like he was calling out the name Louise. Is Louise his girl or possibly his mother?"

SELRIDGE He's full of crap.

WYKOWSKI Who's Louise?

SELRIDGE My mother. But he's full of crap. I never called my mother Louise.

WYKOWSKI Poor baby, wants his mother.
  (*He continues reading*)

CARNEY I don't want to hear any more of this. I don't like being spied on.

WYKOWSKI (*Looks at the book*) Dirty bastard! Wait'll you hear what he writes about me.
  (*Suddenly* EUGENE *appears, coming back from town*)

SELRIDGE It's him. Put it away.
  (WYKOWSKI *slips the book under his bunk, pretends to play cards with* SELRIDGE. EUGENE *enters with a big, self-satisfied smile on his face and a very "cocky" walk*)

EUGENE Hi, guys! (*They all look up, mutter their hellos and resume their activities.* EUGENE *waits expectantly for someone to ask about his adventure but no one does*) So how was your weekend?

CARNEY Fine.

WYKOWSKI   Great.

SELRIDGE   The best.

EUGENE   Good—good—good—good—good.

CARNEY (*To* EUGENE)   Well?

EUGENE   Well what?

CARNEY   What was it like? Give us details . . . Was it "Empty Saddles in the Old Corral" or was it "Swing Swing Swing"?

EUGENE   It was sort of—"Moonlight Cocktails" . . . It was chatty.

WYKOWSKI   Chatty?? Your first time in the sack with a pro was "chatty"?

EUGENE   She's not a pro. She only does it on weekends.

WYKOWSKI   So what does that make her? A semipro?

SELRIDGE (*Laughs*)   Great! That was great. Perfect remark, Kows . . .

EUGENE   At least we talked to each other. I wasn't in and out of there in two seconds. She was a person to me, not a pro.

EPSTEIN (*Still reading his book*)   Self-righteous, Eugene. Be on guard against self-righteousness.

EUGENE (*Unties his tie, starts to unbutton his shirt*)   . . . The second time was "Swing Swing Swing." (*He smiles*)

SELRIDGE   The *second* time? You paid twice?

EUGENE   No. It was a "freebie." On the house.

WYKOWSKI   You're full of it.

CARNEY   Why would she give you a free one?

EUGENE   Maybe I was her one millionth customer. (*He chuckles at his joke*)

WYKOWSKI   Hey, Jerome. Blow it out your barracks bag. (EUGENE *doesn't find what he's looking for. He seems disturbed. He looks through his locker, under his bunk and mattress*)

EUGENE   Has anyone seen my notebook?

WYKOWSKI (*Very deliberate*)   What notebook is that?

EUGENE   The one I'm always writing in . . . Arnold, did you see it?

EPSTEIN   Why did you leave your locker unlocked?

EUGENE   Because I lost my key in the shower drain. There was nothing valuable in there except my book. I thought I could trust people around here.

WYKOWSKI   That's really funny, Jerome, 'cause we thought we could trust you too.

EUGENE   What does that mean?
(WYKOWSKI *reaches under his bunk and takes out the notebook. He opens it up and* EUGENE *makes a move toward it but* WYKOWSKI *jumps on top of his bunk and extends his foot to ward off* EUGENE. *He starts to read*)

WYKOWSKI   "One night a sudden scream from Selridge that sounded like he was calling out the name Louise. Is Louise his girl or possibly his mother?"

EUGENE (*Furiously*)   You had no right to read that. Give it to me, Kowski.

CARNEY   Give it to him. Nobody's interested.

WYKOWSKI   No? You interested in what he thinks about you, Donny baby?

EUGENE (*Lunges for him*)   Give it to me, goddammit!!
(SELRIDGE *reaches quickly and grabs* EUGENE's *arm and bends it behind his back.* EUGENE *knows one move and it's broken*)

SELRIDGE   I'm just gonna hold your arm. If you want it broken, it's up to you.

CARNEY   What does he say about me?

EUGENE   Kowski, please don't read it.

WYKOWSKI   If it gets boring, I'll stop. (*He reads*) "I can't make Don Carney out yet. Basically I like him and we've had some interesting talks, if you don't mind sticking to popular music and baseball. But there's something about him you can't count on and if I was ever in real trouble, Don Carney's the last one I'd turn to."
(CARNEY *and* EUGENE *look at each other. The others are quiet*)

CARNEY   Well, let's just hope you never have to count on me.
(*He is hurt. He gets up, walks to the side, and lights up a cigarette*)

EUGENE (*To* CARNEY)   It doesn't mean anything. It's just the thoughts in my head when I'm writing it. They change every day.

HENNESEY   Let him go, Selridge.

SELRIDGE   You want to take his place? I don't care whose arm I break.

WYKOWSKI   Okay, you ready for the best part? Here's the best part: "Wykowski is pure animal. His basic instincts are all physical and he eats his meals like a horse eating his oats." Hey, Epstein! Can I sue him for defamation of—what is it?

EPSTEIN   Character. Only if his intent is to prove malice and in your case it's not possible.

SELRIDGE   Go on. What else does he say about you?

WYKOWSKI (*Reads on*)   "He masturbates in bed four or five times a night. He has no shame about it and his capacities are inexhaustible. Sometimes when he has a discharge, he announces it to the room. 'Number five torpedo fired! Loading number six!' " (*To the others*) That's really good reporting. This guy should be on *Time* magazine or something.

EUGENE (*Near tears*)   Please stop it. You want to read it, read it to yourself.

WYKOWSKI   What do you mean? You're making me famous. Maybe the movies'll buy this. Great picture for John Wayne.

SELRIDGE   Is there any more?

WYKOWSKI   Yeah. Where was I?

SELRIDGE   You just fired number five.

WYKOWSKI   Oh yeah. Here. (*He reads*) "Despite Wykowski's lack of culture, sensitivity, or the pursuit of anything minutely intellectual, his greatest strength is his consistency of character and his earnest belief that he belongs on the battlefield. He is clearly the best soldier in the platoon, dependable under pressure and it would not surprise me if Wykowski came out of this war with the Medal of Honor." (*He looks at* EUGENE) . . . You really mean that, Jerome?

EUGENE   I told you, I don't mean any of it. I get a
thought and I write it down. Right now I would describe you in three words. "A yellow bastard!"

WYKOWSKI   They don't give the Medal of Honor to yellow bastards ... Let him go, Sel. (SELRIDGE *lets him go.*
EUGENE *rubs his arm in pain*) ... Why do you want
to write this stuff down for? You're just gonna make a
lot of guys unhappy.

EUGENE   What I write is *my* business. Give me my book.
(*He reaches for it*)

EPSTEIN   Wait a minute. (*As* WYKOWSKI *extends the book,*
EPSTEIN *snatches it from his hand*) I think I deserve to
hear *my* life story.

EUGENE   Arnold, I beg you. Don't read it. They're my
private thoughts and if you take them, you steal from
me.

EPSTEIN   I gather then it's unflattering. Don't you know
me by now, Gene? I can't be unflattered. I'm past it
... However, if you don't want me to read it, I won't
read it. But I don't think we'll be able to be truly honest
with each other from this moment on.

EUGENE (*Looks at* EPSTEIN)   ... Put it back when you're
through.
(*He gets up and walks out of the room.* EPSTEIN *opens
the book and starts to read to himself*)

WYKOWSKI   Don't we get to hear it?

EPSTEIN   Sure, Kowski. This is what we're fighting the
war about, isn't it? (*He reads*) "Arnold Epstein is truly
the most complex and fascinating man I've ever met
and his constant and relentless pursuit of truth, logic,
and reason fascinates me in the same proportion as his
obstinacy and unnecessary heroics drive me to distrac-
tion. But I love him for it. In the same manner that I
love Joe DiMaggio for making the gesture of catching
a long fly ball to center seem like the last miracle per-

formed by God in modern times. But often I hold back showing my love and affection for Arnold because I think he might misinterpret it. It just happens to be my instinctive feeling—that Arnold is homosexual, and it bothers me that it bothers me." (*He closes the book. He looks at the others, who are all staring at him*) . . . Do you see why I find life so interesting? Here is a man of my own faith and background, potentially intelligent and talented, who in six weeks has come to the brilliant conclusion that a cretin like Wykowski is going to win the Medal of Honor and that I, his most esteemed and dearest friend, am a fairy. (*He tosses the book on EU-GENE's bunk*) This is a problem worthy of a Talmudic scholar. Goodnight, fellas . . . It is my opinion that no one gets a wink of sleep tonight.

> (*Light up on the steps outside the barracks. A bare light bulb hangs above.* EUGENE *sits on the steps, smoking a cigarette and looking in the depths of despair.*
> *After a few moments,* DON CARNEY *comes out, leans against the post, and lights up a cigarette*)

CARNEY   . . . Did she really give you a second one for free?

> (*There is a moment's silence*)

EUGENE   Listen, I'm sorry about what I wrote in the book. I didn't mean it the way it sounded.

CARNEY   Forget about it. You don't really know me anyway.

EUGENE   No. I suppose I don't.

CARNEY   . . . Is that what you think? That I'm someone who can't be counted on?

EUGENE   I don't know. You're just somebody who can never make up his mind. You say, "Let's go eat Chinese food." We walk in and order and then you say, "No, let's go get some burgers" . . . We play basketball and you never take a shot. You always pass off to somebody.

CARNEY   Because I'm not a good shooter.

EUGENE   You're as good as the rest of us. You just think about it too long. Then it's too late to take the shot . . .

CARNEY   And that's why I can't be counted on?

EUGENE   I wasn't writing about peacetime. I'm sure you're very dependable in peacetime. But we're at war. We're going to be fighting for our lives soon. I mean, somebody throws a grenade into your foxhole, you don't want some guy staring at it for ten minutes saying, "What do you think we ought to do about it?"

CARNEY   Yeah, I can see that.

EUGENE   But you're still sore at me, aren't you?

CARNEY   I don't know. I have to think about it.

EUGENE   I figured you did.

CARNEY   . . . You know what Charlene once said to me? She said the reason she was seeing this other guy in Albany was because she didn't think I was someone she could count on.

EUGENE   You're kidding? Those exact words?

CARNEY   You think I'd ever forget them? She said she really liked me more than him but she wasn't sure I'd ever make up my mind. She didn't want to wait for me forever. So while she's waiting, she sees this guy up in Albany.

EUGENE   You see? That's what I meant.

CARNEY   Except for one thing. I'm not going to be in a foxhole with her with some Jap throwing in a grenade. I *have* to think about this because getting married is more serious.

EUGENE   More serious than being blown up?

CARNEY   Sure. Because if the grenade goes off, it's all over. Two seconds and you're gone. But if you make a mistake in marriage, you've got fifty years of misery. See what I mean?

EUGENE   Yeah. I see. (*He gets up and yawns*) Well, I'm tired. I'm going to turn in. How about you?

CARNEY   I don't know. Maybe.
    (EUGENE *looks at the audience and nods as if to say, "Didn't I tell you?" He starts off*)

EUGENE   G'night.

CARNEY   G'night.
    (EUGENE *goes inside.* CARNEY *sings a chorus of "That Old Feeling," during which time the scenery changes so that by the end of the song he is inside sitting on his bunk. The others wake up, angry.* CARNEY *retreats and lies down.*
    Moonlight is coming in through the barracks window. Suddenly the lights switch on. All six men are in their underwear, in their bunks. TOOMEY *bangs loudly on the bedpost with his clipboard*)

TOOMEY   UP! Everybody UP!! goddammit!!! It is two-fifteen in the morning and I've got a headache, a problem, and a goddamn temper all at the same time. Move your asses, we've got some serious talking to do. MOVE IT! (*He bangs the bedpost again. They all get out of bed, mumbling their surprise and indignation. All stand at attention beside their bunks.* TOOMEY *paces back and forth, silently and angrily*) . . . Is there any among you who does not know the meaning of the word "fellatio"? (*Some of them look at each other*) For the uninformed, fellatio is the act of committing oral intercourse . . . Is there any among you who does not know the meaning of the word "oral" or "intercourse"? . . . It is encouraging to know that my platoon is made up of mental giants. At exactly 0155 this morning, Sergeant Riley of Baker Company entered the darkened latrine situated in his barracks . . . When he hit the light switch, lo and behold, he encountered two members of this regiment in the act of the aforementioned exercise . . . When I was in the Boy Scouts, that kind of thing came under the heading of "experimentation." In the wartime U.S. Army, it is considered a criminal offense, punishable by court-martial, dishonorable discharge, and a possible five-year prison term . . . The soldier in Company B was a (*He looks at his clipboard*)—Private Harvey J. Lindstrom. The other soldier, whose back was to Sergeant Riley, was not seen and made his escape by jumping out an open window with his pants somewhere around his ankles, a feat of dexterity worthy of a paratrooper . . . Sergeant Riley, a man with five pounds of shrapnel in his right leg, gave chase to no avail but reported seeing the man enter this barracks at approximately oh two hundred hours . . . These are the facts, gentlemen. I will be brief. Does the guilty party wish to step forward, admit his indiscretion and save this company what I promise you will be pain, anguish and humiliation beyond the endurance of man. (*No one moves*) No, I didn't think so . . . I'm just going to have to pick him out, won't I? It's amazing what you can find out when you go eyeball to eyeball . . . (*He walks over to* WYKOWSKI *and indeed goes eyeball to eyeball. He moves on and does it with all six men*) Don't blink, Selridge . . . Look at me . . . Stand up, soldier . . . (*No one breathes. No one bats an eye*) There were two eyeballs in there whose shoes I wouldn't want to be in . . . Private Lindstrom will be interrogated in the morning. If he names the man he consorted with tonight, it is very possible Private Lindstrom's sentence will be significantly lessened. A worrisome thought to the gentleman whose eyeballs I just referred to . . . In the meantime all privileges on base are canceled, all weekend leaves are likewise canceled . . . The moral of this story is—when you get real horny, do unto yourself what you would otherwise do unto others . . .

(*He turns and leaves. The others breathe at last and finally look at each other*)

WYKOWSKI   . . . Okay, what are we going to do about this?

EUGENE   Don't say it, Wykowski. Just don't say it.

WYKOWSKI   I don't have to say it. We all know who he's talking about. We all know who it is. You even wrote it down in your book, didn't you? . . . Well, didn't you?

EUGENE   I also wrote down you're an animal. If I'm right, then you should be in the cavalry with a saddle on your back. I'll show it to Toomey, okay? Then Epstein can start serving his five years and you can move into the stables. That should satisfy a horse's ass like you.

CARNEY   Cut it out! Both of you! It's none of our business. Let the army take care of it.

SELRIDGE   No more base privileges? No more weekend passes? You're telling me that's not my business.

HENNESEY   Carney's right. The army'll take care of it.

EUGENE (*To* EPSTEIN)   I'm sorry, Arnold. I swear to God, I'm sorry I ever wrote it.

EPSTEIN (*Cheerfully*)   Actually I'm rather enjoying it. It's like an Agatha Christie story. *Murder by Fellatio.* Title's no good. Sounds like Italian ice cream . . . How about *Murder on the Fellatio Express?*

WYKOWSKI   You think this is funny, Epstein? Let's see if you'll be laughing at Leavenworth . . . And he calls *me* a cretin.

HENNESEY   There's nothing we can do about it tonight. Why don't we hit the sack.
(*He gets into his bunk*)

SELRIDGE (*Getting into his bunk*)   I don't see what's such a big deal. A guy should be able to do what he wants to do . . . Just as long as he doesn't do it to me.

(*He glares at* EPSTEIN. EUGENE *takes a page from his memoirs, tears it out, and rips it up*)

EPSTEIN   That's a mistake, Gene . . . Once you start compromising your thoughts, you're a candidate for mediocrity.
(*They all get into their bunks. The lights go out except a pin spot on* EUGENE, *who sits up and looks at the audience*)

EUGENE   . . . I learned a very important lesson that night. People believe whatever they read. Something magical happens once it's put down on paper. They figure no one would go to the trouble of writing it down if it wasn't the truth. Responsibility was my new watchword. (*We hear a phone ring once*) Anyway, the army must have really scared Private Harvey J. Lindstrom that night because I knew when I heard the phone ring in Sergeant Toomey's room, the poor guy must have talked his guts out. I went out for a smoke because what happened in the next ten seconds was something I didn't want to see or hear.
(*The lights in the barracks go on and* SERGEANT TOOMEY *stands there in his pants, his shirt unbuttoned, strapping on a Sam Browne belt, which holds a pistol in a holster. He stands there a moment. He is not happy about the task he is about to perform. The others sit up and look at him*)

TOOMEY   When the following soldier's name is called, he is requested to dress in his class A uniform . . . and follow me . . . Hennesey, James J.!
(*The others look surprised and turn toward* HENNESEY)

HENNESEY   . . . What for?

TOOMEY   That's a matter you can discuss with the military police . . . Come on, son. I don't like this any better than you do.
(HENNESEY *looks at the others for help. There is none forthcoming. He gets up and slips into his pants. He*

*puts on his shirt and begins to button it. He steps
down front, away from the group, putting his tie on.
He suddenly begins to sob.
Lights out on the barracks.
Light up on* EUGENE *in limbo*)

EUGENE (*To the audience*) . . . I felt real lousy about
Hennesey . . . The next weekend I went to Rowena's
again . . . She didn't even remember me . . . She acted
like I was a stranger . . . I tell her about Hennesey doing
it with another guy and maybe getting five years in jail
and she says, "Well, I haven't got too much sympathy
for their kind, sweetheart. They're just taking the bread
out of the mouths of my babies" . . . I'm never going
to pay for it again . . . It just cheapens the whole idea
of sex . . . (*The sets begin to change into the U.S.O.*)
. . . I was determined to meet the perfect girl. I knew
just what she would be like . . . She's going to be pretty
but not too beautiful. When they're too beautiful, they
love them first and you second . . . And she'll be athletic. Someone I could hit fly balls to and she'd catch
all of them. She'll love to go to the movies and read
books and see plays and we'd never run out of conversation . . . She's out there, I know it. Right now the girl
I'm going to fall in love with is living in New York or
Boston or Philadelphia—walking around the streets,
not even knowing I'm alive. It's crazy. (*Lights up on
U.S.O.* DAISY *is dancing with a soldier*) There she is and
here I am. The both of us just waiting around to meet.
Why doesn't she just yell out, "Eugene! I'm here!
Come and get me" . . .
   (*The dance ends. The soldier goes off.* DAISY *walks
   over to* EUGENE)

DAISY   Hello.

EUGENE (*Turns*) Hi.
   (*He looks to the audience, then back to* DAISY)

DAISY   Would you care to dance?

EUGENE   Me? Oh. Well, I don't dance very well.

DAISY I bet you do.

EUGENE No. I swear. I never dance.

DAISY Then why did you come to a dance?

EUGENE That's a logical question. Because I like to talk. And I was hoping I'd meet someone I felt like talking to.

DAISY We could talk while we dance.

EUGENE It's hard for me because I'm always counting when I dance. Whatever you said, I would answer, "one two, one two."

DAISY (*Laughs*) Well, I'll only ask you mathematical questions. (EUGENE *laughs as well*) I'll bet you didn't know how to march before you got into the army.

EUGENE No, I didn't.

DAISY Well, if you could learn to march, you can learn to dance.

EUGENE Yeah, except if I didn't learn to march, I'd be doing push-ups till I was eighty-three.

DAISY I'm not that strict. But if it makes you that uncomfortable I won't intrude on your privacy. It was very nice meeting you. Goodbye.
      (*She starts to walk away. She gets a few steps when* EUGENE *calls out*)

EUGENE Okay!

DAISY Okay what?

EUGENE One two, one two.

DAISY Are you sure?

EUGENE   Positive.

DAISY   Good.
(*She walks over to him, then stands in front of him and raises her left arm up and right arm in position to hold his wrist*)

EUGENE   All I have to do is step into place, right?

DAISY   Right. (*He tucks his cap in his belt and then steps into place, taking her hand and her waist, and he starts to dance. It's not Fred Astaire but it's not too awkward*) You're doing fine. Except your lips are moving.

EUGENE   If my lips don't move, my feet don't move.

DAISY   Well, try talking instead of counting.

EUGENE   Okay . . . Let's see . . . My name is Gene. (*Softly*) One two, one two . . . Sorry.

DAISY   It's okay. We're making headway. Just plain Gene?

EUGENE   If you want the long version, it's Eugene Morris Jerome. What's yours?

DAISY   Daisy!

EUGENE   Daisy? That's funny because Daisy's my favorite character in literature.

DAISY   Daisy Miller or Daisy Buchanan?

EUGENE   Buchanan. *The Great Gatsby* is one of the all-time great books. Actually I never read *Daisy Miller.* Is it good?

DAISY   It's wonderful. Although I preferred *The Great Gatsby.* New York must have been thrilling in the twenties.

EUGENE   It was, it was . . . That's where I'm from . . . Well, I only saw a little of it from my baby carriage, but it's still a terrific city . . . What else?

DAISY   What else what?

EUGENE   What other books have you read? I mean, you don't just read books with Daisy in the title, do you?

DAISY   No. I like books with Anna in the title too. *Anna Karenina . . . Anna Christie.* That was a play by O'Neill.

EUGENE   *Eugene* O'Neill. Playwrights named Eugene are usually my favorite . . . Listen, can we sit down? I've stepped on your toes three times so far and you haven't said a word. You deserve a rest. (*They sit*) I can't believe I'm having a conversation like this in Biloxi, Mississippi.

DAISY   You don't like Biloxi?

EUGENE   Oh, it's not a bad town. It's all right . . . it's okay . . . I hate it!

DAISY   I'm not that fond of it myself. Actually I'm from Gulfport. We all are.

EUGENE   Gulfport? No kidding? I know a girl from Gulfport.

DAISY   Really? Who is she? Maybe I know her.

EUGENE   Oh no . . . I doubt it. She's in the clothing business . . . Do you go to school there?

DAISY (*Nods*)   Mm-hmm. St. Mary's. It's Catholic. An all girls' school. I really have to move on. We're supposed to mingle. If we're with anyone more than ten minutes, the Sisters get very nervous.

EUGENE   We haven't used up ten minutes yet . . . Please! I really like talking to you.

DAISY   Well . . . just a few minutes.

EUGENE   Would you like a Coke or something?

DAISY   It's way on the other side of the room. You could use up at least a minute and a half getting it.

EUGENE   You're right. Let the next guy get you a Coke . . . Listen, I know this is going to sound a little prejudiced, but I didn't think there were any girls in the South like you . . . I mean so easy to talk to.

DAISY   Oh, there are, believe me. Anyway, I'm not really from the South. I was raised in Chicago. My father used to work on a newspaper there. Then he got a job in New Orleans on the *Examiner* as City Editor, but he took six months off first to write a book.

EUGENE   Your father's a writer? That's incredible because that's what I want to be. Listen, not to get off the subject, but would it offend you very much if I told you that I thought you were extremely pretty?

DAISY   No. Why should it? I like it when boys think I'm pretty.

EUGENE   Do lots of boys think you're pretty?

DAISY   I hope so but they don't always say it. They get very shy around me. My dad thinks I intimidate boys my own age. I'm glad you don't seem intimidated.

EUGENE   Well, no. I told you, I'm from New York.

DAISY   . . . What kind of writer do you want to be?

EUGENE   I don't know yet. So far all I've written is a few short stories and my memoirs. I keep a notebook and write down all my thoughts and what I feel about things. I've been doing it since I was a kid.

DAISY   My father kept a journal the last few years too. That's how he got to write this book. I read that that was a very good way to become a writer.

EUGENE   Well, a few people read my memoirs and they were very impressed.

DAISY   . . . Sister Marissa is glaring at me across the room, so I'd better see if someone else wants to dance. (*She gets up*) I had a very nice time talking to you, Eugene Morris Jerome. I'm trying to remember your whole name in case I ever see it in print someday.

EUGENE   You didn't tell me your whole name in case I ever wanted to write a letter to St. Mary's Catholic All Girl School in Gulfport.

DAISY   Hannigan. Daisy Hannigan.

EUGENE   Daisy Hannigan. Great name. F. Scott Fitzgerald should have thought of that before Buchanan.

DAISY   Well, you have my permission to use it. I wouldn't mind at all being immortalized. (*She extends her hand*) Goodbye, Eugene.

EUGENE   Goodbye, Daisy . . . God, every time I say that name I feel like I'm speaking literature.

DAISY   You say nice things. As a matter of fact, you didn't say one wrong thing in that entire conversation . . . Goodbye.
(*She goes.* EUGENE *watches after her, then turns to the audience*)

EUGENE   At last, something to live for! . . . Daisy Hannigan! . . . Just try saying that name to yourself and see if you don't fall in love . . . I knew I had to see her again. When she smiled at me, I had tiny little heart attacks. Not enough to kill you, but just enough to keep you from walking straight. Daisy Hannigan! Daisy Hannigan!

(*He dances off alone, Astaire-like.*
Lights up on TOOMEY'*s room.* EPSTEIN *sits on the*
stool quietly looking at TOOMEY, *who sits on the bed.*
TOOMEY *takes a long swig from the bourbon bottle.*
He is clearly smashed)

TOOMEY   Have a drink.

EPSTEIN   I don't drink.

TOOMEY   You will tonight.

EPSTEIN   Why?

TOOMEY (*Pulls a .45 pistol and points it*)   Because I say so.

EPSTEIN (*Drinks, sputters*)   Fine!

TOOMEY   You hate the army, don't you, Epstein?

EPSTEIN   Yes, Sergeant, I do.

TOOMEY   Well, I don't blame you. The army hates you
just as much. When they picked you, they picked the
bottom of the dung heap. You are *dung,* Epstein!
. . . You don't mind my saying that, do you? Because
you know that's what you are. Ding dong *dung!*

EPSTEIN   If you say so.

TOOMEY   Damn right I say so . . . I say so because I have
a loaded .45 pistol in my hand . . . And I am also
piss-drunk. If a piss-drunk sergeant has a loaded .45
pointed at the head of a piece of dung that the piss-
drunk sergeant hates and despises, how would you
describe the situation, Epstein?

EPSTEIN   Delicate . . . extremely delicate.

TOOMEY   I would describe it as "fraught with the possibility of crapping in your pants." (*He laughs and drinks*)
I'll be honest with you, Epstein. I have invited you into

my private quarters tonight with every intention of putting this pistol to your ear and blowing a tunnel clear through your head.

EPSTEIN I'm sorry to hear that.

TOOMEY I'll bet you are . . . If I were you, I'd consider that "bad news from home" . . . (*He leans in closer, meaner*) How's the contest going now, Epstein? I'll bet your ass you're sorry you ever took me on, ain't you?

EPSTEIN Some days are not as good as others, I admit.

TOOMEY When you attack a man, never attack his strong points. And my strong point is Discipline. I was weaned on Discipline. I sucked Discipline from my mother's breast and I received it on my bare butt at the age of five from the buckle of my father's Sam Browne army belt . . . And I loved that bastard for it . . . because he made me strong. Damn right . . . He made me a leader of men. And he made me despise the weakness in myself, the weakness that can destroy a man's purpose in life. And the purpose of my life, Epstein, is Victory. Moral victory, spiritual victory, victory over temptation, victory on the battlefield, and victory in a goddamn army barracks in Biloxi, Mississippi . . . That's what my daddy taught me, Epstein. What in hell did your daddy teach you?

EPSTEIN Not much . . . Two things maybe . . . Dignity and Compassion.

TOOMEY (*Incredulously*) Dignity and Compassion??? . . . Are you shittin' me, Epstein?

EPSTEIN A piece of dung would never shit a piss-drunk sergeant with a loaded .45.

TOOMEY (*Puts the gun to* EPSTEIN's *head*) Don't test me, Epstein. I'll bury you with dignity but not much compassion . . . Why the hell do you always take me on, boy? . . . I'll outsmart you, outrank you, and outlast you, you know that.

EPSTEIN I know that, Sergeant.

TOOMEY Do you know what the irony of this situation is, Epstein? Is it Eps*teen* or Eps*tine*?

EPSTEIN Either one.

TOOMEY The irony is, Epsteen or Epstine, that despite the fact that you hate every disciplined bone in my body, you're gonna miss me when I go . . . Miss me like a baby misses her momma's nipple.

EPSTEIN Are you going somewhere, Sergeant?

TOOMEY Didn't I just say that? Didn't I just tell you I was leaving this base?

EPSTEIN No, Sergeant, you didn't. When are you leaving?

TOOMEY At oh seven hundred, April 3, 1943 . . . That's tomorrow morning . . . I know how much you boys are going to miss me. But I don't want anyone making a fuss or anything. No gifts, you understand. If you like, you can clean a couple of latrines for me, but that's about it.

EPSTEIN Where are you going?

TOOMEY I am reporting to Dickerson Veterans Hospital, Camp Rawlings, Roanoke, Virginia . . . I believe, in gratitude, the Army is going to replace my steel plate with sterling silver . . . That means I'll be able to hock my head in any pawn shop in this country, how 'bout that?

EPSTEIN How long will you be gone, Sergeant?

TOOMEY   I just told you, you dumb son of a bitch. I'm going to the Veterans Hospital. They don't send you back from a Veterans Hospital. You become a Veteran. You walk around in a blue bathrobe and at night you listen to Jack Benny and play checkers with the other basket weavers . . . What I'm trying to tell you, you toilet bowl cleanser, is that my active career in the U.S. Army has been terminated.

EPSTEIN   I'm sorry to hear that, Sergeant.

TOOMEY   (*Holds up the gun again*)   Don't give me none of your goddamn compassion, Epstein . . . Compassion is just going to buy you a Star of David at the Arlington Cemetery.

EPSTEIN   Yes, Sergeant.

TOOMEY   They can put sixty-five pounds of nuts and bolts in my head, give me a brown tweed suit and a job pumping gas, I will still be the best damned top sergeant you'll ever meet in your short but sweet life, Epsteen-or-Epstine.

EPSTEIN   I'm sure of that, Sergeant.

TOOMEY   One night from my room here, I heard a game being played in the barracks. I heard Jerome ask each and every man what they would want if they had one last week to live . . . I played the game right along with you and put my five bucks down on my bunk just like the rest of you. (*He takes out a bill*) Here's my money. You tell me if I would have won the game.

EPSTEIN   The game is over, Sergeant.

TOOMEY   Not yet, boy. Not yet . . . All right. You know what I would do with my last week on earth?

EPSTEIN   What's that, Sergeant?

TOOMEY   I would like to take one army rookie, the greatest misfit dumb-ass malcontent sub-human useless son of a bitch I ever came across and turn him into an obedient, disciplined soldier that this army could be proud of. That would be my victory. *You* are that subhuman misfit, Epstein, and by God, before I leave here, I'm gonna do it and pick up my five dollars, you hear me?

EPSTEIN   None of us actually did it, Sergeant. It was just a game.

TOOMEY   Not to me, soldier. On your feet, Epstein!!

EPSTEIN   Really, Sergeant, I don't think you're in any condition to—

TOOMEY   ON   YOUR   FEET!   (EPSTEIN   *stands*) ATTEN-SHUN!! (*He snaps to attention*) . . . A crime has been committed in this room tonight, Epstein. A breach of army regulations. A noncommissioned officer has threatened the life of an enlisted man, brandishing a loaded weapon at him without cause or provocation, the said act being provoked by an inebriated platoon leader while on duty . . . I am that platoon leader, Epstein, and it is your unquestioned duty to report this incident to the proper authorities.

EPSTEIN   Look, that's really not necessary, Sergean—

TOOMEY   As I am piss-drunk and dangerous, Epstein, it is also your duty to relieve me of my loaded weapon.

EPSTEIN   I never really thought you were going to shoot me, Ser—

TOOMEY   TAKE MY WEAPON, GODDAMN IT!

EPSTEIN   What do you mean, take it? How am I going to take it?

TOOMEY *Demand* it, you weasel bastard, or I'll blow your puny brains out.

EPSTEIN (*Calming him*) Okay, okay . . . May I have your gun, Sergeant?

TOOMEY *Pistol,* turd head!

EPSTEIN May I have your pistol, Sergeant?

TOOMEY Force it out of my hand.

EPSTEIN Force it out of your hand?

TOOMEY Grab my wrist! If you dare! (EPSTEIN *leaps for* TOOMEY's *wrist, wrestling for the .45.* TOOMEY *finally allows him to wrest it from him*) Good!

EPSTEIN Okay. Thanks. Now why don't you just try to get a good night's sleep and—

TOOMEY To properly charge me, you'll need witnesses . . . Call in the platoon.

EPSTEIN The platoon? You don't want to do that in front of all—

TOOMEY CALL THEM IN, SOLDIER!!

EPSTEIN (*Sighs, walks to the door, and opens it*) Hey, guys. You want to come in here a minute. (EPSTEIN *comes back in. To* TOOMEY) This is not going to change anything between us, Sergeant. This is just as illogical and insane as before.

TOOMEY Maybe. But it's regulations. And as long as you obey regulations, Epstein, I win. (WYKOWSKI, SEL-RIDGE, CARNEY, *and* EUGENE *enter the room in various states of undress.* EUGENE *is in his Class A's. They all seem confused*) Men . . . as you can see, I'm pissed to the gills and have just threatened to blow Epstein's brains out . . . Private Epstein has relieved me of my weapon and placed me under arrest. You are all witnesses. (*They look at each other*) Private Epstein will now take his prisoner to company headquarters to file charges and complaints . . . I would just like to add that Private Epstein has displayed outstanding courage and has carried out his duty in the manner of a first-rate soldier. I am putting him up for commendation. (*He smiles at* EPSTEIN *triumphantly*) I'm ready when you are, soldier . . . We're wasting time, Epstein. Let's go.

EPSTEIN   I'm not going to do it. I'm not going to file charges!

TOOMEY   Remember what your father taught you, Epstein . . . Show some to a man who's going to Virginia tomorrow.

EPSTEIN (*Looking at* TOOMEY)   . . . Suppose you just get company punishment like the rest of us?

TOOMEY   You can handle this any way you want. As long as justice is served.
(*They all look at* EPSTEIN)

EPSTEIN   . . . Sergeant Toomey! . . .

TOOMEY   Ho!

EPSTEIN   I'll drop all charges and complaints if you give me two hundred push-ups.

TOOMEY   I accept your compassionate offer, Epstein.

EPSTEIN   Thank you. On the floor—please. (TOOMEY *drops*) Count off!!

TOOMEY   Yes, Private Epstein. (*He starts push-ups, first slowly, then rapidly*) One . . . two . . . three . . . four . . . five . . . six . . . seven . . . eight . . .

SELRIDGE   I don't freakin' believe this.

TOOMEY   —nine—ten—eleven—twelve—
(*The lights fade on* TOOMEY'*s room as he continues push-ups.* EUGENE *steps down front*)

EUGENE   Epstein won the fantasy game fair and square because *his* really came true ... In a way they both won because if for only one brief moment, Toomey had turned Arnold into the best soldier in the platoon ... The next day Toomey went to the Veterans Hospital in Virginia and we never saw him again ... Our new sergeant was sane, logical, and a decent man, and after four weeks with him, we realized how much we missed Sergeant Toomey ... One should never underestimate the stimulation of eccentricity ... Daisy and I corresponded three times a week and I visited her twice in Gulfport and the most we ever did was hold hands. I was either too shy or she was too Catholic ... Finally we finished basic training and I knew we'd be shipping out soon. (DAISY *appears, carrying a small wrapped package.* EUGENE *smiles when she appears*) Hi.

DAISY   Hello.
(*They reach out and hold each other's hand*)

EUGENE   Your hand feels cold.

DAISY   Yours feels warm.

EUGENE   Would you like to go somewhere? Down by the lake? Or to Overton's Hotel. They have dancing till midnight ... Or we could just walk.

DAISY   I can't. I've got to be back in ten minutes. I shouldn't even be out now.

EUGENE   *Ten minutes???* ... Are you serious? I came all the way from Biloxi.

DAISY   I know. But it's Good Friday.

EUGENE   Isn't that a holiday?

DAISY   No. It's a Holy Day. It's the day that Christ our Lord died. We have to abstain from parties or movies or dates. It's a day of prayer and mourning.

EUGENE   So why do they call it Good Friday? It sounds like Lousy Friday to me. Ten minutes, Jesus! Sorry, no Jesus. I can't believe it.

DAISY   It's my fault. I should have told you in my last letter . . . We can make up for it next week, can't we?

EUGENE   I'm not sure I'll be here next Friday. We finished basic training yesterday. We could be shipping out any day now.

DAISY   Shipping out? To where?

EUGENE   Europe. The Pacific. They haven't told us yet.

DAISY   Overseas? So soon?

EUGENE   Well, they can't keep us here forever. The army needs reinforcements. We've already lost a private and a sergeant and we're still in Biloxi . . . Can't you stay out a little later? Just tonight? I know I'm Jewish but I don't think Christ your Lord is going to hold it against you personally.

DAISY   I can't, Eugene. I have to be faithful to my beliefs.

EUGENE   What about being faithful to me?

DAISY   I have been. I haven't been to another U.S.O. dance since we met. I just don't feel like dancing with anyone else anymore.

EUGENE   Do you mean that?

DAISY   Cross my heart.
       (*She's about to*)

EUGENE Don't cross it. Religion is always getting in our way. I believe you.

DAISY I think you're a very special person, Eugene. If you want me to, I'll write to you as often as you want.

EUGENE Of course I do. I want you to write me every day. And I want a picture. I don't even have a picture of you.

DAISY What kind of picture?

EUGENE Do you have one where I could feel your skin?

DAISY If I did, I wish I had one where I could squeeze your hand.

EUGENE . . . I'm going to shoot my foot, I swear. I don't want to leave here.

DAISY I'm glad you feel the same way about me, Eugene.

EUGENE You know I do . . . I'd have come tonight even if I knew I only had *five* minutes with you . . . Daisy, I—I—

DAISY What, Eugene?

EUGENE I want to say something but I'm having a lot of trouble with the words.

DAISY That doesn't sound like Eugene the Writer to me.

EUGENE Well, I'm not writing now. I'm Eugene the Talker . . . Daisy, I just want to tell you I—I—goddamn it, why can't I say it? . . . Oooh! I'm sorry. I apologize. I didn't mean to say that. Especially on Good Friday.

DAISY I'll say ten Hail Mary's for you.

EUGENE   You don't have to do that. They're not going to do *me* any good.

DAISY   What is it you wanted to say?

EUGENE   Ah, Daisy, you know what it is. I've never said it to a girl in my life. I don't know what it's going to sound like when it comes out.

DAISY   Say it and I'll tell you.

EUGENE (*Takes a deep breath*)   . . . I love you, Daisy. (*He exhales*) Ah, nuts. It came out wrong. It's not the way I meant it.

DAISY   I've never heard it said so beautifully.

EUGENE   What do you mean? How many other guys have said it to you?

DAISY   None. I meant in the movies. Not Tyrone Power or Robert Taylor or even Clark Gable.

EUGENE   Yeah, well, they get paid for saying it. I'm in business for myself.

DAISY (*Laughs*)   I remember everything you say to me. When I go home at night, I write them all down and I read them over whenever I miss you.

EUGENE   Well, if you're writing your memoirs, keep your locker closed. I don't want to be the talk of St. Mary's.
    (*We hear church bells chime*)

DAISY   It's eight o'clock. I've got to go.

EUGENE   You didn't say it to me yet.

DAISY   That I love you?

EUGENE   No. Not like that. You threw it in too quickly . . . You have to take a breath, prepare for it, and then say it.

DAISY   All right. (*She inhales*) I've taken a breath . . . (*She waits*) Now I'm preparing for it . . . And now I'll say it . . . I love you, Eugene. (*He moves to kiss her*) We can't kiss. It's Good Friday.

EUGENE   You *have* to kiss after you say "I love you." Not even God would forgive you that.

DAISY   All right . . . I love you, Eugene. (*She kisses him lightly on the lips*) I have to go.

EUGENE   Daisy! This is the most important moment of our lives. It's the first time we're in love. That only happens once . . . When I leave tonight, I don't know if we'll ever see each other again.

DAISY   Don't say that, Eugene. Please don't say that.

EUGENE   It's possible. I pray it doesn't happen, but it's possible . . . I need a proper kiss, Daisy. A kiss to commemorate a night I'll never forget as long as I live. (*She looks at him*) I'll even say a hundred Hail Mary's for you on the bus ride back . . . Okay?
      (*She smiles and nods. He takes her in his arms and kisses her warmly and passionately . . . When they part, she seems weak*)

DAISY   I think you'd better say two hundred on the bus . . . Oh. I almost forgot. This is for you. It's a book.

EUGENE   Really? What book? I love your taste in books.

DAISY   It's blank pages. For your memoirs. Page one can start with tonight. (*She hugs* EUGENE) Take care of yourself, Eugene Morris Jerome . . . Even if some other girl gets you, I'll always know I was your first love.
      (*She runs off*)

EUGENE   I knew at that moment I was a long way from becoming a writer because there were no words I could find to describe the happiness I felt in those ten minutes with Daisy Hannigan.

> (*Lights up on the coach train seen at the opening of the play. It is night and the train rattles by in the semidarkness. The same group as we saw in the first scene are in their Class A's, stretched out on the coach seats.* WYKOWSKI, SELRIDGE, *and* CARNEY *are all asleep.* EUGENE *is writing in his new book of memoirs.* EPSTEIN, *once again, is sleeping in the rack above them . . .* ROY's *shoeless foot is practically in* WYKOWSKI's *mouth.* WYKOWSKI *slaps it away*)

WYKOWSKI   Jesus, change your socks, will you? What is that, a new secret weapon?

SELRIDGE   I *did* change them. This one used to be on the other foot.
> (*He giggles*)

CARNEY   You creeps never grow up. I'll tell you one thing. After the war, I'm not having any reunions with you guys.

EUGENE   Hey, Arnold! How do you spell "vicissitude"?

EPSTEIN   You don't! Leave it out. Try for simplicity. The critics will use vicissitude in their reviews.

CARNEY   Did you guys hear about Hennesey?

SELRIDGE   What?

CARNEY   He only got three months in the can. That's not so bad. After that, he's out of this war.

WYKOWSKI   With a dishonorable discharge? He better pray we lose because no one in *this* country's gonna give him a job.

SELRIDGE   The army's nuts. They shouldn't let guys like that out. They should keep them together in one outfit.

"The Fruit Brigade" . . . Make them nurses or something.

EPSTEIN   You hear that, Eugene? We are listening to the generation that will inherit America. It's inevitable that one of these geniuses will someday be President of the United States.

WYKOWSKI   Listen to him, will ya? Thinks he's real tough 'cause he took Toomey's gun away. We'll see how tough he is when he hits the beach.

EPSTEIN   I have to warn you, Kowski, that I expect to be very seasick on the troopship. And wherever you sleep, I'm going to be in the hammock above you.

CARNEY   How about getting some sleep *now?* This may be the best bed we see for a few *years.*
          (*It turns silent as the train rumbles on.* EUGENE *has been writing in his memoirs. He turns to the audience*)

EUGENE   So far, two of my main objectives came true . . . I lost my virginity and I fell in love. Now all I had to do was become a writer and stay alive . . . On that first train ride to Biloxi, we were all nervous . . . On the train now heading for an Atlantic seaport, we were all scared . . . I closed my notebook and tried to sleep . . . (*He closes the notebook*) When I opened the notebook two years later, I was on a train just like this one, heading for Fort Dix, New Jersey, to be discharged . . . I reread what I wrote to see how accurate my predictions were the night Wykowski broke into my locker . . . Roy Selridge served in every campaign in France, was eventually made a sergeant and sent back to Biloxi to train new recruits. He has men doing three hundred push-ups a day . . . Wykowski was wounded at Arnheim by a mortar shell. He lost his right leg straight up to the hip. He didn't get the Medal of Honor, but he was cited for outstanding courage in battle . . . Don Carney, after six months of constant attack by enemy fire, was hospitalized for severe depression and neurological disorders. He never sings any more . . . Arnold Epstein was listed as missing in action and his body was never traced or found. But Arnold's a tricky guy. He might still be alive teaching philosophy in Greece somewhere. He just never liked doing things the army way . . . Daisy Hannigan married a doctor from New Orleans. Her name is now Daisy Horowitz. Oh, well . . . She sends me a postcard every time she has a new baby . . . As for me, I never saw a day's action. I was in a jeep accident my first day in England and my back was so badly injured, they wanted to send me home. Instead they gave me a job writing for *Stars and Stripes,* the G.I. newspaper. I still suffer pangs of guilt because my career was enhanced by World War II . . . I'll tell you one thing, I'm glad I didn't know all that the night our train left Biloxi for places and events unknown!

CARNEY (*Singing*)
    Tangerine, you are all they claim
    With your eyes of night
    And lips as bright as flame
    Tangerine, when she passes by
    Señoritas stare
    And caballeros sigh . . .

Curtain

Broadway
Bound

BROADWAY BOUND *was first presented by Emanuel Azenberg at the Broadhurst Theatre, New York City, on December 4, 1986, with the following cast:*

KATE	Linda Lavin
BEN	John Randolph
EUGENE	Jonathan Silverman
STAN	Jason Alexander
BLANCHE	Phyllis Newman
JACK	Philip Sterling

Radio Voices:

ANNOUNCER	Ed Herlihy
CHUBBY WATERS	MacIntyre Dixon
MRS. PITKIN	Marilyn Cooper

Directed by Gene Saks
Scenery by David Mitchell
Lighting by Tharon Musser
Costumes by Joseph G. Aulisi
Sound by Tom Morse
Production stage manager: Peter Lawrence

SYNOPSIS OF SCENES

ACT ONE

Brighton Beach, Brooklyn, New York
February, late 1940s, 6:00 P.M.

ACT TWO

Saturday evening, a month later, 5:45 P.M.

Act One

The year is 1949.

We are in the Jerome house in Brighton Beach, Brooklyn, New York—a working-class neighborhood about two blocks from the ocean.

It is a two-story frame house. On the first floor we see a living room and dining room, separated only by furniture. Stage right is the front door. Outside is a brick stoop and the surrounding houses. Just inside the door is a staircase that leads to the four upstairs bedrooms. In the living room area are a sofa, an armchair, and a console radio separating the two. Near the front door is a telephone.

In the dining room area is an old, beautiful dining table and five chairs. Just upstage of the table is a breakfront.

The furniture, curtains, wallpaper, and carpeting reflect the small portion of postwar prosperity that has come to the Jerome family.

Upstage center is a swinging door, which leads to the kitchen. Stage left and running up and downstage is a windowed porch. The kitchen is accessible either through the center door or from the dining room through the porch. A door from the porch leads to the backyard.

The second floor bedrooms are arranged as follows: JACK *and* KATE's *room is stage right, and* BEN's *room is stage left. Both are visible only when their doors are open. Fully visible and overhanging the living room are* EUGENE's *and* STANLEY's *rooms. Both rooms contain a single bed and a desk and chair.* EUGENE's *room is filled with books.*

All four bedrooms and the bathroom are connected by a central hallway.

It is about six P.M. *on a cold day in February. Snow covers the streets. It is already dark.*

KATE JEROME, *about fifty and graying, is wearing a sweater to ward off the chill that permeates the house. She is setting five places for dinner.*

As KATE *goes into the kitchen for more dishes,* BEN EPSTEIN, KATE's *father, about seventy-five, comes out of his*

bedroom and starts slowly down the stairs. He is wearing a
heavy cardigan sweater and carrying a brown paper bag. He
is wearing his house slippers over his socks.

    KATE *comes out of the kitchen as* BEN *reaches the closet. She*
speaks louder to BEN *than to anyone else.*

KATE   I didn't call you, Pop. It's not time for dinner yet.

BEN   Is it dinner yet?

KATE *(Setting out the flatware)*   In about a half hour. No one's home yet. Why don't you stay in your room? It's warmer in there.

BEN *(Taking his coat from the closet)*   Maybe I'll walk down to the store and get a cigar.

KATE   There's ice on the street, it's twelve degrees out. Eugene will get you a cigar when he gets home.

BEN   I like cold weather.

KATE   You're always complaining you're freezing.

BEN   I don't like it cold in the house. I like it outside. *(Putting on his hat)* I have nothing to read. Maybe I'll go to the library.

KATE *(Coming to* BEN*)*   It's six o'clock. The library is closed. Eugene has a million books upstairs.

BEN   I don't read what he reads.

KATE   He has everything.

BEN   He doesn't have a book about Trotsky.

KATE   You just finished a book about Trotsky.

BEN   One book doesn't cover Trotsky. Thursdays they stay open till seven.

KATE   This is Friday.

BEN   I'll take a chance.
       (*He starts toward the front door*)

KATE   You want to fall and slip and break your hip
       again? You don't even have shoes on. You were going
       to walk in the snow in your slippers?

BEN   (*Returning to the closet*)   I'll put on my galoshes.

KATE   What's in the brown paper bag?

BEN   (*Sitting on the sofa to put on his galoshes*)   Where?

KATE   In your hand. What have you got there?

BEN   Nothing. It's garbage. I was going to throw it
       away.

KATE   Give it to me. I'll put it in the trash can.

BEN   Will you stop treating me like a child. I'm your
       father, I'll do what I want. When I'm dead, you can
       treat me like a child.

KATE   You're not going to the library. You were going
       someplace else. Where were you going?

BEN   I'll go where I want! (*She grabs his galoshes and
       throws them into the closet*) If you don't like it, I'll move
       in with Blanche. Blanche treats me with respect. Don't
       interfere with me.
       (BEN *goes to the closet.* KATE *stops him at center*)

KATE   You never go out at six o'clock. Something is
       going on here. If there's something in that bag that's
       important, you tell me and I'll bring it there myself.

BEN   The day I can't take care of my own things, they'll
       be praying for me at the synagogue. (KATE *grabs the bag
       from* BEN) Katey, don't!!

KATE (*Looking into the bag*)   What is this? Is this your bed sheet? . . . Where were you taking it?

BEN   To the Chinese laundry. They never close . . . I want it back, please.

KATE   You soiled your sheet and you didn't want to tell me? Why? I've been washing your bed sheets since I'm ten years old . . . So you had an accident. It's all right, Poppa.

BEN   At night I've had accidents. This is the first time during the day.

KATE   So? What else have I got to do with my time? There's no one in this house anymore anyway . . . Take your coat off. You'll catch cold.
(*She goes into the kitchen, taking the bag*)

BEN (*Calling after her*)   Not a word, you promise me? I couldn't stay here if the boys knew.

KATE (*From the kitchen*)   The boys? Who sees the boys? I forgot what they look like.
(BEN *sits on the sofa, still in his hat and coat. He puts his slippers back on and takes a newspaper from his coat pocket and reads.*
EUGENE MORRIS JEROME *comes running down the street, wearing a zip-up jacket with the collar up, and a scarf. He is twenty-three years old. He bursts through the front door and blows on his hands.*
The front door is not locked. Don't forget, this is still only 1949)

EUGENE   Oh my God! Hi, Grandpa! Did you hear? This is the coldest day in the history of the earth. Is Stanley home yet? (*Crossing to the closet and yelling upstairs*) STAN???

BEN   What are you yelling for? I hear you.

EUGENE (*Hanging up his coat*)   I was yelling upstairs for
   Stanley . . . Why are you sitting in your coat?

BEN   What?

EUGENE   Why are you sitting in your coat?

BEN   I was going out. Your mother changed my mind.

EUGENE (*Going to the dining table for an apple*)   You're
   better off. It's freezing. I saw a man kissing his wife on
   the corner and they got stuck to each other. Mr. Jacobs,
   the tailor, is blowing hot steam on them.

BEN (*Looks at him, concerned*)   Two people got stuck?

EUGENE   If they can't get them apart, they're going to
   have to sew all their clothes together.

BEN   They can't get them apart?

EUGENE (*Straddling a dining chair and facing* BEN)   It was
   a joke, Grandpa.

BEN   That was a joke? (*He rises and starts toward the
   closet*) What kind of joke?

EUGENE   I made it up. It's not really a joke. It's just
   funny.

BEN   To who?

EUGENE   To me.

BEN   So if it's funny to you, what are you telling it to
   me for?
       (BEN *goes to the closet and hangs up his coat, but
       leaves his hat on*)

EUGENE (*To audience*)   The strange thing about my
   grandfather is, he has totally no sense of humor. None.
   But everything he says, I think is funny. Maybe be-

cause he doesn't mean it to be. If he tried to be funny, he wouldn't be. (*To* BEN) Where's Mom?

BEN   What kind of animal wears a zipper?

EUGENE   A zipper? I don't know. What kind?

BEN   A horsefly.

EUGENE (*To audience*)   See what I mean?

BEN (*Crossing back to the sofa*)   That's a joke! Not two people got stuck together. You understand?

EUGENE   Yes, Grandpa. Thanks for the priceless information. (*To audience*) My mother and father are the same way. I could say something so funny that the pictures on the wall would get cramps from laughing, but those three just stare at me like dead bodies. I'm trying to become a comedy writer someday, and this is the encouragement I get.

BEN   What kind of fish sings an opera?

EUGENE   What kind of fish sings an opera? . . . I give up. What kind?

BEN   A halibut.

EUGENE   A halibut?

BEN   I got it wrong. I thought it was a halibut, but it doesn't sound right.

EUGENE (*To audience*)   Okay? I guarantee you that a halibut is funnier than the real answer . . . I mean, look at him. Sitting there with a hat on. If he put it on to be funny, it would be dumb. But he doesn't know he's got it on, so it's hysterical.

BEN   Does a mackerel sound right?

EUGENE   Don't work on it, Grandpa. It'll come to you. (*To audience*) My brother, Stanley, is the only one who appreciates my humor. When I make Stanley laugh, I feel like Charles Lindbergh landing in Paris . . . And Stanley comes up with great ideas. That's why the two of us teamed up. We're going to be a comedy writing team . . . (*Like a radio announcer*) "The Jack Benny Show was brought to you by Lucky Strike and was written by Sam Perrin, Nate Monnister, Milt Josephsberg, and Stanley and Eugene M. Jerome."
(*He hums "Love in Bloom" as* KATE *comes in from the kitchen with dinner plates*)

KATE (*Circling the table, setting plates*)   What are you eating an apple for? I made chocolate pudding.

EUGENE   It's not a fatal combination, Mom. Where's Pop? I have to talk to everybody.

KATE   I don't think he'll be home for dinner.

EUGENE   Again? That's twice this week. So what are you setting his place for?

KATE   The hell with him, that's what I'm setting his place for.
(*She returns to the kitchen*)

EUGENE (*Crossing to sit beside* BEN *on the sofa*)   Grandpa? What's wrong with Mom? Did she and Pop have another fight?

BEN   It's none of my business.

EUGENE   You know what's going on. She talks to you. You can tell me.

BEN   She *used* to talk to me. She doesn't talk to me anymore.

EUGENE   She snaps at everybody now. Even Stanley can't get a rise from her . . .

BEN   She was always like that. As a child, she could shut off for a month.

EUGENE   I can't picture her as a girl. Was she really supposed to be such a good dancer?

BEN   I only saw her dance once. I didn't like to go to those places. She used to win cups at the er . . . the er . . . that dance place.

EUGENE   The Primrose Ballroom?

BEN   At the er . . . that place near Long Beach.

EUGENE   The Primrose?

BEN   It was a big dance place in those days . . . the Primrose Ballroom!

EUGENE   Right. (*To audience*) Even his timing was terrific . . . He was the greatest teacher of comedy I ever met . . . Only he didn't even know I was studying him.

BEN   Sure, she was a terrific dancer.

EUGENE   She told me once she danced with George Raft.

BEN   Who?

EUGENE   George Raft. The movie actor.

BEN   I know who he is . . . Yeah, sure, she danced with him. He wasn't a star then. He was just a greasy-looking kid. He used to go around to all the different ballrooms and pick out the best dancer. She was fifteen, sixteen years old. Not pretty. She was never pretty. But she was graceful on her feet.

EUGENE   Why didn't she ever try to become a professional? Wasn't she good enough?

BEN (*Shrugs*)   She had the accident. She burned half the skin off her back. Twelve girls died in that fire. The owner of that shop went to jail. There was no ventilation, no back door. She couldn't walk for a year . . . She never went down to the beach again. Not with her back like that . . . Her sister Blanche was a beautiful girl. There were boys lined up outside the house just to look at her. But Blanche couldn't dance a note.

KATE (*Entering from kitchen with a pitcher of water and water glasses, which she puts on the sideboard*)   What are you two talking about?

EUGENE (*Crossing to* KATE)   About when you used to dance with George Raft.

KATE   You see? He still doesn't believe me, Pop.

EUGENE   Who said? I believe you. One day I'm going to write a movie starring George Raft, and he goes into this club, takes your hand, and dances a tango with you.

KATE   I did the fox-trot better. Make it a fox-trot.

BEN (*Crossing to the table*)   What was the name of that place where you danced?

KATE   The Primrose Ballroom.

BEN (*To* EUGENE)   That was it. The Primrose!

EUGENE   Okay. Listen, everybody. I have major news. This is serious.

KATE   Where's Stanley? The pot roast is almost dry.

EUGENE   Listen to me, will you? I have to talk to you.

KATE   Pop? You want a little wine tonight?

BEN   No wine for me. Too much acid. I'll have a beer.

KATE   We're out of beer.

BEN You got wine?

EUGENE (*To audience*) If I could just get these two on television. (*To* KATE) Will you please come in here and sit down. I have spectacular news for this family.

KATE (*Bringing in relishes from the kitchen*) What family? You see a family in here?

EUGENE Please sit. (*He seats* BEN *upstage of the table and* KATE *at the left end of the table*) Okay . . . ready? I wish to announce that your youngest son, Eugene Morris Jerome—is getting married.
(*A beat of silence*)

BEN A Jewish girl?

KATE He's kidding, Pop. He's not even going with anyone, how's he getting married?

EUGENE True! True! I am not going with her—yet! But I've seen her. Her name is Josie. I talked to her. I had lunch with her. I saw the color of her eyes. This is marriage, Mom. This is the girl for the rest of my life.

KATE This is the same girl you met last summer?

EUGENE No, no! I hate that girl. I never liked her.

KATE You went with her for a whole summer.

EUGENE I had nothing else to do. She was nice on the first date . . . *Part* of the first date. Until nine-thirty.

BEN He liked a girl until nine-thirty?

KATE He's kidding. That's a joke.

BEN That's a joke, too? Ask him to tell you about the people who got stuck together.

EUGENE   This girl is serious. I knew it the minute I saw her. Her father owns a music company on the same floor where I work. She writes poetry. She paints. Her father hung her paintings all over his office. She's incredible. She plays tennis. She plays golf. She plays softball. She's been to Europe. She hums Bach and Beethoven, and she can whistle Rachmaninoff. She has jet black hair and olive skin, and when she walks down the street, construction workers fall into the cement. If I live to be a hundred, I'll never meet a girl like her again.

KATE   She likes you too?

EUGENE   *Likes* me? I took her to lunch, and we ate from the same chopsticks. We couldn't stop talking. Philosophy, literature, sports . . . Yeah, she likes me all right.

KATE   I never heard you so excited about a girl.

EUGENE   There's one minor complication, though. She's engaged to be married.

BEN   She's what?

KATE   He's kidding. It's another joke.

EUGENE   No. Really. She's engaged to a Harvard Law student. But I'm not worried. I think I have the inside track.

KATE (*Getting up and going into the kitchen*)   I have to check the pot roast.

EUGENE (*Calling into the kitchen after* KATE)   She's breaking it off. She's not in love with him. She told him, but he doesn't care. He wants to marry her anyway. That's how great she is. (*As* KATE *comes out of the kitchen with* BEN'*s wine*) If she was marrying him, would she have had lunch with me today?

BEN   Maybe she's looking for wedding gifts.

KATE (*Setting out napkins*)   She sounds fickle, if you ask me.

EUGENE   I want to bring her to dinner next week. I want her to meet the family.

KATE   It's been a long time since this family ate together.

EUGENE   On a Sunday. Everybody's home on Sunday. All right?

KATE   We'll see. Who knows what'll happen by then. I'm sure she's a nice girl, but eat from your own chopsticks.
> (KATE *returns to the kitchen.* EUGENE *crosses toward the stairs*)

EUGENE (*To* BEN)   She never turned down a chance to cook for someone before . . . Something's wrong between her and Pop, isn't there? (*Looks back at* BEN) Grandpa? Did you hear me? (*To audience*) He's sleeping. He's probably working on the halibut joke.

KATE (*Coming out of the kitchen and calling up after* EUGENE)   Where are you going? We're eating soon.

EUGENE   I'm not leaving the country.
> (EUGENE *goes into his bedroom, turns on the light, and begins to write in his journal.*
> KATE *returns to the kitchen.*
> STANLEY JEROME *comes walking briskly down the street. He is twenty-eight, wearing a suit, tie, overcoat, and hat. He wipes his shoes carefully on the front mat, then enters the house. He is very excited*)

STAN (*Hanging his coat in the closet*)   Grandpa? Is Eugene here? (*Screaming upstairs*) GENE!!

BEN (*Waking abruptly*)   What the hell are you screaming for?

STAN   I'm sorry. I didn't know you were sleeping.

BEN   Then ask me. If you asked me, I would have told you.

KATE (*Entering from the kitchen*)   You walk in the snow without rubbers? The pot roast is half dry. Tell Eugene it's dinner.

STAN   We haven't got time, Mom. We'll take a sandwich later.

KATE   What do you mean? No dinner?
(*Upstairs,* EUGENE *puts down his journal and comes downstairs*)

STAN   We have to get right to work. (*Again, shouting upstairs*) GENE!!

KATE   I've been cooking since two o'clock. Your father doesn't come home. You tell me no dinner. What am I, a slave here? . . . Sit down, Poppa! It's ready!

EUGENE (*At the foot of the stairs*)   What's up?

STAN (*To* EUGENE)   What are you doing now? Whatever you're doing, forget about it. Back upstairs. We've got to start in right away. Mom, no calls for us. Take a message, we'll get back to them. We may be up all through the night, so don't get nervous if you hear us yelling. (*To* EUGENE) Come on! Let's go. We're wasting time.
(STAN *starts to dash upstairs*)

EUGENE   You mind telling me what this is about?

STAN (*On the stairs*)   We got a job at CBS! The Columbia Broadcasting System.

EUGENE   *WHAT???*

STAN   I can't believe how much I did today. I was running all over town. I met everybody. I mean, I would make a terrific agent. I talked to these people like they were my friends . . . I met Abe Burrows! He said to me, "Good luck, kid." . . . (*To an uncomprehending* KATE *and* BEN) Abe Burrows, the greatest comedy writer in the business . . . I was on the executive floor, long hallway, pictures of every star in the history of CBS— Jack Benny, Ed Sullivan, Arthur Godfrey, Edward R. Murrow.

KATE   You met them?

STAN   No. Their pictures. (*To* EUGENE) There's too much to tell. I haven't got time. We have to start working. I'm so excited, I'm still shaking. Come on, let's go!

EUGENE (*As* STAN *again starts up the stairs*)   Wait a minute! You mean the regular CBS?

STAN   No, the fake one!

KATE   Can't you talk this over at dinner?

STAN   Is that all you care about? Your dinner? The most important thing that's ever happened in our lives, and you're worried about a lousy pot roast?

KATE (*Obviously hurt, she goes to the kitchen*)   Just like your father. You're getting to be just like your father every day. Next thing you'll turn Eugene against me, too.

STAN   I'm sorry! . . . Mom? Ah, shit! (*To* EUGENE) Come on.
        (EUGENE *and* STAN *run upstairs as* KATE *comes charging out of the kitchen*)

KATE   What did you say?

BEN (*Ushering her back into the kitchen*)   He didn't mean anything.
        (EUGENE *and* STAN *go into* STAN'S *room.* EUGENE *sits in the chair.* STAN *takes off his jacket and tie*)

EUGENE   All right, tell me slow. Tell me everything. What kind of a job did we get? When do we start? How much money do we get paid?

STAN   I didn't discuss details. If they like the sketch we bring in, then they'll hire us.

EUGENE   If they like the sketch, then they'll hire us? You mean it's not a job, it's an audition?

STAN   It's a job. They just have to like it first.

EUGENE   I knew it was too good to be true.

STAN   Let me take care of business. I got us the audition, didn't I?

EUGENE   So it *is* an audition. Why can't you say so? I don't mind an audition, but you make it sound like we're leaving for Hollywood tomorrow.

STAN   We discussed Hollywood. I said we would have no problem in moving to Hollywood. We could leave immediately, if they wanted.

EUGENE   CBS asked if we wanted to go to Hollywood?

STAN   No, I brought it up so they would know how we felt. You have to have confidence when you talk to these people . . . That's why I introduced myself to Abe Burrows.

EUGENE   You introduced yourself?

STAN   In the elevator. I said, "Mr. Burrows, the greatest thing that could ever happen to me is to work as a writer on your staff." And he said, "Good luck, kid." And got off on the twelfth floor.

EUGENE   That's why he said—"Good luck"? You made it sound like you had lunch with him or something.

STAN   Did *you* talk to Abe Burrows?

EUGENE   That's not exactly talking to Abe Burrows. That's like the pope waving to you in the Vatican.

STAN   You say hello to people like that three or four times in the elevator, and after a while they remember you. I'm starving. Do you have anything in your room? Some cookies or something?

EUGENE   Why don't we have dinner first?

STAN   We haven't got time for dinner. We have to work.

EUGENE   If you can eat cookies, you can eat pot roast. It just takes another few minutes to chew it.

STAN (*Pulling* EUGENE *to his feet*)   All right, go get a couple of sandwiches. We can eat here while we work. And some milk. And some dessert. A piece of cake, whatever we've got.

EUGENE (*At the door, turning to* STAN)   How late are we going to work?

STAN (*Sitting in the chair, pads and pencils ready*)   Until we finish. Maybe all night. They want it tomorrow morning at ten o'clock.

EUGENE   They want a finished sketch by ten o'clock in the morning?

STAN   That's how television works. They want it good, but they want it fast. Those shows are on every week, not twice a year.

EUGENE (*Sitting on the ottoman*)   We never wrote a sketch in less than three weeks. And we only wrote one sketch . . . And we didn't even finish it . . . And the first part needs rewriting . . . Maybe we're not ready for CBS yet.

STAN You want me to call them up and tell them that? We'll never hear from them again . . . Once that kind of thing gets around, you're through at *all* the networks.

EUGENE You mean CBS is going to call NBC and ABC and tell them that two guys auditioning from Brighton Beach can't be depended on?

STAN Maybe. Do you want to take that chance?

EUGENE You actually believe that our names are going to come up in a meeting at ABC and NBC? We're not even writers yet. You're the manager of boys' clothing at Abraham and Straus. I'm in the stock room of a music company. Our names don't even come up where we work.

STAN (*Standing*) What is it, Eugene? Are you afraid? If you're afraid, tell me. You have to have confidence in this world. If you don't have confidence, I'll *always* be in boys' clothing and you'll always be in the stock room.

EUGENE Why will *you* always be in boys' clothing if *I* have no confidence? Your career doesn't depend on my confidence.

STAN Yes. It does. We're a team. I need you; you need me. You have a great comic mind. I'm the best editor and idea man in the business.

EUGENE You really believe that?

STAN Absolutely. I have an eye for talent, and we have talent. When Joe DiMaggio came up from San Francisco, didn't I say he'd become one of the greatest ballplayers of all time?

EUGENE Because he was already a great ballplayer in San Francisco. Why are we so great? We sold three comedy monologues to a guy who plays weddings and bar mitzvahs.

STAN   Right. And his salary has tripled in three months. Now all the young comics are starting to come to us. How do you think I got into CBS? My friend Mort Garfield, the press agent, showed the monologues to the head of comedy development . . . Eugene, I'm going to get us everything we ever dreamed of. If you don't have faith in us, I have enough for both . . . Please trust me . . . Now go get the sandwiches. I want to start working on some ideas.

EUGENE   I didn't know we were going to work tonight.

STAN   Well, we are . . . Put some lettuce on my sandwich. And mayonnaise.

EUGENE   The thing is, I wanted to see this girl tonight.

STAN   Well, now you won't see her. And get me some cucumbers.

EUGENE   I could leave by seven and be back by nine. I could write on the subway. I just have to see her.

STAN   You can see her another night. What's wrong with you?

EUGENE   She's engaged to a guy from Harvard. She wants to break it off, but he's coming in tomorrow to talk her back into it. If I don't convince her I'm the guy for her, he's liable to talk her into going through with it.

STAN   If he can talk her into it, what do you want her for?

EUGENE   Because she's perfect. And you only get one chance in your life of meeting a perfect girl.

STAN   You know how many perfect girls there are in Hollywood? They're *all* perfect. In two years you'll be *sick* of perfect girls. You'll be begging for a plain one.

(EUGENE *goes to his own room and begins to dress for his date.* STAN *is in pursuit*)

EUGENE   An hour and a half, that's all I'll be gone. If I don't talk to her face to face, I'll lose her, Stan. I know it.

STAN   Eugene, as much confidence as I have in us, I don't have that much confidence that we can write the sketch by tonight. But we have to try. Remember the story Pop told us? How he had the opportunity to go into his own business with a friend . . . how he stayed up all night thinking about it . . . and he couldn't make up his mind. A week later it was too late. His friend lives on Park Avenue now, and Pop is still cutting raincoats . . . Maybe this is the only chance we'll ever get. Maybe not. But are you willing to risk everything for a girl you might not even be interested in by next week?

EUGENE   I'll be interested in her for the rest of my life.

STAN   Then go out with her. Take as much time as you want. I'll write the sketch myself. (*Storming back to his own room*) I mean it. I'm not going to blow this opportunity.

EUGENE   Never mind. I won't see her.

STAN   I said, I'll do it myself.

EUGENE (*Going downstairs*)   Don't do me any favors.
          (KATE *and* BEN *enter from the kitchen.* KATE *puts* BEN's *soup on the table. He sits down to eat*)

KATE (*To* EUGENE)   Are you eating or not?

EUGENE (*Going into the kitchen*)   We're having sandwiches upstairs, so NBC and ABC won't be mad at us.
          (KATE *follows* EUGENE *into the kitchen.*
          BLANCHE MORTON, KATE's *sister, comes down the street. She wears a mink coat and fur hat. She looks very prosperous. She rings the doorbell. No one an-*

swers. BLANCHE *opens the door and walks in. She crosses into the dining room. We can sense some tension between* BLANCHE *and* BEN)

BLANCHE   Hello, Poppa.

BEN (*Glancing up from his soup*)   Who's that? Blanche? I didn't hear the limousine pull up.

BLANCHE   It's not a limousine, Poppa. It's just a plain Cadillac.
(*She kisses* BEN. *He is clearly uncomfortable*)

BEN   Like John D. Rockefeller is just a plain businessman.

BLANCHE (*Putting her purse and gloves on the sofa*)   It got stuck in the snow, just like other cars. I had to walk the last two blocks . . . Where's Kate?

BEN   What happened to the colored fella who drives you around?

BLANCHE   Robert? He's still with us. He was calling a garage to get us pulled out.

BEN   You pay him enough money, he could have carried you here.

KATE (*Entering from kitchen*)   Why didn't you tell me you were coming? I could have made extra dinner.

BEN (*To* KATE)   Why? Somebody's eating it besides me?

BLANCHE   Thank you, Kate. I didn't come for dinner. I wanted to talk to Poppa.

KATE   You had to come out in this weather? We have a telephone now, too, you know.
(*Everything seems to be an innuendo about the differences in their economic standing.*
EUGENE *enters from the kitchen*)

EUGENE (*Crossing down to* KATE) Mom, I'm having trouble with the pot roast.

KATE What did you do?

EUGENE Hello, Aunt Blanche.

BLANCHE Hello, Eugene.

EUGENE I didn't slice it right. I shredded it. It looks like shoelaces.

KATE I told you to let me do it. What do I bother cooking for?
(KATE *goes into the kitchen*)

EUGENE (*To* BLANCHE) How's Nora?

BLANCHE She's fine. Her children are wonderful. She thinks the new baby looks just like you. He's going to be so handsome.

EUGENE Is that what she said? What did she name him?

BLANCHE Myron Isaac.

EUGENE Myron Isaac.

EUGENE (*To audience*) Myron Isaac Eisenberg. Poor kid. Wait till he tries to date a girl from Mount Holyoke.

KATE (*Shouting from kitchen*) EUGENE! WHAT DID YOU DO TO THIS MEAT??

EUGENE (*Going slowly into the kitchen*) I KILLED IT! IT WAS HIM OR ME, MA!! I KILLED THE POT ROAST!!

BLANCHE (*Waiting for* EUGENE *to disappear into the kitchen, and turning to* BEN) Momma is sick, Pop.

BEN   That's a beautiful coat. What do you need a Cadillac for with a coat like that?

BLANCHE   The doctor tells me if I don't move her to Florida, he can't guarantee what'll happen to her.

BEN   I thought we had a bargain.

BLANCHE (*Sitting on the sofa*)   Not talking about Momma is not a bargain, Poppa. It's a punishment. To me, to Momma, to the whole family. And I'm not leaving here tonight until we talk about her.

BEN (*Rising and crossing to* BLANCHE)   Who's stopping you? Take her to Florida. She'll outlive the palm trees, believe me.

BLANCHE   You can be so cruel sometimes.

BEN   What did I say? I wished her a long life. You come here and aggravate me while I'm eating my dinner, and *I'm* cruel?

BLANCHE   Do you know what she says to me at night? The very last thing before she goes to bed? She says to me, "Why does that man hate me so much?" What do I answer her, Poppa?

BEN (*Crossing to the armchair*)   You don't. Because she'll ask it again tomorrow. Her whole day is built around why do I hate her so much. She sits on park benches and asks strange women why I hate her so much.

BLANCHE   Why do you?

BEN   Who said I did? *She* did, I never said it . . . I have feelings for the woman, I always will . . . But I can't live her kind of life, she knows that. I hope she lives another fifty years, whether it's on Park Avenue or in Miami Beach. But these are my roots. I lived here most of my life, this is where I want to die.
(BEN *sits in the armchair*)

BLANCHE   She's sick, Poppa. This is not the place for her. The cold wind coming off the ocean would kill her in two years. Thank God I can afford to send the both of you to a warm climate. It would make all of us so happy to see the both of you living together in comfort for the rest of your lives.

BEN   Comfort doesn't make me happy. I don't need some place where it's hot twelve months of the year. April till October is all the sun God meant us to have. To want more is a crime against those who were born without. Read your Trotsky.

BLANCHE   Don't turn this political, Poppa. This is *not* political.

BEN   *Everything* is political. The soup in my dish is political. The bread on my plate is political. And the four-thousand-dollar coat on your back is political. (*Rising and going back to his place at the dining table*) Don't tell me about things I was taught from the day I was born.

BLANCHE   (*Rising*) Momma's health is *not* political. Momma's love for you is *not* political . . . When you can't find a reasonable answer for something, you always turn to Trotsky for help. (*She turns angrily away from* BEN)

BEN (*Crossing to the sofa*)   You're angry with me because I won't live in your high-class apartment house where a year's rent could feed everyone on this block for a year? With a man in a uniform opening doors for me who's ten years older than I am? I'm not dead yet, I can still push a door open. Because I don't go to your fancy Park Avenue doctors four times a week? How much money did he get for telling your mother to move to Florida? I got friends who would have told her to move for nothing.
   (BEN *sits on the sofa*)

BLANCHE   And why are you so angry with me? Because you were brought up to despise the rich? I didn't marry

Saul because he was rich. I'm so used to not spending money, he had to teach me how to do it. (*Coming to sit beside* BEN) But if he is loving enough to offer my parents the opportunity to live out their lives without worrying, for the first time in their lives, about where the rent was coming, what in God's name is wrong with it?

BEN (*Lowering his voice*) I can't leave here. Not now.

BLANCHE Not now? Then when?

BEN Are you so blinded by your own life, you don't see what's happening to your sister's? Don't you know what's going on between her and Jack?

BLANCHE No. What are you talking about?

BEN He's getting ready to leave her. Tomorrow, next week, next month, who knows? He stays because he doesn't have the courage yet to go. But he's going, trust me.

BLANCHE I don't believe that. Not Jack.

BEN Not Jack, she says . . . A man gets older, he changes. He suddenly realizes he only has a few years left to do what he thought he had a lifetime to do.

BLANCHE Jack loves Kate. He's always loved her.

BEN Absolutely. But at fifty-five, he can overlook it.

BLANCHE He depends on her. She manages his life.

BEN Lucky for her. Otherwise, he would have left last year.

BLANCHE Oh, God. Don't tell me this. It's the last thing I ever expected to hear.

BEN Do you understand why I'm telling you I can't leave this house? Stanley and Eugene are grown men. Their life is just starting. It's time for them to leave this place. Do you know what it would be like for her to be alone? A woman who doesn't know a thing in this world except how to serve someone? If she can't make dinner for somebody, her life is over . . . You take your mother to Florida. You take care of her. But as long as I'm alive, I'll eat in this house.

EUGENE (*Coming out of the kitchen with a tray of sandwiches*) Your dinner will be ready in a second, Grandpa. Mom is sewing the pot roast back together. (EUGENE *starts up the stairs, stopping at the top*)

BLANCHE Maybe Jack won't leave. Maybe they'll work things out.

BEN Maybe . . . I'll stay here until maybe.

BLANCHE I would do anything in the world for Kate. But I've got to take care of Momma first . . . If I bring her down to Florida, I can only stay a few weeks. I can't leave Saul to spend the winter in New York alone. She doesn't know anyone down there. She cries now when she thinks about it. Stay with her until spring . . . Until April . . . Kate is strong. She can take care of herself.

BEN When did your mother ever have trouble making friends? In two weeks down there she'll be running for mayor . . . If she gets sick, if she needs me, I'll come to her . . . I have my own work to do. This country is getting richer every day from war profits. And whose pockets does it go into? To those who had the money before the war.

BLANCHE Poppa, I'm not equipped to argue these things with you. I don't understand them. I never did. But I respect what you think is right. All I'm saying is, does it have to be in Brighton Beach? Can't you change the world from Florida?

BEN   You can change your bathing suits in Florida. Not the world.

BLANCHE   (*Crossing to the front door and looking out*)   Why do we have so much trouble understanding each other?

EUGENE   (*Entering* STAN's *room with the tray of sandwiches*)   Aunt Blanche is here. She's trying to get Grandpa to . . .

STAN   Shut up! Don't say anything! I'm thinking.

EUGENE   (*Sitting in the chair*)   Have you got an idea?

STAN   Will you shut up?

EUGENE   Tell me so I can think about it, too.

STAN   It's not an idea yet. It's the beginning of an idea. It's just a thought. A germ. A tiny speck in my mind. (*He inspects his sandwich*) You forgot the cucumbers.

EUGENE   How about a college sketch? College sketches are always funny.

STAN   (*Interested. Sitting on the ottoman*)   Like what?

EUGENE   Like this girl, Kathy O'Hara, from Mount Holyoke goes out on a blind date with a guy named Myron Isaac Eisenberg.

STAN   I hate funny names. It's a cheap way of getting a laugh.

EUGENE   I don't know. Why don't you try it out on Aunt Blanche?

BLANCHE   What if, God forbid, Jack *did* leave her? What if the boys moved out? Saul and I can take care of her. She doesn't have to stay here. We could get a place in

Florida for all three of you. Then you wouldn't have to worry, about Kate *or* Momma.

(EUGENE *leaves* STAN's *room and returns to his own*)

BEN (*Rising and returning to his place at the dining table*) You think she would leave this house? You think she would take charity from her own sister?

BLANCHE (*Crossing above the sofa*) I took it from her when I needed it. Where was I going to go when Dave died? There's no shame in it when it's your own family. I would be paying her back for what she did for me and the girls.

BEN Don't you know your own sister better by now? . . . No. I don't think you do.

BLANCHE (*Crossing below the sofa*) Sometimes, Poppa, I think you don't approve of me . . . Sometimes, I think you don't even like me very much.

BEN I have three daughters, and I love them the same. But the one who's in trouble is the one that I help.

BLANCHE Doesn't that include your own wife? Why am I the only one in the family who wants to help Momma?

BEN Because you're the only one who can afford it. Don't ask for too much, Blanche. When you live on Park Avenue, sympathy doesn't come with it.

(BLANCHE *sits on the sofa*)

EUGENE (*Coming back into* STAN's *room*) What's new inside the old brain, Stan?

STAN You're still an infant. I have a goddamn infant for a partner. Why don't you wait in your room. I'll call you when I think of it.

EUGENE I want to help you.

STAN I said, "Come back when I call you."

EUGENE (*At* STAN's *door*) Yes, Heathcliff. I'll be waiting on the moors.
> (EUGENE *returns, again, to his own room and sits at the desk*)

STAN And bring up the cucumbers!

EUGENE (*To audience*) It's very hard writing with your brother, because your whole relationship gets in the way. Can you imagine *Hamlet* written by William and Harvey Shakespeare?
> (KATE *comes out of the kitchen with a hot plate of pot roast and vegetables, which she puts in front of* BEN. *She also has a small box wrapped in gift paper, which she gives to* BLANCHE)

KATE This is for Nora's baby. If Nora doesn't like the color, I can exchange it.

BLANCHE I'm sure she'll love it. She's coming over Sunday with the baby. (*More to* BEN *than to* KATE) It would be a wonderful time for the whole family to get together. Before Momma leaves for Florida . . . Please come.

KATE It's a long trip on the train for Poppa.

BLANCHE I could send a car.

BEN A socialist sitting in the back of a Cadillac with a colored man driving?

BLANCHE You can let me know at the last minute . . .

KATE You sure you can't stay for dinner?

BLANCHE I told her we'd start to pack tonight. If I don't help her, she'd try to get her furniture in the suitcase . . . Poppa? Would you *call* Momma during the week and just say hello?

BEN I have a lot of meetings this week.

KATE   He'll call.

BEN   If I find the time.

KATE   He'll call.

BLANCHE (*Crossing back to* KATE)   I wish I could stay. I wish we had more time to talk. I'll call you tomorrow. (*She collects her things*) Sometimes I miss this house so much. I miss how good we were to each other.
      (BLANCHE *kisses* KATE *on the cheek*)

KATE   Blanche! I need to talk to you. Not on the phone. Can we meet someplace in the city? Let me take you to lunch. Tomorrow, the next day. Whenever you can find time.

BLANCHE   Of course, Kate. Tomorrow. As early as you want.

KATE (*Tears welling in her eyes*)   I hate to ask you this. You know I never like to be obligated to anyone. But you're the only one I . . . (*Suddenly,* BEN, *who appeared to be nodding off at the table, drops his fork onto the plate. His breathing is heavy*) Poppa? What's wrong?
      (*He is holding on to the table to balance himself*)

BLANCHE (*Dropping her bag and package on the sofa*)   Oh my God!

KATE (*Taking* BEN's *hat off*)   What is it, Poppa? Is it a pain? Is it your chest?

BLANCHE (*Rushing to* BEN)   Oh, Poppa!

KATE   Try to breathe slowly. Deep breaths, Poppa.

BEN (*Sitting up straighter*)   It's all right. I'm all right.

KATE   You want some water? (*Pours him a glass of water*) Drink some water.

BLANCHE (*Taking* BEN's *hand*)   His hands are cold as ice.

KATE   Do you want to lie down?

BEN   I got dizzy for a second. (*Now fully recovered. To* KATE) I was hungry. You could wait forever for something to eat around here.

BLANCHE   It's this climate. Two blocks from the ocean in February, how can you keep the cold out of the house?

BEN   It's not the cold. It's not the climate. It's nerves, that's what it is.

KATE   How do you know it's not your heart? You haven't seen a doctor in over a year.

BEN   A heart attack God gives you. Nerves you get from people who worry about you too much.

BLANCHE   Is that meant for me, Poppa?

KATE   It was meant for both of us. You learn not to pay attention. He doesn't mean it.

BLANCHE   He can't stand the winters here any more than Momma. (*She sits at the table*) I don't mean to upset you, Poppa. If you're happier here, then stay. Forget what we talked about. I'll get somebody to stay with Momma. I'll work it out myself.

KATE (*Returning* BEN's *hat to the closet*) All right, Blanche. Leave it alone for now. We've got time yet.

BLANCHE (*To* BEN) Why is it so hard for us to talk to each other? Why is it so hard for you to take anything from me? I'm afraid to kiss you when I see you, I know how uncomfortable it makes you . . . Why is that, Poppa?

BEN (*Banging his fist on the table*) YOU ASK TOO MUCH OF ME! (KATE *and* BLANCHE *are stunned by this outburst*) I am not an affectionate man. I don't trust affection . . . Sometimes people give it to you instead of the truth.

BLANCHE (*Visibly hurt, going to sofa to collect her purse and package*)   I see . . . And what's the truth about me, Poppa? Have I betrayed you because the man I married became wealthy? When I met him, he was on the verge of bankruptcy. Whatever he got, he earned. Whatever he has, he worked for.

KATE   Blanche, stop it. That's enough. Everybody has said enough.

BEN   Let her say what she wants. She's a good girl, my Blanche, but sometimes she forgets where she came from . . . Is it cold outside, Blanche? You bet your life it is . . . Is it hard on the people who live out here? Ask them, they'll tell you . . . Take them *all* to Florida, they'll put up a statue of you on the boardwalk . . . But not even Saul could afford that. They all can't escape, Blanche. They all don't get a ticket to Miami.

BLANCHE   And my sin is that I can afford to buy you one?

BEN   There's no sin, Blanche. You're a generous woman. Even *I* can see that. I thank God you're able to take care of your mother. But I can't enjoy the benefits of a society that made my daughter rich and starves half the people in the country.

BLANCHE   I can't take care of all the people in the country. I didn't ask for all this. I was happier when I had no money and Dave was alive. But I'm not going to curse God because He gave me a kind and loving husband and yes, a mink coat and a Cadillac car. You want them, take them. I didn't ask for it. I found the coat in my closet on my birthday. Some good it does me. It keeps out the cold, but it also stops my father from reaching out and holding me . . . Is that the politics you believe in, Poppa?

BEN   I believe in what I was taught from the day I was born.

BLANCHE   I believe in what I was taught, too . . . I was taught that a family who loves each other takes care of each other . . . You're seventy-seven years old, Poppa, you've done enough. You've worked hard all your life. It's time to play pinochle and walk on the beach. Maybe you'll meet a few retired socialists. (*Going to* KATE) I'll see you tomorrow, Kate?

KATE   Let me see what happens. I'll call you in the morning.

BLANCHE (*Walks to the door, then turns to look at* BEN)   I love you, Poppa . . . and I'll accept whatever affection you can give me. But you're not going to stop me and Momma from giving you ours. We're women, we don't know any better.
(BLANCHE *exits*)

EUGENE (*From his bedroom, to audience*)   Can you see now why I want to write comedy? Even God has a terrific sense of humor. Why else would He make Grandpa a dedicated socialist, fighting against the wealthy class, and then give him a daughter who marries the richest guy in the garment district? I wonder if we could sell it to CBS?
(KATE *clears away* EUGENE's, STAN's, *and her place settings. Then she turns out the porch light*)

KATE   Why don't you finish your dinner?

BEN   I'm not hungry anymore.

KATE   You'll change your mind. I'll leave it in the oven.
(KATE *takes* BEN's *plate and starts toward the kitchen*)

BEN   You think I don't know what's going on between you and Jack? That's what you wanted to talk to Blanche about, wasn't it?

KATE   You spoke to Jack?

BEN   I spoke to nobody. But you don't get to be seventy-seven without noticing a few things.

KATE   Nothing's going on.

BEN   If you can tell your sister, why can't you tell me?

KATE   I don't know. Maybe I'm afraid you'll think it's all my fault.

BEN   Is it?

KATE   You see? That's why I'm afraid to talk to you. (KATE *exits into the kitchen.* BEN *goes upstairs to his bedroom.* EUGENE *speaks from his bedroom to the audience*)

EUGENE   There's so much material in this house. Maybe I don't have to become a writer. If only I could get enough people to pay for seats in the living room.

STAN (*Bursting into* EUGENE's *room, holding a sheet of paper*)   I can't believe it. I cannot believe it!

EUGENE   What?

STAN   I just came up with an idea. One of the funniest ideas I ever heard of in my life. I was hysterical just picturing it.

EUGENE   So what's wrong?

STAN   I just remembered I saw it on the Red Skelton show three weeks ago. (*He throws the paper into the wastebasket*) Can you imagine if we brought that in to CBS? They would grab us by our collars and crotches and throw us out in front of Abe Burrows.

EUGENE   Well, what was the idea? Maybe we could twist it around.

STAN Twist it around? We don't make pretzels, we write comedy. We're supposed to be original, think of *new* things. We don't steal from other people's shows.

EUGENE What are you, the district attorney of comedy?

STAN We're wasting time again. What have you got?

EUGENE *Me?* I don't have anything.

STAN Then what were you doing all this time?

EUGENE I was thinking of a way to grow cucumbers in my bedroom.

STAN God, you are lazy! Let me ask you something.

EUGENE Oh, God! I hate it when you say, "Let me ask you something."

STAN Let me ask you something. Are you serious about writing or not?

EUGENE Yes.

STAN Yes, what?

EUGENE Yes, I am serious about writing.

STAN No, I don't think you are.

EUGENE (*Jumping to his feet*) Oh, Jesus! . . . I am, Stanley. I am serious about writing. I'm kind of footloose and fancy-free about cucumbers, but I'm serious about writing.

STAN You can say what you want, I don't believe you are.

EUGENE I am! I am! (*To the heavens*) Please, Holy Mother, make my blind brother see that I speak the truth.

STAN   All right. Tell me how serious you are about writing.

EUGENE   Let me call a doctor, Stanley. I think you're cracking up.

STAN   I want to know. I want to know just how serious you are about writing.

EUGENE (*Spreading his arms out wide, as though measuring a fish*)   This much!

STAN   Don't get sarcastic with me.

EUGENE   That wasn't sarcastic. I was telling you point-blank I think you're crazy.

STAN   You've been writing your memoirs since you're fourteen years old, and you still don't give a goddamn about your craft.

EUGENE   It's not a craft, Stanley. A craft is Indian rug weaving. My memoirs is putting down the nutty things that have happened in my life. And this conversation is getting a whole chapter of its own.

STAN   That's exactly what I mean. You may say you're serious about it, but you don't *act* serious.

EUGENE   You want me to act serious about writing? . . . Okay. Watch! (*He strikes a very grim pose*) I would rather write a comedy sketch than feed all the starving children in the world.
   (*He falls to the floor at* STAN's *feet*)

STAN   I could kill you right now. You want to forget about this? You want me to call CBS and tell them we're just not ready for this yet? Huh? Huh? All right?

EUGENE   What are you getting so angry about?

STAN   I'm not angry.

EUGENE   Yes you are.

STAN   I'm angry about your attitude.

EUGENE   So why did you say you're not angry?

STAN   Your attitude stinks, you know that?

EUGENE   I can't believe this! Maybe to *you* my attitude stinks. To me, my attitude smells wonderful.

STAN (*Going to the door*)   Listen, let's just forget about it. I don't think we can work together. I'm getting older, I don't have any more time to waste. I'll find somebody else.

EUGENE   How about Abe Burrows? He's probably waiting for you on the elevator.

STAN   No, that's what I'm going to do. I'm going to find somebody else. Someone with a bigger interest in his career than you have.

EUGENE (*Spreading out his arms again*)   You mean bigger than this?

STAN   You've got a lot to learn, my young friend.

EUGENE   "My young friend"? . . . Jesus, now you're Abraham Lincoln! (STAN *storms out, into his own room.* EUGENE *follows*) You know what I think this is all about, Stanley? I think you're scared. I think it's a terrific way to put off sitting down and writing. That's what I think.
     (EUGENE *returns to his own room*)

STAN (*Following* EUGENE)   Go on! Go visit your girlfriend! I just hope to God she's got money and is willing to support you, because you'll never make a penny in this world on your own, you little shit!
     (*He slams* EUGENE's *door, and goes back into his room*)

EUGENE (*To audience*) See what I mean about brothers writing together! . . . They're too busy sibling all the time . . . But in a way, Stan was right. I wasn't concentrating because I was afraid I was losing the greatest girl in the world . . . Being in love is a definite career killer.

(*The door opens and* STAN *comes back in*)

STAN I got another idea.

EUGENE (*To audience*) But lucky for me, Stan was real dedicated. (*To* STAN) What's the idea?

STAN Not an idea for a sketch. But I know what we've been doing wrong.

EUGENE You do?

STAN Tell me what you think we've been doing wrong.

EUGENE What we've been doing wrong?

STAN (*Nods*) What's the essential ingredient in every good sketch we've ever seen?

EUGENE I don't know. What?

STAN Don't say "what" so fast. Think about it.

EUGENE (*Thinks*) What's the essential ingredient in every good sketch we've ever seen.

STAN Right.

EUGENE I don't know. What?

STAN You *do* know. We've talked about it. You're just not thinking.

EUGENE Stan, I don't want to take a high school exam. Tell me so we can write the sketch.

STAN   The ingredient in every good sketch we've ever seen—is conflict! . . . Remember? Remember the night we talked about conflict?

EUGENE   Yes.

STAN   You *do* remember?

EUGENE   Tuesday, September seventh, eight thirty-five P.M.

STAN   All right. Now what's the *other* ingredient in every good comedy sketch we've ever seen?

EUGENE   (*Sighs in exasperation*)   *More* conflict!

STAN   Come on. You know it . . . Think about it . . . Heh? . . . Do you know it?

EUGENE   Yes. It's when one brother wants to kill the other brother.

STAN   YES!!

EUGENE   Yes? That's it?

STAN   It's close. You said it in that sentence. Do you remember what you said in that sentence?

EUGENE   No. It was too long ago.

STAN   One brother wants to kill the other brother. The key word is *wants!* In every comedy, even drama, somebody has to want something and want it bad. He wants money, he wants a girl, he wants to get to Philadelphia. When somebody tries to stop him from getting money or a girl or getting to Philadelphia, that's conflict. Wanting plus conflict equals what?

EUGENE   (*Looking heavenward*)   Oh please, God. Don't let me get it wrong. (*To* STAN) A job at CBS.

STAN   Right.

EUGENE   How do you know all this?

STAN   I watch all the comedy shows. I make notes. I figure it out. I think scientifically. That's why I'm good at gin rummy. I always remember what the other guy picks up.

EUGENE   So now that you know all this, do you have an idea for a sketch?

STAN   No. Do you?

EUGENE   Yeah. I think so.

STAN   When did you think of it?

EUGENE   While you were doing all that explaining to me.

STAN   Well, tell it to me.

EUGENE   Okay . . . there's a guy and a girl. They're in bed together.

STAN   Who are they?

EUGENE   No one. Just a guy and a girl.

STAN   I know, but what do they do? Is he a cop? An insurance salesman? A doctor? What?

EUGENE   It doesn't matter.

STAN   Details are always better for a character. If he's a cop, maybe there's some police jokes in it.

EUGENE   Okay. He's a cop. Patrolman John J. Mahoney. Fourth Precinct, Twenty-seventh District of Manhattan on the night shift, ten to six. His partner is Patrolman Vito Manganezi, and he's married, with . . .

STAN All right, all right. You are some pain in the ass.

EUGENE So this cop is in bed with a girl . . . Maybe they're married.

STAN *Maybe* they're married?

EUGENE THEY'RE MARRIED! They had a wonderful wedding, four hundred guests, catered by the Paramount Caterers . . .

STAN I said all right! . . . Go on.
       (*A loud knock on the bedroom door*)

BEN (*From outside the door*) Will you shut up in there! (STAN *opens the door.* BEN *stands there in his pajamas*) I can't sleep! Go into another business!

EUGENE We're sorry, Grandpa. (*To* STAN) Come on. (EUGENE *and* STAN *run downstairs.* BEN *returns to his room*)

STAN Go on, go on . . . They're both in bed.

EUGENE They're both in bed. She has a broken leg.

STAN I like that.

EUGENE Thank God.
       (*They sit on the sofa*)

STAN What time of year? . . . Winter, spring, summer?

EUGENE Winter. (STAN *stares at him*) Twenty-one degrees, winds fifteen miles per hour, barometer falling . . .

STAN Did I ask you? Go on.

EUGENE It's two A.M. The window is open. It's freezing in the room. She asks him to get up to close the window. He rushes over in his pajamas, but the window is frozen. So he pushes down with all his might—and slips his disk. He can't move. She can't move. The window is still open, and they're both freezing to death. How do they close the window?

STAN How?

EUGENE I don't know. It's only the beginning. I just thought that two people who can't move in a freezing room with the window wide open was a funny idea. Do you like it?

STAN (*Pacing, thinking*) I like some of it.

EUGENE I only *told* you some of it. That's all there *is* is some of it . . . What part didn't you like?

STAN The logic. Why doesn't she call the doctor?

EUGENE (*Sitting in the armchair*) I don't know . . . He's not in. He went to a Broadway show.

STAN At two in the morning?

EUGENE They stole his car in the parking lot.

STAN She could call another doctor.

EUGENE They're at a convention in Cleveland.

STAN Every single doctor in New York?

EUGENE She broke her fingers. She can't dial.

STAN All ten fingers?

EUGENE It's just a comedy sketch. Does it have to be so logical? We're not drawing the plans for the Suez Canal.

STAN Yes, we are. It's not funny if it's not believable.

EUGENE   Oh, you mean the Three Stooges are believable? Moe is fifty-five years old and wears bangs and sticks his fingers in his brother's eyes.

STAN (*Crossing up to* EUGENE)   The Three Stooges? Is that the kind of comedy you want to write? That's for morons.

EUGENE   Really? Well, the morons made it to Hollywood, and the geniuses are freezing in Brighton Beach.

STAN   I'm not going to settle for crap. If we're going to be good, we're going to be the best.

EUGENE   Well, I can't think of anything else.

STAN (*Pacing*)   Let's keep trying.

EUGENE   Their phone is out of order?

STAN   Too easy. Too coincidental.

EUGENE   Too easy? It took me twenty minutes to think of it.

STAN (*Pacing around the sofa*)   Don't give up. Let me tell you the idea again. A guy and a girl are in bed together, okay? It's the middle of winter, and the window is open . . .

EUGENE   What if he's *not* a cop? What if he's a doctor? Then we don't have to worry about calling a doctor.

STAN   If he's a doctor, he fixes them both up. There's no sketch.

BEN (*Shouting from his bedroom*)   THAT'S FINE WITH ME!

STAN   So, she has a broken leg. He gets up. It's freezing in the room. He rushes over to close the window . . .

EUGENE (*Leaping to his feet*) . . . and he trips on the wire and pulls out the telephone cord.

STAN . . . and they *can't* call the doctor! You know what we are, Gene? We're goddamn geniuses. (*He kisses* EU-GENE *and they both run upstairs to* EUGENE'*s room*) Now we can begin! Now we can write the sketch! Come on!
     (STAN *leaps onto the bed, and* EUGENE *sits at his desk.* EUGENE *speaks to the audience*)

EUGENE So at ten to seven in the evening, we had the idea for the sketch that would launch our careers, and we began to write. By eleven-thirty that night we had filled up three pads and had not written a single usable word.
     (KATE *comes out of the kitchen and turns on the dining room lights. She sits at the table, waiting.* STAN *sits up and rubs his eyes*)

STAN I can't keep my eyes open. You want to take a half-hour break?

EUGENE How about an hour?

STAN Thirty minutes. That's all. You have no discipline. Don't let me fall asleep.
     (STAN *exits to his own room, turns off the lights in both rooms. Both lie on their own beds.*
     JACK JEROME, *fifty-five years old and wearing an overcoat, rubbers, and hat, comes down the street and in the front door*)

JACK (*Surprised to see* KATE) You still up?

KATE I thought you might be hungry.

JACK (*Going to the closet to take off his coat and hat*) I had dinner at work. They had food sent in. We have to get the spring line out by next Thursday. (*Sitting on the sofa to take off his rubbers*) Everybody's working over-time. Jacobsen is sleeping in his office.

KATE (*Collecting his rubbers and taking them to the closet*)   Oh, because you said you might be home tonight.

JACK   No, I told you. The whole week. Maybe into Monday or Tuesday. (*Standing and starting toward the stairs*) Everyone's exhausted. It's a wonder they're all not sick.

KATE   I have some tea heated up. Sit with me a few minutes.

JACK   Let me take a shower first. I'm all sweated up. I smell from the cutting room.

KATE   In thirty-three years, it's never bothered me before. I'll get the tea.
(KATE *exits into the kitchen.* JACK *takes off his suit coat and crosses to his seat at the head of the dining table*)

JACK (*Calling into the kitchen*)   How are the boys?

KATE (*From the kitchen*)   I haven't seen them all night. They've been upstairs writing. Stanley thinks they might be able to get something in television.

JACK   Television? Ten people in this country have a television. There's no money unless there's volume. He's better off at Abraham and Straus.

KATE   If he gets this job, he wants to quit. Yesterday he looked for an apartment in the city. I think he and Eugene are getting ready to move out.
(KATE *comes in from the kitchen with a tea service*)

JACK   He's going to pay New York rent on a job he doesn't have yet? He's got a good future at A & S, for God's sake. He's got security there. What do either one of them know about show business?

KATE (*Serving* JACK *his tea*)   It's what they want to do.

JACK What you want to do and making a living are two different things. You don't keep a roof over your head doing what you *want* to do. You do what you *have* to do.

KATE I'm not saying you're wrong. But if they don't try this now, when will they ever have the chance?

JACK A chance at what? It's a one in a million shot. Who knows if they have talent? Did you ever see anything they wrote?

KATE They read me something once. They got upset because I didn't laugh. They didn't tell me it was supposed to be funny.

JACK If *you* didn't laugh, what chance do they have with the ten people with television sets? . . . It's crazy. It's not for them. I'll talk to Stanley tomorrow.

KATE (*Sitting down with her own tea*) It's not your decision, Jack. They're grown boys. They do what they want now . . . We don't need their money. It's only you, me, and Poppa now. And if Blanche can get Poppa to move to Florida, it'll just be the two of us. (*She pauses, looks at* JACK) It's a different world today. They have more opportunities than we did. You never had a chance to look around. You took the first job that came along . . . Sometimes I forget what you gave up to take care of a family.

JACK Was I complaining? Did I say I gave up anything? I wasn't that brilliant or educated to give up anything. But I made the most of what I did. Maybe to some people I didn't accomplish anything important, but as a cutter, I'm one of the best. One of the most respected, ask anybody.

KATE I don't have to ask, Jack. I *know.*

JACK You think I don't know what's on Stanley's mind? You think I don't know what he's looking for? . . .

Actresses! Showgirls! That's what he's looking for. And for *that* he'll give up security and a future.

KATE   Not everybody's looking for showgirls, Jack.

JACK   Is he afraid of hard work? Is he afraid of putting in regular hours? I've done it for a lifetime, it hasn't killed me.

KATE   No, Jack, it hasn't killed you. But the one thing I was always sorry about was that you never did something with your life that you enjoyed more.

JACK   I don't understand you. I've been a cutter for thirty-three years, why do you bring up a thing like that now for?

KATE (*Stacking the empty cups and plates*)   Because you seem different to me now. Because for the first time, I see the unhappiness in your face. You look older to me, Jack.

JACK   I look older because I'm older.

KATE   No. That's not what I see. What I see is disappointment in your eyes.

JACK (*Rising and crossing toward the stairs*)   I'll take a shower and get a good night's sleep. It'll be gone in the morning.

KATE   I look every morning and it's never gone . . . Maybe it's *me* you're disappointed with.

JACK (*Stopping at the sofa*)   What are you talking about?

KATE (*Taking the tea service into the kitchen*)   I don't know what I'm talking about. You tell me, Jack.

JACK (*Calling after her, into the kitchen*)   Tell you what? You have something on your mind, then say it.

KATE (*Coming out of the kitchen, to the dining table*) If I say what I'm thinking, you're liable to tell me what I don't want to hear.

JACK Listen, Kate. I've had a long day. I'm tired. Whatever this is about, we'll talk about it in the morning.

KATE I want to know what you're planning to do.

JACK Planning to do about what?

KATE (*Folding the tablecloth carefully*) Whatever's been going on, I want it to stop. I don't want to know who she is or what she's like. And I don't want to hear any lies. I just want tonight to be the end of it, and I'll never talk about it again, as God is my judge.

JACK You think I'm carrying on with some woman? Where do you get such ideas from?

KATE Two things a woman doesn't have to be told. When she's pregnant and when her husband stops loving her. Maybe we've had enough years of loving each other. But I will not live out the rest of my life being humiliated.

JACK Who's been talking to you? What goddamn liars tell you such things? Nothing is going on. What's happened to us when we can't believe each other anymore?

KATE Maybe it's the way you look at me when you say you're telling me the truth.

JACK (*Deliberately*) There is no other woman.

KATE Why not?

JACK What?

KATE Why not? You're a healthy man, you're affectionate, you're as normal as anyone else. We haven't been together as man and wife since God knows when.

So, if it's not me and you're swearing it's no one else, I'm asking you, Why not?

JACK   Kate, let's not get into this. I beg of you.

KATE   *Don't beg me!!* . . . Don't tell me how trusting we were. We passed all that when our children grew up. Now it's just you and me, Jack, and if I'm not enough for you anymore, then you tell me and get out. Get out, goddamn it! I will not be pointed at from windows as I walk down the street.

JACK   There is no other woman.

KATE   I don't care. Stop it anyway.

JACK   Look, I know I've changed. I know I'm different.

KATE   Yes, you are.

JACK   I've stopped feeling for everything. Getting up in the morning, going to bed at night . . . Why do I do it? Maybe it was the war. The war came along and after that, nothing was the same. I hated poverty, but I knew how to deal with it. I don't know my place anymore. When I was a boy in temple, I looked at the old men and thought, "They're so wise. They must know all the secrets of the world" . . . I'm a middle-aged man and I don't know a damn thing. Wisdom doesn't come with age. It comes with wisdom . . . I'm not wise, and I never will be . . . I don't even lie very well . . . There was a woman. (KATE *stares at him*) About a year ago. I met her in a restaurant on Seventh Avenue. She worked in a bank, a widow. Not all that attractive, but a refined woman, spoke very well, better educated than I was . . . It was a year ago, Kate. It didn't last long. I never thought it would . . . and it's over now. If I've hurt you, and God knows you have every right to be, then I apologize. I'm sorry. But I'll be truthful with you. I didn't tell it to you just now out of a great sense of honesty. I told you because I couldn't carry the weight of all that guilt on my back anymore.
        (JACK *waits quietly for her reaction*)

KATE   How old a woman?

JACK   Don't get into that, Kate. If you want to have your anger, throw something at me. But don't ask me questions about her. Let's talk about you and me. Tell me how we can get through this thing, but who and what she is is not important anymore.

KATE   How old a woman?

JACK   God Almighty, you won't be happy until you dig into it, will you? . . . Forty-four, forty-five, I don't know. I never asked her.

KATE   What did you talk about?

JACK   When?

KATE   That first day in the restaurant.

JACK   I don't remember. We just talked.

KATE   It must have been about something. The soup? The chicken? The fruit cup? How do these things start, Jack? I never heard one before.

JACK   I don't know who you're trying to hurt more, Kate. You or me.

KATE   What did you say in the restaurant, Jack?

JACK   Anything. Everything. We talked about the weather, about politics, about music, our children . . .

KATE   You get forty-five minutes for lunch. Besides eating, that's a lot of ground to cover, wasn't it?

JACK   Yes, it was a lot of ground to cover. Is that the answer you want, Kate?

KATE   Why her? After thirty-three years of marriage, why is she the one you picked?

JACK   Don't! For crise sakes, don't make me say nice things about her. You want me to say she was a tramp? Okay, she was a tramp. I had an affair with a peroxide-blond tramp, Kate. Is that all right?

KATE   I wish to God you did. A tramp I could handle. But that's not your nature, Jack . . . And I want to know why *this* woman was the one.

JACK   This is a mistake, Kate. A mistake we'll both regret, as God is my judge . . . Why this woman? Because she had an interest in life besides working in a bank or taking care of her house. To her, the world was bigger than that. She read books I never heard of, talked about places I never knew existed. When she talked, I just listened. And when *I* talked, I suddenly heard myself say things I never knew I felt. Because she asked questions that I had to answer . . . Learning about yourself can be a very dangerous thing, Kate. Some people, like me, should leave well enough alone . . . The things you were afraid to hear, I won't tell you, because they're true. It lasted less time than you think, but once was enough to hurt, I realize that . . . I never ate in that restaurant again, and I have never once seen her again . . . If either one of us feels better now that I've told you all that, then shame on both of us. (JACK *sits at the table, opposite* KATE. *She turns away from him*) If I killed a man on the street, you would probably stand by me. Maybe even understand it. So why is this the greatest sin that can happen to a man and wife?

KATE   Because I'm not strong enough to forgive it.

JACK   I didn't expect you to.

KATE   What *do* you expect?

JACK   I'm not clever enough to answer that.

KATE   This woman—this refined, educated woman—if I left you, would you go to her?

JACK   She wouldn't have me. She's content with her life the way it is.

KATE   If she *would* have you, would you go to her?

JACK   No.

KATE   Why not?

JACK   Because I know where I belong.

KATE   Here? Is this where you belong, Jack? In a house with a woman who hasn't read the right books or traveled any further in the world than the subway could take her? I take care of a house and I raised a family, but I don't know the questions to ask you that will make you feel things you never felt before. No, I don't think this is where you belong anymore, Jack.

JACK   If I felt that, I would have left last year.

KATE   (*Rising*) You did leave, Jack. You never moved out, but you left.

JACK   I know we've not been the same together. Not for a long time. And for that, I'm sorry.

KATE   So you stay with me because she won't have you . . . I got some bargain, didn't I, Jack?

JACK   . . . So? What do you want to do?

KATE   .What do *I* want to do? Is that how it works? You have an affair, and I get the choice of forgetting about it or living alone for the rest of my life? . . . It's so simple for you, isn't it? I am so angry. I am so hurt by your selfishness. You break what was good between us and leave me to pick up the pieces . . . and *still* you continue to lie to me.

JACK   I told you everything.

KATE (*Sitting in the upstage dining chair*) I knew about that woman a year ago. I got a phone call from a friend, I won't even tell you who . . . "What's going on with you and Jack?" she asks me. "Are you two still together? Who's this woman he's having lunch with every day?" she asks me. . . . I said, "Did you see them together?" . . . She said, "No, but I heard." . . . I said, "Don't believe what you hear. Believe what you see!" and I hung up on her . . . Did I do good, Jack? Did I defend my husband like a good wife? . . . A year I lived with that, hoping to God it wasn't true and, if it was, praying it would go away . . . And God was good to me. No more phone calls, no more stories about Jack and his lunch partner . . . No more wondering why you were coming home late from work even when it wasn't the busy season . . . Until this morning. Guess who calls me? . . . Guess who Jack was having lunch with in the same restaurant twice last week? . . . Last year's lies don't hold up this year, Jack . . . This year you have to deal with it.

(JACK *looks at her, remains silent a moment*)

JACK . . . It's true. I saw her last week. Twice in the same restaurant, once in another restaurant.

KATE And where else, Jack? Do you always sit or do you lie down once in a while? (*Rising*) Twice tonight I went to the phone to see if you were really working, but I was so afraid to hear that you left early, I couldn't dial the number . . . How is it possible I could hate you so much after loving you all my life?

JACK Would you believe me if I told you it was lunch and nothing else?

KATE (*Crossing to the stairs*) I can't talk about this anymore . . . Sleep down here. Anywhere you want except next to me.

JACK She's just a friend now, Kate. That's all.

KATE Is that what you tell her I am? Just a wife?
(*She starts up the stairs*)

JACK   She left her job for six months. I knew what had happened, but I couldn't get in touch with her. Her son was killed in an automobile accident . . . So I have lunch with her and talk about anything else except the accident.

KATE (*Coming back down to the foot of the stairs*)   If you see her again, you take your things and move out of this house.
(*She starts back up the stairs*)

JACK   I slept with her before and you forgave me. Now I buy the woman lunch and offer her compassion and for this you want to end the marriage.

KATE (*Coming back downstairs, close to* JACK)   I didn't expect to get through a lifetime without you touching another woman. But having feelings for her is something I can never forgive.
(KATE *goes upstairs into her bedroom.* JACK *sits at the table for a moment, then goes into the kitchen.*
A subway train is heard in the distance.
STAN *suddenly sits up in bed. He turns on his light and looks at his watch. He rushes into* EUGENE's *room and turns on* EUGENE's *light. He shakes* EUGENE)

STAN   Why didn't you wake me?

EUGENE (*Struggling out of a sound sleep*)   What?

STAN   I told you to wake me at twelve-thirty.

EUGENE   What time is it?

STAN   Twenty-five to one. We overslept.

EUGENE   Five minutes! You're yelling about five minutes?

STAN (*Hopping around the room, slapping his face*)   Come on! Get up! If we fall asleep again, we're dead. Get your blood going. Move! Get oxygen into your brains.

EUGENE (*Sitting up*) Don't slap me. My brains are up.

STAN Read back what we have.

EUGENE The whole thing?

STAN From the beginning.

EUGENE (*Flipping through the pads*) We don't have any-thing.

STAN Read the stuff we crossed out.

EUGENE It's all crossed out.

STAN Read it anyway. If I hear it again, then I'll know why it was wrong. Then we can get it right.

EUGENE There's three pads of it. We'll spend an hour reading back what took us four hours to write what we didn't like.

STAN Stop fighting me all the time. The more you fight me, the more pressure I feel. I need my head clear, I don't need it full of pressure. Just read it, will you, please!

EUGENE (*Reading from the first pad*) "A bedroom, about midnight. It is February and we see frost on the win-dows. One of the windows is open and we see the curtain blowing in. We hear teeth chattering from the bed . . ."

STAN I can't hear it! I can't concentrate! I can't focus on anything! . . . Can you hear it?

EUGENE Yeah, but I'm sitting a lot closer to me.

STAN Let me talk to myself for a minute. (*He walks to a corner of the room*) Stop it, Stanley! Stop and listen to what he's reading. You've waited your whole life for this, don't be a schmuck. (*He takes a deep breath and turns back to* EUGENE) Okay. Read the rest.

EUGENE (*Reading from the first pad*) "A woman speaks. Her name is Shirley. Shirley says—" (*He squints at the page*) I can't read it. The rest is crossed out.

STAN (*Taking the pad from* EUGENE) Let me see it. (*He looks at the pad*) What did you black it out for? When you cross something out, you just put a line through it. (*Pointing a finger at* EUGENE) *Never* black out anything anymore, do you hear me? I want a thin, simple line.

EUGENE   You want me to take a drawing class?

STAN   Let's get another idea. If we're stuck this long, there must be something wrong with it.

EUGENE   It's going to take just as long to get another idea.

STAN   My head is tightening up. I'm all constricted inside. I just can't think. (*He thinks, then looks at* EUGENE) This is hard, Gene. Really hard.

EUGENE   I know.

STAN   I won't give up if you don't give up.

EUGENE   I won't give up.

STAN   I love being a writer.

EUGENE   Me, too.

STAN   It's just the writing that's hard . . . You know what I mean?

EUGENE   Yeah.

STAN Maybe I could be a rewriter . . . I'm terrific at fixing up things that are already written.

EUGENE Like an editor. Every writer needs an editor.

STAN . . . I don't want to hold you back, Gene. If we don't come up with this sketch, if we don't get this job, I don't want it to stop you.

EUGENE We'll come up with it. You just have to relax.

STAN Because there are two writers I know. Marvin Rose and Alan Zweicker. They wrote something for Milton Berle once. They would take you on if I asked them.

EUGENE Don't ask them. I don't want to write with someone else.

STAN No, they're really good. Not as good as us, but you could at least make a living with them.

EUGENE If they're not as good as us, what are we stopping for?

STAN We're not stopping. I'm just planning ahead. Like I do in gin rummy . . . We could be the greatest, Gene. The greatest comedy writers in America . . . I just have to learn to deal with the pressure.

EUGENE So do I. It's not easy for me either.

STAN I'm feeling better. I'm glad we had this talk. It reassures me that you want to stick with me. I'm feeling more relaxed now.

EUGENE So am I.

STAN . . . Now if we can just get an idea.

EUGENE We will. I know we will.

STAN (*Looking up*) Oh, God. Give us an idea, God! I'm here, God. Tell it to me. Give us an idea for a sketch you're not using. Tell me an idea that makes you laugh.
(EUGENE *looks up to see if God is going to do it*)

Curtain

753

BROADWAY

BOUND

Act Two

One month later.

A few minutes before 6:00 P.M. on a Saturday night. It is dark outside and the snow is even higher than before. It's a rough winter.

EUGENE *is sitting up in bed in pajamas, robe, slippers, and white sweat socks. His desk chair serves as a night table and on it are medicine and orange juice. He wipes his nose with an old handkerchief.*

EUGENE (*To audience*)   It was the biggest night of my life and here I was, sick in bed. I took Josie ice skating at Rockefeller Center and fell down seven times and came home with a hundred and two temperature. Jewish guys are never good at sports played between November and April.

> (STAN *leaves his bedroom and comes downstairs. He looks out the front window toward the subway, then sets about rearranging the furniture, the better to hear the radio.* KATE *enters from the kitchen and puts some festive doilies on the dining table*)

... We came in with a finished sketch a few days late, and although CBS didn't think we were ready for big-time television, they did put us on small-time radio. Saturday night at six o'clock, when everyone's getting dressed or eating dinner, but not listening to CBS radio. It was an experimental comedy show to develop new talent and there were six young writers. We knew our future was on the line that night, but it wasn't CBS we were worried about. It was Mom and Pop's approval that meant the most to us.

> (STAN *brings a dining chair next to the sofa as* KATE *enters from the kitchen with a bowl of fruit and a bowl of nuts*)

STAN   No, MA!! No fruit! No nuts! No food at all.

KATE   Why not?

STAN You want a room full of people eating cashew nuts? They won't hear *any*thing!

KATE They could eat fruit. Bananas and oranges don't make noise.
(*She puts the fruit on the table*)

STAN (*Looks at his watch, then dashes to the front door*) Nine minutes to six and Pop's not home. I don't believe it. Of all nights in the world.

KATE (*Going to the foot of the stairs*) I don't know what to do about Eugene. He shouldn't be coming downstairs with the flu.

STAN He'd be down here with leprosy. We'd pile up the pieces in a chair next to the radio. You think he's going to miss this? (KATE *goes to the breakfront and takes out candlesticks, which she puts on the table*) Where's Grandpa? Did you call him?

KATE He's taking his nap. I'll wake him just before it goes on.

STAN We've got nine minutes!! It takes him twelve minutes to get his slippers on. (*Calling up the stairs*) GRANDPA!! . . . Come on down! The show is on!!

KATE (*Returning the dining chair to its proper spot*) What kind of cookies do you want with the tea?

STAN NO TEA! NO COOKIES!! . . . That's all I need is rattling cups and you saying, "Watch your crumbs."

KATE (*Entering the kitchen*) I was doing it for you, not for me.

STAN Then don't do it for me. I want it to be quiet so you can hear the laughs. (*He turns on the radio*) What's the matter with the radio? Is it plugged in? (*He looks behind the radio.* KATE *brings a tray of teacups from the kitchen to the breakfront*) The radio is broken. I can't believe THE RADIO IS BROKEN!!

KATE You have to let it warm up first.

STAN It never takes this long. NO, NO, NO!! IT'S BROKEN!!
(*He throws himself on the floor. The radio comes on. We hear dance music*)

KATE You see!

STAN (*Going to the radio to fine-tune it*) Is that clear: That doesn't sound clear to me. Can you hear it?

KATE I hear it fine.

STAN It's all the ice on the wires. I hate the winter.

KATE (*Coming to* STAN *at the radio*) You're going to get an ulcer, Stanley. You were never this nervous at Abraham and Straus.

STAN Because no one tuned in to listen to me selling boys' clothing. (*He turns off the radio, then crosses to the front door and looks out*) I don't see Pop. I don't even hear the train.

KATE (*Joining* STAN *at the front door*) You told him six o'clock?

STAN Five hundred times. I pinned it on his pajamas last night. Where could he be?

KATE I don't know. I'll go wake up Grandpa.

STAN I'll do it. You turn off the tea. It'll start to whistle in the middle of the program.
(KATE *goes into the kitchen.* STAN *opens the front door and steps out into the cold, looking for his father. Then he comes back in and starts up the stairs*)

EUGENE (*Sneezes. Then, to audience*) Mom and Pop were still together, but you'd never notice it. Almost a month had gone by since the big fight, and they barely spoke to each other. And when they did speak, they spoke in the third person. "Is he coming home for dinner tonight?" "He's not sure. He'll let her know." "She doesn't care. Let him do what he wants." I kept looking around to see if there was another couple there.

STAN (*Opening* EUGENE's *bedroom door*) Let's go. We're on the air. (*Knocking on* BEN's *door*) Grandpa! Come on. This is it! Gene and I are going to become capitalists! (*To* EUGENE, *as they come downstairs*) Pop's not home yet.

EUGENE You're kidding.

STAN (*Coming into the living room and again putting the dining chair next to the sofa*) This is some audience we've got. A mother who doesn't talk to a father who hasn't come home yet, and a grandfather who hasn't laughed since the stock market crashed.

EUGENE (*Coming slowly down the stairs*) My hair hurts. My pajamas hurt.

KATE (*Going to the foot of the stairs and holding up her hand for* EUGENE *to put his forehead on*) You have a hundred and two fever.
   (*She returns the dining chair to its proper place*)

EUGENE Why did they waste years developing the thermometer? You could make a fortune just feeling people in hospitals.
   (BEN *comes down the stairs.* EUGENE *sits in the armchair. In the distance we hear the subway, and* STAN *comes running out of the kitchen to the front door*)

STAN There's the train. (*Looks at his watch*) Even if he runs, he'll never make it on time.

BEN (*At the foot of the stairs*) Have I got time to go to the bathroom?

STAN We're on in three minutes.

KATE (*To* BEN) You go when you have to go. Go on.

BEN You got today's paper?

STAN The *paper?* We won't see you till Tuesday! (*More reasonably*) Didn't I hear you in the bathroom five minutes ago, Gramps?

BEN Was that me? You're right. Forget it. I don't have to go.

STAN (*Seeing* EUGENE *in the armchair*) Not there. That's Pop's chair. Sit over there.

KATE (*Seeing* EUGENE *about to sit on the sofa*) Not there. There's always a draft in that spot.

BEN (*Seeing* EUGENE *about to sit on the other end of the sofa*) Let me sit there. I have to put my feet up. They're swollen again.

EUGENE (*Standing in the middle of the living room*) Boy, this is the toughest seat in town to get.
(KATE *pushes a dining chair next to the sofa for* EU-GENE, *then puts some pillows under* BEN'S *head*)

STAN (*Looking out the front windows*) There's a few people getting off. It's so dark. I can't make out anyone.

BEN (*Stretching out on the sofa. To* EUGENE) So, what kind of a story is this?

EUGENE It's not a story. It's a variety show. It's music and sketches and monologues and comedy interviews. It's entertainment.

BEN Why, because they have nothing to say?

EUGENE It's not *supposed* to say anything.

BEN There's nothing to say? With three quarters of the world in economic slavery, there's nothing to say?

STAN (*Sitting in the armchair*) They didn't want any sketches on economic slavery, Grandpa. They're looking for laughs, not an uprising.

KATE (*Taking her knitting from the breakfront*) There's nothing wrong with a good laugh. We could all use a good laugh these days.

EUGENE What time is it?

STAN (*Looking at his watch*) Jesus! It's almost on. And he's not home yet.
(*He goes to the front door and looks out*)

EUGENE God, my heart is pounding.

KATE (*Taking dates from the breakfront*) Does anyone want some dates? Dates don't make noise.
(*She gives a date to* BEN, *then sits in the armchair*)

STAN NO, MA! Nobody wants anything.

EUGENE Please, God, don't let us be humiliated.

KATE Aunt Blanche has all her friends listening. Grandma has everybody in her apartment in Miami . . . Everybody in Brighton Beach is tuned in.

BEN But try to get them to read a newspaper, they're too busy.

STAN (*At the radio, adjusting the volume. The "Chubby Waters Show" theme music comes on*) Shhh! Here it comes! This is it!

EUGENE Good luck, Stan.

STAN (*Going to* EUGENE, *shaking his hand, then coming back to sit in front of the radio*) Good luck, Eug!
(*From the radio, after the theme music, we hear the announcer*)

ANNOUNCER From New York City, the Columbia Broadcasting System presents "The Chubby Waters Show," starring Chubby Waters and featuring Fred C. Sherman, Grace Dooley, Don Paloma, Sarah Mac-Laren, John Dunninger, Dick Ambrose and his Waldorf-Astoria Orchestra, and special guest star Pepito, the only Spanish-speaking dog in the English-speaking world.
(*The theme music continues under the following*)

BEN (*To* EUGENE) They have a Spanish-speaking dog?

EUGENE Wait'll you hear him. He's hysterical.

BEN He really speaks Spanish, or they taught it to him?

STAN He can bark, "Si, si." Whatever you ask him, he says, "Si, si."

BEN (*To* STAN *and* KATE) If he speaks Spanish, the audience won't understand. They're not as smart as the dog.

KATE Why didn't they say your names?

EUGENE At the end of the program . . . if they have time. Shh. It's on again.

ANNOUNCER (*From the radio*) And now, the star of "The Chubby Waters Show," Mr. Chubby Waters.
(*The studio audience applauds*)

KATE (*To* STAN, *whose head is pressed to the radio grill-work*) Get your head away from there, Stanley. You'll go deaf.

CHUBBY (*From the radio*) Thank you. Thank you, ladies and gentlemen . . . I'm kinda nervous, this being my first big-time New York program. I'm from Decatur, Illinois, and our humor is a lot slower out there . . . I

had my own program in Decatur and when I told a joke, they didn't laugh until next week's show.
(*The studio audience laughs*)

BEN   Oi vay!

CHUBBY   Decatur's kind of a small town. I'll tell you how small it is. Some guys drove through town and threw a snowball at us . . . and we were shoveling it out for a week.
(*The studio audience laughs*)

KATE   Did that really happen?

EUGENE   No, Ma. It's just a joke.

STAN   Shhhh, will you please.

CHUBBY   Decatur's sort of an agricultural town. We sell all the fruit and vegetables that drop offa trucks passing through.
(*The studio audience laughs*)

BEN   Only in America this man makes a living.

STAN (*To* BEN)   Are you going to do this all night?

CHUBBY   The census taker told us the average family in Decatur has about two and a half children. Most families prefer to have two girls and half a boy. (*The studio audience laughs*) The reason being that with half a girl, you still got to buy the whole dress, but with half a boy, you only got to buy the pants.
(*The studio audience laughs and applauds*)

BEN (*To* EUGENE)   You wrote that?

EUGENE   No. One of the other guys.

BEN   Stay away from him. He's crazy.

STAN   Great. Can't even hear the program in my own house.

CHUBBY   When Abe Lincoln left Springfield, Illinois, his first speech was supposed to be Decatur. But his legs were too long, and darned if he didn't step over us.
(*The studio audience laughs*)

BEN   In Russia, he'd be shot by now.

STAN   I can't believe this. My own grandfather.

CHUBBY   The folks back home are really rootin' for me. Because if I don't make good, I'll have to go back to Decatur, but a new baby was born there yesterday, and, well, I lost my space.
(*The studio audience laughs*)

KATE   Why is he telling us all this?
(STAN *gets up and walks to the dining room to calm himself*)

EUGENE   It's a monologue. He's warming up the audience.

BEN   They'd be better off sending up heat.

CHUBBY   'Preciate meetin' ya. I'll be right back, when I make my first tour through New York City and meet the Pitkin family of Coney Island, Brooklyn, New York.

STAN   That's ours! Ours is next. (*Dick Ambrose and his orchestra plays over the radio. The front door opens, and* JACK *rushes in*) Pop! You just made it! You're just in time! Our sketch is next.
(KATE *gets up from the armchair and goes to the dining table and her knitting.* STAN *helps* JACK *off with his coat*)

JACK   I'm sorry I'm late. I couldn't help it.

EUGENE   It's okay. You didn't miss anything. You timed it on the button.

STAN   Sit in the armchair, Pop. You can hear perfectly.

JACK   Three trains were frozen to the tracks. It's some mess out there.

STAN   (*Ushering* JACK *to the armchair, and then sitting in front of the radio*)   Sit down, Pop . . . The comedian's name is Chubby Waters . . . He's a little corny, but the network likes that.

EUGENE   He's about to visit the Pitkin family from Coney Island. That's ours.

KATE   Does he want anything to eat?

JACK   He'll take something after . . . Thank her anyway.

EUGENE   (*To audience*)   You're not going to get big laughs from people who call each other "him" and "her"!
(*Dick Ambrose and his orchestra finish. The studio audience applauds*)

ANNOUNCER (*From the radio*)   . . . Newly arrived in New York, Mr. Charles "Chubby" Waters decides to visit the city he's always dreamed of, ever since he was born half a child in Decatur, Illinois.

STAN   (*To* JACK)   I'll explain that later, Pop.

ANNOUNCER   But it's not the Empire State or the Statue of Liberty or Grant's Tomb that Mr. Waters wants to see. It's the people; for it's the people who make our cities great. And so he decided to take the subway. Being half a person, he walks under the turnstile and rides out to Coney Island. He gets off, smelling the fresh sea water and the stale frankfurter rolls, and walks

through the historic streets . . . and rings the bell of Mr. and Mrs. Morris Pitkin.
(*We hear a doorbell ring*)

EUGENE (*To* BEN)   That's sound effects.
(*We hear a door open*)

MRS. PITKIN (*From the radio*)   Yes?

CHUBBY (*From the radio*)   How do you do? My name is Chubby Waters. May I ask, have you ever heard of me?

MRS. PITKIN   Not that I heard of.
(*A small laugh from the studio audience*)

CHUBBY   Well, I'm a radio comedian, and I have a brand new show on CBS starting this Saturday night at six. Will you be listening to it?

MRS. PITKIN   Only if *you* can make a pot roast.
(*A bigger laugh from the studio audience*)

CHUBBY   Is that anything like a roast ham?

MRS. PITKIN   Not in this neighborhood.
(*A big studio laugh*)

CHUBBY   I'm trying to familiarize myself with New Yorkers, and I wondered if I could come in and say hello to your family.

MRS. PITKIN   Why? My *family* doesn't say hello to my family.
(*Studio laugh*)

CHUBBY   I don't mean to impose, but it would be very helpful to me. I'd be most grateful.

MRS. PITKIN   All right . . . Wipe your feet.

CHUBBY   Certainly. (*Sound effect of wiping feet*) . . . There! They're clean.

MRS. PITKIN   Your *shoes* are clean. I meant the *feet*. Take your socks off too.
   (*Studio laugh*)

CHUBBY   Certainly . . . There! Now everything's clean . . . Oh, what a pretty house. I like your furniture. What style would you call it?

MRS. PITKIN   Sacrifice! That's what you have to do to get it.
   (*Studio laugh*)

KATE   She reminds me of someone, but I can't think who.

CHUBBY   Is that a new rug?

MRS. PITKIN   Where?

CHUBBY   That thing rolled up in the corner.

MRS. PITKIN   No. That's my father-in-law.
   (*Studio laugh*)

CHUBBY   He sleeps on the floor?

MRS. PITKIN   He likes to sleep on newspapers, because if he wakes up in the middle of the night, he's got something to read.
   (*Studio laugh*)

CHUBBY   A well-read bed . . .

MRS. PITKIN   Step over the papers, please. If you get print on your bare feet, it'll be all over my father-in-law.
   (*Studio laugh*)

CHUBBY   I'll put my socks back on . . . Is it possible to meet your husband?

MRS. PITKIN   Sure. Do what I do. Write in for an appointment. (*Studio laugh*) He's in here. But be quiet. He's working.

CHUBBY   What does he do?

MRS. PITKIN   He's in ladies' pajamas.
     (*Studio laugh*)

CHUBBY   How do you feel about your husband being in ladies' pajamas?

MRS. PITKIN   That's the sacrifice I had to make to get the furniture.
     (*Big studio laugh and applause. The sound of the radio show becomes muted, almost inaudible; they all listen, except* EUGENE, *who turns to the audience*)

EUGENE   . . . Practically everything we wrote scored a bull's-eye . . . The only sad note was that although we were a smash at CBS, we came up real short in the living room in Brighton Beach . . . The thirty minutes went by about as quickly as the Middle Ages . . . Finally, our agony was over.
     (*The sound of the radio show comes up again. The theme music is playing at a fast tempo and we hear the* ANNOUNCER *rattling off the credits*)

ANNOUNCER   "The Chubby Waters Show" was a Steve Coleman–Mel Jason Production in association with the Columbia Broadcasting System . . . Pepito the talking dog appeared through the courtesy of R.K.O. Pictures . . . The producer of "The Chubby Waters Show" is Jeff Bishop, directed by Todd Allen and written by Michael Solomon, Larry Shapiro, Frank Connally, Donald Kreiss, and Stanley and Eugene Gerard.

STAN (*As he and* EUGENE *look dumbfounded at the radio*) JEROME!!!

ANNOUNCER   Good night from New York to all of you from all of us.
     (STANLEY *switches off the radio*)

STAN (*Shouting at the radio*)   You couldn't even remember Jerome, you stupid idiot! (*Storming into the dining room*) Gerard doesn't even sound like Jerome. I'm calling a lawyer. I should have been at rehearsals.

EUGENE   It was a great audience, though, wasn't it?

STAN   We got through it, Eug. At least, we got through it.
(*The boys stare at* KATE)

KATE   Well, I liked it. It was lively. The actors were good. Everybody remembered their lines.

STAN   It's radio, Ma. They read them from scripts.

EUGENE (*Returning his dining chair to the table*)   But did you really, really like it, Ma?

KATE   What do you mean, did I like it? Didn't you hear the audience laughing?

EUGENE   That was them, not you.

KATE (*Going to the closet for her coat*)   There were too many funny lines. They came so fast, I couldn't find a place to laugh. Next week make it slower.

STAN   Where are you going?

KATE   I have to go next door to Mrs. Slutsky's to borrow some honey for this one's tea. (*Kissing* EUGENE) I'm very proud of both of you.
(*She kisses* STAN)

STAN   I can go.

KATE   You have a date in half an hour, don't you? It's worth it for me to catch a cold to see you get married.
(*She exits through the back door. The boys turn their gaze on* BEN)

BEN (*Rising slowly*)   I'm going to finish my nap.

STAN   You didn't like it. I can tell.

BEN (*Crossing toward the stairs*)   I didn't hate it either. When I don't hate something, it's not bad.

EUGENE   What was wrong with it?

BEN   To me, comedy has to have a point. What was the point of this?

EUGENE   To make people laugh.

BEN   That's not a point. To make people *aware*, that's a point. Political satire, that's what you should have written. You could change half the world with political satire. Think about that sometime.

EUGENE   Political satire? We're lucky we came up with a few good jokes.

BEN (*On the stairs*)   I'll teach you how to write it. You sneak in a few remarks about what's wrong with this political system. If you make it funny enough, CBS will never notice.

EUGENE (*To* STAN)   Can't you just see it? . . . "The Socialist Revue" starring Chubby Trotsky . . . We'd be writing it from jail.

BEN   I liked the talking dog. "Si, si!" He didn't make any points, but he made me laugh. "Si, si!"
        (BEN *continues up the stairs and to his bedroom*)

STAN   You haven't said anything yet, Pop. Is anything wrong?

JACK   I tell you the truth, I had a hard time listening.

EUGENE   Why?

JACK   Sit down. Both of you. (*They sit on the sofa*) That was us you were writing about tonight, wasn't it? The family.

STAN   No. Not really.

JACK   Not really? You don't think you made fun of this family tonight?

STAN (*After a look to* EUGENE)   No. We weren't thinking of the family. It's all the people we know. Here in Brighton Beach or Coney Island or Brooklyn. People we grew up with. It's no one particular.

JACK   I'm willing to give you the benefit of the doubt. But listen: The woman says to the man, "My family doesn't say hello to my family." That wasn't your mother? If that wasn't your mother, who was it?

EUGENE   It's every mother who lives out here. They all talk like that. That's what happens in neighborhoods. Everyone sounds alike.

JACK   Everyone in this area knows about your grandfather. He falls asleep on buses, on trains, in the library. So you have a grandfather on the show who falls asleep on newspapers on the floor. The people out here who are listening know who you're talking about. And you're not ashamed to put a thing like that on the radio?

STAN   He heard it. He didn't say a word. He never thought it was him.

JACK   I don't care if he said a word or not. *I* knew it was him and *you* knew it was him. It makes no difference who he thought it was. You don't poke fun of your own grandfather in front of the whole world.
(*He takes his rubbers to the closet*)

EUGENE   We'd never poke fun at him. We love Grandpa. But old people fall asleep a lot, so we just wrote it down. It's just a coincidence.

JACK (*Pacing angrily*)   And what about her husband? What did you say about him on the radio?

STAN   Nothing.

JACK   Nothing? . . . Eugene, on the program, what does the woman say her husband does for a living?

EUGENE   He's in ladies' pajamas.

JACK   And I'm in ladies' raincoats, right?

EUGENE   A man being in ladies' pajamas just sounds funny. It's a joke.

JACK   Are you going to pretend you don't know what's going on between your mother and me? . . . Heh? . . . You're not deaf, you're not blind, so you must know something, right? (*The boys say nothing*) I don't know what she tells you. I don't know what stories she fills your head with. God knows what she must say to you about me.

STAN   She never said anything to me, I swear.

JACK   But you know what's going on, don't you?

STAN   In a house with walls like this, you know everything.

JACK   Well, I'll tell you something else. Not only do these walls have ears, the walls on the house next door have them, and the house next to that one have them . . . The whole damn neighborhood has them . . . In a community like this, everybody knows everybody else's business . . . So what do you think happens when the people in Brighton Beach hear a radio program with a woman on it who sounds familiar, tell us her husband's in ladies' pajamas—and they know what that means—they understand the innuendo . . . when they hear that on the radio, what are they thinking when they know that the two sons of the man in ladies' pajamas wrote the program? . . . Heh? . . . Tell me what they're thinking.

EUGENE   I know what you're getting at, but I don't think that's what's going to happen.

JACK   Can you promise me that? Can you give a written guarantee? . . . The only thing people like better than gossip is hearing filth, and that's what those people heard on the radio tonight.

STAN (*Rising*)   What are you talking about? That's crazy.

JACK   I will never forgive either one of you for ridiculing me in front of my neighbors, in front of my friends, in front of strangers. You'll never know how many people I called to tell to turn on the program because I was so proud of my two sons. That's a mistake I won't make again.

STAN   You may have been proud to *them,* but you never encouraged *us.* If it were up to you, I'd still be selling boys' clothing.

JACK   After what I heard tonight, I wish to God you were.

EUGENE   Stan, stop it! Cut it out! . . . I'm sorry you feel this way, Pop. We both are. But I swear, we never thought of you and Mom when we wrote the sketch. We just thought of older couples who lived in this neighborhood, but when it got down on paper, I guess it sounded like the ones we knew best . . . It wasn't intentional, I swear.
     (STAN *sits in the armchair.* JACK *sits between the two boys, but talks to* STAN)

JACK   You know what I thought when I heard it? I swear to God. I thought it was their way of getting back at me for hurting their mother . . . Is that so impossible to imagine?

STAN   No. Not so impossible.

JACK   Ah, maybe we're getting closer to the truth now
. . . What did she tell you about this woman? Did she
tell you what she was like?

STAN   I told you. She never talked to me about any of it.

JACK   But you seem to have feelings about it. Where did
you get them from? Someone you know from New
York? You have lots of friends there, right? Because let
me tell you something . . . No matter what you heard
about this woman, you will never find a kinder or more
decent human being on this earth. You understand me?

STAN   Go to hell.

JACK   What did you say to me?

STAN   I said, "Go to hell!"

EUGENE   Stan. Please. Don't do this.

STAN (*Standing*)   I don't care if she's Joan of Arc, that's
still my mother we're talking about. Do whatever you
goddamn please, but don't blame Gene and me of hu-
miliating you when you're the one who's been humili-
ating *us* . . . You're so damn guilty for what you've
done, you're accusing everyone else of betraying *you*
. . . I never wanted to hear what was happening to you
and Mom. I prayed every night you would both work
it out and it would pass out of our lives. You could have
called each other "him" and "her" forever as long as it
kept you together . . . All my life you taught me about
things like dignity and principles, and I believed them.
I still do, I guess . . . But what kind of principles does
a man have when he tells his sons the woman he's
seeing on the side is a wonderful, decent human being?

JACK (*Stands, composes himself, then walks slowly to*
STAN)   Either you've grown up too fast . . . or I've
outlived my place in this house.
(JACK *looks at both boys, then goes up the stairs to his
bedroom and closes the door*)

EUGENE (*Begins to fold the afghan*) Jesus! I don't believe what just happened . . . I'm shaking, I swear to God.

STAN Do you think what I said was wrong?

EUGENE No. I just don't know if you should have said it.

STAN I didn't bring the subject up, did I? I never accused him of anything. Every one of my friends' fathers screwed around *some* times. Maybe *all* the time. But they don't ask their sons to take the woman into the family.

EUGENE He didn't say it like that.

STAN Screw you, Eugene. What are you taking *his* side for? What are you going to do, buy her a Mother's Day present?

EUGENE I'm not taking his side. Something's happened to him these last few years, I know that. But you don't know his side. You don't know the whole story.

STAN He didn't listen to one word we wrote on that program. He's so paranoid, he thinks it was all about him. Jesus, the one night in our life we wanted his approval, and all he does is tell us what shits we are . . . "Maybe I've outlived this house," he says . . . Is that our fault, too? Another truckload of guilt dumped at our feet . . . He can have the goddamn house because I'm getting out. The both of us. (*He goes to sit beside* EUGENE *on the sofa*) It's time to move, Gene. This is no place for us. We've been waiting for a chance to leave, this is it. They liked our work at CBS, we can afford a place in New York. We should go, Gene, and we should go soon. (EUGENE *stares at him*) If you don't come, I'll go alone.

EUGENE No. You're right. I think we should go . . . I just wish it didn't have to be when everything's so bad here.

STAN   There's two or three places I saw. One over on the West Side, with a little backyard that gets the sun. Great place for parties. It'll be better for us, Eug. You'll be able to see your girlfriend more often. You'll have your own room, she'll be able to stay overnight.

EUGENE   No. She's not that kind.

STAN   Well, you can bring over the kind that do and take your girlfriend to the movies.
     (STAN *goes to straighten the armchair*)

EUGENE   Stan? . . . When we were writing the sketch, did you think we were writing about Mom and Pop?

STAN (*Coming back to sit next to* EUGENE)   No. It was like you said. It's everybody out here. I thought the father was Mr. Greenblatt . . . Joe Pinotti's grandfather once fell asleep in his oatmeal. He almost suffocated.

EUGENE   I did. I thought it was Mom and Pop. And Grandpa. They were the ones I was writing about.

STAN   Okay. So? It was a little bit of them, too.

EUGENE   No. It was only them. The joke about him being in ladies' pajamas . . . I didn't mean it the way he said. To me it was just a joke. But maybe I did it subconsciously, the way Pop said.

STAN   If it's subconscious, it's not a crime, Eugene.

EUGENE   I was the one who should have had the fight with him. Only I didn't know I was so angry. Like there's part of my head that makes me this nice, likable, funny kid . . . and there's the other part, the part that writes, that's an angry, hostile real son of a bitch.
     (*The phone rings*)

STAN (*Going to answer the phone*)   Well, you'd better make friends with the son of a bitch, because he's the one who's going to make you a big living. (*Into the*

phone) Hello? . . . Joe? . . . Did you hear it? What'd you think? . . . Wait a minute, I have to tell Gene. (*Turning to* EUGENE) Joe Pinotti still can't stop laughing. He thought it was better than Jack Benny. (*Back into the phone*) What? You're kidding . . . Wait a minute . . . (*To* EUGENE) His mother and father thought it was about them. They said it was so typical. They loved it. (*Back into the phone*) What? . . . No, they were crazy about it here . . . Yeah, my father thought it was great.
     (KATE *enters through the back door, carrying a jar of honey*)

KATE (*Going to the closet to hang up her coat*) Who's that on the phone?

EUGENE Joe Pinotti, Stan's friend. He loved the show.

KATE Why shouldn't he? . . . Where's your father?

EUGENE Up in his room . . . *your* room.

KATE (*Picking up the tray of sandwiches from the dining table*) The program's over. You shouldn't be downstairs. Get back in bed.

EUGENE Mom, I'm not eight years old.

KATE You are until you move out of this house.
     (*She exits into the kitchen*)

STAN (*Into the phone*) Can I quote you on that? . . . I'll talk to you tomorrow, Joe. Yeah . . . Thanks a lot. (*He hangs up the phone*) The man sells kitchenware at Abraham and Straus. He should be the critic on *The New York Times.*

KATE (*Entering from the kitchen*) What did your father think of the show?

EUGENE (*Crossing to the stairs*) He thought it was very lifelike.

STAN   He'll probably tell you later.

KATE   He tells me hello and goodbye, that's what he tells me. Hurry up and get dressed. Don't keep a girl waiting.
(KATE *exits into the kitchen with a tray of cups and saucers.* EUGENE *and* STAN *go into* EUGENE's *room*)

STAN   I don't get it. How can they sleep in the same bed night after night for a month and not say a word to each other?

EUGENE   I wonder if they say gesundheit if the other one sneezes.

STAN   Jerry Applebaum told me his mother and father didn't talk to each other for over a year, and they still made love three times a week.
(STAN *goes into his own room*)

EUGENE   That's more times than most people who talk to each other. (STAN *dresses for his date.* EUGENE *turns to the audience*) If I ever married Josie, that would never happen to us. How could I sleep in the same bed with her without touching her skin and stroking her hair and telling her how much I love her? Then again, maybe that's what my father said before he married my mother.

STAN (*Coming into* EUGENE's *room*)   How do I look?

EUGENE   Like a Jewish Cary Grant.
(*The phone rings*)

STAN   I've been after this girl for six months, but tonight's the night, kid.

EUGENE   How do you know?

STAN   She loves celebrities. (STAN *goes downstairs as* KATE *comes out of the kitchen to answer the phone*) Get a good night's sleep. We've got a show to write tomorrow morning.

KATE   Not if he's still sick. (*She picks up the phone*) Hello? . . . Who's this? . . . Momma? Oh, my God! I didn't recognize you. You sound wonderful . . . you sound younger.

EUGENE (*Comes out of his room and calls from top of the stairs*)   Is that Josie?

KATE   It's not Josie. Go to bed. (*Back into phone*) No, Momma, it's Eugene.
    (STAN *kisses* KATE *on the cheek, and exits through the front door*)

EUGENE   Ask her if she heard the show.

KATE (*Into phone*)   So, did you make any friends? . . . Uh huh . . . Uh huh . . . Uh huh . . . Momma, you don't have to name them all, I'm glad you made friends.

EUGENE   Ask her if she heard the show.

KATE   Did you hear the radio show? . . . Eugene and Stanley's . . .

EUGENE   Did she like it?

KATE (*To* EUGENE)   She loved it.

EUGENE   Really?

KATE (*Into phone*)   You know *who?* . . . The Pitkin family in Coney Island?

EUGENE   Oh, my God!

KATE   No, Momma. They're actors . . . He's not a dentist. That's a different family . . . These are *actors* . . . All right, Momma. I won't argue with you. If you know them, you know them. (*She shrugs to* EUGENE)

Yes. Everyone else is fine . . . Jack is doing very well . . . Blanche told you what? . . . No, no. That was months ago. Well, I'm telling you different . . . It's fine . . . (*Looks at* EUGENE, *who is sitting on the steps*) What are you sitting there for? I told you to get to bed. (*He moves slowly up the steps, then stops to listen*) . . . Yes. I know you haven't heard from Poppa . . . He's been very busy. He asks for you all the time . . . No. In his room.

EUGENE   You want me to get him?

KATE (*Waving at him to keep quiet*)   Momma, let it alone . . . I don't think it's a good idea . . . When he's ready

to call you, he'll call you . . . I don't think he means to hurt you. He just has to do things in his own way . . . Listen, you told me once yourself. Men are peculiar . . . I'm not defending him, Momma . . . Where am I taking his side? . . . I told him not to go to Florida? . . . Who told you that? . . . *Who told you that?* . . . I'm not yelling at you, but don't accuse me of what you make up in your own head . . . I didn't say—all right. I'm sorry . . . I said I'm sorry . . . All right, Momma . . . Yes . . . Yes . . . I know you do . . . I do too . . . Goodbye, Momma . . . I'll call you next—
(*But Momma's clicked off.* KATE *stands there with the phone in her hand. Then replaces it, wiping the receiver clean. She crosses to the breakfront and puts away the flatware.* EUGENE *watches her*)

EUGENE   How about if I made you one of my famous chocolate milk shakes?

KATE   You put too much Hershey's in it. I don't like it so sweet.

EUGENE (*Coming downstairs, to* KATE)   You know what I thought?

KATE   What?

EUGENE   I thought when you grew up, you stopped having trouble with your parents.

KATE   Yeah? Then be thankful you're still young.
(*She goes into the kitchen.* EUGENE *thinks about this for a moment, then looks in at* KATE *in the kitchen*)

EUGENE   I never see you stop working. When Stanley and I make enough money, we're going to get you a maid, Ma.

KATE   A maid? In Brighton Beach? People would pay admission to come over and look at her. (EUGENE *sits on the corner of the dining table.* KATE *comes out of the kitchen with a cup of tea*) Oh, my God! Get off that table! (*She whacks him with a dish towel*) Are you crazy, sitting on my dining room table?

EUGENE   (*Jumping off the table*)   I'm sorry. I didn't leave any marks.

KATE   Marks I can clean off. But I never want to see you show disrespect to this table.

EUGENE   I didn't mean it . . . I'm sorry, table. I apologize. (*She glares at him*) Is it so expensive?

KATE   My grandfather made this table. With his own hands. For my grandmother . . . (*She stirs honey into the tea, then motions for him to sit and drink it*) Over fifty-two years she had this table . . . When I was a little girl, I'd go to her house and she'd let me help her polish it . . . I didn't know it was work. I thought it was fun . . . Maybe because she and I did it together . . . I was closer to her than I was to my own mother . . . Is that a terrible thing to say?

EUGENE   Not if that's how you felt.

KATE   (*Clearing fruit, candlestick, and doilies from the table*)   When she died, she left a will. She gave away jewelry, dresses, even a little cash. But she knew what I wanted. (*She looks at the table*) The table you eat on means everything. It's the one time in the day the whole family is together . . . This is where you share things . . . People who eat out all the time don't get to be a family . . . (*She sits at the table*) When I'm gone, if you and your Josie get married, this will be your table.

EUGENE   What about Stanley?

KATE   Stanley won't get married so fast. And when he does, you make sure he brings his family to eat at your house.

EUGENE   Maybe you'll let me polish it with you one day.

KATE   When your wife has a little girl, send *her* over. She and I will polish it.
(*She collects* EUGENE's *teacup, and goes into the kitchen*)

EUGENE (*Calling into the kitchen*)   Maybe we'll have twins. You can polish it twice as fast.
(KATE *reenters with furniture polish and a rag. She begins to wipe off the table, with* EUGENE *following closely*)

KATE   Don't follow me around like that. You make me nervous.

EUGENE (*Retreating to the breakfront*)   I'm not following you. I just feel like talking to you . . . I love it when you tell me about the old days.

KATE   I don't remember them anymore. They were such a long time ago.

EUGENE   You just told me about the dining room table, and *that* was a long time ago . . . What was your grandmother like?

KATE (*Stops wiping the table for a moment*)   Tiny. Little bit of a thing. All the women were small in those days. When I was nine years old, I was bigger than she was

... My grandfather had to pick her up to see the Statue of Liberty.

EUGENE   That must have been some day.

KATE   This is what they dreamed of. Their whole life. To get to America. And when they saw that statue, they started to cry. The women were wailing, the men were shaking, everybody praying. You know why?

EUGENE   Because they were free.

KATE   Because they took one look at that statue and said, "That's not a Jewish woman. We're going to have problems again."
(*She goes back to polishing the table*)

EUGENE   That would be a riot. A Jewish Statue of Liberty. In her left hand, she'd be holding a baking pan . . . and in the right hand, held up high, the electric bill.

KATE   And my grandfather, of course, was a socialist. When *he* saw the statue he said, "It's too big. They should have made a small one and given the money to people who needed it."

EUGENE   If your whole family were socialists, Ma, how come you're not?

KATE   Not the whole family. Just the men . . . A man doesn't fight for political causes on an empty stomach.

EUGENE   But you vote. You voted for President Roosevelt.

KATE   I liked his face. I trusted him. I got nervous that he smoked with a cigarette holder, that was a little fancy for me . . . But he had polio. And I figured a man who walked with crutches wasn't out to take advantage of poor people.

EUGENE   You amaze me sometimes.

KATE   And I like Harry Truman. Him I trust, too.

EUGENE   Why?

KATE   Because he walks everywhere. Seven o'clock in the morning, he's out walking the streets. The Secret Service men can't even keep up with him . . . He was once a haberdasher, did you know that? And a man who has to get up early in the morning in the winter to open up a store knows what it's like to be a working man . . . All right. That's enough already. I want you in bed.
   (*She has finished polishing and takes the rag and bottle into the kitchen*)

EUGENE   I will. In a few minutes. First tell me about George Raft.

KATE (*Coming out of the kitchen*)   George Raft . . . If I tell you about George Raft again, you're going to tell me you still don't believe me.
   (*She takes the fruit bowl into the kitchen*)

EUGENE   I believe you. I believe every word you say. So tell me how you met George Raft.

KATE (*From the kitchen*)   You heard it a hundred times.

EUGENE (*Putting a skein of yarn around his hands*)   I know. But every time you tell it, it gets a little better. (*She enters from the kitchen, and sees him with the yarn. He pushes the ball of yarn toward her*) Go on.

KATE (*Slowly taking up the ball of yarn and beginning to wind it*)   The night I danced with him, I committed a sin. I knew God was going to punish me for it, and He did. You pay for your mistakes in this world.

EUGENE   What sin did you commit?

KATE   The day before I was going to the Primrose, my Aunt Sipra died. My mother's sister. The next morning, the whole family went to the funeral. I took the day off from work, and that night we all sat at my grandmother's to sit in mourning . . . But I knew that night George Raft was coming to the Primrose. He was a friend of the owners and he promised he would come. I never dreamed he'd dance with me. I just wanted to watch him. But in the back of my head I thought, if he sees me dance, who knows, he might ask me to get up on the floor with him . . . He wasn't even an actor yet. Just this skinny kid who looked like Rudolph Valentino. But the best ballroom dancer in New York. And to dance with him made you queen of the city.

EUGENE   Did he flip a coin like he does in the movies?

KATE   Never. But he always smoothed down his hair with his right hand. Every two minutes, smoothing his hair down. It got so shiny, you could see your face in it when you danced with him.

EUGENE   So you went to the dance that night.

KATE (*Forgetting the yarn and sitting*)   I told my mother I wasn't feeling well. I told her I just threw up in the bathroom, which I didn't, so she sent me home. I knew she and Poppa and the girls wouldn't be home till midnight. So I ran home and changed my dress and went to the Primrose with my girlfriend Adele Abrams. And all the time I knew that God was going to punish me for this . . . I kept saying to Adele on the way over, I wish I was a Catholic. Then I could go to church, confess my sins, and God would forgive me. But I knew I just committed another sin by wishing I was Catholic . . . I was throwing my whole life away for this one night to see George Raft.

EUGENE   Did you have a—you know—a crush on him?

KATE   On George Raft? You think I'm crazy? He was Italian. I was in enough trouble already. He wasn't my type anyway . . . Your father was the one I had the crush on . . . Since I was thirteen years old. He was five years older than me. He went with a whole other crowd. In those days, young people didn't tell each other they had crushes on them. You had to guess. So you sent messages with your eyes, your face, the way you walked by them.

EUGENE How did you walk by him?

KATE Not too much, not too little. But he was hard to figure out. He was never a show-off, never a fancy Dan. He didn't smile a lot, but when he did, you knew he meant it. Most boys then smiled at everything. They thought it gave them a good personality. Jack was too honest to put on a good personality. He was what he was . . . and to get a smile from Jack Jerome, you knew you had to earn it . . . But it cost him plenty. The smilers got to be the salesmen. The smilers got to be the bosses. The smilers got all the girls. Your father paid the price for not being a phony . . . It was so hard to impress him. That's why I went to the Primrose that night. I thought if Jack heard that I danced with George Raft, maybe I'd get him to notice me.

EUGENE This is a movie. There's a whole movie in this story, Ma. And one day I'm going to write it.

KATE So that night, in a pouring rain, me and Adele Abrams went to the Primrose. My hair got soaking wet, I lost my curls, I wanted to die. But then I got this brilliant idea. Instead of drying it, I combed it straight down and left it wet. Jet black hair. I looked like a Latin from Manhattan . . . The perfect partner for George Raft . . . When I walked out of the ladies' room, my own friends didn't recognize me.

EUGENE I can't believe this is *my mother* you're talking about.

KATE Don't worry. I knew God was going to punish me for the wet hair, too . . . Ten boys must have asked me to dance. But I said no to all of them because I didn't want to tire myself out . . . And then I started to get scared. Because it was ten after eleven and he still didn't show up. If I wasn't home by twelve, my parents would walk in and find out I was lying to them. And with my mother, I didn't need God to punish me.

EUGENE   Twelve o'clock! Cinderella! This story has everything.

KATE   And then, at twenty after eleven, he walks in . . . Like the king of Spain. My heart was beating louder than the drummer in the band . . . He had two friends with him, one on each side, like bodyguards. And I swear, there was something in their inside pockets. I thought to myself, they're either guns or more jars of grease for his hair.

EUGENE   (*To audience*) She actually had a sense of humor. This was a side of my mother I hardly ever saw. (*To* KATE) So, he walks in with these two guys.

KATE (*Taking off her sweater and standing center*)   So, he walks in with these two friends and I know I don't have much time. So I grabbed Bobby Zugetti, a shoe clerk, who was the best dancer at the Primrose, and said, "Bobby, dance with me!" . . . I knew he had a crush on me and I never gave him a tumble before. He didn't know what hit him. So out on the floor we go, and we fox-trotted from one side of the ballroom and back. In and out, bobbing and weaving through the crowd, gliding across the floor like a pair of ice skaters.

EUGENE   "Begin the Beguine" . . . Maybe "Night and Day." That's what I would use in the picture.

KATE   And I never once looked over to see if George Raft was looking at me . . . I wanted to get *his* attention, I didn't want to give him mine . . . The music finishes and Bobby dips me down to the floor. It was a little lower than a nice girl should dip, but I figured one more sin wouldn't kill me . . . And I walk over to Adele, I'm dripping with perspiration, and I said, "Well? Did he watch me?" . . . And she said, "It's hard to tell. His eyes don't move." . . . So I look over and he's sitting at a table with his two friends and Adele is right. His eyes don't move. And it's twenty-five to twelve, and he's never even noticed me. And I said to myself, "Well, if it's not meant to be, it's not meant to be." . . . and Adele and I started for the door.

EUGENE   The tension mounts. The audience is on the edge of their seats.

KATE   And as we pass their table, George Raft stands up and says, "Excuse me." And he's looking right at Adele Abrams. He says, "Could I ask you a question, please?" . . . Adele is shaking like a leaf. And she walks over to him.

EUGENE   Adele? He's talking to Adele Abrams?

KATE   And he says, "I wonder if your friend would care to dance with me?" . . . And she says, "You want *me* to ask her?" . . . And he says, "Please. I'm a little shy."

EUGENE   I don't believe it. I don't believe George Raft said that.

KATE   I swear to God. May I never live to see another day.

EUGENE   Even if it's true, it's out of the picture. An audience would never believe it.

KATE   Fine. So Adele says, "I'll ask her." . . . So she comes back and asks me . . . And I look at him and he smiles at me . . . And his eyes moved for the first time. Not fresh or anything, but he had the look of a man with a lot of confidence and I never saw that before. Scared the life out of me. So I walk over to him and he takes my hand and leads me out to the floor . . . Everyone in the Primrose is watching. Even the band. Someone had to whisper, "Start playing," so they would begin . . . And they began. And we danced around that room. And I held my head high and my back straight as a board . . . And I looked down at the floor and up at the ceiling, but never in his eyes. I saw a professional do that once . . . His hands were so gentle. Hardly touching me at all, but I knew exactly when he wanted me to move and which way he wanted me to turn.

EUGENE (*Dropping the knitting and rushing to the radio*) Wait a minute! Wait a minute!

KATE   What are you doing?

EUGENE   I want you to show me how you danced.
(*He turns on the radio and begins to search for appropriate music*)

KATE (*Sitting down at the table*)   Show you how I danced thirty-five years ago? I don't even *walk* like I did thirty-five years ago.

EUGENE   Come on. You dance every year with Pop at the Garment Industry Affair. Just show me how you danced with George Raft.

KATE   They danced differently in those days. They don't even do those steps anymore.

EUGENE   Not a whole dance. Two steps . . . One turn . . . (*He finds the right music. It is Benny Goodman's recording of "It Had To Be You"*) There! Listen! That's the perfect music . . . (*He crosses to* KATE *at the table*) So he moved you gently around the floor.

KATE   Stop it, Eugene. I'm not in the mood.

EUGENE (*Holding out his arms to her*)   Come on. I'll dance with you . . . I'm George Raft . . . (*He mimes slicking down his hair*) Everybody is watching us . . . Don't let 'em down, Mom.
(KATE *looks at* EUGENE *for a moment, listening to the music. Then she slowly stands and they begin to dance—awkwardly at first, then more gracefully*)

KATE   You're holding me too tight . . . Don't push me
. . . Just with your fingertips.

EUGENE   You're so graceful, Mom . . . I never knew you
were so graceful. There's Adele Abrams. (*He waves*)
Adele? She's wonderful.
(*They continue to dance*)

KATE   Now turn me.

EUGENE   How?

KATE   Just let go. (*He lets go. She does a turn*) Now give
me your hand. (*She is back in his arms for the finish of
the number*) And then it was over.
(EUGENE *turns off the radio.* KATE *is embarrassed,
but flushed with excitement. He smiles at her*)

EUGENE   And then what did he say to you?

KATE   He said, "Thank you. It was my pleasure." And
he walked away.

EUGENE   He didn't even ask for your name?

KATE   I didn't ask for his, why should he ask for mine?
(*She sits at the dining table*) My God, I'm drenched in
perspiration. In the middle of the winter. I don't know
how I let you get me to do such things.

EUGENE (*Sitting on the sofa arm, opposite* KATE)   Because
you liked it. Why do you always stop doing the things
that make you feel good?

KATE   What's the matter? Raising you and Stanley
wasn't something that made me feel good?

EUGENE   There's other things besides raising a family,
Ma.

KATE   Yeah. So I've heard . . . All right. I want you in bed. And no more back talk.
(*She collects the yarn and puts it away*)

EUGENE   You didn't finish the story. Did you get home before twelve?

KATE   No. The trolleys were running late. I came in almost twelve-thirty.

EUGENE   And what did your mom and pop say?

KATE   They didn't know. They decided to sleep over at her sister's house. Only Aunt Blanche came home. And she was fast asleep. I didn't tell anybody what I did . . . But in two days, the news was all over the neighborhood. People were congratulating my mother. They treated her like her daughter was a movie star. She was angry with me, but she knew she couldn't say anything . . . But when I saw my grandmother, she winked at me, squeezed my hand, and said, "I know, darling. I know." (*She turns off the dining room lights*) So now do you believe I danced with George Raft?

EUGENE   Yeah. I believe you.

KATE (*Going up the stairs*)   God, I'm exhausted . . . Never ask me that question again. Telling the story was harder than dancing with him.

EUGENE (*Following her up the stairs*)   I think what you did that night was great . . . And you didn't get caught. So God didn't punish you. The movie has a happy ending.

KATE (*Standing at her bedroom door*)   . . . The movie isn't over yet.

EUGENE (*Going into his bedroom and closing the door. To audience*)   I'll be honest about one thing. Dancing with my mother was very scary. I was doing what my father should have been doing with her but wasn't.

And holding her like that and seeing her smile was too intimate for me to enjoy. Intimacy is a complex thing. You had to be careful who you shared it with . . . but without it, life was just breakfast, lunch, dinner, and a good night's sleep. Most people would settle for that. Most people do . . . I was determined not to be most people.

> (*He leaves his bedroom and goes into the bathroom. A lighting change shows us that the night has passed and the sun is coming up. It is early morning the next day.*
>
> JACK, *all dressed, comes out of his room. He tiptoes down the stairs, crosses to the back porch, and brings out a large suitcase. He brings it into the living room.* BEN, *dressed, comes out of his room and down the steps. He stops when he sees* JACK)

BEN   Since when do you work on Sundays, Jack?

JACK   I didn't expect to see you up so early. I'm sorry, Ben. I haven't got time to talk.

BEN (*Coming into the living room*)   Then take the time. Where are you going, Jack?

JACK   I'm leaving, Ben. I'm moving out.

BEN   I see . . . Did you explain this to Kate?

JACK   I thought I'd call her in a few days. I'd say all the wrong things now.

BEN   You mean in a few days you'll say all the right things? (JACK *goes to the closet for his coat*) When did you pack your bag?

JACK   Friday night . . . when she was out shopping.

BEN   You should have told her, Jack. You could have saved money on food for the week.

JACK (*Coming back to his suitcase, coat on*) I've got to leave before she gets up.

BEN So who tells her? Me? If you want me to tell her, you'd better pay me. And I get top money for telling my daughter her husband walked out on her.

JACK This isn't just happening, Ben. This has been coming for a long time. She may be angry when I leave, but she won't be surprised.

BEN You think she'll be angry? . . . You walk out on her after thirty-three years of marriage and you think all she'll be is *angry??* . . . If that's how much you understand her, then maybe she's better off without you.

JACK What do you know about it? For thirty-three years you were a visitor in this house. You came, you ate dinner, and you went home. You didn't live in that bedroom with us . . . No matter what anyone tells you, what happens to a man and wife happens in the privacy of that room . . . and not even God Himself is there all the time to listen.

BEN You're making a mistake, Jack. No matter what she says, she'll never leave you . . . This thing with the other woman won't last . . . I know, because I've had enough other women in my life . . . Kate will find a way to deal with it. She'll ignore it, she'll pretend it's not happening. She'll live with you and not talk to you to protect her dignity, but she won't leave you . . . I'm her own father and I'm saying to you, *have* your affair until it's over, but don't break up what'll last you the rest of your life.

JACK You don't understand. It's not an affair. I don't sleep with this woman. I did once, not now . . . She's sick. She'll live another five, six more months. Maybe not even that.

BEN (*Nods*) Maybe to you that's a noble gesture, but to me it stinks.

JACK   Don't be so goddamn hypocritical. You've got a seventy-two-year-old wife living alone in Florida, and you stay here pretending you're martyring yourself for a political cause that you haven't been interested in for the last twenty years. I'm the last one to blame you . . . Where is it written that a man must love the same woman until the day he dies?

BEN   In the marriage vow he took.

JACK   If I took it, then you took it too, Ben.

BEN   True. And maybe I don't love anymore. Maybe I am a hypocrite. I don't have another woman, no . . . My mistress is my privacy. I am unfaithful with a room upstairs that lets me do what I want. I'm having an affair with peace and quiet . . . But you're right. I'm no better than you.

JACK (*At the front door with his suitcase*)   I'm fifty-five years old, Ben. I'm not ready for a room yet. I need to run. I need to get away from myself and everything I was. I have no more children to raise. I have nothing waiting out there for me except one thing . . . Something else!
     (JACK *starts to go out the front door*)

BEN   I still think you're making a mistake, Jack. A big, big mistake.

JACK (*Turning back*)   Why?

BEN   . . . Because Kate is my daughter.

JACK   I'll call the boys tomorrow.
     (JACK *goes.*
     BEN *sits on the sofa, then hears* KATE *coming out of her bedroom. He hurries into the kitchen.*
     KATE *comes out in a housedress, goes downstairs and looks out the front door window for a moment.*
     BEN *comes out of the kitchen with a roll on a plate with butter on the side and a knife*)

BEN   How long have you been up?

KATE   A few minutes. I heard Jack coming downstairs, I thought he must be hungry. Did you put up hot water?

BEN (*Sitting at the table*)   Certainly I put up hot water. What am I, an invalid?
(*He butters his roll*)

KATE   You want some eggs?

BEN   No.

KATE (*Crossing to the back porch*)   No eggs?

BEN   Why do you always ask me if I want eggs? If I wanted eggs, wouldn't I ask you?

KATE   It's too early in the morning, Poppa. Don't start in.

BEN   Listen, if it'll make you happy to make me eggs, make them. Scrambled, not too loose.

KATE   You just said you didn't want any.

BEN   I don't. I'm having them for you.

KATE (*Angrily*)   Don't ask me to make you things if you don't want them. (*She catches herself*) I'm sorry. I hardly slept last night.

BEN   I heard the music. I heard you dancing with Eugene. I forgot all about your grandmother giving you the dining room table.

KATE   You forget a lot of things. Poppa. You shouldn't have been listening.

BEN I know. But I enjoyed it. I left my door open a crack . . . Some boys you got, Kate. You raised them good, believe me.

KATE Where is Jack so long? Is he in the kitchen? No one lets me cook here anymore. (*She goes into the kitchen.* BEN *stares at his roll.* KATE *comes back to the table*) Is he in the house?

BEN No.

KATE Where'd he go, for a walk?

BEN No.

KATE He's not in the house and he didn't go for a walk . . . So where'd he go on a Sunday morning? (*She looks at* BEN, *who hasn't moved. And suddenly she realizes . . . She turns away*) Why didn't you tell me? . . . You think I wasn't expecting it?

BEN I didn't know how to say it . . . He's gone, Kate . . . He moved out . . . It's as simple as that.
(*She stands there a moment, not saying a word. Then she goes out to the porch, lights a cigarette, and looks out.*
BEN *goes into the kitchen.*
EUGENE *comes out of the bathroom, fully dressed. His cold is gone. Time is in transition. He stands at the top of the stairs*)

EUGENE (*To audience*) When Mom heard the news about Pop, she didn't cry, she didn't reach for anyone to hug, she didn't make a sound . . . When I was in the army, they told us, in battle, don't bother attending the wounded who were crying for help . . . Go to those who didn't make a sound. They were the ones in real trouble . . . (KATE *finishes her cigarette and goes into the kitchen.* EUGENE *comes down the stairs into the living room. To audience*) . . . The winter moved on and so did our careers. As the temperature grew colder, Stan and I got hotter. They doubled our salary at CBS and we

were washing our hands in the same john as Arthur Godfrey . . .
(STAN *comes running excitedly down the street and into the house. He sees* EUGENE)

STAN   Okay. Don't say a word. Just sit down.

EUGENE   What?

STAN   Will you just sit down. Because you're not going to believe this. Go on. (EUGENE *sits*) No. Stand up. This news is too important to be sitting.

EUGENE (*Getting up again*)   What are you talking about?

STAN   Where's Mom? . . . *Mom!!* Come on inside. Grandpa? . . . Where's Grandpa?

EUGENE   He fell asleep on the kitchen table.
(KATE *comes in from the kitchen and stands by the breakfront, looking at the two boys*)

STAN   Mom! . . . Remember I once told you, you have to have faith in me . . . I knew talent when I see it and I knew right away that Eugene and I had it . . . I never gave up on us, did I? . . . Did I, Eugene?

EUGENE   No. Never . . . Except for the eight times you wanted to commit suicide.

STAN (*Hanging up his coat*)   Except for those eight times, I was like a rock.

EUGENE   And once you smashed the typewriter with my baseball bat.

STAN   Except for the time I smashed the typewriter, I never lost heart, right?

EUGENE   Except for the time you lost heart.

STAN   But otherwise, I never faltered. Never gave up hope. So guess what I'm going to tell you?

EUGENE   You gave up hope.

STAN   We got "The Phil Silvers Show." You, me, and two other writers . . . Two hundred dollars a week . . . Apiece . . . *APIECE!!* . . . That's four hundred dollars a week . . . Do you realize how much money that is?

EUGENE   *Three* hundred dollars a week?

STAN (*Hugging* EUGENE)   Congratulate me, you lousy kid. I negotiated the whole deal myself. We don't even have to pay an agent.

EUGENE   You're incredible . . . When do we start?

STAN   Three weeks from Monday. They wanted to know if we thought we could double on "The Chubby Waters Show," but I turned them down. It's too much work.

EUGENE   We can handle it. Why don't we do it?

STAN   No! Big mistake. We spread ourselves too thin, we'll lose the quality. If we make good here, we'll get the big money later . . . So what do you think about this, Mom?

KATE   What do I think? . . . I got two geniuses, that's what I think.

STAN (*Kissing* KATE)   Three geniuses, because you're the one who gave birth to us . . . That's why I think you should be living in New York, too.

KATE   New York? What are you talking about?

STAN (*Going to stand beside* EUGENE)   Gene and I are moving next week . . . I signed the lease today. We'll be working night and day, it would be murder for us to come out *here* to visit you. The woman showed me a place two blocks away. Perfect for you and Grandpa. Before you say no, come and look at it.

KATE   In the first place, if your grandfather didn't go to Miami, he won't go to New York. In the second place, who do I know in the city?

EUGENE   Aunt Blanche.

KATE   Aunt Blanche lives on Park Avenue. I don't have clothes to visit Park Avenue . . . I have my friends here. I like the stores better. You know what they would charge me for chicken breasts in New York? Forget it.

STAN   I just want you to be happy, Mom.

KATE   You made me happy enough today. Too much happiness and I get scared.

STAN   (*Slapping* EUGENE's *shoulder*)   Come on upstairs. We've got things to talk about.
        (EUGENE *goes upstairs ahead of* STAN)

KATE   What day are you moving?

STAN   Next Monday.

KATE   Did you call the movers?

STAN   (*On the stairs*)   We're not taking any furniture, Mom. We're getting all new stuff. We're just taking our clothes.

KATE   You don't want the bureau? It's a beautiful bureau. Your father and I bought that new in Bamberger's.

STAN   That was twenty-five years ago, Mom.

KATE   You don't want it, don't take it. I'll save it. Maybe your children will want it.

STAN Gene's children. I'm not ready for marriage yet.

KATE Well, get ready. If I don't get grandchildren, what did I need children for?
(KATE *goes into the kitchen.* STAN *and* EUGENE *go into* EUGENE's *room*)

STAN (*Closing the door*) I got other news, too. I saw Pop today. He was waiting for me outside CBS.

EUGENE (*Sitting on the bed*) No kidding. How is he?

STAN The lady he was seeing? Audrey? They took her to the hospital yesterday. He said she won't last out the week.

EUGENE That's too bad. How was Pop taking it?

STAN He looked lousy. He asked about Mom. He asked if she was all right. Then he started to cry. We were in Louie's Restaurant on Madison Avenue. He grabbed my hand and held it. He sat there for half the lunch holding my hand. The waiter looked at us like we were a couple of lovers.

EUGENE You think when this Audrey—you know— you think he'll come back to Mom?

STAN No. I asked him. At least not for now. He said to me, "No, I can't go back to that house . . . Besides, she'd never take me back," he says.

EUGENE Sure she would. She still loves him.

STAN Maybe. But she's stubborn. Like Grandpa.

EUGENE Why are they doing this to each other, Stan?

STAN I don't know. Maybe he explains it all in the letters.

EUGENE What letters?

STAN   He gave me two letters. One for me, one for you.

EUGENE   What's in it?

STAN   (*Handing* EUGENE *a letter*)   I don't know.

EUGENE   You didn't read yours?

STAN   He doesn't want us to. Not yet.

EUGENE   When can we read them?

STAN   After he dies.

EUGENE   After he dies?

STAN   He made me promise him that. I said, "If it's important, Pop, why can't you tell us what's in it now?" He said he just couldn't. We would have to wait.

EUGENE   Suppose he lives to be ninety? They'll turn yellow, we'll never be able to read it.

STAN   They're probably letters of apology. Explaining why he did what he did.

EUGENE   By then I'd be fifty-four. I wouldn't even care.

STAN   Or maybe the letters say he'll never forgive us for what *we* did. For my saying "go to hell" to him.

EUGENE   He already forgave you. He held your hand in the restaurant . . . So? Are you going to wait until he dies to read it?

STAN   I'm going to try . . . What about you?

EUGENE   Suppose I die before him? Does he get his letter back?

STAN   You're funny, Gene. You've got a wonderfully inventive mind, but sometimes it lacks respect.

(STAN *goes into his own room. He looks at his own letter, then puts it in his pocket, takes out a suitcase, and packs.*

EUGENE *turns his envelope over in his hands. Then he looks at the audience*)

EUGENE (*To audience*)   It probably does. I was really confused. I always loved my father, but I didn't like him for leaving my mother and I was really sore at him for leaving me this thing . . . I sure didn't want him to die, but how else would I get to read the damn letter? I knew I was really angry when I thought about sending him a gift on Father's Day and printing on it, "Never Ever To Be Opened" . . . The following Monday was our last day in Brighton Beach. (*He puts on a jacket and puts the letter in the inside pocket. As he speaks, he takes out a suitcase from under the bed and packs.*

(STAN *comes out of his room with the suitcase and crosses downstairs. He gets their coats out of the closet*) Stan and I didn't have much to take. We were going to throw out our old clothes, but Mom put them in a box in the basement. Just in case. Daughters of socialists don't have too much faith in show business.

(EUGENE *leaves his room and brings his suitcase downstairs.* BEN *comes out of the kitchen*)

STAN   Where's Mom?

BEN   In the kitchen baking you two years' worth of cookies.

EUGENE (*Putting on his coat*)   Remember your promise, Gramps. You're going to come to the studio to watch the first show.

BEN   Only if it's about something. If it's just funny, I'm not interested.

EUGENE   No, no. The first show is about a girl from Mount Holyoke. She meets a boy named Myron Trotsky.

STAN (*Sitting on the sofa arm*) Why did you tell him? Now he knows the ending.

BEN You still like to kid me, you two. You think I never knew when you were kidding me? I'll tell you something. When you were kidding me, I was kidding you twice as much.

KATE (*Coming out of the kitchen carrying a large cardboard box tied with string*) Don't jiggle the box too much. It makes crumbs.

EUGENE (*Taking the box*) How much should we ask for them, Mom? We're going to sell them on the train.

STAN No train. We're making *this* trip in a cab.

BEN Don't let my friends see you getting into a cab.

STAN Am I going to get a hug from you, Gramps?

BEN A hug yet. You really want to humiliate me, don't you?

STAN No. I just want to say goodbye.
(STAN *hugs* BEN *and kisses his cheek, then steps away*)

STAN (*To* KATE) Hey! Broadway Momma! (*Opens his arms*) Step right into these arms.

KATE Yesterday he was a writer, today he's Clark Gable.
(STAN *kisses* KATE *and gives her a long hug. Then he steps away*)

EUGENE I just want to say one thing, Ma . . .

KATE Don't say anything. You know me. I don't deal with these things too good.

EUGENE It's not that horrible. And it's quick . . . I love you. Okay? That wasn't so bad, was it?
(EUGENE *kisses* KATE *and gives her a long hug*)

STAN   Okay, come on, let's go! We're not moving to Budapest. We've got a party at four o'clock.
  (EUGENE *steps away from* KATE *and goes to his suitcase at the front door*)

EUGENE   What party?

STAN   At CBS. Do you realize the gorgeous women we're going to meet today.

KATE   Stanley! He's got Josie. You leave him alone.
  (EUGENE *opens the front door and sets his suitcase outside*)

STAN (*In the open door*)   I was kidding, Mom. I won't let a single beautiful showgirl get near him. We'll call you in a few days . . . And, Grandpa, just so you know, I always knew when you were kidding me.

BEN   I knew when you knew.
  (BEN *and* KATE *exit into the kitchen.* STAN *brings his suitcase outside and stands beside* EUGENE)

STAN   Come on. It's freezing.

EUGENE   I just want to look at the house for a minute.

STAN   I'm going to look for a cab. I don't care what it costs, this is one party I'm not missing . . . I told you we'd make it, didn't I? I picked Joe DiMaggio and us. Not bad, huh?
  (*He runs up the street to look for a cab*)

EUGENE (*To audience*)   I knew then that no matter how many times I came back to see this house, it would never be my home again . . . Mom and Pop split up for good and never got back together . . . As a matter of fact, he remarried about two years later, to a pretty nice woman. Mom would really be hurt if she heard me say that, but the truth is the truth . . . Grandpa found it rough going in his seventy-eighth year and finally surrendered to capitalism and Miami Beach . . . He plays pinochle every day and donates half his winnings to the Socialist Party . . . Josie and I got married and we sleep each night with her hand lying gently across my chest. I won't even breathe for fear she'll move it away.

STAN (*Running down the street to* EUGENE) Gene! Come on! I got a cab!

EUGENE I'm coming. I'm coming.

STAN I never realized how cold it was out here before. (STAN *exits up the street, taking* EUGENE'*s box of cookies with him.* KATE *comes out and begins to wax her table under Eugene's speech*)

EUGENE (*To audience*) I didn't keep my promise to Pop. I opened his letter and read it. He didn't apologize, and he wasn't mad at Stan and me for what we wrote. The only thing he wanted was for Stan and me to understand his side of the story . . . Only he never said what his side was . . . Contrary to popular belief, everything in life doesn't come to a clear-cut conclusion. Mom didn't do anything very exciting with the rest of her life except wax her grandmother's table and bask in the joy of her sons' success. But I never got the feeling that Mom felt she sacrificed herself for us. Whatever she gave, she found her own quiet pleasure in. I guess she was never comfortable with words like *I love you.* A hard life can sometimes knock the sentiment out of you . . . But all in all, she considers herself a pretty lucky woman. After all, she did once dance with George Raft.
(EUGENE *turns away from the house, grabs his suitcase, and runs up the street to the cab.* KATE *continues waxing the table*)

Curtain

Since 1960, a Broadway season without a Neil Simon comedy or musical has been a rare one. His first play was *Come Blow Your Horn*, followed by the musical *Little Me*. During the 1966–67 season, *Barefoot in the Park*, *The Odd Couple*, *Sweet Charity*, and *The Star-Spangled Girl* were all running simultaneously; in the 1970–71 season, Broadway theatergoers had their choice of *Plaza Suite*, *Last of the Red Hot Lovers*, and *Promises, Promises*. Next came *The Gingerbread Lady*, *The Prisoner of Second Avenue*, *The Sunshine Boys*, *The Good Doctor*, *God's Favorite*, *California Suite*, *Chapter Two*, *They're Playing Our Song*, *I Ought to Be in Pictures*, *Fools*, a revival of *Little Me*, *Brighton Beach Memoirs*, *Biloxi Blues* (which won the Tony Award for Best Play), the female version of *The Odd Couple*, *Broadway Bound*, *Rumors*, and *Lost in Yonkers* (which won both the Tony Award for Best Play and the Pulitzer Prize for Drama.)

NEIL SIMON began his writing career in television, writing for *The Phil Silvers Show* and Sid Caesar's *Your Show of Shows*. Mr. Simon has also written for the screen: the adaptations of *Barefoot in the Park*, *The Odd Couple*, *Plaza Suite*, *Last of the Red Hot Lovers*, *The Prisoner of Second Avenue*, *The Sunshine Boys*, *California Suite*, *Chapter Two*, *I Ought to Be in Pictures*, *Brighton Beach Memoirs*, and *Biloxi Blues*. His other screenplays include *After the Fox*, *The Out-of-Towners*, *The Heartbreak Kid*, *Murder by Death*, *The Goodbye Girl*, *The Cheap Detective*, *Seems Like Old Times*, *Only When I Laugh*, and *Max Dugan Returns*.

The author lives in California. He is married to Diane Lander and has three daughters, Ellen, Nancy, and Bryn.